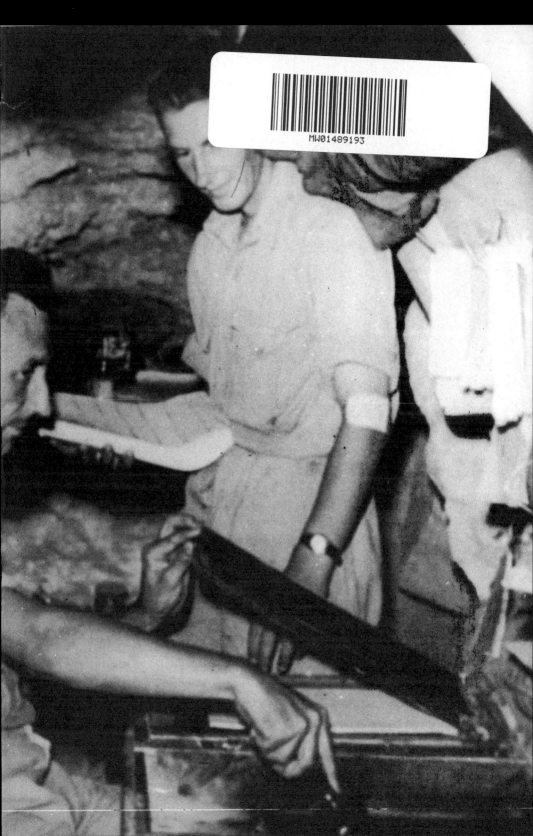

Best Wishes Frank

Pat + Dick Fancke – Dec 1989

MUD and BLOOD IN THE FIELD

This volume contains a full collection of all Newsletters issued by the 2/23 Australian Infantry Battalion, "Albury's Own", 9th Division, from December 1941 until August 1945, and was written and composed by the Officers and Men of the Battalion while on active service.

Compiled by Dick Fancke

PHOTOGRAPHS:

We thank the Australian War Museum, Canberra, for their permission to reproduce photographs as follows:

Dust Jacket Design (front cover) was adapted from photograph No. 20496 and depicts a scene in Tobruk.
The scene on the inside of the front cover, shows Mud & Blood being produced in a cave in Tobruk. The number of the official photograph is 20510 and shows Bill Woods at the typewriter, Jim Mulcahy (Editor) using the duplicator, with Dick Fancke standing.
All other photographs were reproduced from private collections.

ii.

Published 1984 by
John Sissons (Bookseller) Pty. Ltd.
17 Willesden Road, Hughesdale, Victoria, 3166,
in association with the
2/23 Australian Infantry Battalion Association (c)
National Library of Australia
ISBN 0 9590700 0 1
Printed by Prime Print
4/15 James Street, Clayton, Victoria, 3168
Registered in Australia for transmission
by post as a book.

This book is dedicated to all

MUD & BLOODS

We especially remember
those who were killed in action
and those who have died since

"LEST WE FORGET"

They mingle not with their laughing comrades again;
They sit no more at familiar tables of home;
They have no lot in our labour of the day-time;
They sleep beyond England's foam.

For the Fallen
Laurence Binyon

INTRODUCTION

Lieut. Col. F. A. G. Tucker, DSO, ED.

I am delighted to have been asked to introduce Lieut. L. P. Wenborn, who has the honour to write the Foreword of "Mud & Blood in the Field".

When I took command of the 2/23 Battalion in New Guinea late in 1943, the Newsletter Mud & Blood was in recess, the conditions of service making the publication out of the question. However, on the return of the unit to Australia early in 1944, Mud & Blood was again produced, and continued so until the end of the war.

Lieut. Len Wenborn was an original member of the Battalion, and joined the Intelligence Section in Palestine early in 1941. He served in the ranks of this section throughout the siege of Tobruk, with distinction, for which he was Mentioned in Despatches. He later became Sergeant of the Intelligence Section, and subsequently was promoted to Commissioned rank and became the Battalion Intelligence Officer.

He also served with distinction in the Western Desert, New Guinea and Tarakan, and is one of the best known of those who served with the 2/23 Battalion. During the latter part of 1941 and early in 1942, he became Editor of the Mud & Blood Newsletter, and having been directly involved with this publication throughout the war, he is eminently qualified to write the Foreword of this outstanding publication.

FOREWORD

Lieut. L. P. Wenborn

I take it as a compliment to have been asked to offer some comment about this new volume containing reprints of the many issues of wartime "Mud & Blood". I hope my contribution will add to the reader's appreciation of the book.

First let me say that the man whose initiative has given birth to this book thoroughly deserves the commendation of all ex-members of the 2/23 Australian Infantry Battalion. During recent months Dick Fancke has eagerly sought help and information about his project. Luckily his words fell upon more responsive ears than my own. I cheerfully admit that I could have done more than just order a copy, even though I live interstate.

As usual the expert services of Len Wemyss have been secured to produce the dust jacket. His design is more than mere illustration, for it reflects so well the feelings of desert dwellers in the early days of war. It also says: "Remember?"

To revive memories, I have lately referred to the book published by our wartime 2/23 Welfare Association under the title "Mud & Blood 1940 - 1942" wherein Mrs. Edith Simmons and her committee made a valuable gesture toward Battalion tradition. The 1984 book brings together the complete story of "Mud & Blood" for all to enjoy.

Towards the end of our sojourn in Tobruk, I well remember that our respected second in command, Major (then) Bill Birch, handed me the job of editor (when Jim Mulcahy left the unit bound for the "Land of Goshen"). I had some misgivings about such a task, but who could refuse senior rank? Certainly not a private! Until then "Mud & Blood" had emanated from the Orderly Room, where Jim churned out the stuff with gusto. His colourful style made his paras. dance with subtle humour - good stuff for besieged troops. As for me, perhaps I was more at home with a mapping pen than an editor's quill.

I must confess that the publication of Dick's book has rekindled my interest, and indeed my pride in the unit's fortunes. It is good to recall that one served with several thousand others in many different regions. We of the 2/23 came from all walks of life, were lumped together within a framework of platoons, companies, etc., yet we soon became integral parts of a great family whose over-riding passion was to get the war over and done with as soon as possible. Success we did achieve, albeit slowly. Along the hard road toward this end we inevitably grew in stature, learning the while to live in decent harmony with one another. I have come to realize that the sense and the nonsense pervading "Mud & Blood" during the war days helped us all to see beyond the hill.

I believe that the opportunity to re-read "Mud & Blood" will be grasped widely. In convenient book form it should be very suitable for everyone. Above all, to read it will enable one to keep alive the ties of comradeship which were forged so strongly in wartime. Well done D. F.

PREFACE

This Volume contains a complete collection of Newsletters issued in the field by the 2/23rd. Battalion, "Albury's Own" and titled "Mud & Blood".

This Volume contains a complete collection of Newsletters issued in the field by the 2/23rd. Battalion, "Albury's Own", and titled "Mud & Blood". Some of these were produced in better conditions than others; those in Palestine or Australia were done at leisure, and had a wide distribution; others were issued under appalling conditions, such as in the desert where the typewriter and duplicator were clogged up with sand; paper was scarce, and only a minimum of copies could be produced. Early in Tobruk the distribution was approximately 20 only. These were passed round by hand, and woe betide anyone who dallied too long over the reading. Other issues of course, depending on the situation at the time, were given a wider distribution, and in some areas it was even possible to place copies on notice boards for all to read.

Those Mud & Bloods who read these pages will, I am sure, give a nostalgic chuckle here and there; will find many names appearing that will send them back down memory lane, and occasionally there will be a pang as they read of some of their mates who did not make it back. But then again, their spirits will be lifted by the presence all through of that unquenchable humour, the feeling of mateship that nothing can destroy. There are the various competitions; here and there the lines of a budding poet, many with deep emotions they will have experienced in those war torn years.

To the general readers, this volume takes them behind the scenes and into the hearts and feelings of men of an Infantry Battalion during the second world war. It is a chance to share their experiences; happy or sad; humorous or tragic. There may be an item here and there which judged by today's standards and more sophisticated journalism, may seem "corny" or even "juvenile", but if you bear in mind WHEN it was written, under the CONDITIONS it was written, and perhaps more to the point, WHY it was written, you will then doubtless find yourself appreciating every item.

There are approximately 1000 men in an Infantry Battalion, and these are distributed over Battalion Headquarters, HQ Company (comprising specialist Platoons), and four Rifle Companies, A, B, C and D. Each Rifle Company is divided into Platoons, and each Platoon into Sections. Platoon and Company loyalties are strong, and in training, competitions between Companies bring the Battalion together as a Unit. However, in battle, the

Section, Platoon or Company is often isolated, and little is seen or heard of other sections of the Battalion, and the ordinary soldier knows little of what is going on outside his own dugout or his immediate vicinity.

Lack of news is depressing, particularly when under fire, and constantly under stress. Morale can sink very low in these circumstances, and the Mud & Blood Newsletter was distributed and passed from hand to hand around the various dugouts, in an effort to let the men know what was going on in other parts of their Battalion; how their particular part of the war was faring, and give news of the rest of the world.

In these days of transistor radios, it is hard to imagine that generally there was only one "wireless set" to a Battalion, and this was heard by only a few. Any larger than usual group of men would become obvious to the enemy, who would take appropriate action to make them disperse. Its amazing what a few well placed shells, mortar bombs, or stukas will do - dispersal is instant!

The choice of Jim Mulcahy as editor was inspired, as he had a quick Irish wit, and as orderly room Sergeant was well known to most of the men. He made "B" Echelon the butt of most of his humour, and the men in the front line had many a chuckle over the "bomb happy" inmates of that area inhabited as it was by the cooks, the transport, the postal, pay and Regimental Police sections among others. Jim built up a good natured rivalry between "B" Echelon and the forward Companies which provided much humour. Enemy planes attacking Tobruk Harbour, would drop their bombs and then make their way back - threading their way along the wadis looking for choice targets such as "B" Echelon, where they would ground strafe and even drop the occasional bomb they had left over. Sometimes "B" Echelon would be the prime target of such an attack, and bombs would rain down on the luckless inhabitants. This led to much digging, and some of the constructions were quite elaborate. However, it was impossible to remain in these shelters all the time, so when the need arose, speed was required to reach a haven of safety.

Jim built up word pictures of such scenes, and praised the speed of such well known figures as Tich Wynack the postie, Big Bill Marshall the Provost Sergeant, Laurie Folland the RSM, Jack O'Brien the cook, and many others. Everyone took it in good part, and Mud & Blood became the most sought after publication in Tobruk.

When Jim Mulcahy was posted to Officer Cadet Training Unit in Cairo, Len Wenborn of the "Intelligence" Section took over as Editor -

a daunting task, which he fulfilled with distinction while we remained in Tobruk, and then in camp at Julis in Palestine. Jim Mulcahy returned to his job as Editor when we reached Syria, a position he filled until we returned to Australia, and held until we sailed for New Guinea.

On the Unit's return to Australia after the New Guinea campaign, Capt. Ken Lovell, erstwhile Signals Officer and later Quartermaster, took over the reins as Editor, and at Ravenshoe in Queensland, Mud & Blood was reborn, and continued on until the end of the war, even surviving the invasion of Tarakan.

Looking back over those years, the clearest memories that I recall are of the fervent patriotism we had for King and Country, the mateship, and the good humoured optimism of those far off days. Also there's scarcely a "blue" comment, or even a good old fashioned "bloody". This latter until much later in the book, was printed as "b-------", and for that terrible word "bastard" we substituted the much more genteel term "basket". Many readers may find it hard to associate this with the hard swearing, hard fighting Australian diggers of those days, but the fact is that then, the average male did not swear in front of children or ladies, and never swore in print - be it letters home or elsewhere. Also you may notice that the phraseology is sometimes different to that used today, and there are even some words not now in use.

It is now over forty years since these men put pen or pencil to paper and wrote their contributions. The good, the bad, the humorous and the tragic are all emotions mirrored here in the experiences of the Battalion. As such, this book will be a permanent record of the men's day-to-day actions, their thoughts, their hopes and dreams. Many times as I was type-setting the text, I felt the urge to put the notation "killed in action" after the relevant names as they appeared, but its not that sort of book --- rather let us remember them as they were --- our mates, full of life and hope----- and finally, as we turn to the last page and read the poem "War Graves Tarakan", let us remember, and pay tribute.

Dick Fancke.

ACKNOWLEDGEMENTS

Gathering together all the copies of Mud & Blood was a mammoth task, and I must thank all those members of the Association who so generously sent in their valued copies. My thanks also to the staff of the Australian War Museum in Canberra, for making copies available from the War Diary, which helped to make our collection complete. Also for making available the photographs used in the design of the Dust Jacket, and showing the production of Mud & Blood in Tobruk as reproduced inside the front cover. Details of these are given on the title page. Jim Henderson was of tremendous assistance in acting as our Liaison Officer in Canberra and I cannot thank him enough.

To Len Wemyss who designed our Dust Jacket - what can I say? The Jacket he designed for our Official History was terrific, but he has really surpassed himself this time. He just keeps on getting better and better. Thanks a lot Len from myself and all Mud & Bloods; not only for the Jacket, but for all the other support as well.

Ken Lovell generously gave permission to reproduce drawings from his sketch books, and as these were sketched while on active service with the Battalion in the Middle East, New Guinea and Tarakan, they have added considerably to the quality of the volume. These can be readily identified by the signature "KAY".

My thanks also to George Tucker, our Commanding Officer, and to Len Wenborn, for their prompt and efficient help in providing the Introduction and the Foreword at very short notice.

To John Sissons our Publisher who made it all possible, and also the many others who supported me in this project, (there are too many to name them individually) - a big thank-you.

Finally, I must thank the real workers, my wife Pat, my sister Jean, my daughter Janet and her husband Fred, who were all untiring in their efforts to make this production a success, and to meet the deadline.

Dick Fancke

CONTENTS

NEWS EDITOR: Dick Fancke

CARTOONISTS: Tom French, Len Wemyss, Lloyd Jones, Ken Lovell.

xi.

INDEX

xvi.

Volume 1

CHAPTER 1

AT SEA, December, 1940.

Mud & Blood is a magazine for the men of the 2/23rd. Battalion, A.I.F. It has been my earnest wish that the Battalion produce its own little publication.

One thousand men — the equivalent of a small town's population — have come together to fight for their country. You are to a great extent shorn of your normal freedom and associates, wives, fiancees, parents, brothers and sisters — and all the easy pleasures of democracy.

So that this same democracy shall prevail it is necessary for us to be disciplined and orderly, and unlike that same small town which goes its own way, each individual as he pleases, we must become one thing with one mind and one will — the will to win. Every other consideration must be suborned to the fighting efficiency of the 2/23rd Battalion.

But we must have our lighter moments — we must let off a little steam or burst. Hence our magazine. In our midst we have every walk of life represented — as I was proud to put it in Albury, we have everything from cow-cockies down to lawyers.

I feel therefore that 'Mud & Blood' must be very successful. All of you from time to time must contribute to its pages. The more humorous the better. If it is a grouch, then couch it in humorous terms and the editor will no doubt publish it.

The magazine will come out from time to time according to the situation, and I feel sure that every member of the 2/23rd joins with me in wishing it all the best.

— Bernard Evans
Lt. Col.

If England was what England seems,
And not the England of our dreams,
But only putty, brass an' paint,
'Ow quick we'd drop 'er!
But she ain't.   — Kipling

****

FOREWORD

This first effort to record the spirit of the Battalion is due, primarily, to the initiative of a few "diggers".

A.I.F. Units in the past seem invariably to have been able to produce sufficient talent to initiate almost any enterprise. May we prove our ability to emulate their achievements!

Our being able to publish this issue was made possible by the remarkably spontaneous response of certain proprietors and manufacturers of printing material, when they were apprised of our needs. To them gratefully we acknowledge our indebtedness.

They are the Herald, Verona Press, and Messrs. Cooke Pty. Ltd., all of Melbourne; and Messrs. Griffin & Thomas of the Colombo Apothecaries Co. Ltd., Colombo, Ceylon.

The "diggers" who have so readily given up their time and specialised knowledge are G.T. Whitaker, R. Lees, W.C. Hughes, and L. Ash.

J. Alex. Allan, Editor

****

UNION IS STRENGTH

Gunners and Sigs. and P.B.I.,
Each in his turn has had his say,
And shown in friendly rivalry
Though good at their jobs, they're as good at play.

At times when nerves are a trifle taut,
And frayed at the edges, as well may be,
And tempers are -- well, just a wee bit short,
Then one MUST strafe a little impatiently.

Yet their trust in each other will stand the test,
Through the depths to the heights which are
    drawing nigh,
Each at his job will be proved the best,
Gunners and Sigs. and P.B.I.

Duo Oculis Mare

****

ROUTE MARCHING

A tribute to Albury's Own

The magpie's in the messmate, and the sunbaked clay is brown
In the channels where the winter water showed,
And the welkin rocks in answer where the red track ribbons down,
For the Twenty-third are singing on the road.
The haze may shake and shimmer, and the puckered eyelids sting,
And the salty sweat may sting and cake and crust,
Yet the eyes are still a-glimmer, as the jaunty shoulders swing
And the Army boots go pounding through the dust.

(Chorus)
Left — Right — Swing a healthy boot,
Scale the rise and tramp the thirsty plain,
While the jerking side-drums rattle and the cheeky cornets toot,
For the Twenty-Third are on the road again.

There are songs we know of girls and grief and home and hope
    and thirst,
(See the parrot in the hollow of the gum)
There are ditties learned at Bendigo, Toorak, and Darlinghurst,
(O, we'll teach them all to Fritz in days to come!)
Timeless, tuneless — Well, what matter? We shall sing the songs
    of men
To the tune of rushing feet and plunging steel,
And the sudden, rending chatter of the Lewis and the Bren,
When the bugles of the gods of battle peal.

We find our home and hearthstone where hearth and home are not —
(See the rabbits in the bracken by the track)
And the gentle Sergeant-Major cannot tuck us in our cot,
For it's march and rest, then march and bivouac:
And the prayers the Padre knows we know, but never say at night
Torment at times — but what does God require

Of soldiers but to stand and go, and rest and rise and fight,
And hold a soul unshaken under fire?

(Chorus)
Left — Right — Follow where they led —
(O, the First and Twenty-third were gallent men)
"Let us find a road or make one!" 'Twas so the Colonel said —
Sursum corda. Drink in silence — "To the living and the dead —"
The Twenty-third are on the road again.

J.A.A.   Bonegilla

****

ODDS AND SODS

Life's Little Jokes

The bugler who was crimed at Albury, and chased his own bugle.

The private who drew an extortionate rent from the Army every month for allowing his own Brigade H.Q. to use his residence in Olive Street for an office.

The padre who went A.W.L.

The soldier who went on the tear in Perth, changed clothes with a sailor — (both being soused) and completed the business by getting himself jugged by a Navy picquet, while his companion in mirth was pushed into the troopship boob by Big Bill the Sergeant, till things sorted themselves out.

The Mayor of Perth who asked the bandsmen if they were on ticket-of-leave. A sidelight is thrown on this by the regimental barber, who advises that since, at their own request, he ran his clippers over these chaps' heads they are known familiarly as the "Bomb-Headed Bachelors' Sons."

The spruker in the crown-and-anchor game last night who addressed his clients as "gentlemen!"

The bright lad who thought the ship's log was made out of red-gum, and got the idea out of his own head.

****

It is rumoured that the Batmen's Union is subscribing for Christmas presents for the officers

The Chemical Department of our Secret Service Section advises this paper (after a night spent on shore leave in Colombo) that the "perfume of the East" is 80% bad sanitation, 15% B.O., 4% extract of musk, and 1% plain b------ stink. They should know!

It had been a long and weary afternoon, winding up with a visit to the delic-atessen for a glass of milk. "Let me see," said the Fair Maid of Perth coyly, extracting her nose as the last drop gurgled through the straw — "What unit did you say you belonged to?" "Intelligence" said he (just like that) "What a terrible thing . . . . . ." The sweet voice died away, then began again . . . . . "I was just thinking — what if the Germans captured you and sentenced you to death. It's all right dying for Australia and all that, but what a dreadful thing for you to be shot for Intelligence and to have to die an innocent man!"

LIDS

One of the boys on leave in Colombo was steering a somewhat erratic course through the streets, and I was attracted by his extraordinary headgear. It was some sort of cheap white topee. To my amazement I noticed, on getting close, that the headgear was covered with autographs!! But best of all — as he groggily sailed by I looked at the rear of the topee and saw that it bore in large letters the legend - "Keep clear of the propellors!"

The Old Man

Editorial Note: We are assured by "Tich" Weston that the topee referred to above is definitely NOT his.

"Gettin' leave t'morrer," said Bluey, in Cairo. "I reckon I'll go out and see them Gyppie ruins." "Wot's the use of that?" said the Corp., "We can buy postcards of the . . . . . s 'ere in Cairo." "But a man travels for more than to send postcards," said Bluey; "I wanter write me name on the ——— Spinx."

A communique issued by the Perth Dairymen's Assn. admits the capture of one of their chariots by a party under Capt. H.W. Jackson, comprising Lieuts. Grogan, Fallon, Methven, McRae, and Neuendorfs(2). It is understood that mutiny almost ensued when Capt. Jackson, with utter disregard for wastage, despatched the chariot to parts unknown bearing with it a most charming female who had been captured by the party. A special tribute to Lieut. K.O. Neuendorf is the offer by the C.O., Perth Milkmen, of the job of instructor.

Who started the shaven head style? Was it a desire to give the sea-gulls a sporting chance.

LOST, FOUND, STOLEN and SOUVENIRED

Bag, sea-kit, one, containing the following:

2 prs. khaki, socks, marked "J.O.H."
1 pr.   "   "   marked "J.B."
2 F.S. caps, one marked "O.S." and the other "K.E."
1 beer-glass marked Victorian Railways
1 dessert-spoon inscribed Watson's Paragon.
1 dinner-knife marked Globe Hotel, Albury.

also the following articles, all unmarked:

2 khaki shirts (initials obliterated)
4 Blue Light outfits
3 sets summer underwear (initials cut out)
5 hkfs. — 2 khaki, the rest assorted colours.
1 pr. scantees.

Owner of this bag may have it by personal application to Bn.H.Q.

****

"MUD & BLOOD"

WISHES ITS BOYS AND THEIR

FOLKS AT HOME A MERRY

CHRISTMAS AND A

HAPPY NEW YEAR

****

MR. GROUCH – HIS PAGE

LIVING SPACE

The Hun says he's fighting for living space. He ought to talk! I'll change places with him any time he likes. He can sleep all over Europe if he wants to, but let him try sleeping in his tin hat when he can't find room for his hammock. I tried it one night and made a fair job of it, but the two coves who had jumped into the hat first were jammed under me and didn't find things too good. As a matter of fact they were quite cut up, but this was probably because I was wearing my sidearms.

Yes, I'd like to see the Boche trying for awhile to sleep on G deck. I hacked my way to my pack the other day and the poor old sarge-major crept out when I opened it. All he could say was, "Wouldn't it?" "Yes" I said in disgust, "Wouldn't it?"

The only way you can move down there is by groaning horribly and yelling, "I'm sea-sick!" The only trouble with this method is that you're nearly swept overboard by the draught caused by a thousand men trying to get somewhere else before your breakfast turns up again.

I had a great meal the other day. After sweeping three men and one corporal off my plate, I was definitely getting the upper hand after a struggle with a very tasty bone when I took a tumble that I'd eaten my way halfway through the left leg of another company's orderly sergeant. I wish now that he had taken off his socks before entering our bed-mess-sitting room.

I got a bit hungry the other day and went looking for his right leg, but he wears a plaster of paris casting around it now for safe keeping, so I had to stay hungry. And wouldn't that?

Boof Ellis bought a tin of sardines and the tin provided a fairly comfortable bed for himself and two cobbers. They slept with the sardines still in the tin in order to smother the effect of several hundred men with their socks off.

All I seem to be doing lately is fighting my way in and out of our bung hole. I've been four days late for parade every day since we've been on the ship because it takes two days to crash in and another two to get thrown out. I've been told I get a black mark every time I'm late, and there are so many marks against me now that everyone thinks I'm a billiard score.

So wouldn't it?   What do you think?

"Rip"

The Editor, "Mud and Blood"

Dear Sir,

I understand that this paper you're putting over is open to welcome any suggestions for the good of the troops. Well, Sir, I ask you do you think it is a fair thing that officers should make inspections of cabins in rubber shoes when there's army boots to wear, them (the boots) being much more dignified and everything, besides being easier to hear from a distance. Why, I had me door snibbed the other day and just as Lanky Bill was saying "I like these; I'll raise you a tray!" a knock come on the door and a bloke sang out "Don't lock these doors, lad!" Made me feel pretty near as bad as that yell of "Feet on the floor, soldier!" when a bloke is just having a last five minutes after revally. Things like that leave a man pretty lousy.

Hoping you are the same,
I am yours etc.
Belt-holder of No. 4

A careless soldier left his pay book where his wife found it. On being puzzled by three or four entries in red ink she asked him what was meant by —

"A.W.L. 10/-   A.W.L. 1 Pound   A.W.L. 2 Pound"
"Oh!" said the digger "That's the money I've invested in Australian War Loans."

"Cracker" A Coy.

CHAPTER 2

PALESTINE (DIMRA), March, 1941.

HOME LETTER FROM ABROAD

To give people at home a clearer idea of how "Albury's Own" is faring so far away from the lights of Dean Street and the more friendly darkness of certain popular park lands, MUD & BLOOD asked Lieutenant Harry Marshall to make a random choice of a typical Digger's Letter from the pile of uncensored mail that he always keeps handy, just in case he should have a spare moment to fill in.

Unfortunately chance decreed that his choice should fall on the work of one of the army's more hardened and sophisticated sons. So in reading the letter which follows, allowance must be made for the writers obviously vicious nature:

DEAR MUM,

These days I scarcely have time to write to you at all because life here is so full and exciting. But when your 61st letter came with the last mail, leaving me just 59 behind in replies (not counting the Christmas cable which you no doubt received within one hour of my sending it)I felt I owed you an account of this marvellous life and charming fellows who make it so happy for me.

Although I am only a private, my best friend is the Sgt. Major —, such a gentle mannered unassuming man who spends long hours quietly gazing with tear filled eyes at photographs of his grey-haired mother-in-law, wife and lovely children. Every morning about eight he coughs discreetly outside each tent and asks are we ready to get up. We know he would not dream of insisting, but we turn out in our dressing gowns and answer the roll call for his dear sake, because it makes his distasteful task so much easier for him. Then we take breakfast, plenty of nice tasty food so nicely served. But I wish some of these rougher fellows would be more careful not to spill so much on the table cloth and carpets (such rich Eastern Rugs they are) and not to say such rude things to the waiters. I believe the Officers never do this sort of thing, despite the fact that the place where they eat is generally said to be a mess.

Sometimes I play a fascinating game called C.B. — whenever the Bugler sounds a special call the player has to see how quickly he can run to Headquarters.

To fill in the daytime and to keep our weight down, we always have some exercise. The nicest days are those on which the Colonel and all the Officers take us for a lovely long ramble through this pretty country side to admire the entrancing scenery. I always did enjoy picnic lunches in the open air with no Australian ants to worry me you can easily imagine how I love these days out. The local people are so enthusiastic that they hurry out through the gardens of their beautiful homes when they hear us coming to throw us cigarettes and chocolate like they used to in Albury, and the dear tiny children wave flags to cheer us on our way.

We generally have a lie down before dressing for evening dinner, buglers (nice boys) call us with a special call when the sun is going down, and another when dinner is ready. Then we have the lovely evening ahead of us when we have a quiet talk or sit down to thrilling games of Ludo and Animal grab. There are quite a lot of competitors, but the Colonel likes his men to make a small donation before they join in the game, so I cannot afford to play very often. Every now and then I am allowed to go on guard and it is great fun, because I can stay up all night instead of going to bed at 10.30 to please the Sgt. Major.

From this account of the wonderful time I am having, you can quite understand why my hands shake with anxiety when I open the paper each morning fearful lest the war might have finished overnight and I might be faced with the dreadful thought of having to come home. Whenever I think of dirty Melbourne Streets and sudden downpours of rain and crowded trams, I feel so sorry for you all, and realize how lucky I was to receive an invitation for this trip.

Good-bye for the present Mother dear, and you need not bother to write too often, because each mail brings me such heaps of letters that I just cannot find time to read them all.

From your Loving Soldier Son,

WILL. I. GETTON.

FORWARD 2/23rd.

Our second issue from the low lands of Palestine, is published during a period of intensive training. Around us lies the land over which the soldiers of David marched in pursuit of the Philistines, where the Crusaders fought many battles with the Moslems, and where in 1917 the British Forces, including our Australian Light Horse, met with such determined resistance that thousands of lives were lost before supremacy was gained.

With the memory of such deeds of valour in a sacred cause, we are inspired to prepare ourselves to go forward to Victory with honor.

COOKS' TOUR

The 2/23 Battalion Cooks are a strong and happy band
We got on board a Liner, and sailed for other lands
Thirteen cooks and eleven students was the total of the mob
No matter what the going was, we always did our job.

We reached a far off country, and there we made our stand
What made us nearly silly were the fires and the sand
The wood was wet and wouldn't burn, it only made a smoke
And that's the reason why all the builders were very nearly broke.

The biggest pest was Sgt. Jones who worried night and day
For every time he came around he had a lot to say
We chopped up all the boxes and they cut our rations down
And every time he looked at us he had that ugly frown.

We had a game of football while the boys were out one day
We even had the storeman, who thought that he could play
The game was timed to start at ten, it started at eleven
The students first had fourteen men, but finished up with seven.

Bob Annand had broken ribs and Francis had concussion
It was due to Jack O'Brien who was doing all the rushing
Firth and Filler kicked the goals, while Abey did the scouting
Whitney played a rattling game, and Jonesie did the shouting.

Near the end the cooks played hard, and thought they mightn't
    make it
The students went and turned it up, and showed they couldn't
    take it
When the game was over, and we were getting tea
Two student cooks were knocked about, and at the R.A.P.
The playing was erratic, the rules were rather raw
And on the Sunday morning, the Cooks were stiff and sore.

                              C.A. (Longfellow) Jones.

HUT FOR TROOPS

Recent opening of a recreation hut is a further contribution to the comfort of men of the 2/23 Battalion in their first overseas camp. The Colonel's initiative and the Transport Officer's industry resulted in a fine stack of furniture from the Australian Comforts depot at Tel Aviv.

Further team work between the C.O. and the A.C.F. has produced a splendid radio for troops. Towards the monthly rent of 1/7/6 for this set, the A.C.F. contributes 1 Pound, the balance coming from the C.O.'s Fund.

CHURCH NOTICES

Besides the regular Battalion Church Parade, Sunday Services are regularly held by the Padres as follows:-

    0715   HOLY COMMUNION
            in the 2/23rd. Battalion Lines
            Padre R.N. Morrison (C of E)

    0715   HOLY COMMUNION
            in the 2/48th Battalion Lines
            Padre B. Archbold (Methodist)

    0700   Roman Catholic Mass
            HOLY COMMUNION
            in the 2/24th Battalion Lines
            Padre E.J. Conlan (R.C.)

ODDS AND SODS

It happened in Tel Aviv :-

Two Diggers were sitting on the kerbstone very much under the weather, when a young Lieutenant came past. When neither Digger took any notice of him, he turned back and stood in front of them. As no attention was given him he asked -

> Well boys, do you know who I am?
> One Digger looked up, turned to his cobber and said -
> You're drunk Jack and so am I, but Mr. — — doesn't even know who he is.

Military Definitions :-

Q.M.   A bird of strange habits, when attacked, covers itself with indents and talks backwards.

Infantryman:

> An animal of weird habits. It displays a strange aversion to work. It is trained to live underground during the daytime, and to emerge at night seeking what it may devour. When in the open on the move it closely resembles a Camel.

****

It happened just prior to debarkation. Bob Noonan, the little bloke with the big instrument (he plays in the band) was "standing by" near the gangway, helping in the removal of certain equipment belonging to the band, when a pair of pips passed by. A certain nervous Sergeant of the "he'll-get-on variety, wishing to give the pips room to manoeuvre, shouted excitedly to Bob. "One pace step back!" Bob stepped — over the side. It is said that when he finally got rid of the mud, his language set a record that will endure for all time.

****

Private to Sgt. Major:-

> What would you do, if I called you a .?.!.?
> S.M.   "I would crime you"
> Pte.   "What would you do if I thought you were a .?.!.?"
> S.M.   "I could not do anything"
> Pte.   "I think you are a .?.!.?"

Who was the Lance-Corporal, who wrote home and told his wife that a Jackal was a bird?

Favourite Songs:-

The Italian Navy:	Show me the way to go home.
The British People:	Pack up your troubles in your old kit-bag.
Petain:	Prisoners Song.
Hitler:	I'm heading for the last round up.
Laval:	Poor wandering one.
Mr. Spender:	Roll out the barrel.

Fond Mother:-

My boy friend has written home and said he is sending me by boat mail a striped kimona.

"Whatever will you do with it?" asked her mother.

"I don't know I'm sure. I s'pose I can chain it up in the yard, but what I'll feed it on, goodness only knows."

MUD & BLOOD wishes to advise troops that copy of interesting or humorous incidents for the next issue, should be handed to Major Birch.

NOT A HYMN OF HATE

Astonishment, and wonder at the vague possibility of a splendid war time dance tune being regarded as Britain's counter to the Hun's hymn of hate were my reactions when the band of a Cairo night club recently visited declined to play "Till the Lights of London Shine Again." Although perhaps combining somewhat commonplace sentimentality with a quite usual war theme of hopes for peace with victory, this dance number is popularly regarded as one of the only true songs the present conflict has yet produced. Having a particular liking for its melody, I rarely attend any dance or cabaret without requesting the orchestra for it. Sydney and Melbourne gladly played it for me, and Perth showed no greater reluctance.

THEN LEAVE IN CAIRO —

During my time there I visited this particular cabaret, and on each occasion put my request to the band: With hushing whispers and fingers to lips, the leader firmly but politely declined. His attitude almost suggested that one should show more discretion than to ask.

I still wonder whether this Cairo hotspot labors under misapprehension about the song, or can see in it some deep and dark meaning which remains hidden from even its most fervent Australian admirers.

Lieutenant Harry Marshall.

CHAPTER 3

TOBRUK, 28th April, 1941.

     This third issue of the Battalion publication is sent forth with much trepidation, and under circumstances that the preceding two Editors did not have to contend with. Memory brings back envious recollections of Professor Nimbus (J.A. Allan) and Lieut. Harry Marshall, each struggling in the throes of authorship in more or less cosy surroundings, with large foaming tankards to hand, their humour and imagination still further stimulated with the knowledge of the wet canteen just around the corner. Such adjuncts to journalistic effort not being available, you readers will have to be satisfied in these pages with a little dry humour.

James Alexander Allan.

Harry Marshall

Jim Mulcahy

Of all the jobs the C.O. picks out for us, this is about the toughest up to date. "Bring out something humourous in the morning" he said, thinking perhaps he was talking to Lennie Lower. Well, we'll be the first to admit we are no Lennie, although our wit does at times get distinctly Lower and Lower, especially if the company we're in is broadminded enough.

By the way, B Coy. were very disappointed when their fighting patrol went out the other day under George Gardiner and the enemy, after one look at George, decided to see what the weather was like up Derna way. Moral - if you want to get to grips with Jerry, don't let him see George coming.

The whole bad part of the business, though, is that B Coy, unable to get into holts with Adolph's minions, have started shooting each other up. Hope the practice stops soon, as many are wondering whether, if Capt. Gahan allows any more face fungus to accumulate, Major Perry will not perhaps quite excusably mistake him for General Wirewhiskers, and deal with him accordingly.

This practice of collecting little souvenirs from the enemy is becoming a habit. As well as wristlet watches, etc., it is learned that A Coy recently felt the want of a mortar. A small force duly sallied forth and returned with an enemy mortar. Consternation set in when it was discovered there was no ammunition to fit, but not for long, as the same party coolly set forth the next day and captured the necessary bombs, which were duly used (and are still being used) against the people they were captured from. How's that for scrounging, Sgt. McDonald?

Talking about scrounging, A Coy seem to have the poor old Pioneers not to mention the Transport folk, licked to a frazzle. Yesterday, Private Barrett of that Coy calmly proceeded some 3000 yds into enemy territory, took possession of a truck and drove it back into our lines, where no doubt it will be useful. However, the joke is on the Transport platoon, which, after all the assistance in the world had been given, had written the truck off as unattainable. Laugh that off, Mr. Clarke.

Sporting enthusiasts at BHQ are greatly intrigued in an argument that has arisen, and if a match can be arranged between the two concerned, many wagers are sure to be laid if B Echelon are game enough to back their man. Boasts have been made by the said B Echelon that they have a Corporal renowned for his ability to get into a slit trench quicker than the eye can see at the first sound of a plane in the air, and can stick closer to the ground than a stamp to a letter when he gets there. However, BHQ possess a burly sergeant who has the confident backing of all who have seen him in action.

We will be very pleased to hear from anyone in the Battalion who has any item of interest or amusement to offer. Either send in a note or ring the Orderly Room and give details. Remember, it is our aim to bring Mud & Blood to you each day, providing circumstances permit, and our poor old brains won't stand the strain unless a helping hand is given by all and sundry.

Has this happy thought struck you, as it did me today? This is the first time in all my life I have more money than I can possibly spend. Tobruk will be for ever emblazoned on my memory, if only for this unique fact.

Have you heard this one? The cameraman of a well-known newsreel company who has been in the Middle East, ran up an expenses bill for over 400 Pounds, without sending a bill to the firm. At last, urged by cable to send in an itemised bill, he sat down, and after much groaning and moaning, managed to recall a good many items, and sent the bill to London. They wired back saying that his expense sheet had been examined by the firm's accountants, and there was still ten shillings unaccounted for. The cameraman got very enraged, stormed into Marconi House in Cairo, and sent off a cable as follows:-
"Tip to Admiral for manoeuvring battleship so as to give me a good picture - 10/-.

****

INSIDE ITALY

A remarkable account of conditions in Italy is given by a disillusioned Italian who has just arrived in a neutral country after a three weeks tour of Northern Italy. "Within a few days of crossing the frontier, I realised the enormous changes in popular feeling since my previous visit three months ago. It is perhaps best typified in a young cousin of mine brought up a facist who was a fervent worshipper of Mussolini up to the outbreak of war. Now I found that when summoned recently to a Facist rally, he had returned disgusted and torn up and burnt his uniform.

The Trieste hospital and many emergency hospitals are packed with wounded from Albania. Despite the deep sympathy for the wounded, the Fascist collections for them meet with scanty response, owing to the suspicion that the Fascists are embezzling the money. Commerce in Trieste is completely at a standstill for fear of British planes and submarines. In Bari I found the oil refineries terribly damaged by British raids. Everywhere the people are listening to the British broadcasts which they frequently trust more than the Italian.

The wretched food situation throughout the country is well-known. I saw several demonstrations of hungry women with whom the police did not dare to interfere. Germany's monopolising of the former sources of Italian food from German occupied countries is hotly resented."

EPILOGUE

Today you and I are not only part of history. We are history in the making. For years we have enjoyed, almost without effort, freedom, won for us by others who endured, treasures of art and letters not painted or written by ourselves, free speech and enfranchised thought earned by unknown heroes in forgotten days. Today, the guarding and safety of all these things depends on us. The heritage of the ages is in our keeping. We are not creatures of destiny, but destiny itself, for without us all that is decent and kindly and holy, will perish from this earth.

BBC News — 28th April, 1941.

British troops in Greece, it is reported, are continuing their withdrawal. German sources claim that their forces occupied Athens yesterday afternoon, as well as several towns on the coast. No confirmation of this is to hand, but it has been impossible to communicate with Athens since Saturday. The last report to come from Athens stated that German planes had bombed and machine gunned the streets, but it was believed that historic buildings and relics had not been damaged.

German forces have crossed the Egyptian frontier near Sollum. The enemy force is reported as comprising two motorised columns, and is largely composed of Italians. British fighter planes have machine gunned transport at Derna.

In Addis Ababa, houses are being decorated with the national colours in anticipation of the Emperor's homecoming. Elsewhere in Abyssinia, attacks are being pressed home to our advantage, and the South African troops are doing especially good work close to Dessia.

Further contingents of Dominion air force trainees have arrived in England, comprising Canadian, Australian, New Zealand and South Africans, and will go immediately into action

Enemy air action over England was on a small scale. One German bomber dropped bombs over a north-west town. A single raider also dropped bombs over the north-east coast of Scotland. In retaliation, RAF bombers attacked Hamburg on Saturday night. Extensive damage was caused, and many parts of the city were left in flames. Bremerhaven, Emden and LeHavre were also attacked.

Mr. Willmott, former Ambassador to France, declared that present US policy of aid to Britain and China might lead to war, but that would be preferable to peace dictated by the aggressor nations.

Mexico and US have exchanged instruments of ratification of air and military pacts recently negotiated.

Mr. Churchill made an important speech last night to the House of Commons. Difficulties in reception made it impossible to record the speech, but it appeared to concern a decision either taken (or about to be taken) by America to convoy supply ships over the Atlantic by her own battle ships. Should this prove to be the case, it certainly will be the most heartening news we have heard for many weeks, and will assuredly bring closer the time when we can all return to our homes, with the consciousness of a job well and successfully concluded. However, it will be wise to wait until we hear a rebroadcast of the speech before giving complete credence to the above.

TOBRUK, 29th April, 1941.

The writing of this fourth issue of Mud & Blood is a comparatively pleasant affair compared with last night's anguish of soul. Tonight inspiration sits at our elbow, and every now and then a contemplative sip produces a new trend of thought. However, perhaps the most pleasing thought of all is the recollection of how the Transport Section rose to the bait in yesterday's issue. They kicked at our little bit of bandinage, and our heart rejoices in consequence. We've been trying to get a "bite" from Mr. Clarke for a long time now, and were extremely fortunate yesterday to find him at a moment when he had temporarily lost his sense of humour.

By the way, reverting to the abovementioned bottle of inspiration, did you all receive your issue today from the C.O.'s fund. Modesty will not let us claim that we were instrumental in procuring this very acceptable donation, but maybe the C.O. WAS a little touched by the pitiful hint we gave yesterday of how dry we are. Anyhow, the C.O.'s fund has done wonderful work, and has provided many amenities that the boys don't even know about. Hereunder are a few of the items provided which could not otherwise have been enjoyed:-

Xmas cheer	55.872 Pounds P.		
Sewing machine	7.500		
Lamps	4.620		
Coy. funds 5 Pounds each	20.000		
Sports goods	18.075		
Padre's Canteen	8.000		
More beer	17.280		
Still more beer	14.400		
Miscellaneous items			
including advances			Pounds P.
for leave purposes	62.470 GRAND TOTAL		208.217

May the fund continue its good work, and may you all, in your letters home, encourage our good friends in their efforts on behalf of the Fund, by telling them how acceptable have been the various items it has provided.

We heard rather an amusing incident today relating to our old friend Sgt. Jack O'Brien, that famous wielder of the tin opener stationed at B Echelon. Jack, as you may have heard, ranks high amongst the speedsters down there, and in addition has a compact but deep little dugout to which to repair when Jerry looms overhead. Yesterday, some bright lads coaxed a donkey to take up its abode in Jack's little home, and tethered it to a pole in the centre of the dugout. The latter is large as dugouts go, but there wasn't a great deal of room left after the advent of the donk. Anyhow, Jerry shortly afterwards appeared overhead, and there was the usual Stawell Gift imitation amongst the sundry personnel down there. Immediately shelter was gained, grinning faces were poked out and turned expectantly in the direction of Jack's home. We'd cheerfully swop our next free issue of Gyppo cigs for a photo of Jack's face when he went head first into his den and found himself astride the rump of the donkey, with two large lustrous eyes gleaming round at him in the semi-darkness. Anyhow, our B Echelon reporter informs us that the celerity of Jack's exit to the outer world was something to marvel at. We can well believe it.

A horrible thought has just struck us — we are taking a frightful risk baiting one of the cooks. Jack may endeavour to get his revenge on us for publishing his discomforture by forgetting to burn the breakfast porridge, or might even go to the extreme lengths of putting some milk into the "bread and milk". Perish the thought.

Did you see that very nice little bit of work yesterday morning when a lone and very frightened Jerry was chased across the sky by one of our fellows. Jerry was in a deuce of a hurry, and whether by accident or not we can't say, managed to drop his load of bombs ON HIS OWN LINES. We only hope they did a lot more damage than the occasional ones he drops on our side of the fence.

We have wracked our brains all day trying to think up a funny story for today's issue, but alas, owing to the extremely bad company we are forced to keep here in BHQ, couldn't think of one that was printable. However, call around sometime, and if you've one on the hip we will entertain you for hours.

Tomorrow is going to be a very busy one for us - we have decided to go around all our TEETOTAL friends to see how they are shaping. After all, in these uncertain days one should never miss an opportunity of extending a friendly gesture, and it will certainly be a treat (or we hope it will be) renewing old friendships.

Congratulations today to B Coy. for the very excellent little job they did the other night, when a patrol under Lieut. Jess accounted for some 25 of the enemy, with only one minor casualty to ourselves.

Incidentally, during this encounter our chaps were creeping silently towards the enemy, and had got to the stage when voices were heard, amongst other sounds, some 100 yards away. Suddenly a dog started to bark lustily, and most of our chaps nearly had heart failure. They froze to the ground, expecting every moment to see the enemy come charging at them. Nothing happened however, and after about ten minutes the dog stopped, and it was deemed advisable to continue. Imagine the feelings of the Platoon Commander when he discovered that one of his men had fallen sound asleep, and had to be shaken violently by the shoulder before he could be wakened. "A fellow's got to make up his loss of sleep somewhere" he grumbled. Of course, it was his second time out, so perhaps there was an excuse for him being so blase. No, its not true that his O.C., on hearing of this man's propensity for sleeping, immediately nominated him for a position on BHQ staff.

We endeavoured to get the news this morning, but there appeared to be an attempt to jam the broadcast, and we were only able to get snatches here and there. However, with the aid of a little imagination we were able to piece it together, and can vouch for the following as being reasonably accurate.

BBC NEWS — 29th April, 1941.

Our troops are continuing their withdrawal from Greece. Generous praise is given to the Anzacs, who, it was stated, fought a rearguard action for 2½ weeks. Nearly everyone in one party was wearing bandages, but everyone was still cheerful. Our artillery did an excellent job, a team of 21 guns kept firing continuously for over 8 hours at the rate of a shell per gun per minute. Colossal losses in consequence were inflicted on the enemy.

A party of 27 officers and men of the Yugo-Slav army have succeeded in reaching Moscow.

Severe dust storms on the Egyptian border are holding up the enemy advance there. However, it is confirmed that Sollum has been taken. A Curtis fighter machine gunned 21 troop carrying planes in Libya, and it is believed that severe losses were caused.

It is reported from Abyssinia that the Italian stronghold of Dassawa has been captured yesterday. The only places remaining in Abyssinia where Italians are still entrenched are Gondor and Jumma (?). Civilian Italians are being interned at the rate of 1,000 per week.

The RAF has been very active over Holland and other enemy occupied countries, and also inflicted heavy damage on Emden.

TOBRUK, 30th April, 1941.

Well, here we are tonight, replete and satisfied after the best dinner we have yet had in Libya. Congratulations, B Echelon. You have turned out many meals for us under all sorts of adverse conditions, and perhaps we have been unduly critical without properly appreciating your difficulties. However, tonight's was a stout effort, and you would have been amply rewarded had you seen with what gusto the boys cleaned up their mess tins.

Several of the lads have approached us, and asked if our columns could be made available for the purpose of expressing their appreciation of the good work being done so unostentatiously by the Padre. There is nothing that will give us greater pleasure. Padre Morrison, may we, on behalf of the boys of this battalion, express our grateful thanks for your untiring efforts to further their comfort. It may please you to know that you have earned the esteem of every one of us, and we can assure you that your labours have been thoroughly appreciated.

Battalion Headquarters had its first real taste of "bingle bingle" on Monday night. Jerry sent over a few shells and the shrapnel was flying all over the place. After watching some of our more windy merchants, we are more than ever confident we could field a whole team capable of beating the rest of the battalion to the nearest funk hole. And was it a treat to watch them today at their pick and shovel exercises. We could afford to sit back and scoff; we inhabit a cave naturally hewn in the solid rock.

Incidentally, Jerry is getting a little more businesslike every day, and our little bit of chipping of those who take sensible precautions is not meant to be taken seriously. Nobody but a fool goes around looking for trouble, and the best advice we can offer is - KEEP YOUR HEAD DOWN AND YOUR TAIL UP. The tail, by the way, is not nearly so vulnerable a part as the head, and whereas a piece of flying shrapnel might cause a serious hole in the head, another hole or two in the other extremity could easily be sistained without causing disastrous results.

Reverting to Dimra days - A certain member of "Jarvie's Mob", (the wizard of the salute) walked smartly into the office to draw his pay. After signing for the cash and pocketing same he spun round on his heel and began to walk out. Noting the omission of the usual salute, the paying officer halted him and asked "What do you usually do when you receive your pay?". Without a pause came the reply "Spend it, Sir."

A member of a certain B Company fighting patrol on his return from an expedition asked the following:- What popular war song does the effect of a Dinkum Aussie hand grenade remind you of? Hands, Knees and Boomps a Daisy.

We received a phone call from leading B Echelon representatives who have propounded the following queries:-

" We of the Transport Section, location B Echelon (where it is nice and safe) are wondering who the portly BHQ sergeant is · who was so intent on being a change daily girl that, to catch a car for a swim, he left a patient dangling his feet in a dish of Condy's for an hour or so. Mr. Editor - can you help?"

(Certainly, the sergeant in question was Les Allen, but you have your facts mixed up a bit. In the first place, he didn't want to go for the swim - it was us, as his best friend, who insisted on it. Secondly, he informs us that when the said patient removed his boots, he was compelled to vacate the RAP for his own protection. Ed.)

> "We would also like to point out that we think the figures of
> the C..O.'s fund shown in Mud & Blood are just about as
> accurate as the diagnosis of the said sergeant."

(Regretfully we admit that our figures were astray - our attention had already been somewhat tersely drawn to the matter by the C.O., who pointed out that we had omitted to include the primus stoves purchased for the Companies, also the recent issue of chocolate, and many sundry other items. With regard to your implication re the AAMC sergeant, we will leave him to defend himself, but we understand that he hasn't made many mistakes, and only a few of them have proved fatal. Ed.)

> "B Echelon would appreciate Mud & Blood being printed on
> softer paper."

(This is a matter that will have our sympathetic attention, as we are well aware of the great trouble B Echelon is experiencing in finding sufficient paper of the right sort to cope with the epidemic they are suffering down there - an epidemic that always rages at its worst when Jerry is hanging about. In the meantime, we will see if Capt. Morrell cannot issue a few extra rolls - we can never turn a deaf ear to the plea of a friend in distress. Ed.)

> "B Echelon are seriously contemplating, should Mud & Blood
> refuse to publish their sundry contributions, producing
> their own publication, which will be all Mud and no Blood."

(We hardly think, for the reasons mentioned above, that B Echelon will be able to spare the necessary paper, but possibly, if the threat contained in the end sentence is carried out, the paper could be used for both purposes and no one would be any the wiser. Ed.)

By the way, Sgt. Jack O'Brien informs us that he will bake some raspberry tarts for the boys today, if he is supplied with the necessary raspberries. Remembering the numerous dishes of bully stew, the boys will no doubt come to the rescue. Anyhow, on behalf of the boys, thanks a lot, Jack. None of us has seen a tart for a long time, and are wondering if the issue will be on the same lines as the beer - one tart to two men. Such an issue would produce its problems; when the beer is issued, we can always dig up a pal who doesn't drink, but where in the whole battalion would we find a chap who would pass over his tart.

We know you chaps in the front line haven't too much spare time, which probably accounts for the fact that few contributions to this publication have so far come to hand. However, we do want this little paper to be truly representative of the whole battalion, and would urge that each

Company send in daily its little scraps of local news, details of any amusing incident that occurs in their lines, or particulars of any meritorious act of any of their personnel.

CHAPTER 4

TOBRUK, 3rd May, 1941.

The "bingle-bingle" is going strong tonight, and somehow I don't think there will be any great demand tomorrow at the RAP for number 9's. We are looking forward with intense pleasure to tomorrow's spectacle of feverish activity amongst BHQ personnel. Sgt. Marshall will undoubtedly lower his dug-out by another ten feet; the RSM is sure to have his batman looking for another site; and the various drivers, under the able leadership of Dvr. Douglas Innis, will also be continuing their drive down under.

We overheard a conversation the other day as to whether we TOBRUK heroes were likely to get a special medal after the war in recognition of our magnificent stand (modest, aren't we?). The discussion gave us food for thought, and we asked ourselves the question - why wait until after the war? So it is with pleasure we announce that this publication has decided to bestow a special medal - to be known as the Mud & Blood Medal - upon those members of this Battalion adjudged by this paper to be worthy of the honour.

The Medal will be symbolical, and will have stamped upon it a shield, quartered, surmounted by fleas rampant, each quarter bearing respectively a tin opener, plate of bully stew, empty beer bottle, and a dirty singlet. On the obverse side will be carved a grain of dust. We toyed with the idea (the only thing we can toy with these days is ideas) of introducing a bar sinister, but finally decided that any sort of a bar would be singularly inappropriate.

Awards announced in this issue are thoroughly well deserved, and we extend our congratulations to the recipients. Winners of the Medal are as follows, and they are entitled henceforth to use the letters MBM after their names:-

Sgt. G.R.McDonald
>   for introducing the most fantastic furpheys we have ever seen outside the Melbourne Herald.

Sgt. Bill Marshall
>   who has left no stone unturned in his effort to see that the said furpheys are given the widest possible circulation.

Captain Morrell
>   for his magnificent feat in getting rid of the Band Instruments.

Captain Agar
>   for the extraordinary brilliance of his effort in beating the writer at chess seven times in succession.

We would certainly award a Medal to the genius who started the furphy about us taking Sollum if we knew who he was.

Companies are asked to nominate members of their various platoons deemed worthy of receiving this high honour, giving briefly their qualifications. Should this journal approve the nomination, they will be awarded the Medal through these columns.

Have you heard this one, which I believe dates back to the last war. A returned soldier with a decided limp had just arrived back in Australia. Feeling hungry he decided to have a meal, and unwittingly walked into a Vegetarian Cafe without realising the nature of the place he was in. A young and attractive waitress approached, apparently most anxious to be helpful. "Crushed nuts," she enquired. "No, merely a gunshot wound in the leg," replied the soldier.

We heard today about the exploit of a young hopeful in C Coy, who, during their raid on the enemy the other morning, managed to work up quite a hate for Jerry. Running along after a bunch of fleeing Jerries, he saw one of them drop a clip of explosive blue tipped bullets. Stopping in his pursuit, he picked up the bullets, slipped them into his rifle, and let fire at the enemy, by this time a considerable distance away. Seeing a figure topple over, he immediately assumed full credit, and despite the hail of bullets and shrapnel, stopped, took his knife out of his pocket, and calmly cut a nick in the butt of his rifle.

Nature Study - The Bower Bird.

Dear Readers,

As you all know, the Bower Bird is noted for its strange habit of collecting all manner of odd items for its nest, not because it needs them, but because of its peculiar collective nature.

For this reason, its nest is always easy to find by the huge pile of miscellaneous objects strewn around the vicinity. As B Coy. has recently lost several useful articles which they prize highly, they ask all readers to help them in their quest.

i.e. Who is the Regimental Bower Bird?

(Sgd.) Tommy Gun

BBC NEWS — 3rd May, 1941.

A rebellion has broken out in IRAK, apparently largely inspired and encouraged by the Axis. British Forces have recently been sent into the country to protect our interests there, and appear to have control of the situation.

A Turkish statement has been issued to the effect that Turkey will remain loyal to her friendship with Britain.

Evacuation of British Forces from Greece is now complete. There may be still some small bands here and there who will ultimately be able to make their escape. Whilst no official figures are as yet issued, Lieut-General Sir T. Blamey estimates that 43,000 men have been successfully evacuated out of a total number of 60,000. Men lost at sea during the evacuation would not be more than 500.

The Under-Secretary for the Navy in a speech stated that, whilst other theatres of war were important, the only vital sphere was the Atlantic, where it was most essential that our shipping lanes be kept open for the passage of food and other supplies.

President Roosevelt has ordered the mobilisation of all machines in the country to be put into continuous operation night and day, seven days a week, in order to speed up production of war supplies. The question of "freezing" all foreign credits in the United States is at present under consideration.

Authoritative denials have been made of reports that Spain intends shortly to sign the tri-partite pact.

There has only been slight activity in the Sollum area during the past few days. The heaviest enemy onslaught yet experienced has been directed at Tobruk, and has been repulsed. Our troops in Tobruk remain in great heart, and have maintained a great offensive spirit. Their sorties have resulted in heavy casualties on the enemy, and in addition many prisoners and guns have been captured.

Three enemy bombers were shot down over England last night. Raids were not of an extensive nature.

TOBRUK, 9th May, 1941.

Well, Mud'n Bloods, here we are again, after a respite of a few days, occasioned by the fact that we have been moving our residence up nearer to most of you. However, we are now nicely settled in, and are able to give some time to what is happening around us.

Some little delay was caused in sending up the wireless set, with the result that we were unable to get any news for you. As the set has now arrived, we presume that Major Birch must have paid up the instalment arrears. So far we cannot get the plurry thing to work — not even being able to raise our old friend Lord Haw-Haw — but have sent for an axe and a couple of crowbars, and with a little delicate manipulation of the said instruments, we guarantee to make it speak or forever hold its peace.

We have a very cosy little home these days, with all mod cons. The bathroom is a trifle cramped, and we had difficulty in getting the piano down the staircase, but these small annoyances aside, we haven't much to complain about. The many other advantages far outweigh the slight inconveniences mentioned. For instance, we get a better type of dust here than in our former home, and in far greater abundance, whilst the delightful breezes caused by the shells passing overhead are wonderful to behold.

On the night of our arrival, we were greeted by a friendly little horned viper lying outside the front entrance of our dug-out. The dear little pet caused another breeze - at least as far as we were concerned - but Two-gun Tony, our Adjutant, not knowing the little fellow was only there to have a playful nip or two at our ankles, let fly with his .45 and, my word, did that viper get it in the neck.

Another advantage our present home has over our previous one is the much better type of neighbours we have up here. They appear to be a very hospitable crowd, entertaining practically every night, as we can both hear and see them letting off their little fireworks display, big bungers, rockets and fairy lights, etc. The other night it looked so exactly like Henly that we went for a walk to see what we could pick up, but, we might mention, we had our usual Henley luck.

We have never missed our printing press so much as during the past few days. If it were available today we would select the largest type in the box and blazon forth across the front page, in the best Murdoch fashion, - WELL DONE, DON COY. As it is, mere typewriting doesn't do justice to our admiration of the Fighting Dons, not only for the excellent job they did in capturing several posts from the enemy, but for the manful way in which they have held them since.

By the way, we haven't had any more nature studies from our friends down at Sleepy Hollow - B Coy., since they forwarded that interesting little paper on the bower bird. Surely with all the time and opportunities they have at their disposal they could send us a little treatise on the habits of the hibernating animals — you know, those codgers that dig in and then go to sleep for six months or so.

Have you heard this one? No, I don't think you would; its clean. Lieut. Smith had recently been promoted to the rank of Captain. He was greatly annoyed because one of his men kept continually addressing him by the prefix "Mister" Smith. At last he could stand it no longer. "Why do you keep on calling me Mister?" he complained. Quick came the reply — "Well, as a matter of fact, George, I didn't know your first name until this morning."

We have obtained the following stew recipe, and recommend it to our friends Sgts. Leo Jones and Jack O'Brien, of B Echelon (well on the way, I might mention, to being awarded the Mud and Blood Medal), as an improvement on the stew we are getting now. Try it on your primus to-night -

"Take half a tin of bully, drop it several times in the dust, taking care it is well smeared all over; pour one gallon of water over it; insert four peas (one in each corner of the dish); add 3 lbs curry powder; stir well making sure the peas remain separated (so that the stew may be equitably divided later); taste, and if not enough dust and grit chuck in a couple of extra handfuls. Heat over stove until luke warm; serve when it becomes stone cold again."

This is a very tasty dish, and the above quantities will be found sufficient to feed a whole platoon. In fact, we shouldn't be at all surprised to find some left over.

BBC NEWS — 9th May, 1941.

President Roosevelt is still indisposed and confined to bed.

Suez Canal was bombed by enemy aircraft last night. No casualties. Damage inconsiderable.

Features of operations at TOBRUK continues to be offensive spirit of our troops there. Fighting patrols are daily and nightly taking toll of the enemy.

Conditions in IRAK are proceeding satisfactorily in our favour. RAF is doing excellent work bombing enemy strongholds.

Heavy bombing attacks were also delivered by RAF at Benghasi, where landing grounds were plastered.

News from Abyssinia tells of further prisoners and material captured. All other operations in Abyssinia and East Africa continue satisfactorily.

RAF bombed two enemy supply ships in Mediterranean; one ship was left in a sinking condition. Malta was attacked by enemy aircraft yesterday. Damage not yet known.

A letter from the Egyptian Premier was read at a meeting of the Egyptian Chamber of Commerce, London, yesterday, in which he stated that Egypt's feeling of good will and friendship remained unaltered.

It is announced that an agreement between Germany and the Vichy Government has been concluded. In view of the fact that the war has lasted longer than expected when the Armistice was concluded, Germany may have found it necessary to make some modifications of the original Armistice terms. Conversations are still proceeding in regard to the cost of the army of occupation being borne by France.

A White Paper has been issued in London stating that documents seized at Loftofen reveal that Germany is finding difficulty in handling the Norwegian civil population, who still remain strongly pro-British.

Mr. Menzies, Australian Prime Minister, is at present in Canada, and will go to Washington on Thursday.

In the course of a speech in the House of Commons, Mr. Churchill praised the Garrison of Tobruk for their excellent recovery and for the brave stand they were making. He also stated that at Sollum, our army was in a position to hold the enemy, as it was almost impossible for him to move his mechanised army across the desert. Mr. Churchill stated that Britain had in the past month doubled her tank output, and that he hoped that in succeeding months she would continue to double and re-double it.

TOBRUK, 11th May, 1941.

Becoming somewhat bored with the rustic environment that has been our lot for some few weeks, we chortled gleefully yesterday when duty demanded a visit to the big city of TOBRUK. Unfortunately, the place resembled MELBOURNE on a Sunday afternoon; the trams had stopped running, all the pubs were closed, and all the good sorts had gone to the beach, or somewhere. Anyhow, we wandered around admiring the various heaps of stones; saw a big hole in the road that would have provided a week's entertainment for a crowd of MELBOURNE's famed "hole in the road sticky-beaks." At last, in desperation approached a Tommy standing on a corner and hopefully enquired if he knew where we could get a drink. He gave thoughtful consideration to the query, and finally and with all due seriousness volunteered the information that if we waited until five o'clock we might be able to get a "dish of tea" at the Salvation Army hostel. When we recovered from the shock we found ourselves in the A.G. Hospital.

Looked in and saw for a few moments our old friend Sgt. Don Urquhart who, unfortunately, is a patient there with a damaged arm. His many friends in Don Coy., and indeed throughout the Battalion, will be pleased to learn that he is progressing well. His arm will, in time, make a satisfactory recovery, but will probably keep him out of further action, a fact that is causing him no little regret. However, he was pleased to see us, and asked if his good wishes could be conveyed to all his old pals, and his especial thanks to Lieut. Trevor Neuendorf, but for whose timely assistance his wound would have been much more serious.

Then went on to see Pte. John Erswell, of the "I" Section, who stopped a piece or two of shrapnel the other day. John, also, was extremely perturbed because he has been informed he is "for Blighty". Despite the fact that he is a very sick man he nearly wept at the thought of going home and leaving all his cobbers here. He asked us to convey his remembrances and regards to his friends, and in particular to Lieut. McKoy.

Going further, we discovered Pte. J. Coleman of "A" Coy., who was doing very nicely, thank you, and hoped to be back again shortly to have another crack at the blokes who had got him. He also wished to be remembered to his pals in "A" Coy.

The more we saw of the chaps in there, the more we admired their indomitable spirit, their unflinching courage midst conditions not exactly of the best. (there was an air raid during our visit). The thought struck us that the very complimentary messages that have been sent to us recently by Prime Ministers and Generals, have not been altogether undeserved, especially by those of us who have been among the unlucky ones.

Ruminating on the above, it has struck us that we personally belong to the select band of TOBRUK HEROES. What pictures are conjured up of free beers, etc., when we get back again. Fancy walking into Young and Jacksons on a Friday afternoon with the medals (we suppose we'll get about a dozen each) floating proudly a la Goering on our bosom. We'll have a crafty look around, select someone with a Greek medal, and innocently enquire "What's that for?". After imparting the information he is sure to enquire - "What's yours?". Get the idea? We thought it all up ourselves in one of our thirsty moments, but generosity was always our failing, and we pass on the scheme with no thought of reward.

Incidentally, what will the wife say when we write home and tell her she has a hero for a husband? She has never suspected it before, we know. Not that she has ever said so, but our natural sensitivity makes us aware of the fact that she never connected us with heroism in the slightest degree. Hope the "Herald" is giving us a good write-up; then maybe she will believe us and our natural fears engendered by stories of the "man who comes around" will be partly allayed.

At the moment there is a milk strike in full swing in Melbourne. One trusting Mud'n Blood confided to me that he hoped the plurry strike wouldn't be settled until we got back again. Just to be on the safe side we suppose.

Received a letter from our young hopeful last week, and he enquired for a few trophies. Thought if we sent him a set of Iron Crosses he might be pleased. Can anyone in "B" Coy. supply the necessary?

Understand there is a little obstruction being placed on the collection of Iron Crosses, etc., from live Jerries. Well, we ask you, what use are live Jerries anyhow; and what use have dead ones for Iron Crosses?

Duty keeps us chained to a desk and typewriter (nearly all the time anyhow), and so far we haven't had a chance to have a decent whack at anyone. Can we count on any of our friends the next time they are on a fighting patrol, tossing a hefty grenade where it will do the most damage, and say "That one's from the Editor of Mud'n Blood?" We sound bloodthirsty, but we can tell you, the spectacle of those poor chaps in hospital yesterday, maimed and bandaged, and in many cases completely helpless, lying there with tense and strained nerves whilst bombs were dropping in and around them, caused our blood to boil with impotent rage. Think of that, Mud'n Bloods, and also the wanton bombings of our hospital ships, when next you get to grips with the cowardly Hun. Already he has learned to respect the fighting prowess of this Unit; shortly he'll think of us with positive dread. You may, perhaps, think us too emphatic on this subject; we only wish you had been with us when that raid was on yesterday.

The comparative lull we have been experiencing here seems to be almost world-wide, as there is nothing of undue importance in the news, which we give hereunder:-

BBC NEWS — 11th May, 1941.

33 planes were brought down in raids over England last night, making a total of 123 for the first ten days in May. These figures would indicate that the problem of dealing with night raids is on the way to solution.

Further extensive RAF raids have been made over Germany and part of Poland, causing great damage. Dutch pilots took part in these raids as part of the 'commemoration" service on the anniversary of the German invasion of Holland.

Operations at Tobruk continue to be quiet, mainly on account of dust storms, which are hampering both sides. Further RAF and Naval raids have taken place on Benghasi. Our mechanised forces are still active in the Sollum area.

Cleaning up operations continue in Abyssinia, where Rhodesian forces are mopping up the isolated places that have so far not capitulated.

A Cairo communique states that the Iraqi position remains quiet. The Iraqi elements have withdrawn to positions on the Euphrates River. The Rebel leader admits that his losses have been heavy. The Iraqi Airforce has been bombed and shot out of existence.

Shipping losses continue to be heavy, 487,000 tons having been sunk during the month of April. This, however, includes 187,000 tons of shipping sunk off Grecian coast and elsewhere in the Mediterranean. On the other hand, it is estimated that the enemy has lost 600,000 tons of shipping during the past six weeks.

12 Australians have been awarded the DCM, and 46 Australians the MM.

Mr. Roosevelt continues to make progress after his recent illness.

US Government has taken 100 Italians into custody, in addition to 160 Germans arrested last week. It has been announced that shipping services from the US to the Red Sea are to begin.

Reports from France indicate that a number of Municipal Councils have been dissolved - decrees have been published in the French Gazette to this effect. Apparently these councils have not been collaborating sufficiently or satisfactorily enough with the German authorities.

The Opposition Leader (Mr. Curtin) urges Defence Commander in Chief to co-ordinate forces within Australia's strategic area.

TOBRUK, 12th May, 1941.

This morning we are frankly in a sentimental mood - for which fact we sincerely apologise, as we are liable to bore you exceedingly in this issue. Although we admit there is nothing more revolting than a sentimental Staff-Sergeant, we plead as extenuation the fact that yesterday was MOTHER's DAY; and it was the first time for many years that we were unable to send the usual little reminder of our affection that is always to be valued and prized. However, it is a safe bet that none of us were out of HER thoughts yesterday; and, indeed, does a day pass that she does not think of us and breathe a prayer for our safety and well being. We suggest, therefore, Mud'n Bloods, that a spare half hour could very well be employed today in dropping a line to allay her fears, and at the same time let her know that on MOTHER's DAY, even in such a God-forsaken place as TOBRUK, she was not forgotten. We are reminded of a little Kipling verse running something like this -

> "If I were hanged on the highest hill,
>   Mother o'Mine, O Mother o'Mine,
> I know whose love would follow me still,
>   Mother o'Mine, O Mother o'Mine.

> "If I were drowned in the deepest sea,
>   Mother o'Mine, O Mother o'Mine,
> I know whose tears would come down to me,
>   Mother o'Mine, O Mother o'Mine.

"If I were damned of body and soul,
I know whose prayers would make me whole,
Mother o'Mine, O Mother o'Mine."

Talking of Mothers reminds me strongly of Lieut. Clarke, at B Ech., who is conducting a rest home for war-weary warriors down there. Mother was never so kind as Ken is - he soothes the fears of his charges, bathes their bodies, feeds their stomachs, changes their diapers after every air raid, and finally kisses them fondly on the brow and sends them back to their Company new men indeed, fit and refreshed to carry on the good work. Well done, Mr. Clarke, and in recognition of your sterling efforts we have pleasure in bestowing upon you the Mud & Blood Medal. Your career in this unit, Sir, has been followed with interest by the writer ever since the day you pinched the Derna Fire Engine, a feat, we might mention, that puts even Ned Kelly's exploits to shame, and we congratulate you heartily on the distinction that has been bestowed upon you. May you continue to live up to the high standard that the M.B.M. demands from all its recipients.

Complaints have been coming to us that the copies of Mud & Blood sent out are not being circulated. Unfortunately, scarcity of paper prevents us issuing more copies, and it is expected that each person to whom a copy is sent will, after perusal, pass it on to his neighbour. We know this publication is extremely valuable and in years to come will be eagerly sought by millionaire collectors, but in the meantime it is being issued with a view to being circulated amongst as many of the troops as possible.

Just remembered, we received a somewhat incoherent message from B. Echelon yesterday afternoon - am afraid they drink too much Vichy water down there - our shorthand is irreproachable and certainly states that Lieut. Clarke has marital ambitions, Sgt. O'Brien has faded away so much that he is falling through his belt (must be eating some of his own cooking), and someone else has been having so many pills that every time he runs the troops think they are being machine gunned and flee for cover. We know nothing of the pill merchant; we certainly would not believe for a moment that Sgt. O'Brien would be guilty of eating anything he cooked; but we do know for a fact that Lieut. Clarke has been sighing inordinately (he says it is indigestion) for the past week or two, hoping against hope that some nice-looking little blonde will come along and assist him by taking over the duties of Matron of his rest home - amongst other duties of course.

By the way, in a conversation with one of the Company C.S.M.'s the other night, he indicated that he was unaware that the last beer issue was from the C.O.'s Fund, and was under the impression that it was from the Aust. Comforts Fund. We are afraid that many of the issues from the

C.O.'s Fund have been wrongly credited to the A.C.F., and suggest, in all fairness to those who are working so hard back in Melbourne to augment the C.O.'s Fund, that when an issue is made the source from whence it came should be clearly indicated.

Here is today's news:-

BBC NEWS — 12th May, 1941.

British night fighters continue to take heavy toll of enemy planes - last night another seven German bombers were brought down. During the night the raids caused a certain amount of damage, but not many casualties. Many historic buildings - of no military importance whatsoever - were among those damaged. The Houses of Parliament, Westminster Hall, Westminster Abbey, Big Ben and the British Museum were all victims of bombs. In this regard it is pleasing to hear that the main structure of the Abbey still stands, whilst Big Ben is still striking the hours.

The RAF bombed Hamburg and Bremerhaven for the second night in succession, and Emden and Berlin for the third night in succession. Tremendous damage is believed to have been caused, and the flames from burning buildings were a beacon for further bombers. Nine of our bombers failed to return. German fighters engaged our bombers, and at least four of them, and possibly more, were shot down.

Surprise raids were made on enemy air bases in Sicily on Sunday, and considerable damage caused. Many machines on the ground were attacked and set on fire. The enemy was taken completely by surprise, and troops were machine gunned as they ran for shelter. The flames from burning planes and buildings made it easier for our succeeding bombers to find their targets. All our aircraft returned safely.

The RAF was also active in Libya, Tripoli being again heavily attacked. The Mole and shipping in the harbour were hit repeatedly. RAF also attacked aerodromes at Derna and Gazala, where aircraft on the ground were destroyed. Land operations at Tobruk continue unchanged. Further prisoners taken.

Activities in Abyssinia continue satisfactorily.

Our armoured cars have inflicted heavy damage in raids on strategic points in Irak. An aerodrome has been occupied, also a port adjacent to the pipe line, and the whole area in this locality is now under our control. King

Ibn Saud of Saudi Arabia stated that he is unable to give any assistance to the rebel leader in Irak.

Mr. Hoover, former American President, stated that he supported the giving of maximum help to Britain, but thought that to do so it was essential that US remained outside the war.

Union leaders have called a strike in 60 factories of General Motors in USA. Leaders claim strike will not affect contracts for war supplies, but this is denied by the management.

Considerable satisfaction is felt at the great co-operation between British and American scientists and designers of aircraft, who are now pooling their ideas and resources.

Sir Frederick Stewart, Minister for External Affairs, welcomed to Australia a delegation from Netherlands East Indies in Sydney yesterday, to discuss questions of defence matters in the Pacific.

Mechanisation of the British Army is proceeding rapidly, and already is comparable with German mechanised forces in regard to equipment.

TOBRUK, 13th May, 1941.

Today we extend hearty congratulations to Lt.Col. B. Evans, Lieuts. K. and T. Neuendorf, and Lieut. G. G. Anderson, all of whom celebrate their birthday today. We can quite imagine Papa Neuendorf philosophically shrugging his shoulders when advised of the advent of the twins, probably relieved, seeing it was the 13th, that they weren't triplets.

Life is full of little worries, but surely Army life is particularly vexed with those gnawing little feelings of apprehension that lie ever-lastingly at the bottom of one's mind. It's quite a fascinating pastime studying the faces one comes in contact with, and hazarding a guess as to what their particular worry might be. Thoughts something like this would probably never be owned up to, but might nevertheless be true:-

C.O.'s Batman -   Wonder if the Chief remembers how much whisky was left in the bottle last night.

R.M.O. -   Blast this absentmindedness - I hope that squeaky voiced begger never finds out that I really only meant to circumcise him.

R.M.O.'s Batman -   I know my heart won't stand the shock if someone finds he HAS some change when I give him a haircut.

Q.M. -   Good God, down one tin of peaches during April. Hi, Spooner, cut out all fruit issues immediately.

ME -   What the heck are we going to put in Mud & Blood tomorrow.

YOU -   When the blankety blank are we going to be able to BUY some beer again - even if its only as much as the Tommies get.

ALL OF US -   Wonder how long this ruddy war is going to last.

In the issue before last, we had a small paragraph complimenting D Company for their recent valorous efforts. The following reply has been handed in:-

OUR ATTACHMENTS -

Not in the Murdoch fashion, dear Editor of Mud & Blood, which, as you are aware, goes in for size without sincerity, but in our own private fashion, the Dons pay tribute to attached personnel in our recent stunt. A circus has many performers, especially one like ours. The stage is set, and out they come. The Fighting Dons. There's a perfect circus name. Into the spotlight, to the overtures of "Galloping Gertie" and "Sniping Toni" jangled the "Carriers". A youthful act this, with a mechanical twist. The Dons appreciated them. So did the audience. They applauded them loudly and long, showering the ring with everything but the Iron Cross. This was very embarrassing to the poor chaps who were kept busy dodging here and there to avoid getting the mechanical part of their act too twisted. Damn Good Show! Our attached Stretcher Bearers arrived breathless and with many of their bearings somewhat stretched. And our Sigs, positively "reeling" - that's not bad - under their load. Communications are vital. It's good to know that we can talk to someone else occasionally. Our neighbours aren't on speaking terms with us. How we'd love to drop in their back gate just to have a few words with them! A big hand to all who went in with us. Without them we could not have got a laugh out of the whole show.

One prominent Mud'n Blood got in touch with us yesterday and enquired our advertising rates. He wanted a large advt. extolling the merits of his rest home. We were immediately in a quandary, but with presence of mind always on tap, were able to say quite nonchalantly "Two tins of milk or one tin of pineapple." He countered with the offer of one tin of bully which, of course, was turned down flat. A compromise was finally arrived at, the agreed consideration being one tin of milk and half a tin of syrup. The trouble is, we have no circulation figures to quote, and are in consequence hampered in our business transactions. Our minds have been active on the problem, however, and we think the following advertisement assuredly will draw a reply from everyone who reads it. We can then count the replies, multiply them by ten, add five hundred, take away six free copies, and can then issue an audited statement guaranteering our circulation. This is approximately the system followed by all the other great publications, so we had better adopt the standard practice. The catch advertisement is hereunder:-

YOUNG LADY, lonely, attractive, feels it is her duty to give all she has to our brave troops. She accordingly offers a luxurious home, choice viands, and freedom of her cellar to the first handsome Aussie soldier who will supply protection and co-operation. Applications must be addressed to the Editor, Mud & Blood, and should enclose copies of references from previous girl friends, and, if possible, a photograph of his testimonials."

Incidentally, the advertisement that we have agreed to accept will appear in a later issue, AFTER payment has been received and disposed of.

Here's today's news:-

BBC NEWS — 13th May, 1941.

Great excitement has been caused by the announcement that Herr RUDOLPH HESS, Deputy Fuhrer and Leader of the German Socialist Democratic Party, has fled by aeroplane from Germany and landed by parachute in Scotland. He was at once taken prisoner, and is at present in hospital with a broken ankle. German Radio, in announcing his disappearance, stated that fears were felt for his safety, as the Fuhrer had forbidden him to travel by air owing to the fact that he was suffering from hallucinations. Reasons for the flight have not yet been ascertained.

Herr HESS was the third most important man in Germany, and was the only one of Hitler's entourage who was originally with him in the famous 1923 putsch. In consequence he enjoyed the Fuhrer's confidence more than any other man, and his defection will be a severe blow to Hitler. He had been nominated by Hitler as next in line for succession after Goering to leadership of the German nation.

RAF bombers attacked Mannheim last night, also other Rhineland centres.

Enemy activity over England last night was very light, and damage caused was not extensive. One enemy bomber was shot down, making a total of 135 for the first 12 days of May, compared with 133 brought down during the whole of April.

Details of the damage done to Westminster Palace is now announced. The famous debating chamber of the House of Lords is completely ruined, as well as many other historic sections. Yesterday was the anniversary of the Coronation - today the scene of that brilliant ceremony is a heap of rubble, although the High Altar remains intact.

Benghasi was again attacked by units of the Royal Navy yesterday. The enemy resisted with shore batteries and dive bombers, but no casualties were inflicted on us, whilst we caused considerable further damage. Tripoli was again attacked by our bombers.

Troops at Tobruk and Sollum continue to harass the enemy and take prisoners. In Abyssinia there is nothing fresh to report. There is no further news from Irak, but the situation there is becoming more stable.

Japanese Army Journal stated yesterday that Japan could not look on with folded arms while Germany and Russia came to agreements that might be prejudicial to Japan's interests. It stated that a German victory in Europe did not necessarily mean peace in the Pacific.

Moscow Radio reports that bitter fighting in China continues.

Netherlands Foreign Minister, speaking in Sydney, said that the Dutch would fight in the Pacific if and when her interests or territorial integrity were infringed upon.

Lord Halifax stated in Washington that the Battle of the Atlantic was being fiercely waged, and with American help was slowly turning in our favour. On its successful conclusion, Britain would turn her attention to gaining supremacy of the air.

TOBRUK, 28th May, 1941.

Our finer feelings (despite popular belief we still have finer feelings) make us bow our head with shame when we reflect upon the fact that some twelve days have elapsed since our last issue of Mud & Blood. However, the urge to write came upon us in the early hours of this morning and would not be denied. Despite letters written to mother, wife and the little girl friend in Perth, the craving for expression was not satisfied, and the drastic remedy of bringing forth another publication was toyed with until the temptation proved too great and we succumbed. Hence, Mud'n Bloods, this infliction.

Before embarking on our usual course of calumny and persecution, may we take this opportunity of expressing the admiration of the whole of the admin staff for the very gallant, courageous and workmanlike manner in which the boys performed the comewhat stiff tasks asked of them during the past few weeks. One and all, they stood up to the job, when many of less hardy fibre would have wilted. We know the last thing any of them want is praise, but the occasion couldn't be passed without us expressing how proud we are to be associated with you in a Battalion that has not only lived up to the traditions of its illustrious predecessor, but has already in its short fighting career earned for itself a glorious name, adding not only lustre to itself but upon the whole of the second A.I.F. Well done, Mud'n Bloods, you have shown that you can take it, and by heck., you have also shown that you can give it too. In the course of our official duties we come in contact with many personnel from other units, and it is a never failing source of gratification to know that the prowess of this Battalion has won renown and admiration throughout the units in this locality.

We are indebted to a subaltern of one of our battalions who has recently arrived from England, where the officers were billeted in an erstwhile girls' school. His sleeping quarters were in one of the dormitories, and on the first night of their arrival there was a rush to press the bell, over which the following notice was pasted: "If in urgent need of a mistress, ring this bell."

We sit here today, full of well-being, benignity and bully-beef, and a hasty survey of the many blessings of our present position leaves us with the impression that things could be much worse than they are. We contemplate with equanimity all the things we can now do that in our former life were strictly taboo, and congratulate ourselves on the happy fact that, here in Tobruk, life has become a very simple and uncomplicated affair. What's that? What are all the blessings we're burbling about! Here's a few:-

We don't have to pay 7d a pot for beer.

We never wake up in the morning with a hang-over.

We are never faced with the necessity of making that awful decision - whether we'll have a foaming pot of Vic, or merely a small Abbot's out of the bottle and go home early.

Think of having to go back to that terrible period when we used to make a dash, one eye continually on the wristlet watch, and sink about six pots in ten minutes until the time-worn "Time, gentlemen, please" heralded the cessation of our bibulous efforts and the commencement of the inevitable attack of indigestion that followed.

No more the embarassment of having to refuse the occasional "one on the house" that used to spoil our whole evening.

These are some of the things we don't have to do any more. Now for some of the things we can do that we used so often in the past wish we were able to:-

Squat down anywhere we like without worrying about the crease in the old nether garments.

Shave when we can't bear it any longer; wash only when our friends insist on it; boast to one's pals about how long it is since the old shirt had a wash. It's a great thing, this scarcity of water. We get a wonderful kick every time we peer at our singlet and think what the wife's face would look like if she could only see it.

After a hard day's work we can always go straight to bed, without the necessity of having to entertain the particular female in hand. By far the greatest blessing of the lot. Just think of all the wasted time when we used to sit in the park, or on the beach, with some stony-hearted female by our side, just sufficiently responsive to keep hope fluttering faintly in our breast, until finally, after every vestige of hope had vanished, we always discovered that the last tram had gone, and were faced with the usual five miles walk home. Of course, when we got back, being a Tobruk hero, maybe..................

RUMOUR

Actual evidence I have none,
But the Colonel's batman's cousin's son
Heard a sentry on his beat,
Say to a cobber he chanced to meet,
That he had a brother, who had a friend,
Who knew when the war was going to end.

One of the little crosses we have to bear in this life is the constant stream of Mud'n Bloods who come into the orderly room and enquire for Private Ron Lees. When we see a new face we always know he has brought a watch to be repaired. Every time we see him afterwards during the succeeding six months we know he is calling for his watch. Its wonderful how they never give up hope that perhaps, some day, they might get their watch back again. If they could only see the multitudinous piles of springs, wheels and sprockets that literally clumber up the place they would realise that they are more likely to get two or three watches back than only one. The other day we had a stocktaking; records showed that 24 watches had been handed in, 18 had been passed out again presumably, as far as the owner knew, containing all the original bits and pieces, and there were still sufficient works for another 22 watches in hand. We are authorised to state that Ron only requires another three watches to be handed in for repair, and he will have all the necessary pieces for a number 6A Meccano set. Will some kindly disposed persons please oblige. Already he has built a beautiful model fire engine, but still needs a couple of wheels and a mainspring to complete it.

Caution tells us that we really ought to keep this one for another day's issue, when we may be scratching our head in desperation for a story that no one has heard. However, the Scotch in us has got to be stamped out, so here goes:-

Applicants for jobs at a certain advertising agency have to fill out a questionnaire, revealing much about themselves. One applicant got through the first three questions easily - his name, address, and age coming readily to mind; but he got hung up on the fourth. Finally he gripped his fountain pen and wrote opposite the entry "Sex" the frank answer - "Occasionally."

Talking about the handiness of the Private Ron Lees mentioned above reminds us of an incident that occurred some few days ago. Surely everyone in the Battalion knows "Leaping Lena", the somewhat capricious but commodious old I-Ti bus that houses the office of BHQ whilst on tour.

The other day, whilst in the care of the Transport Section, Lena decided she'd had enough and called it a day in the middle of a mine field into which she had accidentally strayed. Sundry pokes in her vitals failing to stir her, she was summarily hauled to the site of BHQ, where the news was imparted by Lieut. Clarke that she would never go again, and that she was to be discarded. Having conceived an affection for Lena, Ronald was naturally disturbed. However, with the aid of a crochet needle (that surgical instrument that has fixed so many troubles) he was able to get her going again, and today, gentlemen, we have pleasure in advising that Lena is as of yore. Incidentally should the Transport Section want to borrow Ron and his crochet needle at any time they have a difficult job on hand, we will at all times be pleased to make him available.

We give hereunder some extracts from a recent pamphlet issued by G.H.Q. Middle East, which requires no explanation:-

HOW AMERICA IS HELPING

The German radio said as recently as March 13th last that the British front line would wait in vain for the arrival of the vitally necessary American supplies. "Britain will be beaten before American help becomes effective," said the announcer.

The Germans said the same thing in the last war. For example, in 1917 a Major Moraht said in the "Berliner Tageblatt", "We have no need to take America's sabre-rattling seriously. The whole American armaments scheme remains for us nothing but a phantom."

Once again Germany is about to get a rude awakening.

As a result of the Lease and Lend Bill, and the companion Appropriations Bill, the strength and resources of the greatest producer in the world are at the disposal of the Allies. There are six basic materials of modern industry - coal, iron, copper, cotton, oil and rubber. Only in rubber is America deficient, and here the British and Dutch Empires between them produce 90% of the world's supplies.

As a manufacturer of finished goods, the United States outstrips all competitors and Mr. Knudson, head of her war production, has told the senate that she can double anyone else's output once the mechanics of the scheme are under way. In the view of experts, the real flow will not begin until the last quarter of 1941, but it is worth remembering that when production begins, it begins at full pressure.

In the last war, American shipyards tripled their output in the single year between 1917 to 1918, and by 1919 had more than quadrupled the 1917 figure. This time they intend to better that performance.

American aeroplanes are the biggest single item in the appropriation. In addition to 11,800 machines already ordered, many of which have been delivered, 10,700 are to be provided under the Bill.

American weapons of all kinds swell the volume of material aid, and an important element in their make-up is that they are being forged for use in both countries, the chief advantage of this interchangeability being that when the crucial stage of the war is reached, it is the key to volume production and keeping the utmost material in use.

American food for British mouths is another of the scheduled supplies. Foods of all description are already being accumulated as a precautionary measure.

"These overwhelming prospects of material aid do not mean that we in Britain are sitting back" said one writer. "We know that our utmost effort is required till the aid arrives and after it arrives; and until victory. We too are in our shirt sleeves."

MESSAGE FROM THE C.O.

Since our little publication broke down temporarily following our big stunt of the 17th May, there has been some delay in my expressing my appreciation other than verbally to all Mud & Bloods, of their magnificent efforts that day.

The General visited the Unit whilst in the rest area, and personally complimented us on the courage, bravery and fighting spirit so pronounced in the 23rd. He visited a number of the men, but, unfortunately, most of you were away swimming at the time.

Mud & Bloods all, it was that spirit which has put the 23rd very much on the map, and made this unit already worthy of its gallant predecessors, the old 23rd. For the sake of our brother Mud & Bloods who have passed on, we will maintain, and possibly intensify this spirit wherever we go, and come what may. For the second time in the past six weeks I have to tell you how proud I am to command the 2/23rd Battalion.

(Signed) B. EVANS, Lt. Col.

BBC NEWS — 28th May, 1941.

President Roosevelt, in a long awaited speech to the Nation, declared a state of UNLIMITED NATIONAL EMERGENCY. He stated that under no circumstances would America stand by and see Hitler achieve his dream of world domination. The recent approach to the shores of America of various war activities had brought home to all that the war lay at the very doorstep of America.

Further details have been given concerning the sinking of the "HOOD". A lucky hit from the German battleship "BISMARCK" on a magazine caused the "HOOD" to blow up. It is feared that there are few survivors. This sinking was soon avenged, however, as the "BISMARCK" was shadowed by cruisers, and also the British battleship "PRINCE OF WALES" which, although slightly damaged, succeeded in registering further hits on the German vessel. This was ultimately sunk at one minute past eleven yesterday morning, when various units of the British Navy closed in on the enemy ship. Further action against the accompanying German cruiser is proceeding.

Mr. Churchill announced that during operations to prevent seaborne enemy troops from landing in Crete, two cruisers and four destroyers had been sunk. Great losses however, had been inflicted on the enemy, and how many thousands of her troops had been drowned it was impossible to say.

The position in the various theatres of war is as under:-

CRETE: The battle proceeds with unabated fury, and the issue lies in the balance. Both sides are being reinforced. Enemy forces have enlarged their penetration of our defensive positions, and our troops have in consequence been forced to withdraw in certain sectors. The losses sustained by the enemy are greatly in excess of our losses.

TOBRUK: Position remains unchanged.

SOLLUM: Enemy forces have penetrated the frontier in three places and our forward troops have fallen back. The enemy advance is similar to the one made three weeks ago which was repulsed. Our forces continue their harassing tactics.

ABYSSINIA: The continued surrender of large bodies of Italians together with enormous quantities of supplies is the main feature in this locality.

IRAK: It is stated that the position here had been largely re-established.

SYRIA: Nothing new to report. British Consuls have left the country, whilst Syria and French Consuls have been asked to leave Palestine.

Mr. Churchill stated that the proposal to introduce conscription in Northern Ireland had been dropped, as the difficulties of enforcing same would be more than the measure would be worth.

TOBRUK, 29th May, 1941.

We have just come from the milling throng around Quarter Hutchinson (he was issuing the rum) and we are left with mingled feelings, predominant being a wave of intense admiration. What a dispenser he would make in the poison department of a large chemist shop. Never a drop too much; if inclined to err at all, it would certainly be on the safe side. His artistry in judging the exact quantity is superb; and his inexorable determination not to deviate from the scale laid down is something to marvel at. When we hinted that AMR & O (Routine Orders) laid down that a Staff-Sgt. was entitled to 10 c.c.'s more than anyone else he actually demanded to see it, knowing full well that our pride would prevent us from producing the written proof. And will we ever forget the look of horror that overspread his countenance when we accidentally joggled his elbow as he was pouring out our issue! Not that we like the stuff. We heard someone say "Hasn't rum got a horrible smell?" Words fail us. Rum doesn't smell. We admit it has an aroma. We'll even go so far as to say a beautiful aroma. In fact, we decided not to drink our issue, but to keep it and have an occasional sniff. Can you imagine our feelings when, after three hearty sniffs, we found there was nothing left. However, we have no complaints; we can certainly vouch for the fact that NO ONE received any more than three whiffs. Tonight we'll finish the composition of a new musical hit entitled "The rum has ended but the aroma lingers on."

The Scotch are a dour, determined race. We are half Scotch on the maternal side, and so are half-dour and half-determined. We wish we were'nt. Why? Well, it's a long story. Major Birch gave one of the orderly room clerks who offended him a long (too long) Italian cigar. He, in turn, having a fancied grievance against us, duly passed it on, and the Scotch in us urged us to the disastrous step of smoking it. The first three inches were sheer hell. If it hadn't been given to us for nothing we would certainly have thrown it away. The next five inches were got through in a sort of coma. Then outraged nature rebelled, and we were reluctantly forced to discard the remaining ten inches. Over the next half hour let us discreetly draw a veil.

Then, somewhat haggard and drawn, and still with a definite greenish appearance round the gills, we staggered back to the orderly room, where we were greeted by our old friend C.S.M. Wiseman, whom we hadn't seen for some time. Casting one concerned look at our sickly countenance, he exclaimed - "I see you have Jimmy Rintoule cooking for you down here."

Someone remarked to us the other day that we were lucky in the orderly room not having to go over the top. We don't quite know what he meant, but if he thinks that the lads in here don't share in the perils of warfare he doesn't know what he is talking about. If anyone doesn't believe the deadly danger the staff encounters almost hourly, we invite them to come along whilst Capt. Kiel is exhibiting his Tommy gun. We also remember the time, not so long ago, when Lieut. Orr was showing us how to de-louse an Italian mortar bomb. He started off with a verbal explanation of the various parts, unscrewing as he talked. His commentary was something like this. "You hold the bomb firmly in the left hand, pressing down on the pin at the top. Next you unscrew the bottom flanges, like this. Now, let me see, I haven't struck this type before, but I think you pull this out and......." We regret exceedingly that we never heard the rest. We were too far away by then.

Have you heard this old bewhiskered one -

A famous hotel in New York, whose clientele includes many salesmen and buyers from other cities, keeps a record of the business houses represented among the guests. A breezy lady buyer from the West, after filling in her name and address on the registration card, seemed to be brought up short by the query - "Firm?". She nibbled her pen a moment, then wrote "Not very," and headed for the bar, ready for anything.

CONFUCIUS SAYS - Strangely enough, when a girl gets into a jam, the boys no longer consider her sweet.

BBC NEWS - 29th May, 1941.

The battle of CRETE has developed into a hand to hand struggle. NZ, Australian and British troops are fighting side by side. It has become an intensive stand-up slogging match, and can be summed up as old style fighting on the ground, with everything new in the air. It is the type of fighting that appeals greatly to the Dominion troops. Germany has employed over 1,000 troop carrying planes. Our troops have been forced back by sheer weight of numbers alone. However, the result of the action still sways in the balance.

World wide interest has been taken in a speech made by President Roosevelt, and various eminent British men, including NZ Prime Minister, have expressed appreciation of the terms of the speech and what it implies. No alteration of the Neutrality Act is necessary to permit the much greater effective assistance that will be given by America to ensure freedom of the seas. Mr. Wendell Wilkie stated he was thoroughly in accord with the President's speech, and called on all Americans to co-operate to give effect to the policy it foreshadowed. American newspapers interpret the speech as meaning that the American Navy will now act without hesitation to safeguard American interests and further the aid that is being given to Britain, even should such action be necessary at DAKAR, GREENLAND, or any other place where America deems it necessary to take action.

Two large enemy supply ships of between 8,000 and 10,000 tons were bombed by our planes off the shores of CRETE. They were last seen enveloped in clouds of black smoke. In addition, one of our submarines has torpedoed four large ships on their way to North Africa. One of these was a liner of approx. 18,000 tons, and contained probably 3,000 troops. The others would be around 4,000 tons each. In all, since hostilities commenced the enemy has lost 2,873,000 tons of shipping, including ships captured, seized, scuttled and sunk. Since the 1st March, we have accounted for 61 enemy supply ships.

It is announced that H.M.S. Submarine "Musk" is overdue, and must be considered lost.

There is little or no news from North Africa, where German troops are reported to have occupied Hell Fire Pass at Sollum. The German forces did not appear to be doing anything more, now that they had reached this point.

There is no change in the position at TOBRUK.

The RAF made further raids on BENGASI and caused considerable damage.

In ABYSSINIA our troops are continuing to mop up isolated bands of Italian forces. Of the total of 300,000 men originally in the Duke of Aosta's army, 90,000 have been taken prisoner. Only two forces of any size remain, one numbering about 25,000 in the north-east, and another force estimated at 17,000 in the Gondor district.

In EAST AFRICA.the position has been cleared up sufficiently to permit our aircraft to be withdrawn and sent to IRAK.

In IRAK there is nothing new to report. No inclination appears amongst surrounding Arab countries to assist the rebel leader.

Only slight spasmodic air raids were made over England during the past 24 hours, and very little damage was done.

The RAF carried out daylight raids over the east coast of France.

The offer made by Australia to provide timber for the rafters of Westminster Abbey when rebuilding commences, was gratefully referred to in the House of Commons. However, it was decided that until hostilities ceased, no consideration would be given to a rebuilding programme.

TOBRUK, 31st May, 1941.

Our own private Gestapo has informed us that today marks a very special event, the anniversary, in fact, of a very important happening in the domestic life of the elder Morrell's a goodly number of years ago. We can well imagine Papa Morrell stroking his Dundreary in ecstatic admiration of what the Nurse was holding, and saying "There is the best future Quartermaster the world will ever see." That his prophecy came to pass is local history. Capt. "Con" Morrell, we offer our heartiest congratulations on this, your ---- (gosh, we nearly let it slip out) birthday. We know that your zeal for the welfare of this Battalion is beyond mere praise; but we do wish that your determination to see that the members of this unit are fed on the fat of the land was not so fixed. For the past seventeen days we have had the fat of the land served up to us for breakfast without a break, and although we know that this is a feat never before equalled by any other Q in the AIF, we suggest something a little less luxurious would be appreciated, something simple like asparagus on toast, f'rinstance.

We promised that a copy of this publication would be sent regularly to that grand soldier and leader, Capt. Ian Malloch, who is away at the moment nursing wounds that, when we saw him last, made him look something like a colander. He was more concerned at the prospect of leaving his men, however, than about his numerous injuries, and it will be a happy day for him (and for us) when he has recovered sufficiently to re-join us. From tales brought back by our re-joined men yesterday, he appears to be making satisfactory progress, as does also Lieuts. Eric McRae and Wally Brown. To all three we send the best wishes of the whole Battalion, and hope they will get some small amusement and interest through reading these columns.

We are minded to write of a little incident that occurred in "A" Company lines last week. Out of the recent issue of BEER (how does one write "beer" to denote bated breath?) the company was given 14 tins, in addition to sundry packets of cigarettes. There being no adequate means of splitting up 14 tins amongst the hundred or so thirsty souls, it was unanimously decided to draw lots; strangely enough, four tins were drawn in one section (don't know whether they were running the raffle or not!); they in turn decided to hold a sub-raffle, and eventually one man was the proud possessor of the four tins. Staff/Sgt. Bob Penhallurick informs me that strong men swooned, whilst weaker ones died a lingering death, at the spectacle of the lucky one swilling his gains. The next morning, we are informed, he had a hangover big enough for an elephant, and was he proud of it?

We had a nightmare last night. We dreamt that a letter had arrived from the wife reading something like this:-

"Darling: (She always calls us "darling" in our dreams).

Today a large hamper arrived for you from the Welfare Association with the request that I forward it on to you. I opened it and found it only contained some nasty tins of beer, chicken, asparagus, lobster, preserved fruit, cake and chocolates. Knowing that you were probably getting plenty of these, I gave the lot away to the bottle-oh, and am sending you instead a nice pair of hand knitted socks and a pair of ear muffs."

We copy the following paragraph quite unblushingly from the columns of Jonathan Swift, in the Melbourne Sun. After all, he is quite at liberty to copy anything of ours, and probably would if he thought he wouldn't be found out. The para referred to is as follows:-

"It may amuse you to know that most American newspapers have featured the story of the Digger who, when asked his opinion about the desert in Libya, replied: "It's all right to fight a war in, but for a nice quiet holiday give me Dudley Flats." Most of the newspapers have been careful to add a footnote to the para informing their readers that Dudley Flats is a noted Australian resort." Can any of you Mud'n Bloods beat this somewhat weak comparison? There's one place comes readily to our mind, although we haven't been there YET, despite copious advice to go there. After all, Dante was an I-ti, and probably had this place in mind when he wrote his famous bed-time story.

BBC NEWS - 31st May, 1941.

Hitler is throwing more and more reinforcements into Crete, with total disregard of the immense losses being sustained. The fighting continues with unabated ferocity, and it is clear that Hitler is determined to permit the slaughter of his men in countless thousands provided he can obtain mastery of Crete. It is clear that our resistance could have been much more formidable had our Air Force not been forced to evacuate the aerodromes on the Island. As it is, our troops are subjected to dive bombing attacks almost continually, whilst German troop carrying planes arrive almost monotonously carrying reinforcements. It is impossible for our forces to withstand such superior numbers, and they have been forced back at Canea, which it is claimed by the enemy has been taken. Man to man, our forces are vastly superior to the enemy, and tremendous losses have been inflicted by our troops. However, the result of the battle is still undecided.

The Admiralty announces the loss of the cruiser "York". This vessel had been damaged in recent operations off Greece, and was being repaired in a bay on the coast of Crete. It was subjected to heavy bombing attacks and has now been written off as a total loss. Casualties, however, were only two killed and five wounded.

In IRAK a Commission of Internal Security has been set up. British troops are nearing BAGHDAD, and in fact at one point are within five miles of the City. The rebel leader, Raschid Ali has fled to IRAN.

Mr. J. G. Winant, American Ambassador to Britain, has been recalled to US by President Roosevelt for consultation. He expects to return to Britain within a few days. He was cheered by a large crowd on alighting from the "clipper" on his arrival.

In US the Curtis-Wright works have set a lead by declaring that all holidays have been voluntarily cut out by the workers. This means that the output of the factories will be increased by 60 more planes, 178 more engines, and many hundreds of propellors and other parts.

Energetic measures are being taken in the US to round up noted Nazi leaders, and various Nazi activities have been curtailed. The notorious leader of the Bund has been arrested.

There were enemy raiders over the west of Britain last night, but in no case was damage caused, and casualties were slight. Raiders also flew over Northern Ireland, but did not drop bombs.

Dublin, in the Irish Free State, was heavily bombed last night, and severe damage to city buildings resulted. In addition, there were many casualties. A large number of city buildings collapsed, burying many inmates in the wreckage.

At Sollum the German forces have remained stationary, and have made no attempt to proceed further than Halfayu Pass.

At Tobruk the position is still unaltered. In a raid over the town earlier in the week, five enemy planes were shot down.

Soviet Russia and Sweden have signed an agreement in which all Swedish claims in the Baltic have been settled.

At Mansion House, the British Minister for Foreign Affairs, Mr. Anthony Eden, spoke of British plans for post-war re-construction. Britain's aim would be to free the post-war world from want, similar to that experienced after the last war - control would be exercised over employment, markets and prices, without interfering, as far as was possible, in the economics of other countries. Germany must play her part in this post war reconstruction, but Germany had proved herself a bad master of Europe. Five times during the past century she had disturbed the peace - terms at the end of the war would be designed to prevent that happening again.

CHAPTER 5

TOBRUK, 2nd June, 1941.

We have heard a lot about the tall tales that were put over by the Diggers of a generation ago, but the humourist responsible for the following despatch to the Melbourne "Sun" has them all licked. Here it is:-

"Stifling sandstorms and temporary exhaustion after last week's attacks are responsible for the easing off in the German attack on Tobruk. The Nazis are preparing for their next assault in a shimmering heat wave, with a temperature well over 100 degrees, and a sand-laden wind like a blast from a furnace. The garrison, by comparison, is luxuriating in cool bungalows and Italian-built underground raid shelters. They have plenty of food and water - and even a daily newspaper, produced by an experienced Australian journalist!"

Whilst admitting the accuracy of the statements about Jerry's difficulties, our imagination baulks at the "luxuriating in cool bungalows." The newspaper clipping was sent by the wife of one of our Mud'n Bloods, who in addition to adding the caption "Home was never like this" wants to know what he is growling about. As the said Mud'n Blood is also a journalist, we suggest he reply in the following strain:-

The daily lot of the Aussie in Tobruk is, in comparison with Jerry's, quite bearable. Awakened about eight o'clock each morning when his morning tea is brought round, he nibbles at a juicy nectarine in between sips, and plans his day's routine. About nine he rises, has a shower in the chromium and onyx bathroom, toys with some grapefruit and an omelette, and is then ready for the day's battle. Ringing on the house telephone for his car, he is driven to his post, where he remains for the greater part of the day. At midday, the tedium is broken when his lunch arrives. An elaborate lunch is not encouraged by the Authorities, and generally it consists merely of a half dozen oysters, portion of cold chicken with salad, and iced cantaloupe to follow. Excessive drinking of alcoholic beverages is strictly frowned upon, and at no meal is a soldier provided with more than a quart of beer; spirits and wines are never served at the midday meal, being reserved for the evening dinner, when rations are not on such a frugal scale.

Some slight compensation for their arduous day is provided after dusk has fallen. In the sure knowledge that Jerry is completely prostrate after the day's heat, it is deemed unnecessary for our men to remain at their posts, and they are at liberty to join the gay throngs in the streets of the town. There they may sit at any of the open air cafes and sip their tankard of cool ale; they may if they so desire, visit one of the numerous theatres or picture houses; or if their tastes lie in other directions, they may frequent one of the many cabarets, where the famed dancing girls vie with each other in seeing that the particular soldier is thoroughly entertained. One rigid rule that the Authorities never relax is the injunction that each soldier has to be back again in his own bed by three o'clock in the morning. Whilst it is admitted that these conditions are not exactly ideal, they are certainly better than Jerry has to put up with, and our troops - noted for their ability to put up with discomforts without grumbling - are happy to carry on, their faith in their leaders telling them that when Jerry is finally vanquished by the heat and sand-storms, their lot will improve considerably.

It's a hell of a job this; writing copy for Mud & Blood. We can never get our minds off the subject of food and drink, and writing paras like the previous one leaves us with our teeth watering, and the memory of the ascorbic tablet and water we had for breakfast ceases to comfort. As for the writing about dancing girls, well, even if our teeth don't water, we are certainly not unaffected in other ways.

TODAY'S BEWHISKERED ONE: (We know it's a bit weak, but don't hold it against us - it's a hot day.)

Digger in car with Cutie - "Well, here we are alone. What shall we do now?"

Cutie -   "You silly fool........."

Digger -   "Give me time, I was just going to."

BBC NEWS - 2nd June, 1941.

It is announced that weight of superior numbers has forced our troops to be evacuated from Crete. Already 15,000 troops have been successfully evacuated. The total number of British forces has not been stated and it is not known if this figure includes Greek forces. A Cairo communique states that we were prepared to pay a certain price to hold Crete, but as soon as this became too costly we decided to withdraw. It is considered a remarkable achievement to evacuate 15,000 troops under such severe enemy pressure as was exercised. RAF fighters maintained patrols over our ships all day on Saturday, and shot down five enemy planes, whilst it is believed that two Italian bombers were also accounted for. A British rearguard force had taken up a position in the hills where there was better cover from dive bombing attacks. A very heavy toll has been taken of the enemy forces, whilst our own losses have also been considerable.

An armistice has been signed between British Military Authorities and the Irakian Commission of Internal Security. The terms provide for the return of all Irakian soldiers to their peace time stations; the return of all British prisoners; the handing over of German agents and rebel leaders. It is announced that the oil fields are now in the hands of Irakians friendly towards Britain. German influence in the oil districts is not likely to cause further trouble.

A further advance is announced by our troops into the Lakes district in Abyssinia. In the past fortnight, our troops have cleared an area of 100,000 sq. miles. 7000 prisoners have been taken in the south, and even more have been taken prisoner in the northern section. Bombers of the South African Air Force have been active in centres of enemy opposition.

Further RAF raids have been made on an Italian vessel sheltering in a harbour in Tunisia. Further raids have also taken place on Bengasi, and hits were scored on the Mole.

One enemy fighter destroyed in yesterday's air activities over England whilst a bomber was destroyed in last night's raids, which were on a more extensive scale than recently. However, casualties and damage were slight.

Bombs were again dropped on neutral territory in Eire last night, when raids were made on Arklow. It is announced that 27 were killed and 80 injured in the raids made on Dublin on Friday night. Investigations reveal that the bombs dropped were of German origin. Germany denies that she was responsible for the raids.

Interesting information has come to hand in regard to the effect-iveness of the RAF raids on Hamburg and Mannheim. Eyewitnesses de-clare that there is scarcely a district in Hamburg that has not been affected. Our new bombs have been causing terrific havoc. Ship building yards and oil refineries have been completely destroyed, as well as many factories and munition works severely damaged.

Extension invasion exercises have just been completed in Britain. These have formed one of the greatest tests of our defences in the south and east that could possibly be devised, and the result of the exercises has given profound satisfaction.

It is announced that the recent drive for 100 million pounds was ex-ceeded by 24 million pounds. This amount was raised in one week, and the money is to be used to purchase war weapons.

TOBRUK, 5th June, 1941.

Official advice has been received that the following members of this unit have been awarded the decoration set out alongside their names. These awards were bestowed in recognition of conspicuous bravery in the action undertaken by "C" Company, supported by "A" Company and Carriers, on the 22nd April last. This, you will remember, was the first action of any size by a company of this unit, and it is indeed pleasing that the many acts of heroism and self-sacrifice so pronounced that day have been suitably re-cognized. Since then, many other acts of gallantry have been performed, and the reputation of this Battalion stands high. However, to the under-mentioned belongs the honour of being the first members of the Battalion to earn decoration, and we extend, on behalf of all Mud'n Bloods, our sin-cere congratulations. It will be our aim during the next few issues to include a paragraph giving some personal particulars of the recipients, and how they reacted to the news of their sudden burst into fame:-

"C" Company	Capt. R. RATTRAY	M.C.
	Sgt. J. BARNARD	D.C.M.
	Pte.. M. O'CONNELL	M.M.
"A" Company	CSM J. DEANE	M.M.
"HQ" Company	Sgt. C.G. RIGG	M.M.
	Sgt. P. HOOK	M.M.

Capt. Rupert Rattray (familiarly called Capt. "Rats" by the lads - behind his back, of course) would indeed be given a tumultuous welcome were he able to return to his native town - Bendigo, or to Port Franklin, South Gippsland, where lies his present home. We can well imagine the congratulations that will be showered upon Mrs. Rattray and six year old sonny in the latter small fishing centre when the news becomes known. Incidentally, Capt. Rattray confided to us that he is not going to tell his wife anything at all about it, but let it come as a pleasant shock when she reads of it in the newspapers. Perhaps it will not be such a surprise to her after all, as anyone who knows Capt. Rattray well would think it the most natural thing in the world that he should so distinguish himself. Naturally, he is a very pleased and proud man, but his natural modesty will not let him discuss the matter at all.

Sgt. Colin Rigg, one of the younger executives of G.J. Coles & Co. Ltd. Melbourne, ignored his firm's maxim "Nothing over 2/6" when he obtained for himself the coveted honour of M.M. Believe us, a large price has to be paid for such honours - a price of blood and sweat and heroic self-sacrifice that is not within the compass of all of us to pay. His many friends will be glad to know that he has been recommended for appointment to Commissioned rank, and no one in the Battalion has earned his promotion more. A bridegroom of only a few months standing before joining the A.I.F., we can well imagine the pride Mrs. Rigg will have in her husband's double achievement. Colin received his education at the Melbourne High School, topped off with a Bachelor of Commerce course at the "Shop", and if he is a typical example of the young man turned out by these two institutions of learning, the more of their students we have in the A.I.F. the better.

Now to tell you of four valiant fighting soldiers whose claims to decoration have so far been overlooked. Much has been written and said lately of terrific battles, great slaughter, and strategic withdrawals. These are matters upon which we can write with conviction, as the knowledge gained over the past few days from personal experience makes us an expert in such matters. Commencing on the night of 31st May, the enemy attacked in great numbers the four members of the orderly room. The attacks at first were sporadic, but gradually, as the enemy increased his forces, they became widespread and continuous, and of a ferocity unequalled by anything since the battle of the Somme. Our front, both flanks and rear were beset incessantly, and the attacks became heavier as darkness grew more intense. Despite lack of ammunition we inflicted heavy casualties, and morning saw us, pale, weary and blasphemous, but still undaunted. On the night of 1st June the attack was resumed with unabated vigour, and at once developed into hand to hand fighting of the closest description possible. Here we had our first serious casualty. Pte. W.D. Woods, after battling valiantly, was the first to retire from the dug-out, leaving us to fight a lonely and futile battle. In the adjoining cave, loud and obscene noises indicated that Pte. Ron Lees was continuing the struggle, also alone, as L/Cpl. R. V. Fancke, through sheer exhaustion, had given in and permitted the enemy to walk all over him, inflicting what punishment they desired. Again, in both posts, the slaughter was tremendous, but seemed to make no impression on the enemy, whose extreme mobility enabled him to attack here, there and everywhere. Despite the great losses sustained, and believe us, there were no prisoners taken, the enemy continued to attack, wave after wave of them seeming to appear from every nook and cranny. However, dawn found us still alive, although very exhausted. We look forward to a resumption of the battle tonight without confidence, and feel that unless reinforcements are despatched by Capt. Morrell in the shape of numerous tins of flea powder, tonight may see the complete capitulation of the Battalion's most redoubtable fighters.

BBC NEWS - 5th June, 1941.

Reports of the arrival of German forces in Syria are to hand. Steady infiltration of German troops continue at the rate of 12 planes full per day. 150 planes (troop carriers, but empty) were landed on one day. Many so called wounded soldiers have been landed, but these are members of a Tank Corps, and are fit and well and ready for action. Syria is apparently becoming a major post for the German Air Force, and possibly for land forces as well.

British troops have re-occupied Mosul in Irak, in the centre of the oil fields. During the recent fighting the pipe line was undamaged.

US Newspapers state that if Britain is compelled to take steps in Syria, the US will approve such action, as it will have been brought about by France herself, who is not only kissing the rod that beat her, but is using it against the only source to which she can look for ultimate salvation.

The Egyptian Government has resigned, and a new Government is being formed under the same Premier.

There is no further news of the fighting in North Africa or Abyssinia.

Mr. Spender states that out of the 6,486 Australians in Crete before the Germans attacked, 2887 are so far known to have been evacuated - these include 218 wounded.

Mr. Nash states that there are 2,800 NZ's not yet accounted for, and will probably be reported as missing.

It was learned that units of the French Air Force, armed with permission of Germany, are leaving for Syria and Tunisia. A message from Vichy states that the Cabinet has decided to defend Syria and Tunisia against a possible British attack.

US ships are to replace British ships on routes between North America and Australia and NZ, releasing British ships for war purposes.

In widespread raids over Britain last night, three enemy bombers were shot down. Damage was not extensive, and casualties were not heavy.

It is announced that Rumania will shortly become a Totalitarian State with a Government under General Antonesque. 136 Rumanian students of both sexes are to be tried by a military court for an anti-German demonstration at a football match, in connection with the widespread conviction in Rumania that the shortage of food is caused by the presence of German soldiers in the country.

TOBRUK, 6th June, 1941.

Certain names have, through frequent use, become linked together so closely that one is never mentioned without the other. Great partnerships come to mind readily, such as Young & Jackson, Woodfull & Ponsford, Hobbs & Sutcliffe, and Speed & Dixon. We have no doubt that in the future, when we meet a cobber and are reminiscensing over a pot of the old amber fluid, if he says "Do you remember George Dixon" we'll look blank, or if he refers to George Speed, no chord of remembrance will be struck. However, no jog to the memory will be required if he refers to Speed & Dixon. These two have been such close pals that one is never seen without the other, and their various deeds and misdeeds are always performed in each other's company. Both old diggers from the previous dust-up, they know the ropes thoroughly, and their exploits both official and unofficial are a shining example to the youngsters in the Signal Platoon. George Speed is the proud possessor of a Military Medal, but is, we believe, loath to acknowledge the fact until his pal gets one also. That this will soon eventuate we are firmly convinced, judging by the display of fortitude and moral courage displayed recently by George Dixon, when he held a tin of beer for ten days during a particularly hot spell, so that he could have the pleasure of having a drink with his cobber on Anzac Day. "Never missed a drink on Anzac Day for over 20 years," he confided.

Recently, Lieut. Harry Orr has been in the habit of coming to the Orderly Room each night, and enquiring if Mud & Blood was to be had. "Always used to look forward to Smith's Weekly coming out," he explained, "and now look forward just as keenly to my copy of Mud & Blood." Haven't heard anything that sounded so nice to our ears since the day the wife murmured "I will," but we are wondering where the catch is. Shouldn't be surprised if tonight or tomorrow he appears with a bunch of notes and says "I wonder, Jim, if you get a chance, will you type this little report for me. There's only about 592 pages and it won't take you a jiff."

It's wonderful what one quarter of a bottle of beer will do. This para can be used as an unsolicited testimonial for Resch's Lager. After one medicine glassful, one bright lad sat down and perpetrated the following. His desire to remain anonymous will be respected, as otherwise we fear he'd be put on a charge report, and probably sent home as a punishment:-

MY THOUGHTS

I am sitting in my dug-out,
    On the outskirts of Tobruk,
And I'm thinking of you, sweetheart,
    And the job I've undertook.

It's for love of home we're fighting,
    There's a job we know to do,
And while there's an Aussie standing,
    You can bet they'll see it through.

Here's why I'm certain, honey,
    So sure we'll see it through,
For I feel now as I'm sitting here,
    That you are beside me too.

Captain "Con" Morrell got ambitious; knowing that after the war the only "professions" open to demobilised officers will be those of janitors, window cleaners, lift-men and truck drivers, he decided to prepare himself for the future. Beseeching Lieut. Ken Clark for a driver's licence, he was promptly taken for a "test" run. The route selected was the road to Tobruk, and as they were nearing the township, Capt. Morrell must have seen a young Lady adjusting her garter, or something, but he missed observing a Tommy bus coming along the road. Anyhow, to cut a long story short, as they crawled from under the overturned truck about ten feet below the road level Lieut. Clark was seen to murmur something to his comrade. We weren't there, but should imagine he would have said something like this. "My dear "Con", your driving is superb; one would think you had been an MT driver for years. Here is your licence, but I sincerely hope you don't do with it what I have in mind." Anyhow, neither of them were hurt much; Captain Morrell fractured his spine in fourteen places, lost an arm and 3 akers which fell out of his pocket, but with the help of a little seccotine he is himself again. Lieut. Clark was equally fortunate, and escaped with a broken neck, and lost nothing but his temper.

SGT. PETER HOOK, M.M. — My word, Peter, we bet those two initials after your name give you a thrill every time you see them. For the benefit of all Mud'n Bloods, we have to advise that we saw Peter this morning, and he is still walking on air. Peter, by the way, hasn't had the good luck to be born in Australia, owing to a deplorable lack of foresight on the part of his parents. Some two and a half years ago, he threw up his job in London, where he had been pushing a pen across policies and things in an Insurance Office, and came out to Australia, where he went on a station in the Hay, NSW, district. When things didn't look so good in the old country a year ago, Peter decided that the sheep could look after themselves for a bit. Now only 21, he has decided that an Army career is just the goods. They never slung any medals around either in the Insurance game or on the sheep station. His family by the way, are still in London, but so far have been amongst the lucky ones, and have been unharmed by the Luftwaffe. They will indeed be proud when they learn of the deserved honour that has been bestowed on Peter, although we fear that in his modesty he will never give them all the details. Here's the best of luck, Pete; remember that Goering finds room for about a score or so of medals on his ample chest, and there's still room on your own bosom for many more.

BBC NEWS — 6th June, 1941.

Germans are still accumulating in Syria. Hotels at Beirut are full of German officers. Three large air bases in Syria are now under German control. More and more planes have arrived in Northern Syria. Syrian towns and villages near the border of Palestine have been evacuated in readiness for war. A French General states that France is prepared, and will meet British force by force.

Germany is reported to have asked Turkey for help in relieving famine conditions in certain islands under German control. Turkey has complied.

It is announced that 450 people were killed in Wednesday night's air raid on Alexandria. This is the first large scale raid on this city. The raiders flew low over the densely populated areas of the city, and many hundreds of homes were damaged.

A statement to the Vichy Government was released by the US Minister, Mr. Cordell Hull. "We are much concerned at the situation that seems to be growing up between Britain and France," he said. "The US has constantly impressed on the Vichy Government that our basic policy is to aid Britain against those forces of aggression that have subjugated France, and it is inconceivable that France should collaborate with her conqueror."

In order to release further supplies of petrol to Britain, it is likely that petrol consumption in the Eastern States of America may be restricted. Cars might not be able to be driven for pleasure.

In three days Canadians have subscribed 384 million dollars towards their War Loan, which aims at raising 600 million dollars for war supplies.

Five enemy aircraft were shot down yesterday over the straits of Dover.

The Japanese Foreign Minister, Mr. Matsouka, stated that his country's relations with Russia had been satisfactorily adjusted, following the completion of the recent non-aggression pact.

It has been announced in the US that if it is necessary to send troops overseas, the first division has already been 100% equipped.

TOBRUK, 7th June, 1941.

There are moments in a man's life when he feels he could with no difficulty whatever crawl into a match-box, stretch himself out, turn over and go to sleep, and not feel in the slightest cramped. Lieut. Alister McKoy, our Intelligence Officer must have had some such feeling the other day. He was proceeding to a point of vantage to observe what Jerry was doing, per medium of the somewhat asthmatic and feeble motor cycle which he favours. Espying a trudging wayfarer, he pulled up and offered a lift. The man accepted with alacrity, and was astride the pillion in no time at all. The road, however, was somewhat bumpy, and the passenger gave no appearance of ease, and finally offered to get off and walk. Mac, the soul of hospitality would have none of it - "You'll soon get the hang of it. Just hang on and

I'll show you how the thing works," he remarked, trying to put his reluctant passenger at ease. Mac, as you know, is a man of few words (his taciturnity and reserve have often been remarked), and in a brief, informative discourse over the next 45 minutes instructed the man in the best way to ride a motor cycle. Finally, the end of the journey arrived, the passenger got off with a relieved air, and gave thanks to God and Mac for having arrived safely. "Have you ever been on a motor-bike before?" enquired Mac. "Oh, yes," was the reply, "I won the dirt track Grand Prix in Sydney last June." The passenger was Eddie Steinbeck, the world famous motor cycle speedster, now Sgt. Steinbeck, of the local "Bush" artillery, and, for all we know, the very man who keeps us awake each night in deadly apprehension that the next one will be that "Drop-short" that is sure to eventuate one of these nights.

We have just returned from a dental parade, and amongst our companions to the torture chamber was that great old battler, Sar-Major Jimmy Dixon. We don't know how many years ago it is since Jimmy arrived in the Doctor's little black bag, but he himself, admits that he is over forty, which is a pretty good indication that he must be around about eighty or ninety. Anyhow, in the course of a chequered career Jimmy has seen much action; his father was a regular soldier in the British Army, and Jimmy was born "on strength". Jimmy was quite voluble about his career in France during the last war, but forbore to tell us about what he had done in the Crimean and Boer wars. Since 1918, he has seen service in India and other eastern countries, and life here in Tobruk is just apple pie to him. His many friends are always amused at the way Jimmy walks around with a chip on his shoulder, and we can never resist having a sly tip at it every time we meet. On the journey to the dentist we had seventeen arguments, and he won every one of them. Knowing Jimmy had seen service during the battle of Mons, we asked him if he had seen the famous Angél of Mons. "No, I can't say that I did personally," he replied regretfully, "but I remember meeting a wonderful little angel at Armentieres and........" Well, Jimmy is a married man and we will not embarrass him by repeating the conversation further.

We were all sitting outside the dentist's tent - the four members of this battalion who were on the parade, and two British Tommies - and being ultra polite to each other inasmuch as we were all prepared to let the other fellow go in first. "My word," one of the Tommies remarked, "you Aussies can certainly fight. If our chaps had as much guts as you fellows, Jerry would have been licked long before this." We never said a word - of the four "Aussies" present, Jimmy Dixon was Scotch, Bill Marshall came from the Tweed country, Wally Newman (the Padre's batman) first saw the light of day in London; whilst I was the result of a bad mistake made in Northern Ireland. We wonder just what percentage of the "fighting Aussies" were born in Australia?

WARRANT OFFICER J. H. DEANE, M.M. : "Tich" Deane seems to have gained in inches during the past week, and we don't wonder at it. One of the smaller men in the Battalion, he has a heart completely out of proportion to his size, a fact that has earned him the distinction of being the first member of "A" Company to be awarded a decoration. Hailing from Coburg, where he first gladdened the hearts of his parents some 26 years ago, he has done the old northern suburb proud. All things considered it is not surprising that Tich has made good in the AIF after some 11 years experience of soldiering in the Militia. Still, as we all know, military knowledge alone does not make a soldier. Tich was working in Melbourne before the war, but we shouldn't be at all surprised if he made the Army his full time job when this little phase is over. However, probably Mrs. Deane and 12 months old Peter John will have something to say about that. Congratulations, Tich old chap, from all Mud'n Bloods.

BBC NEWS — 7th June, 1941.

The Vichy Government has issued more denials that German forces are occupying Syria, but the British Government is in receipt of information that compels her to appraise these denials at their true worth, and her dispositions will be made accordingly.

Reports emanating from Turkish sources say that no faith can be placed in General Dentz's denials of German penetration in Syria, and state that in a fortnight there will be sufficient men and materials in Syria to threaten Palestine.

German pocket submarines have been seen in Beirut harbour during the past week, according to Turkish reports.

It has been announced that the US Government will take over the North American Aviation Co's. works if the strikers do not resume work tomorrow.

President Roosevelt has signed a proclamation authorising America to seize all foreign shipping of countries under Axis domination at present lying in American harbours. In addition to Norwegian, Danish and other enemy occupied countries' shipping, this will include French ships, the lar-

gest of which is the "Normandie" which has been lying at anchor in New York since the commencement of war.

Rumours that Britain was supposed to have sent messages to President Roosevelt by Mr. Winant, American Ambassador, that she could hold out only another three months without increased American assistance could be put down to German propaganda, stated an official White House message. No such statement had been sent.

Mr. Menzies, Australian Prime Minister, who will speak from Melbourne tomorrow night, stated that in future actions in the Middle East, Australian troops would be supported by the largest British Air Force that Britain could possibly produce.

A large contingent of South African troops have reached Egypt. These troops were all seasoned campaigners and had created a most favourable impression in Egypt.

Only a few enemy aircraft flew over Britain last night, and damage caused was slight. There was some activity in the Straits of Dover.

Mr. Ernest Bevin, Minister for Labour, made appeal for greater effort in production of materials of war, stating that the next three months would be the most vital in our history.

No further news in regard to operations at Sollum or Tobruk. Our Air Force has strafed enemy planes in Cyrenaice, and at least three fighters have been destroyed on the ground. Bengazi has been raided several times.

In Germany, 1496 people have been arrested for listening to foreign broadcasts, and one man who distributed pamphlets giving notes from a foreign broadcast was sentenced to death.

More evidence reaching Britain of resistance in occupied countries to Nazi oppression - A Dutch University has been closed for an indefinite period following anti-German riots after the dismissal of a Jewish professor. From Warsaw reports state that an average of 450 people died every day last month from undernourishment. Yet the Germans are publishing long lists of food and other materials being taken from Poland. Five thousand Croat workers have been sent to Germany - more thousands will follow.

It is reported in London that Sir Stafford Cripps, British Ambassador to Russia, will shortly return to London. This is in accordance with the normal procedure to recall ambassadors for reports when necessary.

TOBRUK, 10th June, 1941.

Sitting in the place where we do most of our sitting, and glancing idly at the various scraps of newspaper strewn around, a page headed "Woman's Mirror" caught our eye. How do such publications get sent out to us? And why isn't there a society for the prevention of cruelty to helpless front line soldiers. Fancy having to read this sort of thing on days like these -

> "A delicious salad to eat with cold roast beef can be made from watermelon, thinly sliced, placed on a lettuce-leaf and served with mayonnaise dressing and a finely chopped onion."

No less disturbing is the picture conjured up by the following, although, mind you, we haven't had grass stains on our knees for many years now:-

> "To remove grass-stains from the knees of tennis trousers, steep the affected part in methylated spirit."

This para sounded interesting, but proved disappointing after the first line or two:-

> "If you wish to improve a plain cake and give it a more piquant flavour............."

What's the use of reading this sort of thing? In sheer disgust we disposed of the paper in the most appropriate manner possible.

RQMS George Moore rang through urgently yesterday to warn us that a large and ferocious lioness was at large, and we pass on the grim tidings so that everyone can take steps for their own protection. George was adamant that he saw the animal with his own eyes, and he hadn't been near the rum issue for days and days (well, not very often anyhow). First of all he saw the "spoor" (George is an authority on spoor), and not only did he recognise it as spoor, but it was spoor of a large animal of the cat family. All the old hunting instincts have been aroused in George, instincts that have been lying dormant since the many hunting parties he used to organise on the St. Kilda Esplanade on Sunday nights, when he used to go after other members of the cat family with much success. Now he is fully occupied organising another party, and swears that ere long he will send that lioness up to the orderly room for our edification, and to still forever our mockings. We informed him that if he ever caught a lioness, we would eat it. And

then, in the dim stillness of the night, a thought struck us, and we have re-
pented bitterly of our rash promise ever since. He said "lioness" not
"lion", but the full significance did not dawn on us at first. Knowing
George as we know him, we are fully convinced that any female, no matter
its species, hasn't a hope once he decides to track it down, and, so great is
our faith in his prowess, that already we have reluctantly laid in a large
supply of salt, pepper and mustard.

Returning from dental parade this afternoon in company, amongst
others, with Sgt. Bill Marshall, we were treated to a spectacle of big game
hunting that we are confident would put any efforts of the "B" Echelon
hunters to shame. We were bowling merrily along when all at once came a
terrific banging on the roof of the driver's cab. Looking up, we could see
Bill Marshall nearly purple with excitement, and pointing at something a
little distance away. Thinking of lions, panthers, puma, and what have you,
we followed his pointing finger and there, grazing unconcernedly by the
side of the road, was a large and succulent sheep. Bill at once dismounted
and started stalking the unsuspecting animal, making soft cooing noises
like a dove petting her young. On his face was a look of beatific friendli-
ness, but in his heart was black treachery. Slowly he approached until within a few yards, and the smell of mint sauce was already in our nostrils, before the at last startled sheep commenced to run. Bill's turn of speed, due
to recent exercises, didn't give the poor old thing a chance, and in no time
he had overhauled it. Grabbing it by the tail, he expertly turned it over,
and just as he had lifted it up into his arms came a stentorian roar from an
officer who suddenly appeared from a hole in the ground - "What the
!†+@&*/%? are you doing with my sheep?" Bill never turned a hair as he
set the animal down. "Poor little lamb" he murmured tenderly, brushing
the dust from its wool, "we thought the little thing might have run in front
of the truck and got hurt."

Some base scoundrel has sneaked into the orderly room and swiped
our file copies of Mud & Blood, and we are short of Nos. 3, 5, 6 and 11. If
any Mud & Blood has a copy of any of these issues he will be duly awarded
a Mud & Blood Medal if he loans it to us for a day or two, so that we can
make a copy of same and bring our records up to date. Have a look, will
you?

BBC NEWS — 10th June, 1941.

It is announced that the Free French and British Forces have advan-
ced 35 to 40 miles into Syria. Many French officers and men have gone

over to our forces. Vichy still speaks of heavy opposition, but there is no news of same from any other source.

Work is proceeding normally throughout Palestine, although women and children have been evacuated from the border area, but this is regarded merely as a precautionary measure.

Intensive RAF raids have been carried out in Derna and Bengasi, and the aerodromes at both these places have received special attention. Many planes have been destroyed and damaged on the ground.

The Egyptian Government is organising a scheme for the evacuation of civilian population from Alexandria, following the two recent air raids. It is also announced that compensation will be paid to the sufferers in these raids out of funds from Italian and German property and credits in Egypt.

The Admiralty announces the sinking of the cruiser "Calcutta" and two destroyers during the recent evacuations from Crete. The Italian radio announces that 229 survivors have been picked up and are now prisoners of war.

It is advised by British Naval Authorities that the evacuation of troops from Crete was carried out during the hours of darkness, which meant that the vessels had to travel 360 miles to Egypt during daylight. Under such circumstances it was unavoidable that we should occasion some losses, and it was a tribute to the good organisation and efficient manner in which the operation was carried out that the losses were not more heavy.

A communique from East Africa states another 1,200 Italian prisoners have been taken.

Advice has been received of the sinking of two more of the "Bismarck's" supply ships, making a total of six of these now sunk. When the news came through that the Bismarck was making a dash into the Atlantic to raid shipping, it was realised that she would require constant servicing by supply ships, and plans were accordingly framed by the Admiralty to cope with these. Our Navy has been constantly searching for these vessels ever since.

A Brazil steamer has wirelessed that she has picked up survivors from a torpedoed US vessel in South African waters. No official confirmation of this is yet to hand.

Yesterday the newest type of German Messerschmit plane made determined efforts to penetrate our air defences over the south of England, but our fighters drove them off with ease; two German planes were shot down, and another was last seen losing height rapidly with smoke pouring from the fuselage.

A German supply ship of 7,000 tons was bombed by our RAF yesterday, and when the planes were leaving, the ship was emitting dense clouds of black smoke.

Three Japanese have been arrested in Los Angelos on charges of obtaining information regarding details of national defences likely to prove useful to a foreign power.

TOBRUK, 11th June, 1941.

No further news has come to hand from RQMS George Moore in regard to his lion hunting expedition, and his many friends are apprehensive as to his safety. The last time George was seen, as he was crawling along on his tummy, a bag of spoor in one hand, and a salt shaker in the other. We give hereon a picture of George and the lion, just after George had succeeded in sprinkling it's tail with salt. 'Twas a dastardly thing to do to a poor inoffensive animal. Anyhow we would ask George to be careful in his handling of Leo, bearing in mind the fact that we have to eat him, and after all the salt bacon we have been having lately, we had begun to rather fancy the idea of a little fresh meat. So go easy with that shaker, George. We leave it to our readers to say which is the lion and which George.

You may have noticed that in our issue of yesterday we did not have a paragraph about Pte. M. J. O'Connell, M.M. of "C" Company. Well, the fact of the matter is, Maurie is about as elusive as the famous Pimpernel, and all our efforts to connect up with him have come to naught. He is up in the front line, where nothing very exciting ever happens, but manages to keep from feeling bored by reading war stories and thrillers. The next time the Postal Corporal is up there we will get him to bring back some personal details of Maurie; maybe by that time he will have added the D.C.M. and Victoria Cross to his collection. Anyhow, Maurie, all the best from your fellow Mud'n Bloods.

A man by the name of O. Henry once wrote a yarn entitled "The tale of a shirt". He was a contemporary of ours, only of course, not so good. Anyhow, we relate hereunder another tale of another shirt. Private Rex Spry, AAMC orderly attached, to give him his full official description (he also does a little batting on the side for Capt. Agar, as well as chopping a curl or two off his friends to send home to their mothers) is an extremely tidy, neat sort of person, or so we have been told. It is even related that, in his barber's shop in Geelong, he had been known to brush up all the cut hair, spent matches, butts, and racing tipsters handbills at least once every week. Rex had a shirt, which in itself was not an unusual thing, but this particular shirt was minus a button, and, to one of Rex's fastidious nature, the absence of this button used to keep him awake at nights. Months passed, and Rex was still tormented about that missing button, until one day he had a bright idea - he would sew another one on. Then the trouble commenced; first to find a button; secondly to find needle and cotton. The first was comparitively simple; a quick snip, and off came a button from one of Capt. Agar's shirts; the second offered more difficulty but was finally accomplished. Then to complete the act. Dashing into the dim interior of the R.A.P. (Regimental Aid Post) he picked up the shirt from the back of a chair and started on the job. He was thorough; the Sprys have won renown for their thoroughness in sewing on shirt buttons; that button was put on for keeps. The job completed, Rex rested for awhile, toying with his halo the while. In walked Sergeant Jarvie, picked up the shirt, donned it, and remarked in surprise "Well I never, some kind person has sewn a button on my shirt." Now Rex burns the petrol lamp in the R.A.P. day and night. Never again will he take such risks. "A chap might even go in and wash someone else's mess tin," he told me, with a look of horror on his face.

WRESTLING:

We have been asked to publish the following Challenge from H.Q. Company.

The front line Companies at HQ Cook-house throw out a challenge to the best ten men in the 23rd Militia at "B" Echelon to appear at the above Cook-house on Sunday evening, at 7.30 pm. Everything will be in readiness; the Pioneers are attending to the stadium. If there are any acceptances please send a representative to arrange final details. The bigger they are the easier we can clean them up. Come on, you gazelle eaters and big game hunters, let's hear from you.

(Signed)   Jack O'Brien, Sgt.   A.J. Osmond,
             Promoter.   Secretary.

SPECIAL CHALLENGE:

Cooler Baines, the battling batman

challenges

Skeeter Wynack, the pint pot postman

BBC NEWS — 11th June, 1941.

British forces have penetrated 65 miles from the southern frontier of Syria, and are nearing the Capital, Damascus. Another force is slowly making its way from Irak. A further force is approaching Beirut. It is announced that British Naval Forces are operating off the Syrian coast. RAF and RAAF planes drove off enemy aircraft near Damascus.

Attacks by German bombers on Haifa in Palestine were soon avenged. Our air force immediately attacked enemy aerodromes, and dropped bombs on 50 aircraft on the ground. In all operations in the Middle East, only four of our machines have been lost, and the crew of one of them is safe.

Admiral Darlan broadcast an appeal to the French people to support the Vichy Government, stating that Germany could at any time denounce the terms of the Armistice, and that France was in no position to resist if she did.

The Fleet Air Arm and RAF made further attacks in North Africa, attacks on the Mole at Tripoli and further raids at Derna being announced.

In Abyssinia at least 4 Italian Divisions have been destroyed in fighting in the Lakes area. A further 35,000 sq. miles of territory have come under our control.

Mr. Churchill, in the course of a speech in the House of Commons, stated that the battle of Crete could only be assessed as one phase in the battle of the Middle East, and should not be treated as a battle on its own, but only as a phase of operations as a whole. At least 250 enemy troop carrying planes and many other aircraft were destroyed, he stated. Out of 90,000 killed in the war to date, 85,000 of these came from Great Britain, and 5000 from the Dominions. This gave the lie to German propaganda that Dominions were left to bear the burden.

Mr. Churchill answered criticism of withdrawal of aircraft from Crete. He stated it would have been a fatal mistake to keep our aircraft there without adequate airfields.

Germany has decided to occupy the whole of Greece, including Athens. This was disclosed by Signor Mussolini in a speech. The loss of Abyssinia did not matter, was another of his utterances.

The RAF again raided Brest yesterday. Enemy air action over England was on a limited scale.

In the first four months of the year, Italian and German Air Forces had lost four times as many planes as Britain.

385 killed and 183 wounded in Thursday's air raid on Alexandria. 137 killed and 46 wounded in Wednesday's raid.

Padre Morrison's Summer Residence, with his Fiat runabout parked outside.

TOBRUK, 11th June, 1941.

These days you have only to meet one of the "B" Echelon lads and he immediately commences to tell you of what they have just shot down there, and waxes elequent about the one that got away. We looked up the horoscope of George Moore and find he was born under Taurus the Bull, so we accept with reserve anything he may tell us about his hunting efforts. It is true that a gazelle was eaten down there, but we happen to know that it wasn't shot, but merely died from natural causes, after eating some scones cooked by Sgt. Leo Jones that had been criminally left lying around by some careless person. Even the appended picture of Daddy Gazelle doesn't mean a thing. He only stubbed his toe getting out of George's path. By gosh, George, we're real hungry for a bit of fresh lion these days; what are you doing about it?

Talking about hunting puts us in mind of the very old one about the two city business men who went far up the bush for a quiet holiday, taking with them, in addition to some guns, their golf bags. Each day they would go out with the guns, but the sport was poor, and barring an odd rabbit or two they would come back with empty bags. This soon palled, so one day they took out their golf sticks with them and had some practice hitting the balls all over the landscape. Returning to the pub one of them absentmindedly put down two golf balls on the counter as he called for drinks." What are they?" interestedly enquired the young female beer puller. "Golf balls" was the reply. The same routine was observed the next day, and as the

couple entered the pub the barmaid, endeavouring to be conversational, remarked as a couple of balls were set on the counter "I see you've shot
another golf today."

A few days ago we hurried into the orderly room and saw the younger members of the staff crouched in a corner. Peering over the bent backs
we saw a mouse drinking deeply from a cigarette tin. Every now and then
it would run a few steps backwards, look around, and return to the tin for
another gulp or two. At first the slightest noise would cause it to scamper,
but as it continued drinking it became emboldened, and refused to be
chased away. Finally, it staggered round, looked us fair in the eye, and if
ever a look said anything it said "Bring on your plurry cat." Yes, they were
giving it rum. Such an exhibition of wanton cruelty we have never before
witnessed. Here we were, hadn't had a rum for ages, and they had just
given the last of it to a mouse.

By the way, in yesterday's issue we appealed for the loan of back
numbers of certain Mud & Bloods. Cpl. Freddie Henderson, of HQ Company
came to light with all the missing numbers except number 11. Can anyone
oblige with this number, and we'll buy them a beer the next time we are in
Alex?

Here's rather a weak one, but we have to fill up somehow:-

A patent medicine manufacturing company received the following
letter from a satisfied customer:- "I am very much pleased with your remedy. I had a wart on my chest and after using six bottles of your medicine,
it moved to my neck, and now I use it for a collar stud."

BBC NEWS — 12th June, 1941.

*The British and Free French forces are steadily progressing into
Syria. The main Vichy opposition seems to be along the coastal areas towards Beirut. It is reported from Ankara that two British columns have
entered the country from Irak, in the north east, and have penetrated to
a depth of about 70 miles without meeting with serious opposition. Another report from Ankara that a third British force is operating further north
is unconfirmed from London. Vichy forces are resisting strongly in front
of Damascus, about ten miles outside the town. The RAF is taking a very
active part in the operations.*

*The following announcements have been made in the United States:-
2,000,000 tons of cargo ships and tankers will be provided immediately to*

Britain. Further vessels will be handed over later. American shipyards will be speeded up by completion of the St. Lawrence power scheme, which is now being put into operation.

138,000,000 pounds have been allocated for new shipping. A big scheme for training 7,000 British air pilots in the United States each year has already commenced, and is proceeding steadily every day.

President Roosevelt stated that America would see that all supplies she made available would get to the places where they were most needed, to stiffen resistance.

It has been announced that the output of the Curtis-Wright three factories alone is 60 planes per day, and as production is speeded up, this figure is expected to increase in the near future.

A responsible Government official in the Netherlands East Indies has publicly stated that supplies to Japan of materials likely to be used in war over and above her reasonable needs would not be supplied, and in the event of Japan entering the war against Britain, and rather than allow her sources of supply to fall into hands likely to use them against Britain she would take steps to destroy such sources of supply.

The RAF was active in the Ruhr districts last night. In daylight, RAF attacked a German tanker of 7,000 tons in the Straits of Dover, and scored seven direct hits. When last seen the tanker was burning fiercely and had a heavy list.

Last night German Air Force dropped bombs at many places in England in widely scattered areas. Substantial damage was caused in parts, and in one place it is feared that heavy casualties were caused. Further raids have been made on enemy bases in North Africa.

STOP PRESS:

We have just received the following reply to the challenge issued by HQ Company Cook-house details to "B" Echelon. The reply is addressed to "The renegade Sergeant who was expelled from "B" Echelon owing to not conforming to their high moral and physical standard, and also on account of the undesirable associations he had down there:-

> *"We heard about the challenge that headquarters mob sent out
>   Challenging the "B" Echelon boys to an all-in wrestling bout
> Our boys are game to meet them, at any place they name,*

And when we've finished with them, they'll hang their heads
in shame
We hope O'Brien reads this, and tells his so-called thugs,
That the boys down here all reckon they're a bunch of
punch drunk mugs.

(Signed) C. A. (Longfellow) Jones, on behalf of Basher Morrell,
Kick 'em to death Clark, and the "B" Echelon Terrors.

TOBRUK, 13th June, 1941.

The latest information to hand is that Capt. Geoff Austin of Brigade has seen a leopard in the locality. He swears to it; in fact he was so close that he could count every spot. What we would like to know is, did he count every spot before he saw the leopard. Now all we need is for someone to come in with a tale about frolicsome hippopotami around the lines and we'll really begin to believe we belong to Evan's Circus. The menagerie is pretty complete, but the lads would like to see the little lass in pink tights that rides bareback without which no circus is complete.

Hm! George Moore's lion must have been along this way today!

SPOOR:

o⁰o	-	Lion	)
o⁰o	-	Panther	)
o⁰o	-	Puma	)
o⁰o	-	Cheetah	)
o⁰o	-	Leopard	)
o⁰o	-	Alsatian	)
o⁰o	-	Viper	)

We are indebted to that famous Big Game Hunter RQMS George Moore, of the renowned firm of Morrell & Co., for the appended manual of spoor of the larger native fauna. If any member of this Battalion, during the day's activities, comes across a print in the dust similar to one of these, he will be able at once to identify the animal. In such case he is to immediately send word to "B" Echelon, and an expedition will be sent forth without loss of time. It is essential that the spoor be fresh, as it goes bad in the sun, and in no case can it be considered reliable after say fourteen days, as after that time the animal may get tired of waiting and move elsewhere.

Goody, goody, we cried with glee, when we heard that a parcel of books had been received for distribution to our war weary warriors (that's you and us). Nobody having been bumped off recently or anything, work has slackened off, and a nice browse amidst the dust and flies with the latest thriller was indicated. With a list mentally made out of our favourite authors we hopped in and delved into the small pile of books. First to emerge was a murder thriller entitled "Eric, or little by little." Next brought to light was a harrowing tale, written as recently as 1884, with the title "Her Mistake" in faded gold lettering above a bunch of forget-me-nots. Followed an old medical treatise, a cookery book, and a volume of Victorian ballads written round about the time of the Golden Jubilee. Finally, after surreptiously sneaking under our tunic when nobody was looking, a real corker entitled "Elsie's Rise and Fall," we gave up; we're not selfish, lads; you can have the whole plurry lot. We wonder if it could be made someone's business to see, in future, that no more Sunday School prizes of an earlier vintage than say, 1914, are sent out. As for the kindhearted people who have got the smug satisfaction of doing their bit for the soldiers by delving into attics and old boxes, well, we only wish we knew their addresses so that we could tell them what to do with their literature.

TODAY'S FURPHY (As taken down by ourselves from this morning's BBC broadcast when everyone was talking, and when we weren't listening anyhow)

Feverish activity is being displayed by the British Forces in Egypt in an effort to stem the German offensive from the Belgian Congo. The Suez Canal has been drained, and is being used as an anti-tank ditch.

A request has come from "B" Echelon as to the best way to cook and eat a gazelle. Another one strayed into a nearby mine-field, and apparently the habits of the buzzard and other carrion eaters have been well studied down that way, as the carcase was hastily retrieved and is to form the basis of a meal on Sunday next. Just as, in olden days, a warrior would dine on a lion's heart to give him added courage before a battle, so do the "B" Echelon lads hope that the main features of the gazelle will be assimilated prior to their big wrestling battle on Sunday night. The gazelle it is pointed out, is noted for the swiftness of its flight when danger is scented. The above request is replied to as follows:-

(a)   TO COOK: "B" Echelon will find it an improvement on their last effort if they skin and clean the animal before cooking. If the gazelle is of the male sex, care will be taken to remove all odds and ends that may be found. All unexpended spoor will be carefully extracted and used for basting the animal whilst roasting. Put in a very hot oven and roast fiercely until reduced to a black powder, spread on bread and margarine, and serve when it stops smelling.

(b)   TO EAT: For the fastidious we suggest a knife and fork; otherwise the fingers.

BBC NEWS — 13th June, 1941.

Reports from Syria indicate further important progress in all sectors. Allied troops are closing in on Damascus, Beirut and Aleppo, the 3 chief towns of Syria. For three days our forces have done all in their power to avoid bloodshed in certain areas, and envoys were repeatedly sent to explain our aims. Eventually, as our point of view was ignored, our troops advanced, and some fighting and bloodshed resulted.

One Free French Battalion found that the Vichy Battalion opposing it was a sister Battalion from the same Brigade. Immediately identity was established, both sides ceased fighting.

No damage of a serious nature was caused in Wednesday's air raids on Haifa and Tel Aviv. It is reported that 12 were killed and 27 wounded.

The RAF made further raids in the Ruhr, and also offensive sweeps along German occupied coast line. Extensive damage resulted, but all our aircraft returned safely from these activities.

During the night a small number of enemy aircraft flew low over the SE coast of England. No casualties were reported. One enemy bomber was shot down.

Strong and determined raids were made over Malta, and ten enemy planes were definitely destroyed. Little or no damage was caused. In the 500 or 600 raids that have been made over Malta, the island has suffered very little. No fires have been caused amongst houses owing to the stone construction of the dwellings. Daylight raids were soon dropped by the enemy as he found them too expensive. In all raids, he has suffered approximately 20% losses of aircraft participating.

Further activities of the RAF in North Africa have been directed against enemy MT, and heavy losses have been inflicted. Six seaplanes and a number of merchant ships were observed to be sunk in Bengasi harbour as a result of previous raids.

33,000 out of 50,000 men in the Naval Reserve will be retained in service in the United States until the state of national emergency is declared over.

It is confirmed that the US cargo vessel "Robin Moore" was sunk in the South Atlantic. The submarine commander was aware of the identity of the ship, and the flag she sailed under, as he inspected the ship's register prior to giving the order to torpedo her. The crew were left to their fate in open boats.

A conference of leading statesmen from Allied countries was held Mr. Churchill representing Britain. Poland, Belgium, Checoslovakia, Free France, Greece and Yugoslavia were also represented. Resolutions were passed re-affirming decision to continue the war until freedom was restored to Europe.

TOBRUK, 18th June, 1941.

   This has been a week of outstanding importance in the social and
sporting activities of the Battalion; on Sunday last the Gazelle Eaters at
"B" Echelon entertained guests at luncheon; whilst on Sunday evening the
long awaited wrestling challenge between the Gazelles ("B" Echelon) and
HQ Company personnel was decided amidst the enthusiastic plaudits of
their respective followings.

   Under the fast cooling rays of the setting sun, the stage was set for
an event that will take its place in the history of the Battalion, if only for
the fact that, by their convincing victory, the Gazelles proved themselves
entitled to be classed as front line soldiers. A ring had been constructed
by our busy pioneers, and even if there was no padding or mat under the
stretched canvas, what did that matter to the blood-thirsty spectators;
what if the competitors did look more and more askance at the grazed
elbows, cheekbones and knees as the various bouts on the long programme
proceeded; it was a Roman holiday for the crowd. All the accoutrements
of a well equipped stadium were there, including a press box for the writer.
In opposite corners were the contestants' seats, complete with buckets of
sea water, towels, etc. Stimulants were administered from a bottle from
time to time, but from the disgusted looks of the wrestlers the contents
evidently did not come up to expectations. To goad the combatants on to
greater fury, a box of bully beef tins and biscuits was in each corner. In
the "B" Echelon corner a gazelle skin, recently cured, waved proudly in
the breeze, to the extreme discomfiture of those to windward of it. Every
time a "B" Echelon wrestler looked like weakening, the gazelle skin was
waved aloft as an incentive to greater effort; it not only had the desired
effect, but usually completely overcame the HQ Company representatives,
who have not the immunity that long association with the odorous skin
has conferred upon "B" Echelon.

   The honours of the contest went, by a small margin, to "B" Echelon, and a handsome silver cup (wrought and presented by the local firm
of Ron Lee & Co., Watchwreckers and Jewellers, Tobruk) was handed over
by Major Birch to Sgt. Leo Jones. The event concluded when the defeated
side called for three cheers for the victors, which were heartily given, and
reciprocated by the winners. Supper was then provided, and Sgt. Jack
O'Brien revenged his side's defeat by producing an apple tart that he himself had prepared, and insisting upon the guests eating it.

Results of the various bouts were as follows:-

O'Brien (HQ)	d.	C. Jones ("B")	1 fall(s)
Rentoul M. ("B")	d.	Hand (HQ)	2 "
Summers (HQ)	drew	Abe Armstrong ("B")	
Scott ("B")	d.	Myers (HQ)	2 "
Ouston ("B")	d.	Osmond (HQ)	2 "
Knight (HQ)	d.	Phillips ("B")	1 "
Wynack ("B")	d.	Baines (HQ)	1 "
Jennison (HQ)	d.	Lawrence ("B")	points

EXHIBITION CONTEST:

Goodall (HQ)	d.	Kinross (HQ)	2 falls

We don't know much about wrestling (neither did most of the contestants either for that matter) and so we are unable to give a detailed description of the wrestling. However, one of the highlights was the vigour of the O'Brien - Jones bout, which opened up with a series of arm-jolts, kicks, trips, etc., that looked as fair dinkum as any we have seen in the Melbourne Stadium. Another spectacular hold was provided by Freddy Ouston when he applied a Boston Crab on his opponent that brought the spectators to their feet. By far the greatest surprise, however, was produced by Tich Wynack, the pint-pot postman, when he hoed in and in grim fashion accounted for Cooler Baines, the battling batman. That Tich meant business from the word go was clearly evident. A plane was heard in the distance, and from force of habit the crowd opened up to permit Tich's passage to the nearest hole in the ground. However, Tich never turned a hair. Again, a little later, Jerry started throwing a few shells over, and although they landed within a quarter of a mile away, again Tich stuck to the job in hand, and in the surprise and consternation caused his opponent, succeeded in pinning him for the only fall that occurred in the contest.

To celebrate the slaying of their second gazelle, "B" Echelon staged an elaborate luncheon on Sunday last. Guests invited were Capt. Urquhart and the Editor of Mud & Blood. Capt. Urquhart was unfortunately prevented from attending, and Lieut. G. G. Anderson deputised in his stead. Sgt. Leo Jones heaped coals of fire upon our head by serving a tasty and satisfying lunch, in which roast gazelle played a prominent part. Believe us, lads, that gazelle certainly tasted well, and we have been urging all our friends to see what they can do about it ever since. At the conclusion of the feast, Capt. "Con" Morrell rose and spoke briefly of the pleasure "B" Echelon had in staging the luncheon, which was not only due to the efforts of the skilful hunter, but also to Sgt. Jones and his merry men. He called on Lieut. Clarke to second his remarks, and to endorse his welcome to the visitors.

Lieut. Clarke rose and capably recited After Dinner Speech No. 7 - you know, the one that begins "The previous speaker, by his magnificent effort, has left me nothing to add......." In reply, Lieut. Anderson spoke feelingly and with a full heart (to say nothing of a full stomach) of the pleasure he had in being present. On behalf of Associated Newspapers Inc. Ltd., Tobruk, S/Sgt. Mulcahy arose, amidst thunderous applause which almost completely drowned the catcalls from a small section of irrespons-ibles at one end of the table, and delivered in his usual brilliant style an electrifying oration in which he stated that it was men like those of "B" Echelon who were the backbone of the Empire. Eh? What's that? Well, at any rate he got up and managed to say a few words about how good the gazelle tasted, and that he would be pleased to represent Mud & Blood on all such future occasions. In conclusion of a very memorable event, Sgt. Jones suitably responded to the polite, but for once truthful compliments as to his prowess in the culinary art.

BBC NEWS — 18th June, 1941.

Operations continue in North Africa in the area Halfayu - Sollum - Capuzzo - Sidi Omar. After our initial surprise attacks the enemy strongly counter-attacked, but we were able to hold same. The enemy has brought up reinforcements from the Tobruk area, and is continuing his counter-attacks, but these have been withstood. Operations are at present continu-ing. Further extensive raids have been made by our Air Force on Bengasi, and aerodromes at Benina, Derna and Gazala. Many aircraft on the ground are believed to have been destroyed. M.T. has also been machine-gunned with devastating effect. Considerable casualties are believed to have been inflicted on enemy forces.

In addition to ordering all German consulates in the United States to be closed, a proclamation under the Emergency Act has been issued for-bidding German nationals from leaving the country without permission.

For the seventh night in succession the RAF has carried out exten-sive bombing attacks on West Germany. Much damage has been caused in Cologne, Dusseldorf, and towns in the Ruhr locality.

Activity over England last night was on a small scale. Damage was

*however caused in a south-eastern town and some casualties inflicted. Four
enemy bombers were shot down.*

*In Syria our troops are meeting with stiffer opposition than hither-
to, but operations are proceeding satisfactorily. It is announced from
Vichy that a French destroyer has been sunk off the coast of Syria during
operations. No confirmation of this has yet come from London.*

TOBRUK, 19th June, 1941.

We were helping ourselves yesterday morning to our couple of ascorbic tablets when a Mud'n Blood standing nearby exclaimed in horror "You're
not going to take those, are you?" "Why not?" we enquired. "They're for
the same thing as they used to put bromide in the tea for," he explained.
"Is that so," we replied, cramming a couple of dozen into our mouth. That's
how things are with us these days. Of course, we also miss our beer too.

This mail business is also getting us down a bit too; yesterday we
sat down and wrote four pages to ourselves, posted them, and are now awaiting eagerly for their delivery. At least we know now that there is a letter on
the way. And the things we said to ourselves! Hope the censor doesn't cut
anything out. It's not a bad idea this; you ought to try it. And there is always the chance that the Doc will certify you insane and send you back to
Aussie.

Hope we strike company something like this when we get to Berlin:-
"Good gracious, Adolph," says the great Goering, "You have shrunk to nothing. You must have lost two stone. What's the matter with you?" "Well
my dear Herman, it's this way," says Adolph. "I have to lunch and dine
out every day and, what with talking to the great ladies next to me, I have
no chance to eat." "Ah," says Herman, "That is easily remedied. I have
exactly the same difficulties, but I've invented a formula which lets me
take my meals in peace. I turn first to the woman on my right and I say
'Are you married?' She says 'No'. Then I ask 'Have you any children?' And
she doesn't talk to me any more. Then I turn to the woman on my left and
I say 'Are you married?' She answers 'Yes' I ask again 'Have you any children?' She replied 'Four' and at once I ask 'Whose are they?' And she
doesn't talk to me any more. After that I address the woman opposite me
'Are you married?' She says 'Yes' 'Have you any children?' She says 'No'
And then I ask 'How do you do it?' And she doesn't talk to me any more
and I enjoy my meal." Adolph's face beamed. ' 'Splendid" he says, ."I'll   try
your formula from now on." The two men meet six months later. Adolph's

clothes hang more limply on him than ever. "Heavens, man" says Herman, "You've lost another stone. What's wrong with you?" "Well, you see," says Adolph, "It's these infernal luncheon and dinner parties...." "I know," says Herman, "but didn't you try my formula?" "Yes" said Adolph, "but it doesn't work in the company I keep." "How do you mean, it doesn't work?" "Well, you see, I did everything you told me to do. I turned first to the lady on my right and asked 'Are you married?' She said 'No'. I followed the formula 'Have you any children?' 'Do I look a complete fool' she said. And then she went on talking. Then I addressed the woman on my left. 'Are you married?' 'Yes' 'Have you any children?' 'Four' And then just as you told me I asked 'Whose are they?' 'Well' she said, 'If you want to know the truth I'm not quite sure myself.' And she went on talking. Finally, I turned to the woman opposite me and went through the formula again. 'Are you married?' 'Yes' 'Have you any children?' 'No' 'How do you do it?' All she did was to smile and say 'Well, Your Excellency, if you'd really like to know, you'd better come round at five this afternoon.' And she went on talking. And the trouble is I'm so inquisitive I always have to go round to find out!"

A Home Guard was patrolling his beat when an alert was sounded and he took shelter in the nearest suitable place, which happened to be a grave-yard. When the all-clear sounded he was about to resume his patrol when he saw a shadowy figure coming towards him carrying a tomb-stone under its arm. "Halt," commanded the H.G. "Who goes there?" "A Ghost," came the reply. "Pass, ghost, but what are you carrying that tomb-stone for?" "That," answered the ghost. "Oh, that's my identity disc."

Then there is the one about the two old baldheaded staff officers who thought they could run the war better than anyone else, but when they put their heads together, they made a perfect ass of themselves.

Boy Friend -   "Well, we certainly had a big time last night for 3d."

Girl Friend -   "Yes, I wonder how little brother spent it?"

BBC NEWS — 19th June, 1941.

Allied Forces are now attacking Damascus in Syria. A good deal of opposition is being encountered. Elsewhere our progress continues.

The RAF for the eighth night in succession made determined attacks over West Germany industrial centres. Details of the raid are not yet to hand.

Nine enemy fighters were destroyed and other damaged over the channel yesterday. Our air force that engaged them did not suffer any losses.

A German supply ship of 15,000 tons was attacked by Coastal Command yesterday off Brest. Hits were registered, and the ship was left in a sinking condition.

Enemy air attacks on Britain last night were on a small scale. Damage caused was slight - no casualties were reported.

Germany has admitted responsibility for raids over Dublin a week or so ago. She states a pilot lost his way and thought he was over the English coast. Germany has expressed regret, and offered to pay compensation.

During operations in Libya, the RAF carried on almost continuous patrols over the British and Imperial forces so successfully, that German planes were unable to attack our troops at any stage. Eight Hurricanes dashed into a force of Junkers 87's and shot down at least seven of them. Bombers attacked enemy tanks and vehicles which were stationary, and several of these were tossed into the air like leaves. Several hundred prisoners were taken, and heavy losses in tanks, vehicles and aircraft inflicted. The main purpose of the offensive, to find our enemy strength, was effected, and our troops withdrew to their original forward positions.

Another eight enemy supply vessels have been sunk in the Mediterranean and Agean seas. These are in addition to the seven vessels sunk last week.

Offices have been opened in New York to enrol recruits to work on the new radio locater apparatus that Britain is using for the detection of approaching hostile aircraft.

US has announced that a further 12,000 to 15,000 men will be recruited for her Naval Forces.

Germany has entered a strong protest against American action in closing down German Consulates in US. It is stated that this protest will be rejected by the US Government.

A treaty of friendship was signed yesterday between Turkey and Germany. Both countries bind themselves to respect the territorial integrity of the other. The treaty is for a period of ten years, and a clause provides for renewal after that time. The present treaties and obligations of

*both parties in regard to other countries are not affected. Turkish acknow-
ledgment of her obligations under the Turkish-Anglo Agreement is shown
by the way in which Turkey has at all times advised Britain of the progress
of her negotiations with Germany.*

*At least 23 people were lost when the "St. Patrick", a steamer ply-
ing between England and Ireland, was torpedoed in the Irish Sea by a
German submarine.*

*It is announced officially that the total number of Italian prisoners
in our hands is 230,000.*

*Extensive raids by RAF and South African Air Force continue to
be made on enemy centres in Libya. Yesterday, aerodromes at Benina,
Gazala, Derna and Bengasi were again attacked.*

TOBRUK, 20th June, 1941.

In an uncautious moment we confided to someone that, during a
walk to the beach, we saw an unidentified animal leaping over the brow of
a hill, that might conceivably have been George Moore's lion. This morning George arrived and demanded a public apology for the mockings to
which we have subjected him in previous issues, so we thought we'd better
make the position clear. We have never, at any time, even insinuated that
George did not see some animal of the cat family. Knowing George, we'd
quite believe him if he swore to a herd of pink elephants wearing green
snakes for tails chasing him up and down the wadis with rum jars flourished
aloft in their trunks. What we did doubt was his ability to capture or shoot
said lion. So, as no lion or other animal has yet arrived to grace the larder,
we contend that there is nothing to apologise for.

As a matter of cold fact, we are surprised that George has failed so
far to produce the goods, considering the big game hunters paradise that he
inhabits. On our trip down there last Sunday we would never have found
the place at all if we hadn't come across the spoor of some Morris trucks,
and by following same eventually arrived at our destination. We had no excitement during the journey, as the noise of our vehicle drove most of the
larger fauna away. In the distance we could see a herd of hippopotami
pursuing a couple of giraffes; it was quite interesting watching them race,
but the giraffes eventually won by a long neck. (Sincere apologies for that
one). When we arrived we saw a bulky shape lying on a heap of blankets,
and at first glance throught it was a rhinocerous, but it turned out to be
only George in a slightly amorous mood.

His many friends will regret the departure of Pte. Alan Currie, of "I" section, for Alexandria, owing to a small will-of-the-wisp germ that has eluded the grasping hand of the R.M.O. Alan is far from being a sick man, and a rest, coupled with some good food, will make him right again in about a month's time. He has been informed that his diet is to include a bottle of stout a day, and no doubt other delicacies will be forthcoming. No, we won't tell you what sort of germ it is, nor where you can pick one up. As a matter of fact, we had morning tea with him, and there was a rush to drink out of the same mess tin. We were first, so we have made a date to meet him in Alex. in about a fortnight's time. What's a germ or two, we can always drown the blighter in the first pub we come to.

Pte. Bob Noonan, the C.O"'s batman, is about again, after lying at death's door for several days as the result of an encounter with a scorpion. At any rate, we conclude he must have been at death's door, judging by his appearance. The scorpion sneaked up on him during his sleep, and stung him on the face. Bob tried to brush him off, and the scorp got one home on his hand. Finally, after the third sting, the scorpion started muttering "you're a better man than I am, etc." and curled up and died. So, if any of you chaps ever entertain the idea of "biting" Bob for anything, just think of the fate of the poor scorpion.

There has been a galaxy of parcels lately, and in common with most of you, we have received our share. Have never seen so many cakes, tins of shortbread, biscuits, preserved fruits, etc., outside a grocer's shop before. We have been quite independent the past two or three days, and, even if we haven't said it audibly, we certainly have thought of what the cooks could do with their bully beef and M & V stew. However, even the best of good things begin to pall, and the time will shortly arrive when we will squirm over another slice of cake or biscuit, and begin to think hungrily of a good solid chunk of bully with some pickles and fresh bread.

We are toying with the idea of keeping a "furphey" register from now onwards, and entering the name of the person who arrives with the latest news of how many bags of mail have just arrived; at the moment this one has taken the place of the one about the ship that was just sunk with anything from 50 to 5,000 cases of beer aboard. Strangely enough, we haven't heard that one for quite a couple of days. Hurrah! A driver has just this moment come in and informed us that they are unloading some hundreds of bags of mail at this very minute. No, he didn't exactly see it himself, but he is nearly sure he heard someone say a boat had come in, or was due to come in, and, anyway, isn't that near enough. Lots of "furphs" are started with much less foundation.

BBC NEWS — 20th June, 1941.

There is more evidence of the damage being caused by raids of the RAF over Germany. A Moscow report states that five submarines were sunk in one harbour alone. Another report states that industrial centres have been so badly affected that the production of vital war supplies is being greatly retarded. Direct hits have been made on the great Potsdam Station in Berlin.

In England last night bombs were dropped at widely separated places. Little damage was done, although there were a few casualties. One of the bombers was shot down.

Referring to the recent fighting in Libya, one of the striking features was that we gained definite superiority in the air right from the outset, and never lost it. We never let the enemy planes get off the ground. One observer said it was like shooting a sitting bird. He never saw an enemy plane cross the escarpment without being shot down. In one engagement alone we shot down 11 planes with the loss of only 1 plane ourselves. Fighting has now died down in Libya, and our air force has resumed normal patrols. Our troops returned to their original forward positions with remarkably little interference from the enemy.

In Syria our troops continue their advance and are now within 16 miles of Beirut. 1200 Vichy officers and men have surrendered to the Allies.

Further attempts were made last night to bomb Malta. Our fighters intercepted the enemy planes, and one Italian bomber was shot down into the sea.

In New York yesterday, 250 men and 6 women applied to assist in operating Britain's new radio locater device for approaching hostile aircraft.

More steps are being taken in the US to control commodities of essential materials. Rubber is to be rationed. There is no shortage of supplies, but it is considered advisable to take effective steps to ensure that there will be no shortage in the future.

The Government of India has decided to establish a Purchasing Commission in the United States, on similar lines to the British Purchasing Commission.

A report from an American Steamer which has just reached Shanghai, states that a large fleet of Japanese warships was encountered, num-

bering about 50 ships in all, moving westwards close to the Chinese coast.

The first Canadian Squadron of air bombers has just been manned in Britain. For the ninth successive night the RAF continued their programme of extensive raids on Germany and enemy occupied territory.

There is no further news of happenings at Damascus. Our forces sent a message to the effect that if the town was not surrendered yesterday morning at 5 o'clock, activities would commence. It is not known yet whether the ultimatim was heeded or not.

TOBRUK, 21st June, 1941.

A recent letter from Sgt. Don Urquhart of "D" Company, reveals that the injury he sustained to his arm was more severe than expected, and it was found necessary to amputate it. Don, however, is progressing well, and has taken his misfortune philosophically. He asks that we convey his best wishes to the Battalion generally, and his warm regards to his many personal friends. He'll be on the pier to welcome us back, and even if he will have to do his drinking left-handed, we can scent a real boisterous reunion.

Incidentally, in his letter he mentioned that he had been in touch with Capt. Malloch, who is well on the road to recovery, and looking forward to the time when he will be able to re-join us. No doubt a welcome spell amid the fleshpots of Egypt will be enjoyed before he returns, and he will be able to regale us with all the latest stories of the "naughtiness" of the fair city of Alexandria. He also sends his good wishes and regards to all.

Things are NOT happening these days, with such regular monotony, that it is becoming extremely difficult to find anything to write about. Therefore, Mud'n Bloods, now that you have all sufficient time to let your whilom fancies stray, what about putting on paper some of the doings, funny or otherwise, of the daily round. For all you know, you may have the genius of a Kipling, possess the eloquence and imagination of a Churchill; and, for all we care, you may even employ the methods of Ananias and tell the biggest "whoppers" you can think of. This would only be conforming to the highest traditions of journalism. Try your hand out.

This one was not told us by Padre Morrison, because he wouldn't know whether they did or not, we hope. The vicar of a small country par-

ish had a clergyman friend come to stay the weekend with him. He suggested the visitor should preach at his church at evening service, and the other
agreed. Out walking in the afternoon, the vicar asked him if he had decided
on his subject. The answer was: "Yes, I shall preach on the "widow's
mite." "No, no, I should not do that," said the vicar earnestly, "it is not at
all suitable. Not the widow's mite." "But why not?" asked the other in
surprise. "Well, you see, there are four widows in this parish," replied the
vicar, "and they all DO."

Definition of a barmaid - A girl who keeps the mugs full. Oh, boy,
what a girl. Wonder when we'll ever strike one again? She can be 92 and
as ugly as sin, but as long as she is on the job when we meet up with her,
she'll have an imperishable place in our affections. As a matter of fact, we
were idly scrutinising our pay book the other day, and after looking at the
quite respectable total entered therein, and reflecting on what this figure
will probably stand at by the time the war is over, plus our ten years deferr-
ed pay bearing interest, we decided that we would be able to buy a little
pub somewhere in a back street of Footscray, where custom demands that
the proprietor has one with every "client" that comes in. That'll be the day.

In the lives of all of us, either our private recreations or business
activities entail some phrase being constantly used that will for evermore remain at the back of our consciousness. We personally can see our future
dreams troubled by the sound of a dulcet voice saying "Staff, bring your
notebook, I have an operation order." Others may be troubled with different hallucinations - one phrase that will stick in the minds of many is -
"Struth, he's headed 'em again'. Looking into the dim future we can visualise on some festive gathering of the old Mud'n Bloods, a figure jumping to
it's feet and yelling "18 men in the Jaffa Jail" and the whole multitude
roaring as with one voice "What a shomozzle." We can see the C.O. standing back and saying to Major Birch "Wouldn't it?"

First Chorus Girl -   I believe the magician had his eye on one of the girls
                      last night.

Second   ditto   -   No, dearie, the hand was quicker than the eye.

BBC NEWS — 21st June, 1941.

  *For the tenth successive night the RAF has carried out widespread
raids over German industrial centres. Details of last night's raids are not
yet available.*

A special message sent to Congress by President Roosevelt in regard to the sinking of the American vessel "Robin Moore" by a German submarine a few weeks ago, has caused great excitement in Washington. In his message the President states that this is further proof of Hitler's determination to secure mastery of the seas, as a necessary prelude to which the conquest of Britain is essential. The President states the sinking was an act of outlawry, and wtll be dealt with accordingly.

The US has placed restrictions upon the export of petrol and petroleum products. In future, exports will be permitted only to Britain and Egypt, and other centres of the war where required by the Allied forces.

Enemy air activity over England last night continues on a small scale. No substantial damage was caused, and no casualties were reported. Three enemy aircraft were shot down.

The Prime Minister of New Zealand, Mr. Peter Fraser, has arrived in England for consultation in regard to the prosecution of the war. As when Mr. Menzies was in London, Mr. Fraser will attend Cabinet Meetings.

The Turkish Foreign Minister states that the safeguard clause in the Turkish German treaty of friendship just signed, refers specifically to Turkish obligations under the Anglo-Turkish Pact, which will not be affected. Four other Turkish treaties are also recognised in the treaty. Appreciation is expressed of the British understanding of the extremely difficult situation in which Turkey finds herself.

It is widely felt that the Treaty is directed more against Russia than against England. It is authoritatively stated that Germany did not keep Russia informed of the progress of the negotiations.

Rumours continue to circulate in south Europe of tension between Russia and Germany. It is stated that the tension may be the result of Japanese diplomacy. Reports from Stockholm state that Russia is making feverish preparations on her south-western border. No official comment from Russia on these rumours is available.

In North Africa, dust storms are raging at Sollum and Tobruk, and there has been no further activity by land forces on either side. In the air our Air Force has made further raids on Bengasi harbour, and buildings were demolished and fires started. In addition, enemy MT has been attacked and losses inflicted.

Germany has extended her operations further west and south in the Atlantic, and as a result has achieved some initial success, as is inevitable when there is a change of plans. However, this success will disappear as steps are taken to counter the new move.

In Syria there is little news of operations. Strong opposition appears to be shown on all fronts. A report has been made on the position by General Dentz to Admiral Darlan, and it is expected that the Vichy Government will meet today to consider the report and the position generally.

TOBRUK, 23rd June, 1941.

Not such a bad old war this, and Tobruk isn't such a God-forsaken hole after all, is it? These thoughts appear to be in most minds today, judging by the expansive grins that meet us on all sides. There's no doubt about it, when a mail arrives our whole outlook changes; no beer, no fresh food; dust; heat; flies; what do all these matter so long as our letters come to hand. And what a mail this one was. After such a long interval nearly everyone got a fistful. The record goes to Sgt. Max Dolamore who received 25 and....(well, we'll tell you about that later on). Lieut. Clarke also has joined a pen-friend club, as he received 24 missives. We weren't exactly overlooked ourselves, with 17, and nearly everyone else has enough reading matter for the next few days. There will be many industrious pencils during the next few days inditing replies. At last there will be something to write about, answering the numerous enquiries, and discussing the various items of news that our letters contain. It's a peculiar thing, this "tongue-tiedness" of most of our chaps when a letter has to be written. "What on earch can I write about?" moans a Mud'n Blood in the front lines, looking up at a Jerry plane circling overhead, ducks as a bullet whistles past his ear, and looks with listless eye at shells bursting around and in front of him. "Nothing exciting ever happens round here."

Perhaps a little of our jubilation today is occasioned by the good news from overseas. At long last things seem to be going our way, after a brief spell when reverses were met. Just look at today's news summary and reflect on the various happenings mentioned therein. In Syria we continue to make advances - the capital has fallen to us, and it would seem that the touch of genius that ensured our priority in the race for this important and strategic centre has accomplished its purpose, or is well on the way to doing so. In Abyssinia the last important point of Italian resistance has capitulated. Our dispositions are so healthy that we are able to make demands on French Somaliland to declare either for or against us, and who can doubt the result should she declare for our enemies. At Cappuzzo and Sollum heavy and expensive casualties have been inflicted on enemy forces, whilst our own position at Tobruk remains inviolate. Every indication exists that the enemy has been checkmated in this part of the world, and it is up to us to see that this position remains so. Now comes the joyful tidings that Germany is in such dire straits that she is compelled to attack her powerful neighbour. Whatever the outcome of the present conflict between Russia and Germany, the result must be in our favour. Every shell fired by a German gun in this conflict will be one less fired at us; every German soldier killed will be one less for us to destroy; every German factory bombed and destroyed by Russian means, will augment the nightly toll that our own air forces are exacting. If Germany during the past two years was unable to encompass our downfall with the whole of her resources, how is she going to achieve her ends now that she has to divide them between two strong and implacable foes? Russia may or may not be equal to stemming the German hordes, but she is a first class power, with an air force reputed to be the largest in the world, a Baltic navy of no mean strength, and many hundreds of divisions of trained and equipped troops already on her frontiers. These will not be overcome without severe loss, if they are overcome at all, and now that Britain is in a position to display more initiative and force, with the ever growing volume of American assistance in the background, it would appear not unduly optimistic to hope that at last Hitler has over-reached himself. At any rate, we here in our small sphere, will be following the events of the next few months with breathless interest, and will be fortified in the carrying out of our jobs with the knowledge that, even if in the dim distance, sure indications of a victorious end to this struggle are now apparent. So let us carry on our own operations more grimly and determinedly than ever, striving to make the "Rats of Tobruk" not the least of Hitler's troubles.

BBC NEWS — 23rd June, 1941.

Owing to faulty reception, it was impossible to get details of the German advance into Russia. Such scraps as could be picked up indicate that Germany lost 65 planes in the first day's operations over Russia, whilst the latter country lost 32. Soviet troops are reported to be resisting strongly on the Rumanian Frontier, but Rumanian troops have made advances in the Bessarabia area.

Russian aircraft have bombed ships on the east coast of Finland, and have also attacked from the air, a port there. The Finnish Government has stated that her troops are not participating in the attack on Russia.

The Russian Government has proclaimed a state of siege over the whole of European Russia. Mobilisation for this area has been ordered and will be in operation on Monday.

Moscow radio broadcast Mr. Churchill's speech, cutting out the section that said Britain was not in sympathy with Bolshevist ideals, but stating that Britain would afford every assistance to Russia in her resistance to the invasion.

No official comment has as yet been forthcoming from the US on the new act of aggression of Germany's, but leading newspapers state in leading articles, that now is the time for America to throw everything she has into the struggle to crush Naziism. They state that if Hitler thought that by attacking Russia, looked upon as an enemy of both the US and Britain, he would in any way placate these countries, he was in for a rude awakening. Both countries would oppose him more fiercely than ever before.

It is officially stated that Turkey will remain neutral.

The Japanese Foreign Minister, in discussing the new events, stated that Russia had a formidable army, and it was impossible to forecast the result.

All Swedish ships in the Baltic have been ordered to return to harbour.

The ascendency of the RAF over German air force is being maintained. Yesterday 30 enemy planes were shot down over the English Channel - our losses two. This is in addition to the 28 planes shot down on the previous day, making a total of 58 enemy aircraft destroyed in two days against our total losses of 20.

General Wavell has issued an ultimatum to French Somaliland, stating that it must be declared unequivocably which side she is on. If she declares to adopt the same policy as Syria, time will be allowed to evacuate women and children, and then we will take action. The Vichy Government has protested to Britain against this ultimatum.

In Syria, opposition is being displayed along the whole frontier. Our troops have occupied Damascus, the capital of the country. The RAF and RAAF continue to play an important part in the operations, whilst the Free French Forces have occupied important centres.

In Abyssinia the last remaining centre of strong Italian resistance has fallen - Juma - where Italian troops have capitulated to Patriot forces led by British Officers.

Mr. Churchill, in a fighting speech, stated that Britain would render every assistance to Russia to combat this latest act of aggression on the part of Hitler. He stated that he had repeatedly warned Stalin that this was bound to occur sooner or later, and he only hoped that his warnings had not gone unheeded, and that Russia was prepared.

Leading Statesmen throughout the Dominions, state that this latest act of Hitler's gives us an opportunity to prosecute the war with even greater vigour, and reiterate their decision not to rest until Hitler is destroyed.

TOBRUK, 24th June, 1941.

We have pleasure in advising that, at fabulous cost, we have secured the services of that brilliant journalist and cartoonist, Pte. Lloyd Jones, as a welcome adjunct to the literary staff of this publication. On the assumption that nothing was too good for our readers, we approached Pte. Jones with our offer, and after lengthy negotiations succeeded in inducing him to resign his position as Editor of "The Batman's Truth", that scurrilous and contemptible yellow rag of the gutter that purports to be a contemporary of this journal. It is confidently anticipated that now he is associated with a publication of the high moral standard and dignified bearing of Mud & Blood, his undoubted journalistic ability will be enhanced, and his reputation will assume a new mantle of dignity that his previous association could never have brought about. Pte. Jones is a son of Mr. & Mrs. Jones (we hope) and is connected by marriage with those other families of similar proclivities; we refer to the Smith's and Brown's. It is to be hoped that Pte. Jones' ideas will be as prolific as his clan appears to be. Judging by the number of Jones, Smith's and Brown's that clutter up the landscape, the private hobby of these tribes is not beer drinking. However, the future efforts of Pte. Jones will be watched with critical interest by not only the readers of Mud & Blood, but by its Executive.

This dog will be remembered by you all as the merry little hound that used to scamper around "A" Company lines in Palestine, and has been the centre of more storms than any·other dog alive. Here he is -
THE DOG that has been reviled and blasphemed against by multitudes,
THE DOG that has disgusted 10s and amused 1000s,
THE DOG that - Well, the dog that we can't get rid of because he has become the unit's most outstanding pet.
GENTLEMEN - WE INTRODUCE "CIRCUS", and we hope the little hound's antics in this paper from time to time will amuse you. The little chap originally came from France - at least thats where he learned to "Oui-oui."

COMMENCING IN TOMORROW'S ISSUE - ORDER YOUR COPY NOW.

Despite the colossal expense incurred in obtaining this feature, the price of Mud & Blood remains the same.

* * * * * * * * * * * * *

In certain circumstances the British are an adaptable people, and are not even above learning a lesson or two from the enemy. Eminent economists have studied the totalitarian system of barter, and are prepared to concede that it has its good points. It is proposed to give the exponents of this system an opportunity to put it into practice in Abyssinia, where certain articles in excess of requirements are to be exchanged for more useful items that are not at present available. A table of comparative values is given hereunder:-

1 Italian Corps Commander	equal to	1 roll Toilet Paper
4 Italian Generals	" "	The makings
8 Italian Brigadiers	" "	Four No. 9's.

(To stimulate trade, it is advised that 1 Italian Colonel will be chucked in with every one of the above.)

OFFICIAL ! ! !

We have been requested to call for volunteers to act as escort to a beautiful young female blonde spy, whom it is desired to send to Australia. Two stalwart soldiers, prepared to do their duty, are asked to volunteer for this job, in order to avoid the unpleasant task of having to detail someone for this unpleasant task. Applicants will report to CSM Morrison, who will be in charge of the party. (Yeah, that's the catch - Wouldn't give you a show, would he?)

2/23rd BATTALION WELFARE ASSOCIATION:

Colonel Evans is most anxious that the interests of all Mud & Bloods is looked after at home, as well as at the front, and particularly in the case of casualties which may cause hardship at home. Mrs. Evans presides over the Welfare Association helping the C.O.'s Fund, and also the Young Mud & Bloods. In addition, she represents the Regiment on the Committee of the AIF Womens Association. Much valuable aid can be given to our women-folk through these organisations. Twelve different families of the Regiment have already been helped with their problems - some were legal and others financial troubles. Therefore, the C.O. is most anxious that Mud & Bloods mention this matter to their womenfolk when next writing home. Encourage them to communicate with either our own Committee, or the AIF Womens Association, or if unable to do either, communicate with Mrs. Evans direct.

BBC NEWS — 24th June, 1941.

Reports of the German-Russian conflict indicate that Germany is attacking at eight different and widely separated points, but with only limited success. The Germans have occupied three towns in Russian occupied Polish and Rumanian territory.

Russia claims that in one battle she repulsed a German attack and destroyed 300 enemy tanks mainly through the use of artillery. Several thrusts have been repulsed in other sectors, and the enemy driven back across the frontier. In one part 5,000 German prisoners are claimed to have been taken.

In the air, Russia claims to have shot down 75 planes on the first day, and thirty odd on the second.

The Germans claim that they have penetrated 45 miles in the Rum-

anian sector, and that elsewhere her forces are proceeding according to plan. Germany has bombed Russian towns on the Black Sea, and also important oil centres in the same locality.

Mr. Sumner Welles, American Secretary of State, in a speech stated that any rallying of forces against Nazi Germany must react to the security of the Democracies. He stated that no decision had yet been made as to whether provisions of the Lease and Lend Act would be extended to Russia. However, America would continue and extend her policy of complete opposition to Hitler's dream of world conquest wherever possible. The Russian Ambassador is conferring with American Statesmen.

Finland has protested to Russia against the bombing of Finnish centres and shipping.

RAF continued the air offensive against Germany, and for the 13th night in succession, bombed towns in the Ruhr and also invasion ports. Enemy air activity over England was again on a limited scale; a few casualties were caused, but little damage. As a result of further daylight encounters between the RAF and Luftwaffe, the number of enemy planes definitely destroyed in the past 3 days is 78, at a cost to us of 9 planes. Some of the crews of the latter are known to be safe.

An enemy vessel was damaged by coastal planes off the coast of France.

In Abyssinia, a further 8,000 prisoners have been taken in the Juma area. These included a Corps Commander, 8 Generals, and numerous Brigadiers.

A Cairo statement says that 20 were killed and many injured in an air raid on Alexandria yesterday.

Another supply ship of 4,000 tons has been sunk by the Royal Navy. Its cargo included 1,000 tons of diesel oil.

TOBRUK, 25th June, 1941.

CIRCUS: Initiative,

Well, me lads, look at the news on the other side and rejoice with us. Jerry is not getting it all his own way, and the old Hammer and Sickle seems to be doing a fair job. Things are happening these days with a vengeance. Who would have thought a month ago that we would have another Ally with a population of 200,000,000 helping to fight our battles?

IMPORTANT ANNOUNCEMENT:

In response to numerous requests, we have decided to inaugurate a classified ad section, through which Mud'n Bloods may make known their needs. Send in your advts. accompanied by the trifling sum of 50 akers, which will be used to partly defray expenses when we get to Alex:-

WANTED TO SELL COLUMN:

BHQ has a Wonderful Thunderbox for sale. Guaranteed to hold more flies than any other in the Battalion. Close fitting; stream lined; with latest appliances. A Thunderbox like this compels a good performance.

Don't let your beer get flat. When you open a bottle and can't drink it all at once, don't throw it away. Buy one of our patent BUNGO bottle stoppers. Guaranteed to keep beer fresh for weeks. Buy one now.

R. LEE, Tobruk Watchmaker, has choice collection of watches for sale. Every one guaranteed to go for at least 15 minutes. Each one camouflaged so that its owner will not recognise it. Prices moderate.

REMEMBER THE FIRM'S MOTTO - NO TICK!

AUSSIES

AFTER CRETE DISASTER ANZAC TROOPS ARE
NOW BEING RUTHLESSLY SACRIFICED BY ENG-
LAND IN TOBRUCH AND SYRIA.

TURKEY HAS CONCLUDED PACT OF FRIENDSHIP
WITH GERMANY. ENGLAND WILL SHORTLY BE
DRIVEN OUT OF THE MEDITERRANEAN. OFFEN-
SIVE FROM EGYPT TO RELIEVE YOU TOTALLY
SMASHED.

YOU CANNOT ESCAPE.

OUR DIVE BOMBERS ARE WAITING TO SINK YOUR
TRANSPORTS. THINK OF YOUR FUTURE AND
YOUR PEOPLE AT HOME.

COME FORWARD - SHOW WHITE FLAGS AND YOU
WILL BE OUT OF DANGER !

SURRENDER !!

Come on, you Rats of Tobruk, where are all your white flags?
Down the rat holes, we suppose, and not too white at that. Never mind;
we don't think we'll be needing them. Have you ever seen anything more
amusing than those leaflets Jerry is sending over? Someone must have
told him we were short of paper - probably Schmitt the Spy. Anyhow,
lads, the M.O.'s advice is to only use the side that has no printing on it.
What a wonderful idea Adolph has of the Australian character? - We
thought our deeds of the past few months would have taught him better.
Now, if he only had someone with a brain like ours, his leaflets might produce some results. We'd have sent one over something like this:-

---

AUSSIES

We have been trying to get you out of your "rat holes"
for the past three months, and we're getting a bit fed up
with it. Every one of your chaps we get, costs us about ten,
and it's getting a bit thick.

Do you think that's fair? Play the game, you cads!
Come out and give yourselves up. The German beer is the
best in the world, and we have millions of gallons of it here.
And if you can't stand our Sauerkraut, we'll give you steak
and eggs any time you want them.

We look after our prisoners very well, and every Aussie
is supplied with a Batwoman; this is on the instructions of
the great and farsighted Fuhrer, who hopes in time to improve the fighting quality of the German race.

Our prison camp is the most luxurious in the world -
two-up schools every night, coursing every Wednesday, trots
on Monday afternoons, and the gee-gees every Tuesday,
Thursday and Saturday.

It's all yours, if you..............

PLEASE, PLEASE, LET US TAKE TOBRUK

BBC NEWS – 25th June, 1941.

Reports of the Russo-German fighting are conflicting.

A brief German communique states that operations in the east are proceeding satisfactorily according to plan.

A Russian communique states that at the end of the third day's fighting, German air losses totalled 384 planes. In addition, Russian air attacks on German aerodromes had accounted for a further 220 planes on the ground. In the Baltic, a German submarine was sunk by the Russian Navy.

It is stated that many German forces have been dropped behind the Russian lines by parachute, dressed in Russian uniforms. These were successfully and appropriately dealt with.

Russia accuses Finland of having placed her territory at the disposal of German forces, and is permitting her country to be used as a base for Nazi bombers. Finland has protested her neutrality.

Reports from Scandinavian sources state that German forces are advancing rapidly in Lithuania but Russia says that all attacks in this area have been repulsed.

In a speech in the House of Commons, Mr. Anthony Eden said that all efforts to come to an understanding in the past with Russia had failed, owing to Russia's strict adherence to her pact with Germany. Now Germany had ruthlessly broken this pact when it suited her to do so.

Within the past 24 hours the Turkish Government has assured the British Government that the Anglo-Turkish Pact still remains intact.

Queen Wilhelmina in a broadcast speech declared that the Dutch people throughout the world would give help and assistance to Russia.

Mr. Roosevelt said that the United States would give all possible aid to Russia. How, and in what form this assistance would take, had not yet been worked out.

Again last night the RAF bombed towns in north west Germany. Four enemy bombers are known to have been shot down last night during raids over England. Enemy air activity over England was again light. Some casualties and damage were caused, in a town on the east coast.

Nine enemy planes were shot down in daylight sweeps over occup-

ied France yesterday. 112 planes have now been shot down in the last 3 days compared with a loss of 28 planes of ours.

Vichy forces are reported to have withdrawn to a position about 15 miles north of Damascus. RAF and RAAF planes in a big sweep over Syria have sought out and destroyed or damaged many planes on Vichy aerodromes.

Bengasi has again been bombed by the RAF; also Sicily. In the Mediterranean our submarines have made a successful attack on a 20,000 ton Italian liner, and have also sunk another enemy supply ship.

Our Naval forces have been engaged by units of the French Fleet which tried to interfere with our activities off the Syrian coast. It is believed that one French destroyer has been sunk.

A recent decree prohibits any Italians from leaving the United States without permission. This follows on a similar decree imposed on Germans resident in the US.

In Abyssinia a further 400 prisoners have been taken in mopping up operations in the Juma area.

TOBRUK, 26th June, 1941.

Well, there's nothing anaemic about the news today, is there? Old Joe seems to be more than holding his own, and what with his new air offensive, Adolph must surely be looking round for the old bottle of Aspros; and don't forget, he had the advantage of surprise. We shouldn't wonder if, once Joe gets into his stride, Adolph gets such a kick in the pants that he'll be looking for a little Elba all for himself. Maybe Musso has already reserved some little isle in Mare Nostrum for this purpose.

We have to impart the good news that our Welfare Association has forwarded the sum of 75 pounds to swell the coffers of the C.O.'s Fund. No doubt, when opportunity offers, this amount will be expended upon those little tins of amber fluid that bring such joy to our hearts, or some other comfort that circumstances may make available such as chocolate, writing paper, etc. Most of our womenfolk are working extremely hard to accumulate these funds, and it is up to us to express our appreciation of their efforts when writing home. So don't forget, Mud'n Bloods; it's so easy to take these things for granted, and forget the sacrifice our womenfolk sometimes have to make to permit these funds being sent to us.

LETTER FROM A CORRESPONDENT

Sir,

I wish to complain, through the columns of your worthy paper, about the ineffectiveness of the N.C.I. powder that has been issued to the troops to get rid of troublesome insects. Although I have been sprinkling some round a cubby hole in which a certain NCO sleeps, he is still as healthy as ever; in fact he seems to thrive on it. I am thinking of putting some in his food, and if this fails I know an officer who will give me permission to use the rifle. If insect powder fails, it would be no use trying a booby trap. And talking of insects, could the Quartermaster be reminded that the population of the flea world is doubling and trebling nightly - can't he do something about it? Perhaps he could provide rations for them, and so save me having to provide their sustenance.

Yours etc.

WOULDN'T IT.

CLASSIFIED ADS:

TO LET: Commodious bomb-proof dugout, 40 feet underground, all latest cons, including periscope. No fleas guaranteed. Eminently suitable for postal or provost personnel. Will only let on 3 years' lease.

TROOPS: If your water is not chlorinated don't delay! Let Max Rintoule treat you at once. The man who makes good water bad, and bad water worse. Make appointments at M & B Office, Sharia la Trine, Deliaville.

* * * * * * * * * *

We thought that the new nickname of the RMO (Regimental Medical Officer) - "Adolph" was maybe conferred on account of his moustache, but yesterday learned the real reason. "The greatest 'purge merchant' I've ever come across," grumbled one Mud'n Blood. "A dose of castor oil, two doses of salts, and as many No. 9s as he can cram into me." Yes, does sound a bit drastic treatment for a sprained wrist. "He also gave me some medicine that I have to take three days running," moaned the victim. "He certainly is seeing to it that I follow the directions."

BBC NEWS — 26th June, 1941.

The recent activity of the RAF over Germany and enemy occupied territory is the beginning of what is described as "the greatest air offensive in the world's history." The plan has been carefully worked out and is gigantic in its conception. During the past week our planes have dropped more bombs than during the whole of April. The volume of our bombings exceeds even the worst enemy "blitz" against England last winter.

Last night the RAF again extensively bombed towns in N.W. Germany. In a daylight raid over occupied France, 13 enemy planes were shot down. In addition, two bridges were directly hit, and one was seen to collapse. An ammunition train was blown up.

Air activity over England continues on a light scale. Sporadic raids were made on Scotland and the South of England. Some casualties were caused and damage was not serious.

The names of these Russian towns has got our shorthand completely licked, and we're not even game to have a stab at them.

Today's Russian communique announces destruction of 76 German planes on Wednesday for a loss of 17 Russian planes. In Bessarabia sector, the Red Army is stated to be firmly holding their positions on the eastern bank of the river, repulsing successfully numerous enemy attempts to force a passage across the river. Other attacks in Cernauti (?) area were repulsed. Russian air force dealt a number of devastating blows on German aerodromes in Finland. Enemy shipping was bombed as well as petrol reservoirs in Constanza harbour. Large numbers of German and Rumanian prisoners have been taken. Soviet cavalry drove back German and Rumanian troops which crossed the river Pruth. Russians broke enemy ranks by severe air bombing. Soviet cavalry profited, and charged enemy lines using their sabres, clearing the bridge, and eventually occupied town of Falcin.

Finland states that Russian violation of her territory compels Finland to defend herself with every means within her power.

In Sweden, a number of army, air force, and naval reservists have been called up. Sweden has permitted German forces to cross her territory to Finland.

Mr. Sumner Welles stated that President Roosevelt would not invoke the Neutrality Act against Russia, which meant that American ships would be permitted to carry arms and supplies to Russia.

In Syria, the capture of another town by British and Australian troops was announced. The Navy is supporting our forces by bombarding all Vichy positions accessible. Enemy destroyers in Beirut harbour have been raided by our air force.

Bengasi and Tripoli have again been subjected to heavy raids, and extensive damage has been caused.

TOBRUK, 27th June, 1941.

CIRCUS: Devilry.

More mail today, Mud'n Bloods, and pretty slick too, as this lot only took 15 days to get here. As a matter of fact if we had known a mail was in, we wouldn't have published this issue, as we know from our own experience that your letters will be read and re-read over and over again, and Mud & Blood will not even be missed. Good though this publication is, we are not in the race when letters from home are to hand.

In nearly every mail newspaper cuttings are arriving, which are somewhat embarrassing in regard to their complimentary and laudatory contents.
Hereunder is an extract from the leading article of Albury's Border Morning Mail of 6th June:-

"Proud boast of the men of Albury's Own, up to the time their last
reveille shrilled among the hills of Bonegilla, was that they would pick up
the thread of history where it had been dropped by their predecessors 25
years ago, and write new chapters of glory and adventure.

"They are on the job at Tobruk now, this battalion of magnificent
Australian manhood whom Albury grew to respect so much that it did them
the honour of officially adopting them before they sailed away. The towns-
folk appreciate the incidental fame they are bringing to headquarters by
their stubborn resistance to Nazi Germany in their Libyan stronghold.

"True, they are part of a beleaguered garrison of gallant Anzacs,
but they are very much in the news because they refuse to be dislodged
from a position that is vital to the success of Hitler's ambition to succeed
where Mussolini failed. Over and over again, the enemy has made vicious
assaults against Tobruk; and as often Albury's Own has played its part in
the tossing of them back into the desert.

"Now we learn from the daily communiques that "Mud & Blood,"
the name that the original unit handed on to its 1940 edition, is developing
the art of perimeter pushing. Sorties issue regularly from the garrison to
push back dents in the line miles outside of Tobruk, so as to give it an even
contour. It is not easy work, and it calls for high courage and supreme determination; especially at Tobruk, where those outside the perimeter considerably outnumber those within.

"It is typical of Anzac spirit that, in the stern business of holding
their armed tormentors at bay, our men have found time to publish their
own newspaper. They see nothing incongruous in setting aside a corner of
the battlefield in which to record their impressions of life under fire. This
effervescent little sheet which has found its way back to Australia, is a
pessimist's nightmare. It oozes optimism, bubbles with battlefield humour
and is so very Australian.

"Albury's Own will not always be hemmed in by an arc of enemy steel. But while its duty is to bar the Nazis' progress at the outer ramparts of Tobruk, it is doing a service for the Empire, the importance of which at present lies in the disorganisation it is creating to Nazi strategy."

ALBURY IS PROUD OF "MUD AND BLOOD"

BBC NEWS – 27th June, 1941.

In Tobruk area our troops on Wednesday made further substantial penetrations on a wide front in Salient held by the enemy in outer defences of perimeter, thus considerably strengthening our own positions in this sector.

In Abyssinia, clearing operations in Juma area are nearing completion. South of Sodder, disintegration of Italian forces continuing by desertions of their African troops.

In Syria, British made substantial gains west of Damascus. In coastal sector Damour defences bombarded by our artillery in conjunction with the Navy.

Nine enemy fighters were destroyed yesterday when RAF made another sweep over the Channel and Northern France. Three British fighters missing. Over England there was no enemy activity last night. Very small number of enemy planes came over, but no reports of casualties have been received. Bremen and Kiel were principal objectives of RAF in their relentless offensive for 15 successive nights.

RAF aircraft intercepted a number of Italian planes over Malta on Wednesday, destroying 3 of them and damaging another without loss to themselves. Bazala landing ground, and shipping in Bengasi harbour were attacked.

In Syria, RAF intercepted and shot down 3 Vichy planes and damaged others. Enemy aircraft raided Damascus, causing a number of civilian casualties. Minor raids were also carried out on Haifa and Acre. One British aircraft missing.

Russian-German war communique. Today's Red Army communique announces that Russian troops engaged in fierce fighting with large enemy tank units in Minsk sector and fighting continues. Attempts by Germans to cross river Pruth in Cernai sector were successfully repulsed. In the Bessarabia sector, our units firmly hold their positions along frontier, having thrown back German and Rumanian attacks. Soviet air force yesterday bombed Bucharest,and Ploesti oil refineries are ablaze. No engagement on Soviet-Finnish border. Two enemy submarines sunk by Soviet planes in Baltic. Referring to parachutists, communique claims their groups are being dealt with - captured or destroyed.

On other hand, Berlin says that fighting on eastern front is progressing according to plan, although Soviet troops constantly offer resistance to weight of German attack. It is announced that Italian Motorised Division is being sent to the Russian Frontier.

A recruiting campaign for Spanish volunteers to fight against Russia has started in Madrid.

The Russian Ambassador visited Under Secretary of State who promised favourable consideration of any Russian request for help.

London Minister for Agriculture told Parliament that 3,000 Italian prisoners would shortly arrive in Britain, and would be available for work on the land.

Rumanian Government left Bucharest following Soviet air attacks, says Ankara report.

In broadcast last night, Finnish President said that Finland will fight for freedom of her country, and the creed of her forefathers. He added that Soviet troops had been attacking all along Finnish frontier since yesterday.

It is now revealed that Nazis tried to start intrigues in Ankara. Proposal for collaboration against Russia was flatly rejected.

TOBRUK, 30th June, 1941.

CIRCUS: Hell! Eau de Cologne.

Enquiries have been numerous as to the non-appearance of Mud & Blood during the past two days. In explanation we would advise that we do not go to press on Saturdays or Sundays on religious grounds. We are afraid that the Padre will be down on us if we publish on Sundays, whilst we may offend the susceptibilities of the Hebrew members of the battalion if we issue our paper on Saturdays. We do not know how many of the latter there are in the Battalion, but the R.M.O. has supplied us with figures indicating that there could easily be a considerable number, so we thought we had better be on the safe side. (How's that for a square-off?)

Some few days ago, an unexploded German shell was brought into the "I" (Intelligence) Section for examination. This concluded, the shell was left lying outside BHQ, an object of curiosity to all who passed. Knowing the shell was minus it's nosecap, and was liable to go off if kicked, Provost Sgt. Bill Marshall, with much mental disturbance and, no doubt, secret inner apprehension, picked it up and carried it gently to what he considered a safe distance. Depositing it carefully on the bottom of a deep hole, he reported back to BHQ, where he was duly awarded a Mud & Blood Medal. Today we have been compelled reluctantly to demand the return of said Medal. Yesterday morning, Bill was instructed to supervise the removal of certain rubbish. His not too willing workers toiled ceaselessly under Bill's stern eye, gathering debris from right and left, and disposing of it in a nearby hole. It is against the principles of any provost to do anything that might leave him open to the accusation of working, but taking this risk, Bill produced a box of matches, and set fire to the pile of rubbish. Then he repaired to his nearby shanty to rest and recover from this unwonted activity. Scarcely had he laid his head on his downy pillow than - WHOOSH - outside was a terrific bang, followed by the pitter-patter of tins, bottles, jars, and debris of all description raining from the skies. Yes, you've guessed it in one. Bill's memory is like the old grey mare - not what it used to be, and he had lit a fire over the shell. What! You want to know what his working squad said to him when he asked them to pick up all the rubbish for the second time? Well, we'll have you know this is a respectable paper, and we wouldn't repeat the like.

Cpl. Jimmy Rintoule has been excelling himself lately, and the rank and file of BHQ are going about with dazed expressions. Last Friday night he turned on a dinner that we defy Jack O'Brien, Abe Armstrong or Dick Broderick to better. This was followed by a succession of meals on Saturday and Sunday that showed it was no flash in the pan. Today the boys are talking of presenting him with his portrait done in oils. However, it has been suggested by the creator of our mascot dog "Circus" that if it is decided to do the portrait in water colours, "Circus" will make a generous donation. All we have to say on the subject is that one more dinner like last Friday's, and a Mud & Blood Medal will be immediately pinned on Jimmy's left bosom, with due pomp and ceremony.

News has just come to hand from Lieut. Wally Brown, who in a letter to Major Wall, states he has made a rapid recovery, and is now convalescing. He hopes to rejoin the unit shortly, and sends greetings and good wishes to his many friends in the battalion.

BBC NEWS — 30th June, 1941.

Patrol activity in the frontier area is continuing in Libya.

In Abyssinia our forces advancing from Jimma on 26th June, occupied Dembi, capturing 600 Italian and 100 African prisoners of war.

In all sectors of Syria, local advances were made and fighting is continuing. Six Vichy aircraft which were attacking our troops near Palmyra were shot down by Australian pilots without loss to themselves. RAF also attacked store dumps near Palmyra, and railway lines and other military objectives at Rayak.

Bengasi and Tripoli Harbours were raided, and many hits were made on Moles at both places. No British aircraft missing from these operations. Alexandria had an air raid yesterday morning, several bombs being dropped, causing damage to property, but no casualties.

Lord Beaverbrook, Minister of States, has been appointed Minister of Supply, succeeding Sir Andrew Duncan who becomes President of the Board of Trade. Lord Beaverbrook remains a member of War Cabinet.

No German fighters were encountered when RAF fighters carried out another sweep over French coast yesterday afternoon. All British aircraft returned without incident.

No reports of German planes having crossed the coast of Britain were received until 1600 GMT yesterday.

Axis air losses last week in Europe and Middle East totalled 183 aircraft. Britain lost 65 machines, but a number of pilots were saved. This is believed to be biggest weekly score this year.

Taking Russian claims into consideration, enemy losses for the week must have exceeded 500.

Moscow Red Army communique claims German losses during seven or eight days of fighting to be 2500 tanks, about 1500 planes, and over 30,000 prisoners. Russian losses during same period are 850 planes, 900 tanks, and up to 15,000 men missing. Communique adds that repeated attacks by Finnish and German troops yesterday launched along entire front from Sea of Barents to Gulf of Finland, were repulsed. In Minsk area, Soviet troops and airforce checked any further advance of German mechanised units which had pierced the defences. German mechanised units in Minsk area are cut off from their bases, and are being bombarded and machine gunned by Red Airforce. In Luck area, Soviet tank units and aircraft annihilated a great part of German tank units and motorised troops. Communique says also that real situation is quite different to the captures claimed by German High Command. In Vilnodvonsk area, Northern Poland, Soviet troops retired to new position holding off attempts of mobile units to attack their flank and rear.

Paderwiski, famous pianist and composer, has died in New York after a week of illness.

A few bombs were dropped last night in Eastern England, but no damage reported. One enemy raider was destroyed. British bombers attacked objectives in North West Germany.

In New York, 29 persons were arrested and charged with conspiracy to engage in espionage. It is the biggest round up of spy suspects since passage of espionage act. Twentytwo of those arrested were born in Germany.

Most severe earthquake shocks were recorded at Sydney observatory on Saturday and yesterday. Epicentre was near Finke, Central Australia.

Vichy Hungarian Communique claims that Hungarian planes attacked Soviet objectives.

CHAPTER 6

TOBRUK, 1st July, 1941.

CIRCUS: A job well done.

After a lapse, the old "bingle-bingle" was going this morning with a vengeance. After watching those Stukas diving, followed by the resounding explosion of their out-size "eggs", one was left with the impression that tremendous damage must have been caused. Official reports however, confirm that no damage was done, and once again the accuracy of our ack-ack kept Jerry from getting close enough to his objective to be accurate in his aim. Apparently a new batch of Stukas had arrived; wonder how long it will be before they go the same way as their predecessors.

The shortage of cigarettes is becoming acute, we noticed even the C.O. sporting one of those long bilious looking I-ti cigars this morning. He wasn't looking too happy about it either. The Padre produced a packet for the use of our Editorial selves; don't know what we had been doing to him. We suppose this is the only way a reverend gentleman can work off a bit of hate; in a weak moment we smoked one of the diabolical concoctions, and we have been weak ever since.

We repeat hereunder some lines written by a member of the original 23rd, inspired by the Dawn Service on last Anzac Day, and published in the Melbourne "Sun". Why is it that no member of this Battalion comes forward with an effort worthy of publication. At one time we had hopes that Sgt. Don Renton of "A" Company would lay claim to the poetic laurels of this unit, but he has remained strangely sterile since coming to this country. What about it, Don?

THOUGHTS AT DAWN

Others will gather here and when we pass
    Along that dark'ning road whence no retreat,
New Diggers, now re-born, will tread the grass
    With muffled rhythm as they, halting, meet
            At Dawn.

Let's hope they think of us in terms of song,
    Light hearted, and with laughter in the eye,
And know that we were once alert and strong
    When waiting for the breaking of the sky
            At Dawn.

Hark! Now the last post o'er the Shrine rings clear
March past, new Diggers, you are welcome here.

BBC NEWS — 2nd July, 1941.

Lieut-Gen. Sir Archibald Wavell has been appointed C in C, India. His post as C in C Middle East Forces is being taken by Lieut-Gen. Sir Claude Auchinleck, formerly C in C India Command. This change over is to give General Wavell a well earned rest, as he has borne the brunt of all

Middle East activities since the start of hostilities, and has participated in and directed, five separate campaigns. In addition, he has had the extra burden of all the administrative work entailed by the occupation of various enemy countries.

Another important innovation is the establishment of a Ministry for the Middle East. Mr. Oliver Littlewood has been appointed to this important post, and will probably have his HQ in Cairo. He will be able to relieve the C in C of all matters of administration. He will retain full Cabinet rank.

From the conflicting communiques issued by the Germans and Russians, it would appear that operations are being carried on in five major sectors. German columns are thrusting into Russian territory, but are having to fight bitterly all the way. The German drive through the Minsk area appears to be a most important thrust. The Russians are using artillery on a large scale very effectively and are inflicting heavy losses on the enemy. In the south, the Germans still seem to be held up on the river Pruth, and to be making no progress whatever. In the north, the position is not so satisfactory. It is claimed by Germany that Russian forces in the Murmansk area have been cut off.

The Russian Ambassador has approached Washington, and is endeavouring to place substantial orders for arms and war materials in the United States. Whether these purchases will be on a cash basis or under the Lease and Lend Act has not yet been decided.

Further conferences have been held in Moscow between Russian Military and Naval chiefs, with the British delegation.

During last night RAF attacked strongly the French port of Brest, where three German war vessels are sheltering. In sweeps over France yesterday in daylight, very few enemy aircraft were seen, and there were no casualties on either side. Very few bombers appeared over the coast of England last night.

By agreement with Britain, two French vessels will sail from America to North Africa. These ships will not be permitted to carry arms or other war materials, and will be under the supervision of America.

In Japan, a Military spokesman stated in a broadcast speech that the present war and the "China incident" were a part of the same battle, and could not be separated.

In Syria our forces continue to advance. Normal conditions are be-ginning to prevail in British occupied Syria and Lebanon. Large quantities of food stuffs are being sent into the country daily. Free French sources recognise the independence of Syria, recently proclaimed by Britain when forces first marched into the country.

In Bengasi extensive raids were carried out on shipping in the harbour, and a large troop carrying vessel was severely attacked and troops machine gunned. There is no development in the land situation in North Africa.

German authorities in Belgium have arrested the Burgomaster of Brussels, as well as other municipal leaders in the other towns.

TOBRUK, 3rd July, 1941.

After all, Miss Tomkinson, it was your idea that we come out here and pick bluebells.

Complaints continue to reach us that personnel in forward posts seldom or never see Mud & Blood. We wish to point out that as many copies of this publication are issued as possible, having due regard to availability of paper supplies. However, our circulation provides for a copy being sent to each post, in addition to one for Company HQ. It is, therefore, up to Company clerks to see that this paper receives it's correct circulation. The aim of the paper is, first of all, to acquaint as many of the battalion as possible of current world news, and secondly to discuss battalion matters of interest or amusement. We appreciate the compliment of Mud & Blood being so eagerly sought after as a souvenir, but the main object of its issue is being defeated by this. Let the paper have its normal distribution before socking it away to send to Mary or Gertie or whoever she may be. In time, there will be spare copies for everyone who requires a souvenir to send home.

We are informed that a certain tall Major of this Battalion was much amused recently whilst visiting one of the forward posts. Jerry was doing a spot of shelling, and he was amazed to see two blase soldiers sitting side by side well within range, criticising Jerry's aim. The shells were dropping some fifty to one hundred yards from the post, first on one side and then on the other. The two soldiers applauded or decried each shot, according to where it fell. One of the men was evidently of mature years; the other looked a stripling. The Major approached the two, admiring their cool nonchalence in the face of fairly heavy fire, and had a few words with them. One was evidently a digger with experience of the last war; the other, bearing a strong resemblance to the older man, was a mere youth. Enquiry elicited the information that they were father and son. The latter officially gave his age as 22 years, but admitted unofficially that he had just turned 16, and had come out to look after "Pop". "The old man is too venturesome," he explained, "and needs someone to restrain him, so I try to be with him as much as possible." That the "old man" had not forgotten his parental duties was seen when the Major affably offered his cigarette case to the pair. Pop Wright helped himself, but waved the Major's case away from "sonny" with the statement "He's too young to be smoking yet awhile."

During this quiet period we have been experiencing, much spare time has to be filled in. In an endeavour to help in this, and at the same time assist to cultivate a subject that may be helpful in business life later on, we are prepared to teach, in easy lessons, the rudiments of shorthand. This, contrary to popular belief, is not a difficult subject to learn, and is at least as fascinating a hobby as, say, crossword puzzles. It is a very handy thing to know, and no matter what walk of life the student is in, he will find it a very useful adjunct. All Mud'n Bloods interested in this idea, please send their names to the Orderly Room, and more details will be supplied. It is not proposed to hold classes; lessons and explanations will be supplied and can be worked on in spare time in your own surroundings. If there is sufficient interest shown, we may even give the lessons in these columns. Let's know if you desire to be included amongst those students already enrolled.

BBC NEWS — 3rd July, 1941.

For the loss of two bombers and eight fighters, our RAF shot down 18 enemy planes in a daylight sweep over France yesterday. During a second sweep, no incidents were reported.

A Hungarian communique announces that there are no Russian troops on her frontier, same having been withdrawn as a result of an attack.

Yesterday evening's Red Army communique states that enemy attacked in Srednic Peninsula in direction of Murmansk. Russian troops resisted strongly and inflicted heavy losses on the enemy. In the direction of Dvinsk and Minsk, our troops attacked advanced enemy tank units aiming at their destruction. In direction of Luck, our troops continued their fight against motorised enemy unit inflicting heavy blows. On other parts of front widespread activity took place.

Air lull over England continues. Yesterday no activity was reported over England. British squadrons raided Germany last night when they attacked Ruhr, Rhineland and N.W. Germany.

Today's Red Army communique says that in White Russia Soviet infantry fighting against German tanks, succeeded in cutting off tanks from infantry. In the direction of Brosiov - Luck and Booruise, German attempts to break through were hampered by Russian tank units and dive bombers. In remaining sectors, Soviet troops firmly held State frontiers.

Stalin, broadcasting today, said that enemy occupied Lithuania, greater part of Latvia, western part of White Russia and part of Western Ukraine. He claimed destruction of enemy's best forces, and also declared that Hitler's army will be beaten as Napoleon's was. Stalin appealed to everyone to support the Red Army and Navy for victory. He said "This is a Fatherland war, and also a war for liberation of peoples enslaved by Germany."

In Syria, Allied troops continue to advance, during which several enemy tanks were destroyed and one captured. On coast further local advances made, and no change in central Syria.

In Abyssinia operations continuing satisfactorily; no change in Libya.

RAF HQ announced yesterday that RAAF squadrons machine gunned Rayak aerodrome in Syria destroying two aircraft on ground and damaging four others. Fires were started among dispersed aircraft on Aleppo aerodrome, one of which was destroyed and a number of others damaged.

During the nights of Monday and Tuesday, RAF bombers attacked harbour and shipping at Beirut. Hits were registered on the main docks, at the quays and near ships which are believed to have caused damage. No British machines are missing from these operations.

General Mason-MacFarlane, head of the British Military Mission to

Russia, has reached Soviet Army HQ.

Communique from Chungking - Notification has been delivered to Italian and German Embassies formally announcing China's severance of Diplomatic relations with the Axis powers. This follows recognition by the Axis and Spanish Governments of Japanese sponsored Nanking Government.

An announcement concerning some American action in regard to Monte Video was made, but owing to wireless distortion could not be clearly taken down. Further details regarding this will appear in tomorrow's issue.

* *We wish to asknowledge the valuable help of Pte. John Hall, of Signals, in compiling much of the above news.*

TOBRUK, 5th July, 1941.

According to rumour, so many boatloads of beer have been sunk in the Mediterranean en route to us that a popular misconception has arisen as to the effect this has on tidal influence. Capt. Blaubaum, of Brigade, has gone to considerable pains to allay our fears, and has been giving lectures on the subject. The lectures are timely, as a lot of concern has been felt by the boys in case there was a tidal wave at any time, and they would have been in danger of being drowned in beer, a fate that makes even us shudder. Our tame cartoonist suggests that a suitable and popular lecture might be given on the lines of the illustration alongside. In such a lecture, we have no doubt Capt. Freddy Kiel would be pleased to collaborate with Capt. Blaubaum, as the subject is one on which he can speak with special authority, having in the course of his military career, delved into such matters, with a view of course, to passing his knowledge on to the troops. Oh, yeah!

Lecturer:

The next slide, men, has something of importance to all men in Tobruk.

SPECIAL ANNOUNCEMENT ! ! !

The C.O. has expressed the wish that all men in the Battalion sub-scribe the sum of two "akers" (6d.) for the purchase of tickets in Tatt's. If the Mud & Blood Syndicate were to win a big prize, Mud & Blood Pty. Ltd. would be formed in Australia, with a committee at this end consisting of the three senior officers for the time being, and one other rank per Com-pany, with an Australian Committee of our womenfolk, a banker, and a valuer. Our Australian Committee would be instructed to rent producing property with any winnings, and thereby create a fund to be applied en-tirely for the benefit of Mud & Bloods, or their dependents, after the war. With a bit of luck the Battalion could produce a very fine show, and the C.O. is of the opinion that already the 2/23rd Battalion has done much harder things than merely winning Tatt's. Perhaps these tickets could be purchased say once a month. It is suggested that the first contribution be made on next pay day, and details in regard to collection will be advised later.

MUD & BLOOD P. & A. PARADE.

It is advised that the newly established firm of theatrical entrepan-eurs, Messrs. Jarvie & Mulcahy, have arranged the most stupendous, coloss-al and gigantic assemblage of amateur and professional talent ever to grace the boards in that place of erstwhile entertainment - the Villa Delia. On Sunday evening, 6th July, from 7.30 to 9.00, a high speed concert will be permitted to be given. Ten members from each of the rifle companies will be permitted to attend. In addition, it is expected that "B" Echelon lads will turn up to see what a Sunday evening concert is really like. Brigade personnel have been invited, whilst HQ Company and BHQ lads will be there in force. Hereunder is the programme that has been arranged, and which speaks for itself:-

1. National Anthem
2. Community singing - Accompanist Cyril Fletcher.
3. Roy Read - Vocalist.
4. Tich Deane - Banjo Mandolin.
5. Stan Buswell - Accordeon.
6. Aub. Prowse & Tom Moore - Instrumental Novelty Act.
7. Stretcher-bearers Male Quartette.
8. Stan Graeber - Mouth Organ.
9. Selections by Cyril Fletcher
10. Community Singing.

11.   Rex Spry - Vocalist.
12.   Vic Fauvel - Steel Guitar.
13.   Bill Kemp - Vocalist.
14.   Charlie Challis - Banjo.
15.   Alan Hughes - Vocalist.
16.   English Quintette.
17:    Community Singing.

BBC NEWS — 5th July, 1941.

Activity is reported on both sides in the Tobruk and Frontier areas in Libya.

In Syria remnants of Palmyra's original garrison numbering some 300 Vichy troops surrendered to the British on Thursday. Indian troops occupied DEIR EZ ZOR capturing materials. In other sectors nothing to report.

Italian resistance in Eritrea, Abyssinia and Italian Somaliland has now been brought to a successful close except for the Italian garrison at Gondar, which is now hemmed in by Empire and Patriot forces. General Gazzera, supreme commander remaining Italian forces in Abyssinia has surrendered, together with all Italian forces operating in province of Galla Sidamo.

RAF announced yesterday attacks on enemy shipping at Tripoli on Thursday, and aerodrome. One enemy plane was destroyed, several others were damaged. Bengasi harbour and several enemy aerodromes also heavily raided. Other military targets were attacked in vicinity of Bengasi and Bardia; also enemy motor transport vehicles bombed and destroyed near Derna.

In Syria, Beirut harbour attacked and two enemy aircraft were destroyed whilst others were damaged. Two British aircraft missing from all these operations.

Air Ministry announces that 16 German fighters were destroyed by RAF during yesterday afternoon's sweep over Northern France. Blenheim bombers also attacked objectives near Bethune. Four of our planes missing. Bremen was also bombed from very low level, some aircraft coming down to 50 feet. Frisian Islands also attacked. Over Britain yesterday, for the third day running, no bombs were dropped. Last night, however, enemy was more active than recently. Middle, south-west and east England and south Wales were attacked. No extensive damage was done but some casualties were reported. Three enemy bombers were destroyed during the night. British fighters intercepted and drove off large enemy formation which raided Malta on Friday morning.

German communique states that with Soviet troops falling back on 1938 Soviet frontier, Germans now expect fierce new battles with main Russian forces, which will undoubtedly attempt to hold German advance. Germans also admit that large scale fighting still going on behind German front, as pockets of Soviet troops continue to resist Germans. They also speak of fierce resistance, and there is mention of 52 ton tanks.

Moscow radio announces that the German casualties amount to at least 700,000 killed and wounded. The districts occupied by the Germans were strewn with hundreds of thousands of bodies of German soldiers.

Australian Navy Minister announces loss of the destroyer "Waterhen" in Mediterranean. The "Waterhen" sank while in tow after being damaged. There were no casualties.

Today's Red Army communique reports heavy fighting along the whole front, and enemy attempts to cross BERESINA were repulsed, and fighting developed unfavourably for the Germans.

In North Poland Russian troops fell back on new positions after enemy had thrown his reserves into battle. In South-west Poland our troops have repulsed attacks by superior enemy forces attempting to break the front of our troops. According to later reports, Red Air Force has claimed six enemy planes on Thursday.

Russians claim that the enemy is not standing up to bayonet attacks by our forces. In course of fighting, it was established that enemy tanks are avoiding encounters with Russian heavy and medium tanks.

TOBRUK, 8th July, 1941.

Pressure of work prevented us publishing yesterday (laugh that off, but it is true) so we are giving you a double number today, despite the great amount of work and self-sacrifice involved. We had intended going to the links for a round or two, followed by dinner in town, and a night at the Tivoli. However, our personal desires are always subordinated to the good of the Battalion (who said that?) so here we are.

First of all let us tell you of the greatest show on earth since the day
when Eve dropped her fig leaf in the Garden of Eden; we refer to the magnificent revue produced by Sgt. Jack Jarvie in collaboration with ourselves
on Sunday night last. As time goes on, events of successive importance
continue to occur, that will in due course be inscribed in the annals of the
battalion's history. This event will take its place as an effort not the least
meritorious of the many brilliant functions that this unit has been responsible for, taking into consideration the difficulties that had to be overcome,
and the unique conditions that existed.

A somewhat cold night did not prevent an audience of many thousands from gathering in the vicinity of BHQ (Hush! this is only put in to
trick Jerry). Staging had been erected, natural and other seating accommodation provided, and the superlative organising ability of the business manager of the concert was further evidenced in his arranging for a fine moon-
lit night for the event. Sgt. Jack Jarvie produced the show with his usual
aplomb and despatch, and for a few brief hours could easily have imagined
himself back in Dean Street, Albury, as he expeditiously ushered performer after performer on to the stage. There was never a hitch, and the various items followed each other without pause or delay; altogether it was a
memorable night. J. C. Williamson's please note, in case either Jack or ourselves ever want a job back in Melbourne.

The performance scarcely commenced when there was a scamper,
led by the producer and artists, as a Jerry plane appeared overhead and the
ack-ack opened up. However, it soon passed and the show went on, only
interrupted from time to time by the disconcerting noise of our own artillery as they continued to harrass the Hun. From a distance came the
noise of strife, as our carriers, out on a job of work, hurried on with their
task of annihilating a party of the enemy, so that they could get back before the concert ended.

For an initial effort our local talent was not at all bad, and will improve as a result of the experience. Rex Spry was in particularly good
voice and rendered Road to Mandalay, Tumbledown Shack, and Love
Walked In, to the complete satisfaction of the audience, which was also
convulsed at the antics of Stan Graeber and his Mouthorgan. Another item
of excellence was a novelty instrumental number by Tom Moore and Aub.
Prowse. Tich Deane (Banjo), Bill Kemp (Songster), Vic Fauvel (Guitar),
and Alan Hughes (Songs and Uke) all contributed items of merit and enjoyment. Special mention must be made of the Stretcher-bearers Quartette (Ptes. Newman, Read and Reader, with Stan Graeber) who were par-

ticularly good in their rendering of Silent Night, together with other items of a more serious nature.

However, the honours of the night definitely went to our visitors, who came to assist our own performers and finished up by stealing the show. We refer to Cyril Fletcher and Stan Buswell (9 Div. Sigs) who provided a feast of tuneful melody on their squeeze boxes, and three English friends from the Artillery, Bombadier Clarke, and Gunners Dick and Aaron. Easily the greatest hit of the night was a stirring march song entitled "The Voice of the Middle East" composed and written by Bomb. Clarke. This is one of the most stirring marches that we have so far heard, and will in time, no doubt, rival Roll out the Barrel as the outstanding war hit, just as Tipperary was the outstanding tune of the last war. Gunner Aaron sang this rousing song with verve, and the audience was soon enthusiastic to a degree almost unbelievable. Many requests for the words of the song have been received, and we give them hereunder. It is hoped that Mud'n Bloods will learn this song, so that at future concerts it will continue to give as much enjoyment as it did on Sunday night. The tune is exceptionally "catchy", and all day yesterday around BHQ, batmen, clerks, drivers, cooks, runners, etc., were whistling merrily this new hit.

However, to get on with the performance - Gunner Aaron won the spontaneous applause of the crowd by his rendering of Danny Boy, Rose of Tralee, Shanty in Old Shanty Town, and other numbers. He has a fine voice, and an assured platform manner, and he imparted quite a professional air to his items. Bomb. Clarke was appreciated in a number, The End of the Road. Mention should be made of two fine original compositions of Bomb. Clarke, written after the advance through the desert to the green fields of Barce. These were played by Gnr. Dick and earned great applause for both player and composer. Cyril Fletcher, Stan Buswell and Gnr. Dick, in addition to giving selections on their accordeons, accompanied at various times Community Singing by the audience. Altogether, it was a great night, and it is hoped that it will be repeated in the near future; efforts are now being directed to having another concert next Sunday night, but you will be advised as to that later on.

Just another word before leaving the subject of the concert; we only wish Jerry could have heard our boys as they got up at the conclusion of the show and sang lustily God Save the King. They put all they knew into it, and the effect was striking. As we stood there singing with our English friends, a wave of patriotism seemed to fill every voice with added vigour. We are very apt to take our patriotism for granted, and it is not a bad thing once in a while to stop and reflect on the feeling that brought us into this war. We are all free men, and we are here of our own free choice. We have a justifiable pride in our country, and in our mode of life; otherwise we would not have thought it necessary to give up our liberty and endanger our lives for the preservation of our country and its institutions, and what it stands for. In this environment, we do not think so much of these things, but the fact remains that all the thoughts and aspirations of our pre-army life are still within us. We are here, doing our job, and feeling justifiably proud that we are doing it so well. Who amongst us would be out of it all before its successful conclusion, despite the oft heard wishes that nostalgia causes to be uttered; and the feeling of almost contempt that we all have for the cold-footed blighters that are still tramping the streets of Melbourne may be somewhat complacent, but it is with us all the same. Who'd be one of them?

Having got off our soap box, let us get on with this work of editorial anguish. Where are we? Oh, yes, we promised to give you the words of that song of Bomb. Clarke's; here they are:-

THE VOICE OF THE MIDDLE EAST FORCE

1st Verse -   We are free men always going forward
                   When the hour of need is most at hand
               To do our duty for the Empire's sake
                   For our homes, our country, make a stand
               So that freedom, liberty and honour
                   Is for ever in our motherland
               We will fight again for that cause my lads
                   So now let this song be sung.

Chorus -   We shall march, march all along together
                   With our hearts as ever strong and true
               We'll find that silver lining in the sky
                   There to place the red, white and blue
               We all pledge to our Empire and its freedom
                   And to all who have their parts to play
               Fire away and fight to the last my lads
                   For freedom is ours today.

2nd Verse -   With our Army, Navy and our Air Force
                   Great and faithful Allies with us too
               We have a smile because its well worth while

As we know it means so much to you
For our thoughts are only that of victory
Out the wrong and then to right incline
We will take a toast to our freedom's boast
Our England and Old Lang Syne.

(Written and composed by Bomb. G.W. Clarke)

Since the issue of Mud & Blood in its new form; in other words since we came to Tobruk, we have been expecting a flood of brilliant writings from Lieut. Harry Marshall to add to the lustre of this paper and the entertainment of its readers. Lieut. Marshall, as you know, is one of the Herald's illustrious journalists; we might even go so far as to say he is THE eminent writer on the staff of that newspaper. We do not know what Sir Keith hands out to Harry on pay-day, but we do know that if he was paid what he was worth, his income tax would be based on a figure of around 5000 pounds per annum. So you can imagine how we have fawned upon him in the hope that he would dash off a screed or two for us now and again. Then, yesterday, for the very first time, he showed signs that Mud & Blood existed; in a caustic criticism, he informed us helpfully that, since the inception of this paper, he has noticed four wrongly spelt words. We are overjoyed; at last the great man has unbent; who knows, perhaps within the next six months or so he will forget that he is the Herald's brilliant journalist, and deign to write a line or two to be included amongst the more humble efforts that appear in these columns. In the meantime, whilst he is thinking of something to write about, we will see that at least once in every issue there is a miss-spelt word, so that he can amuse himself by looking for it. We wonder if he will be able to pick it in this issue.

(Incidentally, in case of repercussions from the above, we would advise that the Solicitors for this publication are Messrs. Ellison, Hewison & O'Collins, 352 Collins St., Melbourne, who will receive on our behalf any writ that may be contemplated.)

With regard to the shorthand lessons that we have proposed starting in these columns, we are having a spot of trouble. Difficulty has been experienced in duplicating the shorthand symbols, owing to the fact that the outlines are written in light and heavy signs. The duplicator will not permit this distinction, all outlines coming out in a uniform manner. We have requisitioned for a Stylo pencil which may permit the lessons to be started. Later advice will be given as to this. Incidentally we might mention that over two hundred requests for tuition have come to hand; we can visualize a battalion of shorthand writers in the future. It is not hard to picture a platoon of our chaps, after a bayonet charge and resultant rounding up of prisoners, producing notebooks and enquiring from each other "What's the ruddy outline for Kamerad?" as they interview each succeeding Jerry or I-ti.

In a letter received yesterday from one of our less respectable pals in Melbourne, was a yarnlet that we thought worth repeating:-

EVE: Will I wear my new fig leaf tonight, darling?

ADAM: Well, it might be a rough party. You'd better wear your Scotch thistle.

"C" Company are still chuckling (we are even still smiling a little ourselves) at the experiences of Lieut. Byron-Moore when he took his Platoon on a little patrol into Jerry's lines the other night. They crept slowly, silently, like ghosts, through the wire and well into "no man's land." Nearing the spot marked on their map as likely to be Jerry's position, they were petrified to hear a noise BEHIND them. The patrol stopped dead and fell to earth immediately; no further noise was heard. After a breath-holding pause they proceeded, and again the noise was heard. Once more the patrol went to ground. Byron looked around and was finally able to make out the lines of an inquisitive donkey that wanted to be in the fun. Frantic gestures and "shushings" were of no avail; that donkey followed them everywhere they went, and was not particularly careful as to the amount of noise he made. Eventually, in disgust, the patrol had to call it a night, and they returned to the wire, still followed by the donkey, with most murderous intentions in their hearts. Creeping through on the outskirts of an anti-personnel mine-field, they were startled to see the donk clatter gaily across the field. Suddenly the inevitable happened. A loud bang was followed by clouds of earth, stone, dust and presumably donkey hurled high in the air, and once again the patrol had to fling itself flat on the ground. Great was the amazement, therefore, when the jub-bub had died down to see the donk unconcernedly standing by, stamping impatiently as if wondering when they were going to continue, and getting quite annoyed at their delay. We understand that Byron granted him a reprieve, on condition that he accompanied no more patrols.

BBC NEWS — 8th July, 1941.

Yesterday's war communique announces that Indian troops captured Doomar Kapou in Syria, and British troops continue their advance to-

wards Dorns. *In central sector British forces captured important positions. On the coast, Australians crossed the river and are now in contact with main Vichy position about Damour.*

Nothing to report from Libya and Abyssinia.

Enemy shipping in Palermo harbour was attacked by RAF on Sunday. Two bombs hit 8000 ton ship; other hits registered on three ships. Fifth ship hit by incendiary bomb.

Widespread activity reported Syria, where aircraft were destroyed on Aleppo aerodrome, and Beirut harbour also attacked. Bengasi again raided. Alexandria raided by enemy on Sunday night - 2 people killed, 14 injured; some damage done to property.

RAF continued its offensive in Germany, attacking Munster, Dortsmund, Dusseldorf, Cologne, Emden, Brest and Rotterdam on Sunday night. German warships in Brest harbour were heavily bombed. Six British aircraft missing. Yesterday RAF resumed their attacks on Northern France. Escorting fighters shot down seven enemy fighters for loss of three British fighters. Two of our pilots safe, having been rescued from sea. Blenheims attacked strongly escorted convoy of 8 ships ranging from 2000 to 5000 tons off Dutch coast. Six ships were hit by bombs and left ablaze or sinking. Another convoy off Calais was attacked; one ship of 2000 tons and escorting "E" boat were sunk. 4 British aircraft are missing these operations. Only enemy activity over Britain yesterday was by one enemy plane flying over north-west England. Last night German raiders launched sharp but brief attack on south coast town, dropping first incendiary bombs, followed by high explosives. At south-east coast town, high explosives also fell.

US Naval forces arrived in Iceland. President Roosevelt informed Congress they will eventually replace British forces there. America could not permit strategic Atlantic outposts to be used as air or naval bases against America. This news welcomed by Foreign Office spokesman, and described as one of most important and significant events for some time. British troops there will be gradually withdrawn. Iceland's sovereignty will remain complete.

German newsagency says that German spearheads have reached Stalin line and operations now entering new phase, and violent fighting expected. Fighting on eastern front continues fiercely, and Berlin admits that Red Army fighting power apparently unbroken, and finds its expression in unprecedented Russian counterattacks which caused heavy sacrifices on both sides.

Red Army communique announces that in northern sector, Russian troops inflicted losses on enemy which penetrated our territory. On Latvian front our troops continued fight stubbornly against strong mechanised units containing their advance. On Lithuanian border fierce fighting developed against enemy who attempted to land large forces on northern bank of western Dvina. In central Poland enemy attempted several times to cross Dniper, but fell back with heavy losses to his original positions. Further south our troops are containing advance of strong mechanised forces. Russian troops annihilated an enemy battalion after cutting its retreat.

Germans claim advance in Bessarabian sector and capture of Cernauti. Also advances are claimed in other sectors. Hungarians say their troops carried out flanking attacks.

There were three air raids on Cyprus yesterday morning, enemy attempting to raid port; no damage done but 3 civilians wounded. One enemy bomber was shot down during an attempted raid on Malta, where 4 alarms were sounded on Sunday night. There was little damage done, but a few civilians were injured.

TOBRUK, 9th July, 1941.

Again the famous "firm" of Jarvie & Mulcahy has scooped the theatrical and entertainment field, and has pleasure in announcing that, at colossal expense and after strenuous efforts, the services of that eminent historian and lecturer - Padre Morrison - have been secured for a lecture to be held in the vicinity of BHQ on Thursday evening, at 7.45 p.m. The address will be on LIBYA - Its history since pussy was a kitten. We understand that the Padre will not strictly vouch for the correctness of his data prior to the year 433 B.C., but from then onwards can speak from personal observation. The lecture is given by kind permission of the Bishop of Bendigo (we hope) and in collaboration with the Venerable Archdeacon Best of Ballarat. Prior to, and at the conclusion of the lecture, there will be a spot of Community singing. A silver coin collection will be taken in aid of the Editor of Mud & Blood. Owing to the scarcity of trouser buttons, these will also be welcomed.

One of the latest innovations at the R.A.P. is the "Blue" Room Annexe, (so called on account of the language often heard emanating therefrom) where patients with minor troubles are given accommodation for a few days at a very nominal fee. Here they are under the strict supervision of the staff, which includes the following:-

Capt. J. M. Agar, RMO, SM. (We hope the latter mean Salts Merchant).
Sgt. L. B. Allen, Matron (His figure suits the job admirably).
Sgt. K. N. Roberts, Maternity Sister.
(It is not true that this sister has been abnormally busy lately)
Cpl. Hurricane Dive Bomber Dowel, Chiropodist.
(Swift as his name indicates with scissors and scalpal).
Pte. E. R. Spry, Night Sister.
(He seems to think that this means the sister who sleeps at night).
Pte. J. E. Turner, Slushy.
(This is his own classification, as he moans that he does all the dirty work, and has trouble in getting the right size in pickle bottles).
Sgt. J. Jarvie, T.O.,
(No, you're wrong. This means Tpt. Officer; the initials are not yet T.F.O.)

Back Row: Keith Roberts, Les Allen, Norm Dowell, Jack Jarvie.
Front Row: Jack Turner, Keith Fry.

The R.A.P. advise the correction of a misconception in regard to Sgt. Max Dolamore who was discharged yesterday; he was NOT in the care of Sgt. Roberts; it was nothing like that at all, although the symptoms were not dissimilar.

Then there is the recently established firm of Louse, Louse & Delouse, who have undertaken the unenviable job of operating on any of their friends who are troubled with the above complaint. The treatment is very scientific and very hygienic, and consists of shaving off all hairs and spraying with insecticide and removing clothes to the disinfector. Naturally, this treatment is carried out in the open, and on the last occasion the operations were performed in the wadi, before an appreciative crowd, who "ringed out" in the old manner. This shaving was a touch and go business at times, and the excitement grew so intense that frequently the crowd cheered at the wrong moment, to the obvious discomfiture of the operators and consternation of the patient. We are glad to be able to report that there were no falsetto voices after the show, but in any case, there was no need for the patients to worry, as in the event of any mishap, their money would have been returned.

Shorthand - Pte. Wenborn has offered to collaborate with us in the preparation of these lessons, and is at present working on a scheme by which the duplicator may be able to do the necessary work. More of this anon, when his researches have advanced further.

We are indebted to Pte. F. H. Downs, of "A" Company, for the following. Pte. Downs was aghast at the information contained in yesterday's issue of Lieut. Marshall's apathy in regard to this publication. "I can't let the old Company down" he said. "A Company will never neglect it's duty whilst there's a Downs in it". Well, that's what he would have said, we're sure, if we'd met him.

THE FURPHY MONGER

He said last week the mail is in, I've never seen so much.
I'll kill this lying blighter, if I get him in my clutch.
To think this ruthless bounder said, the mail was never better
   And to our front line section wandered a lonely little letter.
When you see him coming, ignore the rotten cow
   I know a thing or two myself, I'll spill the beans right now
Don't go spreading this around, just keep it in your hat
   Oh! hell, I haven't got the heart, that monger told me that.

BBC NEWS — 9th July, 1941.

Syria - Indian troops made further progress westward from Demir Kapoli, and advance towards Homs continues. On coast, Australians have occupied all objectives south of Damour.

There is no change in Libya and Abyssinia.

RAF yesterday announced widespread air activity over Libya, where raids were carried out on enemy aerodromes and shipping. In Syria, Aleppo Railway Station was bombed, and fuel tanks at Beirut set on fire. Raids also reported from Malta and Cyprus. Five British aircraft are missing.

Jerusalem - It is learned that the food situation at Beirut has become almost intolerable, and Vichy authorities reported to be searching private houses and confiscating food stocks. Allies reached 15 miles east of Homs. On the coast, Allies occupied Elboum, 2 miles south east of Damour.

London - On Monday night, RAF attacked Cologne, Osnabruck, Muenster, Frankfurt, and other towns in western Germany, and Lens and Bethung in northern France, and other attacks made in Belgium and Holland. 9 British aircraft missing. 5 German aircraft were destroyed in raids over Britain on Monday night when they attacked Southhampton.

Moscow yesterday - Red Army communique reports that 58 German planes were destroyed in the air for the loss of 5 Soviet planes. It also claims that fighting continued with undiminished force. In Southern Poland, two enemy infantry battalions were destroyed, including 35 tanks. All enemy attempts to cross river Dnieper were repulsed. On Ukraine border, Soviet troops wiped out two enemy infantry Regiments.

On the other hand, last night's German communique laconically says that operations are proceeding according to plan.

Vichy statement says that Vichy auxiliary vessel "Saint Didier", which was sunk by Fleet Air Arm aircraft in Turkish waters was transporting troops to Syria.

Washington War Department ordered all Air Corps reserve Officers not already on active service to active duty if their civil occupation was not of primary importance in Defence Programme.

London - Yesterday afternoon RAF bombed Wilhelmshaven Naval Base and during sweep over France, 11 German planes destroyed, while 7 British planes missing.

Pretoria - Largest contingent of South African troops to leave Union since embarkation of East African Forces, has now safely reached North Africa, according to official announcement.

Moscow - Todays Moscow communique says that German and Roumanian troops have been driven back in disorder beyond river Pruth as result of Soviet counter attacks. On other sectors, unabaited fighting goes on. German efforts to push forward, but Russians are opposing fiercely.

Madrid - German Submarine was sunk off Gibralta on Tuesday morning by Fleet Air Arm according to Spanish reports. 4 German aircraft were destroyed during raids on Britain last night. Bombs were dropped on Midlands and one point in Scotland. RAF again bombed north west Germany last night, Tuesday.

London - Gracie Fields returned to England yesterday from America. Len Hutton, England, Yorkshire batsman holder of Worlds record Test score, made first appearance of season during weekend, when he scored 58. This performance was very gratifying in cricketing quarters.

TOBRUK, 10th July, 1941.

This war business looks ridiculously easy; at least it appears that way when viewed as Pte. F. A. Stirk views it. This lad, only just arrived with the last bunch of reinforcements, had not previously seen action, but was just aching to get into it. With a small band of comrades - Privates N. L. McDonald, J. W. Slight, R. R. Fedley, A. F. Wallace and F. A. Wilson he determined to start a little war on his own, and received permission to set off last night on a foray into Jerry's country. They took rations for two days, so were evidently of a mind to make quite a jaunt of it. Penetrating approximately two miles into enemy territory, they lost no time in getting to work, and returned this morning with two prisoners - one of them a somewhat dejected looking Italian officer - and news of another left dead behind them. For a start this is not bad, but we feel that Pte. Stirk will consider he is letting his pals and the battalion down if he does not bring the General himself back from the next excursion. Not that this is likely to prove an easy job, as the I-ti C in C will no doubt, when news of this exploit reaches him, remove his HQ another few leagues out into the blue. In the meantime, to keep themselves in form, we suggest that Stirk and his merry men try and bring back a gazelle or two with their next parcel of prisoners - we understand there are plenty of them out there, and they should be easy enough to catch, as they certainly don't run as fast as the I-ti does.

Our grateful thanks to the member of Brigade who so kindly forwarded a Stylus pencil so that our shorthand lessons could be commenced. This will be put into use forthwith.

We are informed that when Herr Hess recently landed in Scotland, he was asked, amongst other things of course, why he had picked the land of the thistle for his escape. He replied that he had come to get a tartan bed. (Bit weak, don't you think? The C.O. told it to us, and we didn't dare refuse to put it in.)

By the way, it is today that the Tatt's Syndicate is due to commence, so please hand your "akers" to the Company clerks, who will record your names and forward same and the cash to us. As soon as the tickets are purchased, the numbers of same will be published in these columns, so that you will all be able to follow the fortunes of the Mud & Blood Syndicate. We've got a sort of hunch we might land that big prize; in fact, so confident are we that already we are planning what gold mine or oil shares we might be albe to submit to the Board of Management. Now, we have a wonderful prospectus of a treacle mine in Fiji that is guaranteed to return 100%. Still we'll talk of that after the marble is drawn.

TODAY'S SHORTHAND LESSON: Pitman's System.

In shorthand, no attention is paid to ordinary spelling. All words are written phonetically. There is a shorthand symbol for each sound. For instance the word "write" would be written in signs signifying R I T; "feel" would be written as F E L; "light" as L I T; and so on. The SOUND of the word only is written down. There is a symbol for each consonant, or main part of a word, as distinct from a vowel. This, for the sake of brevity, we will call the "alphabet". There are about 26 of these main signs, and we will give you them spread over three days. They should be copied out and practiced as much as possible, the sound being audibly uttered as each sign is written. Care will be taken to see that "light" outlines are of uniform appearance, whilst the same applies to "heavy" signs. With practice this will come naturally.

P (pee)   ＼   as in p)et; li(p; le(p)er; etc.

B (bee)   ＼   as in b)ill; ni(b; trou(b)le; etc.

T (tee)   ｜   as in t)in; mea(t; la(t)er; etc.

D (dee)   ｜   as in d)arn; har(d; fa(d)es; etc.

CH (chay) ／   as in ch)ar; ri(ch; en(ch)ant; ch)ur(ch; etc.

J (jay)   ／   as in j)am; le(j (ledge); lo(j)er (lodger); etc.

K (kay)   —   as in k)om; li(k (like); ra(k)et (racquet); etc.

G (gay)   ▬   as in g)irl; la(g; bu(g)le; etc.

BBC NEWS — 10th July, 1941.

Formal application has been received from General Dentz, Vichy High Commissioner in Syria for discussion of terms of armistice. Application was received through Beirut, and reached Cairo just as Australian troops on Syrian coast broke through main Vichy defences of Damour. There is no question of cessation of hostilities now.

A further communique states that Imperial forces have occupied Damour and are now operating north of the town. The advance of our troops towards Aleppo and Homs is proceeding satisfactorily, and further local gains have been made in central sector.

In Libya patrol activity on frontier area renewed. Nothing of importance in Abyssinia.

RAF HQ reported yesterday widespread activity in Syria on Tuesday, while in Cyrenaica RAF bombers attacked Bengasi harbour where fires were started. Elensia in Greece and targets in Crete were also hit. All our planes returned safely from these operations.

Tuesday's enemy activity on Britain rather heavier than usual, and mainly directed against Midlands. Generally, little damage was done and casualties small. 5 enemy planes destroyed. Leaflets were also dropped in East Anglia.

RAF attacked Tuesday night a large number of targets in NW Germany causing widespread damage. 7 British bombers missing. During sweep over Northern France yesterday, RAF fighters destroyed 13 enemy fighters, losing 8 British machines.

It is officially announced that the defence of Iraq has been transferred to India Command, and will thus be the responsibility of General Wavell.

Mr. Churchill announced in the Commons yesterday, that the British Army will be retained in Iceland.

In Washington, Mr. Wendell Wilkie urged establishment of US Military Bases in Northern Ireland and Scotland.

German Official Agency claims German troops occupied Ostrov, 200 miles on road to Leningrad, and captured two other towns in Estonia, and the town of Salla, north of the Arctic Circle in Finland. The same Agency announced last night that considerable forces of the German Army were being maintained in the West in order to safeguard against unpleasant surprises.

The Situation on the Russian Frontier, based on two Russian communiques is as follows:- Generally speaking, the Germans made little or no headway on the whole front. Their main thrust in the direction of Leningrad and Moscow severely contained by Russian troops, while elsewhere Russians give Germans no respite, counter attacking at every opportunity. Throughout Wednesday, fierce fighting continued against large enemy tank and mechanised units trying to break through on Latvian-Russian Frontier, on Lithuanian Frontier in White Russia, and on Ukraine Border. During Tuesday, Soviet Air Force destroyed 102 planes and lost 10, as well as shooting down 7 over Constanza, with the loss of one Soviet aircraft.

Chicago - Answering divorce suit filed against him, Joe Louis denied that he ever struck his wife; he also dismissed allegations of cruelty, and denied that his wife treated him kindly and affectionately.

SPECIAL NOTE:

Perusal of shorthand para on preceding page will reveal that duplicator is not a happy medium for these outlines. Therefore, we will have to devise some other way of imparting these lessons. Those who are available for lessons, communicate with S/Sgt. Mulcahy, who will arrange classes.

TOBRUK, 11th July, 1941.

For those of you who were not able to get along to hear the Padre give his lecture last night on LIBYA, we wish to advise that it was a very interesting and informative little talk. Apparently this land has been fought over and about since 7,000 BC, and, for all the Padre knew, perhaps much earlier than that. Why anyone would want to fight for this benighted area God only knows - our guess is as good as yours. Now, round about the year 3,000 BC, we can quite understand why a decent brawl should develop; at that particular period this country was inhabited by a beautiful fair-haired blue-eyed race, and believe us, if a beautiful blue-eyed blonde should suddenly appear on the horizon these days, we can readily imagine the wave of hostilities that would swamp the place. We've been late for most things all our life, but this is the first time we have been 5,000 years late for anything. Anyhow, if it comes to that, we suppose the whole battalion feels as though 5000 years has passed since they last saw a blue-eyed blonde. Oh, well, cheer up, we have only another 33,000 years to go and we'll be back amongst them again. As the Padre said in his lecture, a jump of a thousand years or so is nothing at all.

There was a goodly crowd at the lecture, and a spot of Community singing was indulged in both before and after the Padre's talk. Unfortunately, we hear that many attended under a misapprehension, as in our announcement in a previous issue of Mud & Blood, we stated that "a spot and Community singing would be indulged in." We hesitate to believe that the cloth would so lower itself as to encourage such a hope, but we have not been able to trace the "furphy" to its source, so can only state that it is up to the Padre to clear his good name. From the "firm's" point of view, the evening was not a success, as due to a little hitch in the organisation, the silver coin collection was overlooked, and we are today, in consequence, poorer by some thousands of "akers". Notice the delicate compliment to the Padre - we are quite convinced that his attentive listeners would have chipped in right royally.

We have often wondered why the Italians are not in favour of wearing shorts, and although we are "still in the dark," we learn from a news item that they are being induced to do so. To our mind, it would be a decided advantage for them to wear the apparel so popular with us, for they would help them to make a speedier retreat when confronted by a bunch of Aussies. Musso's slogan - "short strides for long pants" apparently does not appeal to the I-ti soldier, for his one aim in life seems to be to lengthen his stride, and perhaps this is why he prefers

long strides to shorts. Today our "complaints" are due to Capt. Freddie Kiel, who celebrates his - th birthday. He did confide his age to us, but it is not for publication, and at any rate, it would not interest you. However, we offer him our heartiest congratulations on reaching this ripe old age, and hope that he is with us always, for when we are short of news, we can always have a "shot" at him and thus fill our columns. Undoubtedly you will hail this as a journalistic achievement - this is due to the fact that our editor is down having a swim - and not before time - even his best friends wouldn't tell him, but a label from a Lifebouy Soap carton did the trick. We hope he does not find out who left the label on his desk while he was having his morning nap.

Short pants for long strides.

BBC NEWS — 11th July, 1941.

Cairo RAF announces extensive operations in Libya Wednesday, night attacks being made on Bengasi, Derna, and Gazala. One enemy plane among number which attempted to raid Malta was shot down. Enemy planes attacked in Sicily, three burnt out, others damaged. In Syria RAF attacked Vichy objectives near Beirut and Reacak.

Moscow last nights communique announced destruction of German motorised division, including large quantity of guns and transport. Commun-

ique also reports stubborn fighting all along the front, with the Russians holding their positions everywhere and counter attacking. Russian airforce destroyed 100 enemy tanks on Wednesday. 33 German and 5 Russian planes destroyed. German High Command laconically stated that fighting continued without respite.

It is learned in Cairo that General Maitland-Wilson, C in C Syria addressed an appeal to General Dentz, urging him not to make Beirut an area of combat, thus compelling him to take measures to occupy the town.

American Red Cross announces a ship load of supplies worth roughly half a million dollars, recently arrived in Egypt as a gift from the Red Cross.

RAF continue heavy toll of enemy, both over England and enemy territory. On Wednesday night 6 enemy bombers were destroyed over Britain, and yesterday, 40.

After interview with Roosevelt, Russian Ambassador told press that he told the President good news about the Eastern Front. Navy Dept. advise shipping that mines have been laid in approach to San Francisco Bay.

Moscow today says that no events of importance occurred on the Front throughout yesterday, and Soviet aircraft bombed enemy positions, destroying 25 German planes for loss of 6 of their machines.

Berlin announces that greatest amount of war material in world's history was captured, including over 300,000 prisoners, several Generals, over 300 tanks and 1000 guns. Thus says Berlin, numbers of prisoners exceed 400,000 and Soviet lost over 6000 planes, several thousand tanks and guns.

At least two Nazi planes were shot down last night when enemy activity over Britain was not on a large scale.

TOBRUK, 25th July, 1941.

Greetings, Mud'n Bloods, here we are again back in circulation after a brief period of mental recuperation. However, forgive us if this time we are not our usual bright cheery selves - we have just been in the hands of the R.M.O., and after the numerous doses of salts, etc. that he saw fit to inflict, what is left of us is inclined to look upon the gloomy side, so much so that we are even of a mind to doubt that the war will be ended on the 15th August next, and that we will be home again by Christmas, a belief that seems at the moment to be sweeping the cook-houses and thunderbox areas of the battalion. Anyhow, who wants to be back before Christmas; think of all the presents that would have to be bought; and think also of being deprived of our Christmas dinner here in Tobruk.

News has just come to hand of the continued efforts of our womenfolk back home, who are so busy thinking of our creature comforts these days that they must surely have little time in which to miss us. 500 lbs of luscious home-made cake has just been prepared and sent off in parcels. Numerous packets of sweets have also been despatched, whilst the sum of 20 pounds has been cabled to the Salvation Army Authorities in Egypt asking them to procure sweets for us. This was done to avoid the long delay that ensues before parcels are delivered. In addition, a further sum of 100 pounds has been forwarded to the credit of the C.O.'s Fund, which is beginning to accumulate to quite a healthy figure again, and when circumstances render it possible, a large proportion of this will again be expended upon little items of comfort and cheer that have been conspicuous lately by their absence. Anyhow, on behalf of you lads, we herewith extend our grateful thanks to those responsible for the foregoing valiant efforts. Such tokens of the love and thoughtfulness of our folks at home are an inspiration to continued efforts out here, and leave us with the warm feeling in our hearts that, although so far away, we are certainly not forgotten. Ladies of the Welfare Association, and of the Young Mud & Bloods, we salute you for your untiring work, which we can assure you is deeply appreciated by us all.

Last week we were full of enthusiasm after our little jaunt into the Never-Never in one of the Carriers, and meant to tell you all about it. We decided however, to wait until all the bruises, burns and stiffness had worn away, and in the interim lost some of the said enthusiasm. However, it was a great night, and we certainly take off our hats to those lads of the Carrier Platoon for the efficient and business-like way in which they go about their tasks. There is no doubt or indecision or wondering what to do next; they know their job with text-book thoroughness, and we shudder to think of what Jerry has to put up with whenever he strays within their orbit.

Now for a little bit of Battalion gossip - first of all let us congratulate Capt. Malloch M.C.; L/Sgt. Stuckey M.M.; Pte. Clark M.M. and Pte. Kelly M.M. on the very deserved honours that have been conferred upon them. Decorations are being won for this Battalion so frequently that our folks at home are filled with pride at our doings. Also let us congratulate Lieuts. Fallon, Wilton and Lee, whose wives have conferred the distinguished honour of fatherhood upon them in absentia - a son in each case by the way.

Capt. Jackson has arrived home, and comforted many of our women-folk (hey! have we said the wrong thing?) by tales of our doings in Palestine at a recent meeting of the Welfare Association. Lieut. Hughes has also arrived home, and is at present a patient in the new Military Hospital at Heidelberg. Pte. Keith Woodham is another who has made the return journey.

Recordings of the 2/23rd Battalion Band were made in Tel Aviv just after the Band contest, and these have been sent home. Records are being made, and these may be purchased for 5/- each. Any members of the Battalion who desire to have one of these very interesting mementoes sent to friends or relatives may do so on forwarding 20 akers to the Orderly Room, together with the name and address of the person to whom the record is to be sent. We suggest that one of these records would make an interesting and acceptable Xmas Gift. Two records are being made, the first being "Punchinello" and "Silent Night", whilst the second is equally familiar "Standard of St. George" and "Old Earth".

We have received one or two items of verse from various members of the Unit, and have revised our early opinion that the 2/23rd had no bards of note. We hope to publish these efforts in the course of the next few issues. By the way, the C.O. has offered to donate a bottle of beer to the author of the best Ode - to be entitled "Ode to a Bottle of Beer". No entry is to exceed ten lines. All entries are to be forwarded to Mud & Blood, in which they will be published. So put on your thinking caps - the prize is certainly worth striving for.

BBC NEWS — 23rd July, 1941.

The Vichy Government has agreed to permit Japanese troops to enter Indo-China, and has also agreed that naval and air bases may be maintained there. This permission is believed to be due to German pressure on Vichy.

Mr. Sumner Welles, US Minister for State, has declared this to be an act of aggression, and has named Japan as an aggressor. Reports that troops have already landed in Indo-China have not yet been confirmed, but it is known that a large convoy of transports, escorted by units of the Japanese Fleet is moving southwards. Official statements from British and American sources state that these Nations are fully aware of what is going on, and will not be taken by surprise at any developments.

The German drive against Russia is losing momentum, particularly in the Smolensk area, where Russian troops claim to have completely des-

troyed the German 5th Infantry Division, which recently arrived on that front.

An attempt to raid Moscow was made last night for the fourth succ-essive night. However, only one bomber was able to penetrate the screen of Russian night fighters, and it managed to drop its bombs before being shot down. It is officially stated that damage caused by previous raids was slight.

It is significant that Italian newspapers are preparing the Italian people for a long war in Russia. One newspaper states that a quick decision cannot be hoped for on account of the heavy fighting that has yet to come when Russia's main forces are encountered, and emphasises the enormous distances that have yet to be covered.

Today there is news of the biggest air attack by the RAF since the war began. An enormous flotilla of aircraft, including five different types of bombers took part in the attack, and it is confirmed that seven direct hits with armour piercing bombs were scored on the German Battleship "Gneisnau" as well as other targets. The Battleship "Schonhorst" was also heavily attacked at Brest. Great damage was also done at Brest dockyards where other German warships are sheltering, and at least one German cruiser was straddled with heavy bombs. 15 bombers and 7 fighters of ours were lost during these attacks, whilst 24 German fighters were shot down.

During the past 24 hours, the south-coast town of Dover was heavily shelled from the French coast. No details of damage are to hand.

In the course of a speech in USA, Lord Halifax stated that American bombers would be used to bomb Berlin. "We hope to be able to alter the appearance of that city" he stated, "and make it look something like Lon-don looks today." He was referring to the new long range bombers that are now being delivered by American factories in ever increasing numbers.

A large enemy convoy was practically wiped out yesterday in the Mediterranean by the RAF. Hits were scored on three ships, and two of them at least were certainly sunk. Further attacks later in the day account-ed for the remainder. All our planes returned safely.

In Britain there has been a further call up of men and women for industrial purposes, and men of 46 and upwards now have to register.

Big increases in US armament production were announced last night by the US Secretary for War.

TOBRUK, 29th July, 1941.

Commencing with an abrupt "Good-morning" we will at once go into action and tell you what we think of you Mud'n Bloods. Our spleen this
fair morning is not due to the state of our liver, but to the fact that enquiry
elicits the depressing news that not one of you have stirred yourselves to
make the Battalion Tatt's scheme a success. Indeed, were it not for a few
sporting members of BHQ, the scheme would have fizzled completely.
What's the trouble, Mud'n Bloods? Do you all hail frae Aberdeen, or did
your sojourn in the land of Israel imbue you with the well known character-
istics of that race? The idea was conceived purely as a sporting venture, and
surely 6d. each was not too much to ask you for, even if it was thrown away.
Anyway, think it over and send in your akers to BHQ, as we have not yet
sent away for the tickets, and would like you all to be in it.

Now for a spot of welcome to our latest arrivals who have gone into
residence as "B" Company. We are, we think, speaking for the whole of the
Battalion when we say how glad we are to see the old "circus" functioning
again as a whole, and judging by the calibre of the new Mud'n Bloods, we
fully expect them to take over the illustrious heritage handed down by their
predecessors, with credit and honour to themselves. Very flowery this morning, aren't we? Put it down to the two days we have just had at the beach.
Anyhow, we are sincere in our greetings and good wishes to our new "Reo's"
and hope amongst other things, that they will support this paper with contributions of their wit and wisdom (if any).

We have much pleasure in introducing to our readers, new members
of the Mud'n Blood Staff - Ptes. Len Wemyss and Tom French, who will
henceforth be responsible for all pictorial and cartoon work. As you know,
Pte. Lloyd Jones was previously the perpetrator of those outrages that formerly disgraced these pages, but after he ran out of copies of "Man" he resigned the position. Another innovation is the appointment of L/Cpl. Dick
Fancke to the important post of News Editor, a job which will tax his powers of imagination to their utmost. All this leaves us with more time with
which to swill beer, and otherwise enjoy the leisure that our erstwhile hours
of toil have earned; and who cares whether there is any beer to swill or not,
we can always employ the time in encouraging a still larger thirst against the
happy period when it will be available in immense quantities again?

Referring to the competition commenced in our last issue - "Ode to a Bottle of Beer", the prize for which is a bottle of beer donated by the C.O. we give hereunder the first two entries received, printed in order of receipt only and not, you will notice, in order of merit. This competition is open to you all, and you may send in as many entries as you like. The conditions are simple - No effort is to exceed ten lines, and the winner is compelled to permit the Editor of this paper to sample the prize.

When I survey a cool brown bottle,
I know it is the one thing what'll
    Cure this thirst of mine.

Ah! pint divine, could I but win you,
This ode to you I would continue
    Beyond the set tenth line.

How can one suitably express
The joys which follow your caress
In poems like this little bit
    Wouldn't it?

(VX48595, Capt. J. M. Agar, R.M.O.

To decapitate a bottle of amber fluid
    Would be to me this thirsty day
A reverent act, a rite of ancient Druid
    A sacrifical offering to lay
Upon the altar of intemperance.

Oh! solitary one, you scarce merit attention
    And yet, the thought of Agar gaining thee
Fills my soul with direst apprehension
    To beat him to the prize means much to me
If only to retain you in remembrance.

(VX48676, S/Sgt. J.D. Mulcahy, Ord. Room)

The reputation of Lieut. Boulter as a bard has spread far and wide, and.we are anxiously awaiting the effort that we know the prize will spur him to. Not of course, that it will beat one of the above two efforts (modesty forbids us saying which one). Still, it will be treated on its merits.

Before we close, has anyone ever seen anything more wicked looking than Lieut. Johnny Methven's moustache? Can't somebody do something about it?

BBC NEWS — 29th July, 1941.

Russian communique states that German planes raided Moscow last night. A few planes penetrated the outer defences, but 9 were shot down.

The second German offensive against Russia is losing momentum, and is thought to be petering out. In the Ukraine Sector, the German attack is breaking, owing to the stubborn defence of the Russians. Russia claims to have sunk one destroyer and two patrol vessels, their own losses being one destroyer.

The German radio continues to stress the difficulties that their troops are experiencing on the Russian front. They state that while the Russian Army retains its striking power, territorial gains would be of no use.

Finland has broken off diplomatic relations with Britain.

President Roosevelt has called a conference to discuss the position in the Far East, and several Military authorities will be present.

The Netherlands East Indies have followed the policy of both Britain and United States, and have taken diplomatic action against Japan. In Japan a spokesman urges the Japanese people to be calm, and to await further developments. The strength of the Japanese forces which have landed in Indo China are not yet known, but they have taken over eight aerodromes and other strategic positions.

Last night a few enemy aircraft took part in raids over East Anglia. A small number of bombs were dropped, but little damage done, and only a few people injured.

Mr. Power, the Canadian Air Minister, announced that fifteen Canadian Air Squadrons out of the proposed twentyfive, were already in action overseas, and that eleven of these were being commanded by Canadians.

In England, three new Hospitals provided by America, have been opened.

General De Gaulle is expected to make an important statement after his first visit to the Syrian Capital. While there, he will confer with British and Syrian authorities, with a view to establishing the independence of the country.

A new Cabinet was formed in Trans Jordan yesterday, but the Prime Minister retained office.

TOBRUK, 30th July, 1941.

More entries for the "Ode to a Bottle of Beer" competition. Surely the prize has spurred and enticed reluctant brains to unaccustomed efforts. Also most of the stanzas that have hitherto come to our attention have been about the "female form divine," storms and tempests, glories of warfare etc. Compared to the extravagances of emotion expended in the contemplation of a bottle of beer, all these subjects leave the author cold. In the course of the next few days, we anticipate receiving many more entries, and then we will have to devise a fair and equitable way to decide the winner. The closing date of the competition will be announced shortly.

Today's Entries:

> O brave shape, with the swan like neck
>> And the luscious promise of the mouth
> How oft have I been at thy call and beck
>> In the days before the drouth.
>
> But I swear once more to possess thee
>> I'll taste thy sweetness to the core
> And leave you folorn and empty
>> Here in the desert's dusty maw.

(VX38821, Wrnt. Offr. G. Moore, RQMS)

> An ode, an ode to a bottle of beer
>> Eighteen ounces of nut brown cheer
> A quencher not so very dear
>> But very seldom seen round here
> Perhaps they think we're old and sere.
>
> Now the C.O.'s got one salted away
>> And he's promised to give it away someday

To someone who will write an ode
    Now, really, shouldn't it be bestowed
Upon someone who dabbles in Code?

(VX32593, Pte. V. Firth, Sigs.)

It is with pleasure that we advise of the receipt of two large cases of sweets that have been forwarded by the Salvation Army Authorities in Egypt, at the request of the ladies of the Welfare Association. You remember we told you in a recent issue that they had forwarded the sum of twenty pounds in the hope that it would expedite delivery, and such has proved to be the case. Immediately we have settled down in our new home these little comforts will be distributed, and judging by the size of the cases, there should be ample to go round.

Yesterday we said good-bye to Capt. Barker, Lieut. Rand, Warrant Officer Deane and Cpl. Rowe, who have gone to Palestine for a brief spell to assist in the onerous duties of training our reinforcements, and carry with them the envious good wishes of those of us who remain behind. If they carry out their intention to have as many drinks as indicated, we are afraid they will drink Palestine dry, and incidentally, all of us here will be gloriously "Shickered" by proxy. The only consolation is that we will also have the hangovers by proxy. Anyhow, reiterating our good wishes, we hope it will not be long before we see them all again, and by that we do not mean we are hoping for their early return to Tobruk.

In the course of a visit to the 2/24th Battalion Orderly Room yesterday, we found them in the throes of compiling the first edition of their Battalion Newspaper - "The Flying Furphey", a copy of which has this day been sent to us. We wish our contemporary every success, and trust that their paper fills the same place in their Battalion that, we are assured, this publication fills in the 2/23rd. We notice that they have already experienced the same difficulty as this paper - the hesitancy and sluggishness with which contributions are forwarded, which places quite a burden on the shoulders of a few.

BBC NEWS — 30th July, 1941.

The latest Russian communique reports the complete check of the German advance, and in the Smolensk area, a succession of counter-attacks by Russian forces have driven the Germans from their positions, and inflicted very heavy casualties. On the Leningrad front, very heavy fighting is in progress and the Russians claim that some German units are surrounded.

The Russian Red Star (The voice of the Russian Army) states that the German oil reserves will soon be exhausted.

The Russian Ambassador in London has declared that all the Russian people are behind M. Stalin. Poland has resumed diplomatic relations with Russia.

The terms of the Military Agreement between Vichy and Japan are to be kept secret. However, it is now known that 40,000 Japanese troops have entered Indo China, and that eight aerodromes, and a number of sea bases have been taken over.

The Japanese are throwing out fresh threats against Thailand, and it is noted that they are using the same methods as against Indo China.

A Tokyo Newspaper states that recent moves by United States and Britain have developed into a military threat against Japan.

Mr. Fraser, New Zealand Prime Minister who is now in Scotland, stated that the Democratic Nations in the Pacific are passing through a most critical period.

At a conference with Mr. Sumner Welles, the Netherlands Minister in Washington stated that in extreme emergency, all oil wells in the Netherlands East Indies could be destroyed, and that this could be put into effect at once, and there would be no hesitation in destroying this industry if they were forced to do so.

The Newspapers in Britain comment at length on the debate on production. The Times points out that the greatness of this effort has never, and never has been in doubt, but what is asked is whether the absolute utmost is being done. Many responsible people in this country feel that more can be done, and Mr. Churchill's explanation has not silenced these critics. The Daily Mail sums up by saying that no responsible critic has alleged that production is less than it was twelve months ago, but rather that it has not improved enough.

Mr. Churchill has stated that September 1st is a possible invasion date, and that our forces have been warned to be ready for them.

Mr. Anthony Eden said that a German peace Blitz is imminent, and that we were not prepared to come to terms with Hitler at any time. Any peace with Hitler would only be a cessation of hostilities to allow him to re-

build and oil his war machine,   and would only last as long as Hitler wished.

The Duke of Kent has arrived in Canada by air. He is the first member of the Royal Family to fly across the Atlantic. He will tour every province of the Dominion, and may visit United States before returning to England.

Last night a very small number of enemy aircraft flew short distances over the North coast. Few bombs were dropped, and although some damage was done, casualties were only slight.

In yesterdays attack on aerodromes in Sicily, the RAF destroyed 34 enemy aircraft, damaging many others, and inflicted casualties on ground staffs, all without loss to ourselves.

While a United States destroyer was picking up survivors from a sinking steamer off the coast of Greenland, a submarine was thought to be heard. The destroyer at once proceeded to the spot and dropped 3 depth charges.

In Canada, 300 men took control for a short period, of an aluminium plant, which is the biggest war industry in the country. This was thought to be enemy sabotage, and it has been stated that arrests will be made.

The War Department in Washington has approved of an Air Support Command, which will provide air support for ground troops. Five of these units have been formed, and will be equipped with all the latest types of aircraft.

CHAPTER 7

TOBRUK, 1st August, 1941.

Good morning, lads of the'23rd Battaleeeon' - hope you are all
nicely settled in midst the dust and fleas, as we are. It is always the same
after a move - the first day is spent moaning and bewailing our former luxurious quarters; the second day things do not seem nearly so bad, and by
the time the third day arrives we have become reasonably attached to the
place and are even apprehensive of a further move.

Judging by the size and generally healthy appearance of the fleas
left behind by our friends of the 24th, the latter Battalion must be in great
nick. Staff-Sgt. Burgess left a goodly heritage behind him in his dugout, but
alas, our sense of gratitude failed us during the still watches of the first night,
and there were even moments when we wished that he had taken his tribe
with him. One big fellow, emerging for his midnight supper, looked at us
in surprise, seeming to say "Where's that blasted Burgess gone to? Suppose
you'll have to do." His display of acrobatics, dodgings, somersaults, and sly
nips here and there spoke eloquently of the many little games Staff Burgess
and he must have indulged in. However, the old fighting blood of Albury.'s
Own came surging to the surface, and shame upon us, we have to confess
that this particular little playmate will never more gambol across a hairy chest
with airy abandon, nor, when fatigue compelled, seek refuge and rest on that
little spot in the middle of the back that, from time immemorial, has been
the favourite haunt of tired fleas who think that a little rest and nourishment
is called for.

More entries for the "Ode to a Bottle of Beer" competition. Today's
odes come from very exhalted sources, but despite our very natural desire to

"Get on", we can assure our readers that these entries will be treated strictly on their merits - which you can take as a hint that they will be consigned to the Editorial w.p.b. inasmuch as they do not comply with the requirements "Ode to a Bottle of Beer". However, we are particularly glad to see the entry from the Brig., even if we do not agree with the sentiment expressed at the end of his second entry, but because now the C.O. will not dare to welsh on his offer, as threatened in his effort.

> If you imagine that you are a writer
> > And can even make a living with a book
> If your one ambition now is to get tighter
> > Than you've ever been since settling in Tobruk
> Then accept your Colonel's challenge for a poem
> > Prove to your pals you really are no dud
> Take your pen and ink and paper and just show 'em
> > That you'll win that tin of beer from Mud & Blood.

> > Do you ken Mud'n Blood
> > > With a scheme so queer
> > That for one little ode
> > > You win one tin of beer
> > The prize is so small
> > > Where it ought to be big
> > But I think you'll agree
> > > It's been won by the Brig.

(Brigadier R. W. Tovell, DSO, ED.)

> One day good fellowship and cheer
> > Made me offer some right good beer
> To the Mud & Blood who bravely could
> > Write a stirring ode to one off the wood
> But lack-a-day me! 'Tis poor stuff shown
> > By all the minions of Albury's Own,
> Gadzooks! I thought, a whole bottle of beer
> > Would stir great thoughts and visions dear
> On second thoughts methinks it best
> > To stow the beer down my own chest.

(The Old Man - Lt.Col. B. Evans.)

A number of other entries have been received, including one from Divvy, which will be published in succeeding issues. One from the General has not YET been received, probably because he has not heard of the competition.

BBC NEWS — 1st August, 1941.

Todays Russian communique states that heavy fighting is still in progress in the Smolensk area. During the past two weeks, German forces have launched about 42 heavy attacks on Smolensk, in an attempt to break through to Moscow. The Russians have succeeded in breaking up all these attacks, and are still firmly holding their line. They are now counter-attacking vigorously, and have inflicted very heavy losses on the enemy. Both Russian and German aircraft are supporting their ground forces continuously. Moscow was again raided last night, but once again only a few aircraft managed to break through the outer defences. The Russians state that only very slight damage was done, and no military objectives were hit.

The leader of the Russian Military Mission to America, was yesterday received by President Roosevelt in Washington.

Planes of the Fleet Air Arm yesterday raided ports on the Finnish and Norwegian coast, causing extensive damage to harbour works etc. A German gun-boat and at least four supply ships were hit, and five enemy planes were shot down. Sixteen of our aircraft are missing from these raids.

Finland's decision to break off diplomatic relations with Britain, was met with much regret in official circles.

Japan has offered official apologies for the bombing of the United States Gunboat, and will take measures to prevent any re-occurrence in the future.

Lord Halifax and President Roosevelt met yesterday in Washington to discuss the position in the Far East. Japanese people have been warned that British and United States pressure may be increased.

The latest reports from Indo China, indicate that more Japanese troops are still entering the country, and that the first squadrons of Japanese aircraft have landed. A large Japanese Fleet is also lying off the coast.

The rationing of iron and steel may be introduced in the United States this month, with the object of conserving these essential war materials. Canadian motorists are voluntarily reducing their petrol consumption, and it is thought that petrol rationing will now be unnecessary.

Last night a few enemy aircraft attempted to cross the English Coast, but one was shot down, and very little damage done.

An enemy convoy in the Mediterranean was attacked yesterday by Blenheim bombers of the Bomber Command. One ship was sent straight to the bottom, a second left sinking, and several others were hit. Our losses in this action were seven planes.

The Egyptian Prime Minister has formed a new Cabinet, which includes five members who have been in the opposition since last year.

A report from Ankara states that the Vichy Ambassador has announced that the French ships held in Turkish ports will not be released until the end of the war.

Mr. Fraser, the New Zealand Prime Minister, on his arrival in Aberdeen, declared that if it were possible, all the people of New Zealand would come to Britain to share their difficulties.

TOBRUK, 2nd August, 1941.

Entries are still coming in freely for the "Ode to a Bottle of Beer" Competition, but Mud'n Bloods are warned that the contest will be closed shortly; therefore all further entries should be expedited. Today we include an ode submitted by Lieut. H.J. Boas which will take tossing. We also include a further effort of the Brig's, which makes us think that, if he had contented himself with praising the qualities of the amber fluid, his entry would have made him a hot favourite. Yesterday, we were of the opinion that as a poet, the Brig. was a very good soldier, but this latest entry, especially if put to music, almost puts him in the Gilbert and Sullivan class, which goes to show the unwisdom of making hasty judgements. (Sorry lads, but we've got to put ourselves right again somehow!)

> Disqualified? Me! A Brigadier?
>   All on account of an "Ode to Beer".
> The best of grog, so your Colonel thinks,
>   But whilst in Tobruk the rarest of drinks.
> Then pour your old prize down the C.O.'s chest,
>   I'll drink my whisky along with the rest.
> If your next competition proves such a dud,
>   Then I won't contribute to Mud and Blood.

(Brigadier R. W. Tovell, DSO, ED.)

Oh! Foaming Beverage; Oh! Frothing Juice,
    Worshipped by some; looked on askance by few,
In this parched place, should someone thee produce,
    With pleasure, thy acquaintance, I'd renew.

Product of some fat and wealthy brewer,
    To thee a thirsty soldier tribute pays.
While thoughts of thee strengthen me to endure
    Glory, in bottled form, receive thy praise.

Fosters, Tooths or Abbots, what's in a name,
    All brands, right now, to me would taste the same.

(Lieut. H. J. Boas - A Company).

LIMERICK COMPETITION - EXTRA-ORDINARY ANNOUNCEMENT!!!

The Brigadier offers a cash prize of fifty akers for the best final line for this limerick. The C'O' is the sole judge, and his decision is final. Entries will be published daily, and the competition will close on 15th August 1941.

There was once a young Mud and Blood
Who came from whence cows chew the cud,
    When he got to Tobruk
    They made him a cook
    ....

A reinforcement had just arrived in the front line and was very interested in all the various doings. The following morning he had just settled himself comfortably on the "Thunderbox" when - BANG - a shell exploded right under him with results easy to imagine. A fellow reo rushed up, and seeing his cobber sitting up with the seat draped around his neck like a ruff, enquired "What happened?" "Don't know," replied the unhappy one, "but I think that bully stew we had for breakfast must have disagreed with me."

The thanks of BHQ personnel are tendered to the C.O. for his recent decision to transfer the Postal personnel to headquarters. For months past the fame of the Postal Corporal has spread far and wide, and BHQ are anxiously awaiting to see him in action the next time Jerry comes overhead. Seeing's believing, and we tell you he'll have to go some to beat Pte. Frank Greenfield, of BHQ kitchen. This publication would be pleased to sponsor a match competition between the two; it is the firm conviction of the writer that Frank would win by a street in a 100 yards sprint, although Tich would have it all over him in a digging contest.

BBC NEWS — 2nd August, 1941.

Yesterdays GHQ communique issued from Cairo, says that our patrols from Tobruk again penetrated into enemy lines on Wednesday night, but contact with the enemy was not made. All patrols secured valuable information. A skilful daylight patrol made on Thursday, secured valuable identifications. In the Frontier area, our artillery engaged and inflicted casualties on working parties and mechanical transport in the Halfayer sector.

RAF communique announces that more raids were carried out on Friday on Bengasi harbour, where large fires were caused. Gazala and Bardia were also raided, and a series of explosions were caused. Messina harbour in Sicily was also bombed. All our planes returned safely from these operations.

The Third Canadian Division, commanded by Major General Price, has arrived in Britain to swell the British forces. They arrived in one of the largest convoys ever to cross the Atlantic. Besides thousands of soldiers, the convoy also brought hundreds of technicians, and several hundred airmen trained in Canada. A French Canadian Regiment also arrived. Apart from the dropping of depth charges by one of the escorting vessels, the voyage was uneventful.

Blenheim bombers yesterday attacked enemy shipping off the Belgian coast. Bombs were seen to straddle two ships, and a 2000 ton vessel was left in a sinking condition. Two bombers and one fighter are missing from these raids.

Washington. President Roosevelt has ordered immediate control of exports of all petroleum products from the United States, except to the British Empire and the Western Hemisphere. The complete stoppage of processing of raw silk is also being ordered, and all raw silk stocks in the country are being frozen, and will be used for National defence requirements.

The Madras Government War Fund has reached the One million pound sterling mark today.

Moscow. This mornings Soviet War communique indicated that no change has occurred in the last 24 hours in the position of opposing troops on the Eastern front. It says however, that Russian troops engaged the . enemy along the entire front. In the Baltic Sea, Soviet aircraft attacked and sank an enemy patrol ship and a 5000 ton tanker, and four more ships were heavily damaged. Moscow was again raided last night, but only very few planes managed to break through the outer defences. A number of incen-

diary bombs were dropped causing several small fires. Two enemy aircraft were shot down.

Yesterdays German High Command communique merely stated that fighting on the Eastern front continues to make favourable progress.

Opinion in London, is that at the end of six weeks titanic struggle, the Russians are still holding off the Germans, who are now thought to be preparing for a new offensive. It is estimated that the Germans have used at least half of their armoured divisions in battle, and have suffered very heavy losses in both men and material.

In Sydney, the Minister for the Army, Mr. Spender, stated that as a result of extended Militia training, Australia will always have 150,000 men permanently under arms for home defence.

General Wavell, Commander in Chief of India, presided yesterday at the first meeting of the Defence Advisory Committee. He reviewed the general war situation, and emphasised the magnificant part played by Indians in various war theatres.

TOBRUK, 4th August, 1941.

Introducing our new series - WHO IS IT? No prize to the winner. (Woe betide any member of HQ Company who says this is Major R. E. Wall).

We get terribly homesick when we read the jokes in our contemporary The Flying Furphy, issued by the 24th Battalion. They take us right back to our schooldays.

Wemyss

Tenders called for leasing the spacious, panelled, dugout, shortly to be vacated by the C.O. Honesty compels us to state that the fleas therein are just as big and hungry as those anywhere else, but to compensate, there is a delightful aroma of cognac hanging around, that is worth a few extra akers per week.

He spoils our looks in such a cheerful way that we never go crook at him, and even give him this free advt. in an effort to help him establish his Gent's Salon in the Battalion - We refer to Pte. Alf Cartwright, formerly of Geelong, who will trim the old locks for the modest fee of an envelope and sheet of paper.

OUR "ODE" COMPETITION:

And still they come, and getting better and better too. Am inclined to think there would have been an absolute stampede if the prize had been two bottles instead of one. This one has atmosphere, although it does not comply strictly with the stipulation that the Ode is to "A Bottle of Beer".

> In dusty dugout, stifling, stewing,
>   Sweating soldier restless lies.
> Thirsty thoughts his memory brewing
>   Homewards, beerwards, fancy flies.
> Back to Aussie's ferny fountains,
>
>   Picnics on the Mitta-Mitta,
> Foster's Lager in the mountains,
>   At the races, Melbourne Bitter.
> Then there comes a thought diviner;
>   He dreams each officer shouts a niner,
> I wouldn't be surprised, would you?
>   If this lovely dream came true.
>
> (VX38694, Cpl. J. K. Mullany, D Company)

> When I consider how my throat is dried
>   By desert sand and heat and flies and Sol;
> Then all my soul cries out for alcohol.
>   There's one small can of "Good and Tried"
> I'm told, for him the spirit moves to rhyme.
>   Can the Muse be bought for such small stuff?
> You ask. I hold, in this foul filthy clime,

The price is large; a bottle of good cheer
Above compute. Ten lines in praise of Beer?
Forsooth! the Muse replies "'Tis not enough!"

(Major P. E. Spier, "A" Company).

But, with due apologies to Brigadiers, Colonels, Majors, and other lesser lights, it is our humble opinion that the following effort of a private licks them all -

Oh! Editor, dear Editor, a wretched world perceive,
There's scarce a hotel in it now excepting when on leave.
In soldier-like activities we no doubt do excel
But surely part of soldiering is NOT to thirst like hell.
For liquid drops of amber or of lovely nectar hue,
We long to drink like blazes as the other blighters do,
Who stayed at home to carry on and wisely multiply,
(But that's another tale to which my pen need not apply),
We laugh at death (says you?) but always harbour fear
Lest we be stayed from putting down another pot of beer.

(VX40152, Pte. L. Wenborn, I Section).

Omar Khayam had nothing on one Lieut. Ken Reid, who has dashed our hopes by composing the following lyrical effort. Someone told us he did not drink, and we had marked him down for a visit when the next beer issue was on. Now we think our time would be wasted. Wish they would send up a lot more non-drinkers from the Training Battalion:-

Oh! sleek brown shape! Thou prize of my desiring
Mine inner man cries out for thee.
My eager lips, my thirsty throat aspiring,
To taste thee, brew sublime - and free.

In dreams I see thee held aloft, and shining
Thy sparkling fluid trembleth near,
Ah! bliss divine, what need now my repining,
Soon, soon I'll taste thy precious beer.

Thus dream I, soon 'twill be my lot,
Beneath thy lips to hold my eager pot.

(Lieut. R. K. Reid, "D" Company).

BBC NEWS — 4th August, 1941.

Cairo G.H.Q. Communique reports all quiet at Tobruk and in the
Frontier area. RAF made heavy bombing attacks on Malemi and Candia,
and on enemy shipping at Lampedusa Island. One plane was destroyed, and
others damaged in an attack on Borizzo Aerodrome in Sicily. A large number
of Junkers 88 escorted by Messerschmitts, attempted to damage H.M. Ships
off the North African coast. These were intercepted by British fighters,
which shot down four dive-bombers, and one fighter. Three RAF fighters
are missing. Sir Seymour Hicks, who has spent the last six months in the
Middle East arranging entertainments for the troops, has resigned his posit-
ion as controller of ENSA of Drury Lane. He is going to South Africa this
month to lecture for British Council. Lady Hicks, who has also taken part
in shows arranged for the troops, is accompanying him.

London - Specific objectives in the heart of Berlin were bombed on
Saturday night, in one of the heaviest attacks yet made on the German Cap-
ital. Britain's heaviest bombs were used by a strong force of two and four
engined bombers, and many large fires were left burning. Hamburg and Keil
were also fiercely attacked, and a smaller raid was made on Cherbourg docks.
Four RAF planes are missing from these operations. There was little enemy
air activity over Britain last night, and no casualties.

The Admiralty announces that British submarines in the Mediterran-
ean have sunk two enemy supply ships, and torpedoed a 7000 ton Italian
Cruiser of Condoffieri class. Two hits were scored on another cruiser, but
it is not known whether she sank. Destroyers were observed circling around
the position where the cruiser had been, and laying protective smoke
screens. A floating dock escorted by a destroyer and torpedo boats, was
attacked within less than a mile of the Italian coast. The dock was hit by at
least one torpedo. Four German aircraft were destroyed during the RAF
offensive operations over the Channel in Northern France on Sunday.

Melbourne - Nineteen year old eldest son of the Commonwealth
Premier, Mr. Menzies has enlisted in the Australian Imperial Forces.

Cape Town - Major General J. J. Collier, Military Secretary to Gen-
eral Smutts, died today.

Moscow - Further successes against German shipping in the Baltic
were reported today. The Russians claim to have sunk a submarine, and a
German steamer which was carrying arms for Finnish Army was also sunk
near the Norwegian port of Vardo. Russian planes which raided the Ruman-

ian Airport of Constanza, hit Floating Docks, one enemy destroyer, and ships in the harbour. Fierce fighting continues in the Ukraine, and in the Smolensk area. The Red Airforce claims to have shot down 31 German planes. Their losses were 19 aircraft.

TOBRUK, 5th August, 1941.

Alongside is an illustration of a very beautiful pair of field glasses (extra powerful 8 x 24), sent by the ladies of the Young Mud'n Bloods Association in response to the recent appeal by the C.O. These were sent by airmail - a costly business we can assure you - but the glasses are now in daily use in a sector where they are most required. They are temporarily in the custody of Lieut. C. Rigg, M.M., of the Carrier Platoon but it is the intention of the C.O. to present them to the next Officer who earns and receives a decoration. As you can see, the glasses are of unusual design, and we have no doubt that the lucky recipient will be almost as proud of them as he will be of any decoration that may come along

And now to tell you of the pretty lasses who made the gift possible - we have all their names here - Mesdames B. Evans and Deening; Misses Della Martin, Pat Rattray, Judith Edwards, Ruth Barker, Judith Allen, June Kiel, Olive Goodwin, Nancy Lee, Joan Hewitt, S. McKeisie, L. George, Anna Gahan, Muriel Mullany, Pat Hutchinson, Barker, Morley, Robinson, Betty Jess, Betty Wallace-Mitchell, Page, Allpass, Armstrong and Warren.

Well lads, the sketch alongside is about typical of these girls, who have our welfare so much at heart, so just pick out the one you would like to write to, and we are sure you will get a reply. (Address C/o Mud & Blood Association, C/o Mrs. B. Evans, "Chellowdene", K5 High Street, Windsor, Victoria). Our artist had about four tries before he produced something beautiful enough to please our critical judgement, as we really feel that if the appearance of

these girls in any way matches their goodness of heart, they would all take
first prize in a beauty contest. Anyway, Young Mud & Bloods, our very
heartiest thanks, and we have no doubt you will all be thrilled to await the
final presentation of the glasses - Let's hope he is young and single (we are
all handsome in this Battalion.)

And now to announce the closing of the "Ode to a Bottle of Beer"
competition - This will be concluded tomorrow, so get your entries in tonight or first thing in the morning. Hereunder an entry from the latest I-ti
prisoner brought in -

> I hate-a da Mussa, I wanta no fussa
>   I ain't da good Dago I was,
> No fisha da chippa, I licka da lipa,
>   I crave-a da beer from da Aus.
> Oh! bottle da beera! I love you my deara,
>   So frothy, lak Adolph da Hun,
> All gas lak da Bennie - but I ain't got any
>   I tinka I die in da sun.
>
> I put up my handa and say to da Dig
> Plees take me before da beer's won by da Brig.

> *

> Now it seems to me a pity, that your quest for something witty,
>   Has overlooked the power of the brew,
> It's a weapon very wily, for the troops who use it slyly,
>   Let me tell you what you really ought to do.

> Now all I ask is might I give the bottle to the I-ti
>   Let them guzzle from the muzzle as they will,
> When they taste its malty flavour, they'll put on their best behaviour
>   And they're bound to come in looking for their fill.

> Yes! they'll hail the mighty bottle, they'll surrender never fear,
> And you'll marvel at the power of a bottle filled with beer.

> (Sgt. Don Renton, "A" Company).

Extracts from a letter from Major Birch to the C.O.

"We had a good trip - two raids close by between the lighter and
the destroyer, and a submarine attack a hundred miles or two out. The Sub.

was destroyed by depth charges........I feel very homesick for the Unit - it will do me.........Will you tell Staff Mulcahy that I miss Mud & Blood.

BBC NEWS — 5th August, 1941.

Yesterdays Russian communique states that in spite of the new German offensive in the Smolensk area, their troops are still resisting strongly, and have checked the German advance. The Russians have counter-attacked fiercely, and in one sector, their tanks broke through the German lines, and attacked them from the rear. They claim to have destroyed over 100 tanks, 40 guns, and captured over 1000 prisoners in this action.

Moscow was subjected to a heavy air-raid last night, but once again only a few planes managed to break through the outer defences. Incendiary bombs were dropped, causing a number of fires, but these were quickly extinguished. One German plane was shot down.

The latest Finnish communique announces that all Russian counter-attacks on their front have been successfully repulsed.

The United States has given unlimited licence for goods needed in Russia. This decision was announced by Mr. Sumner Welles in Washington yesterday. He also announced that the Commercial Treaty between Russia and the United States was being extended for another twelve months, and that the shipment of defence materials to Russia was being speeded up.

It is announced in United States that 34 vessels for the US Navy were launched last month, and that 63 more keels were laid. The keels laid were for an Aircraft Carrier, 2 Cruisers, 10 Destroyers, 3 Submarines, and 8 Mine-sweepers.

All United States copper supplies are being placed completely under control as from tomorrow. Most of the leading shops in New York had to call for police assistance, owing to the rush of women shoppers to purchase silk stockings. This followed the recent announcement that all raw silk was being taken over for war requirements.

The United States has sent a warning to Vichy with regard to handing over of further possessions to the Axis Powers, as in the case of Indo China. Vichy has replied to the effect that the agreement with Japan, was for Military protection, as Indo China was almost cut off from Vichy.

Japan is reported to have increased pressure on Thailand, and it is believed that many of the streams of men and material which are pouring into Indo China, are concentrating on the Thailand border.

A New Zealand Airman, Sgt. Thomas Alan Ward of 75 Squadron, has been awarded the V.C. for gallantry in action. After taking part in a bombing raid, the wing of the Wellington bomber in which he was acting as second pilot, caught fire. Sgt. Ward climbed out along the wing, and in spite of terrific difficulties, managed to extinguish the flames.

Britain's new fighter plane, has a range of 1500 miles, and a top speed of over 350 m.p.h. Although this plane was previously announced as a night fighter, a number of them took part in the recent raid over Sicily in which about 40 enemy planes were destroyed.

Further attacks have been carried out by the RAF on targets on the Italian mainland. A large number of Italian fighters were destroyed, but all our planes returned safely. Attacks were also carried out over North Africa, where Benghazi suffered its 107th air-raid, and many fires were left burning. Hanover, Frankfurt, and the docks at Calais were also heavily attacked, and from these raids, one of our fighters is missing.

No enemy aircraft flew over Britain during the hours of darkness last night, but bombs dropped at dusk caused neither casualties nor damage.

Another German vessel has been intercepted while attempting to run the blockade. It was a 5000 ton steamer.

An Official German News Agency states that 98 people were executed after the explosion of four bombs. They say that complete order has now been restored.

TOBRUK, 6th August, 1941.

Our WHO IS IT? Series. Give yourself a pass, and the artist a pat on the back, if you guess who it is within five seconds.

Doings in a large way are in contemplation to celebrate the birthday of the battalion, which will have been in existence one year on the 20th August. It is hoped to have a bumper comforts issue for that day, and no doubt the QM will co-operate with the cooks and ensure that something special in the way of a dinner is provided. And you can bet your last aker that there will be as much to drink as can be got, although this of course, is not saying that there will be anything available.

Also, to commemorate the event, there will be a large six or eight page issue of Mud & Blood, containing items from all sources within the battalion. This publication will be a unique souvenir, and we promise that it will be worth having. As it will be impossible to give a copy to everyone in the battalion, it is proposed to give a special copy to each person who has at any time contributed to the columns of this paper. So if you have not already done so, send in your story, ode or sketch, and it may even gain inclusion in the Birthday Number itself. Those of you who have already contributed, register your names at the Orderly Room, so that your claims to an issue will not be overlooked.

In addition, we will hold a unique competition, details of which will be announced in tomorrow's edition. This competition will be open to all, and will be well within the power of every member of the unit to win. The prize is a box of 500 cigarettes, which are already in our possession, under lock and key.

AWAIT TOMORROW'S PAPER FOR ADDITIONAL DETAILS.

Entries for the Limerick Competition are not coming in too rapidly. Doesn't anyone want 50 akers? By the way, this competition is open to Brigade and the 2/24th Battalion personnel - we are quite confident that

the wit and wisdom of this unit has nothing to fear from outside competitors.
The Limerick is as under, and all you have to do is fill in the missing line:-

> There was once a young Mud'n Blood,
> Who came from where cows chew the cud,
> When he got to Tobruk
> They made him a cook
> ....

And now for the final entries in our "Ode to a Bottle of Beer" contest. The result of this will be announced tomorrow, and all going well, we will be sampling the bottle with the winner tomorrow night:-

> Sweet Mistress! Fount of all delight,
> My senses reel at thoughts of thee.
> Thy charms seduce me day and night,
> My mind from thee is seldom free.
>
> Entrancing beer, within thy bottle,
> Entrust thyself to my caress,
> A rival I would fiercely throttle,
> If to thee his suit did press.
>
> My Love! My eager lips await thy clinging kiss.
> Ah Me! To taste once more such rapturous bliss.
> (VX48676, S/Sgt. J. D. Mulcahy, Orderly Room)

> Oh! haunting love!
> When I espy your entrancing form,
> My palate of insincerities shorn,
> My thoughts in sheer rapture borne,
> Each day, each night, each morn.
>
> Oh! taunting love,
> Your aloof beauty, you've got me in your spell,
> To hold you, caress you, makes my poor heart swell,
> I place my soft lips against yours, Ah! Well,
> You're not for me - but you can never tell.
> (Sgt. Jim Taylor, C Company).

> I'm in this comp. and out to win, I'm partial to a swig,
> But what's a man run into now, an entry from the Brig.

The Colonel too has tried his luck, the Judge can now "get on"
I'm telling privates here and now, their chance to win has gone.

But what a prize this precious ale - Tobruk's most rarest thing,
A tin of beer all to yourself, a man can have his fling.
If luck goes with my entry, my joy will be eternal,
Admitting it would be a shame, to beat the Brig. and Colonel.

(Pte. F. H. Downs, A Company).

BBC NEWS — 6th August, 1941.

After initial successes, the new German offensive of the last two days in the Smolensk and Leningrad sectors, has been checked. Fierce fighting is continuing in the Ukraine. A German broadcast has given a vivid description of the clash of mechanised Units, which is without doubt the heaviest of the war. They claim that Smolensk has been reached, and that fighting is continuing on the Eastern side of the town, and refers to the struggle in this area as being the greatest battle of the war. Hand to hand fighting has taken place in the forests, and terrific artillery duels and tank battles have been fought. The Germans claim that although very heavy losses have been inflicted on the Russian forces, their own losses have been heavy. They also state that in spite of the heaviest losses, German Regiments and Divisions are again preparing for new operations.

A large force of German planes again attempted to raid Moscow. A few aircraft managed to penetrate the outer defences, and although many HE and incendiary bombs were dropped, little damage was done. Five enemy planes were destroyed in this raid. The Germans claim that in raids on Moscow, the great Stalin Motor Works have been completely destroyed, but this is denied by the Russians. The Russians claim that during the last week in July, 41 German planes were destroyed while attempting to raid Moscow, and that not a single bomb was dropped on the city during that period. They also claim that no bombs have fallen on Leningrad proper.

At least four more enemy ships were sunk in the RAF daylight sweep over the North Sea, when a 2000 ton steamer and three patrol ships were attacked. One of our fighters is missing from these raids. In the Mediterranean, an enemy merchant ship of 8000 tons was blown up off the coast of North Africa by aircraft of the bomber command. All our planes returned safely from this raid. A recce flight, has proved that in Sundays raid on Southern Italy, eleven enemy planes were destroyed and many others damaged. The Italian sea-plane base at Sardinia was successfully attacked by the

Fleet Air Arm yesterday. The base was first of all subjected to a heavy bombardment from H.M. Ships, which was followed up by a bombing raid by aircraft from the aircraft carrier, Ark Royal. Scattered German raiders dropped bombs on the East coast of England and Scotland last night. A considerable amount of damage was done, but casualties were slight.

Russia and Norway have resumed diplomatic relations. This was announced after a meeting of the Foreign Ministers of both countries. Moscow has denied the Japanese reports of a Russian - Chinese Agreement. Japan has denied the reports that she has been exerting pressure on Thailand. Thailand's Eastern Army has been established in the area recently conceded to her by Indo China. British forces in Singapore have been considerably increased. A Free French Para Corps has been formed in Britain.

TOBRUK, 7th August, 1941.

By the way, in yesterday's issue we erred in saying that the first birthday of the unit was the 20th August; actually this occurred on the 1st July last, which was the date upon which the Unit officially came into existence. However, the 20th August was the date, as you all know, when the troops were transferred to the Unit from the Training Battalion, and to all intents and purposes, this was the commencement of the 2/23rd. So our forthcoming celebrations will be termed Anniversary rather than Birthday activities. Not that it matters a tinker's cuss, but it is just as well to be accurate.

Now to tell you of the competition devised by the C.O. in conjunction with your Company Commanders - to wit, a Flea Catching (or other vermin) Contest. The competition will close on the 19th August, and all "bags" will be forwarded to the R.A.P. where they will be counted by the Company Commanders, and the winner declared. The firm of Louse, Louse and Delouse will take care of all entries. The first prize is 500 cigarettes, which have already been handed over, and as the Editor does not smoke, have a reasonable chance of survival - in fact, we guarantee it. The competition is not confined solely to fleas, but to vermin of all kinds, and a table of comparative values is given hereunder:-

One bug equals	3	fleas
One rat equals	10	"
Three lice equal	1	"
(Easier to catch by far)		

One gazelle equals	300	"
One I-ti prisoner equals	200	"
(plus all "catch" found on him)		

In criticising the above table which was laid down by the C.O., we think it an anomaly that 300 fleas are allowed for a gazelle and only 200 for an I-ti, whereas we all know the I-ti is much fleeter of foot than the gazelle, and is consequently harder to catch. Still, we suppose there are more I-ti's about than gazelles, and it is interesting to note that "B" Company has already 400 fleas to their credit after yesterday's bag of two somewhat dirty dagoes.

We might mention that all entries may be composed of either dead or alive specimens. All live exhibits will be treated on strictly humanitarian lines by the R.A.P. staff, which will be hard to believe by all of you who have had boils and sores treated over there. In experimenting how to collect the corpses, we suggest a thin needle and a long piece of cotton as being reasonably efficient. Incidentally, we hope you will all play the game and cut out all shennanigan. We issue this warning through inadvertently coming across a loophole in the conditions. Yesterday we caught four beautiful fat fleas, and put them in a pickle jar; imagine our surprise when, so help us, if there weren't nine in it this morning. So to be strictly honest, you will have to segregate the sexes. Let's hope you have good eyesight.

The award of the Mud & Blood Medal is today conferred upon Capt. Rattray of "C" Company, for the very efficient manner in which he had his Company "stand to" the other night, when sounds indicated the approach of the enemy. The Company got into battle formation, every man was at his post, and with tense nerves awaited the onslaught. Here at last was an opportunity to give the Hun and his satellites a taste of the Mud & Blood quality, without the dreary trudging that has always to be gone through before the enemy can be brought to book. Nearer and nearer came the noise, indicating that the enemy was in a careless, reckless mood, heeding little the noise that he was making. "C" Company, to a man, levelled their weapons and - two inoffensive little gazelles galloped past. No! "C" Company did not eat venison next day; their surprise was so great that they all forgot what good eating roast gazelle makes, and those two animals still live for the day when, who knows, they may grace the table of BHQ personnel. Now, if it had been "D" Company instead of "C", with Warrant Officer George Moore on the job, what a different tale to tell.

The C.O. has just received a letter from Jonathan Swift of the Melbourne Sun, and we give hereunder extracts from same that may be of interest:-

"I was very delighted to receive your letter, together with copies of the 'Mud & Blood' which took just about a month to reach me by airmail. I had previously been appealing on behalf of the Mayor of Albury for some binoculars with which to assist your men, and I am pleased to say that the response was such that you should have a pair for every officer in your unit.

"With regard to the message we published about the way you were 'luxuriating' in Tobruk, I have to inform you that this came through the official war correspondent, who possibly had his leg pulled by one of your troops. I am glad it roused your men and possibly caused them to vent their spite on the first piece of enemy they came across.

".....I am, however, in constant touch with Alderman Padman, who seems to be your fairy godfather, and just as proud of the boys wearing the Mud & Blood as everybody else who is reading of your doings.

"I am sending you a supply of the Sun Pictorial and other papers through my readers, which I would like you to distribute with the request that the recipient will communicate with the sender.

"Please send me any Mud & Blood's with special items. They are all acceptable and make good stuff for the folks here."

And now to tell you the result of our "Ode to a Bottle of Beer" competition which closed yesterday. The C.O. was to have judged the entries, but the uniform excellence of the efforts submitted caused him to tear his hair in despair, and he delegated the job to Padre Morrison, who has tackled the problem with characteristic thoroughness, and with whose decision no one will cavil. The C.O. has endorsed the decision, and has decided to give a bottle of beer to the second and third placing. May we applaud him for the magnificent nobleness of heart, superlative wisdom, and great perspicuity that prompted this generous gesture. We feel sure Major Spier joins us in this expression of appreciation, seeing that he filled second place, whilst we just scraped home in third position. The winning entry was submitted by Lieut. Ken Reid of "D" Company; Second place was taken by Major P. E. Spier of "A" Company; Third place going to our Editorial selves S/Sgt. J. D. Mulcahy, of Orderly Room. The three Odes are repeated hereunder:-

FIRST PLACE:

> Oh! sleek brown shape! thou prize of my desiring,
>> Mine inner man cries out for thee,
> My eager lips, my thirsty throat aspiring,
>> To taste thee, brew sublime - and free.
>
> In dreams I see thee held aloft, and shining,
>> Thy sparkling fluid trembleth near,
> Ah! bliss divine, what need now my repining,
>> Soon, soon I'll taste thy precious beer.
>
> Thus dream I, soon twill be my lot,
> Beneath thy lips to hold my eager pot.

SECOND PLACE:

> When I consider how my throat is dried
>> By desert sand and heat and flies and Sol;
> Then all my soul cries out for alcohol.
>> There's one small can of "Good and Tried"
> I'm told, for him the spirit moves to rhyme.
>> Can the Muse be bought for such small stuff?
> You ask. I hold, in this foul filthy clime,
>> The price is large; a bottle of good cheer
> Above compute. Ten lines in praise of Beer?
>> Forsooth! the Muse replies "Tis not enough!"

THIRD PLACE:

> Sweet Mistress! Fount of all delight,
>> My senses reel at thoughts of thee.
> Thy charms seduce me day and night,
>> My mind from thee is seldom free.
>
> Entrancing beer, within thy bottle,
>> Entrust thyself to my caress,
> A rival I would fiercely throttle,
>> If to thee his suit did press.
>
> My love! my eager lips await thy clinging kiss,
> Ah me! to taste once more such rapturous bliss.

Padre Morrison has made some comments on the Competition, which we are only too pleased to pass on, in the hope that, if a similar competition is ever held in the future, his remarks may be of value. First of all, the Padre stresses the fact that all printed entries were very worthy contributions. He particularly mentions the Brigadier's entry as stimulating interest in the competition, and being accepted by all competitors as a challenge. The criticism contained in the Colonel's entry was also a spur. There were 21 entries printed, and some others submitted that were not classed high enough in quality for publication. Many of the verses were of irregular metre and lost points thereby. Many others did not keep to the point - after all, it was an ode to a BOTTLE OF BEER, whilst many competitors referred more to the Brigadier than to the Beer. Some of the entries were distinctly lyrical and attractive but missed out through not sticking strictly to the subject. The most amusing entry in the Competition was one submitted by Sgt. Don Renton - "I hate-a da Mussa, I wanta no fussa." This was an excellent effort, and deserves special mention, as also does the entry of Pte. F. H. Downs, also of "A" Company.

Of the entries classified N.U.T.S. (not up to standard), particular mention is made of two that only just failed to make the grade - we refer to two submitted by Sig. John D. Hall and Pte. V. O. Bridges. As consolation prizes, these two competitors will be awarded a souvenir copy of the Anniversary Number of Mud & Blood, as will also all other entrants in the competition whose items were published.

Referring to the most discussed entry in the whole competition - we refer to the pathetic screed of Lieut. Ken Clarke, which would we know, have torn at the heart strings of everyone who read it, if they could only have found out what it was all about. Apparently Ken had a thirst, and wanted the world to know about it, but just what the thirst was for, no one can imagine, even though he does vaguely hint "Your chastity will ne'er be mine..........My unquenchable desires the remotest thingest." Maybe it was a bottle of beer he was thinking about, and he only forgot to tell us; on the other hand, knowing Kenneth, maybe he had something else in mind. The Colonel hazarded the guess that it was an "Ode to an Enigma." Anyhow, it certainly deserves some recognition, and thinking of a suitable prize put us to some little mental exercise. Accordingly, we have decided to present our bottle, WHEN EMPTIED, to Lieut. Clarke, as being symbolical of his entry - both containing absolutely nothing. We suggest that he puts it on his mantelpiece or somewhere, and it will always remind him of the time when he fathered an ode so "futuristic" that only posterity will appreciate it.

Now that the competition is ended, we heave a sigh of relief. It became quite a strain to see so many Mud'n Bloods going about with a vacant look, lips moving noiselessly as first one and then another brainwave was considered and mentally rejected. One S/Major Bill Morrison confessed to a sleepless night when, until four in the morning, his brain revolved ceaselessly around his contemplated ode which began "Close to my heart you lay sleeping", but what with one thing and another, his thoughts kept wandering, and the ode was never finished. His bedmate - Cpl. Freddie Henderson - got a horrible shock when he woke up to find Bill muttering in his ear "Your beauty has me in it's thrall" and could only with difficulty and much misgiving be prevailed upon to go back to sleep.

A couple of days ago one - Sgt. Laurie Duncan of Mortar Platoon - received quite an interesting bundle of cablegrams. "What's all the fuss about, Laurie?" enquired one nearby stickybeak, "a visit from the stork?" "Good God, No," replied Laurie with a look of horror, no doubt remembering at once his ten months absence from home, "only my birthday and congratulations on getting my third stripe." We also extend our congrats, Laurie.

In spite of all our efforts, ably assisted by a certain Major in the Battalion, Lieut. Johnny Methven still persists in wearing that horrible atrocity above his upper lip. The other morning, Pte. Alf Cartwright, under instructions from his Major, appeared at the palatial dug-out inhabited by Lieut. Methven armed for the job, but said Lieut. woke up too soon and nipped the deed in the bud, so to speak, before he even knew what it was all about. Now we are perforce compelled to appeal to higher authority - surely the powers that be will not permit such a monstrosity to continue without doing something about it. Think of the morale of the troops, and what would happen to them if they ever came upon him unexpectedly on a dark night? John, it's got to COME OFF.

BBC NEWS — 7th August, 1941.

The latest Moscow communique reports that stubborn fighting is taking place 70 miles north of Leningrad, where German and Finnish troops are endeavouring to force their way through the narrow neck of land near the Gulf of Finland. In the Smolensk and Ukraine sectors, fierce fighting is continuing. The Russians claim that in Tuesdays fighting, 14 German aircraft were shot down, with the loss of only 7 Russian planes.

The Germans issued four Special High Command communiques yesterday. They claim that they have taken 89,500 prisoners, and even a larger number of Russians killed, and the destruction and capture of 20,000 guns and 9000 aircraft. No mention is made of their own losses.

It has been announced in United States that millions of dollars worth of orders have been released to Russia, and that the first shipments have already left.

Polish and Czech armies are being formed in Russia, and will aid that country in the struggle against the common enemy.

Waves of German bombers again launched an attack against Moscow last night. Only a few planes managed to break through the outer defences, but many bombs were dropped. Some damage was done, and a number of people killed. One of the 6 planes brought down was rammed in mid-air by a Russian plane, the pilot of which managed to parachute to safety.

The General Officer Commanding Malaya, has discussed the effect of Japan's occupation of Indo China to the strategic situation in the Far East. He says that the probability of a surprise attack on Malaya has been considerably increased. No one can say what is going to happen. We have no aggressive designs, but British and Australian soldiers are capable of bush warfare which hitherto has seemed impossible. Larger reinforcements have arrived, and will continue to arrive to strengthen our forces in the Far East. It is reported that constant streams of lorries are carrying men and equipment across Indo China to the Thailand frontier. Britain and United States have stated that they will regard any move against Thailand as a threat to their interests. Mr. Cordell Hull has made clear, the interest of United States in any move in the Far East. He referred especially to the fact that Japan was already asking for concessions in Thailand. Mr. Anthony Eden during a debate in the House of Commons, said that Japan should understand that when Britain is outspoken, she means what she says. The Times sums up the whole debate by saying that as far as plain speaking can avert a struggle, Mr. Eden's words should do so, but we should avoid both optimism and pessimism.

Enemy air activity over Britain last night was slight. South and South East England suffered small raids, but only few casualties resulted. Two enemy planes were shot down.

The German Aerodrome near Cherbourg was raided again yesterday in our daylight offensive, and fighters on the field were riddled with mach-

ine gun bullets. Four enemy fighters which tried to intercept our forces, were shot down. One of our fighters is missing. In the Middle East, the RAF has made a further series of attacks on enemy positions in North Africa, including Derna and Benghasi. Malta was raided yesterday by enemy aircraft. Some civilian casualties and a little damage was caused, but military objectives were not damaged. Three enemy aircraft were shot down into the sea during the raid.

The Germans claim to have attacked and sunk a British convoy, but it is stated in London that the German claims are at least 350%, and probably 700% more than the actual losses. It is also stated that only when the enemy submarines are doing well, do they attempt to stick to the truth.

The pilot of a Hurricane plane recently captured an E boat off the coast of Malta. While attacking the E boat, the plane was riddled with bullets, but the pilot machine gunned the men manning the gun, who were instantly replaced. He also machine gunned the second gun crew, but then had to make a forced landing in the sea. The pilot then swam to the boat, and found all the crew either killed or wounded. He then took charge of the boat and took it ashore.

TOBRUK, 8th August, 1941.

Today, as you will notice if you are at all observant, we go to press for the fiftieth time, which is not at all a bad record for these troublous times. This issue should be one out of the box, but unfortunately no contributions have come to hand, and after an almost completely sleepless night, due in part to the fleas, and also contributed to by the artillery blighters, our old bean is not functioning too well at all.

How is the flea hunt progressing? If you are having difficulty at all come along and we will introduce you to our dug-out, which contains more of the little baskets to the square inch than any other part of Libya. If we entered the competition we would win hands down, but after our success in the Ode competition, we thought it inadvisable to take more than an academic interest in this one. However, there is nothing in the rules to prevent us helping our pals, and at any hour of the day or night a cursory inspection of our blanket will reveal several dozen "catch". Constant vigilance and drastic treatment does not seem to reduce their numbers in any way, and apparently there is a never ceasing source of victims for your skill. They are all yours for the taking, and we can even throw in a couple of rats which have, completely uninvited, taken up their abode there.

Incidentally, "B" Company claim another 600 fleas today, by virtue of the fact that three more I'tis were brought in by them this morning. Yesterday's two produced an extra 50 fleas each, the C.O. deciding that they were dirty enough to justify this claim by "B" Company. This Company by the way, is building up a handy lead in the contest, and should be well in front unless other Companies are keeping something up their sleeves.

```
D   O   L     Exotic Libya, strange place of love and sorrow
O   U   A         Thy lure induced us to depart our land;
N   R   S     Adventure beckoned, who thought of the morrow,
T       T         Romantic souls longed for the desert sand.
    L   S     So much for oft told tales of gilded vice,
F   I   L         Of love and laughter neath the desert moon.
O   M   I     Our begrimed bodies, home of vagrant lice,
R   E   N         Sigh for such joys that cannot come too soon.
G   R   E     Of flies and heat and lice we've had enough,
E   I             Thy early promise now we would enjoy.
T   C   C     Our present hardships may have made us tough,
    K   O         But pleasure's softer ways we'd now employ.
        M     A trip to Alex now would be so grand,
        P.        So Brigadier, please see what you can do,
              If you can shift us from the desert sand,
                  You'll earn a Mud & Blood Medal, too!
```

HE: Is there some way of making sure you'll be true to me when I go away?

SHE: Yes! take the rest of the Army with you.

Tom French

Russia has issued a statement of German and Russian losses on the East Front. They claim that German wounded, killed and prisoners, total one million, and their own wounded, killed and missing at 600,000. Enemy destroyed total over 6,000 against Russian losses of 5,000. Enemy guns destroyed, over 8,000, Russian losses about 7,000. Enemy aircraft about 6,000, Russian about 4,000. They also state that when the Germans capture a town, they immediately mobilise all the civilian population, and drive them far behind the lines, declaring them prisoners, and that this is how the German claims of 895,000 Russian prisoners is arrived at. The latest Russian communique refers to stubborn battles to the North of Leningrad half way between Leningrad and Smolensk, at Smolensk itself, and in the Ukraine. The Russian Air Force has been operating with ground forces, and has raided enemy mechanised units and infantry positions along the whole front. They claim that 19 German planes have been shot down, with the loss of 14 Russian aircraft. In the centre of the great front, Russian forces still hold Smolensk, where it is claimed that all parachutists and light tanks which the Germans have tried to land, have been wiped out. It is stated in Moscow that German industrial centres have long since failed to work at full speed owing to the heavy British raids. They also state that letters found on German prisoners, told of the terrible hardships of the people in Germany, and how much the British air attacks were feared.

It is reported that Japan is sending large quantities of men and material to centres in Manchukuo, and are massing men near the Russian border. Extensive air-raid practices have been held in Japan. Russia, who it is known have about a million fit troops along the Japanese Frontier, deny that there have been clashes between Russian and Japanese troops. Japan has stated that no claims have been made on Thailand. The Chinese Government announced that steps are being taken to prevent the Burma road being closed by the Japanese. It is stated in London, that British preparations in Singapore are now complete.

July was Britain's best month in the battle of the Atlantic since May of last year. It was stated in London that although we were taking a heavy toll of submarines, that did not mean that we could relax our efforts. Shipyards in Britain have turned out ¾ million tons of new shipping since the beginning of the war. In Britain, it is predicted that anti-aircraft gunners will have greater success against enemy raiders when the nights grow longer. Britain is producing a new type of light cruiser tank. It is well armed and has a formidable fire power. It has been described as the Rolls Royce of tanks.

Only a small number of enemy aircraft crossed the coast of Britain last night. Few bombs were dropped, and the number of casualties slight.

Fighters operating yesterday from home bases, made repeated swoops over enemy territory, and on two occasions, escorted bomber formations. At least four enemy planes were shot down, and many others damaged. Our losses in this attack, which lasted from dawn to dusk, were ten fighters. An enemy aerodrome in Norway, a supply ship, and many other targets were also attacked, and in these operations we lost 8 bombers and 1 fighter. In the Middle East our planes successfully raided a sea base in Sicily, and targets in North Africa. One of our machines is missing. During the past 3 months, 1057 enemy aircraft, mostly German, have been destroyed in the Middle East. Our losses for the same period were 661, and these figures include planes lost in Syria and Iraq. The enemy losses do not include planes shot down by ships at sea or the Fleet Air Arm. Another unsuccessful attack was launched by enemy aircraft on Malta yesterday. One plane was shot down.

London. The Secretary for War has given the latest information about our operations in Greece and Crete. Our total forces in Greece were 57,757 of which 44,865 were evacuated. The details are as follows:- British - 24,100 of which 16,442 evacuated. Australian - 17,125 of which 14,157 were evacuated, and New Zealand - 16,532 of which 14,266 were evacuated. The Australian forces in Crete totalled 6,450 of which 2,890 were evacuated.

As a result of the strike at the Federal Ship Building and Dry Dock Yards in New Jersey, the launching of the cruiser "Atlantic" has been held up. The launching of a number of merchant vessels has also been delayed.

TOBRUK, 9th August, 1941.

Advising all Mud'n Bloods of another issue of smokes and chocolates today from the C.O.'s Fund. By the way, the issue of beer a few days ago (glorious memory!) was also from this fund, whilst the sweets issued loosely were those sent out by the Welfare Association. The tobacco and boiled lollies were issued by the A.C.F. Altogether, it was an eventful week as far as comforts were concerned.

We are today amused at the antics of those two "old stagers" - Speed & Dixon - to qualify for a copy of the Anniversary Souvenir Number of Mud & Blood. A copy will be given to all those who have contributed to its columns, and this artful pair conceived the idea of copying something from the first paper they came across and sent it in. Needless to say, their claim was rejected with contumely (good word that!). Followed an original "poem" from each, which we immediately classified N.U.T.S. However, not for their contributions, but for their pertinacity, we have included them on the distribution list. We give here a few lines from the efforts of each:-

George Dixon's brainstorm -

I've got a cobber the best of the lot,
Beer is his hobby, the same as I've got.
Women don't worry us like some folks we know
We don't drink their beer and won't have a go.

George Speed should be Court Martialled for this -

Four steps down then enter
The home of the two G's,
It is not very palatial,
But its free from lice and fleas.

There is a lot more to both of them, and anyone can have a peep at them on paying the sum of ten akers into the Editorial Beer Fund.

We have been asked by sundry personnel in BHQ to express their admiration of the culinary prowess of one - JACK O'BRIEN - in these columns. At the risk of being accused of flannel-lifting to the cook, we certainly endorse their remarks. (How is it for an extra rissole now Jack?) If the happy faces, denoting satisfied tummies, indicate anything at all, they tell the world that Jack is doing a good job, and doing it cheerfully too. But that voice of his as he exhorts all and sundry to hurry up! We will hear it in our dreams for ever more. What a glorious R.S.M. has been lost to the Army through putting Jack in the kitchen!

A HINT:

Weary brains we wracked with might,
    To write an ode to beer.
Success achieved, to our delight,
    It's now a haunting fear.
Three thirsty days and nights are past,
    (Excuse this silent tear!)
"Do Colonels ever welsh," we ask,
    For there's still no flaming beer.

We had a look at the three I-ti prisoners that "B" Company brought in yesterday, or should we say two and a half?, and are ashamed to think that "B" Company were unsporting enough to keep them. Haven't they heard of our Game and Fisheries Laws? The little fellow, at least, should have been tossed back as being

undersize. Surely "B" Company are not going to be credited with 600 fleas for this lot! We suggest 100 for the little one and 125 each for the other two. Of course, judging by the look of them, there might easily have been another few hundred fleas on them. Incidentally it might be a good idea if "B" Company "flead" all their prisoners before they send them in, as we picked up 1 or 2 fleas from the Operation Room floor after they had gone, and our native honesty will not permit us taking an unfair advantage of anyone. If the fleas belong to "B" Company, then let "B" Company keep them, say we.

I-ti: Don't
        killa me!

Aussie: Kill be b...!
        You mean about
        700 fleas for the
        M & B Competition.

BBC NEWS — *9th August, 1941.*

Germany has apparently had a taste of bombing from the East as well as the West. Last night, British bombers carried out extensive raids over Western and Northern Germany, and some bombers penetrated as far as Berlin. The RAF concentrated mainly on targets in the Ruhr, where the Krupp's factory at Essen, and the great railway yards at Hamm were heavily attacked. This great attack on the Ruhr was only part of the night's operations, as enemy aerodromes in Denmark, and supply ships were also attacked. From Moscow comes the report that long distance bombers last night raided Berlin for the second night in succession. Heavy bombs were dropped, and considerable damage caused. Enemy aircraft crossed the Eastern coast of Britain last night and dropped a number of bombs. Little damage was done however, and no casualties were reported.

The latest Russian communique denies that Germans have mater-
ially gained any ground, but report that Germany's main efforts are direct-
ed at the Ukraine. Battles are still continuing around Smolensk. A special
German communique from Hitler's GQ claims that more than 200,000
Russian prisoners have been taken in the Rheat (?) area, where their forces
are menacing Russian positions, and that a further 100,000 prisoners have
been taken in the Ukraine. The Commander of the Russian Guerilla forces
has ordered that even more extensive attacks be made on German lines of
communications. This system of warfare has been very successful in har-
assing the enemy, and the Germans have been forced to leave large garrisons
in captured towns to cope with them.

Two thirds of the Japanese forces that are to occupy bases in Indo
China have already entered the country, and the remainder are due to arr-
ive within a week. Japanese newspapers again continue their accusations
that United States and Britain were attempting to encircle Japan, and state
that Japan cannot be indifferent to this situation.

The Fleet Air Arm and the RAF have played havoc with enemy air
and sea bases and convoys in the Mediterranean. An enemy convoy com-
prising 6 merchant vessels and 6 destroyers was attacked. Two merchant
ships were sunk, and two others left sinking, and one destroyer badly dam-
aged. The harbour of Tripoli in North Africa was heavily attacked, and
much damage caused. Bardia was also attacked. All our machines return-
ed safely from these operations.

In Syria, General Dentz and 35 of his Officers have been interned.
This action was taken because 75 British and Indian Officers were flown to
an unknown destination, and have not been released. Since the signing of
the Armistice in Syria, 2,000 Frenchmen have joined General De Gaulle,
and more are joining up at the rate of about 100 a day. General Weygand
has arrived in Vichy from North Africa.

The latest account of aerial combat in the Eastern front is given by
the Russians, who claim that 21 German planes have been destroyed with
the loss of 14 Russian aircraft. Russian aircraft have also carried out att-
acks on enemy land forces. The Russians also state that there were no att-
acks on enemy shipping in the Baltic, but German losses up to date are 13
Submarines, 10 Destroyers, 9 Naval Auxiliary vessels, and more than 13
Transports.

British newspaper correspondents have visited the Flying Fortress
which has carried out 6 raids over enemy territory. The rear gunner said

*that he has not yet sighted an enemy plane in any of the raids, but that any
enemy fighter which attacked it would find it pretty hard to find a blind
spot, as it was very heavily armed. The Flying Fortress is fitted with the
secret bomb sight, which enables it to carry out raids from as high as six
miles. As yet, this giant plane has not been damaged in any of its raids.*

*In United States, a request has been made for the Government to
take over the Ship Building yards in New Jersey, which are out on strike.
Workers have also gone on strike at the Curtis Wright aircraft factory in
New Jersey.*

*In Canada, the Minister for Defence has announced that authority
has been given for the formation of a 6th Division of the Canadian Service
Corps.*

TOBRUK, 11th August, 1941.

Had our usual touch of liver this morning, but the following paragraph found on the typewriter restored the old sense of humour somewhat:-

Was on a visit to Jerusalem; me and my offsider went into one of
those ancient buildings that give you the dingbats, and where visitors have
to sign their moniker in a chained up book. We gave the old barn the once
over and then went to the visitors book to do our stuff. Picking up the pen
my cobber saw he had to write his name under a signature that had DAAG-
OSD after it. Said my cobber to the attendant "What's the string of letters
after his name for?" and the attendant replied "Oh! they mean Deputy
Assistant Adjutant General & Ordnance Supplies Depot." My cobber signed his name in silence and solemnly placed after his signature the letters
BBBIBEC. The attendant asked the meaning of them, and without batting
an eyelid, my cobber replied "Oh! I'm entitled to use them; they stand
for Biggest Bludging B...... in Bernard Evans' Circus."

(Pte. J. Milton Butler - Ack-ack).
(Ed. - Isn't everyone in the ack-ack entitled to use those letters?)

In response to our mild hint yesterday to the Padre, we have to advise that the desired result was attained, as may be gleaned from the following verse sent along with the beer:-

Alac-a-day, what have I done?
My sins come home to roost I vow,
The Colonel's prizes have been won,
I'll just go out and give them now.
One BOTTLE only did he say,
That's easy to fulfil I know,
But "bottle filled with beer" today,
Is scarcer than a fall of snow.
I'll try two cans of beer and see,
If I can put it over them.
Black looks askance they'll cast at me
Two ounces less - they will condemn.

Lesh you and me
go and ring--------
DOORBELLS!

* * * * * * * *

The brew was great, as far as it went,
Indeed a treat, our thanks are sent,
To the Colonel who gave from his small store,
Although he knew he could get no more.
But our thoughts of the Padre are very bitter,
In his position he shot at a "sitter",
He knew very well we wouldn't complain,
So those stolen two ounces have gone down the drain,
If the Colonel but knew of the ounces we're docked,
He'd write to the Bishop and have Padre unfrocked,
Oh! Padre, our faith in the clergy is spoiled,
With a Major, a Loot and a Staff you're embroiled.

* * * * * * * *

A young girl went on a pleasure cruise; the following is an extract from her diary:-

Monday - Went on the ship. Tuesday - Invited to sit Captain's Table.
Wednesday - Invited to visit Captain's cabin to have a cocktail.
Thursday - Captain made suggestions, most improper. Said that if I said "No" he would sink the ship. Do not know what to do, as there are 600 people on board.
Friday - Saved 600 lives last night.

A Staff/Sgt. at a Women's Auxiliary Dance was surprised and a little annoyed at the girls' ignorance of rank. Thus when a gushing young female with whom he had been dancing asked what the crown surmounting the 3 stripes meant, he replied that it showed he was married, and the 3 stripes indicated that he had 3 children. A little later the same girl was dancing with an ordinary Sergeant wearing 3 stripes minus a crown. "Oh! she exclaimed, pointing at the stripes, "You naughty man."

BBC NEWS — 11th August, 1941.

The German onslaught on Russia is now in its eighth week. The latest Russian communique states that heavy fighting is taking place 125 miles South of Leningrad, at Smolensk, and in the Ukraine, where the Russians are stubbornly resisting. Yesterdays German communique however, resorted to the old formula that 'Operations are proceeding according to plan'. The German people have been told that millions of Russians have been killed, and over ten thousand Russian aircraft destroyed in fighting on the Eastern front. They also appear to have been promised a speedy victory in the Ukraine. In spite of the German claims of over four weeks ago, Leningrad and Moscow are still in Russian hands. It is reported that the Germans may attempt to take Crimea, by the sea, as large quantities of men and material have been massed in Rumanian ports. The Germans have found that they now have to contend with difficulties behind their own lines, owing to the guerilla warfare carried on by Russian forces. Besides the Russians employing these methods behind the German and Rumanian lines, Norwegian guerilla bands are operating behind Finnish lines. The Berlin correspondent of a Swiss Newspaper states that nothing is being spared in the great battle on the Eastern Front. Hundreds of thousands of houses have been razed to the ground.

Last night's Russian communique gives the progress of the war in the air. The Russian Air Force operating with land forces, has inflicted much damage on enemy infantry positions, mechanised units, and communications. They also claim that 45 enemy planes were shot down with the loss of 25 Russian aircraft. A German communique claims that in last night's raid on Moscow, over 100 planes took part, and terrific damage was done. In Moscow, however, it is stated that the raids caused some fires, but these were quickly extinguished. They also state that only single planes got through to the City, where bombs were dropped, and a number of people killed and injured. Five German planes were shot down during this raid. The alert in Moscow lasted 4½ hours. In spite of these raids, theatres in Moscow have remained open.

The Rome Radio announces that Russia, with growing assistance from her friends, and with her great territory, may hold out indefinitely. It was also stated that it may be wise to spread the belief that the war may last for ten years.

Yesterday the RAF made another cross Channel sweep. Enemy shipping and targets in Northern France were attacked. An enemy supply ship was left burning, and an enemy fighter shot down. One of our fighters is missing. According to one of a group of Russian Engineers who visited the Ruhr before Russia entered the war, it is now in ruins. He states that while he was there, British bombers appeared every night, and dropped hundreds of bombs. A German plane yesterday made a forced landing near Alexandria, and the four members of the crew were captured.

The Admiralty announces that the destroyer "Defender" has been sunk, but there was no loss of life. The "Defender" was commissioned in 1930, and had a displacement of 1375 tons.

From Vichy comes the news that the postponed meeting of the Vichy Cabinet will take place this afternoon. It is thought that the Vichy leaders have been discussing the German demands, which are probably for strategic African possessions.

Mr. Duff Cooper who is on his way to the Far East on a special mission, has arrived in New York, and is expected to remain there for a fortnight. He stated that the British Government expected great developments in the Far East. He also said that British administration in the Far East would be centralised in Singapore.

India has formed three new Spitfire Squadrons. They have now contributed over 3 million pounds to the Spitfire Funds.

The Duke of Kent is still continuing his tour of Canada, and yesterday visited the big ship building yards in British Columbia.

TOBRUK, 12th August, 1941.

We never include a joke in these columns without much mental disquietude, since the morning the Colonel cast a cold eye at one hoary old chestnut that we thought everyone would have completely forgotten, and frostily remarked "I see the day of resurrection has arrived." So we take no responsibility for this one, but put all the blame on Private J. Milton Butler, B.B.BI.B.E.C., of Ack-ack Platoon, who is responsible for same:-

Three refugees in Tel-Aviv were airing their English. Said the father of seven to another "How many kids vos in your family?" Replied his friend "I haf no children, though I lofe them; alas, my vife is impossible." He was immediately corrected "No, no; your vords are wrong; you should say "She is inconceivable." The third refugee interrupted "You are both wrong; I know, because I've studied English. He should have said "She is impregnable."

The recent epidemic of versification shows no sign of abating, and several more items have come to hand, which will be published in due course. Hereunder an effort of Pte. Jimmy Henderson, of I Section, who just barely qualifies for a copy of our Anniversary Number:-

There's many a man is eager,
    And waiting for the fray,
They're ready lad, they're steady lad,
    They won't be led astray.
The line is long, the smokes are out,
    They've got a job to do,
For "Obie's" bell is clanging now,
    'Tis "eats" at B.H.Q.

Apparently our threat about writing to the Bishop has had its effect, as this morning the following missive has been received from the Padre, acknowledging the fact that two ounces of beer have been "stolen", and proffering the "amende honourable" when we reach Alex. Your offer is accepted, Padre, and how:-

Voices from Hell cry out for a drink
    Of two stolen ounces that "went down the sink."
A Major, a Loot and a Staff feel outdone,
    Where they've had all the pleasure their efforts have won,
When we go to Alex, I'll shout them a bottle!
    An honour! And also their quibbling to throttle.
Of a Judge apparently this is expected,
    And I don't care how soon such a move is effected.
But wherever we meet in dust storm or floods,
    Let us drink to the health of all Mud'n Bloods.

"What a Contract"

According to wireless announcements, men from Tobruk are now enjoying leave in Cairo. All those who heard the news this morning passed out, and it was even too much for the old wireless set, which let out one wild screech and gave up the ghost, and not another word could be got out of it. However, our News Editor is able to rise to all such occasions, and today you will find the usual news of so many planes, etc. shot down, and will be pleased to learn that the fighting still continues with unabated fury in Russia. We haven't read his news sheet yet, but probably dust storms are still raging in Tobruk. Now that L/Cpl Dicky Fancke is letting his imagination run riot a bit more, he is qualifying himself for a journalistic career in the future. Dick has, of recent weeks, been taking down the evidence of sundry Courts of Inquiry, in the course of which he has heard so many "tall tales" that he can now, quite unblushingly, let his pen write what it will, sure in the knowledge that no matter what he says, there will always be someone to believe it.

BBC NEWS — 12th August, 1941.

The third big offensive launched by Germany on the Eastern Front is now in progress. A German announcer stated that unless a decision was gained this week, this offensive would also come to a standstill. However, as yet there is no sign of a Russian collapse. The latest Russian communique states that heavy fighting is taking place about 125 miles south of Leningrad and it is at this point that the main German thrust is directed. Fierce fighting is still continuing in the Smolensk area. The communique goes on to say that the Russian forces are putting up a steady resistance, and also gives a description of how the German troops are being routed at the point of the bayonet. Little was said of fighting in the Ukraine, but Russian aircraft operating in this sector, attacked enemy infantry positions, motorised units and communications, and destroyed bridges. They also claim that 39 enemy aircraft have been shot down with the loss of 25 Russian planes. The Russians appear to be endeavouring to strain the German manpower to the utmost, and in a broadcast at Moscow yesterday, it was stated that technique without manpower is dead - It requires armies of many millions.

A group of German aircraft once again attempted to raid Moscow last night. A Russian communique claims that only isolated planes succeeded in getting through to the town. High explosive and incendiary bombs were dropped, causing a number of casualties. One German plane was shot down during the raid.

Soviet bombers raided Eastern Germany last night, but Germans claim that only two planes reached the Capital. The Berlin radio however, went off the air last night at 1030 p.m.

The Polish Prime Minister revealed that the Polish Military Mission was now in Russia. He also stated that the Polish Division being formed in Russia would be furnished with the most modern American equipment.

After yesterday's special emergency meeting of the Australian Cabinet in Melbourne, it was announced that there would be a further meeting today, and that Chiefs of the Fighting Forces would be called in. Mr. Menzies stated that - "While we desire peace, Australia is prepared to defend herself with her forces, and we cannot ignore the fact that Singapore is part of Australia's defences. The time has come when Australia asks for loyal and devoted service from her sons." Throughout Australia, there has been a rush to recruiting offices. It was stated that Beaufort Bombers are to be Australia's first line of defence.

In Tokyo, it is announced that Japan is now to be fully mobilised on a war basis.

The Government of Thailand has ordered reinforcements to be sent to the Indo China frontier.

It is stated in Vichy that at the Cabinet Meeting yesterday afternoon current affairs were discussed. General Weygand left for Algiers before the meeting commenced.

A second all American Eagle Squadron has been formed in England, and yesterday scored its first victory by shooting down a Junkers 88 over the Channel. The first Eagle Squadron has so far accounted for 7 enemy machines.

A Cairo communique reports small patrol activity in the Frontier area. At Tobruk, Italian forces which attempted to attack our outer defences, were driven off, and suffered many casualties. In spite of Nazi propaganda to the contrary, troops in the garrison of Tobruk are able to visit Cairo on leave.

The Federal Ship Building and Dry Dock Company at New Jersey has asked the Government for assistance. Work at the ship yards is still at a standstill and involves 18,000 workers, and affects many war contracts.

TOBRUK, 13th August, 1941.

Have just come from farewelling Sgt. Mick Kenny of "D" Company who has been selected (poor lad) by Divvy to go back to Australia to talk to the CFB's. What a terrible fate to befall a cobber, and our heart goes out to Mick in his travail. Fancy having to go back to the effete civilisation of Melbourne during the Cup Season? Think of the chattering females who will surround him; the pubs that will beguile the last bob out of his paybook; and the rich food he will be compelled to eat to the detriment of his digestion. Horrible! we wince at thoughts of the trials and hardships Mick will have to go through. Why! he may have to search Melbourne high and low before he will be able to find a tin of bully beef! Anyway, Mick me lad, the best of luck, and may you persuade thousands of the blighters that the only life worth living in times like these is the one we are enduring. And our tongue is not in our cheek as we write this - we mean it!

At last relief from the boredom of life in Tobruk is at hand. A momentous decision has been made, and from now on three deserving Mud & Bloods will go each week to Alex. for seven days' leave. Are we overjoyed? This decision means that sometime during the next five years we will once more taste the delights of civilised society; will be able to dash into a cabaret any evening and pay anything up to 7/6 for a bottle of beer; and also, during the daytime, will be able to walk nonchalantly along the various boulevards with the inevitable dragoman alongside attempting to persuade us to all sorts of indiscretions. After all, five years soon passes and, who knows, we may even be lucky enough to get an early leave during the second five years plan.

"Wouldn't it?" remarks Pte. Vic Bridges, runner at BHQ, as he surveys yesterday's routine orders, "A man can't call his flaming soul his own in this Army." He was referring to the edict in regard to beardless chins, which seemed to distress him somewhat unnecessarily, we thought. Of somewhat tender years, he has never yet managed to grow more than a scant five or six widely separated stubbly hairs at the end of his chin, but possibly he has become attached to them and dislikes the idea of the impending separation. Another baby in the unit, Pte. Bill (Dimra) Roberts will undoubtedly be up in arms at the restriction. Bill also hasn't yet commenced to use a razor as part of his regular routine, but no doubt flatters himself occasionally.

Anyway, why the wherefore? Is the masculinity of the Aussie already so pronounced that Authority deems it necessary to deprive him of the solace of growing a beard? Just one more cross in life we have to bear fellow Mud'n Bloods. Think of all those vanished enchanting moments when we used to caress our hirsute chins and wonder what SHE would think of us if she could only see it. And so the officers are to inspect us to see that we have our daily shave! We want to know who is going to inspect the officers! Lieut. Morrie Wilton for one will be scrutinised carefully each morning by a critical platoon, and we wonder if he will have the crust to accost a bewhiskered one in his command with the query "What happened to the razor this morning?"

The mills of God grind slowly, but when they do they often give good measure, and at last they have risen to the occasion. Capt. (Doc) Agar is suffering from that distressing malady for which he has prescribed so often "A dose of castor oil, followed by a dose of salts every two hours." "Very drastic, weakening, but always effective," used to quoth the RMO. He's telling us! Anyhow, if he had informed us of the hour he was having his dose of castor oil, we are quite sure there would have been an audience of many hundreds of gloating souls

to cheer him on. As it is, every time the Captain has occasion to repair to a certain area, the interest round about is intense, and much spirited wagering as to whether he'd make it has occurred.

You all saw, we presume, copy of the letter received by the C.O. from the school kids in Albury, and to those younger Mud'n Bloods particularly we commend the suggestion that you write to the youngsters. By the time we get home again they will all have reached adult stage, and it will be nice to have a friend or two in Albury, as by that time all the friends we remember will be in the Old Colonists Home, or somewhere similar. However all joking aside, why not adopt one of these youngsters as a "pen pal?" Remember, you are all heroes to these kids, and think what a kick they would get out of a letter from one of Albury's Own in "beleaguered Tobruk," whilst your own pleasure at receiving a reply would not be inconsiderable. Our own letter goes off today to Master John Taylor, who sounds like a true-blue dinkum Aussie chap to us.

BBC NEWS — 13th August, 1941.

In London yesterday, it was announced that Britain and Russia have promised full aid to Turkey if she is attacked by any European Power. The British and Russian Foreign Ministers made this declaration, which served to confirm that neither Britain or Russia have any designs on the Dardenelles, and only wish to preserve the integrity of the Turkish Nation. This step was taken to offset Nazi propaganda, and to re-assure Turkey, and was most warmly received.

On the Eastern Front, the Germans state that they have brought so much pressure to bear on the Russian forces, that they have reached the Black Sea Coast in the vicinity of Odessa. The latest Russian communique however, does not hint at any German advance on any part of the front, but claim the annihilation of the 68th German Division, and a German Regiment. The Germans state that a large scale withdrawal is planned by the Russians in the Ukraine, and say that this would counter the German plan to destroy the Russian Army in this Sector. On other parts of the front, heavy fighting is continuing, but Rheat still stands firm, and the Russians claim to have raided an enemy column and destroyed 60 tanks.

The Russian Air Force again attacked infantry positions, mechanised units, and enemy communications yesterday. They claim to have shot down 41 German planes with the loss of 34 of their own. On the 11th August, Naval and Air units of the Soviet Battle Fleet, attacked and sank four Motor Ships and two transports. The Russians report that in Monday's raid on Berlin, many high explosive and incendiary bombs were dropped, causing considerable damage. All their planes returned safely.

It was announced over the Moscow radio this morning, that German planes had once more attempted to raid the City last night. The attacking planes were engaged by night fighters and ack-ack, which prevented any of them getting through to the Capital.

The RAF yesterday made its biggest daylight raid on Germany. The attack was made from a low level, many of the planes hedge hopping. Northern France, Belgium and Germany were the main targets. Six Squadrons of Blemheim bombers attacked the Power Station at Cologne, causing heavy damage. This is the largest Power Station in Europe, and of immense industrial importance. These bombers were escorted by the new "Whirlwind" fighters. Flying Fortress bombers also took part in this great attack, and operated most successfully. Many bombs were also dropped in Emden and Northern France. Enemy fighters which attempted to intercept our bombers were driven off, and three shot down. In all these raids, we lost ten bombers and eight fighters.

Raiders were reported over several parts of Britain last night. Bombs were dropped in Eastern England and in the East of West Midlands. No casualties have so far been reported, and damage was only slight.

The Air Ministry announces that when taking off for a trans-Atlantic flight, a passenger plane crashed into a hall, killing the crew and the 22 passengers. Fourteen of the passengers were Canadians.

Marshal Petain has announced that following the meeting of the Vichy Cabinet, Admiral Darlan has been given control of the Vichy Air, Sea, and Land Forces.

TOBRUK, 14th August, 1941.

Dear Editor:

I have heard such a lot about a man in your regiment named Sgt. Jack O'Brien, and the wonderful pufftaloons he makes. Could you get him to write and tell me what he puts in them? I once knew a big strong he-man in Essendon; he was in the AIF too, and he made wonderful pufftaloons, in fact, better than those of any other man I know. Maybe it is the same man. This fellow was known as Albury's Own, and I think it was most unfair to the women of Essendon that he should have earned this name. Mr. O'Brien is, I am told, a big brawny virile Aussie, with hair on his chest, and Oh! Mr. Editor, don't you just love big virile men with hairy chests, especially if they make good pufftaloons? As a matter of fact, I left my husband because the pufftaloons he used to make were not much good. So if Mr. O'Brien could give me his recipe, I could teach some of the other soldiers round here how to make them. Will be so glad if you can persuade him. At present am feeling extra well; hoping you are the same.

Yours expectantly,
Mrs. MURPHY.

P.S. My friend next door tells me pufftaloons are things you eat, but I don't believe her, do you? I think she must have got the name mixed up.

We are now compiling our Anniversary Number of Mud & Blood, and wish to tell you that a page has been allocated to each Company, one to "B" Echelon, and the remainder will be taken up by BHQ and general items. It will be interesting to see which of the Companies produces the most amusing page, as well as being a unique issue of the paper, thoroughly representative of all sections. So, Companies and "B" Echelon, get busy right away, as we would like your copy not later than the 17th August, in order to give us requisite time for production. Proofs of each page will be sent to the respective Companies for final approval and correction prior to publication. It is hoped that all Officers, NCO's and men will co-operate to make their section outstanding in the paper, and remember, this special number will have a wide circulation. Indeed, if the paper proves of sufficient merit, it may be worth while getting it printed in Alex, so that every man may procure a copy to send home for souvenir purposes. So let's all make it a bumper number.

A highlight of one of "B" Company's forays into enemy territory last week is described by Pte. C.D. Crane, hereunder:-

During the return trip to their base under heavy enemy artillery, mortar and small arms fire, Pte. D.J. MacGrady was noticed to be falling behind the rest of the party. One of his mates, Pte. Bill Lindner dropped back to see if he could give him a hand with some of his equipment. Reaching MacGrady he said "You seem to be slowing down a lot, Mac!" "Yes, I thought I must have been, Bill," was the somewhat breathless reply, "the bullets seem to be passing me now."

With regard to the adoption of the Albury School youngsters as "pen pals" we have been advised of two kids to be crossed off the list. S/Mjr. Bill Morrison has decided to tell Don Benstead what a big bronzed Aussie soldier feels like in Tobruk, whilst Cpl. Freddie Henderson (with an eye to the future) has selected Margaret Newnham as the repository of his boyish confidences. We don't want to damp your ardour, Freddie, but we have an idea that your pick is only aged about 7 years, and by the time you get home she will still only be 14, which will not be altogether satisfactory, will it? Also, we are informed by Cpl. George Dixon that he is corresponding with Jimmy Fuller, whilst his mate Cpl. George Speed has decided to write to Valda Kelly, possibly in the hope that she has a big sister. Hope we are not doing you an injustice, George! We know your hobby is beer, Oh! yeah! Also John Taylor has to be deleted from the list as he has been set down to receive an occasional copy of Mud & Blood, together with the Editorial remarks anent same. There is, of course, no reason why several of you cannot write to the same kid, but it will be much better if you all pick different youngsters. So advise us of your choice, so that they may be eliminated from the list.

How are you getting along with your flea catching? Remember the contest finishes on the 19th inst., so you have not much further time. Also don't forget that if you are about 1,000 fleas or thereabouts short, I can supply them free for the catching in my dug-out. Fine healthy specimens they are too!

BBC NEWS — 14th August, 1941.

On the Eastern Front, the Russian forces in the Ukraine are still bearing the brunt of the third great German offensive, and very heavy fighting is continuing along the whole front. The latest Russian communique announces that some days ago, their troops evacuated Smolensk, but claim that in spite of this, and repeated German onslaughts, their main army is still intact. The Russians also state that heavy fighting is taking place about 120 miles South of Leningrad. The latest German communique however, reports that the progress of the German forces to the Black Sea Ports has been rapid. They also claim that Odessa has now fallen into their hands, but this has not been confirmed. It is thought that if the Germans manage to gain control of the Black Sea Ports, they may attempt to attack Crimea from the sea. It is stated in Russia however, that the Soviet Baltic Fleet is ready to deal with any such attempt. It is stated in Berlin that Bulgaria has been compelled to raise two Divisions to fight with the German army. It was also announced over the Berlin Radio, that Russia must have been equipped with a tremendous supply of tanks, for as fast as the Germans knocked out one lot of Russian tanks, others took their place.

The Soviet Air Force is still operating successfully with their land forces, and have continued their fierce attacks on German infantry positions, mechanised units, and lines of communication. Many enemy aerodromes have also been attacked. They claim that 43 German aircraft have been destroyed, and place their own losses at 35. An enemy tanker of 1300 tons has been sunk in the Baltic. The Russian Air Force has been successfully intercepting enemy raiders, and so far Leningrad has been free from bombing. German planes which attempted to raid the City last night were again driven off, and three shot down.

Mr. Duff Cooper, who is on his way to the Far East, conferred yesterday with Mr. Cordell Hull in Washington. He stated that Britain and US could not allow Japan to have her own way in the Pacific. A spokesman in Tokyo stated that Japan would only stand for so much interference, and when that limit was reached, there would be an explosion, and that any Nations that treated Japan lightly, would soon discover their error. It is reported that Japan intends to send 180,000 troops into Indo China. The Japanese Minister without Portfolio, was shot by an assassin this morning. No statement has been given as to his condition. Chungking, the seat of the Chinese Government, was heavily raided by Japanese aircraft last night for the fifth night in succession. The raid is believed to have been very heavy, and much damage was caused. It was announced in the US that their help for China was not temporary, but that it would continue after the war. China were also assured that the US would not attempt to interfere with Chinese internal affairs.

No formal acknowledgement has yet been received from the Turkish Government with regard to the British declaration to aid Turkey against any aggressive European Nation. The Turkish Foreign Minister however, has already expressed his entire satisfaction, and stated that this declaration has strengthened the existing friendship between the two countries. The German Ambassador to Turkey is reported to have left Ankara for Germany.

The Free French Commander in Chief in Syria, has issued a special order of the day, in which he told all ranks, that they could still be repatriated to France if they wished. In Syria, however, Frenchmen are still joining up with General De Gaulle's Free French Forces at the rate of over 100 a day.

Yesterday, the RAF carried out very heavy raids over Germany. Berlin, the Krupp's works at Essen, and Kiel were the main targets. After returning from these great raids, a pilot who had taken part in the raid on the German Capital, said that when he left the City was one mass of flame. The raid lasted over two hours, and the ack-ack barrage was terrific. Another pilot who took part in the raid on Krupp's, said that the great works were on fire for a distance of about two miles. From all these attacks, 13 of our bombers are missing.

It was stated in London, that Mr. Atlee will broadcast an important announcement on behalf of the Government, today.

To facilitate work on important war requirements, President Roosevelt has suspended the eight hour working day.

TOBRUK, 15th August, 1941.

Dear Editor,

You remember introducing me to S/Mjr. Ken Wiseman in the George Hotel, Albury. Well, me and Ken got real matey, and he was so good to me while my old man was away, but for some reason he will not answer my letters, and I have some important news I want you to pass on to him. Something big has come up, and I know he will be interested; in fact it's swell news. When my friend next door heard about it she said I ought to write to Ken right away and find out what he wants to do about it, and I said that this was a good idea, but maybe he doesn't want to be worried where he is, what with bullets and things flying about. But my friend says Ken's got a right to know since he was instrumental in the whole affair and with his legal mind maybe he can think what we ought to do, although my friend says he's done enough already. But you can tell Ken there is nothing for him to be afraid of. There's no ties on him although I do say it is the little things in life that tie people together. This is going to change the whole course of my life, and my only hope is that Ken won't be sorry for the part he played. Now that this has happened to me it seems like I can see the future quite clearly. I remember once I read a book "The Shape of Things to Come" and that's just how I feel now. No matter how things turn out you can tell Ken I will always think kindly of him, for no matter what anyone may say he certainly did everything in his power to show me the right way. In fact I don't know what I would have done without him, although my friend says maybe I did wrong to listen to him. But I told her if you don't take a chance how can you get anything out of life, and so I want Ken to know that because of his representations and willingness to stand good for me, those people we saw together have agreed to let me take over their boarding house and by the time you get this letter I will be in business myself. Ain't that swell?

Yours in sincerity,
Mrs. MURPHY.

P.S. - Don't forget to tell Mr. O'Brien about my boarding house. He can be my star boarder if he makes the pufftaloons.

* * * * * * * * *

Major F.H. Fitzpatrick, Commander of the Fortress, was touched to the quick to read in these columns that when our recent "Ode to a Bottle of Beer" Competition was decided, there was no BOTTLE to present to the winner, who had to be content with a couple of tins. "Who could wax lyrical over a mere tin" he enquired, (Well maybe we could ourselves at this very minute), and out of the goodness of his heart he produced a real dinky-die bottle of Abbot's Lager and presented it to Padre Morrison for competition in the Battalion. The bottle is actually here, lads, we gazed at it ourselves this morning for fully ten minutes, and of all the bottles of beer we've seen, this one is outstanding. We handled it's cool sides, admired it's translucent colour, smelt it carefully and long, and were even prepared at considerable self sacrifice to sample its contents, so that we could describe it to you properly. However, Padre (drat the man) thought we could take Major Fitzpatrick's word for it that it really contained beer, and the bottle remains there intact, with three sentries with fixed bayonets mounting guard over it, and the Padre's batman, with a Mills bomb in hand mounted guard over the sentries. The bottle will be presented to the Mud'n Blood who sends in the best "Tall Tale" by the 20th August. As many of the entries as possible will be published, but owing to shortness of time and lack of space it may not be possible to publish the entire lot prior to the closing date. You can send in as many entries as you like.

TODAY'S TALL STORY (Entered by Pte. Tom French, I Section):-

I was driving along Bardia Road when a Caproni cruising along at 50 ft. spotted me. He started to drop "Eggs" so I stopped the truck, jumped out, and neatly fielded an egg in my tin hat. I took it in my right hand (grenade fashion) and threw it back at the plane, but it did no damage as it exploded two feet short of the plane. I then got a spare tin of petrol, punched a hole in the bottom of the tin and threw it at the plane. I was more successful this time, as the tin landed on the left wing of the plane. I then struck a match and lit the stream of petrol coming from the hole in the tin. The flame ran all the way up to the plane and set it on fire. It crashed a mile or so away. I was later put on a crime sheet for wasting petrol.

ALBURY SCHOOL KIDS:

The RSM has adopted Kathlyn Grove as a "pen pal"; Cpl. Dick Fancke intimates that the name George Joynson appeals to his fancy, whilst Pte. Olly Bridges will in future be corresponding with I. Pankhurst. Cross these names off the list.

* * * * * * * * *

With regard to our Limerick last line competition, owing to the poor response to this, for which the Brigadier has donated the handy sum of 50 akers as a prize, the closing date has been extended to the 20th August. Hurry up and get your entry in right away. What a shame it will be if we collar the prize through having submitted the only entry.

BBC NEWS — 15th August, 1941.

Mr. Atlee speaking from London yesterday, made the momentous announcement that a meeting had taken place between President Roosevelt and Mr. Churchill aboard ship in the battle field of the Atlantic. It was at the request of President Roosevelt that Mr. Churchill set out, and during the three days they conferred, they discussed many problems, including the position in Russia, the Far East situation, and the future of such bases as Dakar. It was stated in New York that this conference between the leaders of two great Democracies, will be the turning point in the history of the war. Lord Beaverbrook who was present at the conference, stated that the two Nations were now even more firmly united, and were determined to continue the war. He went on to say that Britain needed food, tanks and planes, particularly bombers. We must remember that we are engaged in a struggle with an enemy who has been preparing for years to fight. America must send us as much as she can, and as swiftly as possible, under the lease and lend act. We have been using American Bombers over Germany and they have proved very successful. We have plenty of Tank Divisions and Tank Brigades, but in spite of this we want more. As regards food, we like and need bacon, beef, cheese and other food supplies, and we are eating much better through American efforts. So far we have received over 2500 planes from the US. Comment on this historic meeting is world wide. The Times says that news of the meeting will be warmly received in all Neutral and enemy occupied countries, and even in enemy countries themselves, where the people have not forgotten the taste of freedom. In Canada, the Prime Minister, Mr. McKenzie King, said that the declarations indicate a direct understanding between the two countries. The Egyptian Prime Minister stated that this great event would certainly have far reaching results. In Singapore, Mr. Atlee's reference to Governments associated with Germany is interpreted as a direct warning to Japan. Throughout the conference, the Russian Government was kept fully informed. German comments mainly consisted of angry outbursts and abuse, and referred to the meeting as the propaganda bluff of the two war mongers.

Fierce fighting is continuing along the whole of the Eastern front, from the White Sea to the Black Sea. In the Ukraine, the Germans have made sweeping claims, but it is thought that they must certainly be making some progress. They also claim that the Black Sea Port of Odessa has been surrounded, but this is denied by the Russians. The Russians admit however, that Kairovograd and Pirvomaisk in the Ukraine have been evacuated. Kairovograd is a fairly large town, and heavy fighting has been taking place there for the past few days. The latest German communique claims that the German army has reached its objectives, and that Herr Hitler has gone up to the front line, as the campaign is now almost finished. The Soviet Air Force has again been co-operating with land forces and has attacked enemy positions, and raided many enemy aerodromes. They claim that 74 German planes have been brought down and destroyed on aerodromes and place their own losses at 27 aircraft. A Russian ship operating in the Baltic, has sunk an enemy submarine. It is officially stated in Moscow, that in the heavy fighting on the Eastern front, Germany has so far lost one Tank Corps, eleven Divisions, and seven Regiments, and that twenty-one Divisions have lost more than half of their personnel. They state that the battle of Smolensk contributed in no small degree to these losses. From Singapore comes the news that powerful reinforcements for the Australian forces in Malaya have just arrived.

TOBRUK, 16th August, 1941.

Dear Editor,

Have just heard the glorious news that all you Mud & Bloods are in Tobruk. What a lovely time you must be having as I see by the papers here what wonderful conditions you live under, and what a lot of nice things you get to eat. My friend next door says she bets you are all bomb happy, and I do hope she is right as its such a nice thought to think of you all over there so happy and contented like, and I say just don't take any notice of them stuck-up dive bombers. Still, there is a serious side to this business, although I suppose you boys have never thought of that side of it at all, and think it is just one big lark. It isn't all play you know, and its just as well to remember that you are all over there to fight for those who have stopped behind. If you boys continue to play around the way you are doing, it might even be necessary for some of the fellas left here to have to go too. Someone told me that nearly every building in Tobruk is very loose, and I thought I would give you all a few words of advice about drinking and playing around with loose women. You know what its like when young lads get a skinful; they go looking for the first piece of skirt that is about, and I suppose Tobruk is like everywhere else where there are plenty of soldiers - a pub on every corner and sheilas kicking around all over the place. Well, the only way to keep the lads straight is to give them plenty of bromide, but be careful and don't make any terrible mistakes like my friend next door, who accidentally put the bromide in the star boarder's metho instead of her old man's, and he liked the taste of it so much that he won't drink his metho now without it, which is a very serious matter for my friend, the price of bromide being what it is. Am still feeling extra well. Hoping you are the same.

Yours in sincerity,
Mrs. MURPHY.

* * * * * * * * *

TODAY'S TALL STORY (Entered by Pte. W.D. Woods - Orderly Room).

A certain private, as his birthday approached, conceived the idea of giving a small party to one or two of his intimate friends. The Quarter-Master, Capt. Morrell, hearing of the event, sent for the private and asked him what he proposed to give them to eat, as he might be able to help out. The amazed and delighted soldier modestly ventured "If you could spare me a tin of bully beef and a packet of biscuits, I'd be more than satisfied, Sir." "What! biscuits and bully beef?" replied the QM, "no one in this Battalion will ever eat those whilst I'm QM. Try a few tins of this chicken and you'd better have some of this asparagus and celery to go with it. Oh! and here's some oxtail soup. I suppose you are all tired of tinned fruit, but I'm sorry I can't do better than these cherries and cream. Help yourself, lad, and don't forget, anytime you're short call in and see me." As the Mud'n Blood was staggering away under his burden the C.O. saw him and stopped. "I see by my diary it is your birthday tomorrow, lad. Sorry I have no beer, but if a coupla bottles of whisky would be of any use, drop in and tell my batman." Just then the Padre came rushing up and said "I hear you are having a party. If a dozen bottles of beer and some chocolate would be of any use let me know, but if you don't want them don't force yourself." Going back to his dugout he sent a note to his cobbers inviting them to the feast, adding a footnote enumerating what there was to eat and drink. Back came the unanimous reply "Sorry, can't come along, old pal, but Jimmy Rintoule is cooking the dinner tonight and we wouldn't miss it for anything."

* * * * * * * * *

One of the attached Tommy troops had occasion to visit our RMO with foot trouble - no, not that kind of foot trouble, he had an ingrowing toe-nail. Doc got busy with the clippers, and despite Tommy's protests, continued his inexerable way. Tommy thought he could do the job himself just as well, and with less pain, but the Doc was adamant. "Bet he has the best trimmed hedges in Australia," grumbled the scion of our motherland, cut to the quick as the Doc ignored his moans of pain and clipped busily away. However the old British habit of eventually blundering out of trouble persisted, as, having to visit the Doc for a further session two or three days later, he presented for the operation a foot so unbathed that the Doc, without a word, handed Tommy the clippers, and with averted nostrils, indicated that this time he could do the job himself.

BBC NEWS — 16th August, 1941.

It has just been disclosed in London, that the meeting between Mr. Churchill and President Roosevelt took place on the British Battleship "Prince of Wales". Following the conference, a statement was forwarded to M. Stalin assuring him of the joint assistance of both Britain and US in the struggle against the common enemy. We feel that we must not in circumstances fail to act quickly. Many shiploads of war materials have left our shores for Russia, and many more will leave in the near future. We suggest that a conference be held in Moscow to determine the best methods to aid Russia. This applies particularly to food supplies and war materials. The war goes on upon many fronts, and before it is over, there may be further fighting on fronts that may be developed. Lord Beaverbrook is already in Washington with the intention of discussing supply problems with representatives of the US. He also intends to visit Ottawa before returning to Britain. The US Secretary for War in a speech broadcast to the Army yesterday, stated that the World now faces a more dangerous threat to its peace than ever before. No American Expeditionery Force is being trained to fight overseas, but they are getting ready a force to defend US from any aggressor. He added that we have good reason to believe that Hitler may shortly take action against bases in Africa. In concluding, he said that the American Navy, Army and Air Force must be prepared to meet the enemy who may come from North, South, East or West. In replies to queries as to whether any American warships had fired on any enemy shipping, it was stated that not a single shot had been fired, and not an Axis flag sighted, and it is assumed that they are apparently keeping well out of the way.

On the Russian front, the great battle for the Ukraine is apparently still going on, but the Russian midnight communique makes no mention of this sector at all. It refers however, to fierce fighting all along the line from the Black Sea to the White Sea, with the Russian Air Force dealing out severe punishment from the sky to all German troops and aerodromes. Attacks on the Russian Capital by German aircraft last night were dispersed before reaching the City. A number of enemy planes were destroyed. The Germans likewise claim that when Soviet bombers attacked Berlin last night, none of them managed to penetrate to the Capital. So far there is no evidence that the Germans have reached their objectives in the Ukraine, but it is thought that the next few days will show just how successful the German effort to destroy the Russian Army in this sector will be. The Russians claim that the stubborn defence put up by their forces has succeeded in holding up the German advance, and that one of Germany's best Divisions has been annihilated. It is reported that the Finns have started a new offensive on the Northern front. Russian forces are stated to have counter-attacked vigorously in this sector, but as yet neither of these reports have been officially confirmed. That the German theory of a lightning attack against the Russians has been unsuccessful, is shown by the fact that Moscow is now preparing for a Winter war. M. Stalin on receiving the British and US Ambassadors in Moscow, asked them to accept his thanks for the offers of help received from both countries. The Turkish newspapers have given unanimous approval to the pledges to Turkey by Britain and Russia.

The Officer Commanding Australian Forces in Malaya, has announced that a large convoy of 31 transports has arrived in Malaya with reinforcements. He stated that these reinforcements were well trained and well equipped.

In last night's large scale attack on German Industrial Cities, over 300 bombers took part. It was one of the heaviest raids of the war, and considerable damage was caused. In spite of the large numbers of bombers operating, only 12 are missing. There was very little air activity over Britain last night. A few bombs were dropped, but there were no casualties and damage was only slight. German long range guns shelled shipping in the Channel yesterday. This bombardment lasted for nearly an hour.

There have been further street demonstrations in Paris, and yesterday, a bomb exploded in one of the city streets. The rioters have been threatened with death sentence, in an endeavour to stop the disturbances. As a result of sabotage, a 9000 ton food ship was blown up in a German Canal.

TOBRUK, 23rd August, 1941.

Recent adverse weather conditions, coupled with Battalion movement has prevented us from going to press for a few days, and has also in part prevented the issue of our special Anniversary Number. Shortage of paper also has contributed to the delay, whilst the dust storms encountered at our last location put our typewriters almost completely out of action. This issue is only brought forth under extremely unpleasant conditions, and it is hoped that any imperfections be overlooked by our readers.

It is proposed that all items contributed to our Anniversary Number be published daily in our ordinary issue, and at the end of a certain time these items will be extracted and forwarded to Alex for publication. Orders for this printed number will be taken as soon as the cost of printing same has been ascertained.

We re-produce hereunder copy of letter received by the C.O. from Brig. R.W. Tovell, E.D., D.S.O., on the occasion of the birthday of the Unit:

My Dear Colonel,

On the very memorable occasion of your Battalion's anniversary, I deem it a great honour to add my congratulations and good wishes. Actually, the recorded birthday of your unit is 1st July, but so vigorous and lusty a lad could not be born into this world without due pomp and ceremony, and the importance of his arrival required much preparation. Hence, it was 20th August before the nurse was able to announce to the somewhat agitated father that he had acquired a definite outsize in sons.

Whether I may be considered as Grandfather, or Godfather, I know not, but as his Brigadier I have every cause to be proud of him, who was formally christened 2/23, but is affectionately known as Mud'n Blood.

We survivors of the Great War are extremely jealous of the traditions then created and have watched with anxious eyes the progress of our successors in title. In accepting the onerous duty of carrying the torch lit by the original 23rd Battalion, A.I.F., you and your boys undertook a tremendous responsibility, but I am proud to be able to assure the old Mud & Bloods that twelve months of service has proved that their trust has not been misplaced, and that in your unit the spirit which they engendered is being faithfully reproduced.

May you go forward to even greater heights of achievement.

(Signed) R.W. Tovell, Brig.
Comd. 26 Aust. Inf. Bde.

MESSAGE FROM THE C. O.

Men of the 23rd - "Albury's Own" - Mud & Bloods!

One eventual year has passed by; a year crowded with intense endeavour on your part. Upheaval; changed ways of life; hard and rigorous training; battle; From the first day I addressed some of you at Albury, and later others from Colac, until today, you have worked hard for your country. Sometimes the going has been tough, and certainly it has been fast all the time. I am proud to have the honour to command you. I have often said this, and shall never cease repeating it. Today, many of the original faces have gone; old friends have passed on, but new ones are amongst us and are new no longer. The 23rd will go on and on until victory is ours. Already we are veterans; our men have honoured the name "Mud & Blood" with decorations. Yesterday, the C. in C. offered congratulations to members of the 23rd. We have fought some bloody battles; we shall probably fight more, but we shall fight with the spirit of the 23rd Battalion A.I.F., which is second to none. Our motto is a good one - AUT IN VENIAM AUT FACIAM (We find a way or make one), and we are surely finding a way. I congratulate you one and all in the building up of the unit to it's first birthday. Remember, you are making Australian history!

(Signed) Bernard Evans, Lt. Col.

BBC NEWS — 23rd August, 1941.

  The latest Russian communique reports that yesterday, stubborn battles were continuing along the whole of the Eastern front. They also claim that the German offensive against Leningrad is not making any headway. This appears to be correct, as reports from German sources show that an easy victory is not expected. The Russian communique goes on to say that Battalion after Battalion of reinforcements are pouring into Leningrad. Further South, the Germans claim that on the Central Front, very heavy losses have been inflicted on the Russian forces. The assault in this sector seems to be on a very narrow front. The German drive against the Ukraine like the offensive on Leningrad, seems to be making little progress. After two months of heavy fighting on the Eastern front, the Russians have summed up the German losses, and have issued the following figures:- Twelve German Tank Divisions, 26 Infantry Divisions, and 9 Motorised Divisions have been completely annihilated, and the Russians claim that they can give the identification number of each Division. They also claim that two million Germans have been killed, wounded or captured, and place their own losses at 700,000. Enemy tanks destroyed total 8000 as against Russian losses of 5800; German guns 10,000, Russian losses 7,500; German aircraft 7000 as against the loss of 5500 planes. The Russians in this survey, also recall that at the end of the first month of fighting on the Eastern Front, the Germans claimed to have opened the road to Moscow, Leningrad and Rheat, and to have completely destroyed the Russian Air Force. The Russians have officially announced that during enemy raids on Moscow, 736 people have been killed, and 3500 injured. It is stated in Moscow that although the Germans have captured a number of Russian towns, the Russian army is still intact, and resisting strongly, and that the German man-power is steadily dwindling. A very late Russian communique announces that 32 German aircraft were shot down on Wednesday. A large fleet of German transports, carrying reinforcements to their forces in the Ukraine, has been attacked by the Soviet Air Force. At least two transports were sunk, and a third was set on fire. Two torpedo boats were also sunk. The remainder of the convoy was forced to return to a Rumanian Port. All Russian aircraft returned safely from this raid. The Chief of the British Military Mission in Moscow has testified to the excellent morale of the Russian troops. He also stated that close collaboration between the Russian land and Air Forces has proved most successful. He also said that rain had fallen in the Smolensk area, and pointed out that this was very welcome, as it would seriously hamper the enemy's movements, and would strain the long German lines of communication to the utmost. It was stated in authoritative sources in Washington, that War orders for one thousand million dollars had been placed by Russia in the US. It is expected that 10% of this order will be on its way within a few weeks. Russian requests for Aviation petrol from US, have been readily answered, and large shipments have already left. American built planes ordered by Britain, have been released to Russia, and some of these have been delivered.

London. The First Lord of the Admiralty, Mr. Alexander, in a broadcast yesterday, revealed that 190 Allied ships, of which 50 are French, are operating side by side with the British Navy. He added that Allied Merchant shipping has been reinforced by the addition of 480 Dutch vessels, 720 Norwegian, 92 French and 32 Polish ships. The Norwegian Shipping Minister declared that the Atlantic shipping position has been considerably improved during the past two months, and that this was due to the vigorous methods being used to offset the U-Boat menace.

Very few enemy aircraft crossed the English coast last night, and no bombs were reported to have been dropped. One enemy plane was shot down into the sea. British fighters yesterday carried out a series of offensive patrols against enemy shipping. A number of ships were attacked by machine gun and canon, and hits were scored. Enemy aerodromes were also attacked. Two enemy fighters were destroyed, but none of our aircraft are missing.

It has been announced in Paris that all Frenchmen under arrest in occupied France will be held as hostages in the event of any further attacks on German officers. This statement was made after the killing of a German Officer in Paris.

TOBRUK, 24th August, 1941.

On the occasion of the Birthday of the Unit, Padre Morrison has sent the following message to all Mud'n Bloods. During the period he has been with the Battalion, the Padre has been a true friend of all the boys, and has earned their affection and esteem through his untiring efforts to further their welfare. In this moment of our rejoicing therefore, we have particular pleasure in conveying his message:-

To my comrades of the 2/23rd:

What a thrill to think we are all one year old already, and I can extend my congratulations to you all. It has been a momentous year, and one that I hope we shall all look back upon with satisfaction when we return to the peace of our own beloved land.

I am very happy to think that, by a chain of circumstances beyond human control, I have been privileged to serve with so distinguished a unit, and share your lot, whether of strife or pleasure; to be of some small use in your troubles and joys.

I am glad also to notice how wonderfully you have shouldered the immense responsibilities placed upon you; never flinching in the hours of danger; rushing to accomplish tasks almost impossible to man, but which are recorded   in the annals of the Battalion as events which saved the situation. Faced by a foe whose strength and courage was unknown to us, you battled valiantly and held your own. I am also led to believe that the severe lessons you have learnt in warfare have helped to maintain and even improve your behaviour towards others; that when we are relieved from our present position we will go down to Egypt not "to wallow in the flesh-pots", but bearing in mind that the Mud & Blood colours assert our determination not only to defeat our National enemies, but to assure all that the wearers will behave as gentlemen amidst the representatives of the varied races of the world. It is with some pride I recall the courageous fortitude of all who have served under these colours, and I join with you in remembering those of our comrades who have made the supreme sacrifice - May they rest in God's keeping.

May God's richest blessings rest upon those who have the responsibility of leadership, and upon those whose privilege it is to obey. May we all spend our next birthday in a happy reunion at a place of peacefulness.

(Signed) Roland Morrison, Padre.

* * * * * * * * * * * *

Neath glaring sun and brassy skies
    In lonely grave, but hallowed spot,
Many a former comrade lies,
    With us no more, but not forgot.

Today we strut in all our glory,
    When but for those who've gone before,
Perhaps there'd be a different story,
    With birthday glee for us no more.

    So Mud'n Bloods, in today's joys,
       Just pause and think of pals we knew,
    They're still with us in spirit, boys,
       Perhaps just ahead of me and you.
BBC NEWS — 24th August, 1941.

The latest Russian communique states that fierce fighting is continuing along the whole of the Eastern front. The fighting is most severe in the Centre sector near Smolensk, and in the vicinity of Odessa. There seems to be some backing for the report that the German drive on Leningrad is for the present making little progress. In a broadcast from Moscow yesterday, it was stated that Leningrad was threatened by a terrible danger, and it is therefore, the sacred duty of every Russian to defend the City to the last. In some sectors, vigorous counter attacks have been launched by the Russians, and in the last 24 hours, they have re-captured 9 villages. There is little solid news from the Ukraine, but the Russian communique gives some details of the fighting round Odessa. They say that great losses have been inflicted on Rumanian forces in that sector, and claim that some of the Rumanian Regiments have suffered losses of up to three quarters of their strength. The Germans claim that their troops have penetrated to within 9 miles of the town, and have broken the key positions defending the town. They also state that the battle for Odessa is taking place in terrific heat. The Head of the British Mission in Moscow described the Russian counter attacks that he witnessed some few weeks ago. He said that there were large numbers of Russian tanks, and more Russian aircraft in the sky, than there were German. He also said that the traffic control behind the Russian lines was excellent, and he was greatly impressed by all that he saw. It is reported that the Russians have placed large orders for war materials with the US for delivery next Spring. These orders are said to include large quantities of tanks, some of which are to be flown to Russia in tank carrying aircraft.

The US proposes to build $250,000,000 worth of tanks, and these are to be manufactured under joint co-operation of Britain and US. The Ship Building Yards and Dry Docks at New Jersey, have been taken over by the US Government. This was announced yesterday, and work is expected to be resumed within a few days. The strike at these great yards has seriously impeded the Ship Building Industry of America, but it is hoped that they will soon be working at full speed again. A spokesman in Washington has stated that if the Vichy Government allows German control of any French possessions in Western Africa, the US will seize this territory, and hold it by armed force.

The Japanese Ambassador in Washington yesterday conferred with Mr. Cordell Hull. He said afterwards, that the gap between US and Japan's relations in the Far East, must be bridged. At the conference, problems in the Pacific were discussed, but no agreement was reached. It has been announced in the US, that licences will now be needed for the exportation of goods to Japan and China. The restriction on the exportation of goods to China, is to prevent goods in occupied China falling into Japanese hands. It was also stated however, that there would be no restriction on goods to China through the Burma Road. The Japanese Air Force last night carried out a very large raid on Chungking, and extensive damage is believed to have been caused.

The biggest delivery of food and arms from the US to Britain, was shipped on a convoy of over 8 miles in length. The convoy included passenger liners, and the passengers have stated that the trip was a real pleasure cruise, as swimming, and all deck sports were allowed. As this convoy was crossing the Atlantic, the Battleship "Prince of Wales" with Mr. Churchill on board, passed through the lines of shipping, which had moved into position for the inspection.

The US has promised that their troops will be withdrawn from Iceland at the end of the war. The Prime Minister of Denmark has expressed his appreciation of this announcement. A British merchant ship has arrived safely in Port after an eventful voyage, during which a German submarine was encountered and sunk. In Germany, Nazi newspapers are warning the people against British raids which are expected to be very heavy during the next few months. The D.F.C. has been awarded to a Victorian and an Auckland Pilot. It has been announced in Portugal that motor tyres will in future be rationed.

TOBRUK, 25th August, 1941.

We are indeed sorry to say Good-bye to our genial Adjutant, Capt. Freddie Kiel who leaves the Battalion tomorrow for other parts. However our regret is tempered by the knowledge that what is our loss is distinctly his gain, as he goes to a Staff School in Haifa for four months, during which time he will imbibe (amongst other things) additional knowledge to fit him for a higher appointment. Capt. Kiel is extremely popular throughout the Battalion, but nowhere more so than in the Orderly Room, and no greater words of praise could be uttered than to say that he exacted maximum efficiency from the staff, and at the same time retained his place in their affectionate esteem. On behalf of all Mud'n Bloods, and of the Orderly

Room personnel in particular, we congratulate Capt. Kiel on his selection for this important school, and trust that it will be the forerunner of a still more brilliant military career. We append hereunder a message from him:-

"On the occasion of my impending departure from the Unit, I would deem it a favour if you would pass on the following message to all ranks.

"It has been my honour and privilege to have been Adjutant of this unit, designated 'Albury's Own', from its inception to the present time. I have watched with intense interest and ever increasing pride the amazingly rapid progress of this Battalion from its birth to its first birthday, and its development from a mere infant which could hardly even march, to a fighting machine which Albury, the town of its birth and adoption, might well feel proud. There is now that profound comradeship and perfect understanding between all ranks which can only be found amongst men who have experienced the severe hardships, terrific strains, and ever present dangers of active service.

"My parting grieves me to no small degree, not because I am leaving Tobruk, that could never be, but because it will mean separation from my firm friends and comrades. I desire to express my sincere thanks and appreciation to all ranks for their valuable assistance and co-operation given me at all times during my tour of duty as Adjutant of Mud'n Bloods.

"Wherever I may go, whatever my lot, I will closely follow every action and every movement of Albury's Own, and will share with you your triumphs and disappointments, as this will always be my parent unit. I wish you all the best of good fortune, and in parting, commend to you the watchwords - Loyalty and Co-operation."

(Signed) F. E. Kiel, Capt.

* * * * * * * * * *

No doubt you will be wondering how our various competitions are progressing. We refer to the Flea Catching Contest; the Tall Story Competition; and the Limerick Last Line Competition. These were all scheduled to close on the 20th August, but recent unexpected moves have slightly gummed up our works. In tomorrow's issue, we hope to be able to advise you further as to these various activities.

Recent advice from our Welfare Association discloses that those womenfolk of ours are doing a wonderful job - and how well they know us and our needs. By dint of persuasive means we know nought of, they

have succeeded in having donated to us the magnificent total of 4,800
bottles of beer - equivalent to about six bottles per man. The generous
donor is, we understand, Mr. Grant Hays. That he wins both Derbies and
the Melbourne Cup this year, will we know, be the grateful wish of all Mud
& Bloods after hearing the above news. However, there is a fly in the ointment (there nearly always is in these cases). The A.C.F. are of the opinion
that such a large number of bottles is too much to go to any one unit, and
our Association is hotly debating the point with them. We hope the ladies
win, and in fact, judging by the splendid results they have up to the present achieved, our money is on them. We will advise you later, as soon as
we learn what happens. In the meantime, just think of those 4,800 bottles
of frothy, cool, thirst quencher, lying in some murky store in Melbourne,
whilst here we are, in the heat and dust of Libya, with our tongues literally hanging out. Colonel Eugene Gorman, have you no bowels of com-
passion?

BBC NEWS — 25th August, 1941.

*The broadcast by Mr. Churchill yesterday, has met with World-wide
comment. An idea of the American opinion, can be gleaned from the following remarks. The Chairman of the House of Representatives in Washington, said that throughout this speech, new hope has been given to the
enslaved people of the World. Another speaker stated that if Americans
are compelled to fight, they will not prove less responsive than they have
been in the past. The New York Times states that Mr. Churchill spoke as a
prophet who has seen his prophesy fulfilled. America and England have become full partners in a war to end aggression. Comment in Canada is unanimous, and it is stated there that when the full story of the conference
is told, it will probably go down as a milestone in the History of the World.
In London it was stated that the decisions emerging from the conference,
were most impressive at first sight, but what lies underneath the surface
would probably be even more so. Lord Beaverbrook, the British Minister
for Supply, who has been in the US, has returned to England. Shortly after
his return he had a discussion with Mr. Churchill.*

*The latest Russian communique shows very little change in the sit-
uation on the entire Eastern front. Fierce fighting is taking place about
200 miles from the Black Sea in the Ukraine. German communications
will be strained to the utmost in this Sector, as the river there is over a mile
in width. Although this is mentioned in the Russian communique, it is
stated in London that it does not necessarily mean that the Germans have
reached this Sector. In other parts of the Ukraine, Russian forces have*

been counter attacking. One Cavalry Regiment counter attacked fiercely, re-captured a village, and killed 700 Germans. Heavy fighting is also reported in the Northern Sector near Finland. The German drive on Leningrad from the South, is still handicapped by heavy fighting in Estonia, where German and Russian heavy tanks are engaged. About a hundred Russian pillboxes are also holding out in this Sector. Inside Leningrad, the peoples army is daily increasing in size, and are undergoing special training. All streets in the city are being prepared for barricading. The Russians state that the armament factories in the City will be able to keep the peoples army fully supplied. A War Correspondent in Moscow, says that in the Sectors where the Russians are counter attacking, the battle fields are strewn with dead and wounded. He also states that the Russian Air Force is operating brilliantly, and has given valuable aid to the ground forces. From Berlin comes the news that the Spanish Blue Division is expected to arrive at the Eastern Front very shortly. This Division has been undergoing severe training in German camps. The Russian Ambassador in London yesterday said that he would like to express his thanks for the magnificent assistance given the Russians by the Royal Air Force, whose repeated attacks on the German industrial centres has hampered the Germans considerably.

Yesterday the RAF continued its offensive patrols over the Channel and Northern France. Very few enemy fighters were encountered, and all of our fighters returned safely. During the past week, 5 enemy bombers and 30 fighters have been destroyed. Our losses for the same period being 16 bombers and 30 fighters. It is noted that during the same week last year when the enemy had the offensive, their losses were 241 aircraft as against 61 British. A British trawler has just returned to Port after an eventful voyage, during which it shot down a twin engined bomber which attacked it. When the ship was attacked, the Ack-ack gunners held their fire until the plane was almost on them, and then opened up, scoring a direct hit on the plane which burst into flames and crashed into the sea. Britain has just issued the latest casualty list of the British Merchant Navy. 134 lives have been lost through enemy action, and these include 4 Masters, 3 Chief Engineers, and 3 Stewardesses. The Tokyo newspapers are once again attempting to stir up more trouble, and have brought up the old claim of encirclement. They state that Japan will not stand by while Britain and the US stir up provocative action against her. The Canadian Government has banned the export of coal to French Territories. The extent of sabotage in occupied France is steadily increasing, and 5 cases of sabotage have occurred in Paris alone. As a result, the Vichy Government has called on all rail-

*way employees to put a stop to these outrages, and put the cause down to
lack of food and Communist movements.*

TOBRUK, 28th August, 1941.

The recent move of the Battalion to its new sector has, to a certain
extent, interfered with the progress of our various competitions, but today
we are able to announce that "B" Company are the winners of the 500
cigarettes - first prize in the Flea Catching Competition. The respectable
total of fleas they accumulated was augmented by the allowance of 200
fleas each for the five I-ti prisoners they captured, plus all the fleas found
on the said prisoners. In case other Companies feel aggrieved, we might
mention that the little I-ti runt that they brought in was not allowed for
in full, and we docked their total by 50 fleas. Incidentally, both in our
last habitation and in our present one, we are quite confident that we possessed winning qualifications, but the little blighters would only come out
at night, and we expended, in rather futile manner, the battery of an electric torch catching them. The grand total of fleas accounted for by "B"
Company, everything in, was 16,183, and this figure has been audited and
found correct by the firm of Louse, Louse and Delouse, although the Principal, Sgt. Les Allen, was somewhat perturbed by the fact that during the
counting, one of them got away. Now it is up to the O.C. "B" Company
to decide in what manner he will dispose of the 500 cigarettes, which the
Padre will hand over in the course of a few days.

Now, to submit a few more entries for the Limerick Last Line Competition. As you know, the limerick was -

> There was once a young Mud'n Blood
> Who came from where cows chew the cud,
> > When he got to Tobruk
> > They made him a cook
> ....

Entries received are:-

1.   He's so good he's been sent to the stud.
2.   Though the cow couldn't cook even a spud.
3.   No one's seen such a "Mess" since the Flood.
4.   And the rest of them all came a thud.
5.   He's now dishing out stew in the mud.
6.   Now his plans have been nipped in the bud.
7.   And the stew that he makes tastes like mud.

8.   Now his plight would wring tears from a spud.
9.   With some mud and a spud he's no dud.
10.   And his efforts bring tears to the eyes of a spud.
11.   And his pies could be used as a stud.
12.   What a husband-to-be in the bud.
13.   Even a cow wouldn't chew for the dud.

This contest will be decided today, and the winner announced in the next issue.

In announcing our Tall Story Competition, for which a prize of a glorious bottle of beer was donated by Major F.H. Fitzpatrick, we in error referred to the genial Major as "Commander of the Fortress" - (Padre, consider yourself admonished for giving wrong information). Our error has apparently got the Major into a spot of domestic strife, as revealed in the following letter:-

"Your publication having made me Commander of the Fortress, I can tell the G.O.C. where he gets off; but I want your assistance in framing an .effective and convincing reply to the undermentioned cable received from my better half - "GOOD NEWS. WHEN DO I DRAW EXTRA ALLOTMENT?"

"Congratulations on your paper. If I, as an outsider, can appreciate it so much, then how much more enjoyable it must be to members of the Unit. Good Luck.

Yours Sincerely,

(Signed) F. Fitzpatrick, Major,
Commander Tobruk Sub-Area.

P.S. -   For the information of your lads, it was a lone bottle, and the
         B..............at Base have NOT got a supply of beer.

Incidentally, the Major has forwarded his entry for the Tall Story Competition, which will be printed in tomorrow's issue. Don't forget - send in your entry today - the Competition will close shortly.

BBC NEWS — 28th August, 1941.

A report from Iran, states that the Shah has accepted the resignation of the Iran Cabinet. They will however, remain on duty until another Cabinet is formed. It is stated in Turkey that a peaceful settlement of the conflict in Iran is close at hand. Another Turkish report states that the

*Shah is expected to expel all Germans from the country, with the except-
ion of a few indispensable technicians, and that even these technicians will
be expelled as soon as they can be replaced.*

*Further reports state that there will be no peace in Iran until the
British and Soviet Governments are satisfied that the menace of Nazism
has been removed. Following the advance of British troops into Iran, 600
tons of wheat have been taken across the frontier in an effort to ease the
food situation, as the people are nearly starving. The Moscow radio states
that Russian troops have captured four more towns in Iran, and have now
advanced over 100 miles from the Russian frontier. The Russians, it is
reported, are still advancing, and are meeting with no opposition whatever.
A Cairo report states that the British advance is being covered by the Royal
Air Force, and that in the south, our troops have penetrated 40 miles within the frontier.*

*The latest Russian communique states that stubborn fighting con-
tinued throughout yesterday along the whole front. No mention is made
by the Russians of the German claims to have advanced still further, and to
have captured the Leningrad - Moscow railway junction. In the Ukraine,
the Germans are also making new claims. The Russians there are fighting
fiercely, and there is no doubt that the Germans are being made to pay
dearly for any advance that they make. The Russians state that after one
battle in the Ukraine, they buried over 600 German dead. An official report from Moscow, states that Guerilla troops operating behind the Finnish lines, are hampering the enemy's activities considerably.*

*According to an official German News Agency, British aircraft were
over South Western Germany last night. Our bombers are also believed to
have been attacking the invasion ports on the French coast, as many explosions were heard, and large fires seen from the English coast. Yesterday
many squadrons of our Spitfire and Hurricane fighters made a series of
sorties over the French coast. Ten enemy fighters were shot down, but
eight of our aircraft are missing. The Fleet Air Arm, and the Royal Air
Force have combined in a series of attacks on shipping in the Mediterranean, and targets in North Africa. Bardia was raided, and a number of enemy
ships hit. Railway yards and camps were bombed at Benghasi, and attacks
made on troop concentrations in Libya. A convoy in the central Mediterranean was attacked by our bombers, and direct hits were scored. One ship
was left sinking. From all these operations, including Iran, only three of
our aircraft are missing.*

The shooting of Pierre Laval in France, is stated to be part of an immense plot to undermine the Vichy Government, and it is thought that a number of assassinations may be attempted. It was stated in Paris after the incident, that the only way to check these activities, is by force. Laval, who is now said to be out of danger, was wounded in the arm and in the body. The Vichy News Agency reports that after he was shot, Laval continued walking, got into his car, and was driven off. Later, he rang up his wife to assure her that he was not badly injured. A short time after the shooting, a man was arrested, and later admitted that he had fired five shots at Laval.

Striking figures of the increase in strength of the fighting forces of the Free French, on the occasion of the first Anniversary of the Free French Movement, have been announced by General De Gaulle. Their fighting strength at Sea and in the Air, is at least double that of three months ago, and the number of troops has increased from 35,000 to 60,000. The Free French Merchant Fleet has also increased from 60 to 100 ships.

Mr. Fraser, the New Zealand Prime Minister has accepted an invitation to visit Canada. He is expected to spend five days there, and will visit New Zealand airmen at their training camp.

TOBRUK, 29th August, 1941.

We do not know who was the most pleased - the men of the Battalion or Major Birch, when the latter returned yesterday to the ranks of the "desert rats of Tobruk". The popular Second-in-Command confessed that his sojourn in Egypt was, contrary to all our fond hopes, not altogether an enjoyable episode, and in fact, he was quite homesick for the old familiar Mud'n Blood faces. At the time of his departure, the Battalion was suffering an acute shortage of chocolates and cigarette papers, and the Major went to extreme lengths to ensure that he did not return empty-handed. He broke practically every rule and regulation in the Army and Navy, but finally succeeded in having a couple of cases placed on board the destroyer. Imagine his annoyance and chagrin therefore, to discover that the cases were quietly pilfered during the time he was below decks. Well, we were not there to see it, but we can well imagine the picture as the Major went into action. Single-handed, he took on the whole of the destroyer personnel, and eventually, from numerous nooks and crannies of the ship, the contents of the cases were recovered more or less intact. For this valiant action, (the first time in history that a Mud'n Blood has engaged a vessel of His Majesty's Royal Navy), we bestow upon Major Birch the coveted award of Mud'n Blood Medal.

Not for a minute would we think of criticising the judgment of a superior officer, and especially that of the C.O. (We'll get on!), but, in announcing his decision in the best last line in the Limerick Competition, we are still amazed how the C.O. could possibly have overlooked our own entry, which surely was obviously the best in the whole competition. However we have always been the victim of circumstances, and can only stand aside and congratulate Pte. Vic Bridges of "C" Company for his winning entry. The completed Limerick reads as follows:-

There was once a young Mud'n Blood,
Who came from where cows chew the cud,
    When he got to Tobruk,
    They made him a cook,
With some mud and a spud he's no dud.

In welcoming Capt. Bill Haworth back to the Unit, our mind is taken back nearly nine months ago when, prior to our embarkation, the C.O. in humorous vein referred to our trip as a "Cook's Tour". Strangely enough, Capt. Haworth was almost the only one to take this injunction literally, and he has just returned to the Battalion after many interesting sightseeing tours around Egypt, Palestine, Lebanon, and Syria, and has now come along for a look at "Hell Spot Tobruk." We envy him the many interesting journeys he has made, but are consoled by the fact that, when the Unit ultimately leaves Tobruk, Capt. Haworth will undoubtedly insist upon remaining behind for another six months, so that he may catch up.

Make a note of this Mr. Hitler! Here is a true "V for Victory" story. This morning the NCO's of a certain platoon in this Unit were lined up and advised by their O.C. that one of them would be detailed to return to Australia for instructional purposes. The news was received in stony silence and no enthusiasm was displayed. The O.C. asked each of the seven NCO's assembled if he was prepared to return to Australia, and six of them politely but firmly declined. The seventh was doubtful, and only consented when informed that it was mandatory that this unit provide an NCO. No! they are not all "bomb happy", nor are they suffering from desert madness, but rather they came over here to do a job, and that job has not been completed yet. So their attitude is completely logical, and only typical of the determination of the A.I.F. in general, and this unit in particular, not to waver until Victory is to hand. So, Mr. Hitler, not only cannot you drive the "rats" out of their holes, but they will not even leave them with the consent of their own Authorities. Beleaguered? Laugh that off!

Medical Professor: Give me three reasons why Mothers' milk is the best.

Nervous Student: (1)   It is the most nourishing.
                   (2)   The cat can't get at it.
                   (3)   Er, Er, - It comes in such attractive containers.

BBC NEWS — 29th August, 1941.

The latest Russian communique mentions heavy fighting in the Ukraine, and states that their troops in that Sector have evacuated a town on the South East of the Dniepner River after terrific fighting. The occupation of this town proved very costly to the Germans, as the Russians defended every house, in every street. Streets in this town were mined, and these destroyed many enemy tanks. The Russians estimate the German losses in this battle to be over 5000 Officers and men, 40 tanks and armoured cars, 10 guns, and over 100 trucks and lorries. The Head of the Soviet Information Bureau in Moscow has announced that Russian troops have destroyed the great Dniepner Dam, which was built during the first Five Year Plan. He stated that this great sacrifice was made to prevent the Dam from falling into enemy hands. It is expected that the blowing up of this great Dam will release flood waters on the surrounding country. According to Russian reports, the Germans advancing through the Ukraine, will find nothing but waste land and derelict farming vehicles, as everything of any value at all to the invader has been destroyed. The German drive on Leningrad appears to have speeded up, and according to German reports, their troops are now only 30 miles from Leningrad. The Russians claim that during the last two days, their Air Force has destroyed 78 Nazi planes. They also claim that a number of German ships have been sunk in the Baltic.

Fighting has ceased in Iran. This was announced in London last night, and it was added that the Germans there are at present taking refuge in the German Legation, where all papers are being burnt. The decision of the Iran Government to stop fighting was warmly welcomed in London. Royal Air Force bombers escorted by fighters, carried out another big daylight raid on Rotterdam. There was very heavy fire from the ground defences, but in spite of this, our bombers scored direct hits on ships, wharves and dockside buildings. Our fighters also carried out a number of offensive patrols during the day. From all these activities, 7 bombers and 5 fighters are missing. It has been announced that 140,000 tons of enemy shipping was put out of action last week. The Fleet Air Arm and the RAF have again carried out extensive raids in the Middle East. Three ships were sunk in the Mediterranean, and Tripoli and Benghasi were heavily raided.

After the raid on Tripoli, the fires started could be seen for a distance of 130 miles.

President Roosevelt has announced that a Board will be formed to put the entire United States Defence Programme on a new footing. The Board will handle all problems of supply, and is expected to accelerate the entire re-armament programme. A number of prominent US Statesmen are on the Board, including Mr. Simpson and Colonel Knox. The composition of the British Industrial Mission was announced this morning, and is expected to arrive in US next month.

An increase in the strength of the Canadian Army from 10,000 to over 200,000 in two years, was disclosed by the Minister for Defence yesterday. He said that there must be no slackening in our efforts. All we have done up to date, is to avoid losing the war, and a time will come when we have to take the offensive, and we must prepare for that. Mr. Cordell Hull has stated that the United States may hold a series of talks with Japan with a view to discussing the difficulties arising between the two countries. It is reported that Pro-Axis forces in Japan are once again trying to stir up trouble. M. Molotov's reply to the Japanese protest as to the manner in which American goods are being delivered to Russia, is warmly received in China. Following on recent reports that Japanese troops are being concentrated near Malaya, it has been announced that Chinese forces have delivered strong attacks against the Japanese, and have captured two towns, and demolished Japanese defence works.

From Australia comes the report that Mr. Menzies has handed in his resignation, and is to be replaced by Mr. Fadden. There is nothing to show that Mr. Menzies will accept the position of Minister to London, but strong requests have been made for him to do so.

The German News Agency has just announced that British aircraft dropped bombs on Western Germany last night. A Netherlands passenger liner of 11,000 tons, which was serving as a transport, has been sunk by enemy action in the Mediterranean. A report from Paris states that Pierre Laval is as well as can be expected, but his condition will be in doubt for a few days.

TOBRUK, 30th August, 1941.

S/Major Bill Morrison of HQ Company, is running a Sweep on the Melbourne Cup. First Prize 100 Pounds; Second 25 Pounds; Third 18 Pounds ten. Already he has more than 230 entries, and as there are 287 nominations, he requires another forty odd entries at 50 akers each. Everyone will get a horse, and the money is being paid into Battalion funds, it having been made the responsibility of the Pay Sgt. to see that the winners receive the prizes. In the event of casualty or evacuation of the person concerned, the prize will be paid into his pay book. Bill is anxious to fill the Sweep, so asks that Company Clerks advise him of all entries from the respective Companies. The money can be collected next pay day.

A couple of days ago an observation pole was erected in a fairly conspicuous position during the night. Next morning Jerry saw same, and commenced wasting valuable ammunition trying to knock it over. His 32nd shell did the trick. The following night the pole was re-erected, and there was spirited betting as to how many shots he would have to expend before toppling it. Pte. Len Wenborn took 10 akers off us, greatly to our disgust. Why we always fall into these "sucker" roles we cannot imagine, but he offered the liberal odds of 10 to 1 no hit in 20 shots, and 5 to 1 no hit in 30 shots. Our reasoning proved, as always where our bets are concerned, completely unsound. We argued that after his first day's practice, Jerry would be on the mark. Alas! yesterday he had 117 shots, and the pole still stands. We have a feeling we have been taken on, but cannot just locate how or where, and I. Layem Wenborn is going around with such a self-satisfied grin every time we encounter him that we seriously suggest to the C.O. that he detail Len to sit at the top of the pole during the next shoot, so that he will be able to count the various shells more accurately. However, our chagrin is somewhat tempered by the calculation that Jerry has expended some 169 shells on these useless poles up to the present, and at an estimated cost of 5 Pounds per shell his expenditure has already been considerable. We understand that the C.O. is ambitious to make him waste at least 25,000 Pounds of ammunition before we get tired of re-erecting the poles. We will keep you advised of progress.

Lieut. Norm McMaster swears that the following is true, and believe you us, when Norm swears he swears with conviction and vehemence. We suggested that he enter the story in our Tall Tale Competition, but he treated our advice with contumely. Anyhow, to get on with the yarn - In our front areas, Jerry's FDLs are only a few yards away from ours, and without being too technical, through induction, etc., the various telephone conversations of both sides are often picked up. The other night Norm was conversing with someone and discovered that he was talking to a Jerry who spoke very good English. After polite exchanges anent the weather and the state of each other's thirst, Norm laid his cards on the table - "What about giving us a go at dinner-time tonight," he asked, 'Every time we start to eat you commence chucking stuff at us, and its getting a bit thick." "What time do you eat?" enquired Jerry. "Nine-thirty." "Why, that's the same time as we ourselves eat," replied Jerry, "If you call it off tonight until 10.30, we'll do the same." "Right, it's a bargain," replied Norm. And for that night both sides supped in peace. IF it's true, we suggest Norm be immediately despatched to Berlin, a la Hess if you like, and we are quite sure that some satisfactory peace settlement would ensue, whilst even if things went wrong, no great harm would be done, as we would be relieved from having to listen to any more such "McMasterisms" for the duration.

TALL TALE ENTRY:

Bluey was watching two Minniwerfers coming through the air to either side of him, and did not know which way to duck. They exploded similtaneously, and in coming to, he found his eyes had set, each looking to the outside instead of straight ahead. The hospital doctor sent him back to Australia as being unfit for further duties, as he could not see straight, and privately hinted that Bluey was a good thing for a pension. The Medical Board at home duly examined him, and the President said to Bluey - "I'd like to help you, but although your vision is distorted the sight is good, and we cannot recommend you for a pension." This bitter blow was too much for Bluey, who was banking on a pension, and he broke down and wept; and such was the position of his eyes that the tears ran down his back. On seeing this the President said "It is alright lad, you'll get a pension. I'll certify you are suffering from Bacteria."

(Entered by Major F. Fitzpatrick)
Commander Tobruk Sub-Area.

BBC NEWS — 30th August, 1941.

Yesterday's GHQ communique issued in Cairo, stated that at Tobruk, enemy artillery was more active than usual, and that several dive bombing attacks had been made on the town during the day. It is however reported that no damage was done. Our own artillery at Tobruk was also active, and successfully engaged a large enemy working party. In the Frontier area, there has been some exchange in artillery fire. At Jarabub, enemy aircraft dropped a number of bombs causing slight damage to the Senussi Mosque.

A communique issued from Iran states that after the Iranian order to cease hostilities, Indian infantry operating in the Southern sector, con-

tinued to advance up both banks of the Karain river. The South West advance of the Russian forces is still continuing. It is stated that our policy is to assist the Iranian people by providing foodstuffs to lessen the general shortage of food in the country. Already arrangements have been made to send about 700 tons of wheat into the area occupied in Southern Iran. It is also reported that despite the cessation of hostilities, it is presumed that British and Russian troops will continue their advance, mainly in order to protect installations and troops who have been stationed there.

Royal Air Force bombers operating on Thursday night, successfully carried out heavy attacks on Duisburg, where several fires were started, and explosions observed. Ostend Docks were also attacked, and a number of other targets in Western Germany were also bombed. From all these raids nine of our aircraft are missing. Ten enemy fighters were destroyed by our fighters during a series of offensive operations on Friday. Ten British fighters are missing, but the pilot of one is safe.

A report from Tokyo states that the Japanese Government is adopting certain labour measures, aiming at full mobilisation of the Nation's man power. This will affect one hundred million men. The Japanese Premier, Prince Konoye, has sent a personal message to President Roosevelt, giving Japan's views on outstanding issues affecting the situation in the Pacific.

The latest Moscow communique states that there were no fresh important developments reported from the Russo-German front last night. Stubborn fighting is still continuing along the whole front. The Germans yesterday claimed the capture of Talin, the Estonian Capital. The Russian Air Force claims the destruction of over 500 German aircraft during the past week, and state that their own losses for the same period were 262 planes.

It has been announced in Berlin, that Hitler and Mussolini held a meeting at Hitler's headquarters between August 24th and 28th. They were accompanied by their army and political chiefs. A notable absentee was the Duce's son in law, Count Ciano, who it is stated was prevented from attending by sickness.

New York. Mussolini's latest Battleships are already destined to stick in Port. Reports reaching America show that lack of materials has caused Italy to halt the construction of two 35,000 ton Battleships, namely the Impero and Roma.

TOBRUK, 31st August, 1941.

"A" Company can claim the proud title of "First in last out." In training days they were the first to start any new scheme on guard. On active service they were the last out of Barce; first in the Battalion to go into action; and first into the line. They have been well and ably represented in every stunt of any size carried out in the Battalion. Good work, "A" Company. Keep up the tradition!

(Major P.E. Spier - O.C. "A" Company)

A REO'S ANGLE:

"Be ready to move at 0400 hrs." "Where are we going, Adjutant? Up the line?" "You're going to join your unit." The last sentence I repeated to myself almost incredulously. "You're going to join your unit." YOUR unit! For months and months we Reo's had been thinking of nothing else. "When can we get to our unit?" "Plenty of time; you won't be so anxious when you get there." But no amount of warnings as to the dangers and discomforts of the battle line could quell our urgent desire to become members of our Battalion, and cease to be just spare parts. At last, however, it had really come, and the journey on the fast little destroyer, the entrance into the harbour at night, the disembarkation at the broken stone pier, and the trip down the escarpment in motor transports in the dark (mine toppled over, by the way), are memories which will be clear to me 50 years hence (I hope). From the Staging Camp next day, by M.T. again (no one walks in this war --- much) to Battalion HQ, where the C.O. said a few words of welcome and encouragement to us. Not too much; not too little. He made us feel at home immediately, and told us to forget that we were Reo's, and to remember only and always that we were members of the 2/23rd. If we played the game he said, the old hands would welcome us as one of themselves. And he was right. I don't want to "get on" or to "crawl", but I must say this. The old hands didn't adopt a patronising air towards us, or harp on what they had been through, but instead they quickly adopted us as it were, and helped in every way to make us feel part of the show. Members of the original 2/23rd, whose collective anniversary we now celebrate, we your reinforcements, thank you and want you to know that this is our earnest wish - May we do our duty well while we are in this unit. If the time comes when we must face the ordeal, may we conduct ourselves as gallantly as you did, and thus earn for ourselves the envied cognomen which is surely yours - VETERANS.

(Lieut. H.J. Boas - "A" Company)

(Lieut. H.J. Boas - "A" Company)

* * * * * * * * *

The Assyrian came down like a wolf on the fold,
  His cohorts all gleaming in purple and gold,
The flash of his spears was as brilliant as stars,
  He didn't know the first bloody thing about camouflage.

I shot an arrow into the air,
  It fell to earth I know not where,
That's ten of the damn things I've lost that way.

(The bomb-happy genius responsible for the above did not add his name -
  but we suspect his initials are Boulter - "A" Company).

Thank Heaven "A" Company can face misfortune. We just about
had the flea competition in the bag (or rather bottle), when we drew an
unlucky card from Fate. At least somebody drew the cork from our bottle,
possibly to replace the one from his water bottle which had served for the
rats' supper. All we saw on arrival was an empty bottle and a track leading
thence through the cook-house, and heading south-west. On investigation,
a witness confessed that he had passed a vast concourse of hurrying fleas,
one of whom, on being asked, had said "We're going back to Poppah!" The
witness had noticed that the informant and his companions were large,
blonde, and inflicted with Oxford accents. If only we had a little more
time, a fighting patrol would be despatched to re-collect our entry. We are
sure that it would win hands down. Wow! I mean, Wah!

(Lieut. H.J. Boas - "A" Company).

Here is an authentic story of a recent happening at a large business house in Melbourne. At present in Australia, whenever you ring up, you hear "V for Victory - number please." One morning the phone went in said business office, and the girl said "V for Victory - Who do you wish to speak to?" The man on the other end said "Oh! N for Nuts," and hung up.

(Pte. I. Arthur, 8 Platoon, "A" Company)

Though we haven't caught a prisoner,
    Since the days when out west,
I'm sure that Mud'n Bloods will say,
    Well, 8 Section did it's best.
For we had our share at Barce,
    And at Derna too, I fear,
Then on May the Seventeenth,
    We thought our end was near.
But then we came up smiling,
    With the other Mud'n Bloods,
And thanked the Lord and enemy,
    For meeting so many duds.

(Cpl. W. Brownrigg - 8 Sec. "A" Coy.)

It has occurred to me that you may be able to find a corner in your Anniversary issue for a word from we "Poms." Some of us have had long connections with Aussie, and others (myself included) much shorter, but I know I am speaking for all of us when I say that we have most certainly been made to feel at home in the Unit. For our part, we have been able to spread abroad the doings of "Albury's Own" both in London and throughout the Provinces, and our doings are followed there with as great eagerness as at home. Let me say in conclusion, that the incidence of birth has nothing to do with the question when it comes to a showdown, and that we are proud indeed to be able to claim that we are as "fair dinkum" as the next man.

(Lieut. R.B. Boulter - "A" Company).

BBC NEWS — 31st August, 1941.

This mornings Soviet communique reports fierce fighting along the whole front and claims that 66 German planes have been destroyed. It is estimated in London, that roughly about 5 million men of Germany's Army's total strength of 7 million, are now engaged on the Russian Frontier, and that roughly 90% of the Red Army is also engaged.

A large force of British bombers raided Manneiheim and Frankfurt on Friday night. Docks and Railways at Le Havre were also attacked. Five of our planes are missing from these raids. In January last, British bombers made 1000 raids or sorties, but these figures jumped to 3900 raids in July, when 4400 bombs were dropped. The average of fighter sorties has jumped from 200 to 1500. RAF carried out powerful raids on enemy aerodromes in Greece and Crete on Thursday night. 30 tons of high explosive and incendiary bombs were dropped causing considerable damage to hangars and dispersed aircraft. On the same night, the Fleet Air Arm bombed Bardia. From all these operations, all of our planes returned safely. Few enemy planes crossed the English coast last night, but one was shot down.

A British evacuation vessel is shortly calling at Japanese Ports, and British Consulates are again advising Britishers to take this opportunity of leaving the country.

It is stated in London that eight more Frenchmen have been guilotined in Paris for participating in Communistic demonstrations and espionage against the German Army.

It has been announced in Cairo that the remainder of the British and Imperial Officers who were wrongfully removed from Syria after being made prisoners, have now arrived safely in Beirut. Fighting in Iran has now ceased everywhere, and the situation in areas occupied by our troops is fast returning to normal. Our troops have now reached Kermanshap.

CHAPTER 8

TOBRUK, 1st September, 1941.

Well, Wouldn't it? That briefly describes our feelings in the last fortnight. Here we are, mostly all new to this game of war, and we have met with so much success that perhaps there is a tendency to think ourselves no longer "cow-cockies." However, that feeling is not really apparent. I who am also a beginner to this Company routine, feel that I would not swap this Company for any other. We are very proud of our Corporal Hayes and Private Bennett, and thank them for showing us how it can be done. We are proud of the way all work has been carried out right from the start. "B" Company hasn't finished yet, and we sincerely hope that success will be ours again. We have yet another success coming to us, and that is the Flea Competition. We consider that it is a certainty.

(Signed) K.O. Neuendorf, Lieut.
Acting O.C. "B" Company.

We read in the Albury Border Mail about a stirring appeal put forth to the manhood of Australia by W.O. Ulbrick - "Come back with me to Bardia and Tobruk!" Tobruk, the place that was, and now 'a has been;' a city of gay romance, with wine, women and song, but we did not have the satisfaction of partaking of these pleasures, although we experienced many novelties that we did not know existed. What fun we have swatting flies all day long, and then a battle royal every night with the fleas, to see who does have ownership of the bed. We can even walk down the street now without suffering the pangs of alcoholic remorse every time we pass a pub. And, above all, even though we are not on speaking terms with the neighbours, we do not have to suffer the indignity and insolence of hearing their scathing remarks. So when we partake of all the little pleasures that come our way over here, we are able to understand a man having the enthusiasm to send forth that stirring appeal - "Come back WITH ME to Bardia and Tobruk." But.............Will HE?

(Pte. J. Smith - "B" Coy. Ord. Room)

Overheard at a Company Inspection:

Officer: I like the cut of that man over there; he has the look of a man that would have the firmness of character to go on doing his duty in the face of ingratitude, criticism and ridicule.

Company Commander:
    Yes! that is Casey Jones, the Company cook.

(Pte. D. Crane - "B" Company).

A Mud'n Blood, whilst in Barce, tried to bargain with a Libyan woman for some eggs, but after calling the eggs everything from eggwu to musphe, could not make the woman understand. But the Digger at last, in desperation, squatted down, pointed to his stern, and made a mark on the ground like an egg. The woman smiled her understanding; took the soldier by the arm, and led him into the LITTLE HOUSE. It was bully and biscuits for tea.

Extract from a letter home -

"The trouble here is that we have always got to go and visit Jerry and Musso; they never pay us a visit. Some of our visits are just visits; others get a bit argumentative, and in the hustle and bustle we grab a prisoner or two and get back to our own back-yard. There are other times when things get really damn hot, and we have to run for it. When I say run, I mean RUN, and believe me, the bullets and shells here are FAST, and if a man lags behind and lets them catch up with him, he's asking for trouble."

* * * * * * * *

Since occupying our post in this sector, we have been greatly troubled by rats which consistently persist in performing hand springs on the boys faces at night. Naturally, this has caused them to seriously consider some means of bringing the rats to understand that this sort of thing cannot be tolerated. Now, one Pte. A. Carey, considers he has devised an ingenious method of bringing them to their destruction. This is his idea, which incidentally, caused the death of two rats last night. Firstly, these pests were noticed by him making a regular exit between two sandbags, and running straight through and down to the concrete floor, so he arranged a piece of string with a slip-knot loop and hung it from a nail just in front of the rats' hole. This is where the creature makes its final exit, for as it pokes its head through the loop and heads downwards, it is startled to find itself suspended in mid-air, squealing like one of Musso's minions. Now the only trouble is that the incessant squealing also keeps the boys awake, so it will be appreciated if anyone can advise him of a better system without infringing on patent rights.

Another person found that these pests were affectionately taking to his stock of postage stamps, apparently finding the gum to their liking. However, he is happy again, as he found that by placing the stamps in an envelope marked "SECRET", they were no longer frequented. What! of course its true.

(Lieut. G.W. Lukey - "B" Company)

After partaking of that glorious repast given in honour of the Battalion's birthday, the boys are now looking forward with more confidence to the future, and hope that the next celebration can be held as a re-union, at a rendezvous somewhere back home. On behalf of this Company, I offer sincere thanks to those of the Administration side who made the splendid repast possible.

(Lieut. G.M. Thirlwell - "B" Company).

BBC NEWS — 1st September, 1941.

The latest news of the great Russian battle, which is now in its 11th week, shows that the Russians are counter attacking strongly. These counter attacks are claimed to have broken through the German fortifications, and were launched after a heavy artillery barrage. The Germans themselves admit these attacks, and also report heavy counter attacks in the South. The Soviet Army Newspaper, says that the Germans are facing exhaustion, but the Russian Army is getting stronger, and is gathering its forces for a heavy blow against the enemy. There is no news of fighting in the Leningrad area. The Soviet Air Force has attacked enemy infantry positions, mechanised columns, and lines of communication. They claim to have destroyed 125 German aircraft on Friday.

Yesterday, RAF fighters kept up a non-stop offensive all day over the French Coast, but very few German planes were sighted. Extensive bombing raids were also made, and one flying fortress carried out a daylight raid on Bremen. The pilot stated that the attack was made from a great height and they had a perfect view of the Port. The bombs dropped right on the target. No ack-ack fire was encountered, and no enemy fighters engaged. August has been a raid free month for London. In the Middle East, our airmen are hitting the enemy just as hard as in the West. Yesterday, they delivered a low flying attack on Benghasi from a height of 50 feet. Shipping was also attacked, and the Navy and Air Force have accounted for 12 more enemy ships. Four of them were attacked by our bombers off Tripoli, and 25 tons of bombs were dropped. Torpedo planes accounted for another two off the coast of Sicily.

The presence of Anti Vichy movements in France were admitted by Marshal Petain yesterday, who said that they were pro-British and anti-German. The settlement of all outstanding military problems in Iran is expected within 48 hours. It is reported from reliable quarters that Iran has been asked to grant permission for goods to be transported through Iran to Russia. Other terms are stated to be as follows:- Iran to be declared forbidden territory for all Germans, with the exception of the Legation Staff and a few technicians. Meanwhile, Moscow announced this morning that Russian troops had captured another series of towns in Iran. In London, the call up of all women is to be speeded up. Women selected after interviews, will be given the opportunity of joining up one of the auxiliary movements, but if they decline to do this, they will be detailed for duty.

A new Polish Army has been formed to serve in Russia. The Commander of this Army has stated that the first of his men to join, were now on their way to a training camp. He stated that Russia will fight until both Hitler and Germany are crushed.

TOBRUK, 2nd September, 1941.

Breaking away for the nonce from publishing Company contributions in order to keep up-to-date with local gossip ("C" Company efforts will be published tomorrow), we have first of all to announce the winner of the Tall Tale Competition. Major Birch kindly consented to act as Adjudicator, and in his wisdom chose the effort of one, Pte. Bill Woods, as entitling him to be classed the biggest liar in the Battalion. Therefore, to Bill goes the coveted bottle of beer, and will we be hanging around when the prize is handed over - We'll say!

We conceived the bright idea of running a competition entitled "Leave to Alex", the winner of which will be the person who states briefly and humorously, in not more than 100 words, the best reason for being granted a week's leave to that fair City. We put the proposition up to the C.O., and he has stated that he will use all his efforts to see that the winner of the contest is granted a week's leave, although of course, for obvious reasons, this cannot be guaranteed. In any case, the sum of 50 akers has been donated by a recent prize winner - Pte. Vic Bridges - as prize for this effort. However, here at last is a prize worth striving for - Just think, a week's glorious cut-up in Alex, with wine, women, and song for as long as the old pay-book holds out. We give hereunder the first entry received in this Competition:-

Dear Alexandria:

Can you imagine being blown up by a shell? That happened to me some time back, and being considerably knocked about around the stomach region, was so I am told, left for dead. However, Aspro Jack happened along, and seeing a sheep grazing nearby, transferred the whole of the sheep's intestines into me in lieu of my own. I recovered, but lately have had pains in the little Mary, and on seeking expert advice have been told to move nearer to a Maternity Hospital, as I am about to lamb.

Uncomfortably yours,

AKORANGEPIP.

* * * * * * *

In spite of the recent edict against gambling, we are pained to confess that the nefarious practice still persists, and in fact, is even encouraged by that stalwart of the ring - Pte. Len Wenborn, who not being satisfied with relieving us of ten akers the other day, has just enticed us with a couple of bets we couldn't resist. To place beyond indisputable argument any later developments, we put on record the fact that we have taken 75 akers to 5 Kindergarten for the Caulfield Cup, and 60 akers to 5 Lucrative for the Melbourne Cup. In this particular case we hope Len lives up to his business motto - "I layem: I payem." His stand is just north of BHQ Orderly Room, but we are quite sure that he will have brought down his prices considerably, as by now he has perhaps realised that the two horses mentioned above are favourites for the respective races, and at the present time are being quoted at prices probably about half or less than those he so generously offered us. Ha! Leonard, we scent our revenge!

There is a little private contest going on in the Battalion between two men that not many outsiders know about. We refer to the moustache growing struggle between Lieuts. Maurie Wilton and Dick Boulter. Since the dignity of fatherhood descended upon Mr. Wilton, his moustache has flourished to a degree beyond comprehension, and although Mr. Boulter has not, as far as we know, the same compulsion to provide something for the kid to swing on when he gets back home, he already sports a hirsute adornment on the upper lip, the ends of which could be tied together at the back of his neck. Go to it lads. Now that we have mentioned the matter, Len Wenborn will probably quote prices on the ultimate result. But our money is on the blonde Englishman!

The decoy observation poles that were erected, continue to do their good job of wasting enemy ammunition. Yesterday, we are informed by the I Section, approximately 68 shells were hurled over at them by Jerry. Not only are these poles causing wastage to the enemy, but they are doubtless preventing the said ammunition from being directed at other points where they might conceivably be doing some damage. Keep it up Jerry.

Reference Major Spier's para in a recent issue claiming "A" Company as "First in, last out" both in training and in battle times, I would draw to memory certain facts that he has apparently overlooked. The cognomen earned in training days "The Marching Dons" was altered at Tobruk to "The Fighting Dons." On arrival of the 23rd Battalion at Tobruk, the safekeeping of the town was handed over to Don Company, under the leadership of Capt. G.I. Malloch, M.C. When the Benghasi Derby started, Don Company marched from Tobruk to the Perimeter between Derna Road and the sea, and formed a front line defence whilst the inner defences of Tobruk were put in order. Who turned Jerry's onslaught at the Perimeter with his AFVs? - the "Fighting Dons"; and Tobruk still stands. Surely one weary Captain will never forget where he rested his little head after the sprint from Barce. The Fighting Dons have delivered two large scale counter attacks, one of which was one of the most successful in the perimeter. Has any other Company in this Battalion a better record?

(Pte. E. Stuart - I Section - Ex Don Coy.)

BBC NEWS — 2nd September, 1941.

The latest communique reports fighting along the whole front. The German radio admits widespread Russian counter attacks in the Ukraine, in which the Russians are using gunboats to help them in raids across the Dniepner River. The Russians claim that the total number of German cas-

ualties in fighting up to date is 2,500,000, including 1,000,000 dead. They also claim that between August 1st and 22nd, the Germans lost twelve Armoured Divisions, 37 Infantry Divisions, 8 Motorised Divisions, 17 Infantry Regiments, and several Storm Troop Divisions. Russian planes are reported to have raided Berlin, Koenigsberg, Danzig, and Memel, dropping incendiary and high explosive bombs. One Soviet plane is missing from these raids.

A communique from Cairo reports that the RAF bombed Tripoli Harbour on Saturday night, causing large fires. The Fleet Air Arm was also active, and bombed dumps near Bardia. Hangars and aircraft were hit in RAF raids on aerodromes on Rhodes. One RAF plane is missing.

A communique issued from London states that on Sunday night, the RAF attacked Krupps Armament Works at Essen, and targets at Cologne and Bologne, and laid mines in enemy waters. On Sunday afternoon, a Flying Fortress bomber raided Bremen Harbour, and met with no opposition. It is also reported that record figures for the aircraft industry were achieved last week.

It is stated in Simla that first contact has been established between Russian and British forces in Iran. The British forces entered Hamadan on Saturday, and found the situation peaceful, and British residents safe and sound. From Moscow it is reported that Russian troops in Iran have been ordered to stop their advance, in view of the Anglo Soviet negotiations with Iran. Another report from Simla states that General Wavell has telegraphed to General Quinan, Commanding British and Indian Forces in Iran, congratulating him and his troops on the successful outcome of Iran operations.

Mr. Churchill has sent a message of congratulations to Air Marshal Sir Richard Peirce, Commanding the Bomber Command, for recent successful daylight attacks on enemy territory.

It is reported from Paris, that two men accused of attempting to establish Communist Societies, were sentenced to 20 years hard labour, and that two women were sentenced to 12 years hard labour for distributing Communist propaganda.

Mr. Churchill has cabled his congratulations to Mr. Fadden on his appointment as Commonwealth Premier. From Australia, it is reported that the Army Minister, Mr. Spender, may shortly leave for Malaya to visit Australians stationed there.

A Cairo communique reports a considerable amount of enemy shelling in the Frontier area. At Tobruk, enemy artillery activity was less than usual. In the Wolkefit area of Italian East Africa, a small party of Patriots supported by a few light guns, successfully attacked an enemy position, capturing a few prisoners.

TOBRUK, 4th September, 1941.

"C" Company's contributions towards our Anniversary Number are published below:-

Dear Mother:

You ask me which is the bigger nuisance - fleas or bugs. Well, Mum I'm not too sure, because they are both crook, but the fleas certainly provide plenty of exercise. It's amazing the knots you can tie yourself into when one flea is parading up and down your spine, and his big brother is nibbling the calf of your left leg. It's better than ju-jitsu. Of course bugs are easier to catch, but when you have caught one you wish you hadn't, because the smell, Mum, is something horrible. You would think even a bug would have more self-respect. I mean, none of us is perfect, and after six months in the desert, one can't be sure, but I did have a hot bath on January 26th, and I have had several swims since, so you can't say I don't try. Of course they say even your best friends won't tell you, but what I say is that anything that smells like that hasn't any friends. Our Colonel has a stunt on in which he reckons one I-ti is worth 200 fleas - well, anyone who has spent a night in a dugout with 10 fleas will tell you how silly that is - 10 fleas can cause a lot more trouble than 200 I-tis. And you have to go looking for I-tis, while the fleas come looking for you; so you can guess how much the Colonel knows about fleas. Anyway, Mum, it doesn't matter which are the worst - they are all fair bug-gers.

Your affectionate son,

RUPERT.

We, of "C" Company (firm, but not often) supporters of Mud & Blood, have been grossly insulted by the aspersions cast upon our beloved Sar/Major, Ken Wiseman. He himself denies knowledge of the said Mrs. Murphy, and demands vindication. On the night in question, in company with a Staff/Sgt. well known amongst those stalwarts behind us (well behind us) in every action, he was busily engaged in elbow bending in a popular hotel just outside Albury. If the said Staff/Sgt. were questioned regarding the doings that evening, and the whereabouts of a certain key, that locked a certain door and then disappeared (much to the Sar/Major's gratification), we feel sure that he could not help but substantiate this alibi. A full (perhaps overfull) Captain, and a beauteous blonde might also be called upon to give evidence - but we fear it would be superfluous. What about it, Staff?

WE WONDER —

Little things that puzzle us are listed below, and any solutions to our problems will be appreciated. No notice (except of a hostile character) will be taken of replies from cooks, signallers or the ration truck personnel.

What "D" Company saw that caused the "stand to" the other night: Why "C" Company was not notified of the "stand down" until the small hours of the morning; and, adding insult to injury, who was the author of the foul rumour that "C" Company started the whole shemozzle?

Who the lads were who took a bearing on the moon as it poked over the horizon in order to bring "the artillery to bear?"

How BHQ, who rave about the quality of the meals served to them, always manage to have the largest eaters amongst their personnel attached to the forward Companies?

What are our chances of breaking our record of "18 men in the Jaffa Jail" when we next get leave?

(18 Men in the Jaffa Jail - What a schemozzle?)

Where these damn flies go in the wintertime - so that we can go somewhere else?

Who has had a nightmare in which the whole of the following have featured at one and the same time - Dust, dirt; sand, sun; flies, fleas; chits, chats; bugs, beetles; bully, bacon; and, of course, beer, no beer.

ITEMS OF NEWS GATHERED HERE AND THERE —

That Scotsmen are roaming the streets of Melbourne today looking for the Free French women.

"Look, Snowy—Free French!"

That a housemaid was recently awarded the V.C. for bringing down 10 Jerries before breakfast.

That when a strange gun was heard during a recent artillery barrage, a dashing young Loot remarked "It must be a 6 inch How". And it turned out to be a 15 inch gun from the Navy. Wouldn't it?

CAN ANYONE REMEMBER THIS? —

Scene in "C" Company lines at Dimra - 2300 hours.
Planes were raiding EL KANTARA - only four hundred miles away. The light turns red - loud banging on kero tins - whistles blowing - men shouting. A voice (louder than the rest) "Come on, "C" Company NCO's, get your men out. How are you going to control men in action if you can't control them here." And into the slit trenches we go - with tin hats and RESPIRATORS. Whose was that voice? And where is it's owner now?

BBC NEWS — 4th September, 1941.

Moscow - German boasts that Nazi forces are 15 miles from Leningrad are not confirmed, and Leningrad's defences have been thoroughly organised by Marshal Vorosholiv, and are expected to immobilise the larger German forces for many months. Russians destroyed 11 of 70 German aircraft which attacked Soviet aerodromes near Leningrad. The latest Soviet communique says fighting continues along entire front. Thirtynine German planes are claimed to have been destroyed, as against 27 Russian aircraft.

London - The Air Minister said yesterday that the RAF are now inflicting on Germans and Italians, greater shipping losses than they are inflicting on us. In July, we damaged or destroyed 92 ships in the North, Adriatic, and Mediterranean Seas, totalling nearly 500,000 tons. British shipping losses in July were the lowest for any month for more than a year.

Frankfurt and Berlin were the main targets of the RAF on Tuesday night. Industrial buildings were attacked in Berlin and large fires were left burning. Mannheim and Ports of Ostend and Dunkirk were also attacked. Enemy activity over Britain was very slight, and no casualties are reported. Two ack-ack guns were put out of action in RAF raids on Tripoli Monday night, when Benghasi was also raided. Fleet Air Arm attacked aerodromes in Sicily. One of our planes is missing.

A British submarine followed, and successfully attacked an enemy convoy proceeding down the Libyan coast to Benghasi. Two large schooners were sunk. One ship thought to have been sunk in a submarine attack off Sicily. British submarines also attacked shipping in approaches to Benghasi harbour.

Lord Beaverbrook will head the British Delegation on joint Anglo American Mission which is going to Moscow to discuss material aid to Russia.

In a message to GOC Middle East, General Dill says that as we enter the third year of the war, the Army can look with pride upon what has passed, and with confidence into the future. From Singapore, it is reported that strong Indian reinforcements have arrived there. General Mackay, the new GOC of Australian Home Forces, discussed the Middle East war position with the War Cabinet and members of Labour War Council. General Wavell has disclosed that there are well over 100,000 Indian troops serving abroad, and that the Indian's total fighting forces are approaching the million mark.

Simla - British and Soviet Commanders in Iran operations, met on Tuesday at Kazvin, 100 miles north west of Teheran. It is reported in London, that Anglo Soviet negotiations with the Iran Government in Teheran are still continuing.

TOBRUK, 5th September, 1941.

Hereunder are Don Company's contributions towards the Anniversary Number:-

Dear Editor:

Do you remember how we used to recite at school "How we brought the good news from Ghent to Aix," where somebody, it doesn't matter who, rode up on a horse all lathered and sweaty------? Well! that's something like the condition this message will turn up to you. Now, if the poem went "How we carried the good brews from Alexandria to Tobruk," we wouldn't worry about the sweat, or even worry about who the devil Alexandria was; whether she was a North African Venus or a Southern Italian Venerable.

Something worries me, Mr. Editor! It is this - Regulation 7001, sub-para IV, line 3, says that I may not praise any unit. Therefore I can only run the show down - and if I do that I'll forfeit my leave in Beirut. Your imagination can grasp that my wishes are thwarted both ways, and though I'd like to sing the praises of the men of the 23rd, and of "D" Company in particular, who have marched and fought and cursed and laughed and suffered and died and held and stormed and held again the British line, and in doing this, have by their valour enshrined our name in the esteem of other men, and in our hearts forever implanted three words that will do us, through thick and thin; through hell and heaven; through gain and loss; through life and death; three words - MUD AND BLOOD - but, you see, I cannot do that here. Suffice it then, for me to say - Many, many happy returns, and offer from Don Company to our fellow comrades in arms felicitations and good wishes for another great year together.

(Signed) G.F. Urquhart, Capt. OC Don Coy.

Oh! Jovial Hour; Thou joy so long awaited,
    We lift the brimming cup to thee,
We pour the wine - give thanks, those of us fated
    This first recurring day to see.

Then up with the cup! Down with the wine!
    Raise high the mirth and jollity,

For in this glowing hour divine,
  We toast our Anniversary.

The "Old Man" spoke, quaffed down the flood,
  The gath'ring echoed "MUD and BLOOD."

(Lieut. R. K. Reid - "D" Company)

It is a far cry to the Albury Showgrounds enclosure and the green fields of Bonegilla, but thought of them revives wonderful memories of all sorts - not the least of which is one associated with that word cry - "Swing those arms, Don Company," which was a familiar phrase in those days, and later in Dimra, but it built more than we knew then. That was the period of the "Red Horse Shoe", which the Dons held so long that it even appeared amongst the Q's gear here in Libya, but there is a rumour that he committed it to the earth one April morning lest it fall into enemy hands - or was it a question of space?

Yes! What memories are stirred at the first Anniversary of the Battalion, or shall we say - the Regiment, to embrace all in the way of tradition, loyalty and institutionalism that belongs to that word! We may have said something about the "tie of the Regiment," but, lurking in the corner of the mind, is some thought that this particular article of adornment was taboo to O.R.'s. We recall last winter when recruits from Training Battalions at Albury and Colac looked over the initial officers of the 2/23rd and wondered with whom their destiny would be cast. The allotments proved happy ones, and soon Don Company settled down to its own corporate existence, and in the months that followed, many associations blossomed · into firm friendships that have now been tested and cemented by the touch of danger. Looking back over the year, there have been many changes in personnel. We will always remember with pride and gratitude J.J. Egan, W.T. Evans, G.R. Greckie, G.A. Johnson, G.H. Osborne, J. Spencer and E.V. Wallis, who have given themselves in the cause of freedom and justice they came to further. Some who were with us at the first now serve the A.I.F. in other Units; a few are engaged in other sections of this Battalion, and we see them from time to time, while others of the Company are away sick or wounded, and not a few are prisoners of war. Our complement has been made up by men who have become one of us, and now call the 2/23rd Battalion "their Battalion," but when peace comes again - as it will - all will be gathered into our Company and our peace "State" for reunions and celebrations will put our "War Establishment" in the shade.

Space prevents recounting the various activities and successes of individual members of this Company, so I can only conclude by giving utterance to the thought that we enter a new year with a familiar and trusted leader, and who knows what tales of achievement there will be to tell in the second Anniversary Number.

(S/Sgt. A.P. Reynolds - CQMS "D" Company).

BBC NEWS — 5th September, 1941.

Neither the Russian or German communiques make any specific mention of Leningrad, but the Soviet Press Chief stated that it had developed into an immense bloody battle. The Germans have been held beyond the outer defences of the City, and they are suffering heavy losses. Berlin last night was claiming that Leningrad had been completely cut off, but this is denied in Moscow, where it is stated that the rail service is still open to the City. One Nazi spokesman said that it is still not clear to what extent the German Army is willing to go for the capture of Leningrad. Moscow reports that a combined air and sea attack was made on enemy shipping in the Baltic. Two transports were badly damaged and went aground. The Leningrad Volunteer Force is stated to have shown great skill and courage in the great battle for the City. Official news shows that the Finnish Army has not penetrated beyond its former Frontier, and that here they are meeting with heavy Russian resistance. In the centre sector, the Germans claim to have captured the key railway junction betweenKiev and Moscow. The Russians claim that a number of German attempts to cross the River Dniepner have been beaten off. The Germans while attempting to cross the river were caught in the light of many flares, and suffered very heavy casualties. In the South, the Rumanians have also suffered very heavily. It has been announced in Moscow that the first shipment of American oil, including 95,000 barrels of aviation petrol, has arrived in Vladivostok. According to the German radio this morning, Russian bombers were over Berlin last night.

Once again RAF bombers and fighters spent the day over the Channel and occupied Europe. The Docks at Rotterdam and Cherbourg were the main targets, and bombs were seen to make direct hits. During the raid the escorting fighters accounted for 11 enemy fighters. Our losses were 7 fighters and 1 Blenheim bomber. A Flying Fortress also carried out an attack over Germany, and on returning, was attacked by two enemy fighters. The Fortress immediately climbed rapidly, and left the fighters far below. The plane returned undamaged. In most of our fighter sweeps, fairly strong opposition was encountered. In the Middle East, South African pilots have distinguished themselves, and 5 Italian planes have been shot down. The Fleet Air Arm has carried out an attack on a strongly escorted convoy off Sardinia. Our planes attacked in two rows of three, and their torpedoes were launched from as close as a few hundred yards. One ship was probably carrying ammunition, and this was blown up, and two others were badly hit. The convoy then became completely disordered. One ship made a complete turn and nearly rammed the ship behind it. From this attack, all of our aircraft returned safely. The United States Navy Department has announced that a destroyer of 1090 tons was attacked with torpedoes by a submarine, on her way to Iceland. The torpedoes missed the destroyer, which immediately dropped depth charges.

Mr. Fadden, the Commonwealth Prime Minister, has stated that he will announce the name of the Australian Minister to go to London within the next 24 hours. In the Far East, the Japanese have evacuated a town on the Coast, which is now occupied by the Chinese troops. In explaining this loss, the Tokyo radio states that the Port was not important. It is announced in Washington that the production of Military aircraft was higher in August than for any other month this year, but it is not stated how many were sent to Britain.

M idst the heat, the trials, and desert dust,
U nder the blue and cloud specked Libyan sky.
D irt begrimed, but still defiant of the lust
A nd threats of those who sit outside and try
N azi methods, in a vain effort to retard
D etermined men, who stand inside on guard,
B lessed with a carefree attitude towards life,
L aughing always at the end of each day's strife.
O r maybe watching the bombing of the town
O f Tobruk, and wondering why that alien clown,
D oes not seem to see, the old red white and blue
S till flies, and that this time he'll not get through.

(Pte. V. Firth - Sigs Platoon HQ Coy.)

TOBRUK, 6th September, 1941.

> If a few words of praise in your paper I'm allowed,
> To have formed and commanded HQ Company I'm proud.
>
>   (Major R.E. Wall - OC HQ Company)

> If our efforts don't please in this Souvenir Issue,
> Remember, the paper is hard and not tissue.
>
>   (Cpl. F. Henderson - HQ Coy. Ord. Room)

> Take the Pyramids and divide by two,
>   Sun, moon and stars, and a kangaroo,
> Mix this fine lot, and steam till hot,
>   And at half past two there'll be news for you.
> The Pyramids say, that the sixteenth day,
>   Of the year next May, will be Armistice Day.

> Although the metre gives us fright,
>   We hope like hell the Major's right.
>
>   (Anonymous)

I've been reading in some papers just sent to me from home,
   The stories that were written by a writer on the roam,
About a lot of coves who came from what is called "down under,"
   To a land of hectic pleasures and good things one scarce could number.
Now, this is what rotates me, Strike! They think a bloke's a goat,
   To sit and read such "spieling" and take it on the coat.
Of course, a digger makes the best of every place he finds,
   We're doing fine, but we're the ones to write the paper lines.
Not reporters who catch aeroplanes, and come here for a flip,
   Instead of living with us in the bowels of a ship.
We may look fine in summer shorts and famous digger hats,
   But we live in deep-dug holes and are known as "Tobruk rats."
It seems this Tourist visited the Canteens day by day,
   And found them well stocked up with goods, but that's just by the way,
For when I go to purchase stuff, with chips I have to borrow,
   I hear once more the words "All gone - come back again tomorrow,"
There's something about Comforts - now this is past a joke,
   Especially when I want a smoke, but can't because I'm broke.
And so I read a lot of guff that fair gives me the pip,
   For we've seldom seen a comfort since we started on the trip.

         (S/Mjr. W. Morrison - CSM HQ Company).

We've given of our very best, in the sector on the west,
  Night and day, we've fought and prayed, and passed a bloody test.
Many months have come and passed, battles fought and won,
  Each show revealed not one would yield before a Jerry gun.
And we'll still go "Forward Undeterred," withdraw with equal grace,
  What matter reverses, we'll come again, like the fathers of our race.

                    (Pte. John D. Hall - Sigs Pl. HQ Company).

A man who stuttered badly joined the Golf Club and told the Secretary that he loved Golf, but was shy about his stuttering, and found it lonesome to be on the links without a companion. The Secretary said "I know the solution - there's a lady member here who stutters too, and I'm sure you would get along fine together." A match was arranged, and they met on the green and prepared to play. The man said he would like to introduce himself first. "M-m-m-my name's P-p-p-p-Peter," he said smilingly, "but I'm not a sus-sus-sus-saint!" She smiled in response. "M-m-m-my name's M-m-m-Mary," she said, "but I'm not a v-v-v-v-very good player."

BBC NEWS — 6th September, 1941.

Although the latest Russian communique makes no specific mention of the great battle raging round Leningrad, there is nothing to indicate that the Germans have succeeded in breaking through the outer defences of the City. Powerful Russian counter attacks have been launched, and the enemy have been dislodged from several villages in the great battle area. A German report states that Leningrad was under shell fire, but a Press correspondent in the City makes no mention of this. It is stated in Moscow, however, that the shelling was probably some 30 miles East of Leningrad. The Germans admit that there have been some counter attacks by Russian tanks in the Leningrad sector. It has been stated in Odessa, that all attacks on this important Black Sea Port have been broken. The Russian troops have counter attacked with bayonets, and left thousands of Rumanian dead on the ground. The Russians in Odessa, like the Army in Leningrad, declare that they will fight to the death to stop the City from falling into enemy hands. It is reported in Moscow, that a group of Cossacks have been operating behind the German lines. Their activities have been particularly successful, and they have smashed a German Regiment, destroyed Radio Stations, and wrecked railway lines. The enemy, in an endeavour to put a stop to their activities, have sent out tanks to round them up, but so far, these have been eluded. Berlin was bombed again on Thursday night by Russian aircraft, all of which returned safely. The Soviet air force, operating along the Black Sea Coast, has destroyed 35 German tanks, 100 lorries, and 3 troop trains.

The attempt made by a German submarine to sink an American destroyer off the coast of Greenland has been met with widespread disfavour by the American people. The American public have taken the news calmly, and a survey taken by a New York newspaper shows public opinion as follows: "Wait and see" and "It is high time something of the sort happened to put America in the War." It was reported from the destroyer that the instruments on board at one time showed that it was immediately above the submarine, which attacked more than once. It would be impossible to miss the American markings on the destroyer in daylight, said President Roosevelt, and it is fortunate that the destroyer was not hit. The American Navy is certainly on the alert, and when the submarine is found, it will be destroyed, that is unless it is already on the bottom through the depth charges dropped by the destroyer. The President also stated that if the attack was intentional, we accept the challenge.

The Australian Prime Minister speaking from Canberra, announced that Sir Earle Page has been chosen to go to England. Mr. Fadden said that Sir Earle Page would not leave for London until after the meeting of Parliament on September 15th.

In the most recent attacks on enemy shipping in the Mediterranean by our aircraft and submarines, the enemy has suffered heavy losses. One destroyer has been sunk, a 10,000 ton Cruiser damaged, a 30,000 ton liner sunk, and four other large ships sunk or damaged. A big Italian attack which was launched on Malta, was broken up by the RAF, which shot down 9 enemy planes. Our bombers are continuing to hammer Benghasi and Tripoli, and both of the Libyan Ports have hardly had a raid free night

Sabotage is still continuing in Vichy. Twelve cases have occurred recently, and two German soldiers have died as a result of bullet wounds. Hitler has warned the Norwegian people that opposition to the New Order would be crushed by force.

TOBRUK, 7th September, 1941.

The following communications from "B" Echelon are published for general interest and information. In wishing Capt. "Con" Morrell every success in his new post, we are we feel sure, echoing the unspoken wish of every man in the Unit. Lieut. Ken Clarke, also a "B" Echelon landmark for so long, is now seeing service in the front line, and carries with him the good wishes not only of all "B" Echelon personnel, but of his many friends throughout the Battalion. Incidentally, Ken, congratulations on the recent additions to your family. We had a feeling that once you were sent up in front, you might draw the crabs.

* * * * * * * * * *

I thank you, Mr. Editor, for the opportunity to pen my impressions of "B" Echelon.

I leave to take over my duties with "B" Company, fully appreciating that I must try to maintain its excellent fighting record. Whilst I am deeply conscious of my responsibility, I am also aware that I have an excellent team of Officers, NCO's and men, that have proved themselves to be equal to any task that they may be given.

I should like to place on record my deep appreciation for the loyal co-operation and assistance that has been a feature with "B" Echelon. Whilst I can recall by the score, acts of true comradeship, I am unable to obtain the slightest evidence of one unpleasant incident since the formation of the Battalion. One could easily give details covering the services rendered by the various branches of this Echelon that have just been accepted. Have you ever fully recognised the value of your cooks, who never have considered anything but giving you the best. Those transport drivers that bump over the escarpment day by day, so that you may have a meal; and they always get there, irrespective of enemy activity. The Armourer, who does fix that gun, whatever its brand. The Battalion L.A.D. and drivers, with maintenance that keeps our vehicles on the road.

Just one story that may illustrate this latter point. Prior to the Derna Derby, the C.O. was obliged to send his command to various points from Tobruk to Barce. The whole of the Battalion's equipment normally is carried on 55 vehicles, but when the C.O. was ordered to move to Tobruk to collect his Battalion and defend Tobruk, his equipment, etc., was in Derna, and only 2 motor cars and 2 one-ton vans were available. This meant the loss of practically the whole of our war outfit. It also provided a poser to our C.O., but he still appeared to be confident. The position briefly was - the Battalion would move back to Tobruk to establish a position and hold all attacks, but no means of taking with us the necessary stores for the job. The drivers and Battalion L.A.D. then took a hand. They obtained by every means, defective trucks and repaired them, trailers of all types, including the Derna Fire Brigade Engine. In the dark this work went on, and at 0830 hours on the following morning, every scrap had been loaded, and the most remarkable collection of vehicles ever seen started its journey up the Derna Pass, with tired but contented drivers at the wheels.

When this transport was attacked and partly destroyed, back went several of the boys to collect anything that could be salvaged. I have condensed this story as most of you know of it, but it serves my purpose to illustrate, if such is necessary, how these boys will get you out of a "jam" when the pressure is on.

Whilst I am unable to adequately express myself, I must ask you to accept my sincere thanks to my pals of "B" Echelon. If good fellowship and spirit count for anything - then we must get somewhere.

(Signed) Francis G. Morrell, Captain.

We have been specially asked by Sgt. Leo Jones to suitably express on his behalf, his thanks and admiration for the body of cooks who worked so hard to make our Anniversary Dinner throughout the different sections of the Battalion, so noteworthy. Not only on this occasion, but indeed since the inception of the Unit, these men have done worthy work, and Sgt. Jones can be excused for feeling so proud of them. It is his boast that there is no more willing body of cooks elsewhere in the A.I.F., and for that matter, the cooks can be well satisfied that they have a man of the calibre of Sgt. Leo Jones as their mentor.

LEO JONES

A further interesting fact about one of "B" Echelon's personnel is not generally known, and in fact, must be clearly unique. Sgt. Freddie Carleton (formerly of "B" Company) has served in the present war in the whole four Divisions that Australia has produced so far. Originally joining up in the Sixth, he was discharged for health reasons. His condition improving, he later joined up in the Eighth Division, and entered the Seventh when he came to us. Now our Unit is part and parcel of the Ninth Division, but we hope that Freddie's wanderings have ended, as even if Tenth, Eleventh, and Umpteenth Divvys are formed, Freddie is doing such a good job at "B" Echelon that this Unit will surely prevent him adding to his record.

BBC NEWS — 7th September, 1941.

The battle for Leningrad daily grows fiercer, with a great tank battle raging south of the City. The Germans are now throwing in the great weight of the Luftwaffe, but in spite of this, all their attempts to reach the City have been thwarted, and dozens of Nazi planes have been destroyed. The Russians claim that their Air Force has been dealing out massive blows at the German Panzer Units. It was reported from Moscow last night, that in one sector, the Russian forces during the past few days had dislodged the Germans from a village. They also claim that 117 German aircraft have been destroyed in two days. It is reported from Leningrad, that 20 enemy bombers tried to attack a battery of heavy Ack-ack guns located in a Forest close to the City. This attack was smashed and 14 planes were shot down. Although the Germans still claim that their Artillery is bombarding Leningrad, it is thought in London that the enemy cannot be near enough to do so. Moscow claims that Leningrad is not completely cut off, and that the road is still open. A supplement to the Moscow communique describes the enemy's losses in the fighting on Thursday: 15,000 German officers and men killed, and 100 guns, 18 pontoon bridges, 940 motor vehicles, 180 tanks and Armoured cars destroyed. In the Central and Ukraine sectors, one Russian Battery foiled four German attempts to build a pontoon bridge, and killed over 500 Sappers and infantrymen. A River Flotilla and an armoured train also thwarted attacks to cross the Dnieper. At Odessa, the number of Rumanian wounded is so large, that it is impossible for all of them to be removed. A report received early this morning describes life in the beseiged City of Odessa. Shops, markets, and Post Offices are still open, and the people are still going to the pictures, regardless of the air raids. Newspapers arrive regularly from Moscow, and a daily newspaper is also being published from inside Odessa. Meat is a little scarce, as most of the cattle were driven away when the Germans advanced. Fighting is still continuing only ten miles outside the City. It is reported that Russia has requested the United States to supply aluminium, to offset the losses caused by the destruction of the great Dnieper Dam.

The subject of President Roosevelt's broadcast next Tuesday has not yet been disclosed. It will be broadcast in 14 different languages, and its importance is obvious.

Germany's official explanation of the attempted torpedoing of an American destroyer has been received in Washington, where it is stated that Germany has tried to make it a case of the submarine having been first attacked, and then firing in defence of itself. This explanation has been flatly turned down by the United States, who state definitely that the destroyer was attacked first, and then, and only then, dropped depth charges. In Japan it is stated that this incident could only be expected, as America was not neutral anyway. It is added that a beligerent destroyer was attacked in beligerent waters, and thats that. America is willing enough to supply the tools, but is not prepared to finish the job if it comes to shooting. Mr. Wendel Wilkie's opinion is that the incident was definitely a challenge to the American freedom of the seas, and he urges the President to take up the challenge.

The United States War Department has announced numerous new contracts with aircraft factories, for a thousand bigger and better Flying Fortresses. When these planes fly over Germany, they attack from such a height, that their presence is not known until the bombs whistle down.

TOBRUK, 10th September, 1941.

What a mixed lot of feelings one mail day engenders, the predominant one, of course, being disappointment when no mail arrives from "the one." However, after scanning our recent correspondence our feelings covered a wide gamut - interest, amusement, gladness, and exasperation. An extract from a letter from an old friend reading "...........was so relieved to learn that you were safe in Tobruk, and so had been spared the horrors of warfare......." left us speechless. Our very eloquently expressed "Wouldn't it?" just about sums up what we felt. Apparently there are still those in Australia who feel that we are merely 5/- a day tourists, enjoying a galaxy of good things in sunny Tobruk. However, our ruffled feelings were somewhat smoothed by receipt of a letter from a little lady who has been dispensing beers to us in Phair's Hotel for more years than either of us care to remember. Her letter reads in part - "......by what I read and hear, life is not altogether a bed of roses where you are. What a great job you are all doing; it will certainly make history when this show is over." All very flattering, no doubt, but who isn't susceptible to a little flattery, and it is such letters that are an inspiration to all of us to continue giving of our best, knowing that in the estimation of many we have much to live up to, and determined not to let that good opinion be unwarranted.

We were amused, and perhaps just a little annoyed too, to read a leading article in the Border Morning Mail that this unit had gone through the Syrian Campaign with great success and glory. This particular newspaper has always been an exceptionally good friend to the Battalion, and it is regrettable that its leg has been so pulled. Maybe, we had better charitably say that some mistake has occurred, and let it go at that.

There will be many in the Unit pleased to learn that Official news has come through that Major Perry, and Lieuts. T.O. Neuendorf and Sheldrick are officially declared Prisoners of War. Unfortunately, confirmation has also come to hand of the regrettable news that Lieut. George Gardiner has died from wounds. In addition, comes the sad tidings that Cpl. A. Spinks and Pte. G.M. Matthews, both of whom were previously reported Missing, have died as the result of wounds. Good soldiers all, their names and memory will not be forgotten by Mud'n Bloods throughout the Battalion. As a foil to this bad news, comes the official advice that Pte. J.T. Waterhouse, previously reported Missing - Believed Killed, is now a prisoner of war in Italy.

A Bond salesman, in his search for another means of livelihood, bethought himself of a friend who owned a small travelling circus. The circus owner was obliged to say he had no vacancy on his staff, but he added: "There is one thing that might possibly be a chance. Our gorilla died last week, but we saved his hide - we thought we might stuff it some time. What would you think of putting it on and going into the gorilla cage?" The salesman, pressed by necessity, put on the hide and went into the cage. There he performed his role with exceptional elan. He growled, he roared, he leaped from side to side, he rattled the bars. In these horrendous cavortings he accidentally loosened the door to the adjoining cage. Through the door, presently, came the circus lion. With feline stealth, the lion walked toward the corner occupied by the gorilla, to the vast suspense and alarm of the audience.

The exciting drama became no less intense when the expected victim, catching sight of the lion, lost utterly his gorilla ferocity and cried, "Help! Help!" This strange interruption of anticipated tragedy became complete when the lion was heard to exclaim, "Shut up, you damn fool - you're not the only Bond salesman out of a job."

A large and luscious fruit cake, weighing several pounds, has been given to the Battalion by Major Mawson, of the Salvation Army, for distribution in the Battalion. An equitable distribution would scarcely mean a current each, so for the moment the powers that be are somewhat exercised in their minds as to what to do with it. Any suggestions?

BBC NEWS — 10th September, 1941.

Although the latest Moscow communique is confined to the usual cautious comment that fighting is continuing along the whole front, some indication of the importance of the fighting at Smolensk is shown by the statement that the Russian offensive near Smolensk is continuing. It is significant to note that this is the first time the word offensive has been used to describe Russian engagements. They claim to have smashed 8 German Divisions, which is no mean achievement. The Germans deny that the Russians have recaptured Smolensk. In Moscow, it is stated that the Russians have immense reserves of men and material, and that they are not only capable of defence, but also of counter attack. Despatches from the Central front describe the sector as a mincing machine for German troops. The Germans admit that their troops are engaged against superior Russian forces in that area. There is no change in the situation around Leningrad. The Germans are continuing their claim that they have completed their ring round the City, but this is denied by the Russians who state that there are small coastal strips still open on the East and West. The Germans also claim to have captured a town to the east of Leningrad, but this is also denied by the Russians. The Russian communique makes no mention of Odessa, but a German report admits that the Rumanian offensive against this important Black Sea Port has been completely halted.

The Canadian Expeditionary Force which landed on the Spitzbergen Island have returned, bringing with them the entire population. Before leaving they completely destroyed the coal deposits and radio stations on the Island, and left nothing which would be of any use to the enemy. Norwegian troops also took part in the raid. The Canadian troops were bitterly disappointed at not meeting with any German opposition.

The following figures in regard to our shipping losses were announced in London last night. During July and August, we lost only one third of the amount of shipping lost by the Germans and Italians for the same period. The first British Naval engagement in support of our Allies has taken place in the North Sea. In this latest exploit, our light force smashed German warships convoying supplies in the far north. Four enemy ships were sunk - 1 cruiser, 1 destroyer, 1 armed trawler, and 1 other vessel. We had no casualties at all in this engagement. At the same time, successful attacks were made on 7 other vessels. One was torpedoed off the Norweg-

ian coast, and another supply ship was destroyed in the English Channel. Enemy shipping in the Middle East was also attacked, and a large Italian Schooner was sunk in the Red Sea, and 4 other ships sunk in the Mediterranean.

A Cairo communique reports that our aircraft have been active in the Middle East. Sicily was attacked, and bombs dropped on the docks and jetties. In another flight over Sicily, it was discovered that the merchant ship which was torpedoed some time ago, is now under water. Derna, Capuzzo and Bardia were also attacked. The enemy air force has also been active, and Malta was subjected to three raids yesterday. Bombs were dropped over a wide area, causing some casualties and some civilian damage. Our fighters shot down one bomber. Attacks were also made on the Suez Canal zone, Alexandria, Haifa and Cypress, but there was only one casualty and no material damage was caused.

The Germans have not yet made any statement about the sinking of the American ship in the Atlantic, as well as the sinking of another American ship in the Red Sea. This was announced by the State Department in Washington yesterday. The ship sunk in the Atlantic had a crew of 27, of which three have been picked up after three weeks. The other 24 members of the crew are thought to be lost. It has been officially stated that this vessel was not carrying the implements of war of any sort. Complete facts of the incident have been asked, from Germany. All of the crew of the ship sunk in the Red Sea have now been picked up. They state that a plane attacked the ship, landed a bomb in the centre of it, and then roared away into the distance. They also said that the ship was well lit, and the identity could not have been mistaken. It was stated in Berlin after the incident, that the Suez Canal and the Red Sea are in the war zone, even if President Roosevelt does not think so.

At the time of the Syrian Armistice, there were 27,000 Frenchmen in Syria, and it has now been announced that of these troops, nearly 13,000 have now joined the Free French Forces.

TOBRUK, 18th September, 1941.

It is with feelings not untinged with regret that we sit down to type this issue of "Mud & Blood". For the past five months it has been our task to present to you the daily news, coupled with little items of gossip, local news, and badinage, and the doing so has seemed to bind us in some intimate way, with the doings of the Battalion generally. This issue will be the last edited by us, and in future Pte. Len Wenborn of the "I" Section will be in charge of the paper. In saying our farewell to you all, we hope that the efforts of the magazine have interested, and at times, amused you, and we certainly hope that Len will get all the fun out of publishing it that we did. That the paper has attained some little success is due entirely to your own co-operation, and your ready acceptance of it has been an encouragement to its producer. We would ask you, therefore, to be as tolerant with your new Editor as you were with us, and to assist him as much as possible by sending in scraps of company news, articles, humorous stories, and details of little incidents that occur from time to time.

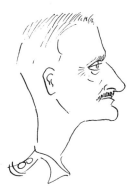

Our new Editor:
Len Wenborn - I Section.

As for us, we are off to a school in Cairo for a considerable period, and without a shadow of doubt the war will be over long before the school terminates. It would be hypocritical to say that we regret leaving TOBRUK, but we can modestly say that we will miss the cheery faces of all our friends and associates, and our only wish is that you were all coming with us. Perhaps it will not be long before we will have the pleasure of sinking a few pots with our cobbers either in Alex or Cairo, and believe you us, on such a happy occasion, we will look upon one and every member of the Battalion as our special "cobber".

Someone asked us one day what the "B" stood for in "B" Echelon and we were unable to give a satisfactory answer. However, spending a day down there recently threw some light on the subject, and we are now able to assure you that it means "Bomb-happy". They are nearly all that way down there these days, and not without sufficient reason. As a matter of fact we have it on the best of authority, that the C.O. is considering establishing a "rest camp" for "B" Echelon personnel up in the forward Company areas, in order to give them a welcome respite from Jerry's attentions.

Have never heard such an enticing lot of "furpheys" as have been circulating during the past week or ten days. Nearly everyone had a friend who knew someone who was acquainted with the batman of an officer in Divvy or Brigade, and they had it on the best of authority that we were all going back to Australia to do a big recruiting stunt; others stoutly maintained that we were going straight to Malaya; whilst we suspect one stout and burly Sergeant not unconnected with the healing profession of being responsible for the one that we were all going off to America to talk them into lending us another hundred akers or so. Well, Mud'n Bloods, they all make nice listening to, but don't believe a word of them, as we happen to be in the know, and we tell you in strict confidence that we are destined to go to the North Pole shortly, in case Hitler considers launching a surprise attack there from the shores of Northern Norway. When we get to Cairo, we will send up a few booklets on the "Love Life of the Penguin," etc.

By the way, no doubt you are all wondering how the bumper Anniversary Number of Mud & Blood is getting on. Well, it is all completed, and should be in print by the end of next week. It will make a very interesting souvenir, and will, with all due modesty, be worth sending home to your friends or families, and should reach them by Christmas. The cost of printing has not yet been ascertained, but it should not be high, so will you all advise your Company clerks how many copies you will require, so that an approximate idea may be obtained of the number to get printed. Also, an attractive Christmas Card has been designed, with an artist's sketch of Tobruk on the frontispiece, and your requirements should also be stated to the Company clerk in regard to this. The cost of this, also, should be reasonable, and the article will be an interesting little momento of this place, even though the Battalion may well be domiciled elsewhere when Christmas arrives, which we sincerely trust will be the case.

Newspaper cuttings just received advise of the arrival in Australia of Capt. G.I. Malloch, Cpl. Mitchell, Pte. Padey, and others, who have all made the headlines by their vivid description of life in Tobruk, and the many actions and forays that they have engaged in. Some of the tales seem a little strong, but then, we will have to envisage all the elbow-bending that probably accompanied their telling, and make allowances accordingly. Still, what a nice sensation to be standing at the bar of Young & Jackson's telling all and sundry "HOW I SAVED TOBRUK." Someday, perhaps, we'll all experience it.

BBC NEWS — 18th September, 1941.

This mornings Cairo communique announces that following our raids in Tobruk, enemy shelling on our forward positions was heavy in the Eastern Sector, but decreased against Southern and Western Sectors. In the Frontier area, advanced elements of British and South African mechanised forces continued patrolling activities. Weather conditions in Abyssinia now permit the resumption of offensive activities in Gondar area. During the past few days, patrols of our troops made several deep penetrations, and in one case reconnoitring lines of approach a considerable distance behind the enemy's front line.

London - The failure of the Iran Government to fulfill their undertaking to eliminate German influence is explained in a Simla communique, which also explains the resumption of the Allied advance on the Iran Capital. Several hundred German women and children have left Teheran, and have embarked for India. The new Shah took oath to Constitution before Parliament yesterday. The Chief of the Police has been dismissed.

It is reported in London that while the German communique says that on the Eastern Front, offensive actions are developing into one operation on a very large scale, the Russian communique states that Russian troops were engaged in stubborn fighting along the whole front. The situation round Smolensk is improving, and Moscow radio yesterday announced that Soviet troops were in a position to invest Smolensk. In a battle north east of Smolensk which lasted for several days, Soviet troops defeated the Germans, whose losses are estimated to total ten thousand men. However, the situation in the Ukraine is still serious, and the threat to Leningrad closer. The Royal Air Force Wing now in Russia, has already been in contact with the Germans, and of hundreds of British machines sent, large numbers have already arrived.

Washington - The Navy Secretary has confirmed that the United States is using all methods, including convoys, to ensure safe arrival of Lease and Lend goods to Britain. Colonel Knox added, that to assume that only convoys would be employed, would be to take a very narrow construction of what President Roosevelt has said.

TOBRUK, 19th September, 1941.

First a cheerio to our 'departed' Editor, Staff-Sgt. Jim Mulcahy, who is soon to taste a spot of civilisation in the Land of Goshen. Doubtless the least civilised portion of his business there will be the attendance at lectures and whatnot, for it is well known that the disciplinary standards at Army schools are extremely high. Can any of you Mud'n Bloods picture our Jim sitting at attention? No, we cannot, either. However, the many and widely distributed people who have derived some pleasure from the reading of Jim's daily prattle, will render him thanks for his job in bringing "Mud & Blood" to its present popularity.

We wish him every success, and may those long, cool ales be satisfying. And don't forget Jim, that we expect some news from time to time.

* * * * * * * * * * * * * * * * * * *

Staff-Sgt. J. D. Mulcahy.

We must ask our readers to continue to offer the ready co-operation which they have shown up to the present. In short, this is your rag, and without assistance from all and sundry, it cannot be produced. When you have a spare moment, scribble out your jokes, your stories or what have you, on a slip of paper and send them in. For instance, we have already heard that there is a cove in Don Company who has some special notions regarding the fortifications of his future home back in Aussie. What about letting us have your plans and specifications for a future issue?

Who said Tobruk, or this part of it, was dusty? If there's anyone who could yesterday have exceeded the writer in dirtiness, he deserves a week's leave. "WHAT'S THAT?" we fondly ask. Yesterday we had the feeling of regret that our paper is read in such delicate circles, for otherwise, some very fruity comments would have made their appearance in today's issue concerning our discomfort from dust. So thick was the atmosphere, that one Sgt. Keith Benson missed the way to his mouth! Those who know Keith will sympathize with him and agree that it was a big mistake. Methinks the Companies will yet be having a most self-satisfying gloat over the fact that the dust did not miss BHQ.

This story was brought to us by our daily blonde visitor from Brigade, Lieut. Jock Cudlipp. WHY ARE FIRE ENGINES RED? It's like this. Twelve inches make a ruler, a ruler is a king, and a king likes fish. Fish have fins, Finns hate the Russians, and the Russians are red. Fire Engines are always rushin' hither and thither, so that's why they are red.

The following is published with a view to identification of the person mentioned therein: A certain Company of this Battalion has not seen its QM for a considerable time, and inquiries are often made concerning his location. Latest report hath it that the gentleman is now 150 feet down and still digging.

A contributor wonders, among other things, what the C.O. thinks of -

1. The acute shortage of beer;
2. Our chances of getting leave; and
3. Our chances when we do go on leave, of breaking the "18 men in the Jaffa Gaol" record.

Well, Sir, these columns are at your service whenever you can give us a ray of hope.

Mention of beer reminds us that the Battalion Orderly Room has the distinction to closely resemble a cellar. Would that it were furnished as was the 'Cellar Cool', where we, in days of yore, were wont to sip at leisure. Cannot you imagine what a genial host Pte. Ron Lees would make? As a matter of fact, Pte. Lees intends to advertise the history of ye ancient 'Orderly Inn' where cobwebbed boards and hanging door keys tell of musty age. It is understood too, that he can turn on Maraschino at least 150 years old, whenever suitable visitors arrive. 'Suitable visitors' include only those who can bring with them a drop of the doings. (Officers, please note.)

The lack of 'furpheys' in this number, is due to the fact that the Editor failed to contact the fountainhead - Sgt. Bill. Of course, it is part of this gentleman's duty when recounting tales to make himself difficult to understand, so we would have been disappointed anyway. Just as well old Bill the bomb-burier NEVER gets excited.

Judging by the appearance of one (now very much disused) truck, it seems that the driver thereof would be well advised to buy a ticket in 'Tatt's', for Driver Claffey was, early on Thursday morning, mighty lucky not to have broken any bones. Maybe THE lucky one is Major H.R. Birch, who had not long alighted from the vehicle. Yes, we feel that it is up to the Major to provide two Tatt's tickets, for it was his side of the truck which was knocked about.

BBC NEWS — 19th September, 1941.

Thursday's Cairo communique states that there was considerable patrol activity at both Tobruk and the Frontier area. On Sunday, British and South African mechanised units captured ten German tanks, for the loss of only one armoured car.

It has been announced in Moscow that all men in Russia between the ages of sixteen and fifty, are to undergo compulsory military training. Training will take place outside working hours, and will not interfere with war production.

A London Air Force communique states that one bomber is missing from the RAF raid on Karlsruhe in the Rhineland on Wednesday night. RAF fighters operating late on Thursday afternoon, sank two enemy mine-sweepers off the Belgian coast, and damaged two others.

The British Government has not yet received confirmation of reports that Italian Warships may be transferred to Bulgaria in order to invoke non-beligerency clause for passage through the Dardanelles into the Black Sea. However, since Bulgaria is at war with Yugoslavia and Greece, it is not expected that Turkey would countenance any such manoeuvre.

Teheran - The new Shah took oath of Constitution yesterday, and has promised co-operation of Iranian Government with Britain and Russia, whose interests lie close to Irans. The Shah undertook to work in concert with Parliament.

London - General Sikorski, the Polish Commander in Chief, broad-casting to Moscow, said that he will shortly be visiting Poles in Russia.

It has been reported in London, that Crimea has been cut off by the German thrust towards Perekop, but the Naval Base of Sebastopol is strongly fortified, and is expected to constitute a strong point for Crimean garrisons who can be supplied and reinforced by sea.

Cairo - Tripoli and Benghasi were raided by the RAF and Fleet Air Arm on Tuesday night. RAF bombers also raided munition factories at Licata in Sicily in daylight on Wednesday. Dumps and stores at Bardia were also attacked. All of our aircraft returned safely from these operations.

Washington - President Roosevelt has asked Congress for an additional 6 thousand million dollars for Lease and Lend purposes, bringing Lease and Lend Funds up to thirteen thousand million dollars. Eighteen hundred million dollars of the new allocation will be for agricultural and industrial products, and twelve hundred million dollars for Ordnance.

London - Sixteen enemy fighters were destroyed in RAF daylight operations over the Channel and Enemy occupied territory on Thursday, during which five enemy ships were sunk, and two damaged. Two British bombers and nine fighters are missing, but two fighter pilots are safe.

It is announced in Berlin, that the German occupation authorities have imposed a three day curfew in Paris, following attempts on lives of German soldiers. In Ankara, it is estimated that 400,000 men are now mobilised in Bulgaria, in addition to 3 German Divisions. Turkey has received no formal Bulgarian request for passage of warships through the Dardanelles.

TOBRUK, 21st September, 1941.

The Battalion is indeed fortunate in possessing, back in Australia, an organisation such as the Welfare Association, which works unceasingly and untiringly for our benefit. In conversation with the Padre yesterday, it was learned that since our arrival here, many hundreds of pounds have been made available by them to the C.O.'s Fund for the purchase of comforts for us troops. It must be remembered, that to make a free issue to a Battalion of men, requires a considerable amount of money. For instance, a distribution of goods worth 2/6, would cost the Fund approximately one hundred pounds, and it takes some work in collecting an amount like that, especially at a time when there is so great a strain on our folks resources. The Padre indicated that there is to be another distribution very soon, and indeed, no less than 50 parcels of cake arrived here last night. When we write home, let us not forget to include that expression of our appreciation of the fine work done for us by the Welfare Association.

Have an apology to offer Lieut. Jock Cudlipp, as portion of the story he gave us yesterday was inadvertently omitted. Although this omission rather spoiled the sequence of his joke, it fortunately did not ruin it altogether. Do you now Sir, feel entirely placated? And will you again contribute to our columns?

Since so many of our readers are vitally interested, it is hoped to gather from time to time, information regarding the performance and prospects of some of the horses included in the Melbourne Cup. Today, little such is available, but there will be more later. We must extend our sympathy to Pte. R. Rowe of "C" Company, whose horse Methuen has passed away. Actually we now know that the animal was dead before our sweep was drawn. Saul, we believe has broken down, and will not race again, while Apostrophe - and this is straight from the stable door - is considered to have too much weight. Whether he has run to fat, or whether it is excess allotment of weight, we cannot quite decide. Burhan Ali seems capable of winning a race or two in these early stages, but will most likely be left at the post. For some of these items, we are indebted to "Matty the News Hound" of HQ Company. Keep up the good work Matty, say we. In fact, HQ Company seems most helpful - even to the loan of a typewriter. In fairness to the owner, Cpl. Fred Henderson, we admit that yesterday the machine became detached from its letter U for at least three minutes. Or was it the hallucination of a raw typist?

The C.O. received a letter yesterday from Cpl. Max Froud of "D" Company, written from hospital, where he had encountered a member of the original 23rd Battalion - one L/Cpl. A. Thomson. Along with his two brothers he joined our parent unit, and he himself has the distinction of having earned a M.M. and Bar. Unfortunately both his brothers were killed. It's grand to make contacts of this nature, and we intend to send L/Cpl. Thomson a copy or two of Mud & Blood for old time's sake. No doubt there are many of the Original 23rd who follow our progress with the utmost interest.

Representatives of B Echelon, inform us that the successor to Pay Sgt. Max Dolamore is equally fleet of foot, so the pay-postal trio will still be an undefeated combination. Little is now heard of Leaping Lena, who has obviously reached her last resting place, where she can browse amongst the stones, or gaze contentedly into the blue Mediterranean. Bombs can do her no harm, anyhow.

Did you hear what an Aussie said in a letter home from Greece, in recent months? He had just visited the Parthenon which overlooks Athens, and had remembered that the guide of his party had said that a certain portion of the sculptured reliefs represented the Birth of the

Goddess Athena. The digger wrote "The birth of the Athena was a great relief". Would be, we think.

As a result of enemy action recently, a quantity of tinned sausages were destroyed. Our guess is that Herr Adolf, not being satisfied with brutal attacks on millions of human beings, has now decided to bring down his wrath upon the defenceless stray dogs of the world. That reminds us - what has become of the one or two canine pets which have previously romped in the Battalion area?

BBC NEWS — 21st September, 1941.

RAF fighters yesterday had their biggest day since we took the offensive. Hundreds of Spitfires were in action all day from Cherbourg to the Netherlands. Our Blemheim bombers were also active, and attacked targets in North Western Germany, at sea, and in Norway. A Flying Fortress carried out an attack on Emden in Western Germany, and dropped many bombs from a great height. On return, the pilot of the Fortress said that they met with no opposition whatever. Two separate attacks were made on strongly protected enemy convoys in the North Sea. In the first attack, our Blenheim bombers roared down within 20 feet of the targets. Bombs were dropped on one ship, which heeled over, and another ship was left burning fiercely. Blenheims also took part in the second raid in which six ships were hit. The back of one was broken, and four others were seen to be on fire. Many of the Spitfire and Hurricane pilots who took part in the days operations, complained that they had nothing to do, and that they did not even sight an enemy plane. On the other hand, one Australian Squadron destroyed six MEs. During the day the total number of enemy planes shot down by our fighters was 15. Our losses were 3 bombers and 7 fighters. One enemy bomber was destroyed in minor raids on this country last night.

The Moscow communique issued at midnight, reports very fierce fighting at Kiev, but although the Germans previously claimed to have captured the City, they now say that the Russians there are putting up a fierce resistance. The Russian Home Guards stand firm under a hail of fire and bombs from Stukas and high level bombers. The Russian aircraft however, are hitting back at the enemy, and on Thursday, 36 German planes were shot down and destroyed on the ground, with the loss of only 14 Russian machines. In the meantime, fighting continues along the whole front, and in the extreme North, it is reported that two Regiments of Finns have been annihilated. Russian warships have sunk a large German transport.

German aircraft attempted to carry out a heavy raid on Leningrad, but the attack was broken up by Russian fighter planes and Ack-ack, which accounted for 17 of them. Odd planes however, did manage to break through to the City, and a number of bombs were dropped, and some damage caused. Further Russian counter attacks in the Centre Sector have resulted in the re-capture of 14 villages. It was reported over the Moscow radio, that Soviet Marines who were landed near Odessa, routed the enemy and forced them to withdraw to the mouth of the River Dnieper.

It has been announced in United States, that hundreds of US planes and tanks have been sent to Russia, and that supplies of all kinds were on their way. It was also stated that the supply is only limited to the transport. The German commander of Paris has ordered that 12 Frenchmen be shot, as a reprisal for the death of one German soldier. These 12 deaths will bring the total number of Murders for the week up to 35. A Rome newspaper reports that a number of arrests have been made in Greece, following disturbances directed against the Axis.

A representative of the enslaved Czech people, has sent a note to Britain, in which he asks for information as to when the "V" Army is to strike. He has, however, been assured that when the time arrives for the Army to strike, the orders will be unmistakable.

The Bulgarian Government has declared a state of emergency, and the Prime Minister has once again expressed his readiness to carry out Axis wishes. President Roosevelt has signed the largest Bill for the National Defence and Lease and Lend programme. The Bill was for 890,000,000 pounds. It was also stated in the US that 16,000,000 pounds worth of machine tools have been shipped to Britain during August, which is 60% more than in August last year. British planes in the Middle East have done more damage to enemy shipping. In an attack on Tripoli, at least 3 hits were scored on a large liner, and a large merchant ship was also hit at least twice. An enemy convoy in central Mediterranean was attacked, and hits scored on one ship. Benghasi harbour was also bombed.

TOBRUK, 22nd September, 1941.

Yesterday, mention was made of our Welfare Association's excellent work. Today, we have further concrete evidence of their support. Cigarettes, chocolate, fruit juice cordial, and fruit cake. Has the war become a picnic? And even the Army has given us rum!

Rum! What a loosener of tongues. Here's a rum story from Old Irish:- Well, we're not one to spread a scandal (much), but we stumbled across something last night that made us raise our eyebrows. Wandering hopefully into Sar/Major Morrison's dug-out, just as he had finished dishing out the rum, we were, strangely enough, in time to partake of a little hospitality. Casting our eye round the place to see if there was anything worth "scrounging" as we went out (a little trick we learnt from Bill), we were intrigued to see a tin marked "Benger's Food". "Hey! put that down, it belongs to Major Wall," remarked Bill as he grabbed the tin. "I'm just about to make some now. It's not bad." As he busied himself, we picked up the tin and read the directions with some curiosity. In large letters was the announcement - For Expectant Mothers - Guaranteed to ensure a plentiful supply of Mothers' Milk if taken during Pregnancy. Then followed a table showing the amount to be taken at different stages of that interesting condition. Watching Bill prepare the dish, it was easy to deduce that the Major is about 4½ months "gone", whilst Bill himself and Freddy Henderson would appear to have been in a spot of bother for the past 3 months. We politely declined to participate in the mixture, as, as far as we know, we are not in need of such stimulants.

L/Cpl. Maurie O'Connell of "C" Company, who won his M.M. on 22nd April, has been written up in Melbourne's "Sporting Globe", complete with photograph. His brother is also mentioned, and we want to make sure whether the photograph is of Maurice or of brother O'Connell. As the photograph shows such a handsome fellow, we are inclined toward the latter view.

What we in Tobruk are missing is just nobody's business. We learn that the folks at home have conductresses on some suburban tram services. As one private to another, could you refuse to pay tram fares under such circumstances?

Ref our comment on sausages in the last issue, we are informed that the A.I.F. overseas is eating 19,000 miles of them per month!

That lengthy slab of humanity with OS feet (otherwise Pte. M.W. Ferguson) has had an appauling piece of bad luck, which unfortunately penetrates as far as his drinking companions. In a parcel which he received from a friend in the Navy, were some tinned foods, a bottle of ink, AND a bottle of lunch. In spite of the careful packing, would you believe that the only damaged portion was the lunch, the bottle being slightly bent. To make matters worse, we read in our lime juice labels today that contents make a delicious mixture with Gin. O Murray Misere.

Following is an extract from a blonde Australian admirer: "I've had lots of fun reading through the pages of Mud & Blood. It was like a tonic to me. I think it is a wonderful effort and must help tremendously to keep up the boys' spirits. I was amazed how they were able in the face of such dangers to recollect the poems from which many took their cues. How well some have been schooled. Surely Shelly, Wordsworth, and other famous poets would be bucked no end if they knew. The Brigadier put up a stout effort. He must be a good sport."

Lieut. Ken Clarke sent in this amusing story which he has recently received from a cobber in Malaya. The friend said: "Last month I shot a tiger. Last week I slept with a blonde. Last night I wished I had shot the blonde and slept with the tiger." Sounds as if Malaya is a place for Aussies in preference to Tobruk. We haven't any wild animals other than "lions" ("B" Echelon variety), nor do we have any wild women. In fact, life is very dull.

Many Don Company boys will feel sorry for Pte. Alan Curry, who is an old Don-ite. Alan has been back in hospital in Egypt for some months, and has now lost his moustache. He suffered from creeping baldness, and when one side of his beloved whiskers was attacked, the whole lot had to come off.

BBC NEWS — 22nd September, 1941.

Cairo - Major General Morshead, Tobruk Commander, has sent a telegram to the Military Commander in Chief of Odessa, which is also described as the Russian Tobruk, stating - "We in beseiged Tobruk, salute the resolution and fighting spirit which we have learned to associate with your country, and with which your gallant garrison is facing its great task. From our African stronghold, we follow your fortunes with admiration, and wish you all good luck and continuation of your success. May the enemy soon be overthrown."

Russia - The ruins of Kiev are now in German hands, after days of fierce fighting. The Russian forces have now finally withdrawn from the City, but before they left, they made sure that the capture of the City would be of no use to the enemy. Several days ago, the Germans claimed that the garrison at Kiev had surrendered, and left the City intact. This mornings German communique, however, admits that when their troops entered the City, they found that all vital supplies had been removed, and that everything of any use had been wrecked. According to the latest Russian communique, the other two great Russian Cities which are threatened, are still

*more than holding their own. At Leningrad and Odessa, the Russian forces
have not only prevented the enemy from breaking through their defences,
but have forced them back with heavy losses to the enemy. The Russian
Air Force has also been active, and on Friday, 60 German aircraft were destroyed in the air and on the ground, as against the loss of 24 Russian machines. Generally, the fighting on the whole of the Eastern Front has been on
a less intense scale, but in the Central Sector, the Russians are still keeping
up their local offensive.*

*London - Today sees the start of the Britain "Tanks for Russia"
drive. It was stated in Moscow that Russia needs tanks, more tanks, and
yet more tanks. "We produce many ourselves, but the requirements of a
2000 mile front are great. We require many more to reinforce our own
efforts. Your tanks are needed, and we know how to use them. The greater the number of tanks we can produce, the sooner the Nazi war machine
will be broken. Send speedily, and as many as possible, to the part of the
front which is most hard pressed." While churches of all denominations
throughout Britain yesterday held special thanksgiving services, the RAF
celebrated the anniversary of the Battle of Britain by another great sweep
over enemy occupied territory. Our bombers attacked targets in Western
Germany, escorted by large numbers of our fighters. During the attacks our
fighters kept off strong opposition, and brought every bomber home safely. Our bombers scored many hits on the targets, and left many columns
of black smoke rising into the air. During the day, 24 enemy planes were
shot down. Last night our bombers attacked Lille, Frankfurt, Berlin, and
other targets in Germany. Four of our bombers are missing.*

*United States - President Roosevelt has called a conference of
Congress leaders, to emphasise the need for the approval of the new Lease
and Lend Bill.*

*Far East - The Chinese Ambassador in London said in a broadcast
that Chinese soldiers had fought the mighty war machine of Japan to a
standstill. He added that the tide seems to be turning definitely in the way
of China. After years of war, the Chinese people are still steadfastly determined to win the war against Japan. Today it is the Japanese who want
the war to end quickly. The Ambassador went on to say that to win the
war quickly, China needs increased aid from Britain and America. According to a communique issued from Tokyo last night, the Japanese claim to
have started another large series of operations against the Chinese forces
in Southern China.*

London - German "E" boats, which tried to attack British convoys in the North Sea, were driven off by our Naval escorts. Two "E" boats were damaged, but there were no casualties or damage to any of our ships.

Vichy - Vichy reports that in future, German troops equipped with machine guns and armoured cars will take over the City if there is any attempt to rise against them. Marshal Petain has warned the French people against any attacks on German soldiers. The German Commander in Paris, states that he intends to increase the number of hostages shot, for the death of every German soldier.

Cairo - It was revealed today that General Sir Claude Auchinleck and the Air Marshal for the Middle East, have sent special messages of congratulation to the Forces in the Western Desert for their recent action, in which they drove the enemy forces back across the Egyptian border into Libya.

TOBRUK, 23rd September, 1941.

We feel very proud of the ten "Mud'n Bloods" who recently were recipients of Commander in Chief's Cards. It is interesting to note that of the ten men, only one is at present absent from the Battalion. This one, of course, is Lieut. Colin Rigg of the Carrier Platoon, who was evacuated about two months ago, after an engagement with the enemy. The list is as follows:

VX33476	Sgt. Carleton F.L.	HQ Company
VX48151	Pte. Clark H.P.	HQ Company
VX42081	Sgt. Hook P.R.	HQ Company
VX40144	Pte. Kelly J.McG.	A Company
VX27678	L/Cpl. O'Connell M.J.	C Company
VX38937	Capt. Rattray R.	C Company
VX19116	Lieut. Rigg C.G.	HQ Company
VX40269	Sgt. Stuckey G.A.	A Company
VX46920	Pte. Coutts D.E.D.	B Company
VX36501	WOII Morrison W.G.	HQ Company

News has come to hand that in an office in Melbourne where many hundreds of young ladies are employed, there is now a noticeable tendency for some of the girls to grow fat. On closer examination, it is also found that the girls in question are almost without exception, those who have their men friends away at the war. What, we wonder, can be the cause of such a strange thing? At least, we can expect this condition to add weight to their affections.

Now would you like a furphey? Somewhere along one of the dusty roads of Tobruk, there must be a secret spot where all the best stories originate. Strangely, our only contact with this interesting place, is per water cart, and we begin to think that water attracts furpheys as readily as it does flies. Didn't the water carriers meet one of the mythical 7th Armoured Div. people, who gave him a Jerry tank as a souvenir? Yes, that's right, and he sent the thing home by airmail. How the representative of the 7th Armoured Div. came to be inside the perimeter is not too clear, but we reckon its safe to assume that he was bound for Abyssinia and got lost. Other items from "B" Echelon include a challenge from the Kitchen staff to the Pay-Postal champs. The former, since the addition of new and rather dark blood, feel satisfied that theirs is an even chance of beating the favourites.

Talking of being lost, we must in honesty say that the only being in BHQ who has not been lost in this area must surely be the Battalion cat. Even our Adjutant had his life saved by a stalwart R.P. who directed him to his flat many chains away. For such deeds of gallantry needs must we begin to think of awarding further "Mud & Blood Medals". Anyone who can truthfully say that they have not at any time been uncertain of their whereabouts is invited to give us their story. Two guesses who will be our first customer - the Battalion I.O. of course.

Last night was so dark that the C.O. and the 2 i/c were unfortunate enough to collide with one another, and both fell to the ground. After regaining his feet and his composure, one was heard to say: "Don't apologise, but be good enough to tell me if you can, which way I was facing before you knocked me over."

At the moment of writing this, the sounds of a popular song come swinging through the still night air. It is "There'll Always be an England", and we want to make known to you an additional verse which, the Padre informs us, is now taught to the school children throughout Australia: Do you remember how lustily we sang the song at our Birthday Concert?

"There'll always be Australia: where wattle blossoms bloom,
Where gum trees rear their shady boughs neath skies that know no gloom,
There'll always be Australia while plains wide to the sky,
Reveal the spirit of our men who dare to do and die,

The Anzac soul inspired our men of old,
Heroes who gave our land a name none dare defame,
Our Motherland we'll give a helping hand,
Ready to start - To do our part - With all our heart,
There'll always be Australia while homes and hearts are free,
As England is so dear to you - Australia is to me."

BBC NEWS — 23rd September, 1941.

Russia - Unshaken by the loss of Kiev, the Russian forces are counter attacking fiercely along the whole of the Eastern Front. Around Smolensk, the Russian counter attacks are gradually taking the form of a large counter-offensive. In this area during the last few days, the Russians claim to have smashed eight German Divisions, and at one point, to have thrown them back twenty miles. This counter-offensive is on a front of sixty miles, and the Russians have advanced an average of 8 to 10 miles, and state that the Germans are still on the run. A correspondent at present on the Eastern Front, has stated that the Russians are cheerful and confident. He states that in the Smolensk area, there is ample proof of the hurried retreat of the Germans, who had built strong defences, and left them intact. The Russian Artillery had been particularly accurate, and many direct hits had been scored on the defences. The Russian armies near Kiev have also launched a counter attack, and the Germans even refer to the fierce fighting there. At Odessa, heavy losses have been inflicted on the enemy, and the outer defences of the City have been improved. At Leningrad in the far north of the front, there is no sign that the enemy is any nearer the City, but a report from Moscow, states that the Russians there have pushed the enemy back 6 miles at one point. During Sunday, the Russians claim to have destroyed 100 German machines, both in the air and on the ground, with the loss of only 21 Russian aircraft.

Bulgaria - It has been reported that Russian parachute troops have landed in Bulgaria, but this is strongly denied by the Russians, who state that this story has been concocted by the Bulgarian Police.

United States - A 7000 ton US vessel, which was travelling to Iceland, has been sunk, and so far there has been no news of the crew of

34. It is thought in America that the sinking of this vessel is probably Hitler's answer to President Roosevelt's statement that American shipping must be left alone. Colonel Knox in a broadcast, stated that the National Motto should be "Step on the Gas", as our defences must be improved. Mr. Cordell Hull commenting on the incident, said that he has told everyone for some time that the Neutrality Act should be changed. It is also reported from the US, that twelve more British warships are at present in American Ports, and that these include the Rodney and the Malaya. The British warships mentioned a few days ago as being in American Ports, have already left.

Middle East - Two Italian liners of about 21,000 tons, which were carrying supplies to Libya, have been intercepted and sunk by our submarines. These ships were travelling at a high speed, and were escorted by a strong force. Our Submarines also attacked another ship, which is thought to have probably sunk. Our Air Force has also been active, and raids were carried out on shipping off Tripoli. Two large Schooners were sunk, and one, which was probably carrying ammunition, blew up with a terrific explosion which destroyed both the ship and the attacking plane. On Saturday night, hits were scored on another enemy ship of about 8000 tons, by our Air Force, which was operating off Tripoli. In this attack, our aircraft attacked a Cruiser, and one plane which dived to within 12 feet of the deck dropped bombs, scoring a direct hit. As the pilot swerved to avoid the mast of the Cruiser, the observer could see where the bombs had landed.

The Ex Shah of Iran, has left his son all his property, in order that he may use it to the interest of the country. The new Shah has in turn, given the property to the State. A new Cabinet was formed in Iran yesterday. A British communique from Simla states that our forces have not yet occupied Teheran. They are remaining outside the City, and our Commanders who entered the City for a conference, left as soon as it was over.

TOBRUK, 25th September, 1941.

Yesterday, we mentioned names of ten men who have brought honour to the Battalion, and today, we have to add the names of two men from "B" Company, who have been awarded the Military Medal. During the last month, these two men, Cpl. Hayes C.B. and Pte. Bennett L., together with an Englishman, Capt. Leakey, successfully held off an attack by approximately 30 Italians, on one of our outposts known then as 'JIM'. Not only did they withstand the attack, but inflicted grievous casualties on the enemy.

It is with interest, that we note that the two medal winners mentioned above, are the first of our reinforcements to make a name for themselves, and we congratulate them accordingly. To be perfectly truthful, we don't use the term reinforcements more than we can help, for once such men reach us, they become full blown 'Mud'n Bloods'.

We have some news of Melbourne football, which has reached its closing stages for 1941. Scores in the League Semi-finals were:-

| ESSENDON | 21 Gls | 9 | defeated | RICHMOND | 11 Gls 15 |
| MELBOURNE | 16 Gls | 13 | defeated | CARLTON | 11 Gls 16 |

Which leaves Carlton now to play Essendon for the right to meet Melbourne in the Grand Final.

Association Semi-final result:-

| COBURG | 15 Gls 17 | defeated | PRESTON | 15 Gls 12 |

Port Melbourne has yet to meet Prahran. The Recorder Cup for the Best and Fairest in Association Clubs has been won by Des Fothergill, formerly of Collingwood.

If anyone has Aug. 6 issue of Mud & Blood, they will see another sketch of the same gentleman as shown here. It must be flattering him too much to give our readers such an unwarranted overdose of his slender form, but there is such a marked change in his appearance, that we are now uncertain whether he comes from Mexico, Madrid, or Mirboo North. It is quite noticeable amongst our Subalterns, that their appearance is on the improve, as they are anxious, (so are we) to throw off their mantle of Libyan dust, in preparation for a triumphant introduction to fresh Senoritas in the M.E.

THREE CHEERS!

Having read the foregoing par, you now know that we are leaving Tobruk.................Xmas is coming, too. Did you know? Were we to publish all reports as to date of our proposed departure, 'Mud'n Blood' No. 79 would be simply reduced to a calendar for 1942.

In a letter from the I.T.B., we learn that Pte. Alan Currie, mentioned in a recent issue, has been declared fit, and expects to rejoin us at an early date. He should be able to give Mud & Blood some rare stories, we think.

In our modern age, it was without amazement that we saw two mechanical robot figures silhouetted against the evening moon. We listened carefully for a minute, and this is what we heard:-

"Darling, I wish you'd have your nuts counter-sunk,
they're scratching my chromium."

BBC NEWS — 25th September, 1941.

Russia - Yesterdays Russian communique states that part of their forces have successfully withdrawn from the Kiev Sector, and that the remainder are attempting to fight their way out. In the Leningrad area, the Germans claim to have entered the suburbs of the City. In a broadcast from Leningrad to Moscow last night, they stated that the enemy was at the gates of the City. The population of Leningrad is faced with the fate of Warsaw, but the Russians are making constant counter attacks, in an endeavour to keep the enemy out. In one of these counter attacks, Soviet troops charged through a curtain of fire, stormed a bridge, and put the Germans to flight at bayonet point. The Germans wavered and broke at the sight of cold steel, and were driven back seven miles. The communique also claims that Soviet forces in besieged Odessa, have thrown the enemy back several miles after a series of counter attacks. They claim that the Rumanian troops in Russia have lost half of their army since the beginning of the war. An offensive in the Northern Front by a German Mountain Division, was broken up by Russian troops, who enveloped the German flanks, and the enemy retreated in dis-order, leaving 700 officers and men dead on the battlefield. On the Central front, Russian troops who have held the initiative for the past three weeks, are now within 25 miles of Smolensk. The Russian Ambassador in London, said yesterday, that at a moderate estimate, German losses in the East were some three million killed, wounded and missing, and in the three months, the number of German planes destroyed, total something like 8500. About one third of the whole

German Army, according to the Ambassador, is now out of action. He went on to say that the fate of humanity for many generations to come, is being decided around Leningrad, Momensk, and in the Ukraine. He warned that too much reliance should not be placed on such uncertainties as General Winter and General Mud, which with modern techniques of war, are considerably minimised, and have been reduced to Colonel Winter and Major Mud. The war won't stand still until winter stops. The German machine is still strong, and Russia faces a difficult situation. He concluded by urging more aid to Russia, who has lost important industrial districts, and a number of factories and plants. Finnish aircraft have been active on the Northern front, and claim to have destroyed an important railway centre, which links up with Leningrad and Moscow. With the aid of British machines, the Russian Air Force has caused serious losses to the Germans.

Cairo - Tuesdays war communique reports that as a result of their vigorous patrolling activities, our forces at Tobruk are steadily enlarging the area outside our Perimeter defences, which the enemy has been forced to evacuate. In the Frontier area, aggressive action by our patrols continues. RAF Headquarters announce that during Sunday, a large enemy liner with its escort was attacked in central Mediterranean, and 8 direct hits were scored amidships, which brought the liner to a standstill. Monday night the Fleet Air Arm attacked an enemy convoy in the same area and machine gunned one of the merchant ships. The harbour at Benghasi and Moles at Tripoli were again attacked yesterday by heavy bombers of the RAF. The attacks lasted far into the night, and hits were scored on the mole and buildings near the wireless station at Tripoli. The Fleet Air Arm attacked enemy merchant ships in the Mediterranean. One torpedo hit a large ship, and another hit the ship following it. Further hits were scored on another vessel. From all these operations, only one of our aircraft is missing. Our submarines have also been active in the Mediterranean, and have torpedoed 5 more enemy ships. Two supply ships, a transport, a mine layer, and a large schooner. The latter was attacked within range of shore batteries, but in spite of this, the attack was pressed home.

Washington - The Secretary of the Navy, Colonel Knox, has declared that the Neutrality Act should be immediately repealed. According to President Roosevelt's Secretary, a revision of the Neutrality Act, and the arming of merchant ships, is likely next week. He added that nineteen million pounds has been requested for the arming of the American Merchant Fleet.

Far East - The following warning in regard to the Far East has just been given by the Commander of the British Forces there. He said that - "The present temporary lull is not the time for sleep. Full opportunity should be taken of the time that is now ours. Japan is watching Russia, and Russia's battle is our battle."

South Africa - General Smutts yesterday reviewed South Africa's wartime and military achievements. He said "I sometimes wonder how it has been possible for this small country, unprepared, to have accomplished so much. We have more than 150,000 men on active service. From an industrial point of view we have accomplished wonders. Even our Mint is manufacturing small arms ammunition.

TOBRUK, 26th September, 1941.

Read about ourselves as do the people in Albury.

Following is a par from Albury's famous daily, "The Border Mail".

"Mud & Blood is the kind of paper I'd like to edit. No ads, no split second decisions to be made about some old hen's reaction to a bit of very necessary sub-editing of daughter Daisy's fifth 21st birthday jag - and no news! True, "Mud & Blood" publishes the communiques of the belligerents as a matter of routine (I almost said respectability), but the mob we used to see in Dean Street are realists by now.

"As there's no hope of dissecting the truth from propaganda, 'Albury's Own' prefers to write about itself - and how!! "

"Another suggestion the 'Mail' makes is "If its (Tobruk's) gaolers had as much sense of humour as their 'prisoners', they'd call it a day and leave their beer behind".

From today, we shall see to it that Jerry is added to our distribution list. Runner!

Of course many of our readers are mentioned in the article, and all of them can claim world wide fame. Especially Tich Wynach for his amazing speed, and Lieut. Harry Marshall for his ability in picking the errors in spelling. By the way, have you noticed how this latter practice has ceased since he became Adjutant?

Items of sporting news received from Aussie, tell of Carlton's defeat at the hands of Essendon, who will now meet Melbourne in the grand final, on Saturday next, September 27th. The Brownlow Medal winner for 1941 was Norman Ware, Captain of Footscray, and some of our readers will rejoice that Ware comes from Sale in Gippsland. Port Melbourne scored a narrow victory over Prahran, winning by 2 points in the second semi-final. W. Elliott, well known champion jockey died recently as the result of an accident.

Anyone interested in the collection of stamps will be pleased to know that the Australian Government contemplates the issue of special stamps to commemorate the Siege of Tobruk and other A.I.F. doings.

Well, wouldn't that! A certain RSM just indicated that he had something which might interest us, so we hasten respectfully to his dug-out, mug in hand. We repeat, respectfully, for after all, he DOES issue the rum (although, we think, in rather small quantities). Just quietly, have you noticed a wicked look in that gentleman's eye of late? Wouldn't be the result of over-running, we suppose? Whoever it was had the effront-ery to write the above para, we cannot say, but now, some 24 hours later, we can assure our readers that the suggestions therein are quite incorrect. Our RSM has found his true vocation at last, and we are forwarding under separate cover, a letter, recommending his ability to Bertie the Cellarman. We are told too, that Bertie and his alcoholic acquaintances are eagerly awaiting all Mud & Bloods at Alex.

HQ Company Mud & Bloods will be particularly pleased to learn that Sgt. Jack O'Brien and Pte. W. Myers have now proceeded to the Con-valescent Depot, having made a good recovery from their unfortunate accident. In a letter from a staff nurse at the AGH where they were, she says Jack and his 2 i/c were most helpful to her. Say we "Who wouldn't be". It appears that when an unusually large number of men arrived at AGH, our cooking experts, led by cheery Jack, took charge of the business and provided the meal for them. Were it to assist a damsel in distress, there is no doubt that each and all of us would have acted likewise (after six months in this dump, anyway).

Well Mud'n Bloods, we don't believe in astrology and all that non-sense, BUT there was a rainbow in the sky this morning. If that's not a good omen, we'll consume our khaki fur felt.

> There was a young maid from Peru,
> Who decided her loves were too few,
>   So she walked from her door
>   With a fig leaf, no more,
> And now she's in bed with the 'flu.

BBC NEWS — 26th September, 1941.

 Russia - On the Russian front, heavy fighting is still in progress, and there is some indication of a new development in the German plan of campaign. Last nights Russian communique states that their troops fought the enemy along the entire front. They claim that in air battles yesterday, Soviet planes shot down 70 German machines, and destroyed a further 68 on the ground. Russian losses were 36 aircraft. Last night several German planes attempted to penetrate to Moscow, but they were driven off with heavy ack-ack fire. It has been reported that the Germans have launched an attack on the Crimea, but this has not been confirmed in either the Russian or German communiques. The report states that 4 German Divisions are taking part in the attack, and that they are advancing from recently gained bases on the coast. To invest the Crimea, the Germans would first have to batter their way across the Isthmus, and here, their usual practice of throwing wave after wave of men into the battle, would be impossible. Crimea has an area three times that of Crete, and during the past three years, it has been made into an almost impregnable fortress, and should be able to give a good account of itself. Odessa is still standing up to the heavy German attacks, and the whole of the City is virtually in the front line of the battle. The Germans are still making big claims as to the encirclement of the Russian troops near Kiev, but it is not yet clear as to how many men the Russians have been able to withdraw from this area. A large Russian City to the east of Kiev is now preparing to defend itself against the German hordes. In the Leningrad Sector, the defences of the City have withstood many attacks by both infantry and tanks. A few tanks managed to break through, but these were destroyed, and in a fierce counter attack, the defenders threw the enemy back six miles. According to yesterdays German communique, their troops were in the suburbs of Leningrad, but today, they merely mention that their troops are nearing the outskirts of the City. A correspondent in Russia, states that the morale of the Russians is high, and that he has no doubt that they can stand the strain of the German onslaught.

 United States - A Bill to repeal the Neutrality Act, was introduced into the Senate yesterday. Most American people understood that when President Roosevelt issued his famous order to the Navy to shoot on sight, he had shot the Neutrality Act right through the vitals. The US Navy Chief has arrived at Hamilton, Bermuda, and has begun an inspection of the country's defences. The Duke and Dutchess of Windsor paid a visit to President Roosevelt yesterday.

Albania - The Serbian revolt has turned into almost a battle in Albania, and this is even mentioned over the Berlin Radio, which announced that the fighting there lasted for several hours. The Italians also admit the open revolt of the Serbian people, and state that there are 1½ million patriots there to be dealt with by the Axis.

Norway - A German sentry in Norway has been found dead at a quayside. The Germans there, immediately arrested a number of dock workers, and sentenced them to long terms of imprisonment with hard labour.

Cairo - The latest Air communique from Cairo reports further effective bombing of Tripoli and Benghasi on Tuesday night. At Benghasi, one vessel was hit and blew up, and hits were also scored on the mole, and ships in the harbour were straddled. Traffic on the road to Benghasi was also attacked. Bardia was raided, and our fighters attacked a number of enemy planes in the Frontier area. Five of our aircraft are missing from all these operations, but two of the pilots are safe.

Far East - Fierce fighting is reported in China, where the Japanese are driving southwards. A Tokyo report states that 300,000 picked Chinese troops are fighting desperately to hold the Japanese offensive. Chinese officials admit that the situation is critical.

London - The 12 German Diplomats who are being exchanged for a similar number of British Diplomats, have arrived in Lisbon.

TOBRUK, 27th September, 1941.

All of us, and particularly "C" Company, will be pleased to learn that Lieut. J.A. Hutchinson, who distinguished himself on April 22nd in the Battalion's first scrum, has now recovered from his wounds. He was in hospital at Derna, but has now been transferred to Sulmona Camp, near Rome.

Reading in a news sheet, it is discovered that teachers at home are now forbidden to use the cane. That's a bit tough on young Australians, because after the war, some of our Mud & Bloods will have to pack a gun to gain control of their pupils. Lieut. Ken Reid will no doubt still have that ugly six shooter of his dangling on an I-ti belt. Which we wonder would be the more frightening - his revolver or his moustache? And unless the army has produced a similar armament for Lieut. Tom Matthews, he'll have to carry a rifle into his classroom. The butt stroke should be very efficient, though. There's another, too - one Pte. Vic Bennett from HQ Company. We can see him supplanting the cane with a range finder. Instead of three with the cane, Vic will deliver one with the range finder - end on, we suggest.

A recent cutting from the 'Argus' reveals the interesting fact that evidently the German officials can't take it, as they are considering a vigorous campaign for an increase in the birth rate. Now hold hard, Mud & Bloods, the road to Berlin is not yet open, but perhaps after reading through these extracts we can help them out with a few bright suggestions. Evidently there must be some other reason why Goering is bedecked with all those medals. First we find Himmler announcing that, "For the pure blooded German, there exists a war duty outside marriage, and which has nothing to do with marriage. This duty consists of becoming a mother by a soldier going to the war." (What with petrol rationing, we guess the village bicycles are now coming into their own).

Then the Stormtroop Journal - that fine example of bulldust - appeals to all Jerries in general, and enamel ones in particular, "to show you are ready, not only to give your life for your country, but present your girl with a new life before you go to your death." Who could refuse to help Hitler and his henchmen out of such a problem? Is it any wonder there has been such a rush to arms? Recalling whispers of internal tumult inside Germany, we think the Army, in pushing out on new fronts, is not looking for strife, but rather running away from it. Mr. Hitler, if you are having so much trouble, why not send all your soldiers out to Tobruk for 6 months, then we can assure you your troubles will be over (and more economically too).

"For shame" is the cry when we read such a heart touching appeal as this advertisement - "I am a soldier, 22, fair, blue eyed. Before sacrificing my life for the Fuhrer and Fatherland, I desire to meet a German woman by whom I can leave a child as legacy for German glory". This must be the answer to a fraulein's prayer, which also appears in the article as - "A German girl wishes to be the mother of a child whose father is a German soldier fighting for Nazism". The Hun seems well aware his life is being sacrificed, and taken all round it is a damn poor show. Once again the Aussies will have to show 'em.

The popularity of WO George Moore is easy to explain, for since he has been handling the Q side, we have been getting a daily rum issue.

George, keep those precious jars away from the Stukas' eggs, which Jerry so frequently lays in 'Bomb Happy Valley'.

It is against our rules to make insinuations; but we have received many queries like this:- "What did Capt. C. Morrell do with the rum when he was QM?"

Just to show how the desert gets you, we publish today, a poem written by Sgt. D. Renton of "A" Company:-

TO A REAL SWEETHEART

You are not here to soothe my sorry plight,
    As on my bed I lay my body nude.
In paltry pit all through the desert night,
    I sleep my sleep of lonely solitude.

Ah me! If I could leave this fiery field,
    While yet I have this precious life to live;
Not meekly to the Siren would I yield,
    To you alone my body I would give.

No more for me the Wanton with her wiles,
    Just you for me and I to serve you true.
All joy is mine and mine the happy smiles,
    As night draws nigh and leads me on to you.

Ah! Rest you there upon my welcome bed,
    While swiftly I throw off my clothes of strife;
And as I stand with all my garments shed,
    My inner soul sings praise to joyous life.

Now come to me; Ah! Sweetness so divine!
    Caress my neck! my breast! Ah! joy supreme!
Oh thrill me as your legs round mine entwine!
    And warmly clasp my waist - my sweet! my dream!

What heav'n is this! What richness of delight!
    What woe was mine when you were far away!
So stay PYJAMAS, sweetheart of the night,
    And leave me not until the dawn of day.

BBC NEWS — 27th September, 1941.

Russia - According to a Moscow spokesman, the German thrust in Crimea has been underway since Thursday, and first reports indicate that the Russians have the situation well in hand. Large scale parachute operations were also carried out, but the Russians, anticipating these moves, waited behind minefields and blew entire German Battalions into the air. Germans attacked again later, but so far no news of German penetration in Soviet lines reported. In Leningrad Sector, Marshal Voroshilov's forces continue smashing at Germans, and during the last few days, Russian forces have managed to move forward, capturing four large villages. Over the whole of this front, one steady battle is raging, with Soviet troops attacking in mass formations. On Finnish frontier, the Finns claim to have reached the River Sher and cut off some power stations supplying Leningrad. No fresh news from Murmansk area, where the Germans appear to be making no progress.

London - Fighter Command Aircraft yesterday afternoon attacked four enemy mine-sweepers and two Anti-aircraft ships off Dunkirk. Both ack-ack ships were damaged, and two minesweepers were set on fire. No British aircraft are missing. Other fighters sank an enemy supply ship off Cherbourg. A statement made in London yesterday, says that co-operation between British and Russian Forces in Iran has not been marred by the least friction. Complete liaison has been established, and both personal and official relations leave nothing to be desired. This denies German propaganda to the contrary.

Moscow - German and Rumanian troops attacking Odessa, suffered 50,000 casualties in killed, wounded, and prisoners, in first fortnight of September. Odessa's defenders have driven the enemy out of two strategically important towns after a two day offensive around the north of Dnieper. London Air Ministry communique states that reports from the Russian front, show that RAF fighters continue to escort Russian bombers on offensive operations. British fighters shot down two more enemy planes without loss to themselves.

South Africa - South Africa has built two 45 ton Anti-submarine vessels for the Royal Navy, and has undertaken further orders for Naval craft. These two vessels which will be launched shortly, are the largest sea-going vessels built in the Union.

Cyprus - Many pilots who fought in the Battle of Britain, are now flying Hurricanes in increasing RAF activity from Cyprus. Several new aerodromes have been built, and within a few weeks, the possibilities of Cyprus have been transformed.

Australia - The Australian representative on the Eastern Supply Council, at present in Malaya, said yesterday that Australia was in the war up to the hilt. We have 600,000 fighting men, and 200,000 munition workers. We have built 50 new ships for the Navy, and we will soon be turning out dive-bombers.

Far East - Japan's drive into South China is reported to be held up by very heavy Chinese counter attacks over the past 48 hours. The fighting is very heavy, and there have been enormous casualties on both sides. The Japanese claim to have smashed 4 of the 7 Chinese Armies in that Sector.

Cairo - A report from Cairo tells of the heroism of South African pilots serving near the Libyan border. Two of our fighters patrolling in that area, were engaged by enemy fighters. One of our planes was badly damaged, and the pilot forced to bail out over enemy territory. The pilot of the other fighter machine gunned enemy moving to the spot, landed, dragged the wounded pilot onto the wing of his plane, and took off.

TOBRUK, 29th September, 1941.

When we read of a crowd of 60,000 odd at a football match in Melbourne, we begin to wonder whether they know there's a war on. Certainly many of them are assisting the prosecution of the war in a manner of which we know nought. However, we reckon that this little verse, written by Ann, the 14 year old daughter of our popular Brig. R. W. Tovell, may do some good.

JOIN UP

Answer the call when it comes to you,
    Don't let others do the job for you,
You're just the fella for whom they plead,
    So don't shirk your duty in hour of need.

Your boy cobbers have gone away -
    Do you really want to stay?
Our brothers, fathers and uncles too,
    Are waiting now for help from you.

The Army, the Navy and the Air Force too,
    Are calling, ever calling you,
The King and country need you,
    To join up right away,
Remember, you've a free will, so join up today.

We Australians are supposed to have a reputation for resourcefulness. Can any of you lads in other Companies beat this "C" Company example? A lad who in normal life is a butcher, was whittling away at a piece of wood from the butt of an old I-ti rifle. The toasting fork was used to burn the small hole in the stem, and believe it or not, our contributor asserts that he has smoked worse pipes than the one "Butch" turned out! We think it is rather late by now, but previously, "Mousey" the body snatcher was taking orders for these I-ti Specials at 15 akers.

Talking of souvenirs, reminds us of our worthy Pioneer Platoon - any one of whom would make a grand souvenir!

Pioneer Bob Scott's thoughts were evidently far away when he and his mates were busy recently doing some blasting for the new R.A.P. During the process, a tall slim gentleman remarked to him: "I suppose you'll be making dugouts in your own backyard, after the war?" "No, Sir," was Scotty's reply "not dugouts, but alternative positions ready in case of an argument with the wife!" What we'd like to know is - who is going to occupy them, Pte. Scott or Mrs. Scott?

Our Sigs have been reading the 'Good Book', and have produced their own 'Ten Commandments' which we publish. God grant that our dearly beloved and useful Sigs obey them to the letter!

To all Whom it May Concern -

These are the standards which a good Sig lives by, and we herewith give them to posterity or a "Mud & Blood". Verily it is writ within the pages of the good book of words, that ye who are followers of the code of Morse, shall keep these Commandments -

1. Thou shalt be courteous, calm and patient, and shall not tell the subscriber to "GO TO HELL", neither shalt thou call the CO, nor any of his officers by the name of a fool.

2. Thou shalt not speak as with a plum in thy mouth, lest the multitude who listen, curse thee.

3. Thou shalt not gossip on the phone lest it be said of thee - "He gossipeth and worketh not".

4. Thou shalt not listen in on any conversation, lest thine ears be burned and thy pride wounded, neither shalt thou repeat anything which thou hearest on the phone.

5. Thou shalt not swing the lead, neither shalt thou be late when called upon for thy shift.

6. Thou shalt have one job, and one job alone; and beware that thy mind wandereth not therefrom.

7. Thou shalt not, when called for cable party, hide thy talent behind a bushel, and be numbered among the missing.

8. Thou shalt not covet thy neighbour's phones, nor his cable, nor anything that is thy neighbours.

9. Thou shalt not be caught stealing anything that is thy neighbours, lest thou be in everlasting danger of being called stupid, but rather shouldst thou at all times be qualified to scrounge, therefore let not thy conscience trouble thee.

10. If thine enemy should slice thy line, curse him not; but rather inform thine own arty, that he may heap coals of fire on thine enemy's head.

N.B. All these things thou shalt do, remembering that whilst an army marches on its stomach, it requireth also the life line of its signals.

"CERTA CITO"

BBC NEWS — 29th September, 1941.

Russia - The Soviet Fleet has scored spectacular successes. A Russian communique states that units of the Soviet Northerr Fleet, have sunk 2 supply ships of 8000 and 5000 tons. Coastal batteries and the Baltic Fleet, have sunk 1 enemy Cruiser, and 1 Destroyer, and damaged two other Destroyers. An enemy tanker was also sunk in the Black Sea. The latest Russian communique reports that every day, the resistance of Leningrad grows stronger. Fighting continued along the entire 2000 mile front, with the Soviet forces claiming a number of important local successes, including the recapture of 10 villages in the Central Sector, and the destruction of German tanks, armoured cars, artillery and transports. Soviet guer-

illa troops wrecked a German troop train. Moscow had its first fall of snow on Saturday. The Russians claim that on Sunday, they destroyed 98 Nazi planes, and place their own losses at 31. American aircraft and aviation petrol, have already arrived in Russia, and the American delegate to the 3 Power Conference in Moscow, declared that the Conference will work fast, because time is vital.

Cairo - The American journalist, Ralph Ingersoll, who arrived in Cairo from Moscow, said that the Russians are extremely confident. They call German soldiers "bums", and say they are only able to fight with immense numbers of tanks. Successful attacks on enemy aircraft bases in Sardinia and Sicily were carried out by RAF on Saturday. The RAF bombed Bardia by daylight, destroying Messerschmitts and damaging others. From all these operations five of our aircraft are missing. The Italian Garrison at Wolchefit in Abyssinia has surrendered to British and Patriot forces.

Rome - Mussolini has announced that bread rationing is to be introduced in Italy.

Berlin - It was announced over the Berlin Radio, that Germans have arrested the Premier of the Protectorate of Bohemia and Moravia, on the charge of high treason. Nazis admit arrests in Czechoslovakia, where sabotage of German war effort has reached considerable proportions, and have appointed notorious Gestapo Chief, Heydrich, to put down the spirit of resistance.

New York - It is stated in New York, that Britain's legless pilot, Douglas Bader, who is a prisoner of war in Germany, and who recently received an aluminium leg dropped by parachute to replace the one broken when he crashed, promptly tried to escape. He was recaptured however, and the Nazis now remove his legs every night.

France - Twenty more Frenchmen have been executed, as a reprisal for the death of German soldiers.

Belgium - An aged couple and their daughter, have been put to death, because they gave refuge to British troops.

Far East - The Japanese News Agency repeats the claim that the Capital of a Chinese Province has been captured, but this is denied by the Chinese.

Australia - Don Bradman, who was discharged from the Australian Air Force on account of ill health, is unlikely to play cricket this season, although his health has improved.

Cairo - Apart from some ineffective enemy artillery fire, the situation at Tobruk throughout Saturday, was generally quiet. In the Frontier area, our patrols are continuing their aggressive activities. On Saturday a South African patrol captured a staff car containing four Italian Officers.

TOBRUK, 30th September, 1941.

In our issue of 26th September, we published a poem by one of "A" Company's Sergeants. Evidently the trend of his verses has touched a soft spot in another Mud & Blood, who writes:-

A certain sergeant; names need not be mentioned,
　An ode has writ, which may be well intentioned.
Five verses picturing his sensuous charmers,
　Then tells us that it's all about Pyjamas.

Nay, Sergeant, Nay! Why spoil thy lusty song?
　We realise that thou'st been here over long.
No need for sudden shame, sixth verse repeal;
　Hold head up lad; We all know how you feel.

H.J. Boas, Lieut.

Curiosity has got the better of us, since we heard that Lieut. Morrie Goldstone has taken to wearing dark glasses. Owing to his rather burly dimensions, we think maybe, that it's a rather futile attempt at concealment or camouflage, or is it perhaps, his way of viewing Libya through rose-tinted glasses?

Pte. Norm Spooner seems to have recovered his composure now that he has been up at the front line for a few restful days. Doubtless, he is the envy of all the bomb happy family at "B" Echelon. Must apologize to him, however, for the spot of bingle bingle during the night before last.

These Don Company fellows are most mysterious, for we don't altogether catch on to the full weight of their most recent contribution. However, we trust that the Dons will see the hidden meaning, should there be one. Here's the yarn:-

There seems to be some healthy rivalry in Don Company, between the CQMS and his driver, Ron Ben (son of) McKenzie and Mrs. Burnett's little boy Norman, whose friends call him "Burnie", and the new storeman, Pte. Len Williams, who succeeded Roy Clark on his transfer to the inner circle at "B" Echelon. At least we gather there is something of the kind concerning the time of their return to "B" Echelon, or else why would the CSM and the Orderly Room Corporal, with the assistance of Tich Allen, meet the truck bearing the food, water and the precious CQMS, and sing that old music hall song "Three o'clock in the Morning" or some parody thereon?   The said CQ hasn't got a suspicious mind, but he was heard to mutter something about talking to that so and so driver, and teaching him some song about the sun breaking the eastern sky; so we are left to make our own deductions about who was late and who was later.

We are unable to say from which Post this anecdote has come, but it's a bloody story —

RATS EAT RATS

This saying proved true the other night, when one of us so called Tobruk Rats awoke to find a rat nibbling at the top of his finger, and blood running everywhere. Lo and behold if the same thing didn't occur the next night, only this time in the dugout of another Tobruk Rat, the operation being performed on the upper arm.

We noticed today that in an Australian Pictorial, was a complete chart and descriptive article headed "WORLD'S BEST FED SOLDIERS", and believe it or not, that's US. Of course, only our modesty prevents us from deleting the word "FED". While we never make a habit of grumbling - not much - we reckon that there's a great day in store for us when we ultimately get back again to Aussie rationing. Amongst other things, we shall taste, (so says the Pictorial) REAL eggs, fresh meat, bread that IS bread, and numerous other things for which our palate craves...........
What a day!

What a popular chap will the cook become, and with what eagerness will the men accept their mess orderly duties. Oh yeah! Forgive us if we whet your appetite with a glimpse of a typical Monday morning snack:-

Rolled oats, fresh milk, bacon and 2 fried eggs, Mashed spud, bread and butter, honey and tea.

BBC NEWS — 30th September, 1941.

Russia - The Three Power Conference in Moscow, had its first
meeting yesterday. A special Russian communique has been issued, giving details of what was discussed at the conference. It was decided to
appoint 6 Committees, to deal with Navy, Army, Medical, Transport, Production and Finance problems. The Commander of the Leningrad defences, and one of the Russian delegates were present at the Conference.
The latest Russian communique claims that the Soviet Air Force has
accounted for 263 German machines during Friday and Saturday. The
RAF Wing which is operating on the Eastern Front, also accounted for
12 enemy planes, for the loss of one British machine. On the Central
front, the German Panzer Regiments, according to the Russians, are in
full retreat. A Military correspondent in Moscow stated that the German
idea had been to batter a way through to Moscow from the North West,
but when the Russians counter attacked and stopped this plan, they
tried a new plan, and wheeled to the South East. This was also unsuccessful, and the Russians have advanced on a 60 mile front, and the whole
area has been turned into a tank cemetery. It is also claimed by the Russians, that in this Sector, 13 German Divisions have been routed, and suffered 20,000 casualties. The German attack on Crimea has developed into a
terrific battle. German planes are constantly raiding the Russian forces,
and it is reported that a great German land force is attacking the isthmus.
It is reported from Leningrad, that a tank battle has been raging outside
the City for the last 7 days. One Russian Tank Unit has destroyed 12
tanks, and put a large amount of the enemy's vital equipment out of action. Here, the Russians claim that the Germans have lost 1500 Officers
and men.

Britain - It was announced in London last night, that British workers have turned out more tanks in the last 3 months, than in the whole of
last year. Last week, more armoured carriers were turned out than ever
before. Spitfires and Hurricanes were in action yesterday over the Channel,
and the French Coast. They succeeded in sinking a sea-going barge, set an
anti-aircraft ship ablaze, and put batteries on the coast out of action. One
of our planes is missing, but the pilot is safe. A convoy of German lorries
was also attacked, and 5 vehicles were left in flames. Our heavy bombers
also carried out raids over Italy, and reached their objectives by flying high
over the Alps. Several people were killed, and a number seriously injured,
when bombs were dropped on a town in North East Scotland. Mr. Anthony
Eden yesterday broadcast to the Czechoslavakian people, telling them to
hold on. No one, he said, would forget the tragic sacrifice by which it was

hoped to avoid the tragedy of war. He went on to say that the Czech people were far from being beaten down, and had only been more united by their terrible experiences. Today, he added, after 3 years, the Czech Nation was far from being destroyed, and is stronger and more united than ever before. Another important British convoy has been escorted safely to Port, despite numerous attacks from enemy planes. The convoy reached its destination, although one ship was damaged, and had to be sunk by our own gunfire. None of the crew of this vessel, however, were lost. A Warship was also slightly damaged.

Cairo - Men of the Tobruk Garrison have made a daring assault on the enemy. They attacked a strong post, and dealt with an unspecified number of Italians. In the Frontier area, our fighting patrols are still harassing the enemy.

Far East - Chungsha, Capital of a Chinese Province, is still in Chinese hands, in spite of Japanese claims to the contrary. The Chinese claim that 100,000 Japanese troops are trapped near the City, and it is stated by Chinese Officials, that the situation is very hopeful.

Teheran - Messages from Teheran say that General Wavell has told newspaper correspondents that he does not think it will be necessary to make a combined British and Russian Command in that area. Asked whether he would visit Russia, he said "Well, not yet". The Commander of the Russian Forces in Teheran, had a 90 minute conference with General Wavell yesterday. General Wavell also conferred with General Auchinleck at Baghdad, and it has been reported that they discussed in full details of co-operation between India and the Middle East.

United States - President Roosevelt is expected to return to Washington to confer with Mr. Cordell Hull re the arming of American Merchant vessels. It is stated that Mr. Cordell Hull favoured modification, rather than the repeal, of the Neutrality Act.

London - It is reported in London that more Czech Patriots have been executed, and at least 20 men were shot on the day that the new German Commander took over. It is also stated that thousands of arrests have been made in Bohemia, and that 2 retired Generals have been shot.

CHAPTER 9

TOBRUK, 2nd October, 1941.

We take the liberty today of offering our readers a word or two concerning one of our Mud & Bloods.

If you've not heard of "The Old Gentleman with the Grey Shirt", it's about time we introduced you. Now, we must admit that Pte. Eric Stuart (Stewy) has achieved more fame than many of us Mud & Bloods, for he has powers of vision that far excel those of any other observer we have ever met.

Of course, this ability comes as a result of his pre-war experience in the Western District of Victoria, where his major sport was that of finding out what went on in the surrounding country side. He as much as told us that he used to be a kind of bush 'oracle' whither the neighbouring lads of the village (and the lasses too, yes?) were wont to gather the local scandal. He kept his secret well, for only recently has he confessed that he did not confine his use of his telescope to the rifle range, but spotted from his back verandah. Sunday morning sights, we believe, were the most exciting. Woe to thee, Eric, if this paper reaches your native haunts.

Since he joined the army, this oracle business has remained his chief hobby, for after pottering about in Don Company for some months, he comes to the I Section, and soon, with the aid of binoculars instead of 'scope, he finds himself explaining the landscape to none the less than the General himself. The way he treats us privates is just too bad, as we are small fry in comparison with his usual associates - field officers, brigadiers etc. Even if he performs no other deed, Eric will go down in history as the only private who has told a Divisional Commander to "Sit down, or you'll draw the crabs on my pole". You see, even Brass Hats are chicken feed to him!

Mention of chicken feed reminds us of home, and there, we can visualise our eagle-eyed observer erecting poles on his property, (with dug-outs for safety) from which he will be able to give map references for the positions of any and all of his own cows, and at least 12 figure refs for those of his neighbours!

It's just as well there are no rabbits in Libya, for the poor creatures would have little chance of finding homes in the vicinity of BHQ, anyway. Local inhabitants - lizards, jerbons and the like - have long since been crowded out. Just the same, if the burrowing abilities of these creatures could be utilized, what a help to the Pioneer Platoon would they be. First job we suggest, would be to dig holes for poles!

Some amusing sights have been seen in and around Tobruk, and probably many of them will be unrecorded. Do you remember our first introduction to the Tommy pattern shorts - or bloomer pants you might call them? Rusty Norton and Jimmy Cook of "C" Company, seem to have started a tailoring competition for remodelling these queer garments. This is the picture:- "Two beefy boys from the bush hopping into these narrow-gutted Tommy shorts with needle, cotton and scissors. The legs cut off and hemmed, and large pieces of the 'cut-off' inserted in the back. Two days and three nights' toil". Incidentally, those 'cut-offs' have proved very useful for a hundred and one things, including pockets, patches, and parcel wrapping.

Have you heard that there's a move in Aussie to increase our pay by about 1/- per day? If the question survives the forthcoming budget wrangling, then we'll be that much better off.

 We remind you that our Christmas Cards should soon be available, and that those who will require them should let their Company Clerks have the necessary numbers. At the same time, the 1st Anniversary issue of Mud & Blood is in process of production, and should also be ready soon. Although only a rough estimate, we reckon that the Cards will cost about two or three akers each, and the Birthday Issue about 5 akers each.

What does this sketch represent?
Western aspect of cat walking eastward. Like to come along?

STOP PRESS: Melbourne 19 - 13 defeated Essendon 13 - 20.
Rivette now favourite for the Caulfield Cup.

BBC NEWS — 2nd October, 1941.

Russia - It was announced in Moscow, that the Three Power Conference held in Moscow, has come to an end. As a result of this Conference, it is reported that Russia is to get practically everything she has asked for from Britain and the United States. The Conference lasted three days, and the Special Russian communique issued at its conclusion, stated that it had accomplished everything which was expected of it. Lord Beaverbrook and Mr. O'Halloran also issued statements that at the Conference, it was decided to place at Russia's disposal, the great production capacity of the United States and Britain, and supply her with everything asked for. They added that Russia on her part, has supplied both Britain and the United States with large supplies of raw materials which had been urgently required. The latest Russian communique issued on fighting on the Eastern Front, states that in the Leningrad area and in the Ukraine, snow is falling, but these two areas remain the crucial parts of the battle. There is no lull whatever in the fighting along the whole front. East of Leningrad, successful Russian counter attacks have been made, and these are confirmed by a German report. Odessa has been smashing Rumanian attacks, and have shot down a number of troop carrying gliders. The Chairman of the Odessa Defence Council, says that the farms around about are still furnishing supplies to the City, and the factories are still working at top speed. In the battle for the Crimea, the enemy seems to have gained some ground. A German report states that their planes have bombed Moscow again, but in Moscow, it is merely stated that 170 enemy planes have been destroyed during the past two months in attempts to raid the City.

London - Lord Beaverbrook yesterday cabled a message to British factories - "Boy Oh Boy, you've raised the roof, and beaten the band! Let's show them what we can do for a 'Tanks for Britain week'." Our new Hurricane fighters yesterday carried out extensive patrols over the Channel. They sighted 8 enemy E Boats off the French Coast, and attacked them with shells and machine gun bullets. Every E boat was brought to a standstill after direct hits had been scored. One was left in flames, and smoke was pouring out of another when our planes left. There was further activity over the French Coast last night, and distant explosions could be heard. Numbers of enemy planes were heard crossing the English coast last night, and our night fighters are reported to have been in action. A number of bombs were dropped, but as yet no casualties have been re-

ported. The Minister for Air explained yesterday, how our offensive fighter sweeps were helping Russia. He said that large forces of enemy fighters had been taken away from the Eastern front to cope with our activities over Germany. He added that since February last, we have destroyed 668 enemy planes with the loss of 428 British planes. During September, we shot down 123 enemy planes for the loss of 73 British machines. In concluding, the Air Minister warned that Britain must expect heavy raids this winter, but said that we would drop heavier bombs on Germany than they have ever dropped on us.

Cairo - British Light Naval Forces in the Mediterranean paid a surprise visit to an Italian occupied Island near Malta, which is an E boat base. The Italians were taken by surprise, and their coastal batteries did not reply until our heavy bombardment, which lasted about five minutes, had finished, and our ships were steaming off. An officer on board one of our vessels, stated that the bombardment lasted for a "furious five minutes". In North Africa, Tripoli has received one of its most effective raids from our heavy bombers. Widespread damage was caused, and a fire was started at an MT park, which could be seen hundreds of miles away. Direct hits were also scored on other buildings. Benghasi was also attacked, and hits scored on the harbour. From all of these raids, only one of our planes is missing.

Far East - Tokyo Radio announced yesterday that the Japanese troops are now withdrawing from Chungsha, as their full objective has been completed. The Chinese, however, say that the Japanese are retreating in great disorder, and have suffered great losses, stating that it was a sweeping victory for the Chinese troops.

London - The new reign of terror in Czechoslovakia, launched by the new Nazi Commander, shows no sign of abating. Two more Czech Brigadier Generals have been executed, and many other Czechs await the firing squad.

TOBRUK, 7th October, 1941.

We won't admit that we're guilty of prying into dark secrets, but a few days ago, in the dugout of one of our (previously) most respected Lieuts, we came upon one of the most striking contrasts which we have seen since our arrival in Tobruk on 17th March. Set side by side, and just conveniently above the bed, were two pictures, each presumably illustrating the sleepers most cherished dreams. These pictures, (and I guess the dreams too) were strangely different, for where one illustrated the most modern developments in warfare, the other showed the female form divine, which incidentally, has been good enough for us since Adam was a boy -

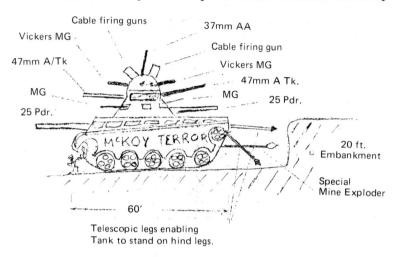

Cable firing guns
Vickers MG
37mm AA
47mm A/Tk
Cable firing gun
Vickers MG
47mm A Tk.
MG
MG
25 Pdr.
25 Pdr.
McKOY TERROR
20 ft.
Embankment
Special
Mine Exploder
60'
Telescopic legs enabling
Tank to stand on hind legs.

The sketch indicates just what a tremendous affair the tank is, for you can see the designer leaning up against the rear, and you can see (we hope) how the name McKOY'S TERROR fits it to a T. Now our task, is to tell you just what the other picture is about, but we cannot do justice on a stencil to such an appealing subject. Hence the table of measurements from which you may draw your own conclusions. Mr. Mac will surely be pleased to add further details, on request, of either one or the other, or both.

Whereas this wonder tank has modern arms,
The creature by its side hath subtler charms.

Height	5'4"	Waist	22½"
Weight	7-11	Hips	35"
Bust	34"	& etc.	

LOST: On night 3/4 October, 1941, one section of "B" Company. Will the finder please return same to Capt. F. G. Morrell. Reward.

The Tobruk rats and mice don't intend to let the grass grow under their feet. Read the latest of their tricks:-

The CO tells us a true story of the startling behaviour of a lucky little mouse which he entertained the other night. The cheeky fellow had evidently learned that the tastiest mouthfuls might be had in a Colonel's dugout, for, to the CO's amazement, the mouse climbed up on to the table and helped itself to half a dozen or so nips of whisky and water. Subsequently its procedure was to rush around in circles - followed by the CO's other guests in order of seniority. Having tried on the CO's boots, his nibs the mouse saluted and slowly walked away.

There's a dearth of up to date information regarding the forthcoming Melbourne races. The Caulfield Cup will be run on Saturday week, 18th October, and all we can tell you is that Rivette has come into the line for favourite, and will again be in charge of E. Preston, who caused a sensation two years ago by winning both the Caulfield and Melbourne Cups.

If Pte. R.A. Myers of HQ Company will call at BHQ, we will offer him a good price for his horse in our sweep. He is the lucky one to have drawn Rivette.

In a recent broadcast, it was stated that an Australian Squadron in England had for the second month in succession, topped the 'bag' of German planes. Tally for September was 18 Jerry machines.

Have you ever heard what syncopation really is? Some of our Mud'n Bloods are looking forward to a piece of it. Definition says - "An unsteady movement from bar to bar."

BBC NEWS — 7th October, 1941.

Russia - It was reported from Russia today that the Germans have launched a desperate offensive along the whole of the front, from Leningrad to the Crimea. The offensive is now in full swing. The Germans are throwing everything they have got into the attack, on the land and in the air. This attack is probably a development of events mentioned by Hitler in his speech last Friday. Moscow said today that there were battles all along the front, and that the Russians were defending every yard of ground. The German High Command today claimed successes, and early reports suggest that the Germans have made some progress. The strongest attacks seem to be in the Central (Smolensk) Sector, with Moscow as the objective. With attacks from the North and the South, the Germans are trying to get to the rear of the strong Russian forces driving towards Smolensk. One German force is attacking between Leningrad and Smolensk. Round Leningrad itself, the German pressure seems to have slackened. There have been various reports of Russian landings on the coast of the Gulf of Finland. The Germans claim these attacks were repulsed. In the Ukraine, the Germans are striving hard to reach the industrial centre of Kharkov, east of Kiev. Further south, where the Germans are attacking the Crimea, they are facing a strong Russian offensive. It is pointed out in London that the position near the Crimea may become critical for the Germans, as they face a strong flank attack. Reliable reports indicate that the Germans are using Bulgarian flags on their ships - Bulgaria is neutral. Hitler's speech last Friday seemed to indicate that the Germans could expect an early end to the Russian war. Goebbels seems to think otherwise. German papers have warned against unjustified optimism, one paper stating that the war remained the greatest test for Hitler and every German - the utmost hatred must be directed against the US and Britain, who had forced Germany into war against Russia. The latest Russian communique states that stubborn fighting is continuing along the whole of the Eastern front. On Friday, 41 German planes were destroyed for the loss of 18 Russian planes. The Isthmus of Perekop, along the approaches to the Crimea, is still the scene of the fiercest fighting. There is also heavy fighting in the approaches to Leningrad, where German attacks have been defeated. A Moscow statement declares that strong German divisions storming the approaches to the Crimea had been unable to penetrate the Russian lines, and had suffered heavily. The Russian attacks on the German flank (presumably NE of Perekop), are reported to have met with success; in some instances the Russians have advanced 20 miles in 36 hours. "Red Star" reports that German parachute troops who invaded Crete have been rested, re-formed, and are now ready for an attack on the Crimea. A correspondent has described a 3 day battle in the approaches to Leningrad. The Germans massed large concentrations of tanks and guns, and used their dive-bombers against the Russian positions, but when the German columns advanced, they were thrown back by the Russians. Units of the Russian Baltic Fleet have been pounding German positions. Defenders of Odessa have repulsed fresh Rumanian attacks, following up with counter attacks, in one place advancing several miles.

Australia - The New Australian Cabinet has been formed. The Prime Minister (Mr. Curtin) announced his new Ministers today. There is a special War Cabinet that includes Mr. Curtin as Prime Minister and Mr. Ford as Minister for the Army. Mr. Evatt is the new Attorney General, and Mr. Beasley is the Minister for Supply and Development. Mr. Dedman has been appointed to the newly created post of Minister of War Organisation of Industry. The BBC Observer in Canberra states that the new Cabinet is taken to mean that Australia's attitude to the war is realistic - the best men available have been chosen. Mr. Curtin has extended an invitation to Mr. Duff Cooper to visit Australia; he will probably arrive in Australia on November 1.

Moscow - Moscow radio yesterday told Russian children the story of Albert John Lewis, 23 year old South African airman, who fought during the Battle of Britain so well that the Germans organised up to a dozen planes to defeat him. He escaped from a burning plane, and after months in hospital, was now over the Russian front fighting the Germans again. A message from Rio de Janeiro reports a battle in the South Atlantic between 2 unknown warships. The fight lasted 20 minutes, flashes being seen from the shore. There was a cloud of smoke, and one vessel was thought to have been sunk.

A Conference has been held in Manilla between American and British leaders. No official comment yet on the talks, but one commentator said that the talks were a warning to Tokyo that the old Axis trick of "picking off victims one by one" would not work in the Pacific. Conscription in the Phillipines has raised 150,000 men for the Army, who have been heavily reinforced with men and equipment from the US.

TOBRUK, 9th October, 1941.

It was only yesterday that we discovered the real origin of this 'V' for Victory business when we happened to visit the RAP for a prick or two. Sgt. Les Allen (you couldn't miss him, could you?) provided the information, which we shall divulge later on. This portly gentleman spins a gruesome greeting to his long suffering customers which sounds to us very much like the old story: "Will you come into my parlour?" said the spider to the fly. As the Medical Officer's offsider, the Sgt. inserts a cunning needle, but as he turned to sharpen it up ready for the stab, we suddenly caught sight of the 'V' for Victory, neatly sewn into the seat of his shorts.

We are not sure, but possibly Les scored a victory over the M.O., who, we regret to report, has since been taken to hospital. Was it a battle with the lance, Sgt.? What about giving us the inside story? Look to your laurels, Capt. Mercer, or maybe we shall be bidding you goodbye, too.

One thing leads to another, so here we insert a conversation overheard between two Mud and Bloods.

Sgt. Allen, emerging from his dugout, met lanky Sgt. Bluey Jackson of Don Company. Said Les: "You look as if there's a famine in Tobruk". "And you look very much like the cause of it." retorted Bluey.

Many and crude were the remarks passed by the onlooking eaters about the crazy truck driver who caused a terrific dust cloud near the HQ Cookhouse the other evening. When he ran over someone's dugout, most of us, including the I Sgt, were amused; but all sign of amusement quickly disappeared when the Sgt. realised that the truck had just about wrecked his own home.

The Battalion has had many associations with the Royal Horse Artillery, and now we find a group of them firing an I-ti 6" How. almost from our front door. In conversation with them, we find that they have, by their own ingenuity and Aust. Ordnance's assistance, repaired the old gun. A couple of days ago the recoil was about twice normal, consequently firing was carried out by a pretty long wire; but with true RHA form they can report some accurate shoots. One target in particular is popular with them ---- "Virgin's Breast, 3 rounds, FIRE'" We, being more proper, would refer to this as "Twin Pimples".

STOP PRESS

BATTALION CONCERT ON SATURDAY NIGHT NEXT 11th

EACH COMPANY TO PROVIDE THREE ITEMS — BY ORDER

100 Akers Prize for best comedy Sketch

"Drunk again" is the obvious solution to our puzzle this morning when we caught sight of the little I-ti tourer which so often brings us comforts. Instead of thumping along at a rattling pace, the car was resting quietly by the roadside, and looking very, very lonely.

No wonder we haven't caught sight of the Padre, this morning!

After a few weeks absence, Lieut. N. McMaster rejoined us yesterday complete with song book, and walking stick. He looked so well that he was selected from numerous applicants for the job of Duty Officer during night 8/9 October. As is the custom in these things, his outstanding success at this important task was rewarded with extension of the normal period so, at the moonlight hour of 0300 hours, picture our enthusiastic Lieut. carrying on, assisted only by a sip of hard-won water. Sir, yours is the Mud & Blood Medal for October, 1941. Please call at BHQ in a few days time for presentation thereof.

Lately, we have published a few stories about the local rats and mice. Here, they are damnably numerous ---- in fact we have considered the publication of a specially ratified issue. In our dugout, their chief delight is to play about in the ceiling with the obvious intention of pouring a stream of Tobruk dirt down our necks. Dammit, it is hard enough to keep clean without having the rodent hordes against us.

BBC NEWS — 9th October, 1941.

Russia - Terrific battles are raging along the roads to Moscow, east of Smolensk. Russians reported fierce fighting all yesterday and last night round Viazma and Briansk. Viazma is on the Napoleonic road to Moscow. Briansk is an important railway junction. "Red Star" states that the tense battles have not abated, night or day - battles of armour and planes. The paper adds that it is evident that Hitler is striving hard to make his drive into the heart of Russia a success - the enemy has been moving from one point to another trying to break through the Russian forces. It is not clear, from reports reaching London, whether the Russians have withdrawn some of their forces in the Central sector, or whether the Germans have driven two big wedges into the Russian lines. The Germans claim that they first made a breach in the Russian lines in the Central sector last Thursday, and now "battles of annihilation" of large Russian forces surrounded near Viazma are taking place. Foreign correspondents in Berlin speak of a big increase in German losses in men and materials. Both sides claim successes from the bombing of each other's supply lines. The Germans lost six bombers in an attempted daylight raid on Moscow. In the Ukraine the Germans say that their offensive and pursuit operations are in full swing, and claim to have reached the Sea of Azov. Although there is no confirmation of these claims, considerable German forces are known to be in the Southern Ukraine. The Hungarians state that the Russian Black Sea Fleet has been evacuating troops from the coast of the Sea of Azov. The Russians are holding the German advance on to the Crimea. The defenders of Odessa are improving their positions; it is reported that the morale of the Rumanians is about broken. Russian attacks in the Leningrad area are preventing the Germans from "digging in" in their recent positions. A German General and a local Gestapo Chief are among the 3000 German Officers and men killed by Guerilla fighters behind the Leningrad front. Snow and sleet have been falling on the Central front; Italian correspondents state that, without warning, the weather along the Eastern front has suddenly changed from summer to winter. The latest Russian communique states that particularly fierce fighting is still taking place near Viazma, 135 miles SW of Moscow and Briansk, 220 miles SW of Moscow. Both these towns are important railway junctions. It was from Briansk that the Germans were thrown back when the Russians started their counter offensive. A Russian spokesman said last night it appeared that Hitler wanted to dig a grave for hundreds of thousands of Germans - he would certainly achieve this. On the Isthmus of Perekop, leading to the Crimea, one German Division has been battered by the guns of Russian warships. Rumanian artillery near Odessa has also been forced back by Russian Naval attacks. The defenders of Odessa have routed four Rumanian Battalions. The Russians are claiming successes near Leningrad, where the Germans are said to be on the defensive. On Sunday 42 German planes were destroyed for the loss of 27 Russian machines. A 7000 ton German transport has been sunk by Russian forces.

London - The British Food Minister states that Britain's supply of wheat and sugar are the best now, than at any time during the war. Mr. Eden the British Foreign Secretary, today told the House of Commons that the British Government had every confidence that the Turkish Government would fulfill to the letter, the Turkish role of guardian to the Dardanelles - it was left to the Turks to supervise the passage of vessels through the Straits.

Australia - The Australian House of Representatives met today, and adjourned until October 29, after passing a Supply Bill for 16 million pounds for two months. After having occupied Opposition Seats for 11 years, Labor members today sat on the Treasury Benches. The former Prime Minister (Mr. Fadden) said he had been unanimously elected leader of the Opposition. The new Prime Minister (Mr. Curtin) has sent a cable to Mr. Churchill assuring him of Australia's part in the war effort.

Berlin - Germany yesterday announced the execution of their 73rd victim for attacks on German troops; 27 more death sentences in Prague. Synagogues throughout Czechoslovakia are to be closed.

United States - President Roosevelt's conference with Government leaders on the revision of the Neutrality Act lasted two and a half hours, and will be resumed today. He refused to comment on the first meeting, but he told his Press Conference that the refusal of the Panama Government to allow ships with the Panama Flag, to carry arms had increased the necessity for the revision of the Neutrality Act. The US petrol co-ordinator (Mr. Ickes) said yesterday that sinkings had decreased so much, that

Britain might now transfer tankers to America. In the 7 months of this year, US has sent to Britain nearly twice as many planes as Britain lost in the defence of the British Isles during the whole of last year. Total value of US planes sent to the British forces this year was 7000 million pounds, mostly paid for with cash.

TOBRUK, 11th October, 1941.

TONIGHT'S THE NIGHT –

ROLL UP TO THE BEST CONCERT YET –

to be held in a spacious cave, complete with stage, electric light, and all mod cons. We are given to understand that during the interval, a bevy of beautiful damsels are to provide sweets and ice cream, and the right to escort these girls home after the performance has been awarded exclusively to other ranks. The only thing missing from the show, will be Sgt. Jack Jarvie's Band, the instruments of which were blasted at Derna.

We have just had a privileged preview of the programme for tonight, and you can take it from us, that you will spend a most hilarious evening, starting at 2000 hours. You will actually hear a piano, and a violin, and other instruments of our long forgotten civilization.

It appears that Lieut. G.G. Anderson's dugout, is blessed with a vent in the top, and in this vent there is a pipe projecting upwards - for the passage of air, NOT water, it is presumed. The other day, during his usual 2 i/c's siesta, he had a most disturbing experience, when he awoke to find water trickling down upon him from the pipe above. Donning his overcoat, he went outside expecting to see the unusual sight of rain in Tobruk; but not a cloud was in sight! Had he been a bit quicker, we think he may have seen a suspicious body receding into a nearby hole. Boys will be boys, eh! The Battalion umbrella is always at your disposal, Mr. Anderson.

For some unaccountable reason, G.G.'s misfortune brings to mind, Cpl. Bluey Hand of the sanitary squad, who goes about BHQ and HQ Company area doing a noble task. He it is, who brings to each and all of us, the greatest relief, and what he can make out of a couple of kero tins, is just nobodys business. Believe us, Bluey, the Battalion is grateful. If ever in the future a revised edition of Chicksale's classic "The Specialist" should be contemplated, we can assure the publishers of a chapter or two from Bluey.

Results of some Melbourne races have reached us. Rinvale won the Epsom event (7-4), Yaralla won the A.J.C. Derby, and Dashing Cavalier won the Metropolitan. Boxing enthusiasts will be pleased to learn of the result of the Louis V Lou Nova contest. Joe Louis won on a technical KO. This news is by courtesy of the Sigs at Brigade, who as usual, are "first with the latest."

We can issue a few more disappointment cards to starters in the Battalion Melbourne Cup Sweepstake, whose horses will not run. In addition to those previously reported, Millie's Hope, Burham Ali, and Bel Buoy may be ruled out. This item may be of interest to Pte. S.A. Mirtschin of HQ Company. We have had an offer of 3 Pounds for his horse's chance of winning the Cup, and the Sweepstake. Evidently his horse Beau Son is gaining popularity. Of course, if Pte. Mirtschin transacts business, we claim a commission for arranging same, and that should be easy enough, since we have not disclosed the person who has 3 Pounds to spare.

"Either I do my own washing or pay YOU for it, or you wash MY clothes for nothing", suggested one of our euchre playing Sergeants to an innocent Private. Having seen the said washing strung up outside the Sergeant's dugout, leads us to believe that the Sergeant's luck at euchre is not in evidence when the coin is tossed. Doubtless Pte. Arthur Hirst himself produced this particular coin. Sounds as if it might be worth borrowing.

Yes, we certainly will reserve an issue for the best of the mouse stories, for they are still coming in from all sources. Today's comes from the Brigadier, who mentions the rat as his particular pet. Each night, a sweet biscuit is left on the shelf above his bed, and the rat in return for this courtesy, consumes his supper without causing any annoyance. However, a few nights ago, the Brigadier was suddenly awakened by an army biscuit which knocked on his face. Next night, although the same procedure was followed, the Brigadier was again disturbed, this time by a few lumps of bully beef. In the morning, there was a tiny note on the shelf explaining these strange events. "That's what I think of your Army food ration. Goodbye for ever.

Yours in disgust,
Mickey Mouse, Senr."

We fully expect to see this wise rodent friend turn up at our concert this evening, followed by the dismissed Private who replaced sweet biscuits with army rations.

BBC NEWS — 11th October, 1941.

The great German pincer movement towards Moscow is reported at some points to have driven a wedge into the Russian lines, but there has been no important break through. Viazma, key town in the path of the Germans, is still holding out, and several attacks have been repulsed. "Red Star" today denied a German report that the Russian Army had been surrounded on the Central Front. The facts are that some Russian forces, surrounded in the Viazma and Briansk areas, have fought their way back to the main Russian Army. The Germans are bringing up vast reinforcements, with masses of tanks and planes, but the Russians are contesting every inch of the way, and inflicting terrible losses on the Germans. The Germans have launched a heavy attack 70 miles North of Viazma, and the main pincer movement is completed at the end of an arc 300 miles to the south, through a line down towards Briansk, and then across to the north of Orel, near where the German advance is being strongly held. Inside the arc, there are smaller pincer movements of a local nature. Russian forces behind the German lines are doing considerable damage. There are fierce battles in the direction of Viazma and Briansk. The Russian civilian population is fighting alongside the Army. The Germans claim further successes along the coast of the Sea of Azov. No change has been reported from the Perekop Isthmus. The Russians claim to have made a series of counter attacks in the Leningrad area - The Germans are holding their positions in the Leningrad area with the greatest difficulty. The German radio today said that the German aim was not so much to capture the territory, but the destruction of the last Russian Division, and states "We must expect a lot of hard work, many a long march, and heavy fighting." The threat to Russia's industries has been emphasised by the Russian Official newspaper. Admiral Stanley, a member of the Mission to Moscow, said today that the German's temporary success would not discourage the Russians. Mr. Halliman, leader of the American Mission that went to Moscow, said today that American aid was being sent to Russia - the US was not giving "lip service" to Russia. The latest communique states that the Russians are fiercely resisting the German threat to Moscow. The battle for the approaches to the City is increasing in intensity. In the three days since their great offensive started, the Germans have thrown in Division after Division, and their losses have been on a proportionate scale. The fierce Russian resistance has cost the Germans thousands of lives, hundreds of tanks and armoured cars, and the Germans have made little, if any, progress during the past 24 hours. There was fierce fighting in the direction of Briansk and Viazma. Due south of Moscow, the German advance was being held north of Orel, from which the Russians have withdrawn in order, after destroying all industrial install-

*ations in the town. Germans claim to have encircled large numbers of Russ-
ian troops; it seems likely that pockets of Russian troops have been left
behind, and that they will still be fighting. The German drive toward Moscow seems to have relieved the pressure on other fronts, with the exception
of the Ukraine, from where there is little reliable news. The Germans claim
to have reached the Sea of Azov, cutting off the Russian forces east of Perekop. There has been no change reported from the Perekoi Isthmus. The
Russians claim to be making many counter attacks at Odessa and Leningrad. Near Leningrad, 40 German planes were destroyed on one drome
within 20 minutes.*

*Cairo today reported another unsuccessful enemy tank attack on
the Garrison at Tobruk. On Wednesday night, the enemy used tanks without seriously affecting our patrol activities. London reports that also on
Wednesday, the enemy used 50 planes in a dive bombing attack at Tobruk,
while the enemy artillery opened fire. There has been no report of any
damage. Four Stukas were hit. On Wednesday night, Naval aircraft scored
two direct hits on a 6000 ton enemy ship in the Mediterranean - the ship
sank in ten minutes. On the same night, RAF bombers left a similar sized
vessel in a sinking condition. Other enemy vessels have been hit both inside Tripoli Harbour and in the approaches to the Harbour.*

*London - The latest American built fighters, now in full operat-
ional service with the RAF, have a range of 1100 miles, and a speed of 400
miles per hour; their cannon fire armour piercing, explosive, and tracer
shells at the rate of 120 per minute, and are capable of stopping light and
medium tanks. The planes also have 4 machine guns. Our bombers last
night attacked targets in Western Norway. A Netherlands Government
broadcast has warned the people of Rotterdam to keep clear of the docks,
as they would be heavily bombed because the Germans had transferred
much of their shipping to that Port. In a daring daylight attack yesterday,
the RAF left one motor vessel ablaze, a seaplane destroyed, and at least
two other vessels seriously damaged at Ostend. A German fighter was completely wrecked as it was taking off from a French drome. Another enemy
plane was destroyed over the Channel.*

TOBRUK, 14th October, 1941.

Our Concert the night before last went with a great swing, and if
applause means anything, every one of the five or six hundred men in the
audience thoroughly enjoyed it - in spite of the heavy atmosphere. The
large cave in which it was held was fitted up with a rough stage, and the

place electrically lit for the occasion. A piano was borrowed from the YMCA in town, and many splendid items were rendered by men from our own, and neighbouring units.

Being Saturday night, some of the married men felt almost as if they were back at home in a theatre or cinema, having their weekly night out with the wife (while ma' in-law looked after the kids) and from these, after the concert, we heard a few unconscious cries of "Hi, taxi" as the crowd emerged from the theatre. Majority of us Privates, of course, went home by train or on foot, and all the young Mud'n Bloods had no option but to go straight home.

The proceedings commenced with community singing, led by Sgt. Jack Jarvie, with Lieut. N. McMaster at the piano, and never has a session of this nature been so successful. Willingness of the men to sing and keep on singing was amazing. Possibly the singing was a ruse to prevent smoking. Then we heard the news broadcast from London, and at the end of this, the show started with Tpr. Turner's announcement of Pte. Rex Spry's song, "Mother Machree". This Tpr. Turner, clad in his special evening shirt of army grey, was a most entertaining M.C. His patter between items kept the boys very amused, and when in the throes of applause, the appearance of the M.C. brought immediate attention in expectation of another joke. Sorry, Mud'n Bloods, we cannot possibly print any of them except the one about Don Bradman breaking a fellow's fingers. You'll have to hand the others on by word of mouth.

So many numbers received thunderous applause, that it would be difficult to single out any one as best. Most of the songs had an Irish flavour - "Mother Machree", "Smiling Irish Eyes", "O'Reilly's Return". All were well received. The men's quartette, accompanied by the accordian provided some splendid numbers, and Cpl. Donnison's song was appreciated - especially by No. 3 Section of "C" Company. The Hill Billies quick time duet was a popular number, as also was the local Paul Robeson's "Swanee River". The catchy song "Hole in the Wall" was written by our Pioneer Officer, we believe.

The instrumental items were highly successful. By this time, Lieut. Ken Reid's strumming hand is probably in a sling, such was the pace of the quartette of ukelele, mouth organ, and swanee whistles. Three mouth organ solos, a duet with the swanee whistles by Aub. Prowse and Tom Moore, and a rapid fyfe solo by a visiting soldier, completed the programme, apart from a recitation by Pte. Ross Trevorrow, and two comedy sketches presented by the Tank boys. Everyone was delighted to see a member of the gentler(?)

sex in the sketch entitled "The Worm Turns". Gentler sex, possibly, but this creature had very muscular shoulders and arms! No wonder she ruled the roost.

Two remarks, which we must not omit - our thanks to all the neighbours who so very ably assisted with their items, and also thanks to Sgt. Jarvie who organised the show. These, we feel sure, are the thoughts of every Mud & Blood who was fortunate enough to attend.

In passing, may we hope for future entertainments of a similar nature? We could, with a little originality, easily make our own amusement. If, for instance, each Section in the Unit would prepare a concert item in advance, the Battalion could turn on a show at a moment's notice.

In a letter from Pte. Bill Woods, who is at a school in Cairo, he tells us that he has had great difficulties in keeping on the straight and narrow path, but (says he) so far, he's managed to do so. That didn't prevent him from enjoying a few cool ales with Pte. Johnny Erswell, formerly of "A" Company and I Section. Johnny Erswell has made a remarkable recovery from a very serious wound, and is likely now to be on the way home. Pte. Woods is in the hands of a young French woman, the lucky dog. According to him, she is teaching him shorthand, but that sounds a bit rich, doesn't it? S/Sgt. Jim Mulcahy - 'Shamrock" as we called him - has also been "Seeing Cairo", Bill tells us, and we suppose his view of it would be tinted with amber, too!

Sorry, Mud'n Bloods, the censor didn't appreciate the Don Bradman joke, so we insert another.

The latest of the enemy's secret weapons is a new gas of such strength that it seeps through your paybook, and injures your next of kin.

BBC NEWS — 14th October, 1941.

The great German drive to Moscow, that has been going on for nearly two weeks, constitutes the most gigantic offensive in the world's history. There has been no news, even from German sources, that the enemy at any point is nearer than 100 miles from Moscow. On the contrary, it is learned in London today that the German offensive has slowed down; it is not known whether this is due to mechanical difficulties, the stubborn Russian resistance, transport problems, or the German necessity of mopping up Russian groups. If the slackening is due to a necessity to "mop-up", this may take two or three weeks; that would bring the enemy to the November snows. The Moscow communique today said that fighting continues, and was particularly fierce in the direction of Viazma, 140 miles west of Moscow. "Pravda" said that the first German break-through in this area was made with a sudden flanking onslaught, but so fierce was the Russian resistance that the Germans are said to have lost 12,000 men, killed and wounded in one day. Russian reinforcements, exceedingly well equipped, and some of whom are already experienced fighters, are ceaselessly marching to the front. A correspondent praises the courage of the Russian troops in facing tank attacks; small parties let the tanks approach to close range before throwing hand grenades and petrol bottles; 50 German tanks were destroyed by one unit in two days in this way. Although the enemy's advance has been slowed down, he is still pushing forward at some points. Berlin radio today spoke of desperate Russian counter attacks in the Briansk and Viazma areas. Viazma, with Briansk, 220 miles SW of Moscow, form the western claw of the German pincer offensive. Russians evacuated Briansk after fighting a fierce rear-guard action, and this withdrawal may have foiled the German plans to encircle Russian troops. Orel, some 200 miles south of Moscow, was evacuated some days ago, making, at the time, Briansk into a dangerous salient. The Germans are being held between Orel and Tula (about 100 miles south of Moscow). Between Orel and Tula are great forests, already white with snow. On the north shore of the sea of Azov, the Germans admit that there are still Russian forces to be fought before the River Don is passed. There is no confirmation of the Berlin report that the German forces are past Rostov, but in London it is believed that if this be so, the German forces can only be motorised units. A supplement to the Moscow communique states that in this area, Russian forces had launched counter attacks, at one point killing 500 Germans in a flanking attack. At Leningrad, Russian counter attacks are keeping the Germans on the defensive. Germans are still being held on the Perekop Isthmus and also at Odessa, although they have made some progress NW of Kharkov. Russian planes destroyed 96 enemy planes in the air in two days in the Viazma area, while Russian dive bombers destroyed over 200 tanks, 600 lorries, 16 batteries, and silenced 50 ack-ack posts. In the approaches to Moscow yesterday, 12 German planes were destroyed, and three others were brought down on Saturday.

Over 300 RAF bombers last night gave Germany one of the biggest hammerings of the war, planes going as far as Nurnberg in Bavaria. Targets along the French and Norwegian coasts, and in occupied territory were also attacked; 11 planes failed to return. In Europe and the Middle East, RAAF planes have destroyed 140 enemy planes, probably destroyed 25 more, and damaged at least 89.

On Saturday night Polish patrols had their first action at Tobruk. Our artillery has dispersed enemy working parties trying to establish posts closer to our lines. In the Mediterranean, six Italian ships have been seriously damaged, and one probably sunk from attacks by Naval aircraft, following up with attacks by RAF bombers. Four of the ships were in a convoy, escorted by five destroyers. The merchant ship attacked at Tripoli on Tuesday night, has since been seen lying sunk in the harbour. On Thursday night, heavy attacks were carried out on Benghasi and Bardia. From all these attacks, five planes are missing. On Friday night considerable numbers of enemy tanks again approached the Tobruk defences. A small listening post, about a mile from our outer defences was "over-run" and we suffered nine casualties. In other sectors of the Tobruk defences, our patrols broke up four enemy parties, inflicting over 100 casualties.

The "Mystery Voice" was again heard on the German Radio last night, telling listeners that Hitler would be "smashed and choked with his own blood-thirsty crimes". A former Italian Minister, broadcasting from US, urged Italians to forsake the Axis and link up politically with the US.

TOBRUK, 15th October, 1941.

Today's issue endeavours to give some encouragement to the troops in their counter attack role against the enemy rodent forces, by advertising a successful method of catching the pests:

1941 MODEL BOOBY MOUSE TRAP – TOBRUK PATTERN
(All rights reserved by Lieut. A. H. Rundle)

Many and varied are the stories being circulated concerning the mice in our present area, but the following tit-bit appears to take the biscuit. A certain Platoon Commander arrived back from the Salient with the rear party to find that his ever efficient Platoon Sergeant had established Platoon HQ in a roomy mud and stone hut. However, during the night in the new quarters, the Platoon Commander was driven frantic by the antics of (so he says) a full brigade of the mouse family. In the morning he told his Sergeant, batman and runner about the new 1941 method of catching the pests; but having been away from the Company for so long, the men looked extremely dubious of his hair brained scheme, and began to wonder what new mania had struck their chief------

A tin of water (dirty washing water, incidentally) was placed on the floor and, on the table above it, a beer bottle, which previously had been covered to the shoulder with a sock, was arranged so that the top directly overhung the tin of water. Then the bait (some lively bunghole) was stuffed into the mouth of the bottle, and all was ready for the mice, being unable to grip the smooth glass of the bottle neck, to fall A over T into the water below.

First night, the Chief set the trap and the catch was, to his disappointment, only 3 bodies. Nevertheless, this small success interested his offsiders immensely and the Sergeant begged to be allowed to try his luck on the following night. He must have made a good job of it for his catch numbered 7, and now he is a stout advocate of the method. Next night it was the Runner's turn, and he equalled the Sergeant's tally of 7. Not to be outdone, the Batman was determined to try his luck, and throughout the night frequent flops and splashes kept the Platoon HQ awake. The Batman's score was 11, and has yet to be exceeded! Probably the record will stand for all time, as the general opinion at 15 Platoon HQ is that the mice are completely rooted (out).

Talk of strange things in Libya, what could be stranger than the discovery of a pet sparrow kept by a couple of neighbouring soldiers, who had brought it from Alex recently. The bird is as tame as can be, but seemed to resent our intrusion, for when we whistled it flew to us and immediately began pecking vigorously at fingers and thumbs. When, however, the whistler lowered his key, the sparrow in appreciation of the change, chirped out a welcome to us. "What next?", we wonder. Pets in Libya now include rats, mice, jerboas, hedgehogs, chamelions, lizards----not to mention cats, dogs, and the latest - a sparrow. We repeat - "What next?"

A LESSON IN SECURITY:

Old Farmer (to soldier son just home from Tobruk); "Well Jim, what be these tanks like, that there's so much talk about?"

Son; "Why, they're just wobbling thingamebobs, full of what-you-may-callums, and they blaze away like billy o' ".

Old Farmer; "Ah, I heard they were wonderful things, but I never could get any details before".

"B" Company personnel will be glad to learn that Pte. C.H. Stuart, who was previously reported killed in action, has now been reported prisoner of war in Italy.

Tobruk weather was particularly unkind to us the day before yesterday, when a vicious wind blew from inland all the dust in creation. This morning we must have bailed out at least ½ a ton of Libya from our tiny dugout. All the appropriate comments about Tobruk which cut the air were decidedly unprintable, but they were truthful, and satisfying to us sufferers. Is there a Mud & Blood who can truthfully say that an oath did not pass his lips? - none in BHQ Wadi, anyhow, could make that claim. At dusk the filthy storm had slightly abated, and when someone mentioned "MAIL", our dust laden spirits soared to a fever of expectation. Bags and bags of mail too, there were. By 8 o'clock we had forgotten about the dust, being much more interested in reading over and over again that our Sweethearts still loved us.

BBC NEWS — 15th October, 1941.

On the Eastern front, the great battle for the approaches to Moscow is moving to a crisis. It is learned in London that German forces penetrated to within 65 miles west of Moscow, but were thrown back. It is believed that this penetration was made in great strength on a narrow front. Apparently the attack was made from a point between Briansk and Viazma - the Western claw of the German pincer offensive. Moscow announced last night that Viazma had been evacuated. It seems that the Russians must have established new defensive positions West of Moscow. Before leaving Viazma, the Russians destroyed everything that could be of possible use to the enemy and mined all the streets. A Berlin spokesman said today that the outer ring of the Moscow defences was now within range of the heavy German artillery; Moscow states that these defences are daily growing stronger. "Red Star" states that the Germans are throwing in tank and infantry reserves supported by planes and artillery in their desire to "break through" quickly. Although Russian reinforcements are going to the front, the Germans have a superiority in manpower and in tanks. The situation remains grave. Another correspondent maintains that the growing Russian resistance seems to be reducing the speed of the German advance. Many instances of skilled action and bravery by Russian Units have been given. The Germans are hurling tanks and motorised infantry from sector to sector. The situation is obscure around Viazma but reports indicate that the Russians have the situation in hand. Moscow says that the withdrawal from Viazma was well organised, although the Germans say they have encircled and split up Russian forces in this area. North of Orel, in spite of intensive attacks the Russians are holding firmly. The countryside is already white with snow - in this area Soviet tanks destroyed 120 German tanks and wiped out a number of enemy infantry. In the Ukraine, Russian counter attacks seem to have checked the enemy's advance; there is continuous fighting North of the Sea of Azov. "Red Star" says that this area is "dangerous", and it describes three big battles, during which the Russians recaptured an important bridge. Russians are maintaining the offensive at Leningrad. Berlin reports a German drive toward the Leningrad - Moscow railway. A Russian paper states the Germans have failed to gain air supremacy. The Soviet Air Force was in action all day yesterday. Further South the Russians claim that the Germans are bringing up Italian, Rumanian and Hungarian troops to the area where heavy losses are inevitable. On Saturday 127 German planes were destroyed for the loss of 27 Russian machines. 7 more German planes were brought down near Moscow yesterday. The German High Command, apart from the claim to have taken 350,000 prisoners in the Central Sector, had little to say apart from the phrase, "Operations on the Eastern Front are proceeding according to plan". Berlin radio commentators have made several references to Russian counter attacks. One said that the Russian troops had left German soldiers in harassed positions by artillery fire preceded by violent air attacks. The commentator admitted that the German infantry had to retreat and take cover. There is little reliable news from the Ukraine, along the North shore of the Sea of Azov; Germans say that Russian formations have been wiped out, and Russians report successful counter attacks. Round Leningrad the Russians have taken the offensive. Last night's Moscow broadcast described a successful raid by Russian Marines landed from Warships, behind the German lines; a section of the German defences were captured.

A German News Agency this morning said that British bombers were over Germany last night. High explosive and incendiary bombs were dropped; there were some casualties. 20 German fighters were destroyed yesterday by the RAF in a series of battles over France. We lost 1 bomber and 12 fighters, but 2 of our pilots are safe. 5 of 12 enemy fighters destroyed in one fight were brought down by Spitfires of the Australian Squadron. RAF planes were again over the Channel last night.

Further enemy losses in the Mediterranean include a Steamship (3000 tons), Motor ship (4000 tons), and another ship of 3000 tons torpedoed by a Dutch Submarine.

Operations at Tobruk and in the Frontier area have been hampered by dust storms, but successful artillery action has been reported near the Frontier. An hour-long tank battle took place outside Tobruk; damage was inflicted on the enemy, but could not be fully observed because of poor visibility. On Sunday 9 enemy tanks came to within 50 yards of one of our patrols at Tobruk, but the patrol still held its ground. Cairo communique again mentions Polish troops in action at Tobruk. On Sunday night a Polish patrol successfully raided a strongpost outside the Eastern defences, showing great gallantry and determination, accounting for 20 enemy dead, while only losing 4 of their own number.

TOBRUK, 18th October, 1941.

This sounds like the most popular theme of the moment:

> A little leave, a little love,
>   A fleeting wish for Peace's dove,
> A little drink, a little song -
>   These are the things for which I long.
>
> Would I be satisfied with these
>   Things simple and few? I think me not
> But floating high on desert breeze
>   Would come my cry "Give me a lot".
>   Lieut. A. Boas, "A" Company.

To think that Tobruk holds a record! It is that of being the only place in the world where dirt tracks for motor cycles are yours for the asking. Read about Hookie, the local champion.

DIRT TRACK COMES TO TOBRUK

Frequently in the evenings just after mess, members of the Carrier Platoon, and those in nearby dugouts, have had the thrill of seeing some very pretty track work on the flats just below the escarpment. The exponent of these finer points of motor cycling, has been that debonair, devil-may-care rider of the dirt track, Sgt. P. R. Hook, M.M., and spectators have been well entertained as they watched him weave his way between the various dugouts and then, make a terrific broadside around the latrines. They have been more than amused, watching some of the novices merely trying to stay with the bike, particularly over some of the treacherous ruts in the sand tracks. Unfortunately this sport has now been denied us, as the massive Carrier Sergeant has been evacuated to hospital. We shall be looking forward to your return Peter.

We don't see a great deal of our aircraft, but we well know that they are causing concern among Jerry's forces. The following verse written by an unknown Sergeant Pilot, gives us a splendid idea of how the other fellow considers his wartime job:

> God give us grace that we,
>> Flying our fighters to eternity,
> May meteor-like before we fall
>> Leave fiery trails of light, that all
> Truth's sons may clutch, and clutching rise
>> To blast Hell's spawn from Heaven's skies.

Our vicinity seems inexhaustible in its supply of strange incidents, for this week on the very day following the dreadful dust storm, the truck which was transporting a swimming party to the beach, became bogged in the mud! Certainly we had a little rain, but not sufficient to prevent some of us from sleeping out. We begin to wonder what kind of place this would be if the weather did really break? Which discomfort would produce the more descriptive comments - the usual driving dust or the quagmire of mud, which an excess of rain would bring?

Who can remember when the Battalion cat produced five kittens back at Delia? She tricked all and sundry, for no one had ever reported the presence of a boy friend for her. No, you could easily miss a tom cat, but could you likewise miss a horse? We had the pleasure this week of seeing a week old foal; a little black chap he was, born of an old white mare! There's something screwy somewhere. Either there's a nigger in the wood-pile, or we don't know our geography.

One of our Sgt. Majors had a letter from home, containing a short poem, which provides an insight into the point of view of the folks at home. WE don't know whether the Sgt. Major was more interested in the poem or the faint tinge of lipstick which appeared on the reverse side. We cannot reproduce the imprint of lipstick, but -

THE HEROES OF TOBRUK

> Today I got a letter from my soldier o'er the sea
>> And I know he's hellish lonely for old Aussie and for me.
> He's way out in the desert among the fleas and sand,
>> Eating mouldy biscuits and stuff thats always canned.
> But you bet he's not complaining of Dagoes and Hitler's crooks,
>> He's a member of a garrison - the Heroes of Tobruk.

Its hard to picture him out there, living in the grime,
    With Jerry bombers overhead - roaring from nine to nine.
He says they're having lots of fun, betting on his shots,
    And they wouldn't even have a spark, if they drank the
                score in pots.
The rats are pretty awful, and the sand storms pretty crook,
    But its just another day for the Heroes of Tobruk.

Then he writes he loves me, that he prays for me each day,
    And wonders what I'm doing, while he's so far away.
I'm sitting on a park seat, listening to the band,
    We've sat here scores and scores of times, and held each
                other's hand.
And when this rotten show is over, and they write of it in books,
    I'll be mighty proud I've loved him, the Hero of Tobruk.

The same Sgt. Major has nearly pestered the life out of us in his anxiety to recover the script of above. Sounds uncommonly like the course of true love, doesn't it?

You have heard of H. G. Wells invisible man? Well, he married an invisible woman, and they had an invisible son. For quite a while they couldn't decide what to do with their son, but eventually they conceived the brilliant idea of putting him in the Italian Navy.

There have been some famous centuries both in sport and war. Take for instance the famous 100 years war, Napoleon's 100 days, Macartney's and Bradman's prior lunch efforts in Test Matches. Captain Bland of "B" Company hopes to be numbered amongst the century getters before he leaves Tobruk. He received his 93rd epistle from his grief and strife the other day, and it is rumoured that his objective will be obtained with a small parcel, even though it be a "fowl" (The remains thereof after undergoing a strong bodyline attack, a few tasty leg glances, a breast high square cut or two, not to mention a few late cuts from under the papal appendage by his friend) should furnish him with a happy memento of that great day.

Mud & Bloods, will you bear in mind that we want to record in our paper all those little incidents which occur day by day? We would like to receive many more contributions, of all kinds, in order to make our rag as representative as possible of all sections of the unit. For instance, what about a story of how you fired your first shot in action.

Here's one -

One night we were holding portion of the Salient, we suffered considerably from the shock of being awakened by such a shot. This one fired from a verey pistol, was the first effort, we believe, by Major R. E. Wall.

Another unique 'shot' was that by Ron Lees, who imbibed a shot or two of rum the other night, and fired himself with snakes and ladders.

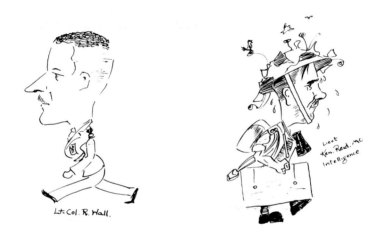

Lt-Col. R. Wall.

Lieut Ken. Reid. MC Intelligence

Great news for bachelor Mud & Bloods! The Government will provide free 3rd class passages to Australia for wives and children of soldiers who marry abroad. If any of the boys take advantage of this concession, we sincerely hope the wife is not sent home on the ship which brought us originally to the Middle East. Let your motto be "Marry the Girl".

Further to our 'V' for Victory suggestion in a recent issue, we have another idea.

"What is the slogan for this 'V' for Victory stunt?"

"Well, Mr. Cohen tells us that it is 'Are V down hearted'".

In eight months of fighting in North Africa and Syria, Australian Pilots have probably destroyed 195 enemy machines, estimated in value at 1½ million pounds.

Volume 2

CHAPTER 10

PALESTINE (JULIS), 30th October, 1941.

A MESSAGE FROM THE C.O.

The 2/23rd. Battalion, A.I.F. is back in Palestine once more - but it is a different Battalion to that which left Palestine 9 months ago.

More dignified - more grim, in the knowledge it has gained, and proud of it's name. It has its spurs in the field - honours have been bestowed - and the name Mud & Blood, for the second time in a quarter of a century, is well known and honoured.

Once again we are, for a while, amongst peace and plenty. Let us make the most of these blessings whilst ours, and enjoy them to the full - but not to excess.

Let us take our leave and our pleasures in the same fine, manly, decent and humorous spirit that prevailed in all our activities in the desert. And while partaking of our pleasures, never must we fail to give thought at odd moments, to those other splendid Mud & Bloods who never came back with us. We have something precious in our keeping. Our ways may yet be hard, but our Motto still stands as ever. We will live up to it.

* * * * * * *

Did you read the number of this issue? We deem it an opportune moment at which to begin a new Volume, because of the feeling of having completed a definite job of work.......... From all sides comes the same reaction to new scenery. How restful it is to gaze upon such a pleasant country-side as that which we view from our camp site. To those who have not yet done so, we recommend a stroll up to the water tower, just to see the panorama which lies beyond, and great will be our surprise if anyone who does so, is not amply repaid.

At the same time, we would do well to reflect that there's another water tower far away, where the surroundings are vastly different. There it was that we bade goodbye to many stout hearts - valiant Mud & Bloods - by whose sacrifice is achieved whatever fame posterity may to us allot.

We have mentioned reaction to new scenery, but never let it be said that we omit to mention the reaction to an altered diet! Alas, many of us have poured luscious ale down our throats until we have been full - even to over-flowing. Too many days have passed since anyone was so delightfully full. We feel certain that not since our Birthday Party in August has a Mud & Blood stomach reached such a satisfied condition.

Don't get the idea that we're here to wax fat, because one glance down the slope will dispel that fancy! Plenty of P.T. and bayonet training, athletics, and etc., won't allow it........ Neither can we look so dreadfully begrimed, as long as the water heater works; and we trust that it does so continuously. If you could have seen what passed through the gully trap last Wednesday, you would have known why our belongings seemed so heavy. It was not so much the gear, as the filth upon it.

Strange it is to hear the bugle again, and strange also that some like it so well that they take a special delight in answering it, and we don't mean the mess call! Anyhow, they say you can be a defaulter as long as you like, so long as you answer the call.

The bandmaster, Sgt. Jarvie is making every effort to procure instruments for his body snatchers to blow and beat, so soon we can expect to be roused, not only by Reveille, but by a tornado of trumpets. The proximity of our own tent to this blasting is rather disconcerting, too.....So far, we believe, the band possesses only one instrument - a cornet - which has a rotary action, introduced of course, to make "The music go round and round".......Since writing the foregoing, there have been some curious sounds emanating from the band tent, proving that their collection has been added to.

How many of you saw Sgt. Jack O'Brien put up the placard "A.I.F. WORLD'S BEST FED ARMY", at lunch time? In ordinary circumstances, we cannot conceive of any army cook, other than Jack, broadcasting his goodness so obviously, and getting away with it, but perhaps we do have a certain amount of inward appreciation of his wares.

On Sunday morning at the cinema, the enemy was again in action. No, we don't mean you, Padre (not this time). A few enemy snipers, cunningly concealed in the rafters, scored at least one very near miss on a perfect target, which was the little round bald patch worn by one of our officers. However, we suppose that its only fair that our Commissioned Gentlemen should occupy the seats rendered dangerous by those feathered creatures above.

Someone had a brilliant idea when they suggested that the A.I.F. observe two minutes silence in aid of the Melbourne footballers, who were injured during the season just concluded. Would we add to that the many men who may be hurt at the Spring race meetings?

The specially designed Christmas Card, and the copy for our Birthday Issue of Mud & Blood are now unfortunately numbered with the missing, as Staff Sgt. J. Mulcahy reports that all the copy for same was stolen from his belongings soon after his arrival in Cairo. Nevertheless, a new Christmas Card has already been designed, and is now in the hands of the printers, who have been instructed to produce 5000 of them. Those who will require the cards should hand in their orders to Company clerks as soon as possible, for they should be available within a week.

With regard to the Birthday Issue of Mud & Blood, the only other copy is on its way to Australia, and so immediate arrangements are being made by the C.O. to have the booklet printed in Australia, and distributed by our indefatigable Womens Committee. We shall have to supply the Committee with a complete list of names and addresses, so here again, Company clerks (those untiring and uncomplaining workers) will, we trust take your orders in this connection. Prices we cannot quote, but a rough estimate of 15/20 mils for cards and 9d or 1/- for the Birthday Issue should not be far wrong.

We have to acknowledge the receipt a few days ago, of "Grubb's Gazette", a publication of one of our sister units, containing an interesting record of their activities during the past six months. We shall send them a copy of our Mud & Blood in the hope of a more frequent exchange.

Yesterday's cross country run provided some thrills for the spectators, but not so many for the participants, for to run approximately 3000 yards, tends to take the sting out of you. The winner, Pte. H.C. McHenry of the Mortars, came home first in the startling time of 10 minutes! He was closely followed by Pte. J.S. Sheppard of "A" Company, and Pte. Eric Stuart of the I Section finished third, just 10 yards behind the leader. Runners found the course a tricky one - with a few stretches of up-grade, which acted as a knockout for those in poorer condition. Speaking person-ally, it might be suggested that a handicap be instituted to encourage the old chaps in the thirties!

Some of you may have noticed that the organiser, Lieut. J. M. Methven, did not take part in the above race; but we can rest assured that he'll not miss his sport, as there's table tennis and whatnot in the Mess (not to mention some charming visitors occasionally).

The two basket ball matches played yesterday (29th October) were our first efforts at the game, and when the players familiarize themselves with rules, the contests will prove very interesting. Men's basketball is very different from the women's game, as players will soon realise. Pte. Rex Spry was the referee, who blew a most impartial whistle. Results were as follows: "A" Company defeated "B" Company, 15 to 5, and "D" Com-pany defeated HQ Company, 7 to 2. Generally scores indicated that goal throwing is an art that requires constant practice. In the first match, Sgt. Trewin threw 8 goals, and Cpl. K. Fox played strongly for "A" Company; but Ptes. W. Herrett and R. Garlick seemed at first to confuse basketball with rugby! Goal throwers for "B" Company were Ptes. L. Bennett 3, A. Coulson 1, L. Lindner 1. In the second match, Pte. Raymer threw both goals for HQ Company, and Pte. Gale was a decided thorn in "D" Com-pany's flesh. For "D" Company, goals were thrown by Ptes. P. Dawson 3, C. Miller 3, G. Thomas 1.

Recently the list of first acceptances for the Melbourne Cup reached us, and we counted 103 horses. All the lucky ones who still hold a chance in our 100 Pound sweepstake must by now have attained a fever of antic-ipation, but news in the next mail, will probably make the list dwindle considerably. By the time the great occasion arrives on 4th November, the field will include the usual 25 or 30 runners. We confidently expect to hear a broadcast of the race, which would occur at 0740 hours on Tuesday next, since we in Palestine are 8 hours behind Melbourne time. (Wireless experts please take this hint).

PALESTINE, 6th November, 1941.

It is with pride that we publish a complete list of the awards gained by members of the Battalion during recent operations:-

DECORATIONS		C in C's CARDS
Capt. G. I. Malloch	MC	Sgt. F. L. Carleton
Capt. R. Rattray	MC	Pte. H.P. Clarke, MM.
Lieut. C.G. Rigg	MM	Sgt. P.R. Hook, MM.
WOII J.E. Deans	MM	Pte. J.M. Kelly, MM.
Sgt. J.W. Barnard	DCM	Pte. M.J.O'Connell, MM.
Sgt. P.R. Hook	MM	Capt. R. Rattray, MC.
Sgt. G.A. Stuckey	MM	Sgt. G.A. Stuckey, MM.
Cpl. C.B. Hayes	MM	Pte. D.E. Coutts.
L/Cpl. M.J. O'Connell	MM	WOII W.G. Morrison
Pte. J. McC. Kelly	MM	
Pte. H.P. Clarke	MM	
Pte. L. Bennett	MM	

We have published in previous issues, the names of the above people together with some stories about their reaction to sudden fame, but to-day's list is intended simply to remind Mud'n Bloods that the Battalion has not up till now, been altogether idle. One of these days we shall have the pleasure of watching some of the medals glisten in the sunlight when they eventually hang upon deserving breasts! We wonder whether any of these gentlemen will ever require the extensive body surface of a Goering to display the decorations of a long war? Strangely, the list is almost entirely composed of men of normal stature; but we can possibly select Pte. M.J. O'Connell (now L/Cpl.) as the one most likely to rival Goering. If you can capture any more maps, Maurie, don't forget to show them to the I Section.

All of us who were at Bonegilla will remember a notable occasion there on 11th October, 1940, when the Battalion was presented with a flag by the 2 AY Womens' Club, and also a list of addresses of Club members who assured us that they would write to any Mud & Blood who cared to start the ball rolling. There must be many lads who would like to receive an extra letter or two from home, and here is their opportunity. You can inspect the long list of addresses of these good people at any time if you call at I Section. Up till now, only a few letters have been sent, and it seems that we have hardly appreciated the generosity of the 2 AY Club members.

If any of the boys look forlorn and lonely, it is certainly one Pte. Max Rintoule, who can be seen moving silently about the vicinity of HQ Company cookhouse. He reminds one of a lost sheep, and we think it would be a kindness if some frequent visitor to Tel Aviv brought him home a toy watercart. Just the same, Max, you can claim an achievement that few can rival - that of having passed 285,000 gallons of water to thirsty Mud'n Bloods.

HQ Company's little mascot "Smiler" comes as regularly to meals as his keeper, Pte. Bruce Venville. The little Rhesus monkey is full of tricks, but none so far are available for publication. There seems to be a danger that Lieut. W.C. Harding will find that the attentions of his batman may be somewhat diverted to the Company pet. In any event, it should be a virtue of every batman that he be kind to animals.

Recently we have had the pleasure of again meeting some old identities, some of whom have been absent from us for many months. Sgt. J.W. Barnard DCM turned up a few days ago looking very fit, as did the remainder of his gang, amongst whom Privates G. Tippett and J. McCartney of the Signallers looked particularly pleased to rejoin their mates, although they must surely be disappointed to discover that Sigs do not now operate in a stuffy cave or a rocky sandbagged dungeon......talking of Sigs reminds us that Lieut. W. C. Harding has just returned from Cairo leave. Since then he has not been much in circulation, so we presume that he is taking the opportunity to relax after a strenuous occasion! Capt. G. Byron Moore and Lieut. K. Reid back from long leave, also appear a wee bit dissipated. Well - what else do you expect?

On Sunday last, we had a word with Lieut. G. G. Anderson who is in hospital with jaundice. He says he has not had much to eat since his arrival there; but probably that's part of the treatment - and a very trying treatment.......... Someone recently asked if there was any connection between the consumption of ale and the contraction of that yellowish bodily hue which indicates jaundice, for the colour of ale does seem likely to produce that effect. Careful now, all you who enjoy a "skinfull".

Other Mud'n Bloods encountered in hospital are Sgt. Thompson who has had a long and troubled time there, and Cpl. George Speed, who is as usual, like a fish out of water when separated from the other George. A day or two ago, Speedy caused consternation in the hospital because he couldn't be found when it was his turn to be attended. After fifteen minutes searching, he was located, and naturally brought down the wrath of the M.O. upon his head. He asked the M.O. how long he would have to wear this so-and-so bandage - "Three months" replied the Doc. "Well" said George, "fifteen minutes won't make much difference, will it?"

Everybody has missed that tall figure which usually makes a tour of the camp area during the morning. In fact, as soon as we heard those bugle blasts, we automatically expect to see Major H. R. Birch's pleasant stride. The Major has been off colour for a few days, and went to hospital on Tuesday last; but we hope for his early return in better health.

Major P.E. Spier, Capt. G. Urquhart, and Lieut. N. Hodges who have recovered from their illnesses, are again with us, and we sincerely trust that all others who are at present in hospital will make a rapid and complete recovery.

"C" Company lads will be interested to learn that Pte. Allan Hughes has left the Battalion to rejoin the unit of which he was originally a member some two years ago.

What wouldn't we give to be in Pte. E.J. Field's shoes? The lucky fellow will now have to his credit an extra 128 Pounds in Australian currency, for his horse SKIPTON came home first in the Melbourne Cup run on Tuesday last. If ever a man had a wonderful treatment while in hospital, Pte. Field is the one. He will be itching to get up and do things. We wonder whether he could be induced to join the writer on a visit to Cairo - that is if the leave really becomes a fact. Pte. Field does not now need our wishes for a quick recovery, but we offer them just the same. Second prize went to Capt. P. Tivey of Brigade, who drew SON OF AUROUS, and we believe he has booked in at BHQ until he collects his dues. At least he should be very popular at the Officers' Mess with 30 Pounds up his sleeve! Third prize went to Pte. T. A. Gooch of the Carriers, and we have heard that he intends to buy a baby carrier. Do you think 13 Pounds would be enough to purchase twins? Marvellous how three men can achieve such rapid popularity, is it not?

First formal night at the Sergeants' Mess was held on Saturday, 1st November. Official guests were WOI R. Alexander from 2/48th Battalion and WOI I.J. Nicols from 2/24th Battalion. Major Birch, 2 i/c who is an honorary Sergeant, was unavoidably absent. This was bad luck, because said Major Birch is an extremely popular member of our mess. Proceedings went according to plan, following a previous recce with the kitchen staff, whose sound tactics provided excellent results. After mess, when the Colonel and his officers arrived, things went with a merry swing, and although George Moore did not repeat his divebombing act of previous days, a very lively time was had by all. Aspirins and light duty were required by many next day, and several Sergeants could be seen sleeping peacefully during the Padre's story telling. A feature of the evening was a minutes silence in memory of fallen comrades, and the sounding of the Last Post by Sgt. Jarvie. With lights out, this was most impressive, and everyone's thoughts were of those of our cobbers who will not come back. Responses by our visitors were well received, and the feelings between the messes of this Brigade are very cordial.

The tote on the Melbourne Cup proved quite a successful venture, particularly for the happy punters who supported Skipton, the winner. Taking into account the scarcity of news regarding latest sporting results, and speed of the thoroughbreds on the training tracks, interest was quite keen. Some of the touts evidently were good judges of form. Lieut. Morrie Goldstone gave out the winner weeks ago, but few availed themselves of his valuable information. Perhaps his previous tips had been a bit out. 133 units of 100 mils each was the total held by the tote, and 7 units were taken out on the winner, which brought an excellent dividend of 19 to 1. Much better than the starting price of 6 to 1. Support of local industries was happily rewarded in this case.

PALESTINE, 15th November, 1941.

Our cartoonist suggests this system between bowler and wicket keeper by BHQ in their future matches.

WANTED —

1 BODY LINE BOWLER.

(apply BHQ Orderly Room)

This paper as a rule, does not cater for classified ads, but occasionally we are approached with a deserving case which merits an exception being made - for example, this one -

LOST -

One morning during the past fortnight, between this camp and Egypt, three large bristling beer-stained moustaches. Finder please return same to Lieuts. M. Wilton, G.G. Anderson, R. Boulter. REWARD.

Whilst musing upon the above par, we came across the following morsel:

"The hair which grew in such profusion,
  Upon the lips of many a 'Loot'
Did cause the owners so much confusion
  When on their leave they did set foot
That, quick as light, their lips they bared,
  Their faces now are unimpared."

You will remember (we hope) that in our last issue, we made mention of Cpl. George Speed being in hospital with a hand injury, and that he was like a fish out of water without his "twin" Cpl. George Dixon. Well, we (and you) should have known what would happen after that. Yes! You've guessed it. George Dixon is an inmate of the hospital, being packed off there after an interview with the M.O. His diagnosis was not as you may think, "fretting for Speedy", but it appears he suffers from a fairly serious chest complaint. We sincerely hope that this won't cause a permanent break in the Speed - Dixon partnership.

Incidentally, Speedy called on us the other day and we noticed that the plaster on his hand between thumb and forefinger was, to say the least of it, badly bent. A remark to that effect evoked the reply - "Oh! that's caused by holding so many mugs of tea". We would like to believe this statement in its entirety but, (our nature being what it is) we strongly suspect that it could be attributed to holding lots of mugs filled not with tea but something rather different - and we don't mean water!

Which brings us to the remembrance that we are glad to see our RMO, Capt. J.M. Agar, amongst us once again, looking none the worse for his stay in hospital. Welcome home Capt. Agar! You must indeed be a popular man judging by the large number of chaps waiting personally to say hello! to you. So we thought anyway, after seeing the crowd outside the RAP a few mornings back. Perhaps this effusive welcome proved too much for the "Doc", as we hear that he is now on leave.

Speaking of leave reminds us that the C.O. arrived back on Wednesday looking very fit and well after an interesting tour of Syria.

All Mud'n Bloods will be pleased to hear that Major Birch, although still in hospital, should be back with us shortly.

Have you heard the tale concerning a certain Sgt. Major in this Battalion being so enamoured with those notorious playmates of ours during recent months, that he decided to smuggle one out with him. But what a peculiar hiding place? First respirator parade and there was this poor rat - forgotten and deader'n mutton. Surely the change must have been too much for it. What we are wondering now is who received the blame for that strange odour about the Company office?

Mud'n Bloods will warmly welcome both new and old faces which we see around us. Among the latter we notice Lieut. Johnny Fallon, and at the next tabloid sports meeting, we are expecting to see a recurrence of his old form over the 100 yards.

The opening round of new sporting fixtures commenced in fine style on Wednesday, when representative basketball and cricket teams from the various Companies vied for the honours. Results to hand are as follows:

BASKETBALL:
Wednesday, 12th November. "A" Company 32 goals defeated BHQ 21 goals. For the winners Broomhead and Fox scored 13 and 8 goals respectively, and Henderson 8 goals for BHQ.
"B" Company 28 goals defeated HQ Company 13 goals.
Selleck 10, Gallagher 8, Darley 5, were kept busy throwing goals for "B" Company, and Raymer 5 for HQ Company.

CRICKET:
Wednesday 12th November. BHQ 7 for 123 defeated "B" Company all out for 83. Best performances were Henderson and Wright 47 and 27 (both retired) and Menzies 6 for 15 (including the "hat trick") on the winning side - Holden 24 and May 2 for 14 in "B" Company.

We are wondering how many Mud'n Bloods have suffered our own sad experiences of late. No, we are not referring to after effects of occasions when we may have "looked upon the wine when it was red". Rather we refer to something much more unpleasant - the ordeal of having a studio photograph taken. Some weeks ago, we received an order from our wives stating that at the first available opportunity we were to obtain and forward photos of ourselves, so that they at home could proudly show to all and sundry what handsome heroes we were. That opportunity presenting itself last week, we very reluctantly allowed ourselves to be coaxed into a studio, and after smiling or grinning - at the 'dicky bird' for what seemed several hours, we were politely told to hand over the cash and to call back on the morrow. Well, we have the results now, and although no oil paint-

ings, we do not think the photos entirely do us justice. Our friends assure
us however, that the camera never lies, so home to Australia they must go.
How many photos have been sent to that fair land in the past few weeks?
We do not know, but their number must be legion, and we are quite sure
that the remuneration from photography must be ample. Perhaps Cpl.
Norm Dowell of the RAP thinks so too, for we understand that after a
recent leave, he returned with one of the latest movie camera models.
Sittings can be arranged for a very moderate fee, but please make all applications through us. Then we will receive a small commission, and every little
helps now that we are again in the land flowing with milk, very little other
liquids, and honey.

NEWS FLASH!

The final results of the TEL AVIV council elections are just to hand
and we have much pleasure in announcing Sgt. Jack Jarvie as the successful
candidate for the Mayoral Chair, closely followed by Lieut. A.N. McKoy,
(Officer's Mess Secretary). Jack is at present on a three day business trip
to HAIFA endeavouring to procure a mouthpiece (for the bugle) he was
unable to obtain in TEL AVIV or JERUSALEM. We hope this is not an
indication of another election, but why did he take all the band with him -
but to act as canvassers?

WOI Laurie Folland, well known to all on Regimental Parades etc.,
today departed the Battalion for a position with another unit. Our loss will
be their gain, and the best wishes of the battalion will go with him for good
soldiering and happy hunting.

Hello! Hello-ello-ello!! Can you hear me mother? Soon wives,
mothers, sweethearts and others will have the thrill of hearing the loved
voices of their soldier heroes in this unit in the "Voice of the Middle East
Session". The ABC have allotted a number of recordings to be made by US
and they are asking for originality. We can envisage the RAP staff doing
good business in throat gargles during the next day or so. Note - crooners
are not barred. So Mud'n Bloods, be prepared!

PALESTINE, 25th November, 1941.

Padre, it is with great regret that we bid you farewell, for you have
been to all of us a true guide, philosopher and friend. We appreciate your
interest in us all the more when we realize that your presence has been made
possible only by a considerable stretching of regulations, for didn't our own
Colonel confess on Sunday week last that your many months of service with
the unit are in reality an unofficial extension of an afternoon visit?

On Sunday, 16th November, our popular Chaplain conducted his last service for Mud'n Bloods (at least until we finish this wretched struggle) and at the conclusion, the C.O. paid a tribute to the untiring efforts of the man who has, during the Battalion's grim initiation, earned the respect and admiration of everyone - Officers, NCO's and men included. Major R. E. Wall, as 2 i/c supported the C.O.'s remarks by saying that we have indeed been fortunate in having had Padre Morrison as Chaplain to the unit, and then led by the Old Man, we Mud'n Bloods gave three very hearty and willing cheers in his honour.

The simple ceremony of farewell was completed when, as we marched past, Chaplain R. N. Morrison took the Salute by the Battalion, and with that, we can assure him, went the good will of every Mud'n Blood.

The following is a message from the Padre for which we made a special request as soon as his impending departure became known:-

Dear Editor,

May I claim a small space in our excellent journal, to say a few words before I leave you for a time. I want to thank the C.O., Officers and all ranks for the very wonderful way in which they have helped me in my work in the Battalion. The hearty co-operation of all has made many extra things possible for which I cannot take the credit to myself. I was proud to be of service among you, and never so humble and grateful as when privileged to take the Salute of the Battalion on the march past on last Sunday. My one wish is that the Almighty Father may be ever present with you in your work and your pleasures, as well as to help and comfort you in the active service which lies in front of this Battalion, with a grand history and tradition to be maintained.

Our days in the West were at times uncomfortable, but your large hearts and courage enabled you to find the will to laugh and enjoy yourselves as I hope you will continue to do - and that our return to Australia will not be long delayed. May I express to you my regret that I could not bring the "Fiat" with me to drive down Collins Street, Melbourne, on our return.

Farewell to all,

Yours ever sincerely,

Roland Morrison.

Heard in the Sergeants' Mess recently: "Who's the stranger, George - the elderly chap with the worried expression?" "Oh, that's our Band Sgt., Jack Jarvie! He was successful recently in the Tel Aviv Mayoral Election, and now, of course, he honours our Mess only occasionally with his presence. If you shout him a drink he will show you his leave pass which gives him permission to arise and walk from his Mayoral Chair!" Since Sgt. Jarvie is commissioned to purchase band instruments and other things less important, he is doubtless very popular in Tel Aviv.

At the end of last week, Capt. R. Rattray MC had the honour to command a special guard in Cairo on the occasion of the presentation to General Morshead of the "Virtuti Militari" (Class V), which is a decoration about on a par with the British C.B.E. To complete the picture, we must also say that our band provided the musical accompaniment which included the Polish National Anthem. (We don't know whether they played oompah as well). Everybody must know why such a decoration should be awarded to General Morshead, and it was particularly fitting that he should receive it from the hand of the Polish C in C, General Sikorski. The personnel of the guard was drawn from our own and sister units, and with Capt. Rattray as O.C., the men evidently performed their duties very satisfactorily, for we have received an appreciation from the General himself. This was published in Routine Orders on Saturday last.

The guard was rehearsed by a Tommy Sgt. Major on the day before, and on Friday 21st November, the big event was completed in a few hours. Capt. Rattray tells us that the 'Present Arms' position was achieved with a 'grand click' and that the whole ceremony was exceedingly well carried out. The party earned a few hours relaxation (?) in Cairo, and on the following morning, the last one to reach the appointed RV was the Officer Commanding! Doubtless this was his reaction after rubbing shoulders with such important personages as Generals and the like. Capt. Rattray has complained too, of a stiff elbow since his return, and his excuse is that he had to give on return a salute with almost every step. Sounds feasible - but we can think of another movement likely to produce a similar disability.

Some time ago, some of us wrote letters to various children in Albury, and by some mischance a letter from Cpl. Freddie Henderson to eleven year old Margaret Newman became lost. Yesterday, Freddie received his reply, for the letter had been recovered as the result of an ad in the "Albury Mail". Margaret's letter was most interesting, and it gave a good indication of how thrilled she was to receive a letter from one of us - (particularly Fred). We cannot remember just what appeared in "Mud &

Blood" at the time, but Margaret evidently received a copy, as she writes: "The Editors who publish your paper are not quite right in saying that I am seven, as I am really eleven, but still that doesn't make much difference, as I am sure I still will not be old enough, and Mum will not do, because she is married." Freddie, what have you been saying?

Well, we have just come in from a tour of the Company offices in search of copy. It's quite refreshing to be made welcome in so many places, and hear the tit bits of news. Had coffee been offered to us at "B" Company, the scene would have closely resembled Arab hospitality, for we had to squat on the floor! As far as that goes, we would not object to a bit of squatting in return for some interesting pars for "Mud & Blood". Perhaps "B" Company's best is this: "One hears about numerous parades for clothing and equipment shortages. The burning question in "B" Company at the moment is 'Is there a paper shortage?' .... The answer must be in the affirmative for, although a reporter is seen lurking around our lines for copy, the other ranks never see the finished article of "Mud & Blood".

In reply, we hasten to tell you that five or six copies of "Mud & Blood" are always sent to each Rifle Company, so a few copies apart from that on your notice board, should be made available for perusal by other ranks. We should also tell you that the paper question has caused the editor some awkward moments, but whoever you may be, our advice is that you complain to your Company, if you do not get a glimpse of every issue of "Mud & Blood".

"B" Company are justly proud of their right to display the "Tin Hat" indicating the best lines in the camp, but we hear that Capt. Haworth's methods are a little motherly. Anyway, the influence of a mother's love is much required hereabouts, especially where our baby Company is concerned. "B" Company had no difficulty on Monday in defeating "C" Company at basketball, scoring 39 goals to 11. The Hayes - Holden - Gallagher combination worked very effectively. Gallagher scored 13 goals, Hayes 9.

"A" Company has lost possession of the "Horseshoe" to "C" Company, but Sgt. Major Ward of HQ Company is quite certain that his lads will win it next week. Possibly the absence of Major Spier, as Battalion 2 i/c, has resulted in "A" Company's loss. However, "A" Company has done well to win three games of basketball, for they have defeated "D" Company 76 -16; "B" Company 15 - 5, and also HQ Company. L/Cpl. Reg Cousins went to Gaza on Sunday to see the cross country run, and was wished into the race. Out of such a large number of starters, he did well to finish 87th. He established an early lead - knowing, we suppose, that just then he would pass the movie camera! More about this contest will be published later.

"D" Company have not had much success in the sporting world, but have greater hopes now that Pte. Chitty has rejoined them. He was captain of the football team in earlier training days. Pte. Chook Fowler has left the Company, and it seems at least one man misses him. Captains we are told, become very well acquainted with the qualities (if any) of their batmen. This same private has an inventive turn of mind, for he has ideas of patenting a special modification of the ack ack gun in order to keep the birds off the raspberry canes. There is more to it than that, because he also knows a modern method of presenting his friends with raspberries. If there are any other Mud'n Bloods so gifted, we want to hear of their inventions, for we would be delighted to commence an "Inventions Column".

A familiar figure rolled into "C" Company today, in the form of one Sgt. Beresford, who when last seen was carrying a troublesome tummy about in the desert, but we will wager he is now punishing the throttle in celebration of his reunion.

PALESTINE, 2nd December, 1941.

We want to remind readers, and especially those who have recently come among us, that our Battalion is fortunate in having a most energetic Ladies Committee working at home on our behalf. Those bottles of ale which you are lately drawing from the Q Store are made available only because of their efforts. We do appreciate their lively interest in us. We begin to wonder whether our efforts of recent months in writing odes to a bottle of beer have influenced the Ladies. Nevertheless, we hasten to assure them that no such motive ever entered our thoughts. However, we would like to make this suggestion, that many, if not all of us, write to the Ladies Committee wishing them the Compliments of the Season, and assuring them of our gratefulness. The address is:- The President, 2/23 Bn. Welfare Club, C/o Legacy Club, Market Street, Melbourne.

HQ and "D" Company each report having received from Albury, a Christmas Card addressed to the Company. The sender was F. Dickenson, and we want to record in our paper, our appreciation of such a thoughtful act.

On Saturday, we saw again the tall figure of Major H.R. Birch, and we trust he is in much better health than when he left us recently. Lately, too, we have said, "welcome home" to Lieut. C.G. Rigg, MM, and Sgt. Peter Hook, MM. The latter may be interested to know that just after he left us in October, a short description of some of his antics was published in "Mud & Blood". We wish also to welcome Chaplain McQuie, who addressed us for the first time on Sunday morning. We might add that we were a step ahead of the Orderly Room in doing this, because our new Padre had not then been officially marched in.

NOTES FROM THE OFFICERS' MESS:

When we were 'up there', most of the officers were heard to express from time to time, the remark 'won't it be great to be all together again?' All looked forward to the time when the Mess would function once more, and they could gather round the bar in an atmosphere of boisterous good fellowship. But, except for the first few days, the Mess has had the appearance of having just come out of battle, in that there has always been a large percentage of cheery faces absent. What with various schools of instruction, some illness, and a sprinkling of leave, there have been few occasions when the C.O. could speak to all his officers at the one time. However, despite this fact, the Mess has run smoothly and quietly (we hope). Since we came back, the officers, in common with the other members of the unit who have 'been through it', have taken their amusements and recreations more soberly than of yore. In other words, though tasting our pleasures more deeply than before, we have 'grown up'.

Talking of schools, these courses must be of absorbing interest. On more than one occasion, a junior officer, having just returned from one, on being asked what it was like, has replied: "Well, the girls in Cairo are........, etc., etc., " or "The beer is such and such......., maybe not as good as it used to be........"; and on being pressed for details of the school itself, has mumbled something like "Oh! the school? Well - er - its like this,........". But, in spite of the fact that boys will be boys, those who have attended these courses have brought back knowledge that will eventually be of great value to the Battalion in future operations.

On 6th November we published the names of those who had won decorations in recent operations. Now, we discover that the names of two men who received C in C's Cards were inadvertently omitted from that list. They are Sgt. J.W. Barnard, DCM, and WOII J.H. Deane, MM.

It seems like old times to hear Sgt. Major Morrison's pleasant word of command float across the "B" Company Parade Ground. Nevertheless, those in the know will detect in his tone a certain strain of despondency.

Lieut. Morrie Goldstone is a well known wit, and his story of our pet monkey's antics indicates this trait. He asserts that the animal is a taxidermist of no mean ability, and if you want further explanation, you must ask him for it. Believe me you will not be disappointed.

It is wonderful what a few pips can do! (You're telling me). We hear that one Lieut. . J.M. M, succeeded in persuading a charming young woman in Tel Aviv to go out with him. Naturally he arrived at the arranged meeting place looking very smart, but when the woman arrived, complete with husband, great was his confusion!! There is one consolation, Sir, for at least you can write a true account of your outing when next you write home.

Last week "C" Company were delighted to exhibit their two trophies - Sword and Horseshoe, but now they have been robbed! Of course, some encouragement has to be extended to HQ Company, so "C" Company kindly allowed them to take the Horseshoe. "A" Company now hold the trophy for the best kept lines, and "D" Company can claim the week's best guard.

Lieut. Ken Clarke, who was a very successful member of the Field Works School, from which he returned recently, has again departed for another course, to gain fresh laurels. "C" Company is justly proud of their blond Lieutenant.

Pte. Vic Bennett of HQ Company, promises to be a most helpful person in the compilation of Mud & Blood. You know, science tells us that it takes considerable energy to overcome the inertia of a heavy body, so when thats done, Vic should be a tower of strength. Once the Bennett body, mind and soul are set in motion, you readers can expect something pretty good.

We cannot let this occasion pass without blowing our own trumpet just a bit. The fact is, we of the I Section feel greatly relieved since the completion of an out-size in maps for the C.O.'s use, because while it was being done, we had almost hourly visits from Brigadiers, Colonels, and lesser stars. We hope the map returns in good order because we as a section felt quite proud of our efforts in the production thereof.

Further details of the 5 mile cross country run - First of those from our Battalion was Pte. Carnham of "B" Company, who finished 39th. Then followed Pte. Eric Stuart (I Section) 64th, L/Cpl. Reg Cousins ("A" Company) 87th, Don Oakley (HQ Company) 106th. We can almost claim to have filled 4th place too, because A/Sgt. Noel Mills from the Infantry Training Battalion ran into that position. Many "C" Company lads will remember Noel back in training days, when his enthusiasm for flourishing a bayonet was quite remarkable.

The highlight of the sporting season occurred last week, when after a very fast game, BHQ defeated HQ Company at Basketball, 32 - 7. Jimmie Henderson threw 15 goals, and thats about all he will ever get, because he has left us for a change of occupation. Sgt. Les Allen also had a big day, scoring 14 goals, but one look at Les, and it is easy to see how he can have a big day!

During the week, the I Section was soundly defeated by the RAP, mainly owing to Sgt. Allen's bulk. Scores were 31 - 16, but of course they don't indicate the quality of the game.

On Saturday afternoon, a Basketball team from the Unit, ("A" Company actually), defeated a neighbouring Artillery Unit. About this match, the referee made the comment that it was one of the best he had ever seen, so it appears that "A" Company can flatter themselves that their team is a strong one.

On Friday, 28th November, "C" Company defeated "D" Company at cricket by 33 runs, Pte. Bridges 39, Pte. Barney Loomes 2/12, and Pte. Page 4/41 were the best performers for "C" Company, while best for "B" were Pte. Nepean 27, Pte. Webster 3/13, and Pte. Morrissey 2/8. This success must have gone to the heads of our "C" Company cricketers, for we overheard one of them suggest that they would do quite well against a Battalion team. At any rate, at least three of them played in the Battalion team against 2/24th Battalion on Monday. In this match 2/24th soundly defeated us. We batted first, and compiled 82 after a hard struggle. Runs were very scarce on such moist ground, and only three boundaries appeared in our 1st innings. Vic Bridges made a valuable 34, and Pte. F. Wise, 15. Collett took 6 of our wickets for 20 runs. 2/24th replied with 127, (McKenzie 30, Enever 24, Collett 44), and our best bowlers were F. Watt 4/34, and Cliff Burrows 3/38. We prospered a little in the second innings, and declared at 5/92 (Keith Benson 47, Jim Cook 20) giving our opponents half an hour to snatch an outright win. 2/24th were quick on the job, making 61 in about 20 minutes, and McKenzie did well with a brisk 43.

PALESTINE, 9th December, 1941.

We have, in this issue, a very pleasant duty to perform in recording our Unit's appreciation of a wonderful gift from Mr. Grant Hays, of the Richmond Brewing Company. He it was who presented us with no less than one hundred crates of beer, and those 4800 bottles of luscious Aussie brew were safely lodged in our QM Store some weeks ago. To transport such a quantity of ale some 9000 miles is no light task, and the good ladies of our Welfare Club have again proved themselves by providing the sum of 70 Pounds to pay for transit expenses of the precious liquid. Now that our throats have actually been warmed by the passage of this delightful beverage, we can assure the donor that our appreciation is all the keener.

In a letter from the Mayor of Albury, Alderman Padman, the C.O. has received word that the sum of 400 Pounds raised by the townspeople, has been paid into the Australian Comforts Fund with the direction that it be spent on Christmas comforts for "Albury's Own".

It cannot be denied that our Unit is extremely lucky to find itself supported back in Aussie by such a wide circle of willing workers, and if ever, in time of war, a unit looked forward to a Merry Christmas, then that one is, without question, our own.

Last week, there was an important addition to the equipment possessed by our famous band. The addition is a mace, which will replace the one lost in the "Derby" many, many months ago. The new one has been made by Mr. Harry Orr's Pioneers, and is mainly the handiwork of Pte. Ken Wilde, whose ability for making useful articles has earned him quite a reputation. The mace is of particular interest, because the head is made from pieces of brass left for us by our generous enemy Musso, when his forces were pushed out of Libya about a year ago. Certainly, you could never guess that the nickel plated head is really portion of 20mm and 149mm shell cases. Our original mace was presented by Mr. Ecker, of the Globe Hotel, Albury, but this, as previously mentioned, was lost along with other equipment. For their recent turnout in Cairo, the band procured a mace of French make, and now they possess one in which everyone must be interested, on account of its association with the Battalion's first battle ground.

At the Church Parade on Sunday, 7th December, the mace was officially presented by the Colonel; and Drum Major Lloyd Jones who received it, proceeded to brandish it with new vigour. We feel tempted here to look into the future, where we can see this same mace twirling its way through the sunny atmosphere of Albury, followed by shining instruments and a Battalion of delighted soldiers who have returned to claim their beautifully worked Colours, which were hung on 3rd November, 1940 in the Albury Town Hall.

A few days ago, Sgt. "Old Bill" Marshall, complete with incomprehensible Scots accent, and smiling countenance, departed from our midst, along with 17 other Mud'n Bloods, all bound for fresh fields and pastures new. Most of these men have been with us for a long time - practically since the unit was formed, so they will have some grand times exchanging yarns with their new mates.

The day of their departure was arranged (?) to fall close to pay day, with the result that much celebration took place - especially the kind which comes out of bottles! One very touching incident occurred when we saw the Regimental Police Sergeant dragged to the bar by his most persistent customer for the "boob" for a goodbye "shout".

When we say cheerio to Sgt. Tommie Lewis, our thoughts are immediately taken back to an early morning some months ago, when some well directed rounds from Tommie's Vickers guns caused a passing Messerschmidt to quickly alter its course.

It would be proper to publish a word or two about each and all of these fellows, but lack of space will not permit it. Let us not forget, however, to wish each one of them all the best in their future activities. Each will be missed, but it is only natural that changes take place. They are veterans all, and indeed, some have fought in two wars.

In addition to the presentation of the new mace on Sunday's parade, there was an event that will go down in history --------

BHQ WINS TIN HAT FOR TIDIEST LINES IN CAMP

And to be perfectly honest, we saw neither hesitancy nor surprise in Mr. McKoy's step as he proudly strode to the C.O. to receive the trophy------ Some suggest that this feat by BHQ is the natural result of Pte. Bill Woods' departure early last week, and his mates lost no time in telling him so!

"C" Company were not long in regaining the Sword for the best guard of the week, although it is believed that this award was a most difficult decision to come to. In "D" Company's lines you will see the Horseshoe telling all that the Dons still know how to march, which reminds us of the days when the Dons claimed almost a mortgage on the thing.

While we're talking of the Dons, let us mention that S/Sgt. Peter Reynolds has had a letter from L/Sgt. Mick Kenny, who in August returned to Australia in order to assist the recruiting campaign. He has given talks to various organizations, and has also been heard at a Pleasant Sunday Afternoon broadcast from Wesley Church. His job at home sounds wonderfully attractive, but would you believe it - he says in his letter that he is already anxious to rejoin the boys in the Middle East.

It may be now, since the war has spread into the Pacific Ocean - closer to our native land than ever before - Australians will need no urging to do their share, and if Mick Kenny's return to us should indicate this, then we sincerely hope that we soon see him.

Is it strange that soldiers in general have a special interest in the opposite sex? No, of course not, and it is not at all strange to see photographs of feminine beauty adorning the walls of various dwellings in camp. BUT, it was a little surprising (and possibly embarrassing) to see such things sitting up like Jackie in front of us when recently we all paid a social visit to the Medical Officer!....... We suppose our M.O. is a keen student of human nature. That is a good thing, and we commend you Sir, upon your originality.

Having renewed our acquaintance with said females, we hasten to introduce them to all newcomers......Elizabeth squats gracefully on a favoured mat looking very attractive, while Hilary delights the eye with her mature form, but critics agree that she suffers slightly from d.t.'s. The third....... Helen.......is just magnificent, perfect in every detail. These three beauties have accompanied our unit through many trials, and until latter days have always been present at all RAP receptions. It is with deep regret that we announce that only Helen remains, as her two companions have been taken prisoner by some unworthy hound. We cannot decide whether lonely Helen is altogether safe in the hands of her keepers, for although we trust Pte. Jack Turner (and some others), we suspect that Sgt. Keith Roberts is likely to let Helen slip through his fingers, as did the other lovelies.

Saturday night at the Sergeants' Mess was an enjoyable one according to reports. Guest of honour was "Sgt." Major H.R. Birch, who was presented with three stripes for the occasion. During the evening, a sporting contest was organized by Sgt. Patt, who defeated all comers in the standing jump contest (weight for age, we believe)......An outstanding performance, this! Whether it was in this competition, or in an earlier scramble caused by Sgt. Tom Lewis and Sgt. Bill Marshall shouting for the Mess, is hard to say, but Sgt. Keith Benson cannot remember how he earned that damaged eye.

The beginnings of a menagerie are in evidence in our lines, for we have a few unusual specimens on hand, including a monkey, a few stray dogs, queer looking Wogs and a bird or two. In addition, we have a fellow with an elusive neck, for he wrote "I wish to notify that I have lost my identity discs that are worn around my neck somewhere in the vicinity of this camp".

PALESTINE, 17th December, 1941.

Today, 17th December, is the first anniversary of our arrival in PALESTINE, when almost everyone saw the Holy Land for the first time. Now, we are thoroughly accustomed to the place, and we have on numerous occasions visited its many places of historic interest. Sent from this land, Christmas Greetings seem to have additional significance; but does that mean we are anxious to stay here? NOT by a long chalk.

Last week saw our indefatigable L/Cpl. Lees despatching Christmas Greetings from the unit to all the bits and pieces that together form a Division. A feeling of goodness seemed to pervade the atmosphere of the Disorderly Room, as Ron included a specially intimate note with the card for the Provos in Tel Aviv. Without wishing to give away secrets, we can publish the text of Ron's addition - "Dear Mr. P.M., I wish to thank you very sincerely, at this season of the year, for your generosity of recent weeks in providing cigarettes for the boys and myself in Jaffa gaol. At the same time, I can assure you that next time I visit you (my next leave is almost due), I shall make a practical effort to return your hospitality by bringing with me a drop of the doings. Your Jaffa residence, Sir, could be made considerably more hospitable by the addition of a wet canteen. No doubt you have many schemes in hand for the welfare of your clientele, but I have taken the liberty to make the above suggestions in case you should have overlooked it." The final touch, perhaps, was the best, when Ron wrote, "Yours affectionately".

Far be it from us to spread rumours, but such things are still to be heard in the vicinity. The following, if not a rumour, must be some homesick OR.

On a date to be fixed we men are to be the honoured hosts to a bevy of VAD's, and all genuine Mud'n Bloods must come prepared to act the part. Ordinary Mess conditions will prevail, except that there will be seats to support all bodies, male and female, kindly lent for the occasion by our more favoured friends at the Brigade men's Mess. All the cooks -

yes, O.B. included, have promised to shave, and have also promised that as the VAD's file past with their shining mess gear (which they will, of course bring with them) they will not handle the promised oyster patties. In case mention of such a menu should sound rather too attractive for such a party, we have an assurance from Cpl. Jimmy Rintoule that with one case of bully beef, he can produce hundreds of such patties. Although liquor must not be served at the Mess, the party will afterwards adjourn to the men's private residences where VAD guests will be offered their choice of Richmond Beer, diluted Rum, and other refreshment, and also invited to join the programme of special parlour games. In this respect, chess, draughts and checkers have been forbidden in order to prevent unseemly disturbance. Dress is optional. It may be that the supply of VAD's will fall short of the demand, consequently the organisers of the party have decided that any man whose name has appeared on a charge sheet during the last month will not be allowed the privilege of entertaining in his own tent. This is somewhat hard on recent offenders in BHQ, but we cannot take risks. One thing more, - your attention, men, is directed to Routine Order No. 29 of the 24th of November, para 148, sub-para (a) and No. 41 of the 16th December, para 190, sub-para (a).

Recently, as you all know, the C.O., accompanied by Lieut. A. N. McKoy and driver Doug Innes, paid a visit to Syria. The object of the visit was to enlighten troops there as to the methods which were employed in the defence of Tobruk, and we have been assured that the series of lectures were highly successful. At any rate, that's the accepted verdict....Another object of the tour was evidently to combine business with pleasure, because it surely cannot take ten days to give a few lectures? Were it not for the fact that this paper is vigorously censored by the Old Man himself, we could publish some more interesting sidelights of this tour, but the truth will out - even if it does come in dribs and drabs. Keep your eyes peeled in expectation of some titbits which our reporters are striving to discover. Perhaps it is indiscreet to mention at this point that the C.O.'s car returned slightly the worse for the tour; so we shall not say any more about it.

On Sunday, Capt. Rattray, MC, stepped modestly out to receive the famous Sword, since "C" Company have again put on the best guard. This Sword is another interesting trophy, for it was made, like the band mace, from pieces of I-ti equipment gathered in by the Pioneer Platoon. The blade was originally a portion of an I-ti truck, and the handguard is made from a shell case. "D" Company again marched off with the Horseshoe, and "B" Company were rewarded with the Tin Hat for being so tidy. With regard to "D" Company's consistently good marching, the suggestion has been made (by them) that groups from other Companies be given tuition in marching - for a small consideration. Charges for same may be had on application to "Tich" Allen, Don Company's diminutive Company clerk.

At last we have discovered why BHQ failed to get a point for the cleanest lines, one day this week. It's a long story; and we cannot afford to go into too much detail; but we must say that we are just a little surprised and disappointed. The food at the Officers' Mess has evidently begun to lack quantity (if not quality) for what did we observe outside Major Birch's window but some remnants of a hot dog! Maybe we shall have to invite the Major to our own Christmas party, for we cannot bear to think of our Major losing weight.

Preparations for Christmas are going apace, and it will not be any fault of the men's, if the celebrations do not reach very merry proportions! By the way, Mud'n Bloods, there is a simple way to bring happiness to at least one member of the Unit, and surely there must be a few men in each Company who would like to do that! Send in some seasonal contributions for our next issue which we expect to publish on Christmas Day, and you will be literally filling the Editor's stocking. Thanks very much, in anticipation.

The Postal people have been kind to us in recent weeks, for the birds which carry the letters have certainly donned their running shoes. We have just examined some letters from Australia, on which the postmark was the 11th December, and the letters were here on Monday night 15th December. Surely that's the shortest time letters have taken in travelling the eight or nine thousand miles from Melbourne? If the new situation in the Pacific has the effect of hastening our mails, we may even think a little less harshly of our Oriental enemies.

Calling on "A" Company this week, our reception was not the warmest, but reporters cannot notice these things if they want news! Pte. Tom Davies almost blushed when he said he had been on leave to Haifa, so the interview with him did not produce anything publishable. We had the decency not to press him.

Major P.E. Spier (also of "A" Company) left camp on Sunday bound for Syria on leave, his companions in crime being Major R.E. Wall and Lieut. M. Goldstone, with Pte. Arthur Hirst as chaperon. Now that we have bade them goodbye, we can say what everyone is thinking - namely, they will be lucky to get back safe and sound, because their ability to drive a motor vehicle is questionable. We shall not easily forget some very anxious mo-

ments which we suffered back at Wadi Delia, when, Major Wall's hand rested
on the wheel of that dilapidated old V8, which was then one of HQ Company's most treasured possessions. Perhaps the Major has improved since
then..........however, we shall soon know.

Of Major Spier's ability in this direction, we know "Sweet Felicity
Arbuckle"; but we are led to believe that Morrie G. is fast approaching his
sixth or seventh motor accident. Beware, Arthur - your very existence is
threatened!

Two of our handsome young Lieutenants called at 7 A.G.H. during
the weekend to visit a certain Sister, who was known to them only by
repute. They duly met the lady and probably enjoyed themselves (they
didn't deny doing so!) but were rather amazed to eventually discover that
they had entertained the wrong person! Not that they have any regrets -
far from it, because the lady had a convenient girl friend, did she not?

Our RSM, along with a few other gallants, visited Tel Aviv on Sunday,
and were very hospitably treated by a couple of maidens, who volunteered
to lend them the light of their torch. This invitation was, of course, gratefully accepted. (Who wouldn't?).......When our heroes courteously suggested
a cup of coffee together, the ladies demurred saying, "We didn't help you
for the sake of favours", but nevertheless were persuaded to partake. We
cannot tell much more about the incident, because neither RSM nor Sgt. R.
Ward will tell. We know, however, that a good time was had by all.

PALESTINE, Christmas Day, 1941.

Today we cannot but allow our thoughts to cross the intervening
seas, and dwell upon our native land, where in spite of the turmoil of nearby
combat on land, on sea and in the air, we can visualise a thousand homes
enriched by the happiness which Christmastide brings. To all our people at
home we say "MERRY CHRISTMAS" from all Mud'n Bloods, and we know
and appreciate just how much their thoughts are with us.

Our festivities this year will differ slightly from those of last year,
because we will consume our Christmas Pudding in our own tents. Instead
of six or seven large parties, we will today have sixty or seventy smaller
ones - none the less merry on that account. Those cheering sounds which
reflect the true Christmas spirit will float merrily throughout the camp area,
replacing for one day the sound of "Slope Arms" shouted by some husky
sergeant.

Xmas, 1940
Dimra, Palestine
The Race Meeting

Xmas, 1941
Julis, Palestine
The Deluge

Remember last year? ....and this year!

And what of New Year's Day? Arrangements for an hilarious day of sports, games and sideshows are well in hand, even to the invitation of Australian nurses and VAD's! Sgt. Jack Jarvie and his merry men will provide an orchestra second to none, and even if the army will not provide dancing pumps for the occasion, most of us will "Trip the light fantastic toe".

****

It was with profound regret that we learned on Thursday, 18th December, of the death of Sgt. A.H. Thompson, who was wounded in April last as we withdrew from Derna. As soon as we returned from the Desert, some of his friends were able to see him again, and all of them looked forward to the time when he would be strong enough to make the journey back to Australia. With traditional ceremony, his remains were laid to rest on Saturday, 29th December, in the Gaza War Cemetery, and at Sunday's parade, the Colonel paid fitting tribute to the splendid service rendered by him to that portion of the unit which left Derna on the eventful day, 5th April, 1941.

****

A year of high adventure, saddened by the parting of comrades, and enriched by friendships made and confirmed in the face of dangers and difficulties, has slipped by since Mud'n Bloods spent their first Christmas Day in Palestine.

It was a new experience to spend Christmas in the land where the festival began almost two thousand years before, and to be near the Bethlehem scenes of the Shepherds' fields, and the Manger itself - also brought closer to many Australian homes because of the nearness of a lad abroad. Ties of kinship and affection thus linked families and dear ones divided voluntarily in freedom's stirring call, at the time when they were accustomed to be together.

The bonds that bind to Home have strengthened in a year abroad, and Mud'n Bloods are now accustomed to service overseas. Messages of greeting and goodwill, sprung from the familiar Christmas story, with its strong quiet note of peace and goodwill, have been sent home as the war extended to the Far East, and brought the scenes of actual conflict nearer home than Mud'n Bloods care for. But this has been done with a confident hope, for the Christmas message is not out of place in a troubled world; it first came to a world that had need of it, and every Mud and Blood is doing his part to make it actual in a new era of peace on earth and goodwill among men.

Contributed by S/Sgt. A.P. Reynolds.

Continuing our reference to the driving ability of one of our respected Majors, we now report that the party (or at least part of it) has returned with battle casualties as follows:

Turkey	1 (total loss; buried at map ref 12345678)
Wog	1 (running wounded)
Wall, Major R.E.	1 (abdominal complaints, now in hospital at Beirut)
Spier, Major P.E.	1 (suffering from severe shock)

It may be mentioned that the last of these casualties has not only had his life shortened by five years, but his previously unblemished hair now turns to grey. An indefinable aura of vagueness and mystery surrounds the respective travellers. They seem willing, nay, even anxious, to talk upon generalities - to describe in detail the countryside, scenery, and etc; but when questioned in respect of social activities they retire discreetly behind a screen of silence. What we want to know is:

(i)   Whose foot depressed the accelerator and NOT the clutch, when about to change down on a dangerous hairpin bend?

(ii)   What were the reactions of his passengers?

(iii)   Is it a fact that of seventeen in the road, only six were actually passed.

Jonathan Swift of the "Sun" Newspaper in Melbourne, has referred recently in his columns to the first reunion and smoke night of returned members of our unit, organised by Cpl. E. R. Alexander, who is at present in the Heidelberg Military Hospital. The date fixed for the reunion was 14 December, hence we expect soon to hear more about it from some Mud'n Blood who may receive letters mentioning the affair. Perhaps some of "C" Company's old hands, amongst whom Cpl. Alexander was numbered, may already have further news of the event, and we will be glad to receive it.

Applications, limited to 50 per company, are invited from personnel wishing to be trained as burglars. No previous experience is necessary, as the camp instructor, Burglar Bill Bowden, assures us that his tuition can transform any honest private in a few days. Returns are due at any time of this or next year.

Last week the Battalion team defeated the 2/8th Field Ambulance at football, scores being 11 goals 13 to 8 goals 11. The play throughout was even, and on our side L/Cpls. Norton and Cousins, and Ptes. Corrigan and Spooner performed their task well. A basketball match against 9 Div. ASC also resulted in a win for Mud'n Bloods - 33 goals to 14. Most successful goal throwers were Swallow 15 and Raymer 10.

The weekly Battalion awards were duly presented on Sunday. "A" Company collected the Tin Hat for best lines, while "C" captured the Horseshoe from "D", but had to allow them the Sword by way of exchange.

And now, some good news about our Birthday Issue. From the numbers of "Mud & Bloods" which the Colonel has sent home, Mrs. Evans has selected sufficient matter for its publication as a newspaper, and the Welfare Committee will have this distributed in Melbourne before Christmas. The well known cartoonist, Mr. Sam Wells, is to provide illustrations, so we can look forward to a bright and interesting souvenir.

Each man in the unit will receive a copy as a gift from the Ladies' Committee. This, let us remember, is another example of the splendid work which the Committee is doing on our behalf.

Everybody knows that "Mud & Blood", although just a humble publication of our various doings, has been read in many parts of the globe. If it has not, up till now, reached the USA we know now that it has done so, for during the week Drum Major Lloyd Jones received a letter from a very important personage - J. Edgar Hoover, who said he had enjoyed perusing our unit publication. By the way, this gentleman is Director of the U.S.

Department of Justice, and doubtless his files contain a full record of Lloyd Jones' past sins. If not, we can soon send him some enlightening information.

On Tuesday night, a team of chess players from 9 Div. ASC braved the weather in order to try their hand against us. There were four boards, our players being Pte. Alan Currie, Capt. J. M. Agar, Sgt. Taylor-Ward, and Pte. L.P. Wenborn, each of whom won. The game between Alan Currie and his opponent Dvr. Mount became a two hour battle, and we were mighty fortunate to win it, since these two players are excellently matched. The social side of the evening was not altogether forgotten, and it is hoped to arrange a return match some time early in the New Year.

This persistent bad weather is something new to us, for not since our arrival in the Middle East twelve months ago, have we encountered such a continued torrent of rain. It's no fun tent-dwelling in these circumstances, but things could be very much worse. Imagine for instance, how dreadful it would be to inhabit trenches at such a time. We have already been labelled "Tobruk Rats", so it does not matter much if we become known as "Drowned Rats".

Perhaps Lieut. Maurie Wilton has chief claim to the new title, because he was washed out of house and home. We cannot be worried about that, however, as we all need a wash occasionally.

Christmas Eve's bonfire was cancelled on account of the rain, and instead we had a very enjoyable hour of fun at the Cinema under the noisy direction of Lieut. Morrie Goldstone. He cut a queer figure on the stage with cool brown bottle in hand vigorously encouraging the boys to sing some of the many songs of questionable virtue.

We have little space left to fully describe the concert, but we must mention that our Pay Sergeant, Dick Clapin, wobbles his stomach most seductively.

Volume 3

CHAPTER 11

SYRIA, 29th April, 1942.

Greetings, Mud'n Bloods! Here's the old firm back again to dish the dirt. After a lapse of several months we celebrate our return to life under canvas by a revival of our battalion scandal sheet, and let all our friends shiver in their shoes from now on! Yes, we do occasionally have a thirst, and, of course, would NEVER DREAM of saying anything about anyone whose salt we had shared, bread we had broken, or beer we had partaken. So here's hoping!

Despite the colossal expense of publication, the price of Mud &
Blood has not been increased. We implored the C.O. to permit the nominal
charge of 3 Syrian Pounds or so per copy, but he thought it would be low-
ering the prestige of the paper by charging so paltry a sum, and we suppose,
after all, he must be right, as very few of your paybooks could stand what
it is really worth. However, what with the price of arak what it is, it is very
hard indeed on the mother bird, so if any of our readers feel inclined to
make a graceful tribute, remember our first choice is Laziza, but don't go
blocking up the entrance to our tent with cases.

Commiserations to Cpl. Kevin O'Shaughnessy, whose friends both
in and outside the Pioneer Platoon will be sorry to learn he has suffered an
accident whilst en route to Beirut. A large armour clad vehicle belonging
to the South African Tunnellers (drat these Springboks!) overcame the resistance offered by our lightly armoured truck, and sent Kev to hospital to
become the pampered pet (he hopes) of the pretty sisters there. We are
hopeful that his injuries are not serious, and that he will make a speedy
recovery. And whilst convalescing, Kev, we wish you luck!

Have you heard the one about the deaf and dumb man who could
only talk with his hands. He got married and his wife made him wear boxing gloves in bed to keep him from talking in his sleep.

Humble apologies, old sons, for the above one. As a matter of fact
we brought back some beauts from Cairo, but we have to try out the Padre
first and see just how far we can go. Remember how Padre Morrison back
in Tobruk days, always just didn't understand anything he thought was a
bit on the nose? He always took our word for it that no double entendre
was meant. Oh, yeah! Incidentally, we saw the grand old chap a few weeks
back, and he sent his warmest regards and good wishes to you all. He has
more than a soft spot in his heart for all you chaps, and we on our part look
back to his work for the boys with grateful recollections. And, whilst we're
discussing the "cloth", just a tip - we don't think our present Padre will
fall far short, if at all, of the high standard of service set up by his predecessor. Padre, those little verses of yours on a Sunday morning strike a
chord that many sermons would fail to reach. So more of them, please!

Talking about poems, what about some of you Mud'n Bloods sending in a few verses for publication in this paper. Understand that our present Laureate is Lieut. Johnny Boas, who perpetrated a few stanzas in his
bomb happy days when we were no longer here to keep a restraining hand
upon him. What about hearing from you again, John? And Sar/Major Don
Renton, you also used to fancy yourself! We can think of a few more who

used to turn our hair grey as we vainly tried to think up nice things to say of their efforts. We distinctly remember one priceless gem that set a standard almost impossible to anyone of lesser genius to reach - we think it took third place in our famous "Ode Competition" (only the most shameless bias on the part of the adjudicator prevented it from occupying first place). Who wrote it, did you ask? Let us think! Oh, yes - now we remember - we did!

Welcome extended to Lieuts. Byron-Moore and George Moore, on their return to the unit. Pay no notice to the similarity of names - they are not related - and, indeed, although they have one pastime in common, their hobbies are different. Byron is a noted swimmer - at least someone told us he was an expert at the breast stroke. As for George - well, you all remember how he used to hunt the gazelles at Tobruk. We understand hunting has still many attractions for him, and we shudder to think of what might happen if anyone tells him of the deers that abound down El Mina way!

Some of you Mud'n Bloods in HQ Company may have come across a chap called Dick Ward. What! Never heard of him? Well, he's the coot who gets you out of bed in the morning at least thirty minutes before Reveille. Not a bad sort of chap, and in many ways has some estimable qualities, but, poor old codger, he suffers under the delusion that he can play chess. If any of you fellows want some easy money, come along and we'll give you two lessons, after which you should be able to clean him up for whatever you are short of. Its a bitter pill for Dick to swallow, but he just has to admit that the Transport Platoon carried the whole of HQ Company - quite often, in fact!

May we suggest that a pair of roller skates be purchased out of Battalion funds for the use of the Orderly Officer accompanying Major Wall on inspection. "Lead the way, Mr. Mulcahy," he instructs, and immediately darts forward at the rate of 85 mph. Even the poor old bugler is often left without enough breath to sound the G, and generally only manages feebly to produce a mere g.

The trials of sharing a tent with anyone! Well, books could be written on the subject - new swear words are generally attributed to this, whilst most bomb happy cases have their origin in the unnatural herding of men together in a small confined space. "Darling," murmers our tent mate, Lieut. Colin Rigg, in his sleep, and we wake up instantly, ready to fly should danger threaten. A glance at his seraphic countenance reassures us that our honour is not being assaulted, and that his dreams have taken him away back to Melbourne, or Alex, or Kantara, or Paradise. Whilst we know what his dreams are about, we are not so good that we can pick out their location. However, we really started out to tell you of last Sunday morning, when we had decided to have a nice long lie in after a strenuous tour of duty in the Officers Club on Saturday night. Around the break of dawn appeared Colin's batman - Pte. Alf Cartwright of haircutting fame - and proceeded to instruct Colin in the art of shaving with a blade razor. For an hour and a quarter, during which we vainly wooed slumber, detailed instructions were given. The thumb under the haft, the first three fingers along the top, the angle of the blade, the long sweeping motion - all these were told, and retold, and told again. At last the operation commenced - we lay in our bed tensed and expectant - we hoped he wouldn't miss the jugular when the inevitable happened. All at once we heard Col speak, and our heart leaped with joy. "Alf", quoth Colin, "where do I put my little finger?" Flesh and blood could stand no more - we rolled over and usurped Alf's privilege - WE told him.

To finish up, we want to say how good it is to be back with you all again, to see all the old faces once more, and to make friends with all the new chaps who have come into the battalion in the meantime. This battalion has never been just a mere association of men - it has been one big family, and everyone who leaves it will tell you of the homesickness that is felt to be back with it again. Whilst we were away, we ran into many old members who had transferred out of the unit, and they were, against all orders and established practice, still wearing the old colours, and wearing them proudly. They are proud of having been with us; they are prouder still of what the unit has done since they were in it, and their faith in our future is unbounded. We have a lot to live up to, Mud'n Bloods.

However, we must confess to a slight feeling of disappointment when we arrived. Everything was changed; so many strange faces; for the first five minutes or so we thought we had arrived at the wrong place. Then in the next ten minutes or so we heard about seventeen different furphies, and at last we really realised we had arrived back home. Even at our junior offshoot at Mughasi, you would seldom hear more than five or six furphies in one day.

Sometimes in the stillness of the night, our mind turns to thoughts of old members of the unit who have gone to other spheres of activity. Sgt. Bill Marshall, for instance. Upon whom has his mantle of chief furphy spreader fallen! Sgt. Bill Bowden would be most indignant that anyone thought he had assumed Bill's position in its entirety. But there are those in and around BHQ who aver that young Bill completely eclipses old Bill in the retailing of juicy tit bits of fiction. And Sar/Major Folland - our heart is sore to think we no longer enjoy his genial presence, and that no more will we hear his sympathetic and musical bass chatting to the men on the parade ground. Capt. John Agar is dealing out aspros and number nines as before, but, alas, not to us. The thought persists - what did M.O.'s do before aspros were invented? Then again, Driver Doug Innes has been away from us for some considerable time. Congratulations, Doug, on your promotion to the dizzy heights of driving the Brigadorial car, and Driver Ron Claffey too has been accused of putting on airs.

Old familiar landmarks are gone - why or where will someone please tell us. We have in mind Major Wall's sun helmet, which, with a little reinforcing, could have been used as an air raid shelter; the enormous soup strainer that Lieut. Dick Boulter sported. Is it a fact Dick that you waxed it so stiff the ends broke off the first time a bint swung on it at Alex, or are we mis-informed?

We propose giving you a brief resume of the daily news, as gleaned from the wireless. Not all of you have access to the daily paper, and even if you have, we fear you will not get much more than we can give you, and indeed, probably not as much, now our news editor, Sgt. Dick Fancke will have his head glued to the radio, and as all the latest news broadcast from Melbourne or Sydney about our blondes and red heads comes to hand, we will issue special editions.

There we go, dropping bricks again! Why did we have to strike such an unfortunate topic. We know of at least one popular Mud'n Blood who has lost his blonde to a Yank, and for all we know, both you and us may be similarly placed. Wouldn't it?

We tender our congratulations to Driver Laurie Froud for breaking our duck at the Field Day last Saturday. Nice work, Laurie! If you ever want to join a good platoon, we can use you in the Transport Section. And congratulations too, to Driver Burnett of the latter section, who, although narrowly defeated, put up a good show. Not that his driving is anything unusual for No. 6 Platoon - we're all like that down there. Whats that? Well, nearly all!

We make casual mention of the fact that a battalion sports meeting is shortly to be held. Our casualness is due to the fact that we know HQ Company is the only one keenly interested in sport, and its a foregone conclusion that most of the events will be won by that Company. HQ Company however, has sportingly declined to nominate competitors in the hop scotch and tiddley winks events, as it is thought the rifle companies should have some appropriate events reserved exclusively for them.

BBC NEWS — 29th April, 1942.

London - Germany and German occupied territories last night again felt the weight of the relentless bombing by the Royal Air Force, for the seventh night in succession. The targets included Trondjheim in Norway and the German Naval Base at Keil. The attack on Keil was very heavy, and large fires were left burning.

It is believed in London that a German battleship and two cruisers are sheltering in Trondjheim Naval Base, threatening our communications with Russia. To carry out this raid, our bombers had to face a gale, and make a round trip of 1200 miles. As on the previous night when this base was attacked, Coastal aircraft made diversional raids on the Norwegian coast, sinking one ship and destroying oil tanks. During the raid on Keil, an enemy fighter was destroyed. In all these operations, nine of our bombers are missing.

Last night twenty enemy aircraft carried out an attack on York. Five of the raiders were shot down. This was a very sharp raid, and parts of the City suffered heavily. Some people were killed.

Our daylight offensive was kept up yesterday, when three big fighter and bomber sweeps were made over Northern France. It is stated in London that the extent of the damage done to Rostok, necessitates the evacuation of the whole town. Nobody is allowed to travel there without a permit, but a visit is being arranged for Foreign correspondents.

America - President Roosevelt has announced that US warships are now operating in the Mediterranean and Indian Ocean. He added that American troops are in South America, Greenland, Iceland, the British Isles, Near East, Far East, Australia, and Pacific Islands. He also stated that there is good reason to believe that in the Far East, Japan's southward advance has been halted. No matter what advances Japan may make, means will be found to send tanks, guns, planes etc., to aid China.

Australia - The Australian Prime Minister, Mr. Curtin, said that Japan was prepared to do anything to make Australia useless as a base. An attack on Australia is a constant danger, and we must be prepared. The Japanese tactics may be to isolate Australia by endeavouring to cut our

*communications with America. He added that the presence of a Japanese
Naval Force in the Indian Ocean also threatens our approaches to Africa
and the Middle East. In concluding, Mr. Curtin stated that strong American
reinforcements had arrived in Australia, including vital war equipment,
which had originally been intended for the Dutch East Indies. Another
Allied attack has been carried out on the enemy aerodrome at Lae, and a
large ammunition dump destroyed. Yesterday twentytwo Japanese planes
raided Port Moresby, but little damage was caused.*

*India - There is no indication so far, that the rapid Japanese advance
to the Burma Road and Mandalay railway is halted. It is not confirmed that
the Japanese have reached the point where the railway ends and the Burma
road begins. This enemy advance towards the supply line of China is being
made in three separate columns, with armoured vehicles. They are moving
well wide of the left flank of the Chinese Forces.*

*Egypt - During a raid on Alexandria, Ack Ack defences shot down
three raiders, and probably a fourth. So far as is known, 58 people are
known to have been killed, and 111 injured in this raid.*

*Moscow - Today's Moscow communique reports no change in the
general situation. The Germans have carried out four counter-attacks in a
section of the Smolensk front. All these were beaten back, and the Russians
claim that 500 Germans were killed, and large booty and valuable documents
captured.*

SYRIA, 30th April, 1942.

Saida, Wogs! We take a dim view of the non-arrival of that beer
we promised ourselves on your behalf. Our thirst and pocket are in such
a state that we are reduced to drinking Enos' Fruit Salts half a dozen times
a day with rather disastrous results. In fact we have worn an entirely fresh
track all to ourselves!

Ever prompt to the call of duty, our tame poet, Lieut. John Boas,
responded nobly to our plea of yesterday, and on his way to the mobile
bath unit, left the undermentioned verses a few minutes ago. We extend
our hearty congratulations John, on a very stout effort in at last bringing
yourself to visit the mobile wallahs, and also, on behalf of your tent mates,
we extend their thanks and appreciation of your somewhat belated consideration.

Revering, my humble eyes adored this thing:
  This perfect, lovely gift: this Syrian spring.
Unwearying, my soul absorbed the scene;
  The snow capped mountains, dignified, serene.
So peacefully remote, so calm, so proud,
  Hiding their naked peaks in misty cloud.

I tore my eyes away, and once again
  Gazed on the beauties of the verdant plain.
A quilt of glory lay upon the earth
    of leaves and grass and flowers, fresh from birth.
The peace and beauty of the lovely whole
  Satisfied the senses; filled the soul.

Unconscious of the signs of coming strife,
  I breathed in all this fresh and vigorous life.
Then, slow, I turned again against my will,
  To see a shameful thing upon the hill.
With trenches and with wire the slopes were scarred,
  Weals and wounds: earth's perfect surface marred.

My dream was shattered. For a while I gazed
  On scenes that thoughts of war and strife erased.
"I shall not look" I cried, and swiftly ran
  From where God's earth was spoilt by jealous man.
"Today, at least, in Paradise I'll stay,
  To dream my dreams, with none to say me nay."

                                        H. J. Boas.

(Qui-ees catere, Johnny - Ed.)

In our official capacity of Transport Officer, we had occasion to
gently chide our old friend Sgt. Les Allen, for his flagrant disobedience in
sitting on the side of a truck with portion of his anatomy overhanging.
However, we had overlooked the fact that our trucks are only six feet wide,
and that it is impossible for him to travel in one without so offending. Anyhow, another truck passed by, as trucks have a habit of doing, but this particular truck neatly scraped Les on his sit-me-down, taking off the hip
pocket, a fair slice of pants, and a not inconsiderable portion of the Allen
hide. Well, the pants were issue, and there was plenty of Les still left, so

he didn't worry, but subsequent investigation revealed that a 25 Pound note that he had in the hip pocket had been torn to shreds. Careful piecing together of the fragments revealed that a fair part was still missing, including the number. Les was in sore plight - mentally and physically - the Cash Office could do nothing for him in regard to the note, and he knew better than to entrust his injured portion to the tender mercies of his own R.A.P. Months passed, and then one day Les decided to have a bath. As he admiringly gazed at his sylph-like figure he gave a whoop of joy. Hastily grabbing a towel and a couple of three tonners, he promptly repaired to the Cash Office, where, to the astonishment of the clerks therein assembled, he displayed his nether portion, and demanded immediate payment - and got it! Or so we are told!

BBC NEWS — 30th April, 1942.

 Cairo - Patrol activity continued in Libya, otherwise there is nothing to report. During an attack on a small convoy in the Gulf of Sirtes on Tuesday, our aircraft shot down two Dorniers, while a direct hit was scored on a tanker. In another part of the Mediterranean, our aircraft attacked a medium sized merchantman, scoring a direct hit with a torpedo. On Tuesday, one enemy aircraft was destroyed in forward areas in Libya. Lorries and petrol bowsers were destroyed when enemy transport was attacked. Aerodromes in Crete were raided on Tuesday night. During a Nazi raid on Alexandria on Tuesday night two enemy aircraft were destroyed by our night fighters, whilst a third was brought down by ack ack. Wednesday morning a Junkers on a recce flight was intercepted and destroyed. Raids on Malta on Monday and Tuesday were on a heavy scale. Two Junkers were shot down by ack ack, and many others severely damaged. Six raiders were damaged on Wednesday during two small attacks. From all operations two of our aircraft are missing.

 London - A large force of RAF bombers attacked enemy naval bases at Trondjheim and Kiel on Tuesday night, starting large fires. Aerodromes in Holland and Norway were also bombed. Two ships and an oil tanker were hit off Norway. Boston bombers with strong fighter escort attacked docks at Dunkirk on Wednesday afternoon, while other fighters made a sweep over Northern France in the course of which two enemy fighters were destroyed. Two RAF fighters are missing. RAF bombers on Wednesday night attacked the important aero engine works at Genhevillie, two miles from Paris. German aircraft again made short, sharp attacks on Norwich.

Havana - Cuba officially recognises the Free French Government under General De Gaulle.

Moscow - Fortyeight German planes were destroyed on the Russian Front on Tuesday, for the loss of fourteen Soviet planes.

Sydney - With Japanese massing troops, aeroplanes and ships in New Guinea, an attack on Port Morsby within the next fortnight is now regarded as probable. Local air superiority which the Allies have maintained throughout April appears to be passing back to the Japanese, who are pouring their latest and best aircraft into the fight. The danger threatening Australia remains constant and undiminished. Strong additional USA reinforcements are reaching Australia.

Chungking - The Japanese reached the suburbs of Lashio at the head of the Burma Road. The Japanese forces are making a rapid advance Northward around the Chinese eastern flank, trying to capture Hsipaw, and thereby cutting the railway between Lashio and Mandalay. American volunteer group pilots destroyed twentytwo Japanese fighters without loss to themselves during enemy raids on Leiwing on the China-Burma border on Tuesday. Fierce air battles took place on Monday and Tuesday.

Turkey - The Turkish paper "Yeni Sabah" says that "Hitler, by his speech, has contributed to Allied propaganda much more than the most active anti-German."

SYRIA, 1st May, 1942.

May Day - The full richness of Spring is upon us, and we sorrow and grieveth, for verily we believeth in the old saying that in the Spring a young man's fancy lightly turns to thoughts of love - and, believe us, not only the young man. Even Uncle Ted was observed the other day sitting with a dreamy look in his eye, sniffing abstractedly at a rosebud, and no doubt regretting that recent changes in duties prevent him from settling any compensation claims down El Mina way.

However, Spring does something to all of us, and in particular makes us personally think more than usual of home, and when we are likely to return there. Not, mind you, that we place the slightest credence on all those stories about the Yanks - doesn't worry us in the slightest - much! Anyhow, if you can keep a secret, we'll let you know when we can expect to return home. The few lines hereunder are published with distinct apologies to Pte. J. Milton Butler, BBBIBEC, whose original poem has been slightly hacked about:-

When skies turn green, and birds are seen,
   To haunt the ocean deep,
And the seas contain, waters fresh as rain,
   And fish climb mountains steep.
When trees bear fruits amidst their roots,
   And flowers grow upside down,
Not till then, will all we men,
   Return to the fair shores of Australia there
   to receive from the enthusiastic populace
   our well earned laurel crown.

A slight touch of liver this morning, (No! We took no part in the party in the Officers' Mess last night) has made us somewhat crabby today, and in such a mood we invariably see our sense of humour take unto itself wings, and leave us in a more or less serious mood. Having thus paved the way, we repeat hereunder the concluding paragraph of our Anniversary number of Mud & Blood, which, by the way, was never published. (Some day, perhaps, if sufficiently under the influence, we may tell you the whole sad story about that episode). We remember we were almost in sobs as we wrote it -

"And so we come to the end of our Souvenir Anniversary Number. What a year it has been. We have had our sorrows, our disappointments, our disillusionments, our moments of fear; but despite all these, who amongst us would not endure them all over again, as indeed, they will have to be endured throughout the period that lies ahead. On the other hand, we have had our joys, our pleasures, and a wealth of interesting experiences that will enrich our memories for the remainder of our lives. We have all gained immensely in stature; in character; in soul; whilst even physically we are improved as compared with our civilian standards. We have proved to others our mettle, and that is of no small consequence compared to the fact that we have put ourselves to the test in our own minds, and can relax in the comforting thought that we came through our ordeal creditably. Therefore, we enter our second year a resolute body of men, ready for anything that may come. We do not know in which direction our path lies, nor against what foe our efforts may be driven, but we will meet what comes with the confidence born of our experience gained during the past twelve months. On, therefore, to our second anniversary."

Well, Mud'n Bloods, the above may all sound like ----- to you, but we offer it to you as showing how little time really affects our position. Already we are close to our second anniversary, and our job is still far from complete. Whether we finish it over here, or in Australia, really matters little, provided we finish it successfully, and in accordance with the ideals that prompted us when we started out on the job. So why worry when we will be going back - rather let us hope that our country will never be in the necessity of having to have us back. This is just a thought to turn over in your minds.

BBC NEWS — 1st May, 1942.

   Cairo - Both sides were active in Libya on Wednesday. British light mobile forces drove off small enemy columns including tanks and armoured cars. There were dust storms throughout the day. Objectives at Benghazi and Heraklion in Crete were bombed Tuesday night. Night attacks were also carried out against enemy transport vehicles in Tendeges, Martuba and Derna areas. Two of our aircraft are missing from these operations. One enemy fighter and one bomber were destroyed and four bombers damaged over Malta yesterday.

   London - Seven major offensives in which targets on a four hundred mile front from Brittany to Flushing were carried out during daylight on Thursday by the RAF. This eighth day of their non stop offensive operations was again highly successful. Targets in Calais area, docks at Le Hague, and aerodromes in Holland received particular attention. Six German fighters were destroyed during the days operations. Four RAF fighters are missing. Three thousand five hundred tons of bombs have been dropped on European targets in night raids alone during April, which is the RAF's greatest offensive month so far.

   Chungking - Japanese forces have captured Lashio terminus on the Burma Road, which the Chinese evacuated, but the Chinese are continuing resistance in Burma. The Burma situation is not hopeless, as the Chinese may counter-attack. Chinese however, recently scored an important victory in southern Hunan Province, central China. Simultaneously, British troops in Burma defeated the Japanese in minor actions 75 miles south of Mandalay - over 100 casualties. British troops are fighting stubbornly south and east of Irrawaddy River.

   Berlin - Germans in Norway on Tuesday, executed 18 Norwegian Patriots accused of sabotage, as reprisal for the death of two German policemen shot in the back on an island off the West Norwegian Coast.

   Moscow - Soviet forces have now reached main German lines in southern sector, north of Kerch Peninsula in the Crimea. 31 German planes were destroyed for the loss of 11 to the Soviet, while a 10,000 ton enemy transport has been sunk in Barents Sea. In a May Day message to fighting services and inhabitants of those parts of the Soviet Union under enemy occupation, Stalin exhorted his troops to make 1942 the year of final victory. The German Army is undoubtedly weaker than some months ago, and its reserves are reaching an end. Sabotage, wrecking war trains and killing German soldiers have become a rule in occupied territory.

SYRIA, 3rd May, 1942.

Good afternoon, Mud'n Bloods! We sit ourselves down this pleasant Sunday afternoon, full of benignity and goodwill (not to mention the M & V with which one so-called cook, Abe Armstrong, strove to spoil our weekend) to write to you of divers happenings within the Unit and elsewhere during the past day or two.

We would take this opportunity of bestowing a pat on the back to those doughty camoufleurs, amongst whom figured prominently Bandsman Leogh, who has been paddling around BHQ, and having a wonderful time spoiling good Government property under our orders. We asked a stranger from another unit passing through the camp if he had noticed the BHQ camouflage, and he replied that he had never even noticed BHQ, which speaks for itself. However, it is NOT a fact that the C.O. has requested his tent to be restored to its original condition owing to his inability to find it, but we understand he got over the difficulty by getting the I Section to take a bearing on the location, and now with the aid of a compass, he can invariably get home without too much difficulty, formal mess nights excepted, of course.

On behalf of his numerous cobbers in "C" Company, and elsewhere throughout the Battalion, we wish God Speed to Pte. Bill Lane, who is leaving the unit en route to Australia. Bill is an original member of "C" Company, but he has recently been with the Transport Section, and is suffering from a painful injury to his knee which has not responded to treatment over here. Bill leaves the Unit with a clean paybook, and his undoubted popularity with his mates and officers, shows that it isn't only the "hard cases" who win the approval of their associates - it is the quiet, clear thinking, hard working type such as Bill that makes most friends in the long run. We all wish him a safe journey back home, and a speedy recovery once he arrives there, after which we know he will be in the thick of it all again. Au Revoir, Bill!

We got such a shock when the C.O. awarded the Horseshoe this morning to HQ Company, that we would have accepted a couple of stiff brandies if anyone had given them to us. Of course, it was the Transport Platoon that really won the trophy, but whilst we knew we were good, we didn't realise we were THAT good. However, now we have it, we are going to keep it. It is perhaps a significant fact that the Company did not have the Ack Ack Platoon during the march past for which the trophy was awarded, and if Lieut. Jones cares to bring his men down to the Transport lines any evening, we will get Cpl. Bird to give them a few wrinkles. It's extra work, of course, but if it's all for the good of the Company, who cares!

We saw the C.O. chatting the other evening to Lieut. Max Thirlwell, and lost ten piastres gambling as to the subject of the conversation, as we saw Max still needed a haircut the following day. We understand Max has forsworn the shingle, and is striving now for a "wind-swept" bob, which gives him such a "careless" appearance, and undoubtedly proves of value to him in his role of the Battalion's GREAT LOVER.

At last there is someone in the Battalion who properly appreciates our worth! Pte. Eric Hamer, of the Mortar Platoon, has sent in a few lines hereunder, someone having apparently told him of our superlative skill at chess. (Curse this modesty of ours, which prevents us from really telling you how good we are!) Under the title "It all sounds like" it reads:-

We know we're good at footy, or drinking Carmel port,
    And even with the lights out, we're good at indoor sport.
But line the chess men on the board, and let the nations cry,
    Oh, who have we that stands a chance, to beat the Great Mulcahy.

Eric, old chap, if you ever have a bottle of aforesaid Carmel port, bring it and come up and see us some time. After an exhibition of such touching faith, we feel we must live up to it by extending a challenge to anyone in the Battalion (Alan Currie of the I Section excepted - with whom we refuse to play owing to him having infringed his amateur status by playing for money.) Never prostitute a noble game, and we can honestly say we have never won any money on chess YET. As for the few paltry pounds we have lost to Sar/Major Dick Ward - doesn't mean a thing - the poor chap looked hard up, so we let him win a few charity games to encourage him.

BBC NEWS — 4th May, 1942.

London - Four enemy raiders were shot down last night during a sharp attack on a town in south west England. It has been reported that considerable damage was caused, and that there were a number of casualties. Agency messages say that many fires were started and a hospital gutted. A few bombs were dropped in another part of south west England, causing slight damage and a few casualties. Two enemy planes were destroyed over aerodromes in Northern France. Our bombers were again over Germany last night according to a Berlin report. The RAF once again carried out daylight sweeps over occupied France. From the English Channel, people watched Spitfires and Hurricane bombers flying over the Channel in the direction of Calais and Dunkirk from dawn to dusk. From these operations only three of our fighters are missing. Of the few German aircraft encountered, four were shot down. Photos taken by our recce machines, show that the German warships Scharnhorst, Gneisnau and Prinz Eugene, are badly damaged, and require extensive repairs. To obtain these photos, our planes made one of the longest flights of the war, covering 1600 miles, round trip. All of these vessels took part in the dash from Brest. The Minister for Home Security yesterday said that Britain's organised fire fighting service did its job splendidly during the recent reprisal raids. He said there is no doubt that it saved a large part of Bath during the recent heavy raids. In conclusion, he stated that Britain was now better equipped for fire fighting than ever before. The British Government has presented Greece with two destroyers and three corvettes, to enable the reforming of her Navy, which suffered heavily in recent operations in the Mediterranean.

America - The Washington Post says that the rising power of the British air fleet is certainly hurting the Germans more than they will admit.

Australia - Today's communique from General McArthur's HQ, reports an attack on Port Morsby by 12 enemy bombers escorted by 8 fighters. Our fighters went up and intercepted them, shooting down 3 bombers and 1 fighter. Our losses were light. Our aircraft raided enemy shipping at Rabaul, scoring direct hits on a transport.

Burma - There are no fresh official details of the fighting in Burma, but there appears to be some confusion. The Chinese were reported to have repulsed a Japanese armoured column, but it was learnt last night that the enemy had penetrated Kweichieh. Later the Chungking radio broadcast the news that the enemy had launched a fierce attack on our forces, who were stubbornly resisting, and went on to say that both sides had suffered heavily. It is understood that the Japanese have recently received reinforcements. The town of Lashio has been heavily raided by Chinese and American aircraft. Buildings were set on fire and a big fuel dump was blown up. A Chinese spokesman said that the Chinese casualties in Burma were between 3/4000 against enemy casualties totalling 13/14000. He also said that 7000 Chinese under command of the Chinese Puppet Government have now joined the Allied forces. General Wavell stated last night that the American Air Force had been co-operating with the RAF in India since the beginning of April. They have made repeated attacks on Rangoon, which the Japanese are using as a base for reinforcements and supplies for their troops in Burma.

SYRIA, 9th May, 1942.

"Sport, sport, beautiful sport" - We can remember the late Alfred Frith singing a little ditty some years ago, commencing something like that. He referred to all kinds of sport, including some varieties that you and we wouldn't know anything about. However, all this preamble is just to tell you that we had a L of a time at HQ Company Sports Meeting yesterday. Such enthusiasm, such prowess, were displayed that we are more than ever convinced of the invincibility of the said Company in the Battalion Sports Meeting shortly to be held. Our blonde terror, Lieut. Ken Lovell, showed a clean pair of heels all afternoon, and, on his own admission, first took an active interest in athletics in Greece, when he won the long distance, 100 yards sprint, and hop step and jump, all at the same time. And he tells us he was wearing full kit, including steel helmet, at the time, which makes his feat of jumping 82' 3¾" on to the stern of the destroyer the more remarkable. This distance cannot be regarded as an official record, however, as no one went back to measure it. No doubt had there been a few Jerries at the other end to lend inspiration and encouragement, a few of the competitors yesterday would have put up times that would defy emulation.

Tragedy reigned supreme in the Transport Office the other morning. One bright young officer, around the witching hour of midnight, conceived the brilliant idea of ringing the Transport Section to see if some trucks he had ordered for the following afternoon were "teed-up". Cpl. Charlie Challis was in bed - (a very good living chap, Charlie - nearly always goes to bed at night if there's nothing else to do!) and in the darkness groped round for the phone. Grasping the mouthpiece he cautioned the caller to hold on whilst he found the ear piece, and the astonished listener heard a choice example of the Australian language when Charlie sleepily clasped the ink bottle and tipped the contents into his ear. We understand it took two packets of Clever Mary, three hours, and much more profanity to restore Chas to his usual state of cherubic rosiness. Bad show, Charlie, what with ink the price it is too!

It's a positive fact! We heard a clean joke the other day, and here it is - we know no one else in the Battalion will have heard it. Jack O'Brien was at the Beirut races. Arriving just before lunch time, the first thing he heard was a coot calling out "Dejeuner 10 to 1." Jack thought that a good tip, put a couple of hundred on it. A little later, as he was sitting in the dining room he heard a waitress call out to the Chef - "Consomme 1". "Wouldn't it," muttered Jack disgustedly, "I would be on the wrong one". Pte. Frank Greenfield is responsible for this one, and if anyone wants to deal suitably with him, we'll gladly point out his tent.

And then, just to show you we haven't joined the Purity League, we might as well tell you about the young bint who had just returned from her honeymoon, and on being questioned by her mother as to whether she had a good time, replied - "I never thought one could have so much fun without laughing". Sgt. Ken Mann, of Don Company, takes the blame for that one!

We found the following gangster story on our pillow one morning, and the writer having wisely and discreetly remained anonymous, we include it to fill up -

"Evans above" cried the gangster leader, the renegade Duke D'Herville, in Bland accents, "Youse guys give me a Paine in the neck. It's perfectly simple. Rigg up a rope on the Birch, climb it until you reach the Vines on the Wall, taking care that you don't Russell the leaves. Drop on the other side - don't worry - you will Fallon some loose earth. Using the church Spier as a landmark, take three steps forward, no Moore, no less. Dig deep and you will find the buried Goldstone. Then walk through the open garden gate, making sure to Boulter after you, and you will find the Buick outside ready for a quick getaway. My Cromie Anderson will both be waiting in it to take you to the fence, Kid McKoy, Orr his Clarke, who will buy the loot from you, but Marshall all your wits as this coot has Dunham brown since he entered the business, and is a weak Reid to rely upon.''

Peter Spier   George Bland   Wally Dunham

G.G. Anderson   Morrie Goldstone

Ted Buick   Ron Cromie

BBC NEWS — 9th May, 1942.

　　Cairo - *There is nothing to report from Libya except normal patrol activity.*

　　Sydney - *The Japanese invasion fleet which was concentrated in the Coral Sea North East of Australia, has been smashed, and the remnants are on the run. The Japanese Navy, in this battle, suffered the greatest defeat in the Pacific war. The great sea and air battle between Allied and Japanese fleets which has been raging for the last 48 hours, has now temporarily ceased, the Japanese having been repulsed, losing 18 ships and 4 damaged. These include the certain destruction of 2 aircraft carriers, one cruiser, 6 or 7 destroyers, and other vessels. Our losses are not known.*

　　New Delhi - *There is no fresh news of the fighting in Burma. It is presumed that General Alexander's forces are continuing their fighting withdrawal up the Chingwyn River valley. United States bombers again attacked docks and other targets in Rangoon area, starting many fires, with no loss to themselves. It is reported that the Japanese have captured Akcyab, which was a former station on the Empire Air Route between Calcutta and Rangoon, the British forces having evacuated some weeks ago. It has been announced that well seasoned East African troops, most of whom have seen service in Abyssinia, have been landed at Ceylon to reinforce the Island.*

　　London - Mr. Churchill will broadcast to the world tomorrow at 19 hours GMT. Sir Archibald Sinclair has disclosed that Britain's victory plan was to smash the German Luftwaffe, and then the European Continent. He also said that the initiative was passing from the Germans to the United Nations, and promised the German airforce a terrible summer. He also praised Sir Arthur Tedder, the RAF Commander in the Middle East, describing him as a man with fire in his belly. It has been announced that the British casualties in Madagascar were only about 500.

　　Edinburgh - The Lord Provost of Edinburgh has called the Admiralty, suggesting that the City should replace the Cruiser Edinburgh which was lost in the Arctic whilst convoying supplies to Russia, with another vessel bearing the same name.

　　London - Today's air communique states that the RAF is unceasingly carrying out offensive sweeps over enemy territory. In daylight on Friday, squadrons of fighters escorted Boston bombers which attacked targets at Dieppe, whilst at night, bombers roared over Germany. Small enemy air activity over East Anglia was reported last night, one German bomber being destroyed.

Moscow - The Soviet official news agency reports that the Germans are using poison gas in the Crimea.

Malta - Over 6000 bombs fell on Malta during April. Ack Ack guns in the same period shot down 101 enemy aircraft. According to General Quade, the German air commentator, Malta is a hard nut to crack. Lord Gort, the new Governor General has arrived in Malta. In a farewell message, he said he left Gibralta knowing the garrison, with determination, would stand firm and steadfast in defence of the Rock.

Chungking - 10,000 Japanese troops have launched a new drive in central China with heavy fighting going on on the North bank of the Yangtse River. Southwest of Hankow, Chinese mobile units and light forces have carried out successful raids, dynamiting Japanese troop and supply trains.

SYRIA, 12th May, 1942.

Remember how we all used to flock around the wireless at Tobruk, and how we used to be cheered when any good news came through? We were reminded of those hectic times by the spectacle of the milling throngs at the RSM's tent during the past few news sessions. Senior officers and men (and even mere Loots) are all one as they thrill to the glad news of our glorious victories. How long and how anxiously we have awaited the turning of the tide! Our hearts are very close to home these days, and who knows, in the light of present events, how soon it will be before we return there. We're now on the "up and up", Mud'n Bloods, and it's our tip that when we return to dear old Aussie it will not be to save her from any invasion, but merely as the vanguard of a victorious army returning to its native land.

The old unit made a name for itself in much grimmer country than this one, and should Hitler decide to have a crack at us down this way, we'll be on the job. So carry on with the good work, Yanks - sailors and soldiers both; we are with you in spirit if not in person, and you can bet your shirt that no matter where we are, or what lies in front of us, we will be giving of our best.

We are pleased to announce that BHQ personnel are taking the forthcoming Sports Meeting very seriously indeed. In fact, starting with the Padre a few days ago, and continuing with the postal staff, the RSM and the Pay Sergeant, they have apparently been practising for the running events - and are they fast! Clutching a scrap of paper to their bosoms, presumably for the purpose of recording their times, you can see them flashing past at any tick of the clock. Evidently they are not training for any of the long distance events, as after covering a mere hundred yards or so they invariably sit down for a breather. Someone told us that it was the Battalion band who had spurred them on to such doings, and we can well believe it, as recently it has affected us in much the same way.

We sympathise with No. 6 Platoon in their chagrin at the Horseshoe going to another company this week. After all, HQ Company is a big company, and one platoon cannot be expected to pull it through all the time. In the absence of the Ack Ack Platoon the previous week, the task was much easier, but with the added burden of the said platoon to carry this week, it proved too much for No. 6. As for the other events, well, we don't like to cast aspersions (whatever they may happen to be), but we did notice the O.C.'s of "B" and "C" Companies buying the C.O. a few drinks in the mess during the week. May we suggest, Capt. Bland, that a little tact and a bottle of beer or two at the right moment might make HQ Company the recipient of all three trophies at one and the same time.

Lieut. Harry Orr has just returned from two days leave in Beirut. He went away, according to his own admission, with 180 Syrian Pounds, and returned with about 50. He declined, despite much pressure, to state what he had done during the two days. However, we know he doesn't drink - much; smoke; go to the races; or play two-up. We also know he has a very sweet tooth, so we can only conjecture as to whether he indulged his fancy for a little bit of Turkish delight, which is a choice but expensive tit-bit down there, we are told.

The dreadful vista conjured by the thought of Lieut. Alister McKoy deprived of speech and talking on his fingers to a blind man is positively appalling. The following limerick is partly responsible for such a gruesome imagining, but the thought has, on different occasions, struck us that Mac would make a jolly good politician. After all, it is not everyone who has the gift of being able to talk all day about Sweet Felicity Arbuckle, as the Padre might be pardoned for putting it -

> A young man came to Albury's Own,
> By the name of McKoy he was known,
>   Had he been born dumb,
>   His fingers he'd numb,
> Through working them to the bone.

BBC NEWS — 13th May, 1942.

Burma - *In Burma, the British troops are meeting a Japanese thrust near the Siam border. The latest communique from Chungking states that our troops north of Mandalay have now been withdrawing beyond the road junction. It is reported that fresh Japanese troops have been brought up to reinforce their spearheads. The communique also states that fighting has flared up with renewed violence. In the air, allied planes are losing no opportunity to strike at the enemy, and appreciation was expressed at Chungking, of the help given to Chinese troops by the RAF and American Volunteer Air Force. Our fighters attacked a Japanese column with devastating effect, and many trucks filled with troops were destroyed.*

Australia - *The shortest communique yet issued from Australia, states that in the North East sector, weather conditions limited air activity throughout the area. After a week in which the Japanese used only fighters in attacks on Port Moresby, bombers made a re-appearance yesterday.*

Russia - *On the Russian Front, the main news is of the German attack in the Crimea, and of the stiff resistance being put up by the Russians. Moscow reports that stubborn fighting continued all through yesterday on the eastern end of the Crimea. The Russians report that since this attack began three days ago, waves of German planes swept over the Russian positions, but that a heavy toll was taken of these raiders. It is also reported that the Black Sea Air Arm has destroyed 20 German planes, and also repulsed a raid on an unknown town. Not only is the Red Air Force defending, but it is hitting back at the enemy. In a raid on an enemy column, 34 vehicles were destroyed and many troops wiped out. A group of Russian dive bombers successfully attacked an enemy aerodrome on the southern front. Moscow reports that there is no major activity on the rest of the front, except at Leningrad, where it is stated that the Russians are slowly pushing back the enemy.*

London - *A number of Norwegian vessels, which for the past two years have been sweeping the English coast for mines, have been escorted to a Russian port where they will continue their minesweeping.*

Malta - *Evidence of Malta's new air strength is given in the latest communique from the Island. In two raids yesterday, 14 enemy planes were either destroyed or crippled. It is stated that the total number of enemy planes destroyed or damaged during the previous three days was 112. In the 72 hours up to midnight on Monday, three Axis planes were destroyed or damaged every two hours.*

Cairo - In the Eastern Mediterranean on Monday, German bombers succeeded in sinking three British destroyers. The vessels were the "Lively", "Jackal" and "Kipling". It is believed that 500 officers and men were saved. British fighters shot down one enemy bomber, and damaged seven others.

SYRIA, 14th May, 1942.

The ancient superstition in regard to the unlucky 13th prevented us from going to press yesterday. Had we done so, we would have extended hearty birthday greetings to our worthy chief, Lt.Col. B. Evans, and also Captains K. Neuendorf and G. G. Anderson, all of whom defied fate by making their bow to humanity on the 13th May, an unspecified number of years ago. Although he is unavoidably absent, our greetings are also extended to Lieut. T. O. Neuendorf, who has just wintered in northern Italy, and who will, if what we hear is true, be doing a spot of celebrating around this time himself. Anyhow, on behalf of all Mud'n Bloods, we wish all the above officers very many Happy Returns of the Day.

Hurrah! After many months another Mud'n Blood Medal is awarded. This time to Cpl. Barney Loomes of "C" Company, and of all the awards of this much sought after honour, Barney's is indeed deserving. We quote verbatim the citation as sent in by Sgt. Jim Taylor:- "It occurred during the recent three-day bivouac of "C" Company. Scene - a charming mountain stream in the valley beyond "Dear Billie" - men bathing - and our one and only Barney drowsily, as usual, sitting on the edge of the pool, dreamily (not unusual) watching the water flowing over and through the log weir. Suddenly bubbles break the surface - more bubbles - so Barney jumps in - and fishes out - what? - none other than "Mousey" Resuggan of RAP infamy - very white about the gills - and very thankful. His feet had been drawn through the logs and he was helpless. Needless to say Barney went back to sleep, but it was a damned good performance." Unfortunately "Mousey" has been evacuated to hospital, the natural result of him submitting himself to his own RAP treatment (he should have known better!). We wish him a speedy recovery, and hope to be around when he buys Barney the drink that we think is indicated.

Talking about "C" Company's bivouac - Pte. Len Wintle tells a beaut story of the 4'6" Viper - not the windscreen or latrine variety - which attacked Company HQ in the form of one elongated 2 i/c, who was caught literally with "his pants down". Len faithfully attacked and despatched the enemy under orders of his superior officer. We understand that it is not unusual for an officer to be doing what Long John was doing whilst originating and directing an attack, but this is definitely the first instance where said officer cannot deny it.

Quite a few of the boys "panicked" when the rain came and stormed the houses of the nearby hospitable natives. With commendable presence of mind, Privates Jack McKinnon and Dick Windley Senior finished up in a double bed - and it is understood that Dick Junior has now got something on the old man. Did they have company? Well, ask them! They say not - but they have applied for leave next weekend to visit the village of Beit Meinda.

Some months ago a very successful competition was conducted in Mud & Blood, which received literally world wide publicity, concerning an "Ode to a Bottle of Beer". This was prompted by a sad lack of the prized fluid, and the verses which graced our pages, indicated that the unit is possessed of considerable poetic talent. Every budding poet will be glad to have another opportunity to express his humour in rhyme, but not this time from any lack of refreshment - rather the opposite in fact. Some months ago our popular RQMS - Peter Reynolds - wrote us as follows, and forwarded the sum of 500 Palestine mils as a prize (said prize being held by the Pay Sergeant - "Didgie" Clapin - who no doubt fondly hoped everyone had forgotten all about it):- "My ACF Christmas Hamper was packed by the Miriam Vale Branch in Queensland, and like all the others, was prepared with a good deal of thought and care. In addition to the card of greeting, another card was enclosed bearing the caption - TEA REVIVES YOU! This was obviously a picture of our handsome Sgt. Leo Jones, as it depicted an anxious cook wondering whether 'one for each person and one for the pot' would be the correct proportion for the morning brew. It may seem strange to you, but the sight of this caricature turned my thoughts to verse, and I have therefore handed the Editor of Mud & Blood 500 mils as a prize to be awarded for the most humourous verse in some way connected with a cup of tea".

Poets through the centuries have written line upon line in praise of Bacchus and his lovers, but all we want are a few rhymes about the trusty teapot. Can you answer the question "Who called the cook a ------------?" If you can, put your reply into a short verse, and don't forget to send it in. By the way, entries for this Tea Competition should not exceed ten lines, and may be as short as you like.

BBC NEWS — 14th May, 1942.

Cairo - *The RAF communique states: Our fighter aircraft on May 12 intercepted a formation of enemy aircraft and shot down into the sea 13 Junkers and 2 Messerschmitt 109's. Other aircraft were probably destroyed. In this engagement we lost one aircraft. One Heinkel 111 was shot down over the Eastern Mediterranean on Monday, May 11. In the course of enemy raids on Malta, in the afternoon of May 11 and on Tuesday morning, 4 Messerschmitt 109's were shot down by our fighters. Besides the aircraft mentioned above, two of our fighters are missing.*

London - *H.M. the King has honoured the Home Guard on the occasion of its second anniversary by assuming the appointment of Colonel-in-Chief of the Force. The action in which 3 British destroyers were recently sunk in the Mediterranean, and which, according to German statements, took place south of Crete, is described in authoritative circles in London as an attack similar to others launched against British ships in that area, and of the type which must always be anticipated. It is pointed out that Crete occupies a very important strategical position. The Axis recognise the value of the Island from the point of view of interrupting British sea communications in that part of the Mediterranean, and have established strong air forces there for such attacks. The Australian Minister, Dr. H.V. Evatt, brought fraternal greetings from the Australian Government to the meeting of the ParliamentaryLabour Party in the House of Commons on Wednesday. He addressed the members on the war problems confronting Australia. At the request of the meeting, Mr. Arthur Greenwood, who presided, sent the following cable to Mr. Curtin. "We send our cordial good wishes to you, and our fullest support in this great struggle which you, and all our kin in the Southern Dominions, are waging for our Commonwealth, which will prevail."*

Chungking - *The Chinese troops in Mienyang Sector, southeast of Hankow, have routed the Japanese force in a five day battle, according to a message received. 1000 Japanese were killed. The remainder are in full retreat to their original base. Large quantities of arms and ammunition were captured by the Chinese. The Japanese, having brought reinforcements, have renewed their push at China's back door, reports from Chungking stated today. They are moving north from Lungling, 50 miles along the Burma Road from the Burma Yunan Frontier, with the object of striking at Poashan, 100 miles inside China. The Chinese appear to have cut in behind the Japanese, who have occupied Myitkina, the northern terminus of the Burma Railroad. Strong Chinese forces today were reported to be engaging the Japanese south of that town.*

New Delhi - RAF bombers carried out a high level attack on Akyab aerodrome early on Wednesday morning. Heavy bombs fell amongst dispersed aircraft, and it is estimated that two enemy bombers were probably destroyed and four damaged. Yesterday our aircraft carried out recces in support of the army in northern Burma.

Moscow - The big news of today is of the German offensive against the Soviet bridgehead in the Kersh Peninsula. The fact that the Germans have thrown several divisions into the attack indicates that they felt that this Russian salient constituted a threat to their position in the Crimea. The actual possession of Kersh is not very material to either side, but it is a greater menace to the Germans, when it is in Russian hands than vice versa. Confidence is expressed in Moscow that the Red Army will defeat the German attempts to drive closer to the Caucasus. The outcome of the present fighting may be apparent in a few days.

Australia - General McArthur states:- "Corregidor needs no comment from me. It has sounded its own story at the mouth of its guns. It has scrolled its own epitaph on enemy tablets. But through the bloody haze of its last reverberating shot, I shall always see a vision of grim, gaunt, ghastly men - still unafraid".

SYRIA, 22nd May, 1942.

Well, Mud'n Bloods, here we are again, after the lapse of a few days occasioned by the move and the big "clean-up" that reminded us so much of spring cleaning days back home. In our contributions bag we notice a wealth of material, so our job today looks to be somewhat easy, for which Praise the Lord!

The following moan was received from an anonymous source, apparently inspired by the early Reveille on the morning of the move:- "In this Army of ours, one can almost judge the importance of an occasion with the time of rising. The underlying idea seems to be to make everyone as tired and as short-tempered as possible, so that when things get into the almost inevitable mess, one can wallow in it for as long as possible, and everyone can talk about the valuable lessons learned. Do you remember leaving Bonegilla, and the amount of beauty sleep we got that night? (Too right, we do, and we have a sort of feeling that if we were back there to-night, we wouldn't be worrying about our beauty sleep either! - Ed.)

We are informed that literally thousands of congratulatory messages have been pouring into "C" Company since the announcement in a recent issue of the signal honour paid to the Company by the bestowal of the Mud & Blood Medal on Cpl. Loomes. Barney wishes us to inform you that he will only sign autograph books between the hours of 0001 to 2358, and if anyone desires his photograph, the cost will be one Syrian pound each - proceeds (after deducting some slight expenses incurred by the Editor) to go towards buying him a new stretcher - the one he has being now almost completely worn out!

Ah, Ha! Another entry in our Tea Verse Competition:-

What amber liquid slakes ones thirst 'neath the desert sun?
    What revives the weary, and, with fresh burst of energy days toiling run.
'Tis plain to see, 'tween you and me,
    The word begins with "T"; (some of course say "B").
So with one accord we cheer - that's torn it -
    I'VE GOT TO SAY — BEER.
                  (Pte. J. Milton Butler - HQ Company).

(Without being unkind - Milton - we scarcely think the mantle of your illustrious namesake has descended upon you. Never mind, lad, perhaps you're good at algebra, or something.)

Just to let you see with what vituperation and abuse we have to put up, we give hereunder a few lines from Sar/Major Dick Ward. We scarce think he means it as a serious entry for our competition, and can only conclude he is hopeful the R.M.O. will see it and "board" him.

The hours you've spent with us, Mulcahy,
    Have been a nightmare and an agony.
We feed you mugs and mugs of tea,
    When you've been on the spree, for your recovery.
The odes that come to you, of Highest Quality,
    In praise and faith in Reynolds Tea,
Should dim your pride and vain frivolity,
    And that ten bob will pass from thee to me.

And now to tell you something of Paine's "Snack Bar" which opened last night with great pomp and eclat for the benefit of all troops in the vicinity of BHQ, and those personnel from Companies who are visiting or passing through. No longer need anyone starve to death on Army rations - as long as you have a few hundred quid in your pocket, you will be able to purchase a tasty repast around supper time. For the meagre sum of half a quid, we regaled ourselves last night on strawberries and ice cream, but had we so wished, we could have had a right royal tuck-in on fried eggs on toast, with a cup of coffee, for 25 piastres, whilst frankfurts on toast also appeared to be much a la mode. A host of willing volunteers helped to make the innovation the conspicuous success it turned out to be. Lieut. Royce Paine was the presiding genius, whilst Sgt. "Didgie" Clapin proved an efficient cashier, and recovered a considerable proportion of the cash he had paid out earlier in the afternoon. Other workers deserving of the thanks of the boys were Jack Kenny, Len Mortimer, Jack Bell, Dave Sparrow, Tom Gooch, Reg Cousins and Jim Willis. Oh! we almost forgot - special thanks are also due to Lieut. J. D. Mulcahy, for his action in generously lending Lieut. Rigg's primus stove to help out in the kitchen department.

BBC NEWS — 22nd May, 1942.

Russia - According to a report from Stockholm, the Russians are now astride the southern railway to the Crimea between Kharkov and Lozovaya. The report adds that the Russians control a portion of the Kharkov-Lozovaya railway link. The Crimea-Kharkov railway feeds Field Marshal von Bock's southern and Crimean armies. It says that the Kharkov battle now seems to be approaching the culminating point. All along the 125 mile front, from Bielgored to Lozovaya, tens of thousands of fighting men are locked in non-stop battles. The Russian pressure is stronger in the north and immediately south of Kharkov. New German counter-attacks in an effort to stop the Russian advance on the Kharkov sector have failed, and have cost the Germans dearly in manpower and equipment. 700 Germans were killed in one sector alone in one attack. At the same time the Russians captured a number of prisoners as well as guns, trench mortars, much ammunition and other supplies. On the Leningrad front two battles are reported. In one, the Russians cut the road between the two German centres of resistance. An unsuccessful German effort to re-establish this line of communications cost them over 600 officers and men. In the second battle, the Germans lost another 300 men as well as a considerable number of supply lorries which were caught by Russian artillery. A Russian town far behind the German lines, in which there is not a single German, was mentioned in a Moscow broadcast today. The broadcast was based on an article in the "Pravda", whose correspondent called the town "Patisansk" (Guerilla Town). There are thousands of Russians in the town, which was under Nazi control for four months, until the Russian Guerillas, after bitter fighting lasting a whole night, dislodged them and took charge. Now "Partisansk" has its own daily newspaper, radio station and postal service. The Guerillas are so popular in the town that the hairdressers, photographers, bakers and other tradesmen render them free service. The town is heartened by the news that the front line is coming nearer, and already the people can hear the canon fire.

Canberra - Efforts made by this country in the last two years have lifted Australia from a fifth rate to a secondary power, said the Minister of Navy and Ammunitions, Mr. Norman Makin, in an interview in Canberra on Thursday. It is almost a miraculous achievement. Apart from the major powers, no country has developed their resources to such a remarkable degree. If Australians could see the tremendous nature of the operations by which Australia's peace time economy was turned to the production of munitions and other defence schemes, they would be astounded. Operatives engaged in munitions, said Mr. Makin, had increased from 5000 to 50000. They would be 100000 in 12 months time.

Stockholm - Germany's reply to Mexico's protest about the sinking of the Mexican tanker off Miami last week is expected to be in the hands of the Mexican Government today, says the Berlin correspondent of Stockholm's "Tidningin". The expectation in Berlin is that it will result in the declaration of war by Mexico on the Axis almost immediately. The other Latin American States are expected to be influenced.

SYRIA, 25th May, 1942.

Sar-Major Don Renton, of "B" Company, has forwarded the enclosed entry for our Ode to Tea Competition. He informs us that it is the effort of the last Hun prisoner his Company took, and was evidently inspired by the Griffiths Tea signs sprinkled along the desert roads:-

> I'm a Jerry in der desert, and I vant a cub of tea,
> But der dirty Pritish puggers dey vont gif a drink to me.
> Dere's a nodice on der building, und I read der vords to youm
> "Nine tousands und a vew odd miles to Griffids vamous brew;"
> "Mein Gott!" I say, "Nine tousand miles! Too pluddy far I tink;"
> Und I ask the goot old twenty-tirds to send me up a drink.
> So I write dis liddle ledder und I make dis liddle plea,
> Blease fill dis liddle Jerry wid your Peder Reynolds tea!

Gestapo George has announced his intention of forwarding to us from time to time confidential reports on the results of his investigations. Apparently G.G. has been snooping around the RAP -

We wonder who received the greater shock a few mornings ago, when Mabel the rabbit, mascot of the Carrier Platoon, poked her head into the RMO's mosquito net. Firstly, it was five minutes before the advertised time of starting sick parade; secondly, the patient hadn't brought a sick report signed by Capt. Bland, and, thirdly, the RAP staff doesn't treat females (or not very often anyhow!). However, it's not true that the RMO sprained his ankle in his fright. (Incidentally, neither is it true that his limp is due to gout, or to that old friend Jack). Will you please scotch these furphies, Mr. Ed? (Scotched - Ed.) To revert to the subject of the rabbit, if same is not claimed by "Silver" or other of its keepers, there looks like being an added tasty dish to "Didgie" specials at the Snack Bar. HQ papers please copy. Mabel's latest fad is drinking the Condy's water - this must be a new treatment of footrot from the inside. However, Mabel and her family of five are a welcome addition to the Circus, which, of course, still has "Smiler" the monk as its No. 1 attraction. What an honour to receive the nickname "Smiler" (Shades of that topee and those long shorts!)

Talking of nicknames, I heard a good one this morning. Col Gall, of Bluey Hand's gang, was nicknamed by his cobbers "I Section". The reason for this nickname is as follows. The boys went on a recce last night to one of the local villages. The return journey was led by Col, who, however, by this time had lost his map, compass and sense of direction; in other words he was lost - hence the nickname. Apologies to Lieut. Ken Reid and his offsiders, but this joke (?) dates back to Dimra days.

Due to the fact that Jack (Slushy) Turner is at a school learning the scientific way to give salts and rip off plaster; that Mosquito Joe (Keith Roberts) is chasing wrigglers up and down the streams of the various companies; that Bill Resuggan is in hospital at Beirut with some good sorts of nurses; and Dive Bomber Dowell is tearing off superficial corns and callouses in his usual gentle style; the staff of the RAP is at present sadly depleted. There remains at BHQ RAP, only the RMO and his "slim" first-mate to deal kindly with the suffering. However, "C" Company is to the fore with the latest innovation. Capt. Rupe Rattray, MC, has gone all medical, and doles out the No. 9's with a careless disregard for supplies, but with wonderful results on his "bludgers". 'Tis rumoured that other OC's Companies are attending the Doc's first aid lectures, not to be outdone by "C" Company.

TODAY'S CHESTNUT:

HE   "What do you weigh, darling?"

SHE   "7 stone 2 lbs stripped for Gym".

HE   "Why worry about him when I'm here?"

BBC NEWS — 26th May, 1942.

Russia - *After 12 days of battle on the Kharkov front, Marshal Timoshenko's Red Army is now locked in a savage struggle with the Germans in a new battle in a pocket south of Kharkov. Having consolidated their positions, the Soviet forces are still engaged in offensive operations, says Monday's Moscow communique. From Stockholm, Axis reports suggest that the farthest point so far reached by Timoshenko's troops is in the neighbourhood of Krasnograd, a strategic town 100 miles southwest of Kharkov. This would mean that since they launched the offensive 12 days ago, the Russians have made a westward advance of over 100 miles. The Soviet communique supplement says: "In the Kharkov direction, the enemy infantry, at the cost of heavy losses, succeeded in driving a wedge into our lines. By flanking attacks, our troops repelled the enemy, inflicting heavy losses. The Germans lost 750 men killed. Booty was captured, including 5 anti tank guns, 11 heavy MGs, and other war material. A Russian unit, operating in the Izyum - Barvenkovo direction repelled a fierce attack by the German infantry and tanks. The Germans suffered heavy losses. 8 tanks were put out of action.*

Burma - *"Burma can and must be retaken from the Japanese. It is a vital point for our re-entry into China, and I am certain that we can get it back" declared General Stillwell, the American Commander of the Chinese forces in Burma, who arrived in New Delhi by air for a conference with General Wavell. Stillwell had flown from Assam after a remarkable 18 day trip, mostly on foot, from Muntho, his HQ in Burma, to the Indian frontier. After his conference with General Wavell, Stillwell is returning to China.*

Canada - *The Government has decided to raise and train an army and air force in Canada, according to the official Gazette of Canada on Sunday.*

Australia - *Allied HQ communique says: "New Guinea, Rabaul: Vunakanua aerodrome was attacked by our air forces, who inflicted severe losses on enemy bombers on the ground. Bombs were dropped on one group of about 20 parked aeroplanes. Two direct hits were observed and many planes were set on fire. One building was set ablaze. Some opposition was encountered, but there was no fighter interception. One of our planes failed to return." Commenting on the Amboina raid on May 23rd. the Commonwealth Air Minister said that after the period of quiescence, this RAAF blow was a particularly good show. Our bombers attacked shipping and the aerodrome, receiving fierce opposition from the enemy fighters, three of which were shot down. Our losses were one plane.*

New York - A new giant army cargo plane, now mass produced in Curtis Wright's plant in an inland City, has been christened Curtiss Commando. The plane is capable of carrying fully equipped soldiers or field artillery, and recce cars, at high speed to points on widely scattered battle fronts.

Mexico - Gigantic crowds gathered on Sunday in Mexico City for the funeral of the Mexican seamen killed by the U-boat attack, and clamoured for war against the Axis. Over 100,000 people took part in a demonstration organised by the Mexican Worker's Federation.

Turkey - The Turkish steamer "Chefac" 550 tons, has been torpedoed and sunk by an unidentified submarine, near Cape Vassilicos, in Bulgarian waters in the Black Sea. The Captain and crew of nine escaped. The "Chefac" was returning from the Bulgarian port of Burgas to Istanbul. This is the second case of the torpedoing of a Turkish ship in five days.

SYRIA, 27th May, 1942.

(As every subaltern knows, the Battalion Guard Commander has simply nothing at all to do while in the long tedious hours of duty; so we impressed Lieut. John Boas (the Battalion Laureate) into producing an entire edition of Mud & Blood all on his ownsome. And in our humble opinion, he has made such a good job of it, that he is certainly going to get the job again before his tour of duty ends. (And will other potential Guard Commanders please note!).

It is no unusual thing for me, as Unit Compensation Officer, to receive a communication like the one below, written for the claimant by some "English Scholar", who, no doubt, makes a small charge for his services. And quite right, too!

Dear Highness,

I beg to notice you to my cosin by merrige Ali Hassan Azziz Bejid Mefiz. Since much years he has proprieted a block of land of 82 hectares measure, of each year one beautiful crop. Before long ago Australian soldiers were on this land for purposes of car parks, which have spoilt crops and amputated other parts. My cosin is very poor and three wives and eight dauters and nine suns. If you will use your condecension of the Military Authorities I am very happy for my poor cosin.

Servant to you Mustapha Leek.

I can't help thinking that a little more personal appeal, couched in the flowery language of the East, might help to relieve the drab monotony of Military correspondence. For instance, instead of an unimaginative, and soul stultifying message like this:

| To: | Guard Officer | | |
| From: | Security Officer | SO 14 | 15 |

| arms | and | amn | ret | awaited |

(Signed) P. Offenon   1400 hrs

couldn't we have:-

I, the Officer of Security in this esteemed unit, have honour to draw attentions to my brother in arms Lord of the Guard. Is it more than too much trouble to address an epistle to myself which tells me of the number of your bullets for your carbines resting with you? Also muskets?

I await hearing your writing me concerning these, being a poor subaltern with much captains and majors to abuse and insult me.

This letter is marked forever by the secret sign of SO 14 which your great wisdom comprehends of.

Your servant, obedient, humble and loving,

P. Offenon.

P.S. I convey to you information of the hour being two hours after midday.

"Sieda George". "Sieda Wog,
Why look you so with eyes agog;
Haven't you ever seen before
An Aussie soldier at your door?"
"Yes, George, Yes", the Wog replied.
"My pretty daughter is inside.
Tomorrow she for wedding is
With Ali Mustapha Azziz,
And so for Aussie she's fineesh
And Mustapha gets his bucksheesh".

NEWS ITEM:

As a result of clothes rationing in Australia, some girls have taken to wearing paper underclothing. We hear that the Yanks think they're tearable.

Sgt: Have a drink?
Pte: You've talked me into it.

Dig: What about it?
Member of Harem:
      Well! Since you press me.

BBC NEWS — 27th May, 1942.

Russia - The battle of the wedge, south of Kharkov, appears to be approaching a crisis. The Germans are hurling masses of tanks and infantry against the Soviet positions between Izyum and Barvenkovo, 75 miles south of Kharkov, in an attempt to cut in behind the Soviet lines towards Krasnograd. The midday communique on Tuesday states that during the night of May 25th, our troops consolidated their positions in the Kharkov direction. In the Izyum-Barvenkovo direction our troops fought defensive engagements with enemy tanks and infantry. In other sectors of the front, nothing of importance took place. Reuter's military correspondent, commenting on the Russian and German communiques, writes: "It appears that the situation on the Kharkov front is rapidly approaching a crisis. The situation is undoubtedly critical. The scale and tempo of the fighting have increased to a very considerable extent. There is no doubt now that masses of men and material are involved. There is still no evidence of any attack at Taganrog or Lake Ilmen."

China - Japanese plans for an all-out offensive against China were reported by the Chinese military spokesman today. The spokesman said that while the battle was raging in the outskirts of Kinhwa, in the Chekiang Province, the Japanese were concentrating troop transports and warships, including aircraft-carriers, at Formosa for an even bigger offensive against Fukein Province. He added that Japanese mechanised units had, in addition, been landed in Indo-China.

Australia - Reports from Port Moresby on Tuesday, reveal that more than 300 Australian soldiers, 4 nurses, and 70 civilians are safe as war prisoners in the Japanese held island of New Britain. This is the first reliable news of the number of prisoners taken, and means that Australian losses during the short, but bitter campaign there, were only a few hundred. The Prime Minister, Mr. Curtin, announced that the War Cabinet has decided on a sweeping new war programme, involving the employment of 318,000 additional men and women for the armed forces and munitions, shipbuilding, aircraft programmes and Allied works, up to December 1942.

He forecast a great increase in the employment of women, and the drastic reduction of the production of goods and of services for civilians, allowing a large diversion of labour to priority works. The Air Minister, Mr. Drakeford, announced that a number of RAAF personnel have been recalled to Australia to buttress the Allied forces defending Australia. The US authorities in Australia are stated to be most gratified at the improvement in the handling of war goods at the ports, brought about by the formation of the Army Dock Operating Companies, enabling the quickest possible "turn-around" of shipping, also by the Central Cargo Control Committee, which is being established in Capital Cities, under the direction of the Minister of Customs, with the intention to reduce to three days the storage time of six days hitherto allowed for private cargo.

London - Further Canadian Army reinforcements, including Engineers, Forestry and Ordnance units have arrived safely at a British Port. Messages of greeting and congratulation from all over the Empire reached Queen Mary on Thursday for her 75th Birthday. She is spending her anniversary quietly in the West country, where she has lived since the beginning of the war. The King and Queen and Princess Elizabeth and Princess Margaret have sent special messages to her.

Local - On Saturday, May 23rd, a slight material accident which took place in the Petrol Refining Station in Tripoli caused an explosion and fire. A certain number of the employees of the Refinery were fatally burned. Among the victims was M. Launay, Director of the Refinery. The funeral service attended by a deeply moved crowd, took place in Tripoli. Repair work is already under way, and will very soon be completed.

Stockholm - It is considered incomprehensible in Berlin that the Russians, despite their losses at Kerch, can throw in so many tanks at Kharkov, says the Berlin correspondent of a Swedish paper. Berlin quarters are denying that the German offensive is now starting. The offensive, they say, will start about the same time as the Germans attacked Russia in 1941, June 22nd.

America - When the Japanese heard of the "Atlanta's" commissioning on December 24, and the "San Diego's" on January 10, they must have winced, for they have no ship that can match the speed or gun-power of the American light cruisers. The best destroyers do only 36 knots against the "Atlanta's" 43, and can oppose their 16 guns with only 6. And 6 more of the Atlanta Class are on the way, a total of 8 ships especially designed to run down and sink enemy destroyers.

SYRIA, 28th May, 1942.

Our "Ode to Tea" contest is not attracting the keen competition that we expected - perhaps the inspiration and imagination of the Battalion would be more stirred by any other beverage. However, that be as it may, there are 500 beautiful Palestinian mils to be won, and here goes our second string for the prize. After all, despite the excellence of Sar/Mjr. Renton's entry, the Padre is the judge, and we suspect he might frown at the bad language contained in that entry!

No sweeter wine e're from the vine is pressed,
    Than that enchanting brew men know as tea.
Sweet solace to tired limbs and nerves sore stressed,
    A boon to all we men who fight on land and sea.
While yet we may, drink deep the sublime brew;
    No nauseous taste of bitter dregs is ours to slay
Fond memories of the morning cup, as we review
    How often such has served to start the toiling day.

As the dew enrich the rose each morn, whilst yet it lives;
Likewise my tea revives my spirit, and fresh life gives.

Howzat, Umpire?

A sad, sad story of trusting innocence basely betrayed is ours to relate this fair morn. Chess-player Alan Currie - of I Section fame - in the sweet simplicity of his nature, allowed himself to be induced to play a game of chess with Sar/Major Dick Ward. Nothing criminally foolish in that, we hear you murmer. We agree with you, but listen! He handicapped himself and PLAYED WITHOUT A QUEEN. Now, we don't know whether any of you have ever played either with or without a queen, but believe you us, a queen can do almost anything, and to deprive oneself of such an important piece is simply suicidal. There was a side wager on the match of 10 Syrian Pounds, and the fact that the Sar/Major was observed smoking one of his own cigarettes the following day shows how the game went. Poor Alan, our heart bleeds for you. No doubt had you been gifted with our genius, you would have lamented somewhat in this strain:-

A certain diminutive Sergeant-Major,
At chess was fond of a wager,
    Now my cash is behind,
    Too late do I find,
That he's just a cunning old stager.

Exactly fifteen minutes after Major Wall had departed his tent en route to Beirut to - (well, we'll leave it at that), a long slim snake crawled from between the flag stones in his tent, where it apparently has been ensconced since the Major's arrival in the area. Our sympathies are entirely with the snake, as in the presence of Majors generally, we always feel much as the snake did, only there are not always flag stones about. Wonder if Major Birch had HIS flag stones turned over, what would be unearthed!

In the act of censoring the thousand odd letters that it seems to us our platoon writes each evening, our heart often yearns for those poor swains who vainly search for some nice sentimental thing to say to their wives, sweethearts and good sorts. We are often tempted to help them out by inserting just the right phrase they are so patently seeking, and have often to restrain ourselves almost forcibly when a very obvious opening is presented. We are toying with the idea of publishing a specimen love letter in these pages that could almost be guaranteed to produce results if we were not so far away. However, here's a few sentimental lines that will please the fair one, and also help to achieve that affectionate ending to a letter that stumps so many of you:-

> "I love you, dear,"
>   Believe me when I say,
> "I love you, dear,"
>   Far more than yesterday.

> "I love you, dear,"
>   Such ancient words I borrow,
> But I love you, dear,
>   Less than I shall tomorrow.

BBC NEWS — 28th May, 1942.

Russia - The Soviet troops have broken through on the flank of the German wedge on the Izyum-Barvenkov front, according to Russian reports. The Soviet troops have thus cut off the spearhead of the main German thrust. In the attempt to check the Soviet advance, the Germans launched two counter-attacks, but were stopped with heavy losses. The German dive-bombing has ceased. The German aircraft are being compelled to jettison their bombs from high altitudes. One Soviet artillery unit destroyed 18 German tanks and 200 lorries. The great struggle on the Kharkov front, transcends in bitterness and intensity, any previous battle during the whole German-Russian war, according to officers of the Russian Guards.

*The latest Soviet despatches give the lie to Berlin's claim that Timoshenko's
drive has come to a complete halt. The fact is that the Russian advance on
the Kharkov front generally, has been slowed down by increased German
resistance. Soviet troops are still gaining ground at certain points on the
Izyum-Barvenkovo sector. Soviet reports today say that the initiative in
air operations is firmly in Russian hands, and cases of contests are rarer
than ever. Both air forces are hitting at troop concentrations, which fact
generally leads to constant dog-fights. The Russians stress the importance
of controlled fire by infantry against the attacking planes, particularly in
open country, like the Ukraine. Latest reports from Moscow indicate that
Timoshenko's troops have gone over to counter-attack in the Kharkov
bulge, and are now advancing, according to a front line despatch from the
Soviet Newsagency received here on Wednesday afternoon. The scene of
the counter-attack is described as an important sector of the Izyum-Barvenkovo front. The Soviet counter-attack it is added, has succeeded in stopping the main German offensive in this area.*

*Libya - A special British GHQ communique on Wednesday states:
During the night large enemy armoured forces advanced from the west to
the south of our positions round Bir Hakeim. Early this morning, the
enemy were being engaged by our armoured forces. No details of the
fighting is yet available. Valuable reinforcements have reached Rommel
in recent months, and it may be taken for granted that the Middle East
forces, despite the reinforcements sent from there to other fronts, are now
up to full strength, says Reuter's military correspondent. With the forces
of both sides so strengthened, the possibility of a major operation can be
regarded as extremely likely. Whether there is likely to be any co-operation
from Italy at the other end of the Mediterranean, remains doubtful. The
massing of troops along the French frontier may be designed to cover possible operations from the Dodecanese in co-operation with the German
troops in Crete. At the same time, it may be recalled that Admiral Cunn-
ingham stated yesterday that the British air forces in the Mediterranean
have increased considerably, and are growing stronger every day.*

*New Guinea - While Allied air forces in the New Guinea sector
appear to have the advantage at least for the present, the lull in the enemy
activity is taken to mean that the Japanese are massing their fighter and
bomber strength, particularly the former. Within the next few weeks,
perhaps sooner, it is expected that they will launch their biggest attack yet.
A new type of Japanese Zero fighter has appeared on this front according
to reports received. It is faster, heavier gunned, and has armour lacking
on earlier models.*

China - The Chinese claim to have halted Japan's drive to isolate China by throwing back the Japanese from two to nine miles in three directions on the outskirts of Kinhwa, killing three thousand of the enemy. Only a few enemy remnants escaped of the Japanese column that reached Wulipai, less than two miles south of Kinwha. During extremely bloody battles, the Chinese threw the Japanese back two miles in the south, nearly eight in the west, and about nine in the northwest. Only two of the four main prongs of the Japanese drive neared Kinhwa, and the Chinese are not only pounding these in frontal attacks, but are also attacking enemy communications, some of which extended eighty miles to the north. Six Japanese warships have been shelling Foochow port for two days, while a strong Japanese expeditionary force, including aircraft carriers, is reported to be massing in Formosa to join the East China offensive.

SYRIA, 30th May, 1942.

Sgt. Len Wenborn, of I Section, having just returned from a week's "duty" in Palestine, we asked him to relate a few of his experiences - below is the result. Whether Len is holding out on us or not, we leave you to judge:

Mr. Editor,

Having been fortunate enough to be sent to Palestine with three others for a brief stay with some of our old friends, I must pass on to you one or two of our experiences. First of all, you'll be awaiting furpheys; but since they were spread in a Palestine tongue, you won't understand them. Neither did we, so that's that, and security wins after all.

Our friends did not have a bugler to call us each morning, which made it necessary sometimes at breakfast time for me to visit one of the cafes in the camp run by civilians, commonly known as "Anne" and "Dorothy Lamour". It costs about 100 mils to look at these attractive creatures over the counter, for there's that much extra in the charges. To come back and discover that two eggs with frills on toast cost only 25 pts in our own canteen is just too amazing!

Capt. "Java", the perfect QM, saw to it that we were farewelled right royally, for he led us surreptitiously to his Q store and there bestowed upon us a dozen of beer, also cigarettes and a tin or two of American beer for future reference. Canned ale is much easier to carry about, as you all know. "Surreptitiously" hardly suits Capt. Java's movements, for he turns a pretty scale - some 20 stone, no less, and he's only 5' 3". His good nature is reflected by the size of his tummy, and he pats it lovingly as he explains the reason - "Tobruk and whisky!" By the way, our own QM seems to be increasing his weight!

On the way home, we had by some stroke of luck to rest in Tel Aviv over-night. Into our boudoir in the morning, at first light, fluttered an elderly gentleman disguised as a barber. I say "fluttered" for he fussed about like a Jew about to make 40 easy mils; and sure enough he did! He whisked the old beard away in grand style, and without the trouble of my getting out of bed! What a roaring trade he could do in camp - when the bugle sounds "No parade today".

Ran short of cash, unfortunately for "Bricky" Beresford, of ITB, for he was stung for a Palestine quid. Bricky was in the Sergeants' Mess at ITB when I met him, some hours after the bar opened. Consequently he doesn't remember lending it to me. I'll bet he misses that quid! Padre McQuie wishes to be remembered to all his friends in Albury's Own. Lieut. Hec Lee would give quids to rejoin us, he says, so perhaps I would have done better to borrow money from him.

And now for some further entries in our "Ode to Tea" contest -

Oh! frothy brew! Oh! malty juice!
    You can't be valued in filoos,
And so, if priceless thus thou be,
      How much more so is hot sweet tea.

Whisky or Gin, of thee a tot
    I place on high with foaming pot;
And if on high thou truly be,
      Higher than high is steaming tea.

To win ten bob I tell this lie,
Business is business - Vat am I?

      (Lieut. John Boas).

A Cup of tea
    So pleases me,
      That I go in
        To ecstacy.

When'ere it's hot,
    Or if it's not,
      War's one delight -
        The steaming pot.

Do what you will, or come
        what may.
Delicious tea suits me, I say.

      (Sgt. Len Wenborn).

Poets have slaved in bygone days
   To tell our race in words of praise,
What joys result in wondrous ways,
   From alcoholic drinks.

But we who know the awful fate,
   Of fellow men, inebriate,
Extol the tea-leaf brew; and state
   That all your liquor stinks!

Why, dammit man, what aileth thee?
You'll be OK with a cup of tea.

(Pte. R. Mitchem, "C" Company)

BBC NEWS — 30th May, 1942.

    Libya - Today's communique gives a slightly clearer, although a still very confused picture of the fighting in Libya. It appears that German armoured units have made a wide sweep round Bir Hakeim, and are concentrated at the road junction about 12 miles south of Acroma (between Bir Hakeim and the coast). Here they are being very heavily engaged by British armoured forces, and the result of the fighting may not be known for some days. It is obvious that the enemy can only carry limited supplies of water, which is as important as petrol. It is satisfactory to note that the enemy supply columns south of El Duda are being successfully attacked by British armoured forces. The enemy's two main immediate objects would seem to be to get Tobruk and to destroy the British armoured units. The British have an equal interest in destroying the German armoured units. The fierce tank battles which started on Wednesday, are still raging tonight northeast of Bir Hakeim in the no-man's land, forty miles south of Tobruk. The Nazi General Nohring, has split his forces into two columns, both of which have been heavily engaged by our armoured forces. The frontal attack against the British defences at Bir Hakeim has been thrown back with heavy losses to the attackers. The third prong of Rommel's thrust struck at British positions south of Gazala, which is about forty miles along the coast west of Tobruk. This also was repulsed with loss. It is authoritatively stated in Cairo, that there is no cause to be dissatisfied with the progress of the battle which has developed on the lines expected by the British command. There are some indications that things have not gone quite according to the Axis plans. The fact that the enemy is tending to split his forces may be an encouraging one. 250 Axis tanks, mostly German, were involved in the first day's sweep around Bir Hakeim. The main tank battle is now proceeding between Acroma, 10 miles south from the coast, and Knights-bridge road junction, 15 miles further south. Free French troops repulsed an Italian attack on Bir Hakeim and claimed to have destroyed 35 Italian tanks.

Australia - The tempo of the air battle is rising swiftly around New Guinea and New Britain, the potential invasion base off northern Australia. After three successive Japanese night raids on Port Moresby, Allied air-craft last night, Thursday, swooped on Rabaul, New Guinea. The fact that the Japanese were able to carry out three raids while sending over heavy fighter forces in daylight against Port Moresby, and maintaining sufficient fighter strength at Lae and Rabaul to meet the Allied attack, is a clear warning that their strength is not affected. Today's communique makes first mention of the fighters on either side going up against the night raiders. The Japanese fighter pilots probably used normal "cat's-eye" tactics against the Allied raiders last night, as they are unlikely to have special night fighters stationed in the New Britain area. Friday's commun-ique states: Our air force carried out a successful night attack on the Rabaul aerodrome, straffing a military camp and starting three large fires. Three enemy planes, attempting interception, were damaged. All our air-craft returned.

Russia - The Russian guns have bombarded Kharkov for the first time in three months, according to the despatch from the Soviet frontier, received at Vichy. The shelling is said to have been carried out at night from the village Danilovkin, 7 miles to the northeast. Marshal Timoshenko has, according to unconfirmed Stockholm reports, surrounded certain German forces, and wiped out two Rumanian Infantry Divisions in the Kharkov battle. The Russians also destroyed 100 tanks, the report adds.

China - Thursday night's Chinese communique states that the Japanese are using poison gas shells and bombs. Kinwha, the Capital of Chekiang, is now encircled by the Japanese, but there is no confirmation here of Japanese reports that the City has fallen. The communique states: On Wednesday at dawn, 10000 Japanese launched simultaneous assaults on Kinhwa from the northeast and south. Heavy fighting is raging. Severe fighting is also in progress to the northeast and east Lanchi, which lies northwest of Kinhwa. A Japanese column from Kienteh got across the Sinan River on Tuesday; they fired many rounds of poison gas shells and also dropped poison gas bombs, thereby enabling the Japanese to cross the river and push on south of Lungyu. A Japanese column to the south of the City, after fighting all day, had lost 1400 killed.

CHAPTER 12

WESTERN DESERT, 6th July, 1942.

Again we greet you, fellow Mud'n Bloods, and in recommencing the issuing of our little paper, are reminded strongly of the almost similar conditions that existed when the Battalion publication reached the height of its popularity way back in Tobruk days; and we earnestly hope that it will again play its part in keeping you amused and in touch with both outside and local affairs. So let's all collaborate, as we did so successfully before, and make Mud & Blood the visible symbol of our pride of unit; the forum in which to express our opinions, our patriotism, our ideals, and our absolute determination to carry on in the tradition the unit has already set, until the day arrives when we can lay aside our arms with the gladness of the conqueror whose cause is just, and whose aims have been secured.

Victory is sweet, and despite local reverses, victory is in the air, and how privileged are we to be in the fight right to the end. Instead of being condemned like so many of our brother warriors in the A.I.F. to a life of intolerable inactivity in some remote corner of Australia, where amenities are probably scarcer even than here, and where they will hear of our doings with envy and regret that they are not with us. Yes, we of the A.I.F. who are still in the Middle East can feel a throb of pride, that in our hands has been placed the honour of carrying on our country's struggle in this part of the world. To us has been allotted the spectacular role, and the eyes of the world are upon us, and the good name of our land will not suffer thereby.

No doubt you are all wondering at our long-windedness, so we may as well tell you that we are filling in the long watches of the night as Duty

Officer. As it is now 0330 hours, you can easily imagine that we have commenced to brood on our wrongs, and during the past half hour, we have
conceived an intense hatred of the powers that be who have ordained such
tours of duty. Commencing with Sir Claude (Auchinleck) himself, our
revilings embrace each successive lower light in the chain of command, and
have at last finished on the Orderly Room Clerk, who is, we suspect, probably the one most culpable. What opportunities for revenge exist did we
only possess sufficient courage. For the past ten minutes we have toyed
with the idea of awakening the C.O. to tell him that all "Sitrep" reports
have come in; or disturb the slumbers of the Adjutant with the information that Pte. Snooks reported for picquet duty three minutes late. Alas,
such diabolical acts are for hardier spirits than us!

Someone asked us the other day had we seen Major Wall in his new
topee. We must admit having seen a topee walking around, but it was news
to us who was under it. Even so, we still acclaim the Tobruk one, which
really fulfilled all the functions of a great-coat, but which, we understand,
was discarded by the Major on account of it exposing too much of his
ankles.

Talking of headgear - what's the general opinion in regard to Capt.
Cumpston's little beret - Sweet, we think! No, we don't think there's any
truth in the rumour that many of the Carrier Platoon have received "walk-
ing-out" invitations since donning their new berets, and if anyone says they
wear lace on their underpants, don't believe it, as he's probably only
annoyed and jealous at getting a knock-back.

Congratulations to Pte. Doug Innes, of (let me whisper it) Transport
Platoon, who has just returned from a four weeks school where he topped
the bill. Doug, as you know, was formerly the C.O.'s driver, and now we
are awaiting the results of the C.O.'s recent school to discover whose really
was the brain running this Battalion.

STOP PRESS:

In the first round of the Western Desert Chess Tourny, Lieut. J.D.
Mulcahy (a young colt of much promise in the Chess world) scored a convincing victory over Sar/Major Dick Ward. The Sar/Major played a sound
game and showed that his faculties are little, if any, impaired with age.
However, youth won the day. Nothing dismayed by his defeat, Sar/Major
Ward accepted it philosophically, and has issued a challenge to all personnel in the A.I.F. over 70, no doubt deeming it wiser to confine his efforts
to his own class.

BBC NEWS — *6th July, 1942.*

Western Desert - *The last three or four days has seen the turning point of the German and Italian thrust into Egypt. Our armoured forces, South Africans and New Zealanders, and the splendid work of the RAF, have caused a general withdrawal westward of the enemy's main forces. The successful fighting on 3 July resulted in the New Zealand Division capturing 300 prisoners, 12 105mm guns, 11 88mm guns, 16 75mm guns, 5 25 pounders with much ammunition, 4 40mm guns, 100 MT, 1 M13 and 1 unidentified tank. Our armoured forces claimed the destruction of 19 tanks of which 18 were German. Our air forces made 116 bomber sorties against enemy concentrations in Daba area and against Tobruk; 155 bomber sorties against the main enemy thrust, and 524 fighter sorties together with valuable reconnaissance reports on enemy dispositions. 6 of our aircraft are missing. Reports on operations for 4 July indicate further thinning out of the enemy's forces to the West. 600 German infantry surrendered to one of our armoured groups, but the officers taking the surrender were fired on, one officer being killed. Several hundred of the enemy were subsequently killed as a result. By 1630 hours the main concentrations of motor transport reported as up to 3000 had moved northwest, protected by a screen of Anti Tank guns and infantry on a 6 kilometer front, 12½ kilometeres south of El Alamein. Throughout the day a further 100 to 200 German prisoners of 115 Lorried Infantry Regiment were captured, at least 10 German and 6 Italian tanks destroyed, and the South Africans claimed a further 3 certain and 5 probable. Stukas were active against our forward forces. 6 were destroyed. Latest reports indicated columns of New Zealanders and Indians were moving north in contact with the enemy, and our patrols were pushing well out to the west.*

Russia - *Moscow communique claims that the Germans have suffered enormous losses in their drive on the Kursh Peninsula. Their forces include 4 Panzer, 5 Infantry and 2 Motorised Infantry Divisions, but the Russians have withstood attempts to force a wedge in their lines. The Soviet Air Force has been active over the battle area and, for the week ending 4 July, they claim the destruction of 380 German aircraft as against 187 Russian machines.*

Australia - *The position remains unchanged. Air operations continue on both sides. Our aircraft carried out attacks against enemy positions at Salamau. One enemy fighter was shot down and four others damaged. Amboina and Lae were also raided. Two waves of enemy bombers attacked Port Moresby causing slight damage and some casualties.*

WESTERN DESERT, 15th July, 1942.

Events have been moving so quickly in the past few weeks that it is hard to realise the great number of changes that have taken place, and as we sat down here cudgelling our brains for items of interest, it dawns on us that for the first time almost in the history of Mud & Blood, there is no scarcity of news.

First, let us wish Good Luck to Sgt. Bert Lazer, who left a few mornings ago for OCTU (Officer Cadet Training Unit), and if keenness is any criterion, then Bert is going to do well down there. All the old Octurnians vied in putting the wind up him, including, we must confess, our humble selves, and Bert left with the mien of one of the old time French aristocrats tumbrilling along to the guillotine.

They come and go, and amongst those in the former category, are Lieuts. Max Simmons and Keith Benson, who have just returned from OCTU, via the Training Battalion, and to these two we extend our hearty congratulations on behalf of all Mud'n Bloods. Lieut. George Moore also made haste to rejoin us, after a bout of illness, when he heard we were into it again. Glad to see you fit again, George, and will be pleased to hear any anecdotes in regard to the pretty VAD's that we feel sure you will have brought back.

Talking about OCTU, we spent a few hours in Cairo last week on the way back to the unit, and looked in on RSM Ken Wiseman and S/Major Barnard. Found them both sitting on their beds industriously polishing their brasses. Yes, they have got right down to the job of being diligent privates again, and believe you us, the OCTU idea of what a good private should be, would make your hair stand on end. The many erstwhile victims of both these Sar/Majors will rejoice, no doubt, to learn that they have each been in trouble for faulty drill, and have each undergone the experience so often meted out by them of being marched in to the dreaded precincts of an Orderly Room. Between sobs of laughter, we informed them how sorry you'd all be to hear of their troubles, and if you want to be really helpful, you can drop Ken and Jack a line telling them just exactly how they should stand at attention, etc.

Poor old Bob Penhallurick had a brief reign as RSM, and rumour has it that his health will prevent him coming back again to the unit, in which case we can only say "Bad luck, Bob". One of our original Sergeants, Bob made friends throughout the whole of the Battalion, and his elevation to No. 1 NCO was very popular. However, time marches on with all of us, and there cannot be many of the old stagers left by this time.

Whilst we're on the topic - congratulations to Acting RSM Dick Ward on his promotion. When the Major left HQ Company, Dick moped visibly, and now that he has gone to BHQ, we shall no doubt see all the old fire and sparkle return. Alas, the old "Brain Trust" has received a double blow in the loss of its formidable pair, but as we mentioned above, time marches on, and such changes are inevitable.

Pte. George Welsh has reported to us having met in Palestine an old friend of the Battalion in Tobruk days - one Cpl. Graves of the King's Royal Rifles, who was attached to "A" Company for some time, and known to them as "the man who came back". He made an attempt to leave Tobruk in May, but his ship was dive-bombed, and after he swam ashore, he did not stop until he reached "A" Company, where he was made more than welcome. He still has in his possession our colour patches, and considers himself a true blue dinkum member of Albury's Own. He sends his regards and wishes to be remembered to all his old friends, and we in turn wish him all the best, and may we meet up with him again soon.

That our doings overseas are watched closely and with pride by our own folks we know, but there's another body who follows our movements with more than interest, as will be seen by the following extract from a recent letter describing the annual dinner of the 23 Battalion A.I.F. Runners' Association.

"In proposing the toast of 2/23 Aust. Inf. Battalion, serving in the Middle East, these old soldiers of the first 23 Battalion spoke, with gratification and pride, of the Unit's very prominent share in the long and heroic defence of Tobruk, 1941. The campaign was described as epic, and every 23 Battalion Runner at this reunion dinner obviously took personal pride in the fact that Mud and Blood colours had once more been well to the fore in A.I.F. action overseas, and against the Jerry.

"Particular mention was made of the large number of decorations won by the unit. Perhaps most telling of all was the statement that 2/23 Aust. Inf. Bn. had, in hard Middle East campaigning, proved itself a more than worthy successor to the original 23rd of the first A.I.F.

"Among the official guests who approvingly heard of this praise of your battalion, were Major General S. G. Savige, who commanded 17 Aust. Inf. Bde. in the Middle East before his return to Australia last Christmas, and Brigadier General Casey of the American Expeditionary Force in Australia."

BBC NEWS — *15th July, 1942.*

Near El Alamein. Monday morning - The Afrika Corps carefully laid plan for mounting another furious attack against the Alamein positions has been frustrated. It has been upset during the past two days by the quickness of General Auchinleck in grasping the opportunity offered by the few hours' hesitation of Rommel, by the Australians who did not lose any time in getting to grips with the enemy, and by the British, New Zealand and South African Artillery, which has been going out and prodding the German and Italian positions continually. Four days ago it became apparent that the enemy intended to attack. There were clear signs that he was moving up into position, and then the Panzers faltered. Suddenly the Australians hit out and took the Italians completely by surprise, capturing an important ridge five miles to the west of the El Alamein positions. Throughout the entire day's hard fighting the Australians, who had made a dramatic appearance in the desert, travelling night and day to reach it, fought off enemy counter attacks against them on the Hill of Jesus. Then the South African First Division under Major-General Dan Pienaar also moved out in a great gun prod of the enemy defences. The Germans, startled by the rapid developments, hurried armour northwards to take proper counter action. They lost about twenty tanks, however, to our guns.

British warships early on Sunday morning delivered a lightening bombardment against Mersa Matruh, and as far as could be seen, "knocked hell" out of this enemy-occupied port. In a quarter of an hour over 700 high explosive shells were rained on to the harbour, containing shipping and E-boats, and on the shore. A medium sized ammunition ship was bombed and shelled near Mersa, going up with a shattering explosion in flames and smoke which rose six thousand feet into the air. Naval aircraft played an important part in the operations. While all this was happening, other Naval flyers dive-bombed a large concentration of tanks and motor transport south of El Alamein. When the ships withdrew after finishing their task, a number of fires were blazing along the shore line, and in the words of one officer who took part, the whole operation was a "lovely job", everything going exactly to plan. Co-operation between aircraft and warships was perfect.

Russia - The situation at Veronezh and the whole of the front west of the Don is described as very serious. Moscow Radio yesterday said that the German crossing of the river near Voronezh was made with several hundred tanks and tens of thousands of troops. Battles on an unprecedented scale are raging between the opposing armies, probably numbering two million men, along a 300 mile front, in which the Germans are paying dearly for every mile they advance. Their losses are huge.

WESTERN DESERT

Information to 2000 hours 14 July - During the day, groups of enemy infantry from 30 to 200 strength were observed carrying weapons and stores and man-handling guns in the NW and Western sectors. Tanks that had been knocked out during the past few days are now being used by the enemy as strong posts. At 1931 hours a major attack was launched on the 2/24th Battalion area - 14 tanks moving toward "D" Company area from the SW, and further tanks supported by infantry and under cover of smoke, from the West. Altogether 20 tanks and 500 infantry attacked Snells Spur. All attacks were repulsed. Two heavy air attacks were launched in conjunction with the land attacks, 30 JU87 and 30 JU88s being in operation, the targets being Snells Spur and the 2/8 Field Regiment battery areas. From the South, it is reported that the New Zealand Division and the 5 Indian Division have successfully attacked the enemy and taken all objectives. Our armoured forces clashed with enemy armour, and was last reported pursuing the enemy in a Westerly direction.

WESTERN DESERT, 18th July, 1942.

Well, Mud'n Bloods, it was a sad awakening this morning for some of us, but a proud awakening for us all. Our grief is occasioned by thoughts of those who are with us no longer, and our pride is justly felt at the splendid deeds of not only the fallen, but of the whole fighting forces of the battalion. Twice now in the history of the unit has it entered a major engagement; each time objectives have been gained, and heavy losses sustained by the enemy, and so will it always be in the future. This unit has set itself a high code to live up to, and yesterday it once again demonstrated its high morale, superlative courage, and skill of arms. We are assured by the C.O. that operations were carried out with text book exactitude, and with skill, spirit and fortitude which, judging by the terrified mien of the many prisoners, must have struck terror in the hearts of the enemy. About six hundred, including three Colonels were taken, and there is no need for us to tell you of the casualties he suffered in killed and wounded - you all saw them for yourselves.

Successes are not gained without penalty, and unfortunately some splendid pals have passed on, whilst others have left us for a while. Capt. Keith Neuendorf went down fighting to the last; already wounded, he dashed back into the fray, a display of courage and heroism quite in keeping with his character as we knew it. We mourn him, but are somewhat consoled with the thought that his end came as he would have desired it - fighting to the last.

"B" and "C" Companies shared the honours of the day, whilst "D" Company, if in a somewhat less spectacular role, did its job capably and well, particularly as it had the misfortune to lose its Company Commander, Capt. Peter Tivey just before the fight commenced, when he was (as far as is known) taken prisoner when in the darkness he mistook his way and wandered into enemy territory. Both "B" and "C" Companies put up a magnificant showing in company with all other arms supporting them, and all the HQ Company Platoons won praise throughout the day. Taken all round it was a darn good show, and one which has added fresh laurels to the unit's reputation.

In an address to the Battalion on the occasion of his receipt of the DSO, the Old Man stated that it had been won by the valour and deeds of his unit. If such was the case we can see him in the future sporting more "bars" than a prison cell, but the first one we contend, will be his own entirely. Yesterday he seemed to be here, there, and everywhere, and the forward Companies were indeed heartened and inspired at his presence when things were thickest. "Lucky" Evans is the cognomen he is known by in Melbourne business circles, and the old luck seems to be holding, as yesterday on at least half a dozen occasions he nearly copped out. Congratulations, Sir, on behalf of all Mud'n Bloods on a damned good display.

There were many individual acts of heroism yesterday, some were seen and noted - but by far the greater number passed unseen. No doubt some of the more spectacular acts will not go unrewarded, but we gathered from the Colonel's exuberant praise of his men this morning that if it were in his power, the most of you would be sporting medals. So, going on that as well as what we ourselves saw, let us personally tender our congrats you ruddy bunch of heroes.

Was amazed at the skill and dexterity of the RAP staff throughout the day. They never once flinched, not even when a Stuka dropped a stick of bombs on the doorstep and killed three men. Within a matter of seconds they were again on the job. And our hats off to the RMO, who carried on with the heart of a lion. One of his first jobs was the amputation of a badly smashed arm, and the feat was performed so deftly and skillfully, despite the adverse conditions that Jimmy Summers has definitely been relegated to second place as the battalion carver. As for Sgt. Les Allen, for the first and only time he wasn't growling at the patients for not coming on "Sick Parade" - he probably would have if he hadn't been so busy. Again, RAP, definitely a good show!

Nor must the Padre be forgotten! All day long he ministered to the creature comforts of the stricken, as well as attending to their spiritual needs. On one occasion he had just given a drink of water to two I-ti prisoners who lay wounded on the ground, and had barely walked away when BANG - right on the spot landed a present from Jerry. What happened to the prisoners you ask? - mafeesh! Which only once again proves a point we always argued - that no good ever comes from drinking water.

In the excitement of more recent events, we must not forget the deeds of "A" Company, nor the spectacular and successful raid carried out by Lieut. Ken Clarke's Platoon earlier in the week, but more about those anon. As no doubt you all know, Capt. "Gee Gee" Anderson was killed almost after moving in, in company with other members of the unit amongst whom were Sar/Major Fred Tambling. We mourn both these popular figures as well as the others who have passed on.

"A" Company has been doing a superlative job right in the thick of it before the rest of the Battalion came to grips with Jerry, and has covered itself with glory. It withstood many attacks, and one particular occasion comes to mind when it was hotly attacked by 14 enemy tanks followed by infantry. The Company stood its ground to a man - allowed the tanks to pass over and through them without budging an inch, and suitably dealt with the following infantry. As for the tanks - we understand they wallowed and bogged and generally offered an excellent target for a little artillery practice. Nice work "A".

BBC NEWS — 18th July, 1942.

EGYPT: The past 24 hours have been generally quiet. Enemy believed to have brought forces North, but no attack has yet developed. Our patrols were out last night, but no contacts were made with the enemy. Our armoured forces in the South report few enemy tanks and movement seen. The RAF have been active over the battle area, the bombers seeking out targets, and the fighters carrying out constant protective sweeps. An enemy attack on the Ruweisat Ridge, mainly by infantry, was beaten off by the Indian defenders. In the late afternoon, the attack shifted to the New Zealand front, where again it was repulsed. In the coastal region we still retain the initiative. Last night the RAF attacked Tobruk. Fires were started amongst shipping in the harbour, and there was a string of explosions.

LONDON: For the first time in 16 months, bombs were dropped in Greater London yesterday. A German bomber was shot down off the East coast. Paddy Finucane, acting Wing Commander, has lost his life in a sweep over France. Leading his Wing in the biggest sweep over France, he was wounded just before attacking the target, but continued the attack and turned for home. His plane crashed into the sea on the return journey. He was 21 years of age, and in his remarkable career, was awarded the DFC and 2 bars and DSO. The number of enemy planes he has shot down was 32.

RUSSIA: In the South the fighting is very heavy, and a despatch last night says that the situation is very grave. The Germans hope to use their superior armament to encircle the retreating Russian Armies. The Russians are trying to reach a defensive line to make a stand. Round Voronzh the position is fair, the attack stopped and the Germans are digging in.

AUSTRALIA: General Blamey has stated that the Australian soldier is the hardiest soldier in the world, and will stand up to Japs, Huns or anyone else. Australian pilots, it is reported, are flying Hudson bombers in England. One of the Jap submarines raised in Sydney Harbour has been placed on exhibition.

MALTA: During a raid yesterday, four enemy fighters were shot down, and others were damaged.

WESTERN DESERT, 31st July, 1942.

Greetings, and a hearty welcome to the unit, to all those new Mud'n Bloods who have just recently arrived. We are pleased to have you with us, and judging by the look of you, it will not be long before you have settled down and become as true-blue members of Albury's Own as any of us. Don't be too critical of us! We are very proud, and justly so, of our show, but possibly we may be a bit boring about our past record and doings, and inclined to forget that there are other units in the A.I.F. who have also done good work. So bear with us until you too become imbued with the Mud'n Blood spirit, after which we venture to suggest you will be as proud of your new unit as we are.

The above remarks have been made as the result of thought engendered by the contents of a letter we were censoring. The letter was written by a new arrival, to a pal belonging to another unit, of which the writer was formerly a member. Roughly speaking, the new arrival thought we weren't a bad bunch of blokes, but could talk of nothing but Tobruk; according to him, we talk too much of what we have done in the past, rather than what we are going to do in the future. So let us take the hint, and instead of eternally boring our new members with talk of our Tobruk experiences, listen instead to some of their Greece and Crete adventures, and we will perhaps learn much thereby.

Amongst our new arrivals were some old familiar faces, and we extend a friendly hand to such old pals as CQMS Harry Beresford, Cpl. Jimmy Rintoule, Pte. D. Coutts, and various other old identities who left the unit many months ago, and are now very glad to be back with us again.

Now, if you coots want to read your favourite paper pretty regularly, you will have to do something about it yourselves. Such old stand-bys as Lieut. Johnny Boas and CSM Don Renton are no longer handy to help us when our flow of inspiration runs out, and now that we are domiciled in the quiet peaceful backwater of B Echelon, where nothing ever happens, (much) we are not au fait with all the Battalion scandal and doings. So please send along all matters in your area of interest, whether incidents of courage or note, or merely ridiculous, matters not. The RAP have promised to donate three Blue Light Outfits weekly to the sender of the best story.

Those mosquitoes that appeared suddenly the night before last, and which the RMO is of the opinion were sent over by Jerry, are progressing rapidly, which does not surprise us in the least. All the ones in our dugout have increased fourfold in stature, whilst we have lost at least a quarter of our avoirdupois. Last night we watched them closely to see if they did display any Teutonic tendencies, and we are almost convinced that the RMO has at last got something. Not only was there a pronounced German accent in their buzzing, but when one landed on the nether limb which we had somewhat immodestly bared to the warm night breeze, we watched it goose-step right from our knee to our...well, almost as far as possible. And goodness only knows what base, dastardly German trick it might have played upon us had we not swatted it in the nick of time.

The many friends of Sgt. Didgie Clapin and Cpl. Tich Wynack will be pleased to know that this redoubtable pair are still functioning well at B Echelon. Tich has applied to the Sigs for a telephone, as he finds it very fatiguing running up the three extension ladders in his dugout every time anyone makes an enquiry about mail. As for Didgie - after our bombing raid the other night, he decided to go down another six feet or so. As he dug, the hole slowly filled with water, and Didgie clambered hastily up the rope we threw down to him. As he emerged, something snapped at him, and along with Didgie we pulled up a fine Tasman barracouta. So keep up your hearts, lads, we're almost home now. Didgie's going to complete the job tomorrow, and then all we'll have to do is syphon the Tasman up into the Mediterranean, and our back door journey home will commence. There's no doubt about it, you can't beat the old Pay Corps.

Have you heard about the digger who applied for home leave on compassionate grounds. He had received a cable from his wife reading - "Not getting any better. Come home at once". His application was refused, investigation revealing that the cable company had made a mistake in punctuation. The cable should have read - "Not getting any. Better come home at once."

BBC NEWS — 31st July, 1942.

Russia - The situation in Russia, particularly on the lower Don, is very serious. Marshal Timoshenko however, is reported to be throwing in more reserves. The great steel city of Stalingrad is threatened by a two-pronged drive, one from the direction of Zemlianskaya, 100 miles SW, and the other from Kletskaya, in the Don elbow, 75 miles NW of the city. The supplement to the Soviet midnight communique tells of stubborn fighting in the SW sector, where a fierce battle has been raging round the crossings at Zemlianskaya for four days. The Germans have finally succeeded in forcing a crossing near the town, where strong Soviet counter-attacks failed to smash their forces. A German break-through is also reported by Moscow between Rostov and Zamlianskaya. Below Rostov, the German drive to the South shows no signs of being slackened, and Nazi Panzer troops are sweeping down on Krasnograd, rich city to the south, and towards the Caucasus oil wells. The Germans are making full use of their superiority in armour, and are pressing forward over the absolutely flat and almost treeless steppes. At the Northern end of the Don front, Russian troops after bitter fighting, have recaptured another village. Moscow claims 10,000 Germans have been killed in the Voronezh area in the past 10 days. The entire Don population has risen against the enemy, acting as guerillas to destroy and interfere with German communications and supply lines.

Egypt - The lull in fighting continues, and in the air there has also been a reduction in activity by both sides. Routine patrols and some artillery duels have taken place in the northern sector, while no change has been reported from the Ruweisat or the southern fronts. Our light bombers and fighter bombers discovered a concentration of about 40 enemy vehicles in the south, and many were destroyed or crippled in a successful attack. Allied bombers and long-range fighters have attacked enemy barges off the coast at Sidi Barrani, and shipping in the Ionian Sea and Suda Bay, in Crete.

London - Our bombers were over enemy territory last night. Berlin says we raided several towns in Western Germany, including Saarbrucken. Yesterday the RAF was over Germany and occupied territory in daylight, our bombers attacking targets in Western Germany, while our Spitfires went for enemy targets in Northern France and the Low Countries. We lost three fighters.

Australia - Relays of Allied planes are keeping up relentless attacks against the Japanese positions in Papua. General McArthur's communique reports that direct hits were scored on an enemy destroyer off the coast of New Guinea, and when last seen the destroyer had smoke pouring from her and was heading for shore. Allied land patrols which repulsed enemy parties in the Kokoda area, roughly halfway between the Japanese landing point and Port Moresby, are pressing home their attacks. Japanese planes have made three light raids on Port Moresby under cover of darkness, while Darwin was raided by two small formations of enemy planes which caused only minor damage.

London - The Admiralty announced yesterday that since the beginning of the war, more than 6,000,000 tons of German and Italian shipping have been sunk, captured or destroyed. This figure does not include losses inflicted by the Russians, estimated at 750,000 tons, nor 44 ships totalling 260,000 tons lying useless in Central and South American ports. Our light naval forces had yet another successful brush with the enemy yesterday, this time off the Dutch coast. Soon after midnight, a patrol of our light coastal forces high speed motor torpedo boats - located an enemy ship with an armed trawler escort. They sank the supply ship, and left the trawler on fire. All of our force returned to harbour, though they suffered some casualties.

United States - Included in a Bill to come before the U.S. Senate today, will be 7,500,000 for a Secret Weapon.

"And he said you can keep the jeep you pinched if you would be so kind as to return the little seude shoe brush in the glove box."

CHAPTER 13

WESTERN DESERT, 3rd August, 1942.

Good morning, me lads! How do you like being down on the Farm? Rather monotonous we admit, and we know how you must all be hankering to be back up above, where life is much more eventful, if shorter. And if you really must be in the fight, there's always the flies; and we might as well tell you that we've been fighting a losing battle with them since yesterday afternoon.

One consolation, we seem to have left our mosquito friends behind, which is rather a good job. Not, mind you, that they weren't the closest of pals. Quite the reverse, in fact. No one could have become more attached to us than they did. But it was rather disconcerting each morning when, at sunrise as they left our dug-out, the Bofors used to open up on them, and there was always the danger of one of them being hit and falling on us.

We haven't yet made our morning round to see if you have all arrived. My old friend, Lieut. Aub Ring, is pretty sure to have a nip left in the little brown jug, and Aub is one of those friendly souls who NEVER greets a pal with the remark - "Much too early in the day for one, Jim old chap."

Then again, we have to resume a friendship with Allan the Lyne-hearted, to wit one Lieut. Allan Lyne, who at last (after two years or so bludge at the I.T.B.) has come up to show us how it's done other than theoretically.

One old cobber we don't expect to see as yet is Lieut. Hippo Hipsley, our pioneering Pioneer Officer. Hippo, we should imagine, is still looking for that pole of his. What! All right, we'll let you in on the story. The CO ordered a dummy OP (Observation Post) pole to be erected in a nice quiet safe spot to draw Jerry's whizz-bangs where they could do no damage. The first day's sport was excellent - about 100 rounds wasted. Then unfortunately for Hippo, the Old Man decided to gild the lily, and ordered some dummy positions to be constructed round the pole. That night Hippo and a party of his henchmen started out, but, alas and alack, couldn't find the pole. Fate has never been kind to us, so we were not present to watch either Hippo's or the CO's faces when the sad news was being imparted. Poor old Hippo, he's up the pole properly now, as the dictum was issued that even if it took till the end of the war, his pole had to be located. Now the wandering Jew pales into insignificance - even he, we have no doubt, could have found his pole without much difficulty. So when you're all back milling round the bar of Young & Jackson's on a Saturday afternoon after the football, drink a silent toast to that poor pathetic figure still wandering around No Man's Land - a figure that will go down in the annals of the Battalion's history as the Man Who Couldn't Find His Pole.

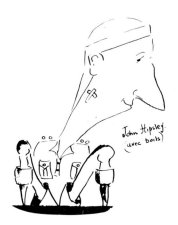

John Hipsley.
(avec boils)

     There's a peculiar, almost magical, family in our midst, and day after day we sit and marvel at the dexterity with which they perform their main trick. The trio we refer to is Sgt. Jack O'Brien, his pa-in-law Cpl. Jimmy Rintoule, and brother-in-law Cpl. Max Rintoule. The stunt they put over in perfect collaboration never varies, and how it is done no one has yet detected. Max, in the course of his duties as water-man, fetches up a large copperful of aqua in its purest form. Jimmy's part is to boil it up ferociously; then, amidst magic incantations, Sgt. Jack shovels spadefuls of what purports to be tea into it, adds gallons of milk, and half-a-teaspoonful of sugar. Then, whether more mystic words are uttered or not, the result is always the same. The boys are issued with perfectly cold, pure water as originally supplied by Max. They have another trick to do with stew, but we'll tell you about that later.

Imagine our feelings when by last mail we received a letter from an erstwhile pal who had the good fortune to return to Australia with another unit some few months back. We said erstwhile intentionally; now he's disowned. We can do nothing better than quote him verbatim - "Here I am back in dull dreary Australia, and already I'm looking back with envy at you chaps enjoying yourselves in the gay cities of the Middle East that I know so well. Cairo, Tel Aviv, Beirut - what memories! How I long for the sunshine and carefree attitude so characteristic of those places. Here I am, returned with so many others to the hazards of warfare, whilst I suppose you will continue to play around without a care until the end of the war. Yes, I am afraid I am frightfully homesick for the dear old Middle East." Well, wouldn't it? Let's be charitable and conclude that, although he's in Melbourne, the sound of those bombs dropping in Darwin has made him bomb-happy.

BBC NEWS — 3rd August, 1942.

The Royal Air Force bombed Germany in daylight yesterday, only a few hours after our night bombers returned from their big raid on Dusseldorf on Friday night. Yesterday's daylight targets for our heavy bombers included Hanover, the naval base at Wilhelmshaven, and Frankfurt. One failed to return. Boston medium bombers raided the docks and shipping at Flushing, in Holland, two of them being missing. Our Hurri-bombers, escorted by Spitfires, bombed German railways and other communications in France. During the day one German fighter was shot down off the Dutch coast, and another off the south coast of England. Friday night's raid on Dusseldorf was probably the most concentrated attack Bomber Command has ever made. It was carried out by a very strong force of bombers, including Lancasters, our biggest bombers, which carry the huge 4000 lb. bombs. The raid was all over in 50 minutes, but in that time, 150 of the 4000 lb. bombs, a great weight of other HE, and hundreds of thousands of incendiaries descended on the city.

In southern Russia, the Germans have penetrated 50 and 100 miles below the lower Don. The midnight Moscow communique speaks of the Soviet troops in fierce fighting around Klopskaya, Zemlianskaya and Salsk. The latter two places are 50 and 100 miles SE of Rostov. Kuchevskaya is on the railway leading from Rostov to Baku, oilfield port on the Caspian. At Salsk on the Caucasus railway from Stalingrad to Novorossisk, the Russians admit a further withdrawal, and the Germans now claim control of the railway between that town and Peschatrokopskaya, about 45 miles to the west. It is believed that this railway is no longer functioning. While the situation in the south continues to be grave, the enemy is being contained along the Don front further north. At Klopskaya, while the Germans are throwing in new reserves and continuing his attacks on the Russian defensive positions, they are being held, and in some sectors, the Russians have taken the offensive. Fighting with stubborn determination, the Russians are safely repelling all German assaults at Zemlianskaya. Russian Home Guards are now reported to be in action on the Don front, and have inflicted considerable casualties on the enemy.

Allied bombers are continuing their offensive against the Japanese north of Australia. Today's communique says that in the Banda Sea, which lies between Timor, the Celebes and the western end of New Guinea, our planes bombed and machine gunned an enemy cruiser south of Amboina. Owing to weather conditions, it was impossible to determine the amount of damage caused. No change is reported in the situation around Kokoda, in Papua. The first eye-witness account of the land fighting in this area between Australian and Japanese troops has been received. It tells of a Japanese patrol of 15 men on recce from Salamau who were ambushed on a clearing by Australian machine gunners and cut to pieces. At least half of the force were killed or wounded. While the Japanese in their flight back to the coast abandoned their equipment and native guides, they stubbornly and courageously insisted on carrying their wounded and dead with them.

More Japanese forces have landed on the coast of Chekiang Province in China, 30 miles south of the port of Henchow. First attempt was made 5 days ago, but repulsed by the Chinese. Later 6 Japanese gunboats reappeared with launches, and gained a foothold ashore. They are reported to have started driving inland. Another Japanese force came out of Wenchow and has recaptured Chingtien, a town in that area. On Friday, a fairly big formation of Japanese bombers - 29 - attempted to break through the air defences of Hongyin, in Hunan Province, but American fighters which went up shot down 9 of the enemy, and one probable. The last two attacks by the Japanese against the American base have cost them 16 bombers.

An RAF fighter squadron has now destroyed 900 enemy aircraft. When the score was 897, three of the pilots each shot down a Fucke-Wulfe 190 at the same time, so no one will know who got the 900th.

No land operations of any importance have been reported from the Egyptian front, where routine patrolling took place during last night, and there was some exchange of artillery fire yesterday evening. There was an increase in air activity following the reduction in operations caused by dust. On Friday our fighter-bombers attacked an enemy HQ and concentrations of motor transport in the Central sector, the HQ probably being that of a German Panzer Division. At least seven bombs fell right on the target.

WESTERN DESERT, 5th August, 1942.

Welcome back you Mud'n Bloods who arrived yesterday. Don't know exactly who did arrive, but already have been greeted by some old friends. And if there are any new-comers amongst you, accept our hearty handshake on behalf of the mob.

Back today after a brief visit to hospital in Alexandria on Court of Inquiry duties. Not many of the lads down there, but saw Cpl. Kenny Wilde, who wished to be remembered to you all, and sent special greetings to his pals in the Pioneer Platoon. Ken is doing fine, but will be away for a while yet. He was running a bit of a temperature the first day or so, but they changed the nurse, and he is now back to normal. Wanted an introduction to his first nurse, but the old luck wasn't holding. She was out with a General, or somebody.

Also saw Pte. "Corney" Myers of the Ack Ack Platoon, and he in turn sent all the best to his cobbers back here. He has a broken finger which does not seem to be responding to treatment, and we imagine he is hopeful that it will continue so, as he is finding the hardships of life in Alex just about bearable. He started mumbling something about a little red-haired VAD, but as we were somewhat preoccupied by a tall and beauteous blonde sister away down the ward, we didn't pay much attention. However, take it from him that everything is fine and dandy, and in spite of our bandinage, we think he will be glad to be back with you all soon.

Called in at that most hospitable place, our LOB's, en route, and literally had hospitality poured into us. Heard all the most fantastic furphies about us - they seem to know more about us than we do ourselves. Everybody wanted to know how everybody else was up here, and we were deluged with messages to all and sundry, so will everyone who has a cobber down at LOB please take it for granted that we were entrusted with a message from him - one big cheerio from them all will just about fill the bill, we think.

So glad to see that Lieut. Johnny Hipsley didn't have to stay behind in No Man's Land after all, his pole having evidently decided to give itself up. Understand that Hippo was just on the point of cabling the proprietors of "Man" begging the services of Snifter to help him locate said pole. We believe Hippo has very strong feelings about poles that run around in the night and simply won't stay put. We may offer him these columns in which to express his views on the subject.

We take off our hat to that Grand Old Man (cigar and all) whom we saw in our midst this morning. What amazing activity for a man of his position and years! And what a compliment to us! Unfortunately we were not on the spot to extend a Mud'n Blood welcome, but Winnie has suffered disasters of greater magnitude than that and still come up smiling. Anyway, to borrow the words of our Yankee cousins, it was mighty nice to see him.

Had some criticism of this paper from a brother officer the other day. He thought the lads were of the opinion that the paper embraced too localised a sphere - in other words, too much HQ Company, "B" Echelon, etc., and not enough about the doings of the Rifle Companies. We quite agree. But how in the hell can we alter it if you Rifle Company wallids do nothing about it yourselves. The officer who offered the criticism incidentally has never yet contributed anything; and that goes for nearly every one of you. We are only too delighted to write up your doings, serious and humorous, if you'll only tell us about them. So snap out of it lads!

Looks as though the indefatigable "Didgie" will be back with a wee drop of the doings some time today. Half a bottle a man we hear is the official dictum, but we have a sort of feeling that it might stretch out a bit further than that. And being strictly teetotal ourselves, we repudiate indignantly the vile rumour that we had anything to do with the RMO ordering our batman to abstain completely from all intoxicants. Not, mind you, that we are pig-headed, and wouldn't break the rule of a lifetime if anyone invited us to have one for medicinal purposes only.

BBC NEWS — 5th August, 1942.

In Russia the main German advance east and south east of the lower Don still continues, but our Allies are holding the enemy further north. Moscow midnight communique spoke of fierce fighting in the Kuchevskaya area, and round the junction on the Trans-Caucasian railway, where for three days there has been furious fighting. The Germans claimed the capture of both towns several days ago, and now say they are well beyond them and approaching the Kuban river, which runs through Krasnograd, and has its mouth at Novorossisk. The Red Army and Red Air Force are disputing every yard of ground, and one place near Kuchevskaya has changed hands three times. Winterton, in a cable from Moscow, says the Nazis have big reserves to throw into the struggle. Higher up the Don, the position is more satisfactory. The direct attack towards Stalingrad has been held in the Don bend at Klopskaya. At Zemlianskaya further south, the Nazis have been waging fierce battles for more than a week, but constant counter-attacks by strong forces of Russian tanks and infantry have prevented any forward movement. The bridgehead established by the enemy more than a week ago is even now not secure. The Germans themselves seem less jubilant than of late, and speak of the extraordinary resources of the Russians. "In face of these, ordinary victories are not enough", they say.

Allied fighter planes have again attacked the Japanese positions at Kokoda, halfway between Gona and Port Moresby, in Papua. This mornings communique from General McArthur's HQ reports many fires started but says there has been no change in the ground situation. Pilots who raided Lae and Salamaua in New Guinea, report that a Japanese cargo ship hit in the previous night's raid could be seen beached and burning. A small British trawler which was recently shelled by an enemy submarine off the east coast of Australia, has now reached port safely. Two of the crew were killed and four wounded. The offensive, rather than the defensive attitude of the people of Australia, as well as of New Zealand, was emphasised yesterday by the New Zealand Prime Minister, Mr. Peter Frazer, who has just returned from a 10 day visit to Australia. Mr. Frazer said the Australian Government stood for an offensive in the Pacific, and he sincerely believed a very strong offensive could be taken. Japanese ambitions for world domination were described in Sydney yesterday by Sir John Latham, Chief Justice of the High Court, and formerly Australian Minister to Tokyo. "In the Japanese way of life, there would be no future for Australians, unless a few were allowed to live as slaves to the Japanese", he declared.

Main news from China is of fighting in the coastal province of Chekiang. Another attempt by the Japanese to land on the coast has been thrown back with heavy loss. In the battle for Wenchow itself, the Chinese say fighting is now going on in the outskirts of the port. American HQ in China has described recent Japanese attempts to attack Henyang and knock out the US Air Corps base there. In raids over several days the Japanese employed 119 planes, of which 17 were shot down, and probably four times that number damaged. American aircraft have put a spoke in Japanese attempts to hold up the supplies now being flown from India to China in big transport planes. Bombers from Chinese bases have co-operated with the RAF from India to devastate Myichinow aerodromes in Burma so that the enemy cannot use it as a base for intercepting the supply planes.

Our patrols were out again last night in front of our positions on the Alamein front in Egypt, but there has been no large scale fighting anywhere on the front. Artillery exchanges have been more lively, particularly on the north and central sectors. In the air, however, activity has been maintained and our fighter bombers have successfully engaged targets over the battle area. In the south, near the Quattara depression, they swooped on a column in which there were 25 trucks, armoured cars, and a few tanks, as well as a wireless van. It is known that 18 of the vehicles were damaged, and 3 were certainly destroyed. Another enemy HQ was raided by our planes, also in the south, while groups of enemy transport were bombed in the central sector. The RAF in the Middle East is now using Britain's big 4-engined Halifax bombers to accompany US Air Corps' Liberators in powerful night attacks on the enemy's supply bases and lines of communication. On Saturday night for instance, targets for our heavy bombers included Tobruk, Sollum, Matruh, Bardia and Sidi Barrani. Naval aircraft are also helping, and have attacked motor barges coming from Italy to the North African coast.

Production of General Grant tanks is 200 per cent ahead of schedule, US production officials announce.

WESTERN DESERT, 7th August, 1942.

Good-day, Mud'n Bloods, here we are again, having decided to call the war off for half an hour or so to dish you the latest dirt. Not, mind you, that we haven't plenty of work to do. (N.B. Have to put this bit in, otherwise the Old Man will put us on another Court of Inquiry or something). Well, how have you been existing for the past week or so without your favourite paper? We have been deliberately refraining from going to press until you sent some contributions in, hoping thereby to cause a storm of protest from all and sundry. To our mortification, no one even noticed the omission. There's no doubt about it, we're slipping. If we're not careful, we'll be nominated for return to Australia.

Now that we've started, we haven't the remotest idea what to write about. Censorship requirements will not allow us to mention that there is a war on, let alone tell you how it is progressing, but take it from us, we've got old Rommel guessing again. So sure are we of this, that in a brief spell from duties (C.O. note!) we penned the following few lines, for which, Padre, pray for our forgiveness.

> They say Rommel's fond of dancing, and to Alex he keeps glancing,
> 　　As he tries to cross this land of flies and sand.
> To reach those bints entrancing, in the cafes ever prancing,
> 　　In the arms of Alexander's Ragtime Band.
>
> Pushing ever to the east, as he sought to join the feast,
> 　　He dreamt not of their present mighty stand.
> Nothing daunted in the least, as they calmly stopped the beast,
> 　　Were the men of Alexander's Ragtime Band.
>
> But old Rommel yet will dance, and his looks will not enhance,
> 　　On a rope swung by many a willing hand,
> For they're leaving nought to chance, not for them the fate of France,
> 　　Is the vow of Alexander's Ragtime Band.

ANY COMPANY — AS VIEWED BY THE QUARTERMASTER.

Scene 1 - Company Office.

"Ah! Sgt/Major. That Quarter bloke wants another blasted return. It says 'Number of Respirators deficient'. Every man must be inspected because this return is important! Now, let me see. I know all the platoons were correct three months ago. Since then 30 men have gone out, and we've had 30, no! 50, reinforcements. That makes - Oh! Never mind, make the usual wild guess. When you give him the return, ask him if he can get us 19 telephones, 73 pairs of coloured spectacles, a pair of Chinese vases, and a grey soft hat with a white band.''

Scene 2 - In the Company Lines.

"Hullo, Bill! What was that I just saw you slinging away?" "Oh! that was my respirator." "That's nothing, yesterday I threw away a great-coat, a pair of boots, and a tin of A/Gas Ointment". "I'll bet you think you're good. Why, I once kicked a spare wheel, 17 water tins, and a camouflage net out of the back of a truck." "Yeah! Let me tell you, I'm the Vice President of the Equipment Slinger Society. I've a trail of stuff all the way from Tobruk to Syria, and back to here. I'm doing pretty good while we're staying here too; if you like I'll show you a big hole where I buried all sorts of stuff last week. For the present I've got my eye on a three ton truck, and I've already eaten three lots of Emergency Rations.''

Scene 3 - The Company Kitchen.

"Well, babbler, what's on tonight?" "We've had a hell of a day with sand and wind, but we've turned out Soup, Fish, Roast Beef and Vegs, Asparagus on toast, Fruit and Custard, Tea, Bread and Butter."

"What! No jam?"

> Oh! Lady Godiva - (away thoughts that are coarse)
> We swear by our beard we'd have nary a peep,
> If instead of riding your bonny white horse,
> You appeared amongst us driving a Jeep.

OH YEAH.

Thursday was the third anniversary of the Declaration of War, and as we paused to make a mental review of these three years, and our own experiences during them, many - confident of victory - could not resist the query - How long? How long?

While it is easy to count the years as they pass, and while confidence courage and determination can mould to some extent, the future, we cannot assess the results of those qualities in terms of years. History records a seven years war, and even a hundred years war, but possibly they were not pursued with vigor for the whole period, and lacked the stress and strain of modern warfare. It is hardly cheering to recall these campaigns from the limbo of history, but much depends on the point of view. Professor Murdoch, the noted West Australian essayist, stated that this war is but the second part of the first world war. This view has much to commend it, and places us in the twenty-ninth year of the World War!

But whether it be the threshold of the fourth or twenty-ninth year of the war, we feel that the time is propitious for high hopes of success for our cause in the near future. On Thursday, we had several Church Parades in the Unit to link us with the National Day of Prayer arranged at the request of the King, and the Colonel, in a short nicely worded address at the conclusion of the service he attended, said history was being made in the desert at the present time; we would have our part in it, and that the Middle East must and would be retained. The following day we received, as part of the Eighth Army, an encouraging message from the King, and with him, we hope that great results will accrue to the United Nations from the campaign in which we are engaged.

A.P. Reynolds, RQMS.

You may not be aware of a short, but very successful campaign recently completed by one of our popular Company Commanders. For (personal) security reasons we cannot give you his name, but we can only state that if he cares to publicly claim it through these columns, a Mud & Blood Medal has been awarded him for the reasons given below. For several days nothing had occurred to disturb the tranquility of the Company Commander's peaceful life. He had altered all his dispositions twice, and the CO had been around and shifted them again, and as the men were digging in again for the fourth time, he felt that nothing f˺ ˻˳er remained for him to do but catch up on his spino. All at once some slight misgivings as to his left flank assailed him. Troubled, and somewhat irritated, he could not say what was wrong, but as the day advanced, the irritation kept pricking him to doubt the security of the aforesaid flank. A hasty survey of the position disclosed nothing to alarm him. Fortunately for his peace of mind, he was not aware of the insidious machinations of the enemy. Presumably whilst he was asleep (we can ascribe to no other cause in this locality) a couple of the enemy infiltrated and took advantage of the very excellent cover afforded on his left flank in which to remain concealed. A day and night passed, and the enemy had increased in numbers to such an extent that their presence, although as yet undetected, caused our Company Commander considerable discomfort. Then all at once the battle commenced. The enemy attacked voraciously, piercing through and strongly entrenching themselves. Burrowing deeply, they quickly consolidated their position, and, rapidly reinforcing their forces to alarming numbers, commenced to exploit their gains. By this time the Company Commander was aware of the menace, and his efforts were at first directed to keeping the attack from spreading to his other flank, front and rear, which, on account of the excellent cover they afforded, were also most vulnerable. Alas, normal methods were unavailing; as fast as the enemy were killed, hundreds more seemed to come from nowhere. Appealing to the writer for advice and assistance - an appeal directed we might say in all humility, to the best and most experienced brain in the unit in just such an emergency - his plea did not go unheard. Desperate situations requiring desperate measures, we rushed him off to a quarter where (despite the Geneva Convention) ample supplies of a certain substance to repel the attackers were available. Thus armed, the result was a foregone conclusion; within a few hours, the spread of the invaders was halted. Another day, and most of them were dead or dying, and with the passing of a further 24 hours, the attack could be considered completely repulsed. It was a great victory, and shows that there is something in this chemical warfare business after all. The secret substance used is not by the way, a new discovery. It has been used in other theatres of war for some time, and is named Blu Eoin Tment. As for the said Company Commander - we may congratulate him on having a very close shave.

WESTERN DESERT, 8th August, 1942.

Another move, and this time down amongst the fig-trees, so the clothing worries of the quartermaster should be considerably lessened. Went down there yesterday on a recce with the QM, and saw him going round counting and measuring the leaves, and making voluminous notes in his pocket book. At the finish he pleasedly informed us that he could supply a clean change for the battalion each morning, and that now Cpl. Reg Cousins was not with us could practically guarantee the fit too. Nature is a very funny thing, you know, and for all his huge bulk, we understand that Sgt. Les Allen only takes a size one in fig leaves.

You all know Cpl. Charlie Challis, who has been away from us for some little time in hospital with jaundice. He sent a letter to the lads in the Transport Section yesterday, and as he mentions many old friends, we repeat the more respectable portions of his letter:-

"I saw Yeoie (Charlie Yeomans) the day after he arrived; he was all fixed up, one leg being in plaster. Then that night I put on a one-act play and got sick again, so they put me back to bed for nearly a fortnight. I am up now though, and getting around, and feel pretty well - a bit too well at times - but so far everything under control. I don't want to make you feel out of it, but I live on fresh fish, chicken, jellies and custard, and there is any amount of fruit. There are dozens of the boys down here, and I can't remember all their names, but Alan Coles seems to be as bad as any I've seen, but he has his chin up high and reckons he is doing alright. Saw Yeoie again yesterday and he is happy - the VAD's are making a fuss of him, so he's right. Macker McKenzie is here, real knocked about, but not nearly as bad as some. Chick Bridges of "A" Company, is next to me with shrapnel in his side, and they're not game to have a go at taking it out. Sunday afternoon we had a Greek Princess here to see us. She's a fair line, but we didn't get a go at her as the officers held the fort."

"Does it hurt, Aussie?" "Only when I laugh!!!"

Also a short note to hand from Lieut. Ken Clarke, who sends his regards and best wishes to the mob. Ken, unfortunately, is wounded in the ankle, and as it has turned septic, he has to undergo an operation. Otherwise, he states he is in the pink, and appears to be in the best of spirits.

Driver Bill Jacobson was down in Alexandria the day before yesterday, taking down some LOB's. He came back with a tale of having picked up a threepenny bit, but is too darned lousy to tell the lads her name.

Pte. Jim Shakespeare Lester of the Transport Platoon, has forwarded the following, for which, we may add, he has been properly disciplined:-

> Out in the Western Desert,
>   At a place they call El Alamein,
> A lonely Div of Australians,
>   Fights steadily on under strain.
> They think of their wives and sweethearts,
>   In the land that they love far away,
> But for the sake of their mates who've died here,
>   They're too proud to call it a day.

They struggle on now more determined,
   Than anyone else has yet done,
And will put in a far better effort,
   To beat up the I-tie and Hun.
They wait for the Yanks and the Tommies,
   To prove just whatever they're worth,
For the Dominions have held back the Nazis,
   From Suez - the key to the earth.
Yes, we want them to get into harness,
   And help us to finish him now.
Then we can dice the deadly old musket,
   And take up the peaceful old plough.

Here's one about a local lad who was serving in the Merchant Navy.
To make a fat story thin, he got shipwrecked, and after twelve months on
a little island, he decided to swim to another island and explore. There he
found a girl who was also shipwrecked. They sympathised with each other.
After a time she said - "Come with me and I'll surprise you with something you haven't had for twelve months." "Strewth", he exclaimed, "You
don't mean to say you've got a bottle of Melbourne Bitter".

BBC NEWS — 8th August, 1942.

*Allied aircraft have made a series of heavy day and night attacks on
Japanese bases in the SW Pacific. General MacArthur's HQ this morning
says that a medium bombing force made a heavy raid in daylight on the
aerodrome, run-ways and dispersal areas at Lae yesterday. Heavy demolit-
ion bombs fell on the target area, and extended harassing raids were made
during the night. During the daylight raid, a number of 2000 lb bombs
exploded on the runways. Another violent attack was carried out on Rabaul
on the island of New Britain. Here Allied bombers met Ack Ack and fighter
opposition, but they plastered an aerodrome with 15 tons of bombs. Seven
enemy fighters were shot down, and one of our machines failed to return.*

*The uneasy lull in land operations on the local front continues, but
there has been increased enemy air activity over the coastal sector of the
battle area. Our own planes have been active in the war of supply and reinforcement going on behind the lines. On Thursday night heavy bombers
of the US Army Air Corps bombed Tobruk, attacking shipping in the harbour, while yesterday morning our light bombers raided the harbour and
supply bases at Mersa Matruh, which the enemy is using as a forward base
for small craft. Our Naval planes have also again attacked Matruh. Every*

day a certain number of Axis troops are being brought by air to the battle front, but most of their equipment has to come by sea, and our air and sea forces are seeing that quite a number of these ships never discharge their cargoes in North Africa. It was stated in Cairo yesterday that enemy aircraft have attacked the oasis of Kufra, 200 miles north of the French Chad territory, and near the border of Libya and Egypt. Fighting French columns captured it early last year.

The German threat to Stalingrad and the Volga is still very serious, and the danger from the area around Kotelnikovo more so than at the other arm of the pincer, at Kletskaya in the Don elbow. Here the Russians are holding firm, and the Moscow midnight communique reports the repulse of many enemy tank attacks, while the Russians have themselves launched counter-attacks. Paul Winterton, in a despatch last night, says·that the news is still satisfactory from the Don Bend, but it is less so in the Kotelnikovo area. Earlier the Russians admitted that another wedge had been driven into their defences, and the midnight communique spoke for the first time of fighting north of the town. This would indicate that the enemy are now straddling the Stalingrad-Black Sea railroad, and are already beyond the town. The Germans are using heavy concentrations of tanks in this sector. South of the lower Don, in the Caucasus, the position is growing steadily worse. After heavy fighting south of Belayaglina, the Russian forces now report having withdrawn to Armavir junction on the Kuban river, where the railway and oil pipe lines branch SW to the Black Sea, and SE to the Caspian. Armavir is only 50 miles from Maikop, important Caucasian oil centre. The Germans last night claimed to be within 30 miles of Maikop itself. The oilfield there is the most northerly of the three main Caucasian fields, but the German thrust south of Voroshilovsk is carrying them closer to a smaller series of wells at Georgievsk.

WESTERN DESERT, 20th August, 1942.

SPECIAL ANNIVERSARY NUMBER.

Another year gone by, and again we settle down to commemorate the date of the battalion's formation, by a special issue of Mud & Blood. How short a time it seems since the last occasion we had a similar task; and yet how much has occurred in that period. As far as outward appearances go, we could still be in the same dusty, hot, fly-ridden atmosphere as Tobruk, the scene of the celebration of our first birthday. Only by looking around at the many new faces, and remarking upon the absence of many old friends are we aware of the eventful happenings that have taken place in the past year. Otherwise, life is much the same; the same job still ahead of us; the same story of effort and achievement behind us that has become traditional of this unit. One long year further away from our homes and loved ones, but, one must not forget, a year nearer to the time when our job will be successfully accomplished, and we will be able to return to them. How often in our dreams do we picture and anticipate that happy time? Who knows, maybe Fate will decree that our next celebration will occur within the confines of our own sunny country, and the memories of the ghastliness of war will be dimmed by our pride in the recollection of the doings of those of our comrades who did not return, and in the deeds of the battalion as a whole, deeds in which each and all of us have played our small part. As we celebrate the conclusion of our second year of existence, we do so in no mood of vain glorious boasting; we have done our job faithfully, and as well as we can, and in the time before us we will continue to do so.

As for this little battalion publication, we hope it has played its part in keeping you interested and amused during trying times, when other amusements and interests were few. We extend our thanks to those who have assisted to make the paper representative and topical, and hope that in the days to come, it will continue to play its part in the daily doings of the unit.

J.D. Mulcahy. Editor.

The Battalion is now two years old. Older than that really, because it was formed on the 1st July. But the first draft marched into the 2/23rd Battalion on the 20th August. That is the day we commemorate.

Since this day last year, many changes have occurred - fearful battles have been fought - old faces have gone - new faces have come. Heavy blows have been struck against the enemy. Glorious deeds have been performed by men of the Battalion, by far the most of them unheralded and unsung from the individual viewpoint. But all adding to the .nighty edifice we have built, and are enlarging - the 2/23rd Battalion Spirit of Mud & Blood. Your deeds set the example for all those thousands of other soldiers back home, as yet untried - but who wait and learn from us. It is our fate to be fighting in the Middle East. It makes no difference. That is why we built the Unit. That is our task.

In our two years of life we have taken greater toll of the enemy than he of us. It MUST always be so. It will be so. Those who have gone spur us on.

I have been spared to remain with you for the whole period - probably a record in Infantry Battalions, and I will conclude, repeating the words I used last year - I am proud to have the honour of commanding you.

BERNARD EVANS, Lt.Col.

I have been asked to contribute to the special issue of Mud & Blood to mark the second anniversary of the unit. For the privilege I am both grateful and proud. My pride is derived from the fact that I have been fortunate enough to help in the ploughing of the second acre; not only the ploughing, but the clearing of the noxious weeds which have threatened to choke the garden of human happiness. "Two ackers an acre" was all that was offered for our delectable present site. Somebody else said "I'd give it away". But we know it is worth more than money could buy, because it is bought at the highest cost. The first acre resembled an arena where you fought the beasts, as Paul fought them at Ephesus 1900 years ago. At that gladiatorial show in Tobruk, the successors of Caesar tossed in all that they had, and had it chucked back. The furrows were stained with our blood, but we value the acre above "two ackers".

The second acre was completed at the same infinite price. That acre is not for sale. It is ours, for it is sown with a seed that shall blossom in all its beauty in the hearts of our children. "Thy Kingdom Come," we pray, and there are two acres of that Kingdom we claim as our very own. Let us then never look back as we plough to the end.

Fredk. Porter, Chaplain.

"B" Echelon -

When Albury's Own is in training, or at rest beyond the areas of actual warfare, our five Company groups, Highest Quality, Ack, Beer, Charley and Don, foregather to the music of the Beer Harry Queen Band, under the watchful gaze of successive RSM's on behalf of BHQ for Ceremonial and Church Parades, and talks by the Old Man.

But when BHQ takes the field, and Ack, Beer, Charley and Don go to action stations with details of Highest Quality, each gives a part to a new entity called "B" Echelon (B for BUSY not BEER) - to be its mother and father, brother and sister - to provide the things expected of those people - and to receive the kicks they take in days when much is taken for granted.

"B" Echelon was a small party in Besieged Tobruk when we had our First Birthday, for some Company groups were 'at home', and (if conditions do not change as quickly as they sometimes do amid the changeful scene of war), it seems as though similar conditions will prevail on our Second Birthday.

But the nucleus is there, and looking across the bridge of a year, one sees some of the changes that TIME has made. Capt. F.G. Morrell, who brought round some good things for our first party, is HOME now, but Lieut. George Moore, who helped him as RQMS, will do the honours this year, and with the willing, untiring services of that good old stalwart, Sgt. Leo Jones, will produce a menu that will indeed be a Western Desert Special. There was no Toc Orange a year ago, but this year Lieut. J.D. Mulcahy holds the reins (or wheel), and the good things will get round all the Companies with the message:-

BIRTHDAY GREETINGS FROM "B" ECHELON.

A.P. Reynolds, RQMS.

R.A.P. BULLETIN:

The R.A.P., after keeping the same staff up to Syria, had a few changes. Capt. Agar moved over to a Field Ambulance, and Capt. Delohery took his place. Capt. Agar (now a Major, what! what!) is doing his bit at the Rest Station patching up blokes so that they can come back "with the boys". (What a shock some of our bludgers must have received to walk into J.McD. A.)

Capt. Delohery received a rather tough initiation to front line first aid, and he takes a poor view of Stuka parades, and their attitude to the Red Cross. Incidentally, he has no connection with that advertisement - "The Cut's the thing."

Rex Spry and his hair clippers left us at the same time. (The boys say they missed the latter most, but I don't agree with that), and I had to get a new loading party for "Medical Stores" on Sundays. Mousie Resuggan joined us at the "Barracks", but whether it was too much "liquid" in Tripoli, or in that river where he nearly drowned, he left us for Hospitals, I.T.B. (and 2-ton Tony), and came back as a Reo. Dive Bomber Dowel still dives on the corns with the same ferocity as of old. Life begins at forty, so look out for next month (remember his 38th birthday on the boat?) Mosquito Joe (Keith Roberts) had his life work in Syria interrupted, but was almost called up for special investigations one night up here, when a specially hungry brand of mosquitoes arrived overnight. Two highlights of Jack (Slushy) Turner's exploits in the Battle of Egypt - (1) The great job he did with "A" Company, dashing around with his Red Cross and his loyal

off-siders, the Stretcher bearers. (2) Caught "with his pants down" and ·
"wounded but remaining on duty". Very difficult to show his wound, or
tell the story of how he copped it. Bob Noonan, after practising on the CO
as his batman last year, reached the height of any batman's ambition -
RMO's batman (his memoirs will be published after the war). Bob is still
available for the band, and was frequently seen almost completely surrounded by his instrument. Dadda Peck and his merry men, the SBs (and it does-
n't mean Silly Beggars), did more than their normal share of work, and did
it well. A few of them are enjoying the administrations of the nurses, due
to getting in the way of some stray metal, but expect to be back with us
soon. The writer of these few lines needs no description - he has frequently
been referred to as that big, fat----------------------Sergeant of the R.A.P.

L.B. Allen - RAP Sgt.

A DAY IN THE LIFE OF THE Q.M. (As seen by others)

It was 1100 hours, and signs of life were at last being shown in the
palatial tent of the QM at "B" Echelon (40 miles behind the line). A figure
dressed in elaborate pyjamas (Comfort Fund Issue) sat up on the edge of
his downy couch, reached under same, and selected from his well stocked
cellar, a bottle of medicinal brandy (justifiably intercepted on way to RAP).
"I must have something for my bed sores", he muttered, downing a hearty
swig. Stepping neatly over the pile of champagne bottles (acquired through
supplementary rations) he nonchalantly lit a cigar from a box presented to
him by the Sullage Contractor, purely as a mark of esteem. His face already
alight with anticipation of the day's sport, he opened a tin of roast chicken
with the dexterity born of long practice, and proceeded to give his orders.
"RQMS, bring me Blue Book No. 4, you know the one - How to Annoy
Company Commanders. I haven't had a return for nearly four hours. -

Armourer, send for a return of all Bren barrels with an inward curvature of more than 1.88mm, and, Oh! Sgt. Cook, hold back half of "A" Company's rations - I've a friend visiting me tonight. Make up the usual parcel for me to sell to the Wogs, and I'll take 20% of the Comfort Fund issue with me when I go to Alex tomorrow. By the way, I don't expect to be back for a week. In the meantime, I'm going up to BHQ to try and upset the Adjutant. While I'm away don't let anyone get away with anything; there was a fellow trying to get a pair of boots yesterday, and although his toes were showing through his left boot, the right was in fair order, and I've only got 500 pairs anyway. About the Bren return - don't be too explicit at first, else it will be too easy for them - you know what to do - just say 'Bren barrels', then send it back and ask about the curvature - then demand triplicate copies, not duplicate, and so on. If you're stuck, consult that booklet from the 'Round Game Department'. I'll be back from BHQ in half an hour or so; tell the batman to fix up my bed - I must try and get some rest. Oh! and remind me to cable home and buy another block of flats." Exit the QM, whistling dolefully his theme song - "Time on my hands".

G. Moore - QM.

Did we tell you about the time Bob Penhalluriack and Bickey Beresford were out on certain duty some distance from their camp, and dropping into a farm for some water, they decided to eat their iron rations? Whilst sitting on the barn step, a hen rushed by, hotly pursued by a large rooster. Bickey threw a lump of bully beef at the hen, which ran faster than ever, but the rooster pulled up and greedily partook of the morsel, whilst the hen reached a place of safety. 'Blimey," remarked Bob to Bickey, "I hope I'm never as hungry as that rooster".

Then there is the one about the man who was given the choice of having 20 evacuee children, or 20 expectant mothers billeted in his house. He chose the 20 expectant mothers, but wrote a note to the Billeting Officer asking him to warn them not to expect too much, as he was over 55 years of age, and feeling a little tired.

Well, Mud'n Bloods, can't think of any more to say at present, except to wish you one and all the very best for the next twelve months, and may we all be celebrating our third birthday together. Keep up the good work, and before you know where you are, the whole damned business will be over. But in any case, no matter what yet lies in front of us, carry on with that feeling of comradeship and pride that we have always known in the old Mud & Blood battalion.

2nd ANNIVERSARY DINNER

2/23 Bn

EGYPT 20 AUG 42

ALBURY'S OWN

Aut Inveniam Viam Aut Faciam

M E N U

Soup	-	Tomato
Roast	-	Roast Beef
Vegetables	-	Roast potatoes
		Peas
		Carrots
Sweets	-	Plum Pudding and
		Brandy Sauce
Savouries	-	Spaghetti on toast
Biscuits	-	Cheese
Tea	-	Coffee

"GOOD LUCK 'RATS"

A U T O G R A P H S :-

WESTERN DESERT, 25th August, 1942.

Well, chaps, here it is almost a week since we celebrated our anniversary, and we don't mind admitting that it has taken all that time to recover from the dinner that Sgt. Leo Jones and his merry men turned on. Felt, as we staggered to our couch to lie down, that Christmas Day feeling when one has eaten far, far too well. Unfortunately, the better half was not there to bring the usual glass of bi-carbonate and water, so we suffered valiantly in the good cause, and in between pangs of heartburn and indigestion, cursed our own greed and the malignancy of the cooks in conspiring to bring about our undoing. Still, it was a great day, and on behalf of the battalion, we extend our thanks and appreciation of the very excellent job, and the great pains taken by the cooks. One and all they rose to the occasion, as they have at similar periods in the past. Good work, lads, call round at "B" Echelon at any time between four and six for your medals!

This is what RQMS Peter Reynolds has to say of the day's events:- Two years old! Two years since that splendid gentleman, the late Lt.Col. Storey transferred a draft of recruits from the 4th Training Battalion in Albury Showgrounds to Lt.Col. Evans for the 2/23 Battalion. A short span in the preparation of an infant for youth and manhood; yet a considerable period in the lives of civilians who have adopted the army, at their Country's call, to fight for freedom; but still short against the centuries in which the touch of human progress is wrought and passed from generation to generation.

It was grand that several foundation members of the Unit, and others who have served for the greater part of the Unit's two years existence - and whose ties of kinship have been quickened by the difficulties of the service and deepened by the touches of danger - were all able to foregather yesterday in a happy anniversary mood with new friends who share our traditions and are preparing to add lustre to them.

In the Army, as in civilian life, it is true that the way to a man's heart is through his stomach, and in this regard the cooks and their helpers won our highest esteem in the excellent birthday dinner they served us last night. The joy of the anniversary occasion was fully shared by every Mud'n Blood in the meal and in the community singing and impromptu entertainments that followed, but no one forgot those who are away from us in hospital and whom we will meet at future celebrations. Nor did anyone fail to remember those absent friends whom we will not see in this world again, but whose memory and service is enshrined in our hearts.

A. P. Reynolds - 21/ 8/42.

Remember seeing a long, long time ago, when we were a wee small laddie completely unversed in the ways of this wicked world, a picture entitled Ben Hur, and to this day have not forgotten the thrill we experienced in a scene depicting several hundred chariots hurtling through the desert into battle. The other night, during the recent exercise, we actually lived through, and participated in something similar, and the old thrill came back again. What a scene to remember in the future when we are all back in our prosaic everyday occupations! As we tore through the night in the centre of that heterogenous mass of vehicles of every description, we seemed to be taking part in some unreal adventure, and we enjoyed every minute of it. What wonderful thrills this giddy old war gives us at times, surpassing anything we ever see in films, and we don't have to pay our ninepence to experience them. Still, much as we enjoy them on these and other days, there are times when the old armchair by the fire, plus book and slippers, would give an even greater thrill.

We were severely admonished by Sar/Major Dick Ward for including those two jokes in our anniversary number, and can only explain that someone took advantage of our youth and innocence, as we certainly did not see the double meaning in them. Having been thus chastened, we cannot include the corker we heard last night, but if you promise not to tell Dick, we might tell it to you some dark night when there's no one about.

BBC NEWS — 26th August, 1942.
Stalingrad continues to hold the front place in the news from Russia. The position of the Soviet forces has grown worse in the past 24 hours, both in the Don arm to the west of the city and on the Ketelmikovo front to the SW. A big battle is now raging on the east bank of the river, where the Germans have formed a bridgehead, and have succeeded in bringing heavy tanks across the Don. The Russians have inflicted serious losses, but so far have been unable to drive the invaders back. The Germans are doing their utmost to force an early decision, regardless of cost. They are throwing in tanks by the hundred, motorised infantry by the thousand, and enormous numbers of planes. To the SW of Stalingrad, the Germans have driven a new wedge through the Russian minefields, and have advanced in the past day or two. German spearheads now extend in two directions from Ketelnikova, one pointing directly to Stalingrad along the railway, while the other is further south and threatens the Volga between Stalingrad and Astrakan. In the Caucasus, the Germans have made another big advance towards Crozny oilfields. They are now at Prokhlydnaya, 70 miles SE of Pyatigorsk, and a little more than that distance from Crozny. Prokhydnaya is an important junction on the Rostov to Baku railway, one line running to

Crozny, and the other linking up with the military road across the mountains from Vladikavkaz to Tiflis, 150 miles to the south. On the Caucasian fronts, more than half of the German forces are not German. Only the spearheads are German, while numerical superiority is given by troops from satellite countries. More than 40 divisions of Hungarians, Rumanians and Italians are now being used in South Russia.

Mr. Churchill has arrived back in London after travelling more than 15,000 miles by air. He spent a considerable time in the Middle East, both before and after his visit to Moscow and, it is now revealed, paid a second visit to the front in the Western Desert. Part of the purpose of the Prime Minister's journey was to see the troops on the front line battle area, and his visits did much good, because of their informality, and the fact that he spoke to as many people as possible. Many people felt better for the sight of his familiar figure, smoking, waving his cigar, giving the Victory sign, thumping his stick on the ground, just as they did in the blitzed towns of England. When he first visited the Desert, Mr. Churchill spent most time with Dominion troops. On his second visit, he spent most time with British troops, and he spent a night with them, in a caravan captured from an Italian General. At a press conference in Cairo, he spoke with confidence of the coming struggle in the Desert, and of Britain's determination to fight for Egypt and the Nile Valley as though it were the soil of England itself. He spoke of Russia's ability to fight on, and of the help coming to her. In the Suez Canal area, Mr. Churchill inspected troops only recently arrived in Egypt, including many famous Scottish Regiments.

The Japanese made another raid on the Australian mainland last night, 3 planes attacking Darwin. All their bombs fell in a swamp area. Over East New Guinea, 4 enemy Zero fighters were shot down and others damaged out of a force of 13 that were attacked by Allied interception units. One of the Allied planes was damaged on the way home. In the Kokoda area, where the Japanese advanced from the NE coast of New Guinea towards Port Moresby, fighting still has not developed into a major action. Our forces based on the Stanley Owen Range guarding the path to Port Moresby, have dispersed an enemy patrol. Destruction of 13 Japanese planes over Darwin during the weekend brought the number of enemy planes shot down by General McArthur's planes to 38. In addition, at least 12 vessels have been hit, several of them sunk. Timor has been one of the principal targets, nine raids having been made on various bases there. There have been 12 raids on New Guinea, 7 on New Britain (Rabaul), and 2 on New Ireland.

CHAPTER 14

WESTERN DESERT, 9th September, 1942.

News to hand today of the doings of those wonderful women of ours back home, who are moving heaven and earth to get comforts for us. The C.O. informs us that he has received a draft for 100 pounds for our comforts fund, and in addition, has been advised of the despatch of 30,000 cigarettes. How they do it beats us, with all the shortage of smokes that exists over there, but you know the old adage - where there's a will there's a way - and who can doubt the determination of our womenfolk to supply us with whatever is in their power to procure for our comfort. These long years have in no way diminished their enthusiasm, and their efforts are indeed practical reminders of their continued love and solicitude for our welfare. On behalf of you Mud'n Bloods, it has been our privilege to extend from time to time our thanks for various benefits received, and once again we have the pleasure of saying a very hearty "Thank You".

By the way, some of you new Mud'n Bloods may not be aware that we have a very enterprising association of our womenfolk and other well-wishers working for us back home, and we would urge you to write to your folks about the desirability of them joining up. They will be more than welcome, and if they communicate with Mrs. B. Evans, K5 High Street, Windsor, either by letter or phone, they will be able to find out when meetings etc., are held. These are sometimes held at the C.O.'s home, and sometimes in a room kindly loaned by the Legacy Club for the occasion. The trend of events in Australia is exemplified in the, to us, rather amusing information that each lady arrives with a teaspoonful of tea, tied up in a little paper bag, and gravely hands same in for inclusion in the communal teapot. We don't know whether the Q.M.'s wife is in charge of this part of the business or not, but have no doubt that this item in the day's affairs is as well organised as all their other activities. Some of the most willing workers in the Association are the nearest and dearest of those comrades who have passed on, and their interest in the welfare of the Battalion is in no whit lessened by the fact that they no longer have anyone actually in the unit. They continue to serve, and that is how the lads would have had it.

Now for the news of our latest competition, which should appeal greatly to all Mud'n Bloods of imagination, and judging by the furphies we hear from minute to minute, who can say that there is a Mud'n Blood devoid of imagination. The C.O. has donated a bottle of sparkling, cool frothy beer, and the Q.M. (for once with the right idea) has promised to provide a specially cooked dinner consisting mainly of large juicy grilled steak, with eggs and chips. This will be the prize for the lucky beggar who sends in the best suggestion as to how the above mentioned sum of 100 pounds should be spent. As a consolation prize, all unsuccessful competitors will be permitted to come to the cookhouse and sniff the steak cooking, and may afterwards stop and watch the winner partake of his dinner. All suggestions will be published in these columns, and may be humorous or serious, but will not necessarily be adopted. The method of adjudicating will be announced later, when we get an appropriate brainwave. So come along, Mud'n Bloods with your suggestions, and if you can't keep them altogether clean, do the best you can. Remember, your Editor's youthful innocence.

Well, we ask you, did you see Ron Claffey yesterday when he got all dressed up to go and collect his M.M. from the General? Nearly everyone in BHQ vicinity, and definitely everyone in the Transport Platoon, assisted in the dressing, and the net result was a vision of sartorial splendour never before equalled in this unit. Were we a fashion reporter, we would probably have described the event on these lines:-

Driver Claffey, pale and subdued in face of the ordeal before him, looked handsome and most, most attractive in Doug Innes' large fur felt hat, turned up at one side, and relieved with a large metallic ornament. His ensemble comprised the Colonel's best shirt, and what would appear to be a pair of Les Allen's shorts, both suitably laundered for the occasion. Socks were kindly loaned by the Adjutant's batman on behalf of the Adjutant, but Claffey, obeying an old superstition, wore his own boots, upon which most of the Transport Officer's boot polish had been used. Stalking up to the General as boldly as a rabbit facing a greyhound, he was duly invested with the ribbon, and afterwards confided to the C.O. that he would rather have gone into action again. It can be definitely denied that during the investiture, he took the General severely to task regarding the recent decision to prohibit beer in the front line. All joking aside, Ron, the boys are tickled pink, and offer their sincere congratulations on a well earned honour.

THIS PAPER WAR - No. 1.

As one whose head is sometimes barely visible above a mountainous heap of returns, etc., I find myself in my forgetful moments caressing the thin slips with my hand, and measuring the heap and comparing it with yesterday's crop. I grow resentful if it is not as big. Now, is that the first faint symptoms of that terrible disease, born of this war, and only now being talked about with bated breath in the offices of the DCMS? As it seems to be a disease confined to British armies, it has been given an English name - Paperitis.

I tremble when I think I may be catching it at last. Full well have I watched its dire effects on a friend of mine. The Adjutant was once a laughing, carefree lad - then I noticed a peculiar gleam in his eye whenever the word "paper" was mentioned. I thought at first that it was but the natural interest of one whose whole waking time is spent in scribbling notes - but no! The gleam deepened as days went on - his trembling hands snatched at every bit of paper he saw. He seemed never happy unless he was surrounded with huge stacks - walls and ramparts of it. Then the other day my worst fears were confirmed - I had delivered the monthly supply of stationery - I came upon him suddenly - his head in a box crooning like a little baby. I suspect him of having a secret hoard in his dugout, in which he bathes and rolls in the stilly watches of the night. I have remonstrated with him - but he still steals away with a guilty look - to be alone. One can but visualise the end - a ceaseless shuttle to and fro of 3 ton trucks - stationery to Adjutant. He, with demoniacal glee, urging his tripled staff to still greater efforts - the ceaseless flow of orders, returns, cascading onto stupified Company Commanders - until they too get the urge and bombard him back again. Then what? One can only think we will be here for life - bogged in a flowing sea of paper.

I am frightened! It might be contagious. Just think of my unlimited resources - and tremble.

G. Moore - QM.

Christmas comes but once a year, but this year surely contains two of the festive periods. This reflection is caused by the intimation, read the other day, that Xmas mails close on the first of November, which is only a comparatively short time ahead. About this time last year we were scratching our heads over designs for a Unit Xmas Card, and then, to our lasting sorrow, we allowed the selected one to be pinched from us at Amiriya. Anyhow, to cut the cackle, the C.O. has directed that a card be designed for this year, and as the time presses, it has to be done pronto. So will any bright Mud'n Blood, with still brighter ideas, come to light with a suggestion or two. A neat drawing, or a rough idea of one which could be worked out by one of our tame artists (sorry Mr. Lovell), together with a couplet or four-line verse of appropriate wording, would meet the bill. Arrangements will have to be made in Alexandria for the printing of whatever card is selected, and in addition to the prize of 1 pound, we will endeavour to obtain permission from the C.O. for the person whose idea is accepted to accompany us to Alex to put the work in hand and spend the quid. Get your old thinking caps and put them on.

Haven't told you a yarn for some little time now; not, in fact since we were chided by S/Major Dick Ward for our Anniversary Number ones. Dick will never forgive us for this one (nor will you, perhaps), but the fact remains that we have been telling it with conspicuous success now for 20 odd years, and we nearly always score someone who hasn't heard it before.

We believe Lieut. Ken Lovell is in the above group.
We think that's him with the superbly horizontal ears!

Two elderly ladies and a young flapper were sitting on the golf house verandah when a noise was heard in the shrubbery alongside. One of the old dears walked over to the rail, glanced over, and came back remarking in horrified tones "There's a naked man outside. I can't see his face but thank goodness he isn't my husband." The second old lass had a peep and remarked "How dreadful - and he isn't my husband". The young flapper in turn had a look and indignantly exclaimed "The cheeky outsider. He isn't even a member of the golf club."

WESTERN DESERT, 14th September, 1942.

Here we sit, frothing at the lips (and it is very seldom that we have froth at the lips these days). Our rage is occasioned by the fact that we have just been chided at our inability to spell. The numerous spelling errors that have lately caused so much comment, however, are not the work of your long-suffering editor, and our world-famous publication will rapidly lose prestige, Sgt. Fancke, unless more care is exercised in the publishing department. Such words as humerous, definately, visable, verander, horified, shubbery, and so on. All of which appeared in our last issue, cannot be found in any well brought up dictionary.

Quite a crop of suggestions for spending the 100 pounds sent by the Welfare Association have come to hand -

Brassieres for Tubby Heard, the C.O.'s batman. Sender of this suggestion remarks that every time he meets Tubby, dressed as at present, he is reminded strongly of his babyhood.

Packets of "Mum" to deodorise the present issue of butter.

Hair clippers for Companies, plus note-books and refills for NCO's.

Beer for the Officers.

Butter-patters for the cooks, who are gravely handicapped at present without these, and have to serve the butter un-patted.

First-class single ticket to Australia, to be raffled.
(N.B. - The Editor to conduct the raffle, we presume?)

Spend the whole ruddy lot on a long cablegram to Mr. Curtin, expressing our grateful appreciation at being left in the Middle East.

From the above, it will be seen that few have taken this vital question seriously, therefore, as the most serious-minded person in the unit, it behoves us to put in our own suggestion, namely -

Most of us, due to the rush of arrival in the desert, came away without many necessaries and little luxuries that could make life more comfortable in these spartan surroundings. In addition, with Xmas approaching, we are all more or less deprived of the pleasure of making those little purchases of gifts to send home that would be so much appreciated by our folks. Our idea is to use the 100 pounds as a fund to purchase a wide range of gifts - one only of each - exhibit same to the lads, and take orders for anything they fancy. The orders could then be classified, and the goods bought in bulk. Arrangements could be made that any articles unsold would be taken back. The scheme has not been worked out in detail, and is only suggested in broad outline. At the conclusion of the business, we would still have the 100 pounds in hand, and this could be spent on extras to augment our Xmas Dinner. What do you think of the idea? And have you any improvements to suggest?

No entries received yet for our Xmas Card contest, so our tame artist - Lieut. Ken Lovell - submits the following to start the ball rolling. He seems to be in a bit of a quandary - which would indicate that he doesn't listen in to the wireless very often.

LETTERS FROM CORRESPONDENTS:

Dear Editor:

We, the undersigned, wish to refute the rumours emanating from BHQ area. It was stated by RSM Penandink, and his "sleeping" partner Tracker Bowden, that they were not drops of rain which fell at about 0530 hours t'other morning, but spray caused by the splash when we two wee lads had our morning dip.

(Signed) Tubby Heard, Les Allen.

P.S.   We don't wish to be rude, or anything like that, but we wish to ask this question - Is it a fact that the beer issue is being put on again for all those who go for that morning swim at 0630 hours? The query was raised in our minds by the sight of "Old Bob", "Tracker" and "Bomber Lees", none of whom are renowned as early risers, but all of whom have that desert thirst. Maybe we're wrong.

EXTRACT - From letter from Sgt. Jim Taylor to Capt. Bill Vines -

"And so we say "Aloha" and sort of "Farewell" to you personally, and to the unit generally - my Board says "C2" - nuff sed - though I really think that there will be an army job for me at home somewhere. Though thoughts of being in Aussie for Xmas are most pleasant, exhilarating almost, and yet strangely unreal, there is more than a slight feeling of "selling out" on one's cobbers. You find that friendships made under such conditions as the unit has experienced, affect you more deeply than you'd realize - and probably more deeply than the rather blase average Australian would care to admit. And it isn't really until you become completely detached from your unit that you realize that, after all, this unit spirit, the good old "esprit......." which you hear so much about, isn't all boloney.

"May it be not very long before we lucky ones are standing, either in Swanston or Dean Streets, as the good old unit struts its stuff before the cheering crowds - and, later on, the meeting of cobbers with one foot on the rail and a jug in the right hand. Wishing you, the C.O. and the unit the very best of luck and health in everything you do."

Well, Jim old chap, in reciprocating your good wishes on behalf of the lads, may we say how sorry we all are that you are not still with us. You go home with the consciousness of having done a fine job, and when you join the growing band of ex-Mud'n Bloods who are already home, we know we will often be in your thoughts. God speed.

Have you ever tried this "jingle" business, it's rather a fascinating pastime. Have a go at it and let's see the results. The trouble is, you can't stop - you have to keep going on. Here's our latest brain-wave, a continuation of "Alexander's Ragtime Band", which, of course, can go on for ever unless someone hits us on the head.

Old Rommel's hopes have faded, and his men are somewhat jaded,
    To push forward more he'd need a magic wand.
For our gallant Air Force raided, and their aims were ably aided,
    By the men of Alexander's Ragtime Band.

Yes! Old Rommel's getting out, and we'll make his flight a rout,
    He's tasting medicine of a very nasty brand.
For there's not the slightest doubt, there's something salutary about
    The bitter pills of Alexander's Ragtime Band.

But the struggle's not yet ended, nor will it be until is mended,
    The break where our former line was manned.
Until his knees are bended, and his strength is all expended,
    Will fight the men of Alexander's Ragtime Band.

And when we've driven out the foe, we'll celebrate with quite a show,
    The best ever seen within this ancient land.
And in the foremost row, there'll be Frankie, Winnie and Joe,
    Applauding the men of Alexander's Ragtime Band.

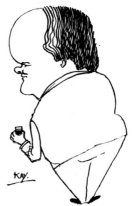

JACK KENDALL   Tich Armfield, "A" Company.

433

CHAPTER 15

WESTERN DESERT, 3rd October, 1942.

Well lads, here we are back again at the old address, with the same old business motto - b------t and more b------t. Alright, you can have three guesses! It is rather nice to leave the hurly-burly of life at "B" Echelon for a time, and come back to the peaceful serenity of BHQ, where one only works 20 hours a day, and has the added joy of listening to the tales of woe of fully 98% of the unit. And one must not forget the ecstatic pleasure of being able to sit back and revile the Transport Officer and "B" Echelon generally, in accordance with the old established unit custom.

Again we apologise for delay in producing issues of this world-famous publication. We were reminded forcibly of our duty t'other day on receipt of a cable from the Foreign Editor of the New York World, whilst it is a fact that Winnie is unable to concentrate on winning the war through having to answer impatient enquiries at question time in the House of Commons, as to the reasons for our non-appearances. So, take it from us, whilst Mud & Blood is being issued - Egypt is safe.

We had a few competitions in full swing the last time we appeared, and we might as well tell you the fate of them all. Firstly, let us deal with the Xmas Card competition. There were many entries, and many of them of a particularly high standard, surprisingly so, indeed. The winning entry was submitted by Pte. Len Wemyss, of the I Section, who won the prize of 1 pound and a trip to Alexandria to arrange the printing of the card. Len has ideas as to how and where he is going to spend that quid, and, come to think of it, what a lot of pleasure one can have for a pound. Consolation prizes of a bottle of beer each have been awarded to some Mud'n Bloods who sent in very excellent entries, so good, in fact, that it was very difficult to adjudge the winner. The consolation prizes go to Pte. Guy ("C" Company), Pte. Flynn ("C" Company), Cpl. Fauvel (HQ Company), Pte. J. Turner (BHQ), Pte. J. Fletcher (HQ Company), and Pte. Stuart (BHQ). To all these winners we extend a hearty invitation to collect their prizes at our dugout at the earliest opportunity; and so long as the sun is well over the yardarm, we don't mind in the slightest producing our two glasses. All joking aside, lads, the above entries were pretty good, and it is a pity that we couldn't adopt them all. Congratulations on a stout effort.

Now, as to our competition for the best suggestion for spending the 100 pounds sent out by the Welfare Association, many ingenious schemes were propounded, but the one adjudged the winner was submitted by Sgt. F.H. McLean, of "A" Company, whose suggestion that 50 pounds be spent on two sets of hair clippers, a pair of scissors and a comb for each platoon. The remaining 50 pounds to be spent on sugar, milk, cocoa and coffee, either to be distributed to the platoons direct, or through the Company cookhouses, so that, now the weather is becoming cold in the evening, the lads could be provided with a hot drink at night.

This scheme will be put into operation as soon as practicable, and we think you will agree that it is an extremely sensible way of spending the money. Sgt. McLean will be sent by his O.C. to "B" Echelon at the first convenient time, after consultation with the QM, to collect his prize of a bottle of beer, plus the best meal that the cooks of this battalion can turn on. The QM will personally supervise the serving of the dinner, and afterwards Sgt. McLean will broadcast his impressions of army cooking over the EBC. (Padres prohibited from listening in!) Capt. Frank Hurley will probably (if he hears about it) be there to take motion pictures of the event. World rights reserved.

Hitler's secret weapon! How long we have heard of it, and awaited its appearance! And now it falls to the lot of our Carrier Platoon (Rigg's Wrigglers) to discover it. We refer to those famous booby traps that Jerry fixes up on such things as abandoned carriers, and that are only visible to carrier personnel. T'other night the carrier platoon reported large numbers of these contraptions, but when a party of Engineers went out the following night, their magical properties had asserted themselves, as the Engineers were totally unable to see them. Hitler must be chagrined to find that the Wrigglers have so soon penetrated his secrets!

By the way, while we think
of it, a cable was received some
little time ago from Major Birch,
(from no less a place than Camber-
well!) reading "Am proud of the
Battalion", so apparently some
news of our recent doings has leaked
home. We can well imagine that
Major Birch will not be alone in
anxiously following our progress
here. In passing on his message we
feel all Mud'n Bloods will be equally
proud - proud that the doings of
their fallen comrades should have
occasioned such a message being
sent.

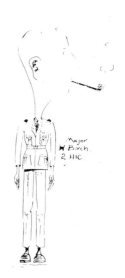

Salvage is the order of the day these times, and what a grand job
most of you are doing about it. However, still more can be and must be
done, and in an endeavour to stimulate a little healthy interest and enthusiasm in this most important matter, a competition between all Companies
and sub-units has been suggested, a prize of 1000 Craven A cigarettes being
awarded to the Company aggregating the greatest number of points, something on the line of our flea hunt competition at Tobruk. For instance a
live Jerry is worth 150 points, an I-ti 100, a carrier 100, tank 150, trucks
100, tyres 5, other rubber goods accordingly, whilst such things as rifles,
jerrycans, tools, etc., will all be assessed and awarded points by the unit
salvage officer. Get to it, boys, and you'll soon be puffing away at those
gaspers. The Carrier Section is going well, but "B" Company, with a
Valentine tank to their credit is not far behind. Progress scores will be
published here from time to time.

Assistant Editor Sgt. Les Allen comes to light with the following:

Well, the worst has happened. We've been having a delightful
bludge while things are so quiet, but alas! it couldn't last. The C.O. trickled
along and saw us playing a quiet game of cards, so he decided that we needed another job. So we are placed in charge of Mud'n Blood Library, and we
ask for the help and co-operation of all troops. Six books will go out to
each Company for a fortnight, and then will be replaced by a different six.
Read them, but look after them, so that they will live to go round the whole
battalion, as they cost the C.O.'s fund quite a packet. And there are some
good ones amongst them too!

A correspondent writes, "Is it possible to call the Rest Camp by that name, when the discipline will be enforced by HQ Company". He then goes on to mention, "that voice known to all on HQ parades". I'm afraid we couldn't publish the remainder of our correspondent's remarks verbatim. After all, ours is a reputable publication, and anyhow the spelling was bad. (We do not associate ourselves with the remarks, Dick! Ed.)

Since when did our friend Capt. Rigg assume charge of salvage, or how long has he aspired to "Q" honours? This inquiry is caused by Col's latest exploit. He led a gang of his pirates in search of treasure in No Man's Land. The result - 8351 tins of Bully Beef, 2947 tins of Marmalade, 1789 tins of cheese and 5796 tins of margarine (be the said numbers a little more or less). Very valuable, indeed, but could we ask a few impertinent questions? (1) Who got down (a) Sugar (b) Milk (c) Tinned fruit?
*   (2) Who was the unlucky "Q" who thought he had successfully "dumped" these commodities, and now will receive them back to his fold?
    (3) Will these articles be used in the Officers' Mess, or will ORs receive some benefit also?

What's this I hear about you, Lieut. Max Simmons? Not content with your successes on the playing fields of Gazira, you bring your athletic prowess to the battlefield of Tel El Eisa. Nice work, my lad - you won easily, even though you had a start. However, the handicapper (B.E.) has noted this effort, and you'll probably be off scratch in your next event. Must have been a decent shock, Max, to see those blighters coming towards you; it's hardly cricket, is it?

All those chaps going on leave to either Alex or Cairo are now reading a long dissertation on what soldiers should do, or rather what they shouldn't do, whilst on leave. T'was written by the Doc, and he paints a lurid picture. The screed is read out in turn by Capt. George Moore (who doubtless could add numerous stories from his own long experience in the Orient); WOII Peter Reynolds (who takes a very poor view of it all); or Sgt. Freddie Carleton (who of course, is so much luckier than the rest of us, who haven't our wives in the Middle East). By the way, Peter's remark after hearing the MO strut his stuff was a beaut - "Hardly worth it, after all that trouble, eh Doc?"

We have received a corker verse from Darkie Downs, of "A" Company, which runs into a mere eleven verses. We have toyed with the idea of running it as a serial entitled "Darkie's Ellegy", but feel it really deserves publishing as a whole. Therefore, look out for our next number! Order your copies in advance! No extra price!

WESTERN DESERT, 3rd October, 1942.

EXTRA - ORDINARY EDITION

Well fellow Mud'n Bloods, we are departing a little from our old policy and custom. We don't need advertisements to buck up our circulation, but here, today, we have something right out of the box; we wish to bring to your notice, another Mud & Blood "First with the latest" -

"THE BATTALION GIFT SHOP"

Under patronage of all the best people.

As not everyone has had the opportunity of getting away to Alexandria or Cairo to purchase those odds and ends that he wishes to send home, we bring them right to your back door, as it were.

We have no expensive shop rent, no costly NEON signs, or heavy advertising expenses, so that we are able to sell at cost price (in fact 5% less, because this is the nett figure at which Capt. Col Rigg was able to purchase in Alex.) I wish I had been a buyer of a large Melbourne Emporium, as I might have been in this trip to Alex, but I can tell you, after a private preview of the stock, that Col has done an excellent job, and you will see lovely gifts that will please those at home.

Our shop is no plate glass fronted structure, its just the usual dugout - Western Desert model, Mark I, and is situated in Sharier Mud Patch (see I Section for map ref.). (Incidentally, the Doc offered his dugout, but it was in liquidation, so we declined his offer). Enter the door of this humble dugout, and you are immediately transported to the basement of one of Cairo's leading emporiums. Well! Thats our story, and we're sticking to it. These goods are available to you by special arrangements with Myers, David Jones, Iky Ikenstein, Saida George, and many other well known firms at home and abroad.

I saw this on one of the invoices:

> "Bought from Hannaux"
> "la marsin de confiane"

Don't know what it all means, but it sounds like the right thing to me.

Shop early and avoid the crush! Travel by train! This old slogan of Harold Clapp's Victorian Railways is not applicable here, I'm afraid, as

Jerry has pinched a few of our carriages. We can't even send the bus to pick you up, so use your feet, remember you are the infantry, after all.

There is no doubt about it. Wars are run on much better lines than previously. It almost takes me back to those old days when they called the war off when it rained. We might even get proper union hours soon, or be paid for war risk. However, what more could you wish for than this unique front line shopping.

Come out of those front line trenches to the comparative safety of BHQ area. Trot along to Didgee Clapin with the old paybook and draw "the necessary". Purchase your gift, with special advice from these well trained shop walkers and assistants. The old QM will come to light with paper and calico (thats more than you get in Aussie). We'll supply greeting cards with every purchase; we'll even provide a censor. We might even get Tich Wynack, the postie, also, but that's asking a lot, the way Jerry has behaved lately. With your purchases completed, back you go to the luxury of your front line homes and Jerry won't even know you've been away. This is what is known as simplicity shopping.

"Very good news this morning. A Mr. Boas, from Australia, is bringing dresses to sell us — the new 'sack-look' too, I believe."

"Fatima! If you must carry watermelons underneath, at least even 'em up."

One speciality which must be excluded from this year's Xmas shopping in the Western Desert. Father Christmas finds it impossible to attend in person, to distribute the gifts to the kids, but platoon commanders can bring their families in, just the same - we'll fix them up.

No ration tickets are needed here, only the old paybook with a few quid on the credit side - we'll do the rest. You can't wrap up and send yourself home (worse luck), but do the next best thing, and send a Christmas gift.

A word of warning - Don't forget that Tracker will be on the lookout, so DISPERSE. We don't want Jerry shells as souvenirs.

Seriously though, this is a great opportunity that nobody should miss, of buying that gift to send home to Mum, Dad, the Missus, the good sort, brothers, sisters, Aunts, Uncles and all the rest. We have concentrated on things of use to those at home, particularly those that the feminine sex require, and find hard to procure in these days of the Ration Book. A good look round Alexandria has convinced us that you couldn't purchase cheaper elsewhere, and we can assure you that these articles are good value.

Among our offerings, you will see the following:
Dress materials
Silks
Cambrics
Woollens
Tobralco cloth
(All of these in plain and pretty floral designs. Just imagine how SHE would look in these).
Ladies pure silk stockings
Handbags in the latest of styles
Cosmetics and toilet articles
(Help HER to look attractive to meet that YANK)
Womens underwear and nighties, etc.
(My vocabulary baulks at the description, and though I'm an old married man with a large family, I still get ideas when I view these things.)
Scarves of fashionable design
Linen table services and handkerchiefs
(By the way, did you hear of the latest scanties - "One Yank and they're down")

As usual we couldn't find much for Dad, but we obtained a few pairs of pyjamas and some swagger dressing gowns; also a few watches and watch straps.

If we haven't got what you need, perhaps we can take your order and purchase it for you. (Another trip, eh Col?)

We've got a few pipes, as long as Dad can get the baccy.

So we ask you to roll up and make your purchases from this, the Western Desert Branch of:

P. K. DOLES & CO. - Nothing under 10 Piastres.

WESTERN DESERT, 26th October, 1942.

Here we are, four days in battle, and finding it so bally monotonous that to fill in time we are producing this issue of your favourite rag. Not that we have anything to tell you that you do not already know, but we thought you might all be short of a bit of paper, and this is a handy way of distributing some.

We are not sure whether it was William Shakespeare, Robbie Burns, or Darkie Downs who wrote those inspiring words - "Be there a man with soul so dead, who never to himself has said, this is my own------" Can't remember the rest, but it was all about the surge of pride and joy that runs through one at times, when the doings of one's country or countrymen are particularly inspiring. And when that terrific barrage opened the other night, it was both awe inspiring and stimulating - a moment when one felt intensely British, and surpassingly proud of it. Old John Bull and his youngsters dishing it out, and how!

In the midst of the colossal bingle, with the sky literally one mass of flame, and the noise something that one will never forget, we stumbled across a Sig, crouching close to the ground with headpiece clapped closely to his ears, and an intent look upon his face. The battle was raging in front, and apparently all round, but no news was coming through, and we felt here at last was a chance to learn how things were progressing. Slapping him on the shoulder, we attracted his impatient attention. "What's the news?" we shouted above the din. "Just getting it now," he shouted back, "Stalingrad's still holding out."

But for sheer nonchalance it would be hard to beat the effort put up by Tubby Heard, the C.O.'s batman, who, when the crescendo was at its peak, was discovered by the Old Man sitting in a slit trench playing checkers with the Adjutant's offsider - Bill Hyland - in the moonlight.

That very interesting looking piece of plaster over the right eyebrow of Capt. Norm McMaster has given rise to a decent crop of furpheys. Norm himself claims the injury was caused when he glanced down the barrel of a

25-pounder, and the blasted thing went off, just grazing his eyebrow. The official explanation, as given to the C.O. is that his binoculars were swinging and suddenly dashed up and socked him one; but we might as well tell you that a little bird whispered to us that Lieut. Max Simmons, aiming with superlative accuracy with a tin of bully beef, taught Norm that it is not always wise to go tossing such things around, as they often boomerang. Anyhow, Norm paraded himself hopefully to the R.A.P. hoping for the best, but was told that he should have been hit a little harder to get sent out. Now, we understand, he is back plaguing the life out of Max, tossing everything but the kitchen sink at him, and inviting retaliation.

What a fine job those two cobber battalions of ours are doing? We refer to the 24th and 48th, who have been in the thick of it for the past four days, and have covered themselves again with laurels. Our turn will come too, and if we acquit ourselves as well, as we undoubtedly will, our new Brigadier will have real reason to be pleased with his command. We can assure our sister battalions that their deeds are a stimulation to us, and we are proud indeed to be with them in the same brigade. May we all three go on to further triumphs together!

In case you are all wondering about those Christmas Cards you have ordered, we wish to advise that they are all ready printed waiting to be picked up, but unfortunately during the present phase of operations it is not possible to send anyone down for them. We, with our usual self-sacrifice, have volunteered to go down for them when movement restrictions are lifted, but the C.O. is reluctant to subject us to the hazards of Alexandria, and Major Wall has been delegated to go at the first opportunity. We still hope to have them in time to catch the Christmas mail, closing on the 1st November, but if we don't - marleesh! They can always go on the next one, and even if they arrive a few days late, our folk will know that we have not forgotten them.

Cheerio, Mud'n Bloods, until our next issue.

CHAPTER 16

PALESTINE, 25th December, 1942.

SPECIAL CHRISTMAS NUMBER

Well, Mud'n Bloods, it is a long time since the last issue of your favourite paper, but what better time than now in which to reintroduce it. First of all, let us wish you all the very best for the festive season;   may you all have stomach-ache tonight, and let's hope you don't get too shickered on that bottle of free beer that we understood is forthcoming.

Not so many of us can remember our first Christmas over this side, or should we perhaps say that we remember it vividly, but there are not so many left nowadays, who celebrated the occasion in a welter of mud and slush. Despite climatic discomforts, it was a very happy festival, and we sincerely trust all you new-comers spending your first Christmas away from home will enjoy yourselves as much as we did two years ago.

Much has happened since then;   old cobbers have passed on;   others have returned home;   newcomers have arrived in the battalion and become old hands. Altogether, it is difficult to recognise the present show as being identical with the happy band who sailed for adventure such a long time ago. However, despite the many changes in personnel, it is still the same happy family;   much better perhaps these days than before. There is nothing like adversity and sacrifice, the sharing of dangers, and the enjoyment of carnival to bind men together;   and all of these are known to members of the 2/23rd. Our old colour patches may have gone, but the proud title of Mud & Blood still remains, and symbolises the fine spirit of camaraderie, courage and determination that imbues every member of this unit, be they old originals, reinforcements, or newcomers.

The new colour patch tricked even the Wogs

Christmas time is not an appropriate occasion for sadness, but we cannot let the occasion pass without a thought for those who are no longer with us. The other day, when the Commemoration Parade was held, who amongst us wasn't inspired, particularly when the Salute to Fallen Comrades was given. The silvery notes of that bugle conjured up many recollections of old pals we have left behind us in the desolate sands of the desert, chaps who were with us last year to celebrate a happy Yuletide. What grand chaps they were, and most of us will never forget the image of those little white crosses in the sandy waste, nor the gallant deeds of those who lie under them. The following lines, quoted in a letter to the RSM by Mrs. Taylor-Ward, express our feelings more aptly than anything we can put into words:-

> They went with songs to the battle, they were young,
>   Straight of limb, true of eye, steady and aglow.
> They were staunch to the end against odds uncountered,
>   They fell with their faces to the foe.

Now, what news have we to give you? Very little indeed we are afraid. Our mind appears somewhat sterile of recent months, leaving us with a feeling of apprehension as to whether only our mind is so affected. Still, iskabibble.

Sgt. Les Allen, who has been lying on a bed of pain (?) for the past few days, has forwarded the following observations:

Having received word that the parcels bought at the Battalion Gift Shoppe had arrived home safely, we remembered that we hadn't chronicled the full doings of that notable show. We'll say that it certainly was a success. We knew that we had a great idea; we knew it really was a winner; but the boys came to light in great style, and supported their own shop to the limit of their paybooks, the credulity of the pay Sergeant, and the outlook of less leave.

The staff consisted of Capt. Col Rigg, the Branch Manager, who was also chief buyer, chief arranger of stock, and chief salesman. (His line of sales talk would sell bathing togs to the eskimos in the middle of winter). Sgt. Allen (of RAP ill-fame) welcomed the guests at the front door, passed them on to the salesmen, then made out the dockets and "fleeced" them for the limit. Pte. J. E. (Slushy) Turner, better known as a bandage artist, was second salesman, and even though he described a pair of scanties as a pair of pyjamas, he must be excused on account of his youthful innocence.

Sgt. Bill Bowden ably performed the duel role of spruiker and "chief mover on". It is hard to say in which role he performed best, but it showed versatility, and his voice improved considerably as the show proceeded. Didgie Clapin started off paying the lads requiring "filoos" to make their purchases, but when he was recalled by higher formation, Len Wintle took over the duties and did good service. An able assistant was "Silver" McClusky. Early in the piece it was he who found the nails, produced a hammer out of thin air, made shop fittings out of the salvage dump, and performed miracles of unravelling of twine. What a man!

Business opened quietly; a good day, but the customers were very shy. Suddenly Jerry entered into affairs. Jealous of the fact that he was precluded from shopping in Alexandria and environs of our up-to-date shop, he petulantly threw over one or two, which landed plop in the mire nearby. At different times, planes (both ours and their's) flew over, but nothing happened to mar the serenity of the show, and business proceeded as usual.

When a few of the officers, such as Major (Now Colonel) Wall, Colonel (Now Brigadier) Evans, and Brigadier Whitehead called round, they were amazed at the show we had, and the display of goods. Each of these gentlemen was prone to remark that of course he knew nothing of these things, but after a few hints from Colin, each one found a mounting parcel of snappy odds and ends as presents for those at home.

It is hard to really realise that this show, the Western Desert Branch of G. J. Coles (as our photos will prove), really was set up and operated some few hundred yards from our own front line, and less than a thousand from Jerry. Can you imagine what Jerry's ideas about those mad Australians must be when they play shop in the midst of war. The success of the show was amply proved with takings of E1100 pounds, and it is good to know that the parcels have arrived home where they will be well appreciated.

Brig. Evans, by the way, visited the Officers' Mess last night, a resplendent vision of scarlet - truly a glittering sight. He asked us, per medium of this paper, to extend his hearty greetings to all in the 2/23rd, and may we, on your behalf, as heartily reciprocate.

We have great pleasure in publishing hereunder, a letter addressed to you all from our popular Padre Porter:

My dear Comrades in Arms,

It is true to say "When springtime comes a young man's thoughts turn to love," and it is equally true also that when Christmas comes, all our thoughts are of home. We often sing the old song "Keep the Home Fires Burning", but it does not require a huge log fire in order to keep real warmth in the home folks' hearts. Unselfish love and devotion of pure hearts means warm hearts that no amount of icicles of bitter cold warfare can affect, really. The ancients of Britain kept "Yuletide" at this season. They heaped up the Yuletide logs on their fires because of the pagan belief that by so doing, they warmed the world when all life was threatened with extinction through extreme cold. Because the Great Creator of mankind gave warmth and love at this season through the Babe of Bethelem, this old world has, and will continue to be, warmed back into sanity through the re-establishment of "Peace and Goodwill among men."

God bless you all, and send us to our hearths and homes in peace in 1943.

Yours sincerely,

Frederick Porter.

Volume 4

CHAPTER 17

AUSTRALIA, 1st May, 1943.

Salutations, fellow Mud'n Bloods! Here we are back again, and this is the first of a new series of attempts to keep you amused by dishing the dirt. This paper has been published in four countries, also at sea, but this is the first time it has been written on Australian soil, and my word, that is a record that gives no end of joyful satisfaction.

It is a vastly changed Battalion to that which used to chuckle over our scandals in Tobruk. Very few old faces left, but in spite of that, we hope all you new Mud'n Bloods will get as much fun out of your Battalion "rag" as the old timers did. See to it that we are kept supplied with contributions. A prize of 10/- will be paid to the contributor of the best item appearing in each issue, and we know of at least one literary Sergeant who is disappointed that Mud & Blood is not going to appear seven times a week. He had reckoned on an extra 3 pounds ten shillings weekly to help pay his grog bill.

By the way, the Padre has received 250 books & novels (classical and modern). The chapel and library is being constructed, and within a few days the books will be available from the bookshelves. It is hoped that the number will be increased from time to time. If you have any books in your possession, and are prepared to loan them to the library, every care of them will be taken. Write to your friends at home for suitable books. ACF will forward parcels to the battalion. For Unit entertainment, books of plays, sketches and dialogues are urgently required. For further information see the Padre.

EARLY THOUGHTS ON THE FUNCTION OF "B" ECHELON —
JUNGLE WARFARE:

Piecing together the stray reports and remarks of the "You'll be
sorry you left the Middle East" variety, one is forced to the conclusion that
at long last nemesis has caught up with, and proposes to smack with a wet
and slimy hand, that portion of the battalion known as "B" Echelon.

Those of you who were forced to sojourn in an area in Tobruk aptly
named Bomb Happy Valley Mark II, will remember the gloomy, hangdog,
tremulous and pouch-eyed sub-humans who were the oldest inhabitants of
that delectable spot, whose sole joy seemed to be in conducting one to view
the bigger and better bomb holes. Apparently they have a counterpart in
New Guinea and environments. Only THEIR contributions to the happiness
and well-being of the warrior is in pointing out wetter water, slimier lime,
junglier jungle, and giving utterance to doleful forbodings as to the playful
habits of the denizen therein.

In this connection it has been remarked that the cooks must be prepared to light a fire under 3 feet of water with one hand, and with the other
ward off attacks by infuriated alligators. A disturbing feature of this pastime
is the noticeable increase in the percentage of treble-voiced cooks in the 7th
Divvy.

These cheerful optimists, whose habit in the past was to apply to the
QM store for anything from a pair of ladies' garters to a 4 engined bomber,
will be chagrined to learn that all stores must now be carried on the shoulders
of a person termed a "Boong". All attempts so far to ascertain whether the
"Boong", like the camel, is divided into the "Pack" and "Riding" varieties
have failed. But surely even the most case hardened General will hesitate
before perpetrating the unpardonable blunder of making a Quartermaster
actually W A L K!! Eager enquiries from a certain section of the cooking
staff re female "Boongs" have met with the rebuffs such premature probes
deserve. Apprehension grows as one hears of the long list of potential playmates ranging from minute multitudinous wrigglers to mosquitoes that keep
cows as pets. One thing is certain, however, and that is that the Round Game
Department will be as firmly entrenched here as on the other side. When
"B" Echelon is up to its eyes in dank wet mud, no fire, no rations, no hope,
and only a few faint bubbles mark the spot where the RQMS and Technical
Sergeant have gone down for the third and last time, at that precise moment
a figure is bound to appear to the besmirched, bemired and bewildered QM
and ask for a return in triplicate, showing the number of tin tacks officially
sentenced US since last Pancake Thursday.

Captain G. Moore.

Went this afternoon, accompanied by their enthusiastic OC, Lieut. Ted Warburton, to inspect the new Auxiliary Platoon. Alas, poor Little Rommel, he has his worries, as has every OC who has a platoon comprising mixed sexes. But his popularity with his troops is unquestioned, as he was literally welcomed with squeals of delight. Was introduced to the leading Lady of the Platoon, who (despite her condition, or maybe because of it) appears to be the apple of Ted's eye. Also met another celebrity up there, but it wouldn't be tactful to tell you anything further concerning him. Cute little individual, however, which probably is responsible for the nomenclature.

Incidentally, Ted is in dire straits looking for a bore (?). We innocently mentioned Lieut. Eric Gibbs' name to him, but it appears that it is another kind of bore that is required. You see, two of the young lady arrivals of yesterday are feeling rather lonesome, and would welcome a little male society. We understand a guard is placed on their lines, however so don't get any ideas.

Talking about the Lady, and her interesting state of health, this paper is running a sweepstakes on the date and number of progeny. Entrance fee 3d. Competition closes 1800 hours Tuesday, 4th May.

Have you ever heard of a cove named PADRE FREDERICK PORTER? Well, he perpetrated the following, and after trial he has been sentenced to recite it at the forthcoming Battalion Concert, that is, if he's finished his CB by then!

When Rommel gave up the Ghost and gathered up his gear
In the East that is called Middle, and next door to Near,
He thought of all the fleshpots, of which his Panzers dreamed
Would be their pighog prize, but, not so it seemed,
Could any so-called invincible Hun break thro' that Ruck
Of tough and tanned young warriors, for they came out from Tobruk.

Then Hitler took up hope in his house in Berchtesgarten,
and called for all his Henchmen, and hastened them to hearten,
Telling them that those same so-called Rats that sat on
His scheme to sack old Cairo, had sailed to sock Nippon.
But Rommel said, "I'm sorry, for us there's no Nile Dancers,
Those darned Australians have kicked the pants from off my Panzers."

Tuning-in to short wave sat Tiger-toothed old Tojo,
Listening-in to lusty cheers bursting from his radio.
"So solly! Curtin has recalled the 9th to fill the cussed gap,
Who join their kith and Yanks to kick back every Jap."
And so the Rats that gnawed and rocked that Little Rommel fellow,
Stand ready now to run rough shod o'er the hide that's always yellow.

ANNOUNCEMENTS:

Today, 1st May (weather permitting) Battalion Camp-fire concert - 1900 hrs.

Sunday - Inter-Unit football match on Atherton Showgrounds, 1400 hrs.
    2/23 v 2 A.G.H.

It is proposed that a MINSTREL PARTY and a CONCERT PARTY be formed in the Unit, names of personnel prepared to take part in either of these parties to be submitted to Sports Officer, giving full particulars as to type of item.

Now, chaps, for a very special announcement in these days of tobacco scarcity. This paper is conducting a competition on the lines of our famous Ode to a Bottle of Beer of Tobruk days. Only this time the Ode is to the Lady Nicotine. Entries must not comprise more than twelve lines. The prize will be a 1 lb. tin of Kentucky Club Pipe or Cigarette tobacco, donated by your Editor. Believe you us, it's a glorious tin of fragrant weed and well worth striving for. Come on, all you budding poets, go to it! And even if you are non smokers, we can get the lucky winner the sum of two pounds for the prize if he prefers. Details of closing date, judging, etc., will be published later. Remember, our last competition attracted entries from Brigadiers downward, but they didn't win it just the same.

Well, cheerio lads, until our next issue, in which we hope to see many of your own contributions. Think of all the beer you can buy with that extra ten bob when you get that local leave that is coming along shortly.

                              J. D. Mulcahy, Editor.

AUSTRALIA, 4th May, 1943.

If not exactly besieged with contributions to this, our second Australian issue of Mud & Blood, we still have a few choice offerings from several contributors of bygone years. Padre Porter, in a spirit of atonement for his last effort, has come to light with the following:-

MARCHING FEET

Were you with us, bygone friends, you Ghosts of Alamein?
Did you gather with us, pals, 'neath trees of the shady lane?
Could you hear those heartening cheers as we swung along the street?
And did your hearts with pride keep time to the big drum's beat?
Were you with us, cobbers all, in the ranks that once were four?
Me thinks you felt the soft caress of confetti thrown from the door.
If so, no doubt your eyes turned right passing the saluting base,
Indeed, then Bill you must have seen the light on your dear one's face.
Proudly she stood in that cheering crowd or did she listen at home?
No matter! we know she does not think you under the sandy loam.

Oh, all you phantoms of Tobruk and Tel el Eisa shades,
March with us yet - lest we forget - as we go down jungle glades,
Your splendid service to our cause, your courage and devotion,
Men sure and steady shall be the Light of Peace on land and ocean.

＊ ＊ ＊ ＊ ＊ ＊ ＊ ＊ ＊ ＊ ＊

Criticism is, no doubt, always welcome, that is when it is construct-
ive, so if we seem a little harsh in our review of Saturday night's Camp Fire
Concert, it is only with an idea of suggesting improvements in future functions of a similar nature. First of all, let us congratulate Lieut. Hughie
McLeod on an excellent job of work under difficult conditions. However,
he committed the unpardonable blunder of not ensuring dry weather, so
off with his head. Sgt. "Dadda" Peck and his merry men were indefatigable
workers, and gave many excellent items, but we suggest that too much use
was made of them. Some of their items were on the long side, and a rendit-
ion of more topical and up to date musical numbers would have been welcomed. Sgt. "Bing" Bridgeford was excellent, and why he was not called
upon for more numbers is beyond us. We could have gone all goofy and
sentimental over such numbers as "Lovely Weekend", and we are quite
sure the boys would have joined in with gusto had he invited them to do so.
Pte. "Speed" Landrigan pleased the boys with his smart recitation re the
steeplechase, and will have to brush up another number, as the boys will
surely want to hear him again. As for the other elocutionist (with the
repertoire of jokes) we suggest he call round and retail some of his cleaner
ones for inclusion in this rag. With better weather, and more time spent in
arranging the programme, we are confident the next concert will be a
whizzer, so all you talented prodigies roll up and give of your best. After
all, even if you are no good, nothing much will happen to you.

HORTICULTURAL NOTE:

Whilst so much work is being put into gardening, a word or two on the old fashioned leek might be useful. There is nothing like having leeks in the garden. You can have them almost anywhere, but they are not very satisfactory facing into the prevailing wind. Many people favour the early morning variety of leek, and often have them in boxes on the window, but having no houses here in the camp, Companies could arrange to have their leeks in cut down kerosene tins outside the door of tents. We do not suggest leeks around cookhouses or orderly rooms, but we would urge them on the weather protected sides of the many trees in the area, or on the camp boundary overlooking the road. Leeks would make a splendid addition to the table at the various messes - We do not advocate the boiling of leeks however. Company gardeners plant now and be assured of an abundance of leeks in the coming cold weather.

"Asphodel"

And now for the first couple of entries in the "Ode to a Smoke" competition. Here they go!

Cigarette! Cigarette!
You are warmer and truer
Than any fond wooer
I've ever met; and yet,
Though I kiss you,
Do you think I will miss you,
With tender regret?

(Not entirely original)

No my friend,
Ere the end,
I will throw you away and forget,
And before you are dead
I've another instead,
For I'm lighting another cigarette.
Oh Yeah?

Major P. E. Spier.

TYRANT MISTRESS

Oh Lady Nicotine, release me from thy spell,
    Much too long I've groaned beneath thy yoke.
Tormented always in this jungle hell,
    Now I'm denied the solace of a smoke.

Sweet tyrant, please have pity on thy slave,
    I assure thee that it is no joke
When every waking hour your joys I crave,
    And beg in vain to be allowed to smoke.

Deep comfort has thou brought me in the past,
But now my weary spirits wrecked and broke,
The future's such, I really feel aghast,
No Love! No beer! No e'en a bloody smoke!

Capt. K. C. Clarke.

Entries are coming only very slowly on the Sweepstake proposed in our last issue. Lieut. Warburton assures us that we'd better not delay the closing date too long, and HE ought to know! Get in your entries. All you need to do is put your name on a piece of paper, together with date, time and number, and enclose 3d. By the way, the Lady is on view outside parade hours, so if an inspection will assist your judgement, go to it. By the way, Doc Davies is debarred from entering this sweep, as he would have a distinct advantage.

In our next issue we will have something to tell you of the "Suggestions Club" and the benefits and amenities that may ensue as a result of their ideas. The C.O. has listened sympathetically and readily to their suggestions, and every effort is being made to put them into effect. More anon about this!

Some of you may remember our vain efforts to teach shorthand to some of the troops in Tobruk. Possibly inspired by our example, the powers that be have inaugurated an Army Educational Scheme. For some months past this scheme has been in operation, and we shall be hearing more about it in our Battalion soon. Facilities whereby men of all ranks may undertake a course by correspondence will be extended, which should prove of inestimable benefit to them after the war is over. Further information will be available soon, and an officer will be appointed to supervise.

To the Editor, Mud'n Blood.

Would you kindly publish the following appeal to all members of 2/23 Aust. Inf. Bn.

Let's provide our own entertainment.

After spending a few weeks in this area, it must be obvious to all that, if we are to have entertainment of an evening, it shall in most cases, have to be provided by ourselves.

Here are a few suggestions. Should they appeal to you, don't just forget them, see your Unit Sports Officer or Padre and help them to make your evenings more enjoyable.

1. Companies to have camp fire concerts - it is here that talent will be found.
2. Inter-company debates.

Come on 2/23rd, let's have the fun of creating our own entertainment!

Sports Officer.

AUSTRALIA, 8th May, 1943.

Onlookers yesterday were somewhat mystified when Capt. Ted Tietyens, whilst crossing the river with his men, suddenly dived into the water, fully clad, and disappeared from view. The majority thought that it was a new and amusing circus trick, whilst a few concluded he had merely fallen in, and stood by grinning broadly. Shortly thereafter the wet and disappointed skipper reappeared, but within a matter of minutes repeated his exploit. This time he emerged triumphant, with a large cat fish clamped firmly in his jaws. No! not for him idle circus capers; he was merely demonstrating how a "bushed" man could obtain sustenance in time of need. It is understood the idea came to him in a dream, when he imagined himself at the Melbourne Acquarium watching the seals feeding. The only drawback he confessed later, was the fact that he swallowed a mouthful of water, a thing he hasn't done for years. As a result of his prowess, he is now hailed throughout the battalion as the amphibian (s)kipper.

OH! YOU BEAUT.

This jungle's a wonderful place, now isn't it? There's birds, snakes, stinging plants and vines which stop your progress like a straight left. And there's leeches, have you ever seen anything like them? Do you know that just the other night a party from "C" Company was bivouaced up in the hills. 0600 hours the next morning and there was a terrific row between two of the boys, one accusing the other of stealing the oil out of his oil bottle and his pullthrough. It was not until the leading scout stumbled over a two-foot-six leech that the mystery of the missing oil and pullthrough was solved. That leech had opened the butt-trap and drawn the oil from the oil bottle. How do we know? Why, the weight of the pullthrough was still hanging from the leech's mouth!

Lieut. H. McLeod.

A FRIEND IN WEED

They speak of a dead man's vengeance,
They whisper a deed of hell,
In the realm of Ali Baba
And this is the thing they tell.

In a dense and a leech ridden jungle,
Neath the blue of a northern sky,
Lie the bones of an Aussie soldier,
Who had crawled away to die.

He had left his wife and dear ones,
To join the bulldog breed,
For he could not soldier onwards,
Without his ounce of weed.

Lieut. Ted Warburton.

R. A. P. CHATTER

It gives us great pleasure to be asked to contribute an article to our popular battalion paper, Mud & Blood.

The R.A.P. has been for the last week a centre of attraction for several reasons. The item of paramount importance seems to be the horticultural effort so ably designed by Tom Lincoln, and believe us, fellows, we are not attempting to compete for the fiver; our effort is to create a rustic setting for you in which to consume that delightful amber beverage (not what you're thinking either!) "Mist Tussi", and the inevitable Aspros guaranteed to cure any disease known to mankind.

WE can't help being "Happy in the service" when we have delightful clients who inform us that urine is as effective as some of our expensive and mysterious lotions. Next we have the B Class Handicap, one of the most popular events of the season, with entrants from most of the well known company stables in the Battalion. I am regretful in informing the cooks that their popular contestant, "Doc" is scratched after witnessing his trials with the hygiene squad, not to mention the inside information we heard about the Doc seriously considering a bromide tonic for their anaemic nomination.

After a strenuous leave, Zubes were on parade for maintenance, with military snap and precision. Some magnificent physical specimens appear on this parade, as at the high port they march in. The inspecting officer casts a critical eye. A sigh of relief. No complaints.

Slushy.

LADY NICOTINE

Dear Lady Nicotine, to me you are the Queen,
Of that fair world of pleasure full of dreams.
What use are hours of leisure, without the fragrant pleasure,
That you bestow upon us, Queen of Queens.

Yet your favours now are few, Oh, what are we to do,
If you deny the joy that we so crave.
A smoke we beg of you, a cigarette or two,
Another we will make from the butts we save.

They say 'tis okey-doke, Gum leaves or tea to smoke,
And from a piece of cane you'll get a draw,
But we upon our knees, Ask you, dear Lady, please,
Do not deny us solace in this war.

VX17445, A. A. Coles.

And the Band played! Nothing unusual about that; but it was good
to hear the strains of their evening harmony a few days ago when they visited
our artillery neighbours just down the road. Nor were the Arty wallers alone
in their appreciation, for our worthy (but, we regret to add, somewhat tact-
less) RMO was heard to remark to his Arty companion, "Well, Major, you've
certainly got a decent band - almost on a par with our own!" Had the Doc
looked closer at the players blowing their trumpets on the improvised Band
Stand, he would have recognised his one and only "Dadda" doing his stuff.
At all events the entertainment was most enjoyable, as also was the hospitality subsequently offered to the visitors. Let us have more of this visiting,
for it engenders a healthy atmosphere of good fellowship between Units.

Lieut. Len Wenborn.

Looking around these days, one finds very few razor blades and
excessive facial fungus, and it does bring vividly to mind thoughts of other
days when enjoying a well earned leave, we allowed ourselves to wander
into the Cairo barbers shop. Remember the day when you walked hesitat-
ingly to the entrance of the barbers shop, there to be seized by a daring
looking piece, over rouged, over powdered and over mascared, and before
you realised where you were, your body was in the prone and the lather
on your face. How the "bint" used to hover around giving very suggestive
and inviting lifts to her eyebrows, and dabbing a bit of scent on your shirt.
The man of tonsorial art, spits upon the strop, and carries on with the job
of sharpening the razor. Then a hot towel is suddenly jammed over your
face and you wriggle like hell, not so much from the heat, as from the
suddenness of the attack, and the endeavour to free your nostrils from the

musty smelling towel. More lather, and the barber swings his razor in a few circles and flips, presses the soap on the side of your head with the ball of his thumb, and sets to, to relieve your face of its bristly fungus. Dangerously he flashes the razor close to your face, grins, showing a mouthful of teeth every colour except red, and breathes garlic, hashish and yoghurt into your face, at the same time enquiring "Good razor, Dig?" Afraid to move for fear of parts other than bristles connecting with the blade, you grunt in the affirmative, despite the fact that the whiskers are being torn or dragged out. The shave is over, and a mixture of lemon juice, cheap eau de cologne and water is splashed on your face. Following immediately on the smarting liquid is a great blob of cream, more lard than anything else, which is very vigorously and none too carefully rubbed into your face. "Massage Sir?" "No" is your answer, but you get the massage just the same. Sparks fly from the glass violet ray outfit, and you jump very uncomfortably in your chair as your "dial" takes current and heat on the isolated patches. Watching out of the corner of your eye, you glimpse a "wallud" with a dirty cracked enamel basin, and a-once-upon-a-time-white towel, and a battered blue kettle of water steaming and sooty on a wheezy old primus. The towel goes into the basin, the water on the towel - two black hands juggle the hot towel across to the chair, and it is flopped without ceremony at nearly boiling point on your face. More of the uncertain eau de cologne mixture and then some powder. Suddenly you shoot upright with the movement of the chair, and before you can protest, clippers are running up the back of your neck and relieving you of your wool. You originally went for a shave. You are getting the whole works. Fussing and fiddling and opening and closing the scissors on empty air, the barber makes a great show of performing a great feat. The scalp is given what it pleases the barber to call "friction" - highly perfumed oil is rubbed into the remaining locks; the hairs in the nose are snipped out, and the space in between the eyebrows lightly touched with clippers or razor. The finishing touches are applied with the corner of the towel dipped in scent. On rising from your seat of suffering you are heavily handled by a lad and a straw brush to relieve you of the pieces of hair. The barber bows and smiles, still showing the awful molars - the boy bows and grins, and the "bint" beams as you walk to the pay desk. It costs you nearly half a quid and you smell like the Monkey's Palace of Scents, and your face feels as if it has been sandpapered and coated with stiffening varnish.

"Asphodel"

It is advised that Sgt. Daines of HQ Company won the prize of 10/- for his contribution "Horticultural Notes - Leeks".

AUSTRALIA, 15th May, 1943.

Quite a lot of news to relate in this issue. First let us tell all those friends of Lieut. Harry Orr, (brother of our Pioneer Sergeant, Jack Orr), who was taken prisoner badly wounded in July last, that word has been received that he is on his way home, having been included in a recent exchange of prisoners. He should be in sunny Australia in a matter of weeks, and it is hoped that with the skilled medical attention he will receive here, he will soon be restored to health. Naturally Sgt. Jack is going around these days with a beaming countenance, and we rejoice with him.

Someone has been whispering of a 2/23 Battalion Ball, to be held in Atherton on Monday evening. We are not quite sure whether our leg was being pulled or not, but if the news is true, then we can easily imagine the furore within the breasts of all our young eligible bachelors. The C.O. mentioned the project a few days back, and stated there would be a goodly array of ladies, and if there were not sufficient to go round, the old pest of "tap" dancing would be resorted to. You know the sort of thing - just as you've exchanged names, complimented her on her dancing, and are just about to suggest that it's much too hot inside - some grinning ape taps you on the shoulder and your partner is whisked away from you, and you have to start the whole business over again with someone else, and with like results. As for us, thank Bacchus, our hobby's beer!

The Battalion Concert last Saturday evening went with a bang from the word go, and a most enjoyable programme ensured the enjoyment of all present. Someone had the foresight to ensure the absence of the Padre, and the wit (if somewhat pungent) was at least refreshing. But then, our idea of humour has always been on the low side.

Following on this function came HQ Company's Concert on Wednesday night, and now, we do know for a certainty, where all the Battalion bawdy jokes emanate. However, despite this, a very varied programme was presented with perhaps the limelight being a Quiz Contest, with teams competing from each Platoon; HQ Platoon collared the dough. The Battalion organ received its initiation, Capt. McMaster making the night air hideous with much wails and caterwaulings in quick time. Someone ought to let Brig. Evans know that the Sig. Platoon is coming good, as for two consecutive nights now, the amplifying system rigged up by them has worked without a hitch. Shades of Lovell!

GERTIE'S STAG PARTY:

By means and methods as yet unknown, Gertie managed to ring in on a stag party held way out in the jungle midst slush, "stanishwire" vines and leeches. Gert led the young bucks out, and they seemed to be a little unhappy as Gert ripped lively, lithesome and none too winningly through the jungle.

Now, as a rule, stags hate to be interfered with, and one huge fellow who had retired to the fastness of a huge tree, attracted Gert's attention. Gert went on the prod contrary to all rules of stagging, and started poking at this big retiring fellow with a huge pole - The old stag stood the insults for a time, but all of a sudden there was a terrific bellow, and the stag came charging down the tree at Gert. It is regretted that we cannot determine as from whence the bellow emanated - from the stag or Gert - as our reporter was well lubricated with some very potent liquid obtainable from the Sergeants' Mess. Had it not been for the timely and spontaneous effort of "Jungle Joe" Wylie, Gert would have most certainly been crushed neath the huge and many antlered and cumbersome body of the once retiring stag.

With great ceremony, pomp, wailing and ho ho ho's, the body was carried back "Wog" funeral fashion, and is now shackled to a large tree in HQ lines, and it is Gert's daily mission to stand with rapturous gaze, so mindful of a cat going up to a salmon tin, at her latest conquest. And Gert's not bulling, either.   "Asphodel".
(Editor's Note)
(Never mind! we share a tent with Lieut. "G" Gibbs, and we think the stag ferns outside the tent are just too sweet!).

We were going to make this a special "jungle" issue, inspired mainly from the doings of the mixed party from BHQ, the QM's department and sundry others (including your worthy editor) who went bivouacing with Capt. Kayler-Thomson (our imported jungle artist) a few nights ago. However, our reflections came to us in verse, and are not yet completed. They will appear in a subsequent issue under the heading "The Tris and Tribs of Jungle Jim". Great idea this being an Editor, you can always get your own stuff published.

Here is our latest entry in the Ode Competition, coming from the highly talented pen of RSM Dick Taylor-Ward.

"CIGARETTE"

Thou ancient boon of comfort loving men,
    Thou satisfier of the hungry heart,
What beauty's in thy shape and thy smoke,
    What silent tribute to the old earth's art,
Thou slow, insidious charmer of the sense,
    Thou slender shape of brownest loveliness,

What rapture fills the simple hearts of men,
  To stroke thy form with tenderest caress,
Now gulp the fragrant incense of thy breath,
  And watch the blue-grey tumbling vapours roll,
Such pleasures cheat mere thought, thou libertine
  And mistress of man's vague and restless soul.

C. Taylor-Ward, RSM.

Original? Well, more or less.

For information re brand of cigarettes that inspired the above, see Editor, contributor is busy!

Inter Company debates are being organised, and all those who would like a good argument, either to participate in, or listen to, should be interested in these ear bashing contests. BHQ are drawn to meet HQ Company on Sunday evening in the recreation hut at 1845 hours. BHQ team will be led by RSM Dick Taylor-Ward, and HQ Company by Sgt. Bill Daines. (Ye Gods! this pair alone could fill the biggest gasometer in Australia). The subject to be discussed is a contentious one that no doubt you have all argued about amongst yourselves - "Is the present strategy 'Beat Hitler First' in the best interests of Australia". BHQ say it is, HQ Company say "No", the spin of a coin having decided their views upon this very important question. We have cabled Messrs. Churchill and Roosevelt not to terminate their conferences pending this debate being held, as it may bring to light new facts that may well determine their future plans.

A Battalion song sheet is being prepared, and will be issued shortly to as many men as possible, so that they may participate in community singing when any of the newer melodies is suggested. At the present time no one seems to know the words of anything more up to date than "Home on the Range", which used to be hummed by Grandma on her honeymoon. Anyone knowing the words of the following, please send them on to the Editor, also the words of any other song they would like included in the song sheet.

1. Deep in the Heart of Texas
2. Tangerine
3. I'll Walk beside you
4. One dozen roses
5. Elmers Tune
6. When they sound the last all clear
7. Yi Yi love you very much
8. Begin the Beguine

9.   Mexicalli Rose
10. A Lovely Weekend
11. White Cliffs of Dover
12. Nightingale Sang in Berkley Square

POST – WAR

I thought when we were torn apart
    The sun would fall from heaven,
The moon be hurled down the abyss
    With stars and planets seven.

How could I dream the time would come
    When I'd murmer casually,
As I came across your photograph
    "I wonder..............which was she?"

Lieut. H. McLeod.

Volume 5

CHAPTER 18

AUSTRALIA, 6th June, 1944.

Despite the interest in this Second Front skirmish, we consider that our "Battalion Paper" must go to press. It is over twelve months since our last publication, but of course that delay was caused by that cruise to the fascinating tropics. We were so impressed with the said tropics, that we are anxious to attend any course of two years duration in Victoria Barracks to further our knowledge of jungle life.

Now that we have dropped the hint (C.O. please note) we will proceed. Many Mud & Blooders are new to us, and we wish you all "welcome". May you flourish, and may your tobacco ration be increased. Jack Carden, the Canteen bloke, has walked so far searching for wood that he has B Classed his fetlock. He didn't want a B Class, but the Doc simply insisted. We think the Doc misunderstood Jack. He really wanted a D.

(Ken Lovell)
(our new Ed.)

Who is this bloke shoving in...........er - "Sorry, sir". The C.O. has something to say chaps.

"After a long vacation whilst the Battalion was engaged in operations in New Guinea, we welcome an old member back to our happy community - MUD & BLOOD. Born en route to the Middle East in 1940, this paper has made fame with the Battalion throughout it's theatres of operations.

"Since the last issue of this publication, the Battalion has suffered

a great loss in the late C.O., Lt.Col. R.E. Wall, officers
and men who gave their lives in the New Guinea oper-
ations---------in silence, we remember them.

"To all new members of the battalion, I extend a hearty welcome to our ranks, and sincerely
trust that you will soon, if not already, be imbued
with the traditional spirit of comradeship shared by
Albury's Own.

"I know that the past cheerfulness and comradeship displayed in the pages of this publication will flourish
in the forthcoming editions, and ask you one and all to
support it to the full, and join with me in wishing it continued success."

> F. A. G. Tucker, Lt.Col.
> Comd. 2/23 Aust. Inf. Bn.

STRANGE AS IT MAY SEEM

After nigh on four years as a Victorian Battalion, although adopted
by New South Wales, something peculiar has at last crept into our midst. We
have noticed this strange practice on such occasions as when we have been
"bludging" at LTD Brisbane, and after watching the antics for a few moments
have sadly shaken our skull and muttered "Poor Cows, they'll learn." We
have in the past few weeks been treated to the spectacle called Rugby. This
game has various objects, the main one of which is (a) to get as dirty as
possible (b) to ignore the fact that a football is used, and (c) to be like a
divorcee, and always get your man. Appropriately enough, the fields odd
man is called the referee. This takes one back to the days of Santell, Meeske,
Hackenschmidt and other such lions of the wrestling era. As far as we can
gather, they score in this game by tries (we'll say they do) which eventually
become converted. A rather dim view of this latter practice is taken by Mr.
Chifley and the Padres' Union.

> A.M.P.

SPORTING NEWS:

28th May: The firsts had a decisive win over 2/43 Bn. and ran out easy
            winners 14 goals 8 to 8 goals 6.
            The seconds upheld the traditions and also tossed their
            opponents, but only just - 8 goals 7 to 8 goals 5.

4th June: In the words of the classics - we got a bath from our old rivals 2/48 Bn. Out played, out marked and out of breath, we were all out in mustering 5 goals 10 to 19 goals 15. But what of the bloke who wagered 6 pounds at quarter time? Maleesh! he will get it back when next we meet them.
The seconds jogged on to another victory, 14 goals 12 to 4 goals 2.

Rugby League:
28 May: Imagine the Battalion fielding a Rugby side! To the cynics it may appear a colossal nerve, but believe it or not, we won 13- 0. Congratulations to these foreigners who play this strange game.

4 June: And just to prove how good they are, the foreigners won again 20 - 0. Experts who understand this peculiar game claim that the premiership is "in the bag".

Cricket:
28 May: We lost the first match of the season after a close game against 2/48 Bn. who scored 84 against our 65. Doug Ikin (HQ) topped our score with 14. Jack Brady (D) and Barney Loomes (C) shared the bowling honours.

3 June: We broke our duck and scored 9 - 197 in 110 minutes. Len Mortimer (HQ) 30, Don Ward (D) 20, Mark Custance (HQ) 28, and J. Moore (C) 22 were our best with the bat. 2/32 Bn. knocked up 180 in 105 minutes. Jack Brady took 6 - 67 and Barney Loomes 3 - 47.

LOCAL FLASHES

HEARD IN "C" COMPANY MESS:

"Ashes to Ashes and Dust to Dust,
If Heaton don't get us - Trickett must!

Is there anyone in "A" Company who can tell us:- "WHO IS ESME?"
We all get behind in these matters sometimes.

Someone asked us if the Row Bird lays blue speckled eggs?

* * * * * * * * * *

The Python of HQ is an amazing creature. It plays a ukelele, and also writes shaggy doggerel. Here's a sample:

THERE'S DOUGH IN IT

We offer a prize of 10/- for the best entry submitted in our contest "Ode to the Atebrine".

Now, you budding Longfellows, Shelleys and Wordsworths, let your imagination run riot, but keep it (fairly) clean. Entries close 22 June 44.

Speaking of keeping it clean, we must tell you of an experience of one of our lads who was courting a sweet young thing. Her mother entered the parlour unexpectedly, "Well I never" she says, and up pipes our S.Y.T. "But mother, you must have." Dear, dear!

GLAMOUR

I wandered to a cafe where the night life sank its port,
A sort got onter me and said "What unit are yer sport?"
I come from 9 Division but I'm going back from leave
Awe, just a Glamour Boy she said, some fightin's what yer need.

You'se gents wot stay around the town with shielas on yer knees
I'm right awake to you'se she said and I ain't 'ard ter please.
Me boy friend in New Guinea put me wise, you'se were not there
Bert's in a mobile laundry and he's done his bloody share.

When I arsk 'im in a letter if you'se blokes 'ad 'ad a fight
'E writes and sez the Glamour Boys had never been in sight
It just shows, yer can't trust papers, 'cause me Berties in the know
E's campaignin' at Port Moresby - where you'se birds oughter go.

Now you all have an idea of what we're looking for, shoot your jokes, verse, articles and what not into:- WOII FOX A Company, Sgt. NUGENT B Company, WOII ROBINSON C Company, Sgt. KENNY D Company, and WOII NETTLETON HQ.

THIS IS YOUR PUBLICATION — USE YOUR TALENT — AND
CONTRIBUTE WEEKLY.
                                                                          Ed.

AUSTRALIA, 16th June, 1944.

We can remember, way back in the days gone by, being swept along Spencer Street in a jostling crowd, groping a path down dark side streets, paying a couple of bob, and passing through turnstiles to sit on hard benches from whence to gaze with bated breath at two pugs pawing the air in the West Melbourne Stadium. Last Thursday night, we didn't have to shove or pay for that great promoter, Darky Edwards stacked on a show worthy of

Dick Lean's best, right on our own doorstep. The talent displayed in the bouts was rather varied, and the boxers seemed to wave to their cobbers in the audience very often. Some of these waves occasionally dashed however, against flesh and bone, and judging by the RAP's line up next day, the gloves weren't filled with feathers.

Someone did suggest that Jerry and Tex were punch drunk, but that's impossible - we haven't any punch in the Mess, and if we did, who the hell would drink it when there is "threepenny dark" to be had.

All in all, a splendid show, and congratulations to the lads who ducked under the ropes and threw the punches. The results are listed below:

Pte. PENS	BHQ	8 - 7	d Pte. HARRIS	HQ	9 - 4	on pts.
Pte. HALEY	B Coy	10 - 7	d Pte. FINLAYSON	B	10 - 1	on pts.
Pte. McQUEEN	HQ	10 - 1	d Pte. PYERS	B	10 - 0	on pts.
Pte. HAYES	HQ	10 - 6	Pte. ELLIS	C	9 -13	Draw
Pte. McEWAN	D	9 -13	d Pte. HOLMES	D	11 - 9	on pts.
Pte. MALOUF	D	13 - 2	d Pte. LADLOW	B	12 -13	on pts.

Company notes are flowing in, and several contain news of (envious) farewells to old-timers who have left to return to industry etc. Some mysterious types tossed the Board and convinced the Doc that they were too old. These latter, too old types, usually get married immediately. "Too Old?" Jimmy (China) Field, Rupe Hickey (HQ), Sgt. Forbes Kemp (D), have gone back to the cactus, whilst Sgts. Abie Armstrong and Vic Bennett have gone to other units, but no doubt will sadly miss their cobbers, who wish 'em all the best. Lieut. Peter Hook hooked a B Class, and has since departed to become a cut-lunch Commando.

And now may we depart from the straight and narrow to tell you of this true happening during a recent lecture by the medical people. The subject was M & B tablets, and it was explained that each step in the experimental chain was numbered hence, M & B 601, 602 etc. One cunning lad remarked "Cripes, they had early success in finding the pill to defeat constipation."

LOCAL FLASHES:

Out of the 102 sizes in uniforms issued by the "Q" Store, who gets the other 100?

TODAY'S CASUALTY LIST:

From recent operations, Sgt. RON LEES did NOT return to base.

In D Company there's a Sergeant who asked an artist bloke to paint him. Unfortunately, this Michaelangelo was sacked as a painter, and heartbroken, turned to verse, and gradually got verser and verser. He calls his lament the "IMMORTAL SERGEANT".

A certain Sergeant haunts our lines
His voice is like a light that shines
Though very short he's always heard
At early morn just like a bird.

We all enjoy his subtle wit
At times, he's rather good at it
Comes out with wise-cracks like a clown
Although he has been known to frown.

His rolling gait and swinging motion
Like a bouncing cork on the rolling ocean
Especially when he's got one under
His voice resembles that of thunder.

At times he shouts and raves aloud
Enough to hold the largest crowd
It just depends on time and mood
He may come out with something crude.

Sometimes he reads us GRO
Para one, oblique stroke so and so
He reels them off just like a book
Enough to make the dumbest look.

Like Bantam Rooster with eyes aglow
He frowns and fossicks to and fro
His brood of fledgings dressed in green
A finer brood he's never seen.

But though he's small his heart is big
Although at times we think he's a gig
In days to come we'll laugh and chortle
Of our little Sergeant. He's IMMORTAL.

A.W.L. Bishop, D Coy.

In response to our quest for poets, we have received a number of entries in the "Ode to the Atebrine". Styles vary, and two are published below as samples:-

Oh! Atebrine, Oh! Atebrine;
To whom the Medico prays;
You Oppressor! You Depressor!
You prolonger of my fevered days
How I hate you! Hate you! Atebrine.

Oh! Atebrine, Oh! Atebrine;
Dressed in your cellophane so gay
You're tempting, alluring, and to my fevered brow
Your hand steals swift and smoothing
Just to prolong my torture till another day.
You are false - My Atebrine.

Oh! Atebrine, Oh! Atebrine,
I devour you every day;
Till my fever has abated, and my senses fairly swim
You are hateful! Distasteful!
But I would not be without you.
My little Yellow - Atebrine.

                                        Sgt. Ron Lees.

An anonymous post submits:-

Oh little pill of yellow hue
We used to laugh and joke at you.
But now we all give you your due,
Dear Atebrine.

When home on leave we were afraid,
Of rumours of your power to jade
A man's desire for escapade
False, Atebrine.

All the smart guys surely warned us
That we would soon be down with jaundice
Your yellow tint it was, adorned us
My Atebrine.

We proved it wrong - or did our best
Letters daily prove the test,
"I'm knitting bootees and a vest"
Oh Atebrine.

With your aid we'll win this war
And keep the Nip from Aussies' shore
We'll shoulder arms no -----------more
Thanks Atebrine!

Shake it up with those entries now, and don't forget the 10/- prize for the best Ode. Cheerio till next week.

Ed.

SPORTING NEWS:

Aussie Rules:

June 11:   After a thrilling game, our senior team just held on long enough to defeat 2/43 Bn. by one point. The outstanding feature of the match was the brilliant exhibition of umpiring. Congrat's "Umpie", we vote it the best seen since Jack McMurray. Unfortunately the seconds lost, but they battled well - 5 goals 16 to the opponents 9 goals 10.

The Officers' team defeated the Officers of 2/48 Bn. - 5 goals 15 and one broken ankle, to 3 goals 4 and 18 broken hearts.

Rugby League:

Well! The foreigners did it again, 15 - 10. Hey! They're not bad. What about giving 'em some support next week?

Cricket:

Against the Field Ambulance, the firsts gained an outright win by an innings and 29 runs. Lieut. Lovell (HQ) 60 not out, Don Ward (D) 29. Jack Brady (D) 25, were the batsmen to score best, and Jack also collected 6 - 20. Don Ward skittled the tail-enders and took 3 - 1, the cad! The seconds won again with 118 against a Field Ambulance 64. Johnston topped the score with 46 - Cornell (HQ) 22. Roger Dowell (HQ) got the hat-trick and finished up with 7 for 20. Good show.

AUSTRALIA, 23rd June, 1944.

Greetings Mud & Blooders. Another week has slipped by, and we have moved a fraction nearer to our Dedman Zoot Suits. 'Tis indeed a slow progress, but a sure one. We were just casting our minds back over the years gone by, when in walked our worthy RQMS, the clever exponent of the art of "chercher la femme". As well as being cunning at "tiggy" (if we can call it such) he is rather versatile in that he has decided to write for us.

FOUR YEARS AGO:

As this month of June draws to a close, the minds of many Mud'n Bloods are looking back through the varied experiences of the years to the parallel month of 1940, when it seemed that the old world in which we had been enjoying ourselves would crumble about us. We never really thought this would happen, and to ensure that it could not, chaps from farms, factories and offices flocked from towns throughout the length and breadth of Victoria for reception points at the Caulfield Race Course and Royal Park. There were similar movements in the other States, and no one counted the cost. If the intervening years have passed slowly to those of us who have moved about: and the time dragged more for the people - especially the womenfolk - at home. At the outset we could not forecast the course or duration of the war; neither could we anticipate that the years would be relieved by opportunities to return home on leave at least twice.

Before the close of June 1940, a thousand men from Caulfield and Royal Park were camped in the Albury Showgrounds. When the 2/23 Aust. Inf. Bn. "Albury's Own" was formed there the following August, there were born those lasting friendships that were the basis of an enduring Unit spirit and tradition. It may be of interest to new Mud'n Bloods to know that the Battalion's first colour patch was made in the shape of a diamond - chocolate over red - hence the well known term, "Mud and Blood". Across the span of years we now look from our "darkest hour" to the invasion of Europe, which now keeps us close to the loud speakers at news time, and which, we have the confidence to believe, will lead to the victorious peace that is the first goal of the United Nations. Although our task is not yet finished, Mud'n Bloods can feel with simple pride that they have shared in the "blood, tears, sweat and toil".

A. P. Reynolds.

So much interest has been aroused in our "Ode to the Atebrine" that the Brigadier has decided to extend the field of competitors, and now there is a Brigade competition with the prizes of 2 pounds and 1 pound for the best entries. In the future, all entries submitted to Mud and Blood will be forwarded to Brigade. Naturally we can't publish them all at once, so we have selected one at random.

ATEBRINE!

A tiny pill so round and small
Although distasteful, loved by all
The way you're loathed is but a sin
For you're immortal, Atebrine.

You're there in almost every place
An honest boon to the Allied Race
From Tropic Hell and Jungle Green
The men you've saved are plainly seen.

The many lives you help to save,
While men in grips of fever rave
With aching limbs and yellow skin
They all adore you - Atebrine.

From forward line to A.G.H.
There's not a doubt you've earned your place
Among the heroes of the Ranks
To you, Oh Atebrine, Our thanks!

And when at last this war is won
We'll not forget a job well done
By you, elusive, yellow pill
Our humble thanks - We love you still.

                              A.W.L. Bishop

We have decided to cancel the closing date of 22nd June, 1944 for our Battalion Competition, so keep sending in your entries.

This week's Battalion Parade was surely a "unique" affair. The RMO's right arm was so tired after taking the salute at the march past, that he had to drink the hospital brandy with the aid of his left arm. A truly sad affair. When the C.O. blasted us poor creatures for the exhibition displayed, one of our mighty Sig. Platoon uttered "What does he want for six bob a day? - the ----------Black Watch!" Looks like a bowler hat for "Sunny".

SPORTING NEWS:

Aussie Rules: The first 18 annihilated RAE 30 goals 13 to 4 goals 6. We might suggest to the Sappers that they use booby traps, mines and bull-dozers next time we meet. The Seconds also had a field day, and defeated 2/7 Field Amb. 19 goals 10 to 2 goals 4.

Rugby: We are so impressed with the efforts being put up by our first and second teams, that we have decided to refrain from referring to them as "foreigners". The foreign cows! The Firsts still go on undefeated. Their latest victims 2/3 Field

Amb. were beaten 5 points to 3. The Seconds in a scratch match (an appropriate name) defeated the gang over the road 10 points to 9.

Cricket: The First XI had another outright victory, defeating 2/43 Bn. by 7 wickets and 5 runs. Our best performers were left-handers Jack Brady (again) 6 for 12, and Roger Dowell 4 for 18. Tom Andrews 34 topped the score of the batsmen.

Boxing: Unfortunately the race meeting upset our boxing programme, but the great Darky provided some good entertainment nevertheless. The results are as follows:

Pte. Harris	(HQ)		Pte. Pens	(BHQ)	Draw.
Pte. McQueen	(HQ)	defeated	Pte. Hamilton	2/43 Bn.	TKO.
Pte. Ladlow	(B)	defeated	Pte. Modie	2/24 Bn.	on points
Pte. Dempsey	(D)	defeated	Pte. Piper	2/24 Bn.	on points
Pte. McEwan	(D)	defeated	Pte. Finlayson	(B)	on points

A letter received from Lieut. Barney Grogan who went "in the bag" at Tobruk, discloses that he, after escaping to Switzerland, has become very interested in ski-ing, in fact he has skied so much that he has married one. A Swiss she, no less. Good hunting Barney, and we hope you never miss your Swiss.

A real jungle man gives us the "griff" on how to become "jungleated"

THE JUNGLE FIGHTER'S LAMENT

Once when we were soldiers bold to Queensland we did go
To learn the art of jungle war in the most modern way they know,
We didn't know when we arrived how hard 'twas going to be
But now, after weeks of bloody hell there's not much left of me.
They double us down to a mountain stream and there's many a curse and sigh
For there's not a man in this jungle heat who wouldn't lay down to die.
We've climbed great cliffs and mountains, swam rivers long and wide,
Crawled through "stanashwy" till the skin wore off our hide.
We've marched over miles of roadway, taken gullies on the run,
Till the bleeding packs upon our backs feel more than half a ton.
Our bones are stiff, our muscles sore, it's quite apparent why
Old soldiers simply fade away - They ain't got time to die!

Here's a shaggy dog to go on with -

A bull picked up a ladies glove and strolled slowly (obviously the old bull) over to a heifer:

"Pardon me, dear --------- you've dropped your brassiere".

Which brings us to the end of this week's issue. Entries are rather slow in coming in, and we would like a bigger effort to be made. Come now "write that down McPherson" and be in it.

Ed.

AUSTRALIA, 7th July, 1944.

Mud'n Bloods all - hear ye! 'Tis a tale of thrilling adventure we are about to tell - still thy nerves and hearken.

Way back in days of old there lived a man who was called Robin Hood. Little did we know that when he died his spirit would live on. But on it has lived, and what is more, has crept into the skin of one of us. He is called Robin Sedgehood, and a better archer ne'er was seen.

One day Robin blew upon his clarion and called together his Merry Men in green. The jungle tingled with suspense. Robin drew himself up and roared, "For inspection port bows"! There was a click and a twang as the bows clipped forward with amazing precision. Poor Friar Chrystal Tuck had a dirty bow, and was so embarrassed that he shot his arrow into the rear of Long John Hjorth, and down went Long John. Maid Marion McMinn dropped her long bow, ripped her jerkin into shreds, and bandaged Long John's wound. Consternation reigned, and there were so many S I Ws (self inflicted wounds) after that, that Maid Marion had to be issued with a new jerkin. The men of Dirty King Ron on the neighbouring hill took advantage of the situation, and attacked. Fortunately the only casualties were the cow that got tangled up with Dirty King Ron's booby traps and curdled her milk, and the poor leech that fell for an anaemic infanteer, and died of starvation.

But soft, let us away from the Forests of Sherwood, and back to camp.

"Saida, George" greets us the moment we poke our nose into the place. "Shove this in your Blood and Thunder"! Why, it's the dear old Python again, and he produces "Bounce out".

BOUNCE OUT

Ah No! what is it I hear
To penetrate this drowsy ear
Thro' misty fog and dew
Tis some rare jest, a merry prank
To draw from our forgotten bank
A battered smile or two
Or three.

It seems but half an hour ago
With daylight coupons running low
I slumbered peacefully
Now something in the atmosphere
Has brought me wide awake with fear
OhGod! it just can't be
Reveille.

Python.

We are a "wake up" to this Reveille business. In fact we know such a lot about life, that we intend to start our Dolly Dicks' column. Our first letter came to us this week from "Worried Curley", who writes:-

Dear Miss Dicks,

Every night I dream I am in a harem surrounded by beautiful girls. I always appear as a Nubian slave in these dreams, and I am worried, and would like to know what to do?

Dear, dear, Curley,

My heart bleeds for you. If you are what I think you are in that Harem, Boy, you just can't do a ------------thing!

D.D. glad to answer questions.

Perhaps we should move to the sporting events of the week after that.

Aussie Rules:	In a fast moving game, our Firsts defeated 2/24 Bn. by 19 goals 5 to 10 goals 9. Best players: Fred Hassett, "Butch" Merton, "Tichy" Ellis, Jack Rice, Bill Meaney and Lieut. "Sunny" Holt. Seconds defeated the Workshop's team 12 goals 16 to 6 goals 11. Officers: Our Officers (minus Sam Brownes) defeated 2/48 Bn. Officers 8 goals to 2 - 3. Best players: The umpire and that red shaggy dog.
Rugby:	You foreigners! What's the meaning of losing a match? Bad luck ----- but it was a closer go than the scores 10 - 0 indicate. We forgive you.
Cricket:	We defeated 2/3 Field Amb. - Scores 2/23 Bn. 2 - 148 to the Field Amb. 9 - 140. Don Ward 62 n.o.; Len Mortimer 47; Jack Brady 3 for 17.

The Ode of the week is published below, and it comes from the pen of Alf Le Serve, who is so friendly with the lady woodchopper.

ODE TO ATEBRINE

You've heard about young Albert
Who got ate by lion at zoo
These verses speak of atebrine
and the men who ate it too.

Our M.O. tells us that you're "hot"
He's the one who's supposed to know
And says that if you're on the spot
The fever will not show.

I don't know if his story's true
But figure's don't often lie
Though science may have made a blue
When giving you a try.

It'll make no difference where we are
We'll face the buzzing terror
And fight the bug called malaria
Till our hides have turned to yeller.

Grams of drug we'll take a day
With plenty in reserve
Our blood content is then OK
Longer fighting days we'll serve.

A. Le Serve.

LOCAL FLASHES

The Dons have a new clerk. The following conversation is reported to have taken place over the phone:-

Blue: (answering the buzz) "Hello" ......
Adjutant: "Is that Don Company? Who's speaking?"..........
Blue: "Bluey Williams here".........
Adjutant: "Oh for Heaven's sake. Is there anyone there with brains?"......
Blue: "Mick Kenney's in the next tent"..........
Adjutant: "In that case I'll ring later".

We are sorry that last week's edition was so delayed. The Rowbird was building a nest somewhere, and used up all the paper. See you next week - Good hunting.

Ed.

AUSTRALIA, 20th July, 1944.

To those members of the Battalion who attended the Church Parade on Sunday, we wish to point out that the Padre's reference to the "Q" side of Heaven aroused our curiosity. We didn't believe that such a thing existed ------ but it does. To prove our statement, we submit a copy of documents which came into our hands in a most unusual fashion. "The Archer" at practice the other day shot an arrow into the air, and lo and behold! it fell to earth - with "bumf" attached.

HEAVENLY COMMAND ORDERS
WAR ESTABLISHMENT OF A SPIRITUAL AID DETACHMENT
TYPE "A" 11/606/1

SECURITY - This establishment is designed to deal with two hundred sinners per day.

PERSONNEL

DETAIL	Offrs.	WO's	Sgts.	Rank & File	Total
Chief Priest	1				1
Samaritan Grade 1		1			1
Artisans (incl. 1 Cpl & 1 L/Cpl)			1	12	13
Interpreters, writing, wall	1				1
Rivetters, soul				1	1
Fitters, wing				1	1
Fitters, halo			1		1
Acolytes			1		·1
Shepherds			1		1
Whiteners, sepulchre				1	1
Galvanisers, activity			1		1
Virgins, wise (a)	2				2
Virgins, foolish	2				2

ATTACHED PERSONNEL		TRANSPORT	
Mobile Font Unit - -		Hearse, one-seater	2
Waterman	2	(1 spare)	
Holders, infant	1	Chariots, fiery	1
Godfathers	1	Clouds, ascending	1
Godmothers	1	Lorry 3-ton, 7 whld uplift	1
Relations, Lachrymatory			
(as required)			

Sanitary dutymen 1
Godmothers, fairy 1

NOTE: (a) To be reviewed after 40 days and 40 nights.

SUBJECT: SPIRITUAL AID DETACHMENT TYPE "A" 11/606/1 - SECURITY

HEAVENLY COMD.
12345/HC
23 Dec. 43 BC.

PROVISIONAL WAR EQUIPMENT TABLE FOR S.A.D. TYPE "A"

Item		
Pearls, castable	Gross	2
Pearls, Grade 1	Gross	2
Paths, straight	Yards	10
Paths, narrow (in lieu of paths primrose)	Yards	1000
Ladders, scaling		1
Boxes, manna		7
Gauges, depth sin		22
Halos, nets, camouflage		22
Crooks, shepherds		1
Lamps, virgin, wise full		2
Lamps, virgin, foolish empty		3
Vices, assorted		7
Chains, retaining body and soul 547		56
Chains. retaining, body and soul tools detaching		5
Bottles, wine old (for new wine)		3
Harps, harping G.S.		200
Gates, pearly, left		1
Gates, pearly, right		1
Walls, collapsible - Jericho pattern	sets	1
Locators, water, rods		1
Dividers, Sea, Red		1
Cymbals, loud	prs	1
Cymbals, well-tuned	prs	1
Rushes, bull fathoms		3
Baskets, rush, infant		1
Rivets, wing ½-inch	lbs	47

RASC SUPPLY

Item		
Loaves (or stones in lieu)		5
Fishes small		3
Wine, new (for old bottles)	Quarts	6
Oil, foolish	Quarts	4567
Oil, wise	Gills	¼
Honey, wild	lbs	10

PROVISIONAL A.F.L. 1098

Item	
Articles 1 - 39	1
Commandments, assorted	10
Pens recorder, gold	1
Glasses, dark	1
Signs, directional, upwards	1
Signs, directional, downwards, asbestos	1
Chisels, tablet, inscribing ½-inch	1
Chisel, tablets, inscribing mallets	1
Tracts, uplift reams	246
Fingers, moving, writing	5
Charts, celestial	280

1 O.R. (without SA) will be trained in spiritual aid (non-alcoholic) and 1 Officer and 6 O.R.'s in wing repair and oil decontamination work.

Trumpets, Archangel brazen		1
Slings, DAVID pattern		1
Slings, Fortune, outrageous		1
Arrows	gross	1
Jawbones, ass	pairs	1

* * * * * * * * * * * *

"ODE TO THE ATEBRINE"

This week we have pleasure in presenting for the first time in the pages of Mud'n Blood, one of the works of the well known HQ personality - John Milton Butler. Do you remember those NUGINNY days.

Where one's red blood ran thin
Where one oft' heard those plaintive lays
"COME BOYS - HERE'S YOUR ATEBRINE"

Do you remember one's frame atremble
And the feel of all known earthly ills
"Thou cursed man, do not dissemble -
When last did you see those yellow pills?"

The M.O. grins a satonic grin
As he says "For the major sin
You will daily take 12 atebrine
May they have mercy on your skin."

J.M.B.

Poetry is a lovely thing, but so is "Abbots", and when the two combine, we find such harmony. Don Company last week, could have well used this as their signature tune -

Starkle, starkle, little twink
    Who the hell you are you think
I'm not under the alchofluence of inkelhol
    Though some thinkle peep I am
I fool so feelish
    I don't know who is me,
That the drunker I sit here
    The longer I get.

"Bertie the Cellarman"

Speaking of signature tunes, we would like to ask "Curley" to play "Paper Doll" sometimes for us. We just love this number, and don't hear enough of it. Major Brown requests that it be played earlier than 0615 for he adores the classics in the morning when he is doing his P.T.

RACE MEETING & RODEO

Rarely have we seen such a colourful and gay gathering as the one that witnessed the races and rodeo held several weeks ago. Rarely too, have we seen such a collection of race horses. We say RACE horses out of respect for the feeling of those gallant four limbed bundles of bony flesh. Those horses my friends, had souls if nothing else. The Officers' horse (named Amounis by Cripes, out of Breath) was trained by Zuperman, and tampered with by the Vet. This horse proved it's worth, and won by a good margin, running a quarter hour in eight minutes. The rider, Rupe McInnes (a National winner) admitted that he got off and ran alongside Amounis at the back of the course to keep it from falling in a dead faint, but tactics is tactics, and we won - that's the main thing. Overheard in the paddock - "Why didn't you come away at the turn as instructed?" - "I couldn't come without the ------- horse, could I?" which explains all.

The rodeo seemed to be a lot of bull. We weren't quite sure who was on who, or who was paying, sort of thing, but it was all clean fun and well worth the walk ---------(?). May there be bigger, better and brighter entertainments like these, and may we train as lorried infantry.

"Centaur"

SPORTING RESULTS:

Last weekend the Battalion once again proved it's superiority in the sporting world, and every team had a victory, with one exception. The Cricket team suffered it's first defeat.

Aussie Rules: We defeated the Arty, 18 goals 11 to 10 goals 8 in the first eighteen's match. Best players: Tich Ellis, Kevin Fox, Harry Lennox, "Ackie" Atkins, Bill Meaney.
In the seconds game we won comfortably, 11 goals 6 to 9 goals 9. Best players: "Bluey" Smith, Maurie Amour, Brindle Brown, and Custard got a few kicks too. Our Officers trounced the Officers from over the road 7 goals 6 to 5 - 2.

Rugby: In a tough game which was watched by a large crowd of our supporters, our lads wrestled more effectively than their opponents. Our kicking in the shins and clawing and scratching, was forceful and we gained by disregarding the ball entirely. Good tactics for the ball (we think) spoils the game. Scores: 6 - 5. Best players: Reeves, Morrish, Malouf.

| Cricket: | The Engineers booby trapped us and won by 46 runs, 148 to our 102. Jack Bradey 5 - 72 and Lieut. Simmons 3 - 11 collected the bowling honours, Captain Lovell 33 and Sgt. Jack Hjorth 30 were our run getters. |

PREMIERSHIP LIST:

Aussie Rules:	1st XVIII	Top
	2nd XVIII	Level fourth
Rugby:	1st	Level first
	2nd	No comment!
Cricket:	1st XI	Top

BOXING:

Once again Darky has triumphed, this Tex Rickard of the 23rd has again proved himself a Prince of Promotors. Saturday night's fight fans were treated to as fine an exhibition of clean fast boxing as Madison Square Garden has ever seen. Not a punch pulled right through the show, lots of holes punched the air, but those which did connect (the Konk seemed to be the target for Saturday night) had plenty behind them, and if the crowd came looking for blood they got it - particularly the ringsiders.

Best fight for the night goes to Pte. Lowe of a CCS, and Pte. Christenson of a neighbouring Battalion. Congrats on an excellent show, boys, and we look forward to having you with us again.

Lieut's Allan "Southpaw" Head and Tommy "Windmill" Atkins· put on a whirlwind show until halfway through the second round one of the contestants discovered his falsies still in place, when in split seconds he miraculously changed from Southpaw to Orthodox, and covered up beautifully.

Congrats to all the lads who donned the gloves to provide a tip top show - we hope to have you back again. Help us to present bigger and better shows each Saturday night, listen to the crowd roar from inside the ropes - Let Darky have your names and weight - he'll do the rest, may even offer to train you - I'll leave that to you. Results listed below:

LIGHT WEIGHT

| Pte. Devlin | 9 stone 7 lbs | def. | Pte. Harris | 9 stone 4 lbs on points |

WELTER WEIGHT

Pte. Slatter   10 stone   KO'D Pte. Luff   10 stone 4 lbs 2nd rnd.

LIGHT HEAVY

Pte. Modie   12 stone 3 lbs   def.   Pte. Ladlow   12 stone 9 lbs on points

WELTER WEIGHT

Pte. McEwan   9 stone 12 lbs KO'D Sgt. Laybourne 10 st. 7 lbs 3rd rnd.

MIDDLE WEIGHT

Pte. Lowe   11 stone   def.   Pte. Christenson 11 st.5lbs   on points
Pte. Williams 11 stone 2 lbs   def.   Pte. Bickley   11 stone 6 lbs on points

HEAVY WEIGHT

Pte. Modie   12 stone 9 lbs   def.   Pte. Levy   13 stone 6 lbs on points

"RINGSIDER"

We must go to press now, so we will say Goodbye now........ Ed.

**Did you hear about the Officer and Gentleman,
home from N.G., who took off his pack?**

AUSTRALIA, 20th August, 1944

BIRTHDAY NUMBER

We apologise for the delay in publication of this number, but the bumf war has been solid, and up till now, no paper has been available.

The Battalion celebrated it's fourth birthday on 20th August 1944. As in previous years the right thing was done, and the W.O. Jones Special Coupon-less Buckshee Mungaree was produced. These meals have been relished under many unusual conditions, but no matter what the difficulties have been, the "babbling brooks" have always triumphed. 1941 found the Battalion celebrating in Tobruk; 1942 at El Alamein; 1943 at Milne Bay; and 1944 in the sunny (?) north of Australia; 1945 Tokyo - ?????????

The C.O. would like to pass on a message to all, and here it is:

"It is with pride and pleasure that I extend to all present and past members, my sincere greetings and good wishes on the fourth anniversary of our Battalion.

"When we cast our minds back through the past four years, we recall with great pride the many gallant deeds performed by our comrades on the battlefields of North Africa and New Guinea - We bow our heads in reverence to those who have sacrificed their lives in order that our cause of freedom and peace may be achieved. "We will remember them".

"May good fortune be with you always, and come what may, I know that the fine spirit of comradeship, courage and determination, which has so characterised the Battalion's past exploits, will continue with its former splendour."

F.A.G. Tucker, Lt. Col.
Comd. 2/23 Aust.Inf.Bn.

The Sergeants at their Birthday Dinner took advantage of the occasion to unveil its War Memorial in a quiet, solemn period before dinner. The Memorial is a replica, in Queensland woods, of the Monument in Tobruk Cemetery, and was finely executed by the Pioneer Platoon. The simple ceremony was performed by Warrant Officer Reynolds, who has been in the Mess since Albury days, and concluded with Sgt. Peck sounding "The Last Post" and "Reveille". In the course of his remarks, the RQMS said:

"Each day we remember them when the bugle sounds "Retreat" and thus link their names with the noble company of men who have given their lives through long years of history to make our Empire the power for good it is today. Because men of our race, in all ages, have been willing to adventure and to sacrifice everything - even their lives - the British Commonwealth of Nations still stands as a bulwark among the Nations of the World."

Many congratulatory letters and telegrams have been received, among them greetings from Brig. Bernard Evans, DSO, our original C.O. 2/23rd Welfare Association, 2/23rd Battalion Association, and sundry personal messages from ex-members of the Battalion. We appreciate these gestures, and thank all our well wishers.

Did we hear someone say, "Who is the 2/23rd Welfare Association, and the 2/23rd Battalion Association?" Gather round and lend us your ears.

The 2/23rd Welfare Association was formed by the Ladies (God Bless 'em) who had an interest in the Battalion. This Association has been most loyal, and has given us great assistance in the past. It is suggested that you blokes tell your wives, mothers, or girl friends of this Association, and to contact the Sec. Mrs. E. E. Simmons, Flat 4, 38 Kingsley Street, Elwood, Victoria.

The 2/23rd Battalion Association is a comparatively new show formed by ex-members of the Battalion who are in a position to gather for meetings, etc., in Melbourne. The object of this Association is to assist Battalion members or their dependants should the necessity arise, either during or after the war. Already many discharged members of the Battalion have been found jobs and received advice and assistance from this source. The entrance fee to this well and worthily recommended Association is 5/-. For further information, see Sgt. Ron Lees at BHQ.

A lot of water (beer and gin) has passed under the bridge since our last publication, and many things have happened. "A" Company has pleasure in announcing to the world that it's a father. Sorry, Wrong! We mean "A" Company has a father. Congratulations to Lieut. Shaw, who has been suffering terrific "synthetic pains" (apologies to "Random Harvest") for the past week or so. It's a boy, Stephen. Young Steve wrote to Dad this week and told him what happened at the hospital the day after he was born. Steve was laid down beside another one day old infant, and Steve, being inquisitive, said "Who are you?" The answer was "I'm a little girl - who are you?" Steve replied "I'm a little boy". She said "How do you know?" and our young protege, being a cunning lad, reached down and pulled up his night dress. "Look", quoth he, "Blue Booties."

SPORTING NEWS:

Aussie Rules: 2/23 Bn. second XVIII and Fitzroy won the two most important Premierships for the season. Our lads put up a magnificant show and provided the spectators with plenty of thrills, particularly in the last quarter. Best players were hard to choose, for everyone played well. We think that "Custard" Reichman and Darky Thomas were our best, with good support given by Eric Hurst, "Bull" Oakes, Billy Ballagh, Jack Ryan and Jerry Braybon. Scores 11 - 15 to 2/43 Bn. 12 - 7.
Our first XVIII was defeated in the semi final by a better team: our old rivals 2/48 Bn who went on to win the Premiership. We offer them our congratulations.

Rugby: Our team was not quite good enough, and were beaten in the semi final. A good effort for the Battalion's first attempt at this strange game.

Cricket: After an exciting finish, we lost the semi final by 5 runs. Scores 2/48 Bn 69 and 82 to our 64 and 82. Best performers Jack Hjorth 29 and Mark Custance 23. Bowlers to shine were Barney Loomes 4 - 19, Tich Ellis 4 - 15, Roger Dowell 4 - 15 and Capt. Tubby Matthews 4 - 5.

Boxing: Great assistance in the sparring practice was given by some U.S. Marines.

* * * * * * * * *

The prize of 10/- for the best "Ode to the Atebrine" was won by A. W. L. Bishop of "D" Company. Thanks to all competitors who showed an interest in this Competition. Try again in our next.

Once again, we have lost some of our old timers to industry. (We wish we had a cow, an acre of ground, and two billy cans). Several of our footballers have gone, but it is pointed out that Billy Tatt is still with us. Evidently there is no "tit for Tatt."

It is some time since we have received a short story for M & B, and we are delighted to publish this dramatic, stark, soul revealing epic.

SECURITY !! NOTE: All characters in this story are entirely fictitious, and resemblance to any living person is purely coincidental!

The C.O. had been successful in touching the cookhouse for a "cupper chey".

Returning from said cookhouse, it could be seen that his mind was not at ease. Dragging his feet, he did not even to attempt to hurdle the railing, his usual custom, which surrounded the sacred precincts of BHQ.

Adjutant!   he said; "I've just heard some shaking news."
"Ah", said the fat one, quite brightly.
"We're moving next Monday" The C.O. pronounced the death sentence on the leave.
"But Brigade definitely told us we would be here another month or more, Sir! Here is their letter X99/F/Y24."
"Sorry Porky" said the C.O. "I overheard one of the cooks state that we were moving on Monday."
"One of the cooks?" queried the Dumpling, his voice hushed and solemn. "Then Brigade must be wrong."
"Marleesh the Condys. Apples will grow again", the C.O. turned to his desk with forced brightness.

In the next room, the Orderly Room Sergeant took his eye from the keyhole of the Adjutant's door, and proceeded to give the BHQ staff, the "griff", to wit - the good oil. A gloom settled.
The day stumbled on -
The Adjutant swept in, his face wreathed in a triumphant smile, nay, a smirk. "It's all 'waffle', sir," he cried, "Brigade were right, we're not moving Monday after all!" The C.O. looked up stealthily sliding Mandrake into his drawer, "What do you mean, 'Pud'?, you know perfectly well that Brigade were wrong." "Sir!" the Adjutant's voice rang like the famed bell of Wareo, "I have just visited the latrines, and Pte. Jones - Lascelles, who was on seat No. 4, told me that we would NOT be moving for at least a month or two. He wouldn't lie to me, Sir!"

The C.O.'s breast heaved tumultuously, a grateful look in his eye, Tubby smirked more expansively, and the Orderly Room Sergeant, (with his eye), flew back to his table.

The sun shone brightly, the birds whistled. Once more all was right with the world.

"Gill"

EDITOR'S NOTE: If Cpl. Len Wintle doesn't lend me some pipe tobacco, I'll let the world (and the C.O.) know who hides behind the name of "Gill".

AUSTRALIA, 2nd November, 1944.

"Are you in the picture?" That is the question of today. One hears
some strange phrases and words whilst out fighting the imaginary Nips, but
this one is really fascinating. One Bright Lad was asked this question, and
he answered "No. 1". Consternation reigned, and the one with the three pips
said "You don't know what you're here for?" "Oh Yes, we're defending
a platoon locality" says the B.L. "Well, you're in the picture" beamed the
three pipper, and up spoke the B.L. "Cripes, I thought someone was taking
a photo." So you see how confusing it all is. But, dear friend, there is
another bright lad who does understand this double talk. It is our Stewie
of "I" Section fame. The RSM asked the worthy Stewie if he "had the
picture", and the answer was "No", "But I've been carrying the ------------
frame for miles." After seeing Betty Grable last week we wish we had been
in the picture too. (Did you notice the brand of shoes she wore?)

You can't keep a good man down, and here's another poem from
"Gill" to prove our statement.

VOTE MAYBE

I weep and I whine, I long and I pine
To get a ride on that railway line.
I want some leave, my breast gives a heave
I think of the grog like a thirsty dog.

Oh, gimme a home, and I'll never roam
Oh, gimme a ruse to get some booze.
I'm all browned off, please dig up some sting
I feel like a WAAF, without a wing.

Do I really think that leaves a moral
'Fore we set sail across the Coral'
Take it from me, she's an even bet
For a tonna dough, you won't get set.

Pumpkin and Fish are in the know
If they are right, we will never go.
They bet on it though it were water
We will never see another mortar.

So now I'll leave you in suspense
I couldn't tell you for pounds or pence
But if I don't get it, I'm gonna grieve
Oh please Mr. Curtin, give me some leave!

"Gill"

This poetry business must be simple if Cpl. Wintle can write it , so we'll have a crack at it. Just to make it different, we will make it into quiz form. We give you the clues, you give us the answers. A purple liver will be awarded to the sender of the correct answer. The answer is a Battalion identity.

He is nearly always out of bounds,
In a final match was chased by hounds.
Does a good job. Some think he's crackers
You know him well, his name is.....................

They seek him here - They seek him there,
They seek him almost everywhere
He buys beer and eggs and vish and jibs
That's a lousy word but it rhymes with................

What about you blokes? Simple isn't it? Send us a few of these "quizs" and we will get your man for you.

SPORTING RESULTS:

Football 1st XVIII - **In the** last three matches we have won two and lost one. We defeated 2/48 Bn for the first time in years.
Scores: 2/23 Bn   11 - 9 def. 2/48 Bn   9 - 10
                 2/7 Fd. Regt.   10 - 8 def. 2/23 Bn   8 - 17
                 2/23 Bn   7 - 11 def. Div.Sigs   5 - 9
Our best players in these matches have been Fred Hassett, Akkie Atkinson, Darkie Thomas, "Titfa" Tatt, Rusty Norton, Chick Jarman and Jack Ryan.

Football 2nd XVIII. We continue our run of successes. Eleven victories straight.
Scores: 2/23 Bn   11 - 13 def. 2/7 Fd.Regt.   8 - 9
                 2/23 Bn   10 - 5 def. 9 Div HQ   6 - 9
Best Players "Custard" Reichman, Jack Ryan, Berris Greaves, Brindle Brown and Buster Brindley.

Basketball: Our firsts   defeated 2/48 Bn   43 - 34
             "   seconds   defeated 2/48 Bn   35 - 27
             26 Brigade   defeated our "A" team   30 - 12
             Our "B" team   defeated 26 Bde "B"s   23 - 16
Best players: Lieut. Heaton and Eric King.

Cricket: Two matches only have been played in the new series.
          2/23 Bn 183 defeated 2/11 Field Amb. 161

Scores: Capt. Lovell 64 n.o. Roger Dowell 28 and 5 for 50.
Barney Loomes 21, Len Mortimer 19.

2/48 Bn 192 defeated 2/23 Bn 107 and 5 - 56.
Don McKinley 18, and 2 for 33; Len Mortimer 30. Capt. Lovell
20; Capt. Matthews 3 for 23; Skeeta Thompson 3 for 51.

JOTTINGS:

Lieut. Gibbs the new Transport Officer ringing the switch, and asking
for the Transport Officer.

Lieut. Jack Orr paid us a visit. Jack's put on weight, and must be at
least 6 stone 7 lbs now.

The Padre's ear-bash last Sunday - "Little man you've had a busy
day."

Max Rintoule having trouble with his water (don't get ahead of us)
cart.

Capt. McMaster feeling "In the Mood" at Reveille this week.

Ackie coming home on the pig's back.

This week we received news from the 2/23 Battalion Association.
They have had several meetings, and the fund is growing. Have you joined
up yet? Five bob isn't much to part with, so how about it? Be in it and
help your cobbers. When the war is over too, there will be an ideal excuse
in the Association for coming home to your wife just a teeny bit "tipsy".

Padre Bryson (the seven dwarfs all rolled into one big lump) rather
startled us the other night with his brilliant rendering (with actions) of
Shakespeare.

> "Thirty days hath Septober
> April, June and no wonder,
> All the rest take coffee, except
> Grandma. She rides a bike" -
>
> "Wouldntit"

Still they go. The old timers I mean. The most recent to leave us
were: Tex Horkings, Ted Nepean, Eric Lawrence, Len Edmonds, Jim
Jackson, Fred Moore, Keith Horsfall, Eric Hollindale, Tom Hollis and
George Lester. Cheerio fellers. We're sorry to see you go, and wish you
the very best...............

Brigade intend holding an exhibition of Arts and Crafts soon, and we want the Battalion to walk off with a few prizes. If you have tendencies arty or crafty, get cracking and be "in at the kill". Of course, limericks, verses, ditties, short stories aren't for that sort of business, so send 'em in to us. By the way, Ack-Willie Bishop won the Brig's two pounds for the best "Ode to the Atebrine" in the Brigade Competition.

Be seeing you...............................Ed.

AUSTRALIA, 8th December, 1944

According to Battalion Routine Orders of 25th November, vacancies now exist in 1 Aust. Dog Pl. RAF. After all these years nothing really surprises us, and so we have set to work to establish a W.E.T. for training stores for this new organization.

WAR EQUIPMENT TABLE (Training Stores)

(Subject to Alteration)

Holders dog left hand	3	Posts aiming (trg) daylight	
Holders dog right hand	3	(Aust)	4
Holders bitch left hand	3	Detectors scent (assorted)	12
Holders bitch right hand	3	Traps flea	36
Splints legs lifting right rear	6	Sticks discipline	24
Splints legs lifting left rear	6	*Warmers nose dogs MkIIX	24

* It will be noted that the feelings of sensitive dogs are considered. Some dogs ARE sensitive, but others are just plain bitches.

* * * * * * * * *

Recent reports advise that among the latest list of names of repatriated prisoners of war, those of five members of the Battalion appear:-

Lieut. Barney Grogan and Jack Fullarton (D Company) taken prisoner in Tobruk. Frank Hayes (C Company) and Lou Johns (A Company) and Kid Moloney (B Company) taken at El Alamein. Great news, and the battalion wishes them all the best. Barney Grogan has been seen wandering the streets of Melbourne. Let's hope he doesn't meet up with Harry Orr. Can you imagine the result?

"Who's Who" has created an interest and outlet for those who want to get their man. Unfortunately some verses are too strong, and can't be printed ------ but they're right on the dot, nevertheless; here are a couple of the less "vivid type".

"On Admin matters he's a wizard,
Conducts his staff as a roaring blizzard
At times pink elephants he sees
You've guessed in one it's SGT...................."

"With Sam Browne on, and brasswork bright
His manly form the eyes delight
To miss his wrath you must be lucky
He's a fiery man is Bluey.................."

Dolly Dicks has returned from her holiday, and she has improved her knowledge and technique even more. We welcome her back, and ask if she can assist a little lady who writes -

"I am engaged to a L/Cpl. Recently I met a nice boy from my fiance's battalion. He is a part owner of some sort of school from which he gets a lot of money. He says he gets on well with the kids. I like to think I am loved by a man who conducts a school because I am fond of children and all that. My fiancee says this boy is a "bodger" which means I expect, he will soon be an officer. Am I wrong in giving up my L/Cpl. and going after the more cultured man with the good position and prospects?"

"Moonshine Mary"

Dear Mary,

I think your new boy friend is a spinner of tales, and may become "too uppity" in his outlook on life. Go for the Lance Jack, and good luck.

Dolly Dicks.

SPORTING RESULTS:

Aussie Rules: 1st XVIII - Our team combined magnificently to defeat 2/7 Field Regt. 11 - 13 to 17 - 14. All members of the team played well, and we do not dare name the best players. There were 18 of 'em. This match was the first semi-final, and judging by our form, it would seem that "it's in the bag".

2nd XVIII - The juniors had an off the record match and defeated 2/24 Bn. Best players: Butch Merton, Bill Hearn, Billy Ballagh and Bluey Smith.

Cricket: 2/48 Bn 207 defeated 2/23 Bn 186. Don McKinley 48 and 4 - 26; Roger Dowell 40 and 6; Barney Loomes 28.

IDLE GOSSIP:

SPECIAL - The results of the Atebrine N. G. Handicap are to hand:

1st	The LOVELL filly
2nd	The DYSON colt
3rd	The APLIN colt
4th	The McMASTER filly

Butch MURTON won 4th place, but a protest was upheld. His filly was not eligible, as the Atebrine penalty weight was not carried.

"Never have so few babies had their heads wet by so many with so little."

Watch this column for further news. There is no stopping the 2/23rd Battalion.

Lieut. "Sunny" Holt is southbound. Musclebound - Poor Charlie!

Company dinners have been great successes, and most impressive speakers have been usually too full for words.

It was pleasing to see such wonderful co-operation and good feeling between the battalion and the Air Force on recent operations. It was a pity that the male members of the Air Arm were not present, and you fellows, despite your disappointments, are to be congratulated on the sportsmanship displayed in the way you carried on with the WAAFs.

Have you fellows decided on your Xmas presents yet?
Lieut. Wenborn has some good suggestions at the Education Hut.

That's all for now fellers, CHEERIO - Ed.

STOP PRESS: HQ Company 2/23 Bn defeated HQ Company 2/48 Bn in the final of the inter-company football competition.

AUSTRALIA, 17th March, 1945.

Here's mud in your eye, Mud & Blooders! The blood of Mud & Blood is circulating freely again after an unavoidable sluggish interlude.

Veteran of Middle East and New Guinea campaigns, faithful recorder in a hundred and more editions of the sayings and doings of "Albury's Own" in this war, Mud & Blood has recently been in the public eye.

In a four column article in a recent edition of the "Melbourne Herald", Capt. Harry Marshall, one time Adjutant of 2/23 Bn in the M.E., has written an informative and interesting article on our unit paper. The highlight is an inset facsimile of a personal acknowledgement by Field Marshal B.L. Montgomery, of a leather bound inscribed volume of Middle East issues of Mud & Blood, forwarded to him by Mrs. Simmons, the President of the Ladies 2/23 Welfare Association. Here it is:-

> TAC Headquarters
> 21 Army Group
> B.L.A.
> 15 October, 1944

"Dear Mrs. Simmons,

I would like to thank the ladies of 2/23 Welfare Association for sending me a copy of "Mud & Blood". I look forward with much interest to reading this book, and about the men who fought so gallantly during those years.

> Yours Sincerely,
> B.L. MONTGOMERY
> Field Marshal.

Mud & Blood has done the 2/23rd Battalion another signal service in eliciting from so great a soldier such a warm tribute to those of the unit who, under "Monty's" distinguished command, "fought so gallantly during those years."

An epitath to our fallen comrades; just cause for pride to those who remain.

It is interesting to trace the paper's progress. First issue in the Indian Ocean, 1940....... Destruction of the handpress by a Jerry ground-strafe near Derna Pass, April 1941 ...... Kept in circulation by means of typewriter and duplicator ...... A morale lifter in the seven months siege of Tobruk............. Edited and published under all conceivable conditions of modern warfare ... Living always up to the Battalion's motto: "Either find a way or make one" ..... Successfully edited by Sgt. (now Capt.) J.D. Mulcahy; Sgt. (now Lieut.) Wenborn, and latterly Capt. Lovell. Humorous in the main, yet capable on occasion of interpreting authoritatively the deeper and finer things of the Battalion spirit. Who can read unstirred, an editorial written in July 1942 before the El Alamein battle, pledging the Battalion's absolute determination to carry on the tradition the unit has already set, until the day when we can lay aside our arms with the gladness of the conqueror whose cause is just, and whose aims have been secured?

CONGRATULATIONS to our C.O., Lt.Col. F.A.G. Tucker on his well merited decoration, a distinguished honour to him and the Battalion.

MENTION IN DESPATCHES: Our 2 i/c Major E.H. McRae, O.C. Don Company, Capt. W.J. Vines, Pte. D.S. Mollenhagen, Cpl. N. Coventry, Pte. N. De Forrest, (Posthumous).

COMINGS & GOINGS:
After SPRING comes the "MENACE" in the Autumn of our days. Welcome Capt. Minnis!
Our C.O. a fine bouncing boy. Good luck to you sir, and your son and heir.

A happy Benedict - Major McRae, Congratulations.
Capt. Vines, a lovely daughter - Congratulations.
George Thomas, a girl. What about this Atebrine theory?
"Johnno" (Corp) - a boy. Good plumbing!
"Stick" Evans, a B Class, and prospects.
"Phippsy" & Dead Eye?

Capt. Vines still clings to the battalion, and the battalion to him. Don Company will see to that!

Lieut. Jack Orr returned to us for a while, and 'turned on the heat'. Blazes! Incidentally, our sincerest sympathy to Jack on the recent sad loss of his mother.

Lieut. A. Lyne back from Brigade. Cheers.

THOUGHT OF THE WEEK:
"The best place to find a helping hand, is at the end of your own arms."

TIT-BITS FROM OUR ROVING REPORTER:
Good show Transport! Topped the Brigade, eh? No wonder you've been well-oiled lately.
The electric light plant has done a stout job for the duration - 5 days.

Kit inspection has been very thorough of late. It is rumoured that CSM's of B & D Companies even picqueted evacuation points.

Since our last edition, the Sergeants have been in an hospitable mood. At a famous blow-out about a couple of months back, spirits were so high octane they nearly blew up. Their last 'do' was but a week back. Catering a high order; giggle-juice flowed freely.

The Sergeants' Amateur Theatrical Society presented "Cinderella" the same night, when time and the actors were ripe.... a display of histrionic talent as polished as sand-paper. 'Lucky Joe' as 'Cinderella' was rather the worse for wear, but a game battler. Prince 'Stalk' found his teeth instead of the Princess's glass slipper. Baron 'Porky' breathed beer and fatherly benediction, but not on poor 'Cinders'. Fairy Godmother PEEL forgot her cue, and presented 'Cinderella' with a couple of glasses of gin instead of glass slippers, which left the poor Princess flat-footed and 'Stinko' at the ball. 'Foxy' and 'Baby-face' were well cast as the Ugly Sisters. No wonder the Prince gave them a miss in baulk.

LEGEND OF LIGHT

The C.O. sent for Fred one day,
To send him on a mission -
"Trot off and buy a lighting plant;
We have the Brig's permission."

So Freddie packed his bags and went
As soon as he was able.
If you want to know the time it took
Then glance at the following table.

September month hath thirty days,
It's quite a handy figure
To measure out the time it takes
To buy a lighting jigger.

"WONDERING"

FLASHES FROM THE HOME FRONT:

BHQ: It was nearly the 'Last Post' for the bugler who boxed on with the tree instead of his mate - a case of mistaken identity or a Brown-out? BHQ's kit inspection was so thoroughly carried out that the inspecting officer's own hat was salvaged when he put it down for a second. Tit - for - hat.

HQ Coy: Sgt. Mortimer is on his way south to wage war on the wily females at the Battle of Records.
SPOONER take note for future reference!
Your silversmith, closely related to 'Argus the Boy Wonder' gave a good display of his work at the recent kit inspection. -
One dozen knives, forks and spoons beautifully laid out on a blanket.
More hair for the MGs. Go to it 'Samson' DRAKE.
In the hurly-burly of late, the Q store has given birth to three kittens. What of the three blind mice?
Since the dry season has set in 'Bubbles' is resting peacefully of nights.

'A' Coy. Strange evacuation - a shirt with AAB 83. Owner still angling for it. Nice work!
'A' Company were recently amazed to find that they had a tripple champion in their midst, hiding his talent in the proverbial paper bag - heavy, light and featherweight champion of Australia. Only fights with a good head of steam, and socks deep in the mud to keep him on balance. Atta boy, 'Spike'!
'Walter Raleigh' and colleague repeated the cloak act the other night, but things came to a 'head', and they might have been clocked, only Ralph passed judgement.
Has anyone found 'Slogger's' trousers?
Why will 'Robbie never starve in the desert? Because of the sand which is there'.

'B' Coy. Seen in the lines - a walking kit bag Mk III in the shape of a person wearing three shirts.
As no AWAS are included on establishment, the RQM cannot supply 'B' Company's indent for 'brassieres', or was it 'stays'?

'C' Coy. Dark Waters flow deep when Amoore and his swooners exercise the pipes of an evening. The mighty Atom Riley had a spot of bother fitting Ray Bryant with hats, tin, but finally made it by enlarging one of Pinkie's Dixies. Incidentally, Pinky is a little annoyed as it has cut down his brewing necessities; but Ray has promised to lend it to him when he wants to make an extra nine gall.
Hobson's choice was tit for Tatts when wily Will handed out the bugle the other day.
Burky was disappointed at lecture on evasive tactics - hints on dodging Japs, not MPs - Look out Burky, we're on you.

Snaky Sid, the Orderly Room Lizard had a tough trot without the molar for a week, but still managed to bite a few heads off. 'Nuji' the Stooge still having trouble with his runner; hope Orderly Room will quieten down now 'Basher' Brindley is on the job.

'Wilt' had ants in pants the other day; tent over-run with them, even woke him at 1500. Have to start getting up for meals, crumbs in the bed brings 'em, you know!

'D' Coy.   Tommy is having trouble in KEEPING HIS PLATOON together OR apart - judging by the noise from Company lines recently. The Skipper appreciated the situation when the Stork flew over 'D' Company.

Congratulations from all.

Cricket: 17 Platoon & 16 Platoon. Owing to the excellent umpiring by Platoon Commander of 17 Platoon, they lost. He has since turned his attention to TENNIS.

The nightly 'housey' game in the Company Mess hut 'mecca' for eager speculators. Nick Balaglou says the scene is reminiscent of pre-war Monte Carlo, less the females and the free Champagne. The highlight of recent 'Soldier Speaks' session was OMAR's colourful account of 'Life in a Circus' - says he's undecided at times whom he's working for - the Nation or Barnum & Bailey. A few new faces in the Company lately, hearty welcome to all, especially Lieut. Lyne and Sgt. Palmer. 'AMBIE' beware! we bar 'The face on the Bar Room Floor', unless it is your own prone body.

Welcome, yes - but, alas farewell too, to some old-timers, especially CSM 'Dunc' Duncan, an original, and a soldier with a fine record. So long 'Dunc' till the big parade in ALBURY apres la guerre.

After a bevy of good Formal Dinners, we're having a SOAK, sorry, A SMOKE NIGHT. TO-NIGHT'S THE NIGHT! The C.O. will be waiting with carts, hand, jungle, and wheel barrows to escort the revellers home.

CHEERIO fellows until next time.......... Ed.

Volume 6

CHAPTER 19

TARAKAN, 21st May, 1945.

We go to press under fire. The RAAF have heard a cat walk through the bush and "it's on!" TARAKAN. Ain't it Paradise. We must tell Fitzpatrick to bring his technicolour film and camera along. Ambrose Palmer can give him the good oil, seeing it doesn't cost a bean, and there's gallons of it here. Ambrose is big-hearted that way - always giving things away - even Tarakan itself.

And, sir! These are Tarakan's best. Before the war, 2 million gallons per year.

New Guinea produced some troppo cases, but here there are some which make the N.G. outbreaks look very tame. Ron Lees has a pet chicken which is allergic to mosquitoes, so the worthy Lees built a mosquito net, and there-under roosts Daphne. We noticed him stroking her leg the other night, and when challenged, he said he was putting repellent on it. Cute, eh!

America has it's Bob Hope who keeps 'em amused, but "A" Company has it's Pongo. His brand of humour is popular with the Nips, for whenever he takes his Owen to a party, Nips chatter with delight, and many are heard to say "Boy, you're killing me." And How! "B" Company's heavies have the title of "pill-box busters." Perhaps the Jardine leg theory has Nip rattled. "B" Company also boasts of the stalwart who played peek-a-boo for hours with an ape.

Is there a Doctor in the house?

"Pill Box" Bill Jardine

Keith Chrystal and "Why WIEBRECHT Why", had some target practice this week. Hearing movement on the Base perimeter, they both fired. Whamee! Next morning we found a cow prostrate on the ground. Evidently the poor brute had been backing into the perimeter, for there were three neat "inners" in her hide. Just missed the bull's eye by a whisker.

There will be no free canteen issue this week.

Did he fall or was he pushed? Skipper Maurie Wilton certainly performed brilliantly when he fell into that oil swamp.

George Henderson is giving free instruction on "Booby traps" and "Strong Boxes". Bring your own rope, but no rice, please.

The fighting Dons regret the losing of Skipper Bill Vines, who has gone south to a Staff School. In fact the whole Battalion misses him. Good luck, Bill. Jack'o and Woosh saw some of the local lasses in pyjamas, and thought that they were walking in their sleep. Try 'em and see --- they're a wake up.

The Ex Mud & Bloods who receive this will be proud to know that the Battalion has excelled itself again, and Tarakan will go down on record as another triumph. Tobruk, El Alamein, Lae and Finschhafen.............. Tarakan. The glorious deeds and achievements in campaigns make history, and we silently remember those lads who gave their all to bring Victory one step nearer.

The "I" Section is furious. Old Acorn, or Skinny to you, refutes the statement that he questioned an ape for hours, and fed bananas to a Jap prisoner. Off the beam again.

It's a strange world you know. Here we have stories of apes and chickens. Remember Cairo ---- Monkey and the chook?

I remember those bright boys in the "I" Section questioning
on ape and feeding bananas to a Nip prisoner at Tarakan.

Someone said to Peter Reynolds yesterday, "How's your Malayan?" and Peter blushed and said "How did you know?" ---- "Anyway she's Chinese, not Malayan". We asked him if it was true that ..... (alright, we know that one .... Ed.)

And now chaps, we close the press for a spell. Good hunting......
Cads.

TARAKAN, 5th June, 1945.

                                                                        Editor.

Hi ya fellers! We have much pleasure an inouncing that the beersere. We have anpicitated it for weeks, and at last our hopes have been filfulled. Fillemupagain ---------- and here's eye in your mud.

Looking down through history we see many famous names. Women's names. Cleopatra, Tiger Lill, Queen Anne, Nell Gwynne, Tilly Devine, Killarney Kate -----. The Battalion has another name to add to this list - MARGY.. This little lady was found on Tarakan, and was wooed by many men. Her curves fascinated them, and as her covering was shed little by little her charms revealed became increasingly seductive. Men wanted MARGY - men sought MARGY, but MARGY remained alouf. She was pure, and despite the subtle advances, she stood firm. One day as she lay reclining in the sun, her limbs bare, her twin pimples pointing to the sky, she was attacked. MARGY fell, and, struggle as she did, she could not resist. (That bitch JANET was hard to toss too).

Perhaps it is some form of psychology having names like Margy, Janet, Clarice and Freda given to ridges. We venture to suggest (we NOT being interested in women) that a greater result would be gained if names such as Castlemaine, Abbots, Cascade, West End, etc., were substituted.

Well, its on again. Ron Lees' chicken was off colour (we think she's working up to an egg) and he dosed it with crushed aspro.

The RAP is becoming a 'Minnis' to Tac HQ. The fighting patrol called for, discovered an ape looking for an apesse. Fair go Charlie, you were young yourself once.

Dost thou know one 'Pucka' Sherry. To see him with his boongs is a rare and amazing sight. The boongs don't speak English - 'Pucka' doesn't speak Malayan, but somehow he gets results. Of course, if his arms were tied to his side there would be nothing done at all. We hope his ears aren't burning, for everything else around him is.

You have heard no doubt of a man wrestling with a steak. Darky Byron of "A" Company had a real catch-as-catch-can the other night when he obtained one fall to none against the box of rations that dropped on him in his doover. Munga Murphy of the Sigs has challenged the loser.

We have heard that quite a number of the old blokes have drawn the crow down below. Can you imagine how unhappy Kevin Fox must be ------ living at home at his pub and toiling for three hours a day at LTD Melbourne. Laurie Duncan soldiering on at Darley, with AWAS fluttering around him. To you Laurie, we pass on the knowledge that here in Tarakan, the Malayan word for 'beware' is AWAS. Leo Jones is teaching cooks to cook cookies at Royal Park. It is said that he has started a second front already.

18 Platoon is still chuckling at the remembrance of the sight of Tottie Tottle tossing grenades delicately on to the Nips. STIFF luck for the Sons of Heaven.

Hoot Gibson has asked us to insert an ad in the Wanted to Sell column. We are sorry we cannot comply with his request, as we have sold the space in the papers to the Yanks.

Fishy Salmon has disclosed that he has a controlling interest in a business in Albury. It produces bone dust and chloride. Fishy is anxious to know if any bald bloke has suddenly sprouted hair. If so, he will change the powder he is already putting in our water.

Be seeing you ----- Ed.

TARAKAN, 2nd July, 1945.

Off they went, rifles, owens, and grenades at the alert, faces grim, searching eyes flashing into every bush. The dusk patrol was on its way. They crept out silently, and faded into the rosy dimness of the dying day. Silence. We, who remained, sat listening, nerves taut - listening for the crackle of death from the Owen, and the "spang" of the bursting grenades. Time dragged on, maddeningly slow. "What was that?" A branch snapped, and into sight came the dauntless patrol. We counted them in - One - Two - Three. "Thank God all safe". "How many did you get?" asked Ron Lees and Peter. 'Six" came the laconic answer. The crowd gathered around and gazed in rapturous admiration at the six white gardenias recovered from the village behind "B" Echelon. This was the cue for Keith Chrystal. He went into the Canteen and produced one bottle of hair-oil, for successful patrols always meant hair-oil. Yep my friends, its the old time game of "cherchez la femme". For those not already in the know, certain members of the battalion are miles in front, and nearly every night these Romeos (with in support, hair-oil) visit the CCS and present flowers to the sisters there. Lofty Cameron has been so moved by these events that he has written some shaggy doggeral.

"SPRING IN TARAKAN" by Lofty

There's a commendable spirit amongst gallant Twenty Third's
Thats given them new zest in life and happiness in Birds.
They've started up a salvage task thats raising many blisters,
But its worthwhile for just a smile from charming local sisters.
Each heart and mind is set to find something by any measure,
To grace a room or cause a swoon and bring our "Sisters" pleasure
The Competition's getting warm, in front is Leo Shield,
   but not by much, since mortars went a scrounging battlefields.
There are meetings in the jungles, forming working bees, to try
    outdo the enterprise of "Wonder Boy" Ron Lees.
The drivers do enjoy this craze in spite of others banter,
Delivering spoils "Light Heartedly" just like Father SANTA.
This fashion started off with flowers by W.O. our "Don Juan"
And I'm wondering just where this will end in ....

WAR TORN TARAKAN.

Dedicated to our "SISTERS" - 110 CCS, TARAKAN.

But nevertheless the war goes on. "C" Company insists that "still waters run deep". Darky Waters, that is. It is said that he ran half an hour in twentyfive minutes to beat that landslide. Lieut. Bert Goon is asking for a Bloodhound GS Mk I (cold nose type) to assist in tracking down the phantom near Janet. There was another phantom around "C" Company cookhouse last week. The gremlin insisted on pushing men off balance. Perhaps it was the jungle juice, but we leave it to you.

> One Hoye, with initials B.T.
> Drank of jungle juice rather ME.T.
> When questioned by all
> Said "twasn't a fall"
> Twas PT not plural of DT.

The RAAF are dancing around madly these days to the tune of "The Strip Polka", but Jack Gilmore, "A" Company, is more refined, and glides along to the tune of "Where is my wandering boy, tonight?" Lieut. Thorburn is working out a beam for his boong trains to come in on. "A" Company specialise in wanderers - even Company HQ has a phantom wanderer who raids the munga box at midnight. It is said that the phantom dealt in eggs on the Tablelands, and is still suffering from shell shock. There are many ways of "getting Nips", but Darky Roberts takes ? the cake. The story goes that Darky held up a piece of cake to a Nip, and lured him into captivity. Try 'em on gold fish next time Darky.

Gunga Holbrook has gone to Morotai and left "B" Company. The Company could still hear Gunga singing the Maori's farewell when the boat sailed over the horizon. Can you imagine the embarrassment of Lieut. Kinnane's patrol when they investigated a Nip whom they had bowled over and found that he was not peering around a bush at them, but was crouched down for other purposes. This yellow Son of Heaven, to make matters worse, was about to use a surrender leaflet to complete the job.

It is pleasing to see the comradeship (despite their 3 ton trucks) shown by the boys of the RAAF. Our lads, who have been entertained by them, certainly have been well cared for, and Mud'n Blood wishes to thank the airforce for their generosity and goodwill.

THESE WE REMEMBER

Now that "organised resistance has ended", time permits us to give fuller thought to those of our Comrades no longer with us. Naturally our deepest sorrow leans to those who so gallantly gave their lives - and to their folks at home and close friends within the battalion, we extend humble and sincere sympathy. Then there are the others - the wounded. They too call for our sympathy and to our pride in a job well done. To them, we can but express the fervent hope that they will soon be on the road to good health, and gladly look forward to the day when we shall see them again.

In response to letters that have been forwarded to relatives and to the wounded expressing the sympathies of the battalion, the passing days bring mail to the C.O., which is indicative of the marvellous spirit of these people. We give you the following messages and extracts:-

Mr. R. Mackie, of O.K. Apartments, Barry Parade, Valley, Brisbane - an old Digger himself - sends his best wishes to all, and would appreciate a letter from his son's (Bill) mates. He hopes parcels forwarded to Bill will be accepted by "B" Company, and enjoyed.

Major Issell - now at Heidelberg, writes - "I've been having some trouble with my leg and have just let writing slide, however I've just had an injection to quieten it down a bit, so am taking the opportunity to get this letter away. Lieut. Smith is in my ward, and has been given leave while his artificial arm is being made. Capt. Simmons and Lieut. Rees arrived a couple of days ago, but as they are in another ward I've not seen much of them. Lieut. Edwards has been sent to a convalescent camp pending further treatment. Quite a lot of our lads are arriving, and I often have a couple of them up here. I'm confined to bed so haven't been able to contact the non-walkers yet. You can imagine with what interest we read the newspaper accounts of the battalion's activities, and it is great to read of the doings of our lads. It seems that our battalion has done its share of the job - that, of course, reflects great credit on both you and the unit. Would you please let me know if there is anything I can do for you at this end - are there any magazines etc., you would like forwarded, as an instance?"

Bill Ogilvie of "B" Company, who is not far away, expects to be back with the unit in a few weeks time.

Denny Johnson of "D" Company, is improving every day, and hopes too, to return ere long. Cpl. Jack Fisher now at Heidelberg, "still with a tube inside me" - obviously maintaining his usual manly spirit, desires to be remembered to his many friends.

Lieut. Smith, a patient of the 115 AGH, but at the moment enjoying a spot of leave at Mildura (Good luck to him) writes that his arm healed very quickly and apart from his "phantom left hand" is feeling very fit. He extends to all ranks the best of luck.

Capt. Bill Vines (doing a school at Cabarlah, Queensland) writing in his inimitable easy style tells of a brief visit to Melbourne where he was able to take the opportunity of contacting by phone, letter or person, the next of kin of most casualties known to him.

Amongst other matters he writes:

"Needless to say, I've followed your doings since my departure with very considerable interest, and have thought a good deal about all of you as individuals, and hoped like hell that very few more would become casualties. Have been here two weeks now, and am almost on the point of going under for the third time in a mighty sea of bumph. You've never seen the like of it - by the time the course ends on the 27th October, I'll need a 3 tonner to cart it all away.

"Please remember me to old friends, and especially to the blokes in "D" Company. The thing I'm proudest of in this war is having commanded them in a scrap."

Culture

NEWS FROM SOUTH

Most members of the unit are aware of the close bond that exists between the Second Twenty-Third and the people of Albury, but for those unfamiliar with the battalion's history, it is pointed out that it was in this border town the unit was formed and did its initial training. There, a truly remarkable interest and friendship for the unit sprang into being, and ere long the phrase "ALBURY'S OWN" became widespread. Since those far off days, Albury has continued to take a keen interest in the unit's movements and operations, and as evidence of their lasting enthusiasm, we quote firstly a letter from the Mayor, Alderman Padman, Esq., and secondly a leading article from the Border Morning Mail.

> "Mayor's Room, Town Hall,
> Albury, N.S.W.
> 20/ 6/45.

Dear Colonel Tucker,

Please accept my very sincere thanks for the continued supply to me of your Regimental Paper "MUD AND BLOOD". It is particularly pleasing to receive this paper, as it helps to keep us in touch with the battalion and its doings, and it is very interesting to note the many personal pars in regard to members of the battalion. A few days ago I heard from Mrs. Simmons, that you were in need of face washers. I immediately made this known to the Albury people, and believe me the washers rolled in, in a constant stream. The result is that our women-folk have packed one thousand of these, and I am forwarding these on addressed to you today.

I trust that they get through without undue delay. May I point out that we here in Albury, sincerely welcome the opportunity to be of service to our battalion, and if there is anything we can do for you all at any time, please let us know, and I assure you that, that which lies within our power to do, will be done very gladly indeed.

We know of course that "Albury's Own" is in the thick of things again, and we know that the same grand service which has characterised the activities of the 2/23 in various theatres of war is being given again. For this we are indeed grateful and proud in that this town is honoured by having the battalion known as "Albury's Own".

On behalf of all our people here I send to you all our very kindest regards and best wishes.

                                        Sincerely yours,

                                        (Signed) D.G. Padman."

BORDER MORNING MAIL
Friday, June 22, 1945
A Message to "ALBURY'S OWN"

Names in recent casualty lists recognisable as belonging to personnel
of "Albury's Own" are a sober reminder that this unit, which brought such
fame to our district, still is paying the price of service. About this time,
five years ago the history of the battalion began when, as a training unit on
the Albury Show Ground, the late Col. Storey was charged with the responsibility of preparing the raw material for Col. Evans, its first Commanding
Officer, to take over and bring to the stage where it dropped automatically
into the honourable ranks of the Second A.I.F. The 2/23rd left Australia
carrying the rich blessings of a town to which it had endeared itself, and a
vow that, come what may, the link between them never would weaken by
the dimness of memory.

The Colours of "Albury's Own", blessed before embarkation, and
committed to the trusteeship of the citizens of Albury, remain in an honoured position in the Council Chambers awaiting the day when their reclamation
will write another proud chapter in the unit's history - and in Albury hearts.

From Albury to Borneo via the Middle East and New Guinea is a
long journey, and the five years of its completion have produced a pageant
of human glory second to none in the A.I.F. The battalion's journal "Mud
and Blood" cites Tobruk, El Alamein, Lae, Finschhafen, and now Tarakan,
as the epics of its illustrious record, the effulgence of which has intensified
the pride of Albury in its fighting namesake. The pageant, however, has
not been without a sorrowful side to both parties. The battalion has suffered grievously by the death of scores of gallant comrades, and the town
has been affected deeply by the battlefield severance of priceless friendships.

Nevertheless, the fact that "Albury's Own" contains now but a
small proportion of its original personnel, has in no way lessened the burning
interest in the old unit of the survivors who returned to the Albury district
to pick up the threads of civilian life, or of the towns-people's sense of concern for the welfare of their successors in Borneo. Among 1945 "Mud and
Bloods" are many to whom the birthplace of their battalion is but a name.
To them, Albury offers an assurance that the traditional hospitality of the
towns-people is theirs for the invocation. At all times, Albury is ready to
respond to requests for comforts beyond the capacity of the A.C.F. to
supply, and which will help to make the conditions of tropic warfare more

bearable. The town asks the Commanding Officer to bear this in mind when he feels that his men could do with that little "something extra" to promote contentment among all ranks.

For the part "Albury's Own played in the grim business of breaking into the enemy's stronghold in Borneo, the town offers its congratulations. The feat was the natural sequence to others of like daring and valor, and another example of the traditions established at Tobruk when the battalion was the hunted, not the hunter. In both roles, it has been Albury's honour to have been associated, hence its admiration for the men who wear the distinguished "Mud and Blood" shoulder patch".

* * * * * * * * *

Many thanks Mr. Mayor and Citizens of Albury. We trust we may continue to be worthy of your confidence and pride.

Cheerio fellers. Send in your stories to Editor, Mud & Blood, C/o "B" Echelon, Tarakan, B.O. 2.

TARAKAN, 31st July, 1945.

Last week we had a visitor, one Robert Nelson, War Correspondent. Quite a splendid type of bloke, for when we met him the second thing he said was "You can call me Bob if you like". The first thing he said of course was "Got any grog?" Bob, we believe, came to get the GG on the doings of the battalion, and judging by the wadding in his ears, he was fairly well ear bashed. He has travelled round a bit. Sydney, Melbourne, Brisbane, Darlinghurst, King's Cross (then nipped back to Darlinghurst), N.G. and covered other tropic paradises including the Phillipines. We, not having been to the Phillipines, asked him to tell us the facts of life as found in Manilla, so hence the following article -

"The poor Australian soldier on his six and six a day, and the poor war correspondent (who, as everyone knows, always has less dough than the penniless private) has a mighty lean time in the ruined Phillipines capital of Manilla. But there are compensations - for instance, the women ..... and, well, and the women. You'd think the Phillipines (known to the troops as 'Flips') would be gratefully showing their liberators a good time - "turning things on". Not so. The Flip's happy at his liberation alright, because never before in his history has he been able to get his hands on anyone as easy to fleece as the Yanks. As you know, our Allies are kinda weak about women.

"Naturally, Australians have no interest in that sort of thing, so you make for the nearest pub, where you sit yourself down on a packing case chair and a packing case table, and drink native gin at nine bob a nip, and listen to an unwashed string band play "As Time Goes By". Time eventually goes by at such a rate that its lunchtime, so you seek yourself out a cafe that looks slightly less dirty than the rest. If you happen to find one that's got clean table-cloths, the steak you order will cost you twentyone bob, plus another ten bob should you decide on a slice of paw-paw as a sweet.

"But, inevitably, lets get back to the women. There are thousands of American WACs in the ruined city, whom the Yanks have completely given away in favour of glamorous Flip and Spanish girls - not that you can blame them. The Flip and Spanish women with their lace mantillas over their sleek hair, and their ...... and their ..... well, anyway, they're really something. But the WACs - they fall back on the next best thing, the Aussies. They'll corner you in a street and listen wide-eyed as you tell 'em about your goanna farm and they'll let you buy 'em gin, etc, etc. Well, anyway, as I said at the beginning, the Australian has a lean time in Manilla, but any of you big, battered blokes of the fighting twenty-third who may be planning a tourist holiday in the "open" city, should remember that even the Digger and even the poor war correspondent can manage to chip a few more bits of plaster from the ruined walls - if he tries, and if, of course, he can get his hairy hands on some dough ....."

As a sort of P.S., I might add that its been my experience that the gin was much cheaper (both ways) and no less plentiful at BHQ. Besides, at BHQ you can drink it in peace - without the bother of having to make love to Spanish glamor girls and WACs."

Bob Nelson.

That was quite a fruity story, but we can tell you another one. Staff Lousada's banana plantation has been done over again by the "boongs". The few of them who do not own dixies persist in stripping the leaves off the plants and using them as dishes. Lou Lou is an efficient fellow really, for he is breeding these plants for a duel purpose. Of course, the first is for the fruit, but the second is quite a novel idea. As you know the trouser issue is rather grave, and old Lou is cashing in on the brains of Adam and Eve. Yes, he is going to issue banana leaves in lieu. He is a trifle worried about how to tuck one banana leaf into two gaiters, but never fear, for he will solve the problem eventually.

Bluey Johnstone of "A" Company came up for a bit of a chat the other night, and said "Hullo" with the accent on the "Huh". Three of the group who collapsed were evacuated with alcoholic poisoning. Pity!

Speaking of alcohol reminds us of that beaut brew offered to us last week. It was a trifle bitter, and we said so. "That's funny" said the moonshiner, "I'm sure I put everything in - let me see - dried apricots, chlorinated water, raspberry jam, blue boiler peas (germinated) boot polish (Dark Tan) ... Ah, I've got it! I forgot the mosquito repellent." Tut tut! You will notice the famous vitamin giver outer, the blue boiler pea, has been used in the above recipe, but please don't think that abused little vegetable has only one use. "B" Company, well known as the archery Company, has been unable to find suitable wood for bows, so that secret weapon man has evolved a super stunt. He has issued native blow pipes and blue boiler peas. At the moment he is experimenting on air bursts (he has no doubts as to their armour piercing qualities).

Manilla, we were told, is a strange city, but Melbourne seems to be developing a war neurosis all of its own. A denizen of that Victorian village (that squares off the insults hurled at Rugby on the Tablelands - Wally Bagley please note - Ed.) has expressed his views on the matter and writes -

"MELBOURNE, MY MELBOURNE!! VX88668.

The "News from Home" we saw last week of jitterbugs "hepping" in Melbourne's streets and dance halls practically caused an uproar amongst the large audience at DJOEATA. After the reel had finished, the din of heated argument and jibes made many a Melbournite struggle for an apology. "What about your Melbourne now, Blue" shouted an NX; - "Do you want to go home now Fred?" yelled a WX. VX's had some awkward moments. It appears that while we have been away, our younger brothers and sisters have advanced from being "swing fans" to addicts to youth's new craze the world over - "Jitterbugism". Those from Melbourne will remember on their last leaves, how the cult of Jitterbugism was developing in our dance halls - at the "Palm Grove", "Trocadero", "The Dugout" and "Palais Royale". At some, roped off portions divided the "heppers" from the more dignified dancers. Our American Allies set the tempo in 1942, and Australian Youth rapidly caught on. There is not one state in our homeland that is now immune. When we go home this will be a new problem for us in our re-education to civilian life. The younger set language will be in those strange terms "Jumpin' Jive", "In the groove" and "bounce me brother". This has set conservative VXs thinking - "Melbourne, my Melbourne, what madness is this?"

"A" Company reporter has brought in some local news, but he insists that we keep his name out of the press so to protect Cpl. Quinn, we will not disclose his name. That sounds "fishy" but as "A" Company only has one fisherman, he's on pretty safe ground. The shark in the creek didn't catch on, but we think Ted Bayard may. Why not stick to the pink elephants Ted - sharks - Tida bagoes.

It has been claimed that Darky Roberts is "bomb happy". Anyone wishing to claim the above complaint please bring your own bomb.

Don't go down the mine Daddy is our advice to Gunga O'Neill. We are a trifle vague about this mine business, but we do know that you will probably strike trouble, Gunga, but who knows? You might pick up the lode first try.

Is it true that the red-head of 7 platoon is about to "cut a groove". Why don't you go in for the classics? The ballet is the place for you. We believe Ballerinas are pretty good.

"B" Company are usually too busy to write articles, but for this edition they have induced their poet to "Hep that quill".

"B" COMPANY

Now when I joined this company
T'was easy to be seen
That I was just a raw Reo,
Just another one in green.

I didn't get to know the boys,
Even some I didn't see,
For a 'Blue' was on that evening -
Quite a nasty one for "B".

To me it was a mystery,
The attack made me feel weak.
I guess I learnt a lot that day
On Satelberg's high peak.

I saw what jungle fighting meant,
And then it came to me
How proud I was to be a bloke
Who'd fought with good old "B".

I've met some fellows in my time
Who were good pals to me,
But they were never in the race
With mates I made in "B".

Though some of them are missing now
And just a memory,
All of you who knew them well,
I'm sure you will agree,
That where so ere you journey
By land, by air, by sea,
You'll never meet a stauncher mob
Than you did in good old "B".

"Ex Bagman"

STOP PRESS from "B" Company:

George (keep it clean) Hamdorf, ex gold miner from W.A. did some panning in the creek. Remember George "all that glitters is not gold". That was the sun shining on the water. We suggest you use some of the water next time George, and weaken your spirit a trifle. Fancy turning catherine wheels down a cliff at your age.

"D" Company has been in the wars (strange). Last week a patrol with Ross Mathewson in command, sallied forth to "do over" any wandering Nips. Seeing the quarry in the swamp (its usually a swamp in a quarry - but you know "D" Company) the patrol set an ambush and waited. Just as the Nips were about to be despatched to their Gods, the patrol was attacked - by wasps. It was said that the Marx Bros. could not have stacked on a better turn. The ambush 'shot through' and raced back up the track. The Nips also "beat it", frightened by the noise, and the wasps just stayed there and did whatever wasps do in moments like those. Total casualties - 57 stings.

The same Company had the unique experience of seeing a Jap "bludger" putting on a turn worthy of our best. A patrol spotted three Nips walking down a track. One of them was hobbling on two crutches. The patrol opened up, and the two-crutch man dropped his oars, up-anchored and headed for the sea. It is reported that he broke evens. How odd!

Some heartless wretch has suggested that the two man band from the Rec. Hut should go up and serenade Margy or Freda - what have they done to deserve that?

We vote this one the joke of the week. A certain gent airing his Malayan, said to a native making his way to the "Stork" cafe, "Makanan". The native, looking very serious, shook his head and answered "Munga".

Charlie Company's newshound has spilled the beans about Skipper Bateson's birthday celebration. Apparently the heights of Joyce bamboozled

Arthur Bateson

him into thinking he was in the Tyrol. The Yodelling was superb, and audible for over 1000 yards. But that still doesn't excuse that fowl from attempting to lay eggs on his bed. Poor attempts, indeed, from what we can hear, but in our faith in the ability of this bird we do believe that one day an egg will come. We and the hen are "expecting".

Jimmy Guy, the RAP bloke with "C" Company, is a harsh brute. We cannot fully disclose what he does to them, but the butterflies he treats all die with a smile on their faces.

This month we welcome back two blokes to the battalion, namely Lieuts. Barney Grogan and Jim King. Barney went into the bag at Tobruk and later escaped from Jerry only to be captured by a little Swiss Miss at a later date. Barney did a lot of ski-ing, but nevertheless he has a daughter. Jim was "pinged" by a straffing plane during the landing at Lae two years ago. The game was a bit rough too, and though it was not soft ball, the umpire called "Strike one - ball one".

The mentioning of softball reminds us to let you know of the talented team which the Officers field. In the two matches played to date they have been victorious. They defeated 2/24 Bn team 15 - 11, and 2/48 Bn HQ Company 6 - 4. Anyone wishing to issue a challenge just let rip - but be warned. They're hot.

We have pleasure in announcing that some decorations have been awarded to several of the boys of the 2/23rd. We offer our heartiest congratulations to Lieut. Tommy Atkins, MC; Lieut. Stan Smith, MC; Sgt. Laurie Froud, DCM; Cpl. Noel Dingle, MM, and Pte. "Dutchy" Holland, MM.

Tommy Atkins M.C. Tarakan.

Stan Smith M.C. Tarakan.

The band has laid a counter complaint against the Padre's choir. Actually we must overrule the complaint on the grounds of professional jealousy. Another factor in favour of the Parson man's singers, is that they only practice for an hour at a time (that band goes from morning till night and up to now they haven't played one piece right through). The Padre needs more voices, and Mud and Blood suggests that you budding tenors and baritones lend a hand. There's not much opportunity to "shout" here, so be in it. Rally round fellers!

Letters and messages from various sources indicate that the following wounded lads are well on the mend: Colin Johnson, Dudley Hill, Dave Macauley, Frank O'Brien, Graeme Stabell, Bill Woodorf, Cpl. David Tottle, Ken Bartel and Bill Ogilvie.

The C.O. has received a letter from Lt.Comd. Nettleford of HMAS ...., a corvette which recently visited Tarakan. In his letter the Lt. Comd. expressed his appreciation and gratitude for the kindness shown to him and his ships company by the officers and men of this battalion.

Just in case you blokes are not sure of how your mothers, wives or sweethearts can contact the 2/23rd Battalion Welfare Association, here is the address: Mrs. E. E. Simmons, Hon. Sec., 2/23 Aust. Inf. Bn. Ladies Welfare Association, Flat 4, 38 Kingsley Street, Elwood, Victoria.

The ladies of the battalion have always done a magnificent job, and they are worth their weight in gold. Their latest effort is the contribution of over 22 gross of razor blades. They also advise that there are some more face washers on the way. Write home chaps, and tell your womenfolk to contact Mrs. Simmons if they think they can help the Association along.

And for all you optimistic five year blokes. Have you considered joining the 2/23rd Bn. Association. This club has grown up from an idea in a fertile brain, to a big organization. You will meet the old gang there, and from information gleaned, the meetings are merry and bright. The paper the club produces is called Mud'n Blood Junior, and we enclose a story taken home by Percy Tait and published by "Junior".

TARZAN OF TARAKAN

Some of the lads of the Battalion had a pet ape (not the RSM) - they tied it to a tree. As time went on the ape (not the RSM) got a gutful of captivity, and those soft hearted young Australian warriors, ever mindful of the welfare of the wogs and the fauna, decided to return the aforesaid ape (not the RSM) to its jungle haunts. The first step, the unleashing, was successfully accomplished - the ape (not the RSM) was free. Unfortunately (for Tich) Tich Wynack the battalion postmaster came strolling by - he could not have had his hat on, for the ape (not the RSM) up and at him. Tich was off - head and tail they raced for the cactus - Tich breaking all records (and he has some good ones) for cover. And so our story ends - what happened in the cactus will forever remain a secret. Tich and the RSM (not the ape) are still with the unit - Tich happy with his sheets of stamps - RSM happy with his sheet of charges.

And that, dear readers, is the end of this edition. Don't forget to send in the dirt on your cobbers. We have no compunction, and will risk any libel suits. Send articles, verses etc, to Capt. Lovell, "B" Company, and after that, hope for the worst.

Cheerio blokes - Ed.

STOP PRESS:

They're off to a flying start. The first batch of war weary veterans left for Aussie after an impromptu farewell party held at the RQ Store. The C.O. and a crowd of five yearers wished them Bon voyage. The Bn. will miss their services, but everyone, we're sure, wishes them all the best, so we say cheerio to WOII Peter Reynolds, Tichy Wynack and Nugget Hughes, all original members of the battalion.

Peter Reynolds

TARAKAN, 21st August, 1945.

MUD & BLOOD BIRTHDAY ISSUE

Well fellers, it's all over, and the 2/23 Bn. has fought its last campaign in World War II. The traditions handed down by the old warriors of the 1914-18 War have been upheld. A word from the C.O. fellers:

Dear Mud and Bloods,

On this, our fifth birthday, I wish to congratulate all ranks who have served with the battalion during these five years. You have served your King and Country with great courage, determination and loyalty and have played an important role in the great Allied task, which has at last ended in complete victory over the enemies of the peace loving peoples of the world. I am proud of you all, and proud indeed to have served with you.

Some of you will be serving on with the battalion in its future role; I wish you good luck, happier days, and keep up the good name which has been so dearly won, and to those whose service will soon be terminated, I wish a safe and speedy return to your loved ones, and a happy, peaceful life.

Let us all remember our life's duty to remain united in peace as we have in war, to ensure, firstly the security of those ideals for which we have fought on the battlefields, secondly the peace and comfort of the loved ones of those whom we have left behind, and finally the preservation of the glorious memories of those who gallantly gave their all.

F.A.G. Tucker, Lt.Col.

BATTALION CAVALCADE:

The 2/23 Bn. was formed in Albury on 20 August 1940. As part of 26 Brigade, side by side with 2/24 and 2/48 Bns, the battalion has performed its duties worthily and well. With pride it remembers Tobruk, an epic of the Western Desert where the Huns were halted for the first time in their mad surge towards world domination.

Syria was not a battle ground for the battalion, but there it stood ready to help defend the approaches to Palestine and the Suez Canal, at a time when the enemy was forcing the Russians back towards the Caucasian Mountains. After the German advances had been decisively checked by the Red Army, Syria became a training ground. We can add too, that the battalion became vitally interested in the "joie de vie" available in Beirut, Tripoli, Damascus and other delightful Syrian towns. Yes, Syria was a country never to be forgotten.

Rumours have always been abundant, but never has there been such a varied collection as those circulated when the Ninth Division left Syria suddenly, and passed through Palestine down into Egypt. It wasn't until the Suez Canal was crossed that the truth was known. The Western Desert again. And so, early in July 1942, the Division found itself face to face with a victory flushed German Army (the Ities were there also).

The fighting was fierce, and at Tel el Eisa and El Alamein, the battalion fought magnificently. Those were the battles that began the victory march for the Allies into the heart of Germany, and the 2/23 Bn can be proud - it is proud - of having fought and played its part under the leadership of Lt.Gen. Montgomery (now Field Marshal).

Churchill and Montgomery still praise the NINTH DIVISION.

He said of the Ninth Division "they fought until flesh and blood could stand no more - and then they still went on fighting" - and blokes, the 2/23rd Battalion was right in that fighting.

After having spent over two years in the Middle East, the battalion arrived home in February 1943. All the weddings, etc. having been celebrated the Battalion moved to Kairi on the Atherton Tablelands where it learned jungle fighting, and in September 1943, put its training to the test in the attack on Lae. Apparently the training was good, for the Japs were handed out a severe thrashing, and a lesson in tactics. The same results came from the actions at Satelberg and Wareo.

Who called it "Easy Street" ? (Remember?)

And last, but not least, came Tarakan. This little island proved a very tough nut to crack. The Japs fought fanatically, but fanaticism cannot stop determination and courage; once again the battalion triumphed.

'Me catchee good conclact," 2/23 Laundry

As our thoughts turn towards home, we must think of those whose loved ones remain here and in New Guinea and the Middle East. We must - we will remember them. We can help them too. This is not sales talk, for sales talk should be unnecessary. Join the 2/23rd Battalion Association. It has already helped out needy cases, and it's our duty to keep the flag flying after the war, as it was before. Men of the 2/23rd Battalion, we must stick together, and help those who can't help themselves.

The investiture of awards to members of Tarakan Force by Lt.Gen. Sir Leslie Morshead was a stirring ceremony, and we were proud of the Battalion's representatives. During the war the 2/23rd has won - DSO 3, MC 10, DCM 4, MM 18, with many MID awards and GOC Cards (ME) - a splendid record.

SALUTE TO GRACIE

With a "Ba Goom lads" and a cheery wave, we were introduced to OUR GRACIE. Yes, Miss Gracie Fields arrived amid cheers from over 8000 troops and for 45 minutes entertained us as we have never been entertained before.

She sang, joked and switched from comic opera to dialogue and back again to straight singing without batting an eyelid, and in such a manner that left most Mud and Bloods spellbound.

We thank you Gracie most sincerely and enthusiastically, and wish you "Bon Voyage", and drop in and see us again some time.

GREETINGS AND FAREWELLS:

Last week we said goodbye to the sole remaining original officer of the battalion - Major McRae, the 2 i/c. Good luck, Sir, and for goodness sake, don't rush round too much and overdo things.

More 'bomb happies', five yearers, have been released, and amongst them are some original Mud and Bloods. Bon voyage, and may we all be having one together at the City Club in the near future.

The mail bag has been full lately bringing to the C.O. messages of congratulations and good wishes to the Battalion. We give you the following extracts:

Accept congratulations, convey to all lads of battalion our thanks, lovely news..........Mrs. G.G. Anderson.

Congratulations and Best Wishes to you and the unit for future operations. .... John Turner.

Sincerest congratulations and Best Wishes to yourself and battalion on the final knockout.............. Max Simmons.

My thoughts are specially with you all on occasion of fifth anniversary celebrations. Rejoice greatly these festivities fall within octave of VP day. .... Peter Reynolds.

Many thanks, dear friends; all Mud and Bloods join with the C.O. in expressing their appreciation of your good wishes.

"THE DIRT"

What's wrong with Bubbles Dunstan? He is always at the RAP. "Just kicking on" he says, but we think he likes to feel the Doc's stethoscope on his left breast. Have you noticed his development lately. My Oh My, Bubbles, watch all those points.

Gunga of "A" Company is mortified. Since the Company has begun playing shuttlecock, he finds that his pet bantam is bald in a most embarrassing place. Who are the cads that sing "Rip the feathers away?"

Butch Ohl, "A" Company cook, disturbed a Nip so we are told, and hurled a bottle of vinegar at him. The Nip gave him such a sour look and said "What! No pickles?"

Our old friend Tubby Painter came in on Victory Night "On a Wing and a Prayer". He stooged around "B" Company's parade ground, but finally "pranged". He was asked how he felt, but did not say "wizard".

If any five year man is feeling down in the dumps, apply to Capt. A.M.R. and Row for his delightful book of verse entitled "How to be happy on Tarakan?" Another lively little booklet he has published "hari-kiri" is really good - you will die laughing.

"B" Company's lighting plant is controlled by "Swazzle" Beckley. It's usually a toss up between Swazzle and the lights as to who will blackout first. It is said the reason for the blackouts that do occur is that there is water in the petrol. Someone should keep Swazzle away from the water truck.

WAR GRAVES - TARAKAN

Will you walk with me in the heat of day,
Till we come at the crossroads on the way
Of a dusty road on Tarakan,
To a scene in the scheme of the war's mad plan.

There are soldiers there in a little square,
Who will breathe no more of the dust-filled air.
On the trails they died, by the road they rest,
With the foreign soil on each manly chest.

On the crosses which mark the arid mounds
Are the tales of courage which knew no bounds.
"Killed in Action" and "Died of Wounds";
But the wasted lives are the war's worst ruins.

You will see their mates at the gravesides stand
Quietly, slouch hats held in hand,
And you may grieve, as they will too,
For the hopes and dreams which will not come true.

In death these men have but simple needs,
No separate tracts for differing creeds;
For the shoulders which never were cold in life
Are together in death as they were in strife.

You may gaze at the flag which hangs from the mast
To honour the men who were staunch till the last,
And fancy you hear a quiet voice say -
"Australia, my country, will you repay?"

"Will you warm my hearth, give daily bread
To the hungry mouths which once were fed
Through the sweat and toil of a fallen man,
Who sleeps by the road on Tarakan?"

So when you return, by the dusty road,
You may bear your share of a sacred load,
With a pride whose flame ignited then,
Will burn till the sound of the last Amen.

                         F/O A.T. Latham.

ORDER OF THE DAY

by Gen. Sir Thomas Blamey, C in C. Adv. LHQ Borneo; 15 Aug 45.

SURRENDER OF JAPANESE

The Japanese have surrendered.
Our long and arduous struggle has ended in complete victory.

The climax has come at the time when all six Australian Divisions are fighting strenuously each on its own area, in the far flung battle lines. No divisions amongst the Allies have contributed more to the downfall of our enemies than ours.

Our General Officers and our Commanders of all grades, our Regimental Officers and our Warrant and Non-commissioned Officers have led you unfalteringly to victory. Under their guidance, the troops have been formed into a magnificent army to the pride and glory of Australia.

We have fought through the burning days and freezing nights of the desert. We have fought through the ooze and sweat of tropical jungles. We have defeated the Italians and the Germans, and we would soon have destroyed completely the Japanese before us.

We are now to go to our homes, having done our part in ensuring freedom for all peoples. We will not forget this freedom, for which we have fought so long and successfully, and so let us stand together in future years to ensure that it remains the crowning heritage of Australian people. Above all, we give thanks to the Almighty for His greatest and crowning mercy, that marks for all people the total downfall of tyranny.

(Signed) T.A. Blamey, General
C in C, Australian Military Forces.